METROLINK

METROLINK

by
John Senior
and
Eric Ogden

Transport Publishing Co Ltd : Glossop : Derbyshire : England

© Transport Publishing Co Ltd July 1992

ISBN 086317 155 9

This book is dedicated to the many people who have worked to create the Greater Manchester Metrolink System.

Their efforts have put Greater Manchester once again in the forefront of British transport and their achievements will be recognised by the many millions of people who will ride on the new Light Rail Vehicles – conceivably some 100 million by the turn of the century.

We wish to record our absolute conviction that an integrated LRT system has a vital role to play in improving public transport and reducing congestion and pollution in our towns and cities.

We have sought to record the process of developing the concept of Metrolink, justifying it, meeting the government's requirements for a private sector involvement in funding and managing a complex contract in full. Our account therefore includes the problems as well as the achievements. Viewed from this point in time, however, it is inevitable that we must reserve judgement on some features of the Metrolink process especially its use of the first Design Build Operate and Maintain (DBOM) contract to be applied to a modern public transport system.

Eric Ogden	John Senior
Saddleworth	Simmondley
Oldham	Glossop

Produced electronically for the Publishers by
Mopok Graphics, 128 Pikes Lane, Glossop, Derbyshire
Printed and bound in Great Britain

Acknowledgements

We would like to record our grateful thanks to the many people who have helped to make possible the production of this history of the Metrolink project – from conception through construction up to the opening of the system.

The late David Graham, former Director General of the Passenger Transport Executive, gave the project his blessing and encouragement and in so doing "lent us the key" to open many doors. His successor, Chris Mulligan, has been equally supportive. Bill Tyson, the Executive's Director of Planning and Promotion has given us considerable assistance – not only by providing information on contractual and financial aspects but also by acting as co-ordinator at proof stage. Whilst any errors are ours, we are pleased to acknowledge the work done by Bill in helping us to ensure that accuracy and a fair balance went hand-in-hand. The reporting of matters affecting all three parties – the Executive, GMML and GMA – where each often had a different perspective – was not always easy but we believe our work is indeed fair and balanced.

Others within the Executive to whom we owe a debt of gratitude include Deputy Director General Roger Hall and the whole of his Metrolink team, especially Tony Young who has helped in so many ways, and Jane Nearney, Press and Public Affairs Manager, and her team, including Bill Maddocks and particularly Ann Baslingdon.

Scott Hellewell, first in his capacity within the Passenger Transport Executive and subsequently as Operations Director at GMML, "lent another key" and has – like Bill Tyson – spent many hours in his "spare time" at weekends reading drafts and checking proofs. We have burnt the midnight oil together – and we've seen the dawn together on several occasions too! Scott and his co-directors – Eric Black, Chelvin Hibbert and Don Kenny – have helped enormously and we thank them and all their staff at Metrolink. Paul Neal and Andy Morris have coped with our many photographic and video sessions, Margaret Hyde and Alison Rushton have kept us informed of events and provided a steady flow of press and PR items. Phil Robinson deserves a special mention for co-ordinating all our requests and phone calls in such a friendly and efficient way.

Councillors Clarke and Flanagan each provided an insight into the background of the scheme and we are most grateful for their co-operation and for their interest in the project. From the City of Manchester viewpoint, Sinclair McLeod, City Engineer, helped us with much background information and through his staff, notably Keith Williams, gave insights to aspects which we could not otherwise have perceived. Major Holden (IOR) was most helpful as also was Geoffrey Claydon.

We also wish to acknowledge the assistance of various individuals from many companies, including: W. S. Atkins – Roger Hull and Allan Woodgates; Balfour Beatty – Noel Duffy, Steve Pont, Steve Shudall, Bev Waterhouse; BR – Chris Leah; CMDC – John Glestor; Faircloughs – David Horn and Keith Hick; Firema's management including Aldo Agosto and all the staff at their Bologna factory; GEC – Jeff Done, Brian Middleton and Mike Scott; GMA – David Cox; GM Buses – Val Stevens and Alan Westwell; Mott MacDonald – David Rumney and Dick Carr;   Mowlem – Nicholas Hopkins and Jim McDermott; STIB – Yvan Flecin, Paul Gijselings and Marc Thienpont; Transmark – John Berry.

Mark and Geoffrey Senior spent many hours patiently tracking down items which needed photographing, often in the very early hours of the morning, whilst Margaret Robinson kept a steady stream of prints flowing to us through Jane Nearney and Margaret Hyde. John Fox of the Manchester Evening News responded to our requests for particular items with alacrity and enthusiasm and his wide angle lens literally added another dimension to some of the pictures. Janine Booth designed the book and prepared many of the graphics. We thank the advertisers who have supported us, and if we have inadvertently omitted anyone, we trust they will forgive us.

Finally we acknowledge our gratitude to our families who have put up with disruptions in various ways over a period of three years, together with other ongoing commitments. Their good humour, interest and active co-operation have made our work possible. We trust that the general reader will find much of interest, the professional reader much of help, and that all readers will enjoy this book as much as we have enjoyed compiling it.

Photographers

Buchan, C. V. Ltd	91 (upper)	Salford Art Galleries	18 (lower)
Central Manchester		Senior, Carolyn	17
Development Corporation	69	Senior, Geoffrey	14 (lower), 15 (lower), 18 (upper),
Chatburn, Victor	138 (centre)		55 (lower left), 63 (lower), 70, 71
Department of Transport	146		(both), 77 (lower), 80 (both), 93
Fox, John, courtesy			(lower), 95 (both), 96, 97 (all), 112
Manchester Evening News	9, 62, 90 (lower), 94 (upper), 100		(upper left), 114 (upper), 123 (right),
	(upper & centre), 103 (lower), 110,		139 (lower)
	113, 114 (lower), 125, 133, 134	Senior, John A.	20 (lower), 23 (lower right), 30, 56,
GECA TPL	104		57 (lower), 58 (both), 59, 60 (upper),
Gee Photography, Hale	74		61 (both), 63 (upper), 65 (both), 66,
Greater Manchester Metro Ltd	119, 128 (both), 143 (upper)		67, 68 (all), 73, 75, 76 (all), 77
Greater Manchester			(upper & centre), 78 (all), 79 (all),
Passenger Transport Executive	21, 24, 38 (both), 39, 47, 50		81 (lower), 82 (upper), 84, 85
Hyde, W. G. S.	42		(upper), 86 (centre & lower), 87
Manchester City Engineers	55 (upper right), 55 (lower right), 86		(upper), 88 (all), 89 (both), 90
	(upper), 87 (lower)		(upper), 91 (centre & lower), 92, 94
MTMS Archive	19, 22, 64 (both),		(centre & lower), 103 (upper), 105
			(centre & lower right), 107 (upper),
Manchester Museum of Transport	23 (upper)		109 (all), 111 (both), 112 (lower),
Ogden, Eric	20 (upper), 23 (lower left), 81		115, 122 (upper), 127, 130, 135
	(upper), 105 (lower left), 112 (upper		(upper), 136 (upper), 138 (upper),
	right), 136 (lower right)		139 (upper), 143 (lower two), 152
Robinson, Margaret	11, 28, 34, 41, 45, 55 (upper left),	Senior, Mark	124
	60 (lower), 82 (lower), 85 (lower),	STIB	121
	98 (both), 99 (upper), 100 (both	Transport Publishing Co Ltd	
	lower), 101 (both), 105 (upper), 117,	Archive	14 (upper), 15 (upper & centre), 23
	120, 122 (lower), 123 (left & centre),		(centre)
	135 (lower), 138 (lower), 136 (lower	Transport Publishing Co Ltd	
	left), 137, 141, 144 (both), 145	Studio	25, 57 (upper), 93 (left), 102, 126
	(lower), 146, 147, 148, 150, cover		

The Authors, seen with the TPC team, to whom they extend their grateful thanks for coping with what turned out to be – in true Metrolink fashion – a slightly bigger job than had been expected! Left to right Eric Ogden, Shirley Gregg, Mike Cowx, Carolyn Senior, Mark Senior, Margaret Davies, Geoffrey Senior and Author/Publisher John Senior.

Eric Ogden trained as an accountant with the North Western Electricity Board and subsequently worked for 21 years at the University of Manchester where he became Assistant Accountant. He was ordained Priest in the Church of England in 1977 and serves in the parochial ministry at St. Anne's, Lydgate, in the Diocese of Manchester. Apart from Army Service, he has always lived in the Greater Manchester area. Born in Bolton, he now lives in Saddleworth with his wife and son. Perhaps because both his parents worked in the motor industry he has always possessed a keen interest in motor vehicles, specialising in the history of road passenger transport. His connection with TPC dates from 1974 when his first title, Lancashire United Transport, became TPC's first bus book. This is his eleventh title in a range covering histories of manufacturers and operators through to Metrolink, Britain's most modern passenger transport system.

John Senior has a long standing interest in tramways and light rail. He first joined the then Light Railway Transport League in 1954 and is a founder member of the National Tramway Museum. When time permits he drives vintage trams in Manchester's Heaton Park. Business and holiday travel abroad over the intervening years has allowed him to pursue his interest in modern light rail developments and, like many others, he never thought he would see on-street light rail return to British cities. In 1973 he founded TPC in the middle of the infamous "three-day week". Since then he has produced many books on British transport including the Commemorative Volume marking the demise of the erstwhile National Bus Company. Having returned to his native Manchester in 1971 with his wife and two sons, all of whom are involved with the business, he salutes all those whose efforts are transforming the City, particularly in the Castlefield area.

Contents

Foreword

by Councillor Joe Clarke,
Chairman,
Greater Manchester Passenger Transport Authority

This book writes a new and fascinating chapter into the history of Greater Manchester. It tells the story of Metrolink, the most modern and exciting transport system in Great Britain.

From the dawn of the railway age people have dreamed of a transport system which would carry passengers rapidly, comfortably and safely across Manchester. In 1839, before the two stations were even built, there was talk of a tunnel which would link Piccadilly (then called London Road) with Victoria.

Plans for underground railway systems then followed, each one bigger than the last as the City itself expanded. All were abandoned on economic grounds. A proposed monorail and a new plan for a "Picc-Vic" tunnel met the same fate.

In 1982 came a plan for a 100km light rapid transit system, to be created from a number of locally significant passenger railway lines, with surface links across the City. Six years later The Queen gave the Royal Assent to the proposed new system – Metrolink.

In April this year the dream became a reality – a dream which included the 150-year old wish for a link between Piccadilly and Victoria.

To achieve this, many people worked long and hard. Members of the Passenger Transport Authority lobbied Ministers for funding, supported by all ten metropolitan district councils in Greater Manchester. Members of all three main political parties united to ensure the success of the campaign. Though

a Government grant was obtained, most of the funding for Metrolink came from the ten district councils.

I cannot praise too highly the co-operation which the Passenger Transport Executive has received from the Department of Transport; Bury, Manchester and Trafford Councils; the City's Highways and Planning Departments; the Central Manchester Development Corporation; the chambers of commerce and trade; community groups and many others.

Lastly I would like to acknowledge the patience, support and good humour of the people of Greater Manchester, to whom Metrolink belongs.

PASSENGER ENQUIRIES
please ring

GREATER MANCHESTER PASSENGER TRANSPORT EXECUTIVE ENQUIRY NUMBER – 061 228 7811 – FOR BUS, LOCAL TRAIN AND METROLINK INFORMATION IN GREATER MANCHESTER

or

GMML METROLINK PASSENGER ENQUIRIES 061 205 2000

Empty streets at the height of a spectacular storm on 1st June 1992. Photograph by John Fox courtesy of Manchester Evening News

Who put the transport of the future on the streets of Britain?

Metrolink is the first street-operating light rapid transit system in Britain.

It will travel right through the heart of city centre Manchester, linking Bury, in the North, with Altrincham in the South. Travelling on existing railway lines and then onto the City's streets, Metrolink has not only revolutionised passenger transport, but it has set the standard for future public transport in Britain.

Work started on Metrolink as early as 1982, with draft proposals and planned routes. Now the project has come to fruition with the opening of the system, Greater Manchester has the most advanced passenger transport system in Great Britain.

The Greater Manchester Transport Authority gratefully acknowledges the co-operation of the ten Councils of Greater Manchester, the Department of Transport, the Department of the Environment, the European Community, the City's Highways and Planning Authority, Central Manchester Development Corporation, the community groups and the chambers of commerce and trade, to name but a few.

Together we have succeeded in putting Metrolink on to the streets of Manchester, the benefits of which, are already transforming the city centre.

It's an achievement that we can all be very proud of. Yet ultimately Metrolink belongs to the people who use it. The people of Greater Manchester.

Greater Manchester Passenger Transport Authority

9 Portland Street, Manchester M60 1HX.

FUNDED BY THE COUNCILS OF BOLTON, BURY, MANCHESTER, OLDHAM, ROCHDALE, SALFORD, STOCKPORT, TAMESIDE, TRAFFORD, WIGAN AND THE DEPARTMENT OF TRANSPORT.

David Graham
AN APPRECIATION

by
Councillor Jack Flanagan,
Chairman Metrolink Working Party

Metrolink is a lasting memorial to the work of David Graham, former Director General of Greater Manchester Passenger Transport Executive, who died in April 1991.

Among David's many talents the most outstanding was, in my view, his ability to manage complex tasks. He was a man of vision who fully understood the political and economic realities. His expertise enabled him to analyse seemingly intractable problems. On Metrolink he devised solutions which appeared impossible to those who doubted that the scheme could ever be brought to fruition. As Chairman of the Metrolink Members' Working Party, I was able to closely observe the way David led the team which achieved these objectives on behalf of the Authority. Metrolink would not be here today without a tremendous amount of work by many people within the Authority and Executive. Above all, however, David led the team. The scheme had to be justified to the Government, the form of the contract had to be agreed, the contract needed to be drafted and approved and the bids evaluated before construction on the ground. Each of these tasks was a project in itself. That the supertrams are running on the streets of Manchester today, after what must be the shortest construction period on record for a new transport system, is largely due to their efforts.

When the Government rejected our proposal for a publicly-funded light rapid transit system they made it clear to us that no grant would be forthcoming without private sector involvement in the project. We met that requirement, and as a result of finding this support we now have a system which will, I believe, be the cornerstone of public transport throughout Britain in the years to come.

It is sad that David Graham is not with us to see Metrolink supertrams in action, but no doubt he is looking down on them with a wry smile as he remembers the battles which were fought to put them on the rails. After an outstanding career in public transport Metrolink is his lasting memorial.

Manchester gets it first.

Metrolink, operated by Greater Manchester Metro Ltd., is the first street running Light Rapid Transit System in Great Britain and one of the most advanced anywhere in the world.

METROLINK

Britain's most advanced passenger transport system. Get going. Get the **ET**

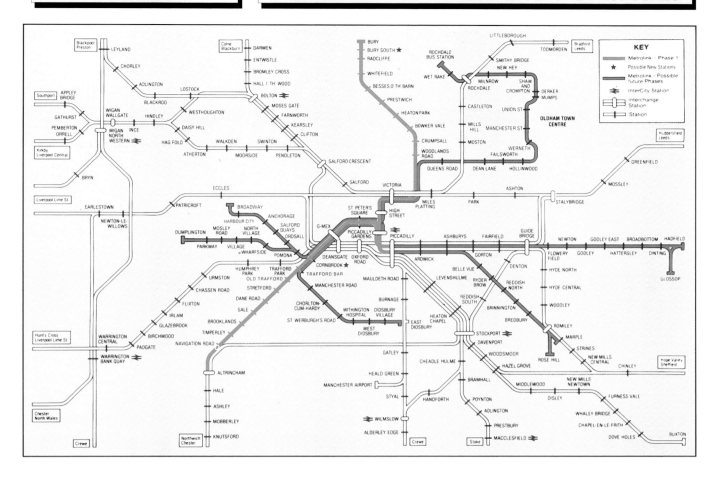

Metrolink's relationship with the local and main line railway network is shown on the above diagram. Phase 1, the blue line, between Altrincham and Bury is expected to carry some 10 million passengers per year. The City Centre section forms the spine onto which the proposed extensions (shown in red) will be grafted, thereby greatly increasing the system's potential capacity and also offering greater scope for reducing the number of cars in the City Centre.

When the Altrincham section of the line reopened on 15th June 1992 the first train was greeted with due ceremony – and yet very appropriately – by Altrincham's Town Crier. The accessibility of the Metrolink system and its Light Rail Vehicles will be appreciated by all whose mobility is impaired or who cannot use other means of public transport when they are shopping or have young children with them.

The appearance of the sleek Metrolink Supertrams in Manchester's streets in Spring 1992 confirmed Greater Manchester Passenger Transport Authority's determination to lead public transport out of the doldrums, and to demonstrate that clean and attractive modern vehicles running frequently and reliably through the shopping and business areas will attract ever-increasing numbers of passengers as they do in cities in other countries throughout the world.

Office workers on the fringe of the city centre will be able to gain easier access to the commercial areas during their lunch hour, just to take one example of improved facilities.

Pedestrians and passengers alike will soon appreciate the benefits that follow reductions in numbers of cars, vans and lorries in the city centre. Although deregulation has meant that more buses than ever now use the streets of Manchester and other cities, the LRVs or Supertrams will play their part in calming the road traffic.

Investment in high technology equipment to drive – and stop – these vehicles, and the special treatment of the track fixing in the streets, will ensure that their passage from G-Mex to Piccadilly and Victoria Stations will be almost silent and free from vibration. Whilst Manchester will be the first UK city to experience this new form of transport it is, of course, commonplace outside our islands.

The appearance of these Supertrams has, naturally, aroused much comment. Many of those watching the progress of the new system can remember the original trams (abandoned in January 1949) and three questions are raised time and again, "why are we bringing the trams back to the streets?" or, from the more enlightened perhaps, "why did we do away with them in the first place?" and, "why has it taken so long to bring them back?"

There are no simple answers. The original trams fell from favour in Manchester around 1929, an early date for a major system to be proposing wholesale changeover to buses, though some towns had already made the change prior to 1929. Lack of investment, resulting in slow, uncomfortable, noisy, old-fashioned

On 10th January 1949 the first generation of Manchester's trams made their final run through the city's streets.

Former British Rail train operating between Manchester and Bury and photographed at Crumpsall in July 1991.

Investment in new trams in Sheffield in 1953 and Glasgow up to 1954 was against the prevailing climate. Scrapping of these vehicles some 6-8 years later was an unfortunate example of wasted assets – the normal life expectancy for such rolling stock would be at least 20 years.

vehicles guaranteed the new generation of buses introduced from 1927 onwards would make a killing. In 1930 a Royal Commission on Transport advised the abandonment of tramways, considering them to be obsolescent. Notwithstanding this some cities continued to invest in their tramways, creating reserved tracks on which high-speed, comfortable, high-capacity trams transported millions of people safely and cheaply to work and play.

Enforced neglect during World War II produced arrears of maintenance and the need to replace rolling stock which were beyond the scope of most local authority finances. Those systems which might have survived then found that they could no longer benefit from using cheap electricity which they generated in their own power stations. The creation of the nationalised electricity industry resulted in the removal of this major advantage of tramway operations – cheap energy.

By the end of 1960, Blackpool was the sole survivor of some 120 English tramway systems, benefiting from a massive investment in rolling stock in the mid-'thirties almost unmatched by any other system. Two years later the only other remaining UK system, Glasgow, closed. Blackpool and the pioneering tourist line in the Isle of Man – the Manx Electric Railway – were all that remained of an industry which at its peak operated some 14,000 vehicles.

By the time the last trams had been abandoned the buses which had replaced them were themselves running into trouble. In a free market economy no one is isolated from the actions of others. The rise in wages, reduction in cost and easy availability of the motor car, had given rise to another revolution and the era of personal transport had arrived.

As the motor car proceeded to change the face of Britain, with motorways, by-passes, multi-storey car parks, yellow lines, parking meters and traffic wardens proliferating, another nail was knocked into the buses' coffins. Television provided home entertainment and evening traffic levels dropped dramatically, reducing the buses' patronage even further.

Now another cycle has come full turn and the influx of private motor cars into our towns and cities has created traffic jams and congestion to match the worst examples throughout the developed world.

Atmospheric pollution is now also being accepted as a major problem in the UK. Not only Los Angeles, Tokyo and Athens are having to ban cars to reduce exhaust levels – even Edinburgh (September/October 1991) and now Manchester (February 1992) are admitting that noxious emissions are approaching danger

A Metrolink LRV in the same location, after conversion of power and signalling, in April 1992, soon after commercial operation began.

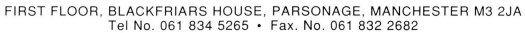

levels and have exceeded EC safety levels.

Between 1969 and 1974 Passenger Transport Authorities were created. Their brief to integrate, operate and improve all public transport in order to reduce congestion and pollution seemed a tall order but history will show that the battle was being won and the networks of buses and express coaches, and trains were demonstrating their ability to entice motorists out of their cars, the first step in the battle against congestion. By 1985 patronage was rising again.

Unfortunately the Government then produced effects even more drastic than electricity nationalisation of 1948 when in 1986 bus deregulation replaced integrated transport. It is too early to quantify fully the financial effects but if one of the main objects was to save money by reducing subsidy it may be hard to justify deregulation and privatisation.

Furthermore a 13% increase in bus mileage in Greater Manchester has to be set against a *reduction* of 20.6% in numbers of passenger journeys. The Passenger Transport Authority believes strongly that a fundamental review of deregulation is needed if the full benefits of Metrolink are to be realised.

Now the LRV has made its comeback with clean, comfortable, quiet transport which virtually eliminates on-street pollution. No one who has seen modern light rail systems operating through pedestrianised areas of cities in Europe or America can be in any doubt as to their efficiency. Their capability as people movers en-masse is without question.

Greater Manchester's initiative is part of an on-going policy to improve the environment and to make travelling within the conurbation a more enjoyable event. It now intends to demonstrate that investment in Light Rapid Transport, and that the extension of its system by building on the spine which the first phase has created, is the only sensible way forward to improve life in our cities. Indeed it firmly believes it is the *only* way forward.

Light rail vehicles operating in European cities clearly show the advantages for pedestrians. In addition to their quiet operation the fact that their precise path is known gives passengers and passers by alike a greater sense of security. This is Basel, a Swiss city served by a modern tramway network.

Greater Manchester has always been at the forefront of public passenger transport. John Greenwood's first British horse bus service of 1824, the Liverpool and Manchester Railway of 1830 with the world's first passenger railway station, the Manchester Ship Canal of 1894 with its unique swinging acqueduct at Barton-on-Irwell, and the airfield at Hough End Fields (named Alexandra Park, after the nearest railway station, and pre-dating the first municipal airport at Barton-on-Irwell, the predecessor of Ringway Airport) from where the world's first airline services commenced in 1919, all combined to place Manchester very firmly on the transport map. As befits the city and the region, Metrolink is in the vanguard of light rail developments and is pioneering much new ground.

Having established Greater Manchester's pre-eminence in public transport, let us now concentrate on rail transport since Metrolink combines running on former heavy rail tracks with tramways in the city's streets. Manchester was a terminus of the world's first passenger railway to be operated by steam locomotive, and retains the world's oldest station in Liverpool Road, which now forms part of the complex of the Museum of Science and Industry within an industrial conservation area.

Until 1969 Manchester was the only English city outside London with four principal railway stations, and the only great city outside London into which as many as seven pre-grouping railway companies had worked regularly. Also until 1969 it claimed the longest station platform in Europe which connected Victoria and Exchange stations. By the Act of 5th May 1826 the Liverpool to Manchester line was to terminate in Salford but fortunately for Manchester the company's fourth Act, of 14th May 1829, gave powers to carry the line across the River Irwell to the Liverpool Road terminus within the Manchester boundary.

John Greenwood's regular horse bus service between Pendleton Toll Gates and Market Street, Manchester, pre-dated Shillibeer's London service by five years. By the time of his death in 1851 Greenwood had become one of the largest horse bus and coach proprietors in the north, with daily services to Chester, Buxton and Sheffield in addition to local routes around and within Manchester and Salford. On John Greenwood's death, control of his business passed to his son, also called John, and he, together with his brother-in-law, John Haworth, introduced rail transport onto the streets of Salford early in 1861. Britain's first street tramway was opened by George Francis Train in Birkenhead in August 1860 but this system suffered from the disadvantage of the rail protruding above the road surface and thus

The world's first passenger railway station at Liverpool Road, Manchester together with the adjacent Agent's house, seen after renovation.

Greenwood's 5-wheeled omnibus.

interfering with other road traffic. Greenwood and Haworth avoided this problem by means of a three-rail system. The two outer rails, or plateways, were made flush with the road surface. The centre rail was grooved to accommodate a small guide wheel fixed under the vehicle which kept the iron-tyred main wheels running on the smooth flat rails or plates. The invention was registered as 'Haworths Patent Perambulating Principle' and it was proposed that it should cover the original 1824 route from Pendleton to Market Street, Manchester. However, permission could only be obtained from the Pendleton and Salford authorities and the line was constructed to terminate at Albert Bridge on the boundary between the two towns. The perambulatory equipment was fitted to existing horse buses and thus they could run either on or off the tramway. Rail running was so successful that it contrasted strongly with the off-rail sections on uneven roads but the venture was not extended, remaining in use until 1872.

The Tramways Act of 1870 allowed local authorities to construct and lease tramways with the option to purchase the undertaking after 21 years at the then value of tramway and equipment. Both Manchester and Salford Corporations obtained Tramway Orders under the terms of the Act to enable them to design, build and lease, but not operate, tramways within their respective areas. The Manchester Suburban Tramways Company was formed in 1877, with John Greenwood as a director, to build and operate its own lines and also to operate on lines constructed by the municipalities. The original leases were signed in 1877 to run for the period of 21 years

A typical Manchester horse tram, double-decked but single-ended. At the terminus the complete body rotated on the turntable incorporated in the truck. By this means it was possible to eliminate the second staircase, so reducing the weight and increasing the passenger carrying capacity. Trams of this type, built at the Carriage Company's workshop in Salford to the Eade's patent, operated throughout the city and its suburbs over a system of 89 route miles.

and these later determined the scale of municipal passenger transport operation in the Greater Manchester area. The first horse tramway operation running on grooved rail commenced on 17th May 1877 between the Grove Inn, Bury New Road, Salford and Deansgate, Manchester.

The Manchester Carriage Company had been formed in 1865 when the Greenwood interests were merged with those of other omnibus operators in the area. John Greenwood became Vice Chairman and Managing Director and remained prominent on the local transport scene until his death in 1886.

In 1880 the Manchester Tramways and Carriage Company, with John Greenwood as Chairman, was formed as an amalgamation of the Manchester Carriage Company and the Manchester Suburban Tramways Company and this organisation expanded to become Greater Manchester's major transport operator in the 1890s with 89 miles of tramway route, 515 cars and 5,300 horses working from twenty depots.

In Salford and Manchester the leases of the Corporation's lines granted to the Company expired between 1898 and 1901. A Bill of 1895 allowed local authorities to operate the tramways themselves and the Corporations decided to take over tramways and operate them as an electric system. Manchester's first section of electric tramway opened on 6th June 1901 between Albert Square and

Cheetham Hill and the Company's last horse tram services operated on 31st March 1903. The meeting held later in 1903 to wind up the affairs of the Manchester Carriage and Tramways Company was chaired by John Greenwood the third, the son of John Greenwood junior, who lived on until 1940.

Municipal trams were also operated by Rochdale, Ashton, Oldham, Bury, Bolton, Stalybridge Hyde Mossley & Dukinfield Joint Board, Wigan and Stockport. Rochdale was the first of these to abandon its system, in 1932, whilst Stockport operated trams in Greater Manchester until 25th August 1951.

Returning to the railways, it is clear that, from its earliest days, Manchester's railway system suffered from two major problems: the main termini were located at the edge of the city's central area, and there was no direct north-south link. While the rapid growth of the railway system quickly established Manchester's regional and national importance, the number of companies building railways into Manchester, the land areas required for termini, and the lack of flexibility in a central area which was fast becoming built up, all combined to preclude the lines from penetrating further towards the city centre. Eventually only two of the four main termini remained, Piccadilly and Victoria.

Piccadilly Station owes its origin to the first short section of the Manchester and Birmingham Railway which opened only as far as Stockport on 4th June 1840. The Manchester terminus was a temporary structure located in Travis Street. In 1842 it was enlarged by bridging over Store Street and the permanent terminus at London Road was brought into use. In its early days the station was variously called Store Street and Bank Top, the latter no doubt due to its construction on a viaduct of sixteen arches.

The area below the station – the Undercroft – was for many years a hive of activity. Goods were loaded and unloaded from railway wagons which were moved by means of ropes powered by hydraulic capstans. Part of this area has been converted to create Metrolink's interchange with British Rail.

To accommodate ever-increasing traffic, London Road was rebuilt and extended in 1865-66 and again in 1880-82. When finally rebuilt and modernised in 1960 (including installation of the 25Kv electric system) it was renamed Manchester Piccadilly.

The predecessor of Victoria Station was Oldham Road, the terminus of the Manchester and Leeds Railway. The section to Littleborough was opened on 4th July 1839, but the nearest the railway ever got to Leeds was Normanton in 1841. In that year the Company constructed a steeply inclined section from Miles Platting to a station at Hunts Bank, closer in to the city centre. This station was enlarged and rebuilt and opened as Victoria Station on 1st January 1844. Later in the same year, the Liverpool and Manchester Railway was extended to run into Victoria. At the time, Victoria was the largest station in the country and the first to be named after the Queen. The original Oldham Road and Liverpool Road stations closed as passenger stations and became major goods depots.

Until the advent of Metrolink, Manchester continued to suffer from these deficiencies of rail communication which were recognised 150 years ago. Indeed, the first plan to link the sites which were to become Piccadilly and Victoria Stations was for a rail tunnel as early as 1839, when Parliamentary powers were obtained, but it was not proceeded with. One major drawback in the plan was considered to be the lift at London Road which would have formed the interchange between the tunnel railway and the main line. Over 150 years later, Metrolink is to incorporate an escalator and lift connection between the undercroft and the concourse at Piccadilly station! A central viaduct link was proposed in 1866 but this also came to nothing as the city centre was already built up by this time.

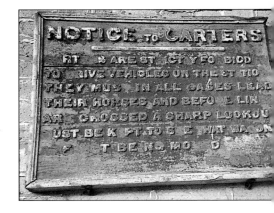

Notices such as this one, warning that "Carters are strictly forbidden to drive vehicles on the station. They must at all times lead their horses and before lines are crossed a sharp look out must be kept ..." abound in the Undercroft. Incorporating hand-cut wooden letters they date from the mid-1880s.

Manchester Victoria Station's imposing facade. Victoria is one of the principal points of interchange with Metrolink.

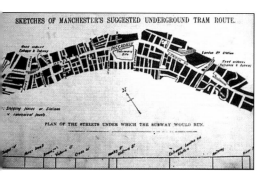

SKETCHES OF MANCHESTER'S SUGGESTED UNDERGROUND TRAM ROUTE.

PLAN OF THE STREETS UNDER WHICH THE SUBWAY WOULD RUN.

The Manchester Guardian printed this sketch showing proposals for an underground tram route linking London Road station (as it then was) with Victoria in 1914.

A proposal for a 'circular' underground railway linking Victoria, London Road, Oxford Road, Central and Exchange stations was made at the turn of the century when London subway building was at its height. Parliamentary powers were sought for this scheme, the cost of which was estimated at £1.5m, but again it failed to proceed. Another 'circle' plan appeared in 1912, partly underground with eight city centre stations and a branch to serve the University of Manchester! World War One caused the abandonment of this project and it was never revived.

In the 1920s Manchester City Council formed an Underground Railway Special Committee and a system of some fourteen miles costing £4m was proposed in 1926 which would have covered the central area with extensions to Salford, Stretford and Prestwich. A more ambitious scheme of 35 miles was proposed in 1928 incorporating an inner and an outer circle linking the main lines radiating from the points on the fringe of the city centre. It was estimated that the inner circle alone would carry 100 million passengers per annum and that the cost of the full scheme would be £20m.

By 1928 the city's tramway network was carrying some 328m passengers per year and running some 24.1 million car miles per year. Its legendary general manager, Henry Mattinson, had produced a scheme combining underground and surface sections. This scheme provided for connections at the outer ends with electrified suburban lines to enable cross-city services to be operated, a similar principle to today's Metrolink. Unlike today's free-for-all, however, the intention was for tram and bus services to be co-ordinated with the cross-city rail services. The two underground sections, totalling seven miles, were planned to run from Old Trafford to Collyhurst and from Ordsall Sidings in Salford to Ardwick with a central interchange near Manchester Town Hall. It was suggested that the underground sections should be constructed by Manchester Corporation, which would then lease them to the railway companies to operate. Here is another similarity with Metrolink, where the Executive owns the system but it is operated as a franchise by GMML (Greater Manchester Metro Ltd), a company owned by the construction consortium.

Nothing came of these schemes, largely due to the costs involved and lack of Government assistance with funding. Unfortunately, Mattinson died in 1928 at the early age of 51 and his scheme died with him. At this time the Manchester-Bury line was the only electric line in the city though the far-sighted Mattinson had recommended more. The Altrincham line was electrified in 1931, albeit by a different system, thus completing the outer routes incorporated in today's Metrolink.

No further proposals appeared for nearly 40 years due to the enthusiasm of Robert Stuart Pilcher – Manchester's next transport general manager – for buses and the intervention of World War Two. In a report to the City Council in 1964 considering the future needs of the city, Pilcher's successor, Albert Neal, recommended the introduction of a rapid transit system. Nothing came of the idea.

The next proposal came in 1966 and was for a suspended monorail between Middleton and Wythenshawe across the city centre also linking with Manchester Airport at Ringway. Taylor Woodrow was promoting the ALWEG monorail system and Manchester Corporation commissioned a study by consultants De Leuw, Hennessey, Chadwick, OhEocha (known as De Leuws!). After considering the ALWEG and Safege monorail systems, the Westinghouse Skybus system and heavy rail, the consultants' recommendation was for a heavyweight electric rapid transit system, initially from Northenden to Blackley via the city centre, a line of eleven miles with fourteen stations, at a cost of £43.5m. The line was to be underground between Fallowfield and Collyhurst and would have linked Oxford Road and Victoria stations. It would then have been extended to link Ringway with Langley giving a total cost of £61m. The intention was to cater for later extensions to include British Rail routes to Bury, Oldham, Hyde, Romiley, Swinton, Eccles, Sale and Altrincham, thus including the present Metrolink route. This ambitious scheme foundered as its predecessors because of the cost.

The 1968 Transport Act led to the setting up of the SELNEC Passenger Transport Authority and Executive with the duties of producing an integrated and efficient transport system within their area. They were the predecessors of the Greater Manchester PTA and PTE. In their long term plan, published in 1973, they proposed a modernised rail and bus network based on a Piccadilly to Victoria tunnel, which became known as 'Picc-Vic', to link suburban electric lines from Stockport and Wilmslow to Bury and Bolton. This had been first developed in 1970 and got Parliamentary approval but once more the cost was considered prohibitive and Government funding was not forthcoming. The scheme was effectively abandoned when the Greater Manchester Council in 1977 decided not to renew the Parliamentary Powers.

The next attempt to develop Manchester's local railway network and link the two main line stations led to the introduction of Metrolink. In 1982 a **Rail Study Group** was set up by the then Greater Manchester Council (in existence from 1974 to 1986 which was the Passenger Transport Authority during those years), the Passenger Transport Executive and British Rail. Its task was to investigate how the railways around Manchester could be improved and expanded and how links to the city centre could be created. The Study Group recommended the construction of three conventional railway links – the Hazel Grove chord, the Windsor link in Salford (both now in use) and a line to Manchester Airport, which is now under construction. A further recommendation was for the conversion of certain British Rail lines to Light Rail Transit, including the construction of a cross-city section, through the streets, linking Victoria and Piccadilly Stations. This proposal provided the link between the stations at a fraction of the cost of the schemes involving tunnels. However, because of the overall cost and restrictions imposed by HM Treasury it was clear that the LRT scheme would have to proceed in phases.

Before leaving the historical background to Metrolink, the various methods of linking the railway stations (by road) should be recorded. The

The inter-station tram service was at everyone's mercy. Passengers complained of delays due to congestion whilst the ever-strong taxi lobby bemoaned their lost fares.

Bristol 'Superbuses' were used for the 1932 inter-station link. Two are seen on the former Exchange Station approach around 1934.

Northern Counties of Wigan built the bodies for the single-decker Leyland Royal Tigers used on the City Circle bus services between 1961 and 1965. Manchester Corporation Transport Department created an effective brand image for the services.

Seddon midi-buses waiting at Piccadilly station approach whilst operating the Centreline service.

Ample shelters are provided at Victoria Station, where this Dennis Domino midi-bus is seen, in contrast to Piccadilly where passengers still wait in the open.

first inter-station service commenced in 1905 by tram route 50, running a circular service from London Road to Knott Mill (now Deansgate) station, then along Deansgate to a point close to Exchange and Victoria stations, and along Market Street and Piccadilly to London Road. By 1932 a single-decker bus service was linking Exchange station approach with Victoria station and London Road station approach. This bus route had a chequered existence, being reduced, revised, withdrawn and re-commenced as the City Council tried to placate the taxi lobby. A service ran spasmodically during the early years of the war and between 1942 and 1945 a service was introduced primarily for military personnel.

The next inter-station service ran from 1958 to 1961 when British Railways asked Manchester Corporation Transport Department to provide a replacement bus service between Oxford Road and London Road Stations while the rail line was re-electrified to 25Kv ac.

The last full-sized single-deck city centre service ran between 1961 and 1965 in the form of a city circle, comprising two circular services, A and B. Four single-deck buses equipped for one-man-operation were reserved for these services. Meanwhile, Central and Exchange stations were closed in 1969, Central station was later converted into the G-Mex Exhibition Centre with its strong present-day association with Metrolink.

The next attempt came in 1974 during the period (1969-1986) when the Passenger Transport Executive was a bus operator. Seddon midi-buses of Greater Manchester Transport operated the Centreline service on an intensive basis at a low flat fare, shuttling between Victoria and Piccadilly stations, via the business area and covering some streets which were not served by full-sized buses. Originally envisaged as a temporary 'stop gap' service until Picc-Vic was built it had the double advantage of linking the two railway stations and taking rail passengers arriving at the stations directly into the city centre. From 1986 the Centreline has been worked by Dennis Domino midi-buses. These vehicles were built to a robust specification for this intensive service, the chassis being, in fact, shortened examples of the full-sized equivalent, with an expected 20 year life.

Following deregulation in October 1986, these heavyweight midibuses passed to Greater Manchester Buses Ltd. and still operate the service.

The Centreline has probably been the best solution to date, though its main deficiencies have been its circuitous route and the inability of the small vehicles to cope with large volumes of luggage, or to take prams and large push chairs. Metrolink will finally close this gap between Victoria and Piccadilly rail stations, linking them directly through the city centre by rail for the first time in over 150 years.

It is somewhat ironic that the Greater Manchester area has had a long and close involvement in rail transport going back to the pioneering Liverpool and Manchester Railway of 1830 and yet it was one of largest conurbations in the developed world without a rapid transit system until the advent of Metrolink. Rolling stock and railway equipment to help move people and goods in all kinds of environment have been produced locally since 1830. Traction equipment is still provided for today's railways around the world. Its local engineers have contributed much to LRT systems in other conurbations but not, until now, in their own.

Greater Manchester's network was created by a dozen or so railway companies between 1830 and 1910 and was a strong influence, together with local tram and bus services, and express coach services, on the pattern of development in the area. Indeed, the local road transport services carried so many people that, having to mix with other traffic, first the slow-moving horse-drawn lorries and later the large numbers of motor vehicles, city centre chaos was experienced virtually from their introduction through to the 1950s, the heyday of road passenger transport.

From the 1960s public transport gradually declined to be replaced by private cars, and with ever-larger road haulage vehicles, the chaotic situation was little improved despite much continuing work on traffic management by the City Engineer & Surveyor's Department. This city centre congestion gradually spread to the surrounding town centres and the Passenger Transport Executive was created in a new initiative to attempt to tackle the problems.

Today's railway network, although much reduced from its earlier status, retains deficiencies which existed 150 years ago, as already mentioned. The central area stations are only on the edge of the central business district and therefore access by rail is poor compared with that provided by car, bus or taxi. But road access is subject to increasing congestion and restriction. Furthermore, the absence of north to south cross-city links resulted in two virtually separate networks. These two factors have inhibited the development of the railway system into a strategic network across the Greater Manchester area and so the railways' potential contribution to efficient passenger transport has not been fully realised. Other major problems were the outdated rolling stock. Some was over 30 years old and various replacements, transferred from other parts of the country such as Glasgow and Devon, did little to help since some were themselves approaching obsolescence. The non-standard 1200 volt dc third rail electrification on the Bury line was life-expired and a considerable amount of track and signalling renewal and bridgework was required. Similarly the Hadfield and Glossop line with its 1500v dc overhead system needed upgrading, a job carried out in 1984 when the standard 25Kv ac was installed and some Glasgow blue trains were cascaded onto the line.

As mentioned in the previous chapter the Rail Study Group, set up in 1982, resolved to take a fresh look at Greater Manchester's railway network. The preferred option – Picc-Vic – was now dead and buried but some legacies remained. The Bury Interchange was the sole visible benefit, though in the Royal Exchange area some work had been done during the redevelopment in the Market Street/Cross Street/Corporation Street complex to make provision for an underground station – Royal Exchange – had the scheme been given approval.

An artists impression of the proposed Royal Exchange Station for the Picc-Vic scheme.

The Group, in examining alternative rail strategies, assumed that the three key BR investments – Hazel Grove Chord (enabling Sheffield trains to reach Manchester via Stockport instead of Marple), the Windsor Link (to enable trains from Bolton, Preston and the north west to reach Piccadilly) and the Manchester Airport link would be approved and built. It was then assumed that on Inter-City routes, local rail services would continue to be provided by BR with financial support from the Passenger Transport Executive.

This then left a number of lines which carried mainly or exclusively local services on which most or all of the costs were borne by the Executive. These are the lines which either received the heaviest subsidies or which would require major investment to replace worn out infrastructure and which would be potential candidates for closure if revenue support was to be severely constrained. They included the lines from Manchester to Altrincham, Bury, Oldham, Rochdale, Glossop/Hadfield and Marple/Rose Hill, all of which are actual or proposed Metrolink routes.

The Study examined two broad options for these lines and each was aimed at overcoming the basic problems of central area accessibility, north-south links, renewal of rolling stock and replacement of non-standard traction systems. The first option was a phased system of cross city centre tunnels in association with electrification of the existing rail system, based on conventional 25Kv ac electrification and standard rolling stock for local services. The second option was for unconventional solutions including vehicles that could run either on existing streets or in tunnel across the regional centre to provide a network with interchange with the main Inter-City network.

The first option was a modified Picc-Vic tunnel project comprising a direct link between Piccadilly and Victoria Stations with one intermediate station at Piccadilly Gardens and a spur to Central Station (later G-Mex) with an intermediate underground station at Albert Square; it would then be linked to the Altrincham line using the former Central Station approach viaducts. This scheme had been developed in an earlier rail study which had examined a number of lower cost heavy rail tunnels.

While heavy rail solutions had been well-researched in previous years, the less conventional solutions, including light rail, had not previously been studied. In order to examine the second option it was therefore necessary to commission a **Feasibility Study** to scrutinise the issues involved in segregating any such system from other BR movements.

In determining whether lines would be suitable for conversion to an unconventional system, they were judged on four main criteria. First the route must be capable of segregation from conventional rail routes (Inter-City and local passenger) with the exception of grade crossings with limited freight movements. Then the routes must be compatible with the development of the conventional rail network. Next, existing or potential traffic must justify the conversion. And finally, routes must provide a logical network and afford adequate interchange with the main BR network.

It was apparent that the Altrincham, Bury, Rochdale via Oldham, Glossop/Hadfield and Marple/Rose Hill lines could satisfy these requirements provided that the Hazel Grove chord was built and if the Chester service was diverted to operate from Altrincham via Stockport to Piccadilly instead of its then route along the Altrincham line, or if it was curtailed at Altrincham. One additional route was added, the former Midland rail line serving Chorlton, Withington and Didsbury. It was felt that the remaining local lines would not meet the criteria although some, for example the Wigan via Atherton line, could possibly be longer-term candidates for segregation.

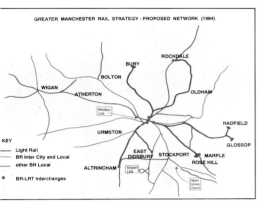

GREATER MANCHESTER RAIL STRATEGY - PROPOSED NETWORK (1984)

Railway network in the Greater Manchester area showing the Windsor Link, Hazel Grove Chord and Airport Links.

A **Transit Systems Options Review** was then undertaken covering rail-based systems including steel-wheeled and rubber-tyred trains, road-based systems including buses and trolleybuses, automatic guideway systems, dual-mode systems including busways, guided buses and rail buses and people-mover systems. The basic system requirements were defined as follows:-

(a) passenger capacity to carry flows in the range 1,000 to 5,000 passengers per hour, with a maximum of about 10,000 passengers per hour over central sections.
(b) maximum speed not less than 80kph with high acceleration/deceleration rates.
(c) ability to operate over existing and proposed alignments without extensive additional engineering costs.
(d) high levels of reliability.
(e) acceptable environmental features.
(f) capability for expansion beyond the study network.

An additional requirement in the case of surface links in the city centre was the ability to operate on-street.

The final report advised that any system not then fully developed should not be considered further because of the protracted time scale for development from prototype to operational acceptance. It was also considered that fully-automated systems, like the driverless London Docklands Light Railway, should not be considered. The review therefore concluded that the only modes that warranted further investigation were light rail, reserved busway and guided busway, and Mott, Hay & Anderson (now Mott MacDonald Group Ltd) were commissioned to undertake feasibility studies of these options. They endorsed the conversion of the suburban rail lines to light rail and extension across the city centre to link Manchester's two main rail termini – Victoria and Piccadilly – thereby establishing the UK's first street running light rail system.

Since the only modern light rail scheme operating in the UK – the Tyne & Wear Metro, opened in 1980 – did not operate on street it was necessary to travel further afield to see the operation of systems with fixed surface links.

In order to gain first-hand knowledge, three Rail Strategy Study Reports were commissioned. In September 1983 a European Study Visit was arranged, with members from Greater Manchester Council, Greater Manchester Passenger Transport Executive, British Rail, Manchester City Council and the Department of Transport. The Study group looked at tramways, metros, trolleybuses and guided busways and visited Rotterdam, Utrecht, Köln, Dusseldorf, Essen, Karlsruhe, Rastatt, Freiburg and Zurich.

In October 1984 a Canadian Study Visit examined transport in Portland, Vancouver, Calgary, Edmonton, Thunder Bay, Toronto and Buffalo. A significant difference which the group members noted was whereas in Europe tramways had, in the main, been retained, updated and extended, a number of the North American systems offered a closer parallel to Greater Manchester by the use of former rail alignments in the suburbs.

The Portland system particularly impressed the group, and many similarities were seen between that system and the proposed scheme for Greater Manchester. Later, Gerald Fox and John Schumann from Portland were commissioned to prepare a study document on Greater Manchester's LRT proposals, and to give their views on these proposals in the light of their own experience. This formed The Portland Report, an invaluable document full of sound comment and advice which was produced following a two week visit to Manchester by its authors.

In October 1985 the Study visit was to the French city of Nantes, with members from Greater Manchester Council, the Joint Passenger Transport

STUDY VISITS

The reports produced by the Study Visit Groups made interesting reading. Their observations are in some cases even more pertinent now that Metrolink has been built.

From the 1983 visit.....

The picture that emerges is nevertheless a consistent one, and makes an interesting comparison with British experience over the past fifty years.

In all the cities visited (with the exception of Utrecht, where we did not view or consider the general transport system), the major element in public transport policy since the war has been the general retention of a tracked (i.e. Tram) system of public transport for the main services into the city centres, and its continuous upgrading.

Buses (with the exception of Essen), were used generally only as suburban feeders.

The retention and development of fixed rail urban transport systems to provide the main form of transport to the city centre has been the continuing policy of national, regional and city governments, generally in parallel with major road building for orbital and inter-urban traffic.

Comfort and passenger "convenience"....With tracks formed generally of continuous welded rail, and with modern suspension systems, sound insulation and often double-glazed windows, the quality of ride is very good, and noise levels (or lack of them) impressive. With smooth ride (compared with buses), many passengers chose to stand, even when seats were available.

In all the cities and conurbations visited, an improved fixed track public transport system appears to be seen as a key element in providing access to the city centre, and help maintain its economic and social role.

One aspect where there is a common approach between England and the Continent is pedestrianization of the town centres, with common tales of initial opposition from shop keepers and motoring organizations, and ultimately a welcome acceptance of the improvements and benefits that such schemes bring.

From the 1984 visit ....

From Portland...... *LRT was seen as the most cost efficient way to carry increasing numbers of passengers compared to an all bus system.*

The 2 section articulated cars........are for low platform operation only. It was considered that high platforms would be too intrusive.

From Calgary....This line has resulted in increases of passengers ranging from 39% to 80% compared to the previous bus system.

From Edmonton..... The construction works for the LRT system were managed by a small project team, with a separate review team to carry out monthly monitoring of the consultants and the management teams. The review team included two senior European managers with extensive LRT experience, one from England and one from Germany.

Financial Policies..... There is now general acceptance that capital investment in public transport should be met entirely or very largely from public funds.

Public transport is now seen as an essential ingredient in city life and is being financed accordingly. This is in complete contrast to the UK where public transport is still subject to political oscillations.

From the 1985 visit to Nantes........

The Government were serious about tramways.

It is obvious that a great deal of attention (and money) has been paid to design detail.

The bus routes that ran parallel to the tramway were re-routed when the tramway was opened. There are bus routes linking points served by the tramway, but the bus takes a more circuitous route and acts as a feeder to the tramway.

With the introduction of the tramway the bus system was gradually reshaped to complement the tramway – not to compete.

The success of the tramway has promoted an order for 20 further articulated trams. Initially these will be used to lower the peak service headway

The Nantes tramway is proving itself to be very successful and immensly popular.

Provided close attention is paid to environmental aspects, detailed design and traffic management, a modern tramway can be introduced successfully within existing highway alignments.

Board, Greater Manchester Passenger Transport Executive, Manchester City Council, British Rail and consulting engineers Mott, Hay & Anderson. The Nantes tramway was of special interest since it was the first completely new tramway in a European urban area for many years when opened in 1985. The Report produced after the Study Visit concluded that 'Successful conurbation-wide public transport provision can only be achieved through co-operation by all local authorities in the area.' This point has never been in doubt in Greater Manchester, where, as already recorded, the 10 City and Borough Councils and all the main political parties have given full backing to the scheme at all times. Some of the more significant of their observations are recorded in the margins of these pages but a number of more fundamental attributes were also clearly recognised.

The two key attractions are flexibility and cost. Light rail is the only mode of transport, public or private, which is equally at home on a road or a railway for the transition from grooved rail in paved track to flat bottom T-rail on ballasted track can be made easily and imperceptibly. The vehicle which glides gently through a pedestrian precinct can also achieve high speed and acceleration on segregated railway. The ability to negotiate curves down to 25m radius or even less, and climb gradients of 6% or even more, make it comparatively easy to create new urban alignments which give good access to areas of major traffic generation. Any combination of different types of alignment can be linked to create new routes – existing or former railways, existing or proposed highways, median strips, landscape strips or other open spaces including derelict land.

The capital costs of new light rail lines depend very much on local conditions, and the level of civil engineering works required. In general, the costs are considerably lower than a fully segregated heavy rail system or metro, and substantially less than a highway with equivalent capacity. The high levels of productivity achieved by light rail make it possible to achieve break-even or even profit on direct operations, a situation unattainable on most urban rail systems. In cost-benefit terms, a well designed light rail line can probably provide a return higher than many other urban transport investments.

Other inherent advantages of light rail are those associated with electric traction. Low noise levels and absence of pollutants make LRT environmentally sympathetic. Smooth acceleration and deceleration contribute to high levels of comfort. Advanced electronics offer improved safety and reliability and reduced energy consumption.

Some or all of these advantages were seen in the various systems visited and members came back in no doubt that LRT clearly had as much to offer Greater Manchester and the rest of the UK as it had in Europe and North America.

Mott, Hay & Anderson subsequently carried out much of the engineering planning for the project. This encompassed aspects such as permanent way, alignment, geometric parameters, structural works, power supply and overhead line equipment, signalling and tele-communications, rolling stock, depot and stabling facilities. A draft working timetable based on the projected travel demand was then established, forming a framework for the operating plan and rolling stock requirements. Working closely with the Executive they also provided estimates of construction and equipping costs for individual routes of the proposed light rail system, together with a suggested programme for implementation.

The next, and crucial part, was the preparation of Parliamentary Plans for the street-running sections and for the conversion to light rail of British Rail's Bury and Altrincham lines. Here again Motts also assisted the Executive with the associated documentation for submission to Parliament in 1984 and 1985

All the pieces were now on the board – all that remained was for the Government to indicate that it would allow the light rail network to proceed.

All eyes are on the Minister of State as he considers the implications of additional costs in the Undercroft. The Passenger Transport Authority and Executive found Michael Portillo was extremely supportive of Greater Manchester's LRT proposals and his enthusiasm and determination to keep things moving forward in Whitehall was crucial to Metrolink's success.

On the opening of the Manchester Metrolink, Mott MacDonald is proud to have been closely involved with this prestigious project since 1982. Our services included preparing all Parliamentary Plans and detailed studies for extensions to Trafford Park, Salfords Quays Oldham and Rochdale town centres.

Our multi-disciplinary strength allows us to address all the civil, structural, electrical, mechanical and environmental aspects of light rail projects, from assessment to detailed design and commissioning - including representation at Public Inquiries and project support at Parliamentary and funding stages.

Other recent light rail commissions include:-

- Preliminary design, Parliamentary Plans and Environmental Statement for Nottingham Light Rapid Transit

- Tyne & Wear Metro Airport Extension and Sunderland Extension Study

- Plymouth LRT Pre-feasibility Study

Mott MacDonald - a commitment to excellence

For further information please contact:

Mr J G Grant
Mott MacDonald Ltd
St Anne House
20-26 Wellesley Road
Croydon CR9 2UL

Tel 081 686 5401

The Parliamentary Process

For centuries Parliament has had two different forms of legislation: Public Bills concerning the country as a whole, and Private Bills which concern more local matters. Private Bills came into prominence in the eighteenth century during the great canal building period because promoters often wished to do things which cut across the private rights of individuals. This has been a particular characteristic of linear developments. After the canals came the railways when the legislative pressures became more intense. From the inauguration of these transportation revolutions it has been possible for particular landowners to frustrate a canal or railway development by refusing to sell without recompense – which amounted to ransom – or because they did not much fancy a nasty, noisy, dirty, dangerous thing (ie a nuisance) on their land. In the case of tramways, rails laid in the road were classed as a 'nuisance'. So the promoter needed what would now be called compulsory purchase powers and protection from common law actions for nuisance. This, briefly then, was largely what the Parliamentary debates on railway schemes were about in the nineteenth century.

During the past 150 years, Parliament has developed ways of lightening its legislative burden. Mindful that more than 40 LRT proposals were under consideration Parliament decided that if its legislative process was not to be completely overtaken by the volume of work involved in those proposals, changes must be made in the method of enabling such schemes to be given approval. Also there was an obvious need to update much of the legislation under which Metrolink, for example, would have to operate. The Inspector in charge of the Metrolink Police at Queens Road may or may not be aware, for instance, that under Section 62 of the Town Police Clauses Act of 1847 he was, until 16th March 1992 'empowered to take the reins of any hackney carriage or tramcar (which within the Act would include LRVs) and drive the said vehicle to the nearest livery stables'. Many people will doubtless regret that neither he nor the members of his force will be able to perform this useful function in the future!

Recognising that whether it liked it or not, the tramcar seemed about to make a grand re-entry to Britain's streets, Parliament therefore decided that the famous 1870 Tramways Act, under which almost all the original tramways were built, should be taken down, dusted and revised or repealed. Since Metrolink was the catalyst for this action it was perhaps not surprising that the new Bill – the Transport & Works Bill of 1991 – got through the Upper Chamber only hours before Parliament was prorogued on the 16th March prior to being dissolved ready for the 1992 General Election.

This Bill was drafted on the recommendation of a Joint Committee of the two Houses and following its enactment as the Transport & Works Act 1992 it will reform the whole Private Bill procedure for obtaining Parliamentary powers for constructing LRT systems. The Private Bills procedure remains for other purposes.

Much railway law is of antiquity. Railways still work to Acts of 1871 and 1933 among others and, as alluded to above, tramway safety is dealt with in the 1870 Act introduced when the motive power was the horse. Other transport modes, such as the monorail once proposed for Manchester, are not properly dealt with at all.

In order to build the Metrolink system, then, it was necessary to obtain a Private Act of Parliament to provide the Passenger Transport Executive with powers to build the city centre sections, to compulsorily acquire land and property if necessary and to take over responsibility for operating the two British Rail lines. The last time a statute authorised a new street tramway in Great Britain was in 1948 to enable Glasgow Corporation to construct the Carnwadric route of its then extensive tramway system. The last Act permitting major street tramway track alterations was in 1949 to allow London Transport to make changes in connection with the 1951 Festival of Britain. The Acts sanctioning the construction of the Tyne & Wear Metro and the Docklands Light Railway treated those systems as railways for legal purposes. It was the street running aspect which made the Manchester system different from its two modern predecessors and made it the pioneer of its type in the country.

The proposals resulted in two Private Bills deposited in November 1984 and November 1985 respectively. Enactment of these on 9th February 1988 created the Greater Manchester (Light Rapid Transit System) Act 1988 and the Greater Manchester (Light Rapid Transit System) (No. 2) Act 1988. They refer to the Tramways Act of 1870 and its distinction between Tramways (on highway) and Tramroads (off highway, as in railway practice).

The first, and longest, Act gives power to make works and lists the various tramway and tramroad sections within the city centre, stating the gauge of 4ft. 8 ins. There is power to deviate, the inclusion of subsidiary works, and the statement that details of rolling stock are to be approved by the Secretary of State. The Act states that the the 1870 Tramways Act shall have effect subject to certain modifications. Other sections cover the

Very little compulsory purchase was necessary for Metrolink to proceed. In the Snow Hill area, below, some demolition of old property took place. The Executive was obliged to purchase the public house, a listed building, but has no plans to re-open it! A major property redevelopment is planned for this area.

distance between passing vehicles (not less than fifteen inches), reduction in the width of footways, stopping up streets, repair of streets, notice to police and provisions as to the use of electrical energy. The Executive is given the power to make byelaws and to charge for the use of the system. All the foregoing covers the Light Rapid Transit system itself. Other parts of the Act cover lands and their acquisition, and protective provisions for British Railways Board and the statutory undertakers.

The No. 2 Bill authorises an extension of the system consisting of a tramroad continuing from the end of the street section (Work 5 of the first Act) on the disused railway viaduct which once carried railway tracks to Central Station. There is a clause to permit British Rail to transfer any part of its existing railway system to the Executive, covering the Bury and Altrincham lines and no doubt with a view to proposals for extensions to Oldham, Rochdale, etc.

To date seven Private Bills have been deposited, though the numerical order is confusing. Numbers 1 and 2 have been referred to above and were enacted as the 1988 Act and the (No. 2) Act 1988. Greater Manchester (Light Rapid Transit System) Bill No. 3 of November 1987, covering the Salford Quays extension, was enacted as the Act of 1990 (un-numbered). The next Bill, of November 1988, (un-numbered) covered extensions to Dumplington via Trafford Park, Didsbury and works on the Oldham/Rochdale route. Mis-description of the Oldham/Rochdale railway led to the Executive effectively seeking to take over British Rail's rights to operate via the 1989 (No. 4) Bill. The 1988 Bill became the (No. 2) Act 1990.

Bill No. 4 of November 1989 was to allow revisions in the alignment on the Dumplington route, work to facilitate a temporary terminal outside of Piccadilly Station Undercroft, and powers to operate over the BR Oldham/Rochdale line. Assent is awaited at the time of writing. Bill No. 5 of November 1989, containing the Rochdale town centre extension, East Didsbury extension and additional land for temporary use during construction of the Salford Quays route was enacted as the Act of 1991. An un-numbered Bill of November 1990 covered the Oldham town centre link and has completed its passage through the House of Lords at the time of writing.

Bill Deposited	Act	Brief Description of Powers
1. Nov 1984	1988	Bury and Altrincham line conversion
2. Nov 1985	1988 No. 2	City Centre
3. Nov 1987	1990	Salford Quays extension
4. Nov 1988	1990 No. 2	Trafford Park, Chorlton, Oldham-Rochdale
5. Nov 1989	*	Revision to Trafford Park
6. Nov 1989	1991	Rochdale Town Centre, East Didsbury
7. Nov 1990	**	Oldham Town Centre

Notes:
*   No. 4 Bill   Awaiting Royal Assent.
**   1990 Bill   All stages in first House (Lords) completed.
                         Commons stages to commence in 1992.
                         Royal Assent expected late 1992/early 1993.

The Economic and Financial Evaluation

Another essential step in obtaining approval from the Government was to carry out economic and financial evaluations. The objective of an economic evaluation is to measure the increase in total benefits to the community from a policy decision such as investing in Metrolink. It is a method used in transport because a purely financial evaluation omits a significant proportion of the total benefits of transport investment. In some areas this is because there is no mechanism for reflecting benefits in terms of revenues received. This applies to roads, for example, where there is no direct charge each time a journey is made. In other areas, many of the benefits are enjoyed by the non-users of the system – often the community as a whole.

The economic evaluation of Metrolink therefore measured its costs and benefits to the community regardless of the source of the costs and the recipient of the benefits. The main sources of cost and benefit were: –

1. The capital cost of Metrolink.
2. The saving in capital expenditure which would have been needed to keep the Bury and Altrincham lines open.
3. The operating costs of Metrolink.
4. The savings in British Rail operating costs on the lines.
5. Some savings in bus operating costs and in the capital cost savings of not replacing buses which will result from service changes likely as a result of the introduction of Metrolink.
6. Time savings to passengers using the existing British Rail services.
7. Time savings to people switching to Metrolink from bus and car.
8. Reduction in congestion.
9. Reduction in accidents.

All of the costs and benefits listed above can be quantified and valued. Besides these there are other benefits which would be much more difficult to quantify, including environmental benefits (less noise, less pollution at the point of use, etc), economic regeneration and job creation.

To justify the scheme the Department of Transport required a full social cost-benefit analysis covering the following options: –

1. A base case in which the rail service would be replaced by buses.
2. Retention and modernisation of the existing railway lines.
3. Light rail transit (LRT).

Comparing modernisation with the 'base' would determine whether the Rail Strategy Study was correct in concluding that investment in retaining and modernising the lines as conventional railways was justified, and comparing LRT with modernisation would determine whether the extra investment in LRT was justified. This involved extensive modelling exercises using the Greater Manchester transportation model to predict the shift in patronage from bus to rail and the benefits passengers would gain from LRT which would take the form of time-saving on their journeys. In essence, a new network of public transport services, including LRT and revised bus services, was put into the model. The model assigned journeys to whichever of bus or LRT gave the lowest journey cost when both time and monetary costs were taken into account. Similarly, benefits to existing rail users were calculated. These comprised savings in journey times, shorter waiting times and, above all, walking time savings in the city centre. Estimates were made of the switch from private car to LRT and the reduction in congestion which would result. Finally, the impact on operating costs and revenues on all public transport (conventional, rail, LRT and buses) was evaluated.

The results formed the basis of the benefit estimates for each of the options and were compared with the estimated capital costs. A 30-year evaluation period was used with future costs and benefits being discounted to the base year using the then standard 7% Treasury rate. It showed that there was a case for retaining the lines as railways and converting them to light rail. Although LRT would involve higher capital expenditure than the existing rail services, this would in part be offset by savings in the costs of replacing the bus fleet, a factor that would become less important in the deregulated climate as more and smaller bus operators make their vehicles last longer and make more use of secondhand vehicles with transfers between associated companies. LRT operating costs were estimated (on the basis of Tyne & Wear Metro figures) to be lower than those of the former rail services even though over 50% more train mileage would be operated. Passenger time savings and additional revenue contributed the remainder of the benefits. This extremely complex work produced a benefit per pound of cost of £1.44 and formed the basis of a formal submission for grant which was made early in 1985 and marked the start of the funding operation.

At this time, however, two major pieces of legislation were being considered by Parliament; the 1985 Local Government Bill (which proposed abolition of the Metropolitan counties) and the 1985 Transport Bill (which proposed deregulation of bus services). Their enactment altered the structure of both the Passenger Transport Authorities and their Executives and changed the function of the Executives. As a result the Executive lost its powers to operate buses and specifically to co-ordinate public transport. It retained its powers to operate all other modes and gained new powers to promote public transport. Its relationship with British Rail and its general powers to promote LRT were essentially unchanged.

The impact on the LRT grant application was, however, fundamental. The Department of Transport, once it had evaluated the application, presented the Executive with a series of requests for further information with the most important area of concern being the effect of bus deregulation on the case for LRT now that the Executive was to lose its powers to determine all bus services. In the initial evaluation the Executive had taken the view that it would not base the case for LRT on major cost savings on the bus network as it appreciated that deregulation would constrain its ability to obtain them. However, the Department's concern was with the effect of deregulation on patronage once buses were free to compete with both British Rail and with the light rail system. This meant that the whole basis of the patronage and revenue estimates had to be re-appraised. In the event this involved a whole new exercise comprising the development of a new model of patronage, and carrying out a new passenger survey and new market research.

The Executive carried out much market research among bus and train passengers and car users making daily journeys to and from Manchester. This was used to 'model' people's reactions to different types of journey and in particular to LRT's penetration into the city centre, a feature the railways have not achieved in 150 years and which was important to motorists because of congestion and difficulty of parking. Buses could conveniently serve this purpose but they too were subject to traffic congestion. Only LRT could bring passengers much closer to their final destinations – offices, shops, entertainment, etc – in central Manchester without the disability of traffic congestion.

The new model of patronage based on research amongst passengers travelling on the Altrincham and Bury corridors used stated preference analysis. This is a research technique in which potential passengers are asked to choose between different journey characteristics which involve a trade off between cost, time and other characteristics. This allowed a corridor-specific demand model to be developed which could be used comparatively quickly to test the sensitivity of the results to a series of assumptions. It was necessary because at the time the effect of deregulation on the frequency and fares of bus services on the corridors was uncertain. The extensive and detailed passenger survey allowed, amongst other things, more accurate revenue estimates to be made. The new market research helped to estimate the likely switch from car to LRT and the number of new trips which might be generated.

Although the walk between Piccadilly and Victoria stations takes only about fifteen minutes, and either station is within ten or fifteen minutes walk of many parts of central Manchester, the research showed that users of the system would value the direct central area penetration more than time-saving alone would indicate. By combining the speed of the train with the access to and within the city centre which the bus provides, but without the congestion, LRT was considered well-placed to compete effectively with the bus and the car.

Whilst this work was being carried out bus deregulation came into effect on 26th October 1986. The impact was beneficial to the case for LRT which was an apparently paradoxical result and an unexpected one. Bus operators reduced the range of services on the corridors, and on the Bury corridor in particular they reduced the range of central area destinations served by direct services. Fares increased in real terms as did rail fares, but this allowed the creation of a firmer revenue base for LRT. In the event, patronage on the two British Rail lines increased by over 10% and this itself improved matters. The revised evaluation submitted in mid-1987 showed that the benefit per pound of cost had increased from £1.44 to £2.66. After many hours of technical discussions between the Executive's Economic Advisor and the Department of Transport's economists, in late 1987, the Secretary of State agreed that the scheme possessed a robust economic and financial justification and that, in principle, it would be able to receive a capital grant under Section 56 of the 1968 Transport Act.

The start of operation through the City Centre was the occasion everyone had been waiting for, and the smiles reflect the atmosphere on that occasion. Left to right are Cllr Jack Flanagan, Geoff Inskip, Cllr Clarke, Roger Hall, Cllr Harkin, Cllr Burns and Bill Tyson. The latter, now the Executive's Director of Planning and Promotion was its Finance Advisor from 1970 to 1990 and was responsible for the economic evaluations described here. "It was the most demanding piece of work I have ever done and on many occasions it felt as if it would never end."

Financial Evaluation

The level of detail obtained from the economic evaluation was insufficient for the purpose of a financial evaluation. It became necessary to obtain much more detailed estimates of revenues and operating costs of the proposed light rail system to determine the risk for private capital investment. This requirement prompted one of the most comprehensive surveys of rail passengers ever carried out in the Greater Manchester area and helped to establish how many people used the train services, their final destinations, whether they were changing to another train service, the type of ticket, rail card, concessionary permit, etc. The results of this survey, together with the market research carried out to estimate the likely transfer of trips from cars and buses, were then passed to the consortia which were to bid to design, build, operate and maintain the system. This data was scrutinised by their own experts and assisted them in the preparation of the bids.

As this preparation proceeded it became apparent that the capital costs were becoming greater than originally estimated for a variety of reasons. At a period of economic recovery, industries such as engineering and rolling stock manufacturing had full order books, causing prices to harden. Raw material prices were also increasing. It became necessary therefore to re-evaluate the project to ensure that the benefits had increased in relation to the costs. This took place in 1989 in close collaboration with the Department of Transport.

The project also required re-evaluation for another reason. The Government had changed its criteria for making grants under Section 56 of the 1968 Transport Act to projects like Metrolink. In the past such projects qualified for grant if they showed a satisfactory economic rate of return and where benefits exceeded their costs. The evaluation agreed in 1987 satisfied this criteria. Grant was given as a percentage of the agreed cost of the project. From 1989, grant was determined by (i) savings on public expenditure (for example as compared with existing rail services or subsidised bus services) and (ii) benefits which the project conferred on non-users (for example reduction in congestion costs, accident costs and contributions to economic regeneration). Metrolink was originally evaluated on the old basis using the economic appraisal; it now had to be examined on the new basis as well. Fortunately, it also passed this test.

The main lessons to be learned from Manchester's experience in making these evaluations are that the time and resources necessary to plan and finance LRT are considerably greater than originally envisaged; it is essential to retain a high degree of flexibility within a plan so that changing circumstances can be used to maximum advantage; and that planning and funding a line need to be done in very close conjunction with each other. Even on the later criteria which the Department of Transport applied to Section 56 grants, the evaluations demonstrated that Metrolink was justified because of the congestion and accident reduction benefits and the substantial savings to public funds from the avoided expenditure on local railway subsidies.

Sadly the European light rail vehicle building industry has passed by Great Britain. From a thriving tramcar industry in the first decade of the century, and a railway building industry which built extensively for export, Britain now experienced a situation in which there was only one British builder willing to bid for the Metrolink vehicles. The virtual elimination of tramway systems in the UK had resulted in the extinction of the tramway manufacturing industry, and the railway building industry was not geared to build small numbers of light rail vehicles at a price which was competitive with European mass-produced products.

The experience of Blackpool Transport Services Ltd, the sole survivor of modern tramway operation in Britain, highlights the problem. In the 1950s it purchased a fleet of single-deckers from railway builders Charles Roberts of Wakefield; in the 1960s it turned to MCW of Birmingham (for trailers); subsequently it was obliged to carry out major rebuilding of pre-war cars itself before undertaking a major exercise in building double-deck vehicles from new bus body components. Eventually it purchased new single-deckers from East Lancashire Coachbuilders of Blackburn (one of its principal bus suppliers) but the lack of volume orders results in a very high unit cost. And even at this latter stage it had to carry out much engineering – including bogie construction – in-house.

It would, of course, still be possible to design and build tramcars or light rail vehicles in this country but the market is so small, and each British LRT proposal envisages differing requirements for rolling stock, creating a situation where unit costs would become prohibitive.

However, increasing interest in light rail transit is being shown by several British cities and towns. By 1986 British Rail Engineering Ltd (BREL) had completed an extensive market research exercise to assess the likely future market for Light Rail Vehicles, and to review the wide variety of specifications then being developed around the world. From the research findings, BREL was convinced that there would be a developing market in the UK for Light Rail and felt that this would be stimulated if a full-sized demonstration could be arranged to show the UK rail industry's faith in British Light Rail. Accordingly, BREL approached the Passenger Transport Executive to seek its co-operation and assistance in staging such a demonstration within its area.

Although the Tyne & Wear Metro had been operating for several years, and the Docklands Light Railway was two thirds of the way through its initial construction contract, a demonstration which would include an indication of street running capabilities would have considerable merit. BREL realised that the chances of developing a British Light Rail design were remote at this time and that any vehicles produced in Britain would, at least initially, have to be to foreign design. This was reinforced by Blackpool's experience.

After reviewing a large number of designs, BREL concluded that the UTDC design being built at that time for the Santa Clara system in California was the closest to the likely requirements of the British systems then being considered. A UTDC car was on demonstration at the World Expo in Vancouver in the autumn of 1986 and plans were made to bring the vehicle to the UK when the exhibition closed. The plan was to run the car in the UK for about three weeks to demonstrate how a modern Light Rail system could be integrated into the urban landscape of a British city. Manchester was chosen as the preferred venue in view of its most advanced light rail proposals, hence the approach to the Executive. It was also planned to have the vehicle available for static displays in a number of other cities.

In its approach to the Executive, BREL indicated that co-operation was being sought also from British Rail, and that involvement was to be invited from a number of interested manufacturers and contractors, with each party being expected to meet its own costs. In the case of the Executive's involvement, this was limited to assistance in planning and demonstration, and in the publicity and public relations arrangements for the three week period.

In the event, the UTDC car was not available to be shipped to Britain and an alternative had to be negotiated with GEC Transportation Projects Ltd, Linke Hofmann Busch and the London Docklands Light Railway. The vehicle concerned was the last of the initial Docklands Light Railway cars, No. 11. This resulted in the demonstration being postponed until the spring of 1987.

Light Rail Vehicles are built extensively in France, Germany and Italy, but in both Britain and North America the lack of a domestic market has inhibited development and reliance has been placed on European technology, especially that from Germany. Accordingly, the DLR vehicles were built by Linke Hofmann Busch of Salzgitter, near Hanover, one of Germany's main builders of main line stock and Light Rail Vehicles.

The three week demonstration was named Project Light Rail and the sponsoring organisations were Balfour Beatty Power Construction Ltd, British Rail, British Rail Engineering Ltd, Fairclough Civil Engineering Ltd, GEC Transportation Projects Ltd and the Passenger Transport Executive. It is significant that all these bodies were to be involved to a greater or lesser degree in the construction of Metrolink.

Various possible locations in the Greater Manchester area were considered. The line finally selected was part of the Fallowfield loop between Gorton and Trafford Park, which was still operational as a freight route with about three freightliners per day. The section chosen for the demonstration was a two kilometre length between Hyde Road Junction and Sandfold Lane, south of the former BR Reddish depot. This section had originally formed part of the Manchester-Sheffield electrification and the overhead masts of the former 1500 volt dc system were still in place. Furthermore, double track was still in position, although by then only a single line was operated.

The original proposal to provide all the site accommodation and stabling facilities at the former Reddish depot was abandoned in favour of a point adjacent to Debdale Park, north of Hyde Road, the site of the former Hyde Road station and goods yard. It was considered that this site, although derelict, would be easier to secure, had good highway access, and would require relatively little preparatory work.

DLR car No. 11 was delivered, like its predecessors, from Hamburg to Kings Lynn and was brought from there by road to Ardwick, Manchester. Here, it was assembled on BR track and towed to the nearby Longsight depot for commissioning before being towed to the demonstration site at Debdale Park. DLR cars are operated by current collection from a third rail, and for the demonstration No. 11 was fitted at Longsight with a temporary pantograph for overhead operation.

New overhead equipment and masts destined for the Tuen Mun Light Rail system in Hong Kong was provided by Balfour Beatty Power Construction Ltd and examples of both span wires and bracket arms were included. Most of the two kilometre test track used the original former Manchester-Sheffield overhead masts with wire provided by Balfour Beatty and erected by BR staff. Emergency overhead structures were erected and bolted to the disused track adjacent to the running line. Power was provided by BR at 750 volt dc using a static class 303 Electric Multiple Unit, parked on the disused branch towards Fairfield Junction, to step down from the 25 Kv ac feeder from the Glossop/Hadfield line at Gorton Junction. The 750 volt dc supply was obtained from the class 303's traction motor circuits.

A low-cost temporary timber station, similar to others provided by the Executive within its area, was erected by Fairclough Civil Engineering Ltd close to the site of the former station. (After the demonstration the platform was moved to form part of a new station at Hag Fold, Atherton.) A selection of static exhibits included a new-style Glasdon passenger shelter, sections of typical sleeper track and grooved rail track, and a section of DLR third rail.

Project Light Rail was formally opened by David Mitchell, Minister of State at the Department of Transport, on Tuesday 10th March 1987 amid an impressive array of politicians and industrialists, including the Chairmen and Managing Directors (or equivalents) of all the sponsoring bodies. A number of officials from the Passenger Transport Authority and Executive were given a preview the previous day. During the following three weeks, over 10,000 people visited the demonstration including official parties from every conurbation in the UK. Several members of the DLR staff came to Manchester to see their own vehicle in service for the first time. On two weekends (14th/15th and 20th/22nd March) the demonstration was open to the public and a special bus service from Piccadilly Station was provided for which a small fare was charged. Media coverage was most encouraging.

During the three week period some 3,000 questionnaires were distributed to visitors who rode on the Docklands car and of these almost 600 were

A comprehensive LRT display area at Debdale Park was visited by several thousand visitors to Project Light Rail who found much of interest there.

There was considerable interest from transport professionals, politicians, enthusiasts and the general public most of whom took the opportunity to ride on the light rail vehicle.

returned for analysis. It was found that the general impression of the vehicle was good and most aspects were well received. Most criticism was directed at the comfort of the seating, but visibility and ease of access were highly rated. The operation and action of the doors was also criticised but these matters had already been recognised as unsatisfactory. The organisers claimed that the vehicle demonstrated a smooth ride, good visibility, a high level of comfort (though this was not borne out by the returned questionnaires!), low noise levels both inside and out, rapid acceleration, and smooth brakes. As such it proved a worthy prelude to Metrolink and a significant event in Manchester's transport history.

At the end of the demonstration the vehicle was towed back to Ardwick for the two halves to be separated and lifted onto low-loading road trailers for the journey to London. One half was taken through Manchester city centre, past the G-Mex centre, through St. Peter's Square and up Mosley Street to Piccadilly so that some initial impressions could be obtained of a Light Rail Vehicle in the City's streets, albeit about a metre above the road surface. Photographs taken during this journey were subsequently used as a basis for further artists' impressions for use in promotional literature. Thereafter, car No. 11 became the 'Royal Train' on the formal opening of the London Docklands system by H.M. The Queen. The dimensions of the Docklands vehicle are: length – 28 metres, width – 2.65 metres, height – 3.40 metres above the rail. Weight is 38.5 tonnes unladen and maximum speed is 80 km/h (50mph). Seating capacity is 84 with space for 139 standing passengers.

Project Light Rail had a significant effect in promoting the awareness of the Greater Manchester scheme, both locally and further afield. It encouraged a number of other cities facing problems from traffic congestion to seriously consider light rail as an option. There are at present over 40 British towns and cities where light rail systems are being actively contemplated with feasibility studies commissioned, Parliamentary powers received and grant applications submitted. Project Light Rail, in pointing the way to Greater Manchester Metrolink, heralded the revival of interest in light rail transport in Great Britain at a most opportune time.

The Docklands car made a good impression during its three-week operation in Manchester though passengers found the automatic (driverless) operation somewhat strange.

Having completed its detailed investigations, considered the findings and reports of the economic evaluation and satisfied itself that LRT was the correct choice the Passenger Transport Executive then waited to take its next step. The passing of the first Parliamentary Bills in February 1988 cleared the way for this. What was needed now was approval from the Government to seek Tenders for the construction of the system.

An announcement to the House by the then Secretary of State for Transport in July 1987 indicated that subject to the Executive involving the private sector in its proposal, and provided that any scheme met its criteria for a grant under Section 56 of the Transport Act of 1968, the Government would meet some of the agreed contract cost of the light rail system.

The final authorisation from the Secretary of State came in January 1988, allowing the Executive to invite tenders for Phase 1 of the LRT scheme which in June of that year became formally known as Metrolink, a name registered and held by the Executive.

Before further progress could be made it was therefore necessary to find a way of involving private sector capital. The ground rules were set by the government and were simple – there had to be a real transfer of risk to the private sector which had to invest its own money with no possibility of the public sector underwriting it.

The Department of Transport engaged Merchant Bankers Schroeders to advise on this matter. At the same time the Authority and Executive jointly commissioned their bankers, Kleinwort Benson, who had been advising the project since 1984, to examine options for introducing private capital. A range of options was produced by Kleinwort Benson, but in the end the Department of Transport adopted a method devised by its advisers which came to be known as DBOM – Design, Build, Operate and Maintain.

The principles of this unique contract are discussed in detail in Chapter 7 but the requirement was for a single contract to:

   – design and build the system

   – operate and maintain it for a period of years

A single price was to be the basis of the bids which would effectively consist of two elements:

   – the construction cost

   – a payment to the Executive for concession to operate the system.

The concession payment was to be used to offset part of the construction cost and was the private sector contribution. The bidders were taking the risk on themselves that they could make enough money out of operating the system to recover the money they had invested in paying for the concession.

The terms of the operating concession were crucial to this process. Again, extensive negotiations with the Department of Transport were necessary and resulted in a concession agreement in which the Authority and Executive specify:

   – minimum service levels

   – operating performance standards including reliability and crowding

whilst the contractor has freedom to set fares and operate a higher service level. The concession will last for 15 years.

To progress this concept the Executive decided to authorise the creation of a **Project Review** which would cover arrangements for tendering for the construction. Because no suitably qualified person was available within the Executive, Roger Hall, then Managing Director of Property Services with Greater Manchester Buses Ltd, was asked early in 1988 by David Graham to draft the project review and to advise how the tendering process should be managed by the Executive. His previous experience as a management consultant, then with large GM Buses contracts and his time with Costain gave him an insight into the contractual aspects.

The draft review proposed two legs to manage the process, one under the Director of Planning and one under a Project Group, to develop the scheme. This report to the Executive was approved and it was agreed that its author, Roger Hall, should work part-time with the Executive on pre-tender documentation and development. It was agreed also that the team members should be chosen on the basis of the skills required linked to the needs of drafting the specification and eventual tender evaluation, and that they should be seconded to the team.

Many hours of negotiations with the Department of Transport were needed to agree specific contract clauses and the many practical problems overcome to achieve the eventual result. In hindsight, the task of converting a tender into a contract was certainly under-estimated in the case of this so far unique 'Design Build Operate & Maintain' (DBOM) form of contract. The DBOM concept is discussed in detail in the next chapter. There were some differences in the views of each party's merchant bankers and advising consultants. For example, whereas the Executive wished for a five to seven year franchise, the Department wanted 30 years. A compromise of fifteen years was, as noted, eventually agreed.

Various forms of contract were examined, including samples from the Royal Institute of Chartered Surveyors. Advice on drafting the technical specification was sought from quantity surveyors Hannaby & Associates, James R. Knowles & Associates, British Rail and Mott, Hay & Anderson, and the Executive's legal department was involved. Many months of negotiation with the Department of Transport took place and the Executive was also discussing service patterns and technical requirements with the elected Passenger Transport Authority.

The Metrolink Project Group seen in May 1992. Left to right (standing): Richard Naylor, Tony Young, John Berry, Steve Burns, Liam McCarthy, Sara Frost, Richard Carr, Geoff Brierley, John Abbott, Phil Burrows, David Rumney, (seated): Mavis Sampson, Roger Hall, Joanne Ross.

During the discussions, the Department of Transport was keen to limit the degree of detail in the contract specification feeling that the bidders should be given maximum scope to produce innovative solutions to problems. The Executive's view was that it would be difficult to evaluate the tenders if there were no definite guidelines. With hindsight the Executive feels certain it was right, and for future schemes would urge the Government to allow it more control at design stage. It also believes that the main advantage of the DBOM contract, namely its ability to create an LRT scheme in remarkably short time, could be retained provided that extra time was made available for design consultation before the contract was let and work began. Many of the problems experienced by the various contractors on Phase 1 could have been avoided if, say, an extra six to nine months had been allowed.

While 'Design & Build' contracts had been used before – indeed the Besses o'th Barn bridge over the M62 is an example – and much experience of them was available, DBOM was largely a venture into the unknown. In the light of its experience so far, the Executive believes that a DBOM contract would be more appropriate on a 'green field' site rather than on a project which was installing a system on existing railways in every day use and into a major city centre. The sheer number of third parties such as statutory undertakers (electricity, gas, water, telephones), British Rail, Local Authorities and property owners imposed constraints which would make the task of building the system complex without a clear design brief being available at the outset. To combine these novel contractual arrangements with an already unique LRT project led to complications which may have been lessened by a more traditional approach. If the pre-design stage had been followed by the Executive's intended full design specification, there would have been far fewer problems at the construction stage, although the project would probably have taken longer to complete.

Options were limited, however, because the Government had taken the view that DBOM was the best solution given its commitment to introducing private risk capital in funding the project. David Graham decided that DBOM was the only course by which Metrolink could be achieved and in the light of these factors the Passenger Transport Authority and Executive felt that in the interests of progressing the system, taking advantage of grant support, it should progress it as rapidly as possible.

Ideally then, given the time, the Executive would have prepared a more detailed design specification with a more traditional form of contract, and the contractor would have built to that specification. There could then have been a separate contract to operate and maintain: this would require one tender for 'DB' and another for 'OM'. The Department of Transport's view was that the design construction with the operation would result in a better quality system.

Besses o'th Barn rail bridge over the M62 and A56 at Whitefield. This inverted T-section bridge is pictured shortly before withdrawal of the British Rail electric trains.

As the contract format developed the Department of Transport thus required the Executive not to specify a detailed design. The Executive came up with the idea of a **Reference Specification,** which was accepted. This was agreed as a basis for pricing, with the contractors being permitted to vary it according to their expertise. It was a matter of stating in outline what was required (for example, a high-floor vehicle with platforms and stations), on the basis that the contractors would know what to build in the light of their experience. There was very little light rail manufacturing experience and even less operating experience available. This would manifest itself throughout the project and is almost certainly one of the main factors contributing most to the delays in the system becoming operational.

A major feature of the bidding stage was the whole mass of information

Light Rapid Transit System Greater Manchester

Applications are invited from suitably experienced companies interested in being included on a select list of tenderers for a contract to Design, Build, Operate and maintain this first phase of the proposed Light Rapid Transit (LRT) system.

The first phase of the LRT system extends from Altrincham to Bury and embraces both the existing rail network and a new City Centre link. In a total length of some 19miles (31 Km) the on-street trackwork to be laid in City streets amounts to 1.7 miles (2.7 Km).

The works will, in addition to City Centre track works, include OHLE, signalling and controls, provision of LRT vehicles and civil works in connection with provision of one new viaduct and refurbishment of existing bridges, tunnels and embankments together with associated works of drainage, fencing and the construction of city centre LRT stations.

The value of the Phase I Capital Works including the provision of LRT rolling stock is anticipated to be in the order of £50m.

The operating concession granted to the successful tenderer will be for a fixed period of years with the ownership of the system, including the infrastructure and all the operating assets, remaining with the Passenger Transport Executive. The operating concession will include responsibility for maintaining these assets in accordance with standards laid down by the Passenger Transport Executive.

It is envisaged that the successful tenderer will be responsible for meeting the costs of operating and maintaining the LRT System and will receive all the operating revenues.

Tenderers will be required to specify the amount of public sector grant they would require. This will be based on the capital costs adjusted for the value attributed to the running of operations for the concession period.

A two stage tender procedure is to be adopted with Stage I tender documentation being available in October 1988 with a short listing of 2 or 3 tenders to be made following evaluation of Stage I submissions as presented in December 1988. Stage 2 tender documentation will be available byFebruary 1989. The Stage 2 tender period to extend to May 1989.

Commencement of the work is scheduled for no later than September 1989.

The Stage 2 tenderers will be required to submit fixed price bids on the basis of a construction period extending over approximately two years.

The intention is that tendering should be restricted to tenderers of proven capacity and experience in the construction and operations of transport systems. It is unlikely that any one company will have all the requisite skills and therefore potential tenderers are advised to consider the formation of a consortium to undertake the project.

An application for tender documents will not automatically ensure inclusions on the Stage I tender list.

An information pack will be sent on request to all prospective tenderers.

This scheme has also been advertised through the medium ofthe Official Journal of the European Communities.

Application for consideration should be made by 30th June 1988 to:

I.E.M Buttress, Director of Administration & Secretary, Greater Manchester Passenger Transport Executive, PO Box 429, 9 Portland Street, Piccadilly Gardens, Manchester M60 1HX. Tel: 061-228 6400

**Greater Manchester
Passenger Transport Executive**

necessary for the bidders, such as details of bridges and the survey of the alignment. All known information was assembled on a databank. As a safeguard for both sides this information was issued on the basis of a non-contractual survey. This databank proved to be a great help to the bidders and it saved them independently compiling essential records for themselves. With its databank of twenty volumes, the Executive believes that it has established more data than in any previous contract for a similar volume of work. It took over twelve months to compile the information for the databank.

The Department of Transport believed that in response to the 'reference specification', the bidders would bring forward new ideas, some of them innovative, hence its desire not to restrict them with a finely detailed specification. In the event there was very little change from specification when the tenders arrived. Although one of the tenderers suggested lowering the railway platforms for use with low-floor cars with street level doors the idea was not cost effective.

EC rules on tendering were followed. First, a pre-tender, enquiry package was advertised in the national and international press. About 140 responses were received, each of which was entitled to receive the package. These ranged from the 'local builder with a handcart,' to contractors of the calibre of the eventually successful consortium members. Following this the Executive decided to carry out a two-stage tender process. Stage 1 would not require fully detailed bids – which were expensive for bidders to compile. It would, however, serve to allow selection of the bidders for Stage 2 – on the basis of which the contract would be awarded. During the Stage 1 tender period, detailed discussions were held with the bidders, all questions and answers being logged to ensure that no later misunderstandings arose. One intriguing incident at this time was the interest expressed in bidding by a major UK vehicle manufacturer. In the event no bid had been received from this manufacturer by the closing date!

The enquiries were whittled down to twelve for Stage 1 tender listing, and of these eight were selected. Three tenderers withdrew, leaving the five consortia which submitted the tenders which were received and opened on 1st February 1989.

Tenders were submitted by:-

(i)   CIE Consult (the Consulting Division of Coras Iompair Eireann, the then national transport system of the Republic of Ireland, covering both rail and road passenger transport operation and the operators of DART).
(ii) The GMA Group (comprising GEC Transportation Projects Ltd, John Mowlem & Co PLC and AMEC plc).
(iii) The Norwest Holst Ltd, Hawker Siddeley Group plc, Rosehaugh plc (developers) and Ribble Motor Services Ltd Consortium.
(iv) The Trafalgar House Construction (Regions) Ltd and BREL (British Rail Engineering Ltd) Consortium.
(v)   The Trans-man RT Systems, Simon Carves Ltd, Alsthom International (Alsace Thomson-Houston Company), Henry Boot & Sons plc and Greater Manchester Buses Ltd Consortium.

The three consortia which withdrew were....

(i)   Transmark (Transportation Systems & Market Research Ltd) with Fairclough Engineering Ltd. [Note: Transmark is a wholly-owned subsidiary of British Railways Board].
(ii) TNT UK Ltd/Tarmac Construction Ltd
(iii) Wimpey Construction (UK) Ltd/ABB Traction AB (Asea Brown Boveri)

The tender evaluation process included consideration by a number of consultants and liaison with the Department of Transport, the Manchester

City Engineer, British Rail and the statutory undertakers responsible for gas, electricity, water and sewerage.

The evaluation was considered on four key elements, namely financial, contractual, operational and technical, for each of which a ranking order was produced. An overall assessment was achieved by bringing these together to form a final matrix which provided the basis for three bidders to go forward to Stage 2.

As it was necessary to work within the constraints of Government, price was clearly a major factor. Of the five tenders received at Stage 1, all from consortia which could be seen to be competent to handle the project, two were considerably higher than the remaining three. This was a major factor against them and, after all the other criteria had also been applied to the bids, the three lower bidders went forward to Stage 2. All the bids were considered to be first class but they ranged from £80-£150m.

The three consortia recommended by the Project Group to proceed to the second stage of tendering were the GMA Group and those led by Norwest Holst and Trafalgar House. These recommendations were accepted by the Authority and Executive.

For Stage 2 of the tender process the three consortia received additional data bank information together with updated tender documentation, and their submissions were opened by the Executive on 25th July 1989. The second stage bids varied only slightly from stage one, being still in the £80m bracket.

The moment of truth as the boxes containing the Stage 2 bids are opened at the Passenger Transport Executive's headquarters.

In January 1988 the Secretary of State for Transport made a statement in the House of Commons which effectively authorised the Passenger Transport Executive to proceed to invite tenders for Phase 1 of Metrolink involving the conversion of the existing British Rail Bury and Altrincham lines and connecting them with a link through Manchester City Centre. Whilst the Executive had anticipated that a separate operating concession would be awarded once the system had been built, in fact the authority to invite tenders was on the basis that the design/build and operate/maintain elements had to be dealt with as one single contract with all the assets, including the rolling stock, remaining in the ownership of the Executive. In preliminary discussions the Department of Transport was originally looking for an operating period of 30 years within the proposed Contract, whereas the Executive wished a shorter period of between five and seven years, as it did not feel that full value would be received in the public sector for a very long period. Eventually, a compromise period of 15 years was agreed. The Government believed that this approach would encourage the greatest private sector involvement. The Executive's Director General believes that the DBOM concept may well have resulted from the Government's unfortunate experience in connection with the funding of the Docklands Light Railway.

Following a two stage tender exercise, on the 27th September 1989, the Passenger Transport Authority, composed of elected members from each of the ten district councils of the greater Manchester area, decided that a contract be awarded to the GMA Consortium for the design, build, operation and maintenance of Phase 1 of the Greater Manchester Light Rail Project (Metrolink). This decision was made subject to the final approval of the Department of Transport being obtained.

As stated in Chapter 6 the concept of a single contract to design, build, operate and maintain (DBOM) a Light Rail Transit System is so far unique in the UK. Furthermore, the method of funding a passenger transport contract from a partnership of Government and private capital is also entirely new. Although it was not its original intention for constructing Metrolink it was because the Passenger Transport Authority accepted these principles that Manchester will have the first of a new generation of British light rail schemes including street running, which, at the present time, over 40 British towns and cities will hope to follow.

It is estimated that the DBOM approach saved between 3 and 6 months in the time taken for Metrolink to become operational. This saving of time and money should be borne in mind in any comment on the delays which occurred in opening the system, delays which were largely due to ensuring that the system would operate safely, delivery and commissioning of vehicles and training of operational staff.

In considering how the DBOM concept has worked to date, it is important to note that the Executive was restricted in what it could specify in the tender in relation to the construction and operating requirements, thus giving the consortium more freedom to design and build what it felt was appropriate. There were certain requirements which the Executive was able to specify including provision to be made for the mobility impaired, the need to utilise

"DBOM is probably the first contract of its type in the world and has, consequently, won world-wide attention" – Chris Mulligan, Director General, Greater Manchester Passenger Transport Executive.

existing stations, to provide new stations in the city centre and to provide power via overhead power lines in the construction phase. In the operation phase the Executive was able to impose on the tenderers the need to cater for the forecast number of passengers, to ensure all aspects were designed with safety and fire precautions in mind, and a requirement to meet certain service frequencies.

Whilst those closely associated with Metrolink appreciate that the DBOM concept has had benefits, not least a substantial reduction in costs due to the reduced number of LRVs required to operate the system (circa £12 million) – there remains the view that the application of the concept could be improved upon in future contracts.

It was hoped by Government that the DBOM concept might lead to the private sector taking all the risks associated with the project whereas in practice this did not happen. There was an option put forward by the tenderers involving full risk transfer to the private sector, which would have cost up to an additional £40 million. One of the most difficult aspects of the full risk scenario was that tenderers were expected to take account of any changes in legislation imposed during the period of the contract. Clearly this caused the tenderers some difficulty, principally because in a 15 year period, when there could be a number of changes of Government, it was impossible to foresee what changes in legislation would be imposed. If an operating concession had been awarded once the system had been constructed then some risks could have been more easily identified.

It is interesting to speculate on the reasons why the Government decided to use this new form of contract hitherto untried in public transport investment projects.

Manchester's experience suggests that if the design elements had been dealt with in a more conventional way and an operating contract had been awarded once the system had been constructed then the whole scheme might have been more manageable. One of the major difficulties with the DBOM approach is the fact that no one organisation had the necessary expertise to both design and build and then operate and maintain a light rail system – hence the consortium approach. In mixing the two it has led to practical difficulties between the various parties, some of which clearly might not have arisen if the contract had been split. However, there were potential benefits from a single consortium building and operating the system as the operator has to bear the risk of any revenue loss or cost increases arising from decisions made during the construction phase.

The DBOM contract, although only one contract, still had to be split between the design/build and operate/maintain elements. The design/build section allowed a two year period within which to have the system ready for commercial operation. The operate/maintain section is effectively the 15 year concession during which the system has to be operated and maintained. The important point to stress is that the two sections clearly are quite separate, but the same Contractor is involved in both.

A justification for separating the elements of the contract is that there is a need for design to be under the control of those with knowledge not only of the proposed LRT system but also the everyday workings of the city and its services. Even with close monitoring by the Executive and its consultants, area engineers and traffic controllers, situations have arisen which might have been foreseen and prevented with closer initial involvement. This, the Executive believes, is the crucial element needing recognition and acceptance for the benefit of future schemes.

One of the practical difficulties with the design and build concept is that concerning relationahips with other parties like British Rail. Detailed design only starts after the contract has been let and in some cases it was only when detailed designs were available that British Rail could subject them to the testing needed to meet its own safety requirements.

British Rail, faced with ever-increasing pressure to meet new safety requirements, had no foreknowledge of the contractors' precise intentions until the plans were available. It considered, rightly, that it must safeguard its own position by insisting on approval of those plans by its own staff and advisers before allowing access for work to begin at Victoria and Piccadilly Stations. This, inevitably, resulted in delay in starting work on crucial schemes – particularly Piccadilly Undercroft. With full design under the Executive's control these matters would probably have been dealt with in a rolling programme which would have benefited all parties and reduced delays.

The City also had a part to play which the contract originally excluded. Investment by the City Council and the Central Manchester Development Corporation will have enhanced Metrolink by a £3.75m upgrading. In the Undercroft at Piccadilly station, CMDC decided that it would provide substantial investment in a scheme to improve the appearance of the 'concrete box' where the LRVs terminate. Over £1.2m has been spent in this area. In Balloon Street the City has spent over £60,000 in upgrading the street paving.

The construction works funded by these contributions have had to be integrated into the original contract.

Writing this account before the building contract is complete makes it too early to judge the merits and demerits of the DBOM concept. Its full impact can only be assessed over the life of the construction period *and* the 15 year operating contract. The DBOM concept has given rise to some problems related in this chapter. Equally it has been the way by which private sector involvement was secured and this helped to strengthen the case for the scheme in the Government's eye. There have also been cost savings – for example from reduced rolling stock requirements.

It is impossible to foresee what problems might have arisen with a conventional contract. These have been avoided by the DBOM concept but, by definition, are impossible to identify.

What is clear is that the experience of the Metrolink contract needs to be evaluated fully by the Authority, Executive, and the Government to ensure that the lessons which can be learned are identified and put into practice on future contracts in Greater Manchester and elsewhere.

When the bids were opened and examined there were no surprises in store. The three bids were very close in financial terms – all around £80m – and it was necessary to scrutinise them closely to find their strengths and weaknesses, advantages and disadvantages. Evaluation reports were prepared and as at Stage 1 these were submitted to the Passenger Transport Authority and Executive.

After considering the reports both bodies gave approval to the recommendation that the GMA Consortium should be invited to undertake the Greater Manchester Metrolink Project, and the award was announced on 27th September 1989. The following 24th October, the then Minister of State for Transport, Michael Portillo, finally approved the scheme for the grant under Section 56 of the Transport Act of 1968 thus enabling the contract with the GMA Consortium to proceed. The formal signing eventually took place on 6th June 1990, itself a significant date, recalling the opening of the original City electric tramway system on 6th June 1901.

The Consortium and the Executive prepared the massive documentation which formed the contract. There were so many documents that the signing alone took some hours! The task of co-ordinating the contract document, agreeing the principles with the Department of Transport and negotiating the detailed contract clauses with the Consortium was led by Geoff Inskip, now Director of Finance at the Executive who comments, "We spent hours and hours, often until after midnight, in hard-headed tough contract meetings. And even when we had agreed the Department of Transport then scrutinised the contents. A big thankyou to all those involved especially for the spirit in which the negotiations were conducted."

Complex negotiations on the DBOM contract were necessary and it was, therefore, impossible to wait for all of it to be completed and signed with the result that construction work began six months before all the signing was completed. The contract is, in fact, in several parts. All the elements of a contract between the Executive and a newly-established consortium, together with a funding package made up of contributions from Central Government, the Authority and the constructing consortium added to the complexity of this unique form of contract.

Geoff Inskip, Director of Finance at Greater Manchester Passenger Transport Executive.

It is necessary to appreciate also the enormous amount of preparatory work, and the cost of that work, which was necessary to achieve the contract. The Passenger Transport Executive estimates that £2m had been spent before it was ready to seek tenders for the construction. Manchester City Council incurred considerable costs (estimated at £0.3m) in planning the co-ordination of Metrolink with its traffic strategy, planning the phasing of its other traffic management schemes, and planning the movement of the statutory services away from the Metrolink tracks to avoid disruption of the system once it is in operation.

The successful consortium affirms that to investigate, prepare design proposals and costings, and to submit these in the form of a tender also cost hundreds of thousands of pounds. There was then a further similar cost to reach the second stage of tender. It is important to record that all this work was speculative up to this point and that the unsuccessful tenderers must have incurred similar costs. It is clear from these figures that a very large amount of time and money was required to be incurred long before any construction work can begin. The investment is only realised when the scheme comes to fruition. Greater Manchester's scheme was unique in many ways and therefore had no precedent for prior consideration.

The detailed method of submitting tenders, examining and considering the documents and then receiving presentations from the hopeful tenderers was time-consuming for the many people involved. This preparatory phase was, however, a vital part of the process and one which might have benefited from even more time and resources than it was possible to make available to ensure that the interests of all parties were fully considered and adequately covered by the contract.

When the GMA Group was originally assembled during the summer of 1988, the leading member was GEC Transportation Projects Ltd. Indeed, at Stage 1, Alsthom was a member of a competing consortium led by Simon Carves Ltd. That consortium also included Greater Manchester Buses Ltd (GMBL) for experience of operating passenger transport. At Stage 1 the GMA Group did not include an operator, and during the Stage 2 tendering period GMBL joined the GMA Group to provide operational experience.

The amalgamation of the power systems interests of GEC and Alsthom formally took place on 1st April 1989 under the company name GEC Alsthom Transportation Projects Ltd. The name Alsthom is derived from the Alsace Thomson-Houston Company, the French counterpart of the British Thomson-Houston Company (BTH) which itself was subsumed into GEC many years ago. It is noteworthy that BTH powered the first electric trams in Manchester in 1901.

The successful tenderer, then, was known as the GMA Group, consisting of GEC Alsthom Transportation Projects Ltd, a subsidiary of the GEC plc; John Mowlem & Company PLC; AMEC plc and GM Buses Ltd. GEC Alsthom was responsible directly or through its sub-contractors for the vehicles, the power supply system, signalling, telecommunications and the fare and ticketing systems. Similarly Mowlem carried out, or sub-contracted, the constructional work on the Cornbrook Viaduct, the G-Mex Viaduct and the bowstring arch bridge over Great Bridgewater Street, and civil and building work on the stations, together with the construction of the city centre track and alignment. AMEC, through its subsidiary Fairclough Civil Engineering Ltd, constructed the Operations and Maintenance Centre, consisting of the depot and offices at Queens Road, Cheetham Hill, Manchester.

GEC and Mowlem had joined forces to bid for London's Docklands Light Railway project in 1983. This was a design and build contract for the London Docklands Development Corporation (LDDC), and it was a condition that the project must be completed for a fixed sum. Whilst LDDC was the client, the operator was to be the Docklands Light Railway Company Ltd, then a subsidiary of London Regional Transport. GEC and Mowlem thus had experience of designing and building a light railway in the UK.

GEC Alsthom Transportation Projects Ltd is based in Trafford Park and is thus a major employer in the area, with another factory in the North West at Preston. AMEC plc is probably better known through its subsidiary Fairclough Civil Engineering Ltd, based at Adlington near Bolton. These companies have extensive interests in the North West and have been associated with many major civil engineering schemes such as the construction of motorways and railway bridgeworks, including the inverted T-section bridge on the Bury line over the M62 at Besses o'th Barn.

Greater Manchester Buses Ltd is a company wholly-owned by Passenger Transport Authority. (As already stated the Executive ceased to be an operator from 26th October 1986 as a result of the Transport Act of 1985 which required, inter alia, a company to be formed under the provisions of the Companies Acts. The shares were then transferred to the Authority.) Although there has been substantial competition in Greater Manchester since bus deregulation in October 1986, GMBL remains the largest operator. It operates extensively in the Altrincham and Bury corridors and into the two interchanges. GMBL worked also on the rail replacement services introduced during the construction period after British Rail operation ceased, together with the North Western Road Car Company Ltd and A. Mayne & Son Ltd on the Altrincham route and Rossendale Transport Ltd on the Bury route.

GEC Transportation Projects Ltd sub-contracted the production of the vehicle bodies and bogies to the Italian Firema Consortium based in Milan, a group of six companies which between them design and produce electric and diesel electric locomotives for heavy rail and electric railcars and trailers for suburban and inter-city services, together with all types of rolling stock. The companies comprising the consortium are Officine di Cittadella spa and Officina Meccanica della Stanga spa, both of Padua; Casaralta spa of Bologna; Fiore spa and Officine Casertane spa of Caserta; and Firema Engineering srl of Naples and Milan.

The GMA Consortium, now including GMBL, together with the Passenger Transport Executive, formed a company with the title Greater Manchester Metro Ltd (GMML), which was incorporated in March 1990 and now forms the operating company. The Executive's involvement in GMML is a minority interest. However, as owner of the system it clearly requires representation and earlier advice from the Merchant Bankers was that an Executive shareholding would be received positively by private sector companies bidding for the concession. GMML will operate the system under contract to the owner, the Executive. The first three executive directors were Eric A. Black OBE, Chief Executive; D. Scott Hellewell, Operations Director and T. Don Kenny, Commercial Director. Following the retirement of Eric Black at the end of March 1992 Chelvin J.Hibbert was appointed to the position of Chief Executive.

GMA had now to set in motion the building of the system and no time was lost – indeed with a scheduled 24 month contract from start to completion there was no time to be lost. Here was one of the weaknesses. Pressures of time would hinder the contractors right through the scheme and some work proved abortive due to the need to keep working against the clock.

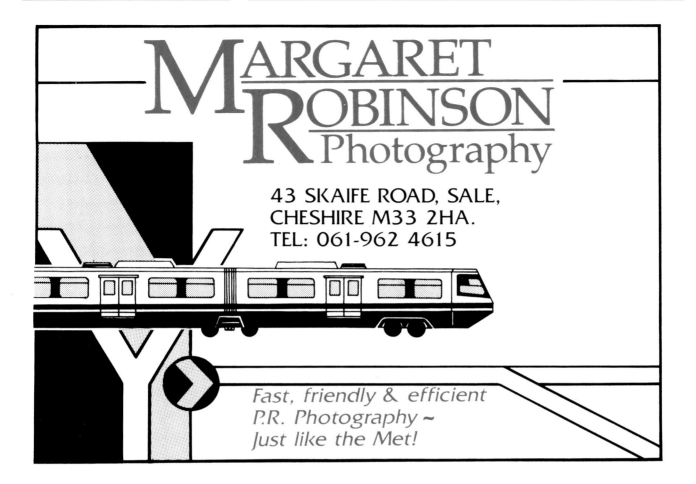

GMA's Project Manager David Cox has been working on the Metrolink project for four years. Previous light rail experience during his 18 years with Mowlem includes his term as Sub-Agent for the cut-and-cover tunnel section of the Tyne & Wear Metro at Byker. David Cox heads the Design and Build team, reporting to the Supervisory Board of GMA comprised of Directors of Mowlem, GEC and AMEC. Input from WS Atkins Design, Architecture and Quality Management divisions is also his responsibility.

He remarks, wryly, that a contract involving £100m of design, build and commission work to be carried out in a two year period "can be regarded as a challenge in anyone's terms" and confirms that "Metrolink has been a very demanding project". He firmly believes that only by having the one (DBOM) contract could the pace have been maintained – "during the first four months of 1992 daily meetings between the various parties have been necessary to keep the project moving".

Recognising that there will always be criticism of any project, he nevertheless finds it annoying that critics ignore the major achievements "on top of everything else 120 existing structures, some of which are multi-span, have been refurbished on the railway lines, for instance. Where high technology is involved there will always be problems, but the solutions pave the way for the future. The DC immunisation of BR signalling circuits is just one example."

He wishes to place on record his recognition of David Graham's vision – "the structure of the scheme that he envisaged and its translation into reality has worked extremely well. He had a very clear idea and it has worked".

Having been involved in Metrolink from the very beginning, even before tenders were invited, David Cox has seen the whole project, from concept to completion, through the builder's eyes. He recalls the division of the DBOM Contract to create GMML as the Operate and Maintain arm, headed by Eric Black, whilst he continued to lead the Design and Build team, and confirms that "the relationships between GMML and GMA have stood the test of time".

In 1989 work began on moving the underground services in the City Centre, thus ensuring that the trackbed of the new tramway should be kept free from roadworks in the future. The upper photograph shows the start of the work, in Piccadilly, in September 1989, whilst the lower picture gives some idea of the network of pipes and cables below the road surface.

The first phase of Metrolink comprises three sections; the existing railway between Bury and Victoria Station, the new City Centre sections, and the rail alignment from G-Mex to Altrincham. The Bury and Altrincham lines unlike most other suburban lines in Greater Manchester were constructed primarily to serve local suburban journeys, and for that reason are well located in relation to the development in those two corridors.

The Bury line formed part of the original Lancashire and Yorkshire Railway, but for over 20 years was operated independently from the rest of the British Rail network, in effect as a segregated rapid transit line.

The Altrincham line originally formed the Manchester South Junction and Altrincham Railway, built jointly by the London and North Western Railway and the Great Central Railway. The City Centre sections follow mainly highway alignments, with a few short sections off highway across land which was either semi-derelict, or used for car parking, or where some demolition was required. However for the length of system, a remarkably small number of buildings had to be demolished.

The Bury Line

The northern terminal is at Bury Interchange, opened in 1980 to replace the former Bolton Street Station to the west of the town centre. Bury Interchange stands on land formerly occupied by the market and abattoir which were closed and demolished in the 1970's. It was originally conceived as one of the northern terminals of the Picc-Vic tunnel network, and was the only major component to be retained when Picc-Vic was finally abandoned in 1977. Bury Interchange is now regarded as a showpiece, and has received visitors from all over the world. Relatively little change has been necessary to convert it to the northern terminal of Metrolink.

From the Interchange, adjacent to the pedestrianised town centre shopping area, the line heads southwards using part of an old rail alignment under Manchester Road to join the former line to Bolton Street at Bury South Junction which is still in place giving access to the Bury Electric Motive Power Depot. This depot was due to close with the opening of Metrolink, but

Interior of Bury Electric MPD. Note the absence of the third rail – the car sets were hauled in by capstan-driven ropes and rolled out under gravity.

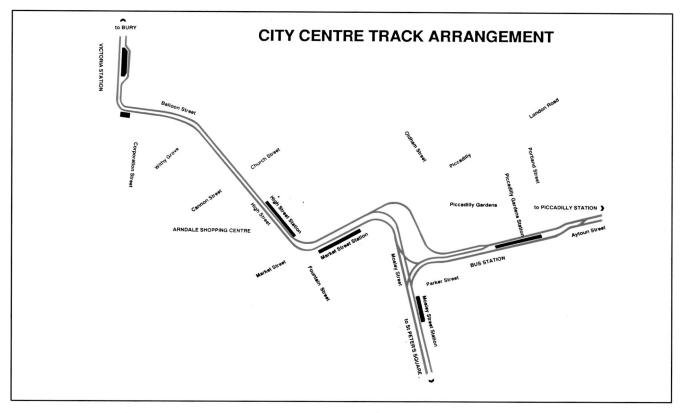

CITY CENTRE TRACK ARRANGEMENT

A schematic diagram of the City Centre layout from G-Mex to Victoria, with the spur to Piccadilly Undercroft.

LRV number 1013 at Bowker Vale during a training run. Note how low the pantograph is on this section when compared to photographs taken in the city centre where double-decker buses and high box vans need clearance below the overhead wires.

The above view, taken from the roof of the CIS building, shows three LRVs on the Bury line, outside Victoria Station. The centre vehicle is held in the siding waiting for a path through the station. It will then continue driver training duties between Victoria and G-Mex.

The exit from Victoria Station, through the 'hole-in-the-wall', showing the wide paved area between the station and Corporation Street.

was retained for commissioning and modifying the Metrolink LRVs after their arrival from Italy. The amount of work required in a restricted timescale meant that insufficient workshop space was available within the Operation & Maintenance Centre at Queens Road. Part of the land may be used for a proposed new park and ride station to be called Bury South to be built to the southeast of the existing depot. This station would also serve the residential area and schools within a short walking distance.

The line continues southwards through relatively open country, crossing the River Irwell, and Hagside level crossing, one of three vehicular crossings on the existing rail alignments. The next station is Radcliffe where extended park and ride facilities have been provided and, like all other existing stations, facilities for access by disabled people are included as part of the Metrolink contract. In this case, as in most others this is achieved by providing ramps. From Radcliffe the line recrosses the River Irwell on viaduct and then enters a long cutting to reach Whitefield Station after a short tunnel beneath Bury New Road. In the early days of the Executive, Whitefield had been considered as a major bus/rail interchange with a bus station built over the railway in the manner adopted in Hamburg and Toronto. This proved to be too expensive, and a cheaper bus station was provided on the north side of Stanley Road. A new car park is planned alongside the station.

The line continues through Whitefield to Besses o'th Barn, the only intermediate island platform station, and one that requires lift access for mobility impaired people. Although it is close to the M62 Motorway, and would be an ideal location for a major park and ride facility, there is unfortunately no spare land in the area.

An unusual design of an inverted 'T' section concrete structure carries the Bury line on a single span across the M62 Motorway to head for Prestwich and on to Heaton Park. Lifts have been provided at Heaton Park station to facilitate access. The line enters a tunnel beneath Heaton Park itself, where the sole survivors of Manchester's original tramway operate on Sunday afternoons, before emerging to reach Bowker Vale Station. After crossing over the A576 Middleton Road the line continues through residential areas to Crumpsall and on to Woodlands Road, passing within a short walk of the Cheetham Hill shopping area, and the Abraham Moss Centre (AMC) where an additional station may be provided in the future. This would replace the next station at Woodlands Road, and a further new station has been considered for Smedley, near Queens Road. The line passes under Queens Road, Manchester's intermediate ring road, at a point where the depot lead gives access to the O&MC which has been built on the former British Rail Queens Road sidings.

A brick and steel viaduct carries the Bury line over the Victoria-Thorpes Bridge line, part of which would form the proposed light rail alignment to Oldham and Rochdale. This will link in to the Bury line at Irk Valley Junction using a short section of abandoned viaduct, where the line crosses the River Irk. It then descends into Collyhurst Tunnel, alongside the A664 Rochdale Road, before emerging adjacent to the main line between Miles Platting and Victoria to approach Victoria Station under Cheetham Hill Road Bridge. The Bury line terminated in Platform 5 at Victoria, Platforms 1 to 4 having been cleared as a Picc-Vic working site back in the early 1970s, although an emergency electrified bay was retained into Platform 4. At this point the realigned Metrolink tracks swing further north towards platforms 7 and 8, before swinging southwards to leave Victoria station at Long Millgate, crossing Corporation Street to the start of the first street track in Balloon Street.

The sole survivor of Manchester's tram fleet, 953 strong at its maximum, is based in the City's Heaton Park and operates on the tourist/museum line on Sunday afternoons during the summer season. Number 765 was built in 1914 and was restored in the 1970s. It was withdrawn from service in 1930 shortly after the arrival of the new General Manager, Robert Stuart Pilcher, and his decision to replace the tram fleet with buses. The success of his conversion of the busy 53 route, almost encircling the city centre (and passing what is now the entrance to GMML's Operations Centre), paved the way for wholesale abandonment, only interrupted by World War 2, and completed shortly afterwards.

Balloon Street's impressive Victorian buildings contrast with the modern LRVs. This is the most steeply graded section of the Metrolink system, and the area is scheduled for future redevelopment which, if achieved, will result in the tramway passing through the new Galleria complex.

Nicholas Croft is too narrow to allow complete segregation of road and rail vehicles. Buses share the roadway with other traffic here, and traffic filtering in from Back Turner Street and High Street finds itself alongside the LRVs.

The raised section of the platform, giving direct access to the saloon of the LRVs, can be seen in this view in Market Street, Manchester. Where pedestrians will regularly cross the road and wish to have access behind the platform a continuous step has been provided along the front of the lower section, as shown.

Mosley Street at its junction with Market Street shortly after operation began between Bury and G-Mex.

Manchester City Centre

A number of options for City Centre routes were considered in the Rail Strategy Study between 1982 and 1985. Streets considered as possible light rail routes included Cross Street, Corporation Street, Cannon Street and Piccadilly. Having examined all the relevant factors, particularly the effect that light rail operation would have on other traffic movements including those of buses and pedestrians, a three-leg route was defined with a central triangular junction at Piccadilly Gardens which forms the hub of the Metrolink network.

From Balloon Street opposite Victoria Station the line runs on-street for a short distance. Other traffic will be permitted although only for local access as Balloon Street was closed at its junction with Corporation Street many years ago. The line then crosses Dantzic Street to Snow Hill where demolition of a number of old properties was required. This was the only area of significant demolition in the first phase. The alignment has been designed to enable an additional station to be provided at Shudehill in the future, in the event of the proposed major redevelopment taking place in this area. This would also provide a convenient interchange location for the Arndale Bus Station, on the opposite side of Shudehill.

The line re-enters the street at the Shudehill/Nicholas Croft junction to gain access to High Street where the tracks run in the centre, but segregated from most other traffic movements. At the Cannon Street/Church Street junction the tracks swing to the east side of High Street with a platform provided for southbound trains, adjacent to Debenhams Store and opposite the Arndale Shopping Centre. The tracks curve sharply into Market Street, between the two major department stores, Lewis's and Debenhams, to reach the triangular junction at Piccadilly Gardens. A platform for northbound LRVs is located in Market Street adjacent to Lewis's. There is insufficient space to have allowed both stations to be built in Market Street.

The spur to Piccadilly Station leaves the triangular junction to run along

Manchester's City Centre showing the track layout from Market Street, lower right, leading down Mosley Street, centre right, and also through Piccadilly Gardens (using the delta junction) in the centre of the illustration. The line to Piccadilly BR Station crosses Portland Street alongside the Passenger Transport Executive's offices (outside which four buses stand in line waiting to enter the bus station) and comes out of our picture at the top left. Photograph by John Fox reproduced by courtesy of Manchester Evening News.

Contrasting shades of block paving indicate the areas where pedestrians may walk at all times, coloured red, and the LRV's swept path, coloured buff/grey.

One of the trials before operation could begin entailed running two LRVs side-by-side over the whole of the City section in order to check that all clearances were correct. Here the two vehicles in question wait to leave Aytoun Street, both bound for Piccadilly Gardens.

the north side of Piccadilly Bus Station, adjacent to Piccadilly Gardens, with an island platform to give interchange to the large number of bus services serving this area. Some 3,000 buses per day pass through this bus station.

The line crosses Portland Street opposite the former County Hall, now ironically named Westminster House, and alongside the Executive's headquarters where Metrolink was conceived. This will be one of the most complex signal-controlled junctions on the system. The tracks run in side reservation on the southwest side of Aytoun Street, to the junction with Auburn Street where they swing south-eastwards to cross vacant land, previously used for car parking, to cross Shepley Street, now closed, before reaching London Road near its junction with Blaydon Street, also now closed at this point. This section of London Road had a complex tidal flow traffic management scheme incorporating kerb side bus lanes in both directions, withflow southbound, withflow northbound as far as Whitworth Street, and contraflow north of Whitworth Street. This section of London Road had to be redesigned, removing the tidal flow scheme but retaining a northbound bus lane. The Metrolink tracks run down the west side of London Road for a short distance before crossing the main traffic flow under signal control to gain access to Piccadilly Station Undercroft opposite the junction with Whitworth Street. The Undercroft station has lift and escalator links to the BR mainline concourse and also a pedestrian link to Platforms 13 and 14. The Metrolink tracks continue for a short distance into the Ashton Street Tunnel which will eventually give access underneath the mainline BR platforms to emerge at Sheffield Street for the eastern extensions, the details of which are yet to be determined.

From the Piccadilly Gardens triangle the third leg of the City Centre system runs along Mosley Street as pure street tramway, although most other vehicular traffic has been removed apart from northbound buses. After crossing Princess Street and running alongside the Peace Gardens the tracks reach St Peters' Square where a new station with individual platforms is provided between the Cenotaph and the Central Library, and close to Manchester's Town Hall. This station has been finished in Portland Stone to complement its surroundings. Most traffic around the square has been

removed, apart from a northbound busway, and a single lane for southbound traffic from Princess Street. In addition to providing for Metrolink, the pedestrianised areas have been extended.

After crossing the Oxford Street/Peter Street junction, the tracks run along Lower Mosley Street alongside the former Midland Hotel, crossing Windmill Street and then leaving the highway alignment to join a new ramped viaduct alongside G-Mex, to reach the high level viaduct structure across Great Bridgewater Street to the south of G-Mex itself. Design in this

Mosley Street in more leisurely days, before the Great War. A southbound open topped tram passes the Art Gallery.

St. Peter's Square in the mid-'thirties. A tram from Didsbury makes its way to Piccadilly, passing the almost complete Town Hall extension.

area was subject to approval by the Royal Fine Arts Commission and the viaduct ramp has been carefully designed to match the original structure of Central Station as now restored to form the G-Mex Exhibition Centre. The pre-cast concrete structure of the viaduct was subsequently brick faced to complement the existing building and arches and C. V. Buchan, an AMEC company, manufactured the infill panels. Mowlem submitted the scheme for a design award in April 1992.

The tracks then skirt the southern edge of the high level area, formerly

Mosley Street in March 1992. The LRV is on driver training duties

St. Peter's Square in May 1992 soon after City Centre operation began.

Facing page: The impressive outline of the Town Hall Extension forms the backdrop to this view of cars entering and leaving St. Peter's Square. During this pre-operational period a full timetable service was operated, without passengers, to ensure that everything was functioning correctly.

Lower Mosley Street was widened and its traffic flows amended to allow vehicular access to the car parks on the left. The new home for the Hallé Orchestra will be built here. Only buses or road vehicles requiring access to the Casino in the Midland Hotel are allowed to use the roadway shared with the LRVs. The Bowstring bridge and its access ramp are prominent alongside the G-Mex centre.

On 28th April 1007, still decorated from inaugurating the service through the City the previous day, became a 'Special Car' and undertook a proving run to test the feasibility of running private charter vehicles in amongst normal service operation. The Railway Inspector (right) joined the party which included left to right, Geoff Brierley, Steve Firth, Paul Neal, John Hart, Andy Morris (hidden), Keith Williams, Scott Hellewell, Tony Young, Richard Naylor, Geoff Inskip, John Berry and Kit Holden. A Silver Wedding Anniversary and four birthdays all falling that week had prompted the idea. Enquiries for Charter Cars will be welcomed by GMML.

First of the fleet leaves the G-Mex ramp at the point where the girder rail of the street tramway begins. The fleet numbers are still positioned as applied in building before sponsorship required their re-positioning to allow name transfers to be fitted.

used for car parking, to reach a new Metrolink station at G-Mex, at the northern end of the Deansgate Station footbridge providing interchange with British Rail services on the Warrington and Windsor Link lines to the north west, and all services eastwards to Oxford Road, Piccadilly and beyond.

The Altrincham Line

The former Central Station approach viaduct, which was built for the Cheshire Lines Committee and closed in 1969, is used by Metrolink to reach Cornbrook Junction. There are in fact three parallel viaducts over this route, the southerly line being used by the existing British Rail services, the central viaduct now used by Metrolink, and the northern viaduct which is not proposed to be used at present.

After passing over the Castlefield line at Castlefield Junction, crossing Egerton Street and the Bridgewater Canal, the line runs alongside Pomona Docks where a new station may be built in conjunction with future developments. At Cornbrook Junction, an under-pass takes the Metrolink tracks beneath a realigned Warrington line before rejoining the Altrincham line itself. As part of the Metrolink Phase 1 works, some preliminary works have been provided for a grade separated junction with the branch to serve Salford Quays and/or Trafford Park.

From Old Trafford the tracks follow the existing railway, crossing the former Cheshire Lines Fallowfield Loop and Midland main line, part of which is earmarked as the Metrolink line to serve Chorlton and Didsbury. It will be reached by ramps down from the Altrincham line just south of Old Trafford Station, which has been renamed Trafford Bar. The next station at Warwick Road serves the Old Trafford Cricket Ground and Manchester United Football Ground and has been renamed Old Trafford. The line carries on to Stretford where it runs parallel to the Bridgewater Canal for much of

Facing page: Castlefield, showing the railway viaducts, Bridgewater and Rochdale canals and the area currently being redeveloped through financial assistance obtained by the Central Manchester Development Corporation.

Cornbrook Underpass nearing completion as Balfour Beatty level the track and ballast for the Metrolink LRVs. A British Rail class 158 Sprinter passes overhead heading towards Manchester on the line serving Warrington and Liverpool.

its journey to Altrincham, crossing over the River Mersey flood plain and underneath the M63 Motorway to reach Dane Road Station, Sale. The possibilities of providing strategic park-and-ride sites in this location are being examined. The next station, at Sale, serves the town centre, while the line heads on southwards to Brooklands and Timperley. Another possible new station, roughly midway between Brooklands and Timperley, at South Brooklands is being investigated.

South of Timperley the short section of single-line starts because of the restricted alignment width between Deansgate Lane level crossing, where the British Rail line from Stockport runs parallel to Metrolink, and Navigation Road. This is operated as two single-line sections side by side, an operation further complicated by the level crossings at Deansgate Lane and Navigation Road. South of Navigation Road a four-track formation enables both BR and Metrolink to revert to double-track.

The station at Navigation Road now operates as a single platform on the west side used by Metrolink trains in both directions whilst the east side platform is used by BR trains on the Chester service, again in both directions. Additional car parking is to be provided with provision for further expansion should demand increase in the future.

The line passes under the A560 Woodlands Road to reach Altrincham Interchange, a four platform station which remains in BR's ownership, with two platforms for the passenger service between Stockport and Chester and two platforms for Metrolink trains. The Metrolink platforms on the west side of the station are adjacent to the bus station which forms part of the interchange and was the Executive's first major bus/rail interchange when opened in 1978. Proposals for a major shopping development may eventually provide the opportunity to create direct access between the Metrolink platforms and an upper-level shopping concourse.

End of the line – Altrincham station with a Chester-bound BR sprinter in the background. The photograph was taken on 14th May 1992 on the occasion of the official inspection by the Railway Inspector.

Work began at Timperley before withdrawal of the British Rail trains, and the lift installations can be seen in the course of construction in the upper photograph. The scaffolding and steps to the right provided temporary access to the canal towpath. In the lower photograph little has changed since the BR trains were withdrawn on Christmas Eve 1991. New station signs together with the application of insulating membrane on the station platform are the most obvious items. A different colour is used to indicate the disabled loading point. The passenger shelter and projecting platform edge for easy wheelchair access are also noteworthy.

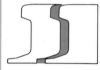

Extent of the system

This first phase Metrolink system is 31km of route, comprising 15.86km (9.86 miles) of the Bury line, 12.33km (7.66 miles) of the Altrincham line including the former Central Station Approach viaduct, and 1.98km (1.23 miles) of street section between G-Mex and Victoria making a total between Altrincham and Bury of 30.17km (18.75 miles). The spur to Piccadilly Station is an additional 0.73km (0.45 miles).

Provision for extensions has been made for the Oldham and Rochdale line at Irk Valley Junction, for the east side lines to Ashton, Glossop/Hadfield and Marple at Piccadilly Undercroft, for the Salford Quays and Trafford Park lines at Cornbrook Junction, and for the Chorlton/Didsbury line south of Old Trafford. If all these lines come to fruition, the Metrolink network could ultimately extend to some 120km.

The polymer-bonded rail gives way to sleeper track at the head of the G-Mex ramp although the rail within the concrete base is flat-bottomed railway section rail down to the foot of the ramp.

The decision by the Passenger Transport Authority to go for an on-street LRT – or tramway – system was, as we have seen, taken after considerable investigation of alternative options, and the evaluation of the LRT concept.

The crucial link in the chain, however, would be the Railway Inspectorate (RI). The examination of the system, in all its aspects, and in effect subsequent granting or withholding permission to operate, would be the sole responsibility of the appointed Inspector. He would be concerned with the safety of the system, from design, through construction, to the competence of the operating staff and their management.

Much of the work of the Railway Inspectorate rests on co-operation or general powers in the Health and Safety at Work Act and the old railway and tramway legislation has been found wanting on occasion. Private Bills have been used in the past to give additional powers especially for the approval of rolling stock as it was known that existing primary legislation did not provide all the statutory powers required by the Inspectorate to inspect works and receive reports on accidents or 'near misses'. The Transport and Works Act of 1992 (See Chapter 4) provides for comprehensive powers to make regulations in all these areas.

It was necessary, therefore, to involve the RI from the earliest days and Tony Young, in his capacity as Principal Planning Officer with the Passenger Transport Executive, had regular meetings with various Inspectors. He recalls that the RI came under the jurisdiction of the Department of Transport at that time (since 1991 the RI has been placed under the jurisdiction of the Health & Safety Executive and has become Her Majesty's Railway Inspectorate [HMRI]). Existing tramways were originally the responsibility of Major Tony King and then of Major Peter Olver but the LRT proposal was first dealt with by the late Lt Col Tony Townsend-Rose. However, as the proposals became more definite, the man who was to see the project through to operation came on the scene.

Major C. B. ('Kit') Holden had joined the RI after entering the army through National Service and spent his initial period of training on the Longmoor Military Railway. In 1985 he found himself involved in the Manchester LRT proposals. He recalls that, like many others, he was perhaps slightly surprised when the Bill to create Metrolink received Royal Assent, but since he had by then spent over two years working towards creating a working document for the benefit of those who would be involved he was naturally pleased.

The *Provisional Guidance Note on the Highway and Vehicle Engineering Aspects of Street Running Light Rapid Transit Systems* (PGN for short) was the outcome of meetings of a Working Party set up and chaired by Kit Holden and which included David Overton (formerly of the Manchester City Engineer's Department but nmow with Oscar Faber Traffic Ltd), Howard Saffer (Highways Engineer, Sheffield City Council) and representatives of various branches in the Department of Transport concerned with Traffic Policy, Road Safety, Traffic Signs, Traffic Communications and Control and Roads Engineering. Other members, particularly Tom Turner from the Department's Regional Office in Manchester, were co-opted as necessary and advice was sought from the Transport and Road Research Laboratory. Tony Young was used as a technical consultant to make sure that the discussions remained strictly practical and user-

Major C. B. Holden, HM Assistant Chief Inspecting Officer of Railways. He has spent many hundred hours walking, testing and checking alignments, clearances, pointwork, communications, vehicle details and a host of other items to satisfy himself as to Metrolink's ability to meet all the requisite safety requirements. The Major's career had taken him to Germany and to the Far East, to the Royal Military College of Science (Shrivenham) and to the British Transport Staff College, to working with the Royal Navy for two years, to the Ministry of Defence and to command of the first new Garrison Transport Squadron in Aldershot. He had been concerned with railways of all kinds, with ports, ships and water transport, and with all manner of road transport from bicycles to tank transporters. After joining RI he has again been to the Far East and has been the Inspectorate's principal man advising the Department of the Environment (Northern Ireland) on railway safety matters on NIR.

friendly. The PGN provided advice on Traffic Signs, Design Construction and Control of Traffic Signals, Highway layouts and markings, Intersections between the LRT system and other roads and pedestrian crossings, Stations and Stops, Overhead Electrification, and Vehicles. Its purpose was to ensure equally the safety of LRT systems and of other road users.

The Study Visits referred to in Chapter 3 included members of the RI, and Tony Young recalls stimulating their interest by showing how the various items raised in discussion by the Working Parties were dealt with in operating situations in Europe and North America.

Major Holden's intention was to have the *Provisional Guidance Note* available to be sent out with the Tender Documents, thus ensuring that the various contractors and their sub-contractors would be fully aware of the RI's thinking, and likely requirements. Although this was not possible, sufficient guidance was available at tender stage and a paper presented to the Symposium of Civil Engineers in Nottingham in 1990 was also useful.

The Major recognises that, inevitably with such a new concept, there were some omissions. Nevertheless the document codified the Inspectorate's opinions and has stood the test of time. It is currently being revised to take account of experience gained in Metrolink so as to be available for future LRT proposals.

The first practical involvement for the Inspector was the Project Light Rail demonstration (see Chapter 5) where he had to approve the use of the platform and wiring, and operation of the Docklands car. His work on the Metrolink project brought him into contact with many of the people he had dealt with on the Docklands Light Railway – for which he is responsible – from Mowlems, GEC and the various consultants.

He has been involved right through the planning and creation of Metrolink and knows the system inside out. His job has involved many dawn walks through the streets and he was part of the inspection team on the day the Bury line was vested with the Executive – a day he will not forget.

Jeff Done, GEC Project Manager, Kit Holden and Scott Hellewell, Metrolink's Operations Director, on one of their many forays whilst inspecting the system. Their relaxed attitude gives no hint of their activities the night before when they were checking the delta junction until 3am!

As each part of the project came on stream the RI monitored progress and checked that the work carried out met the DTp safety requirements.

Once the trial running and staff training progressed, Kit Holden was able to judge the competence of the team who would be responsible for the safe carriage of 10 million people per year on the first phase. Only when he could be seen to be satisfied did GMML seek his authorisation to begin operation between Victoria and Bury – and he was pleased then to be able to confirm his satisfaction and approval. Each section has required his approval and he has spent many hundred hours on Metrolink territory with something approaching a season ticket in the city hotels!

As an impartial observer the Inspector is in a good position to form a balanced view of the overall project. He recognises the different aspirations and requirements of the various parties and considers it his responsibility to guide them to avoid taking actions which he would later be compelled to refuse to accept, whilst at the same time avoiding direct involvement. Recognising the large sums of public money involved he is anxious to avoid abortive work and is on record as saying that he feels "there is not much wrong with the Metrolink project".

That is not to say everything is perfect. "With a DBOM contract built down to a price no one is going to waste money looking for better solutions to problems if the first solution is acceptable".

Major Holden recalls many interesting and enjoyable situations during Metrolink's construction and commissioning but one he particularly relishes is the inability of the Capcis consultants retained by the Executive to advise on eletrolytic and other matters to find sufficient current leaking to earth to be able to measure it. He sees that as a marvellous tribute to the track construction and a good omen for the future.

It was apparent from the earliest days of the Metrolink project that conversion of the Bury line would be problematical. The need to keep the British Rail service running as long as possible, thus creating the shortest possible changeover period – and least disruption to passengers – was clearly the ideal. Attempting to achieve this was another matter.

The shut-down period began, as planned, on 13th July 1991 from which date trains from Bury terminated at Crumpsall. A temporary bus service took passengers on to Manchester Victoria Station. From 17th August all service on the line ceased, with Metrolink operation expected to begin in November.

Recognising with hindsight the enormous amount of work which had to be done in that short changeover period Eric Black, then GMML's Chief Executive, acknowledged that a gross underestimate had been made by the consortium. He made this view public at a Press Conference held at Queen's Road on 13th January 1992. Since Mr Black was speaking on behalf of the same contractors and sub-contractors who were signatories to the contract not everyone was fully sympathetic.

Six main areas had to be addressed by GMML and its sub-contractors before the LRVs would be able to operate -

(i)   Removal of the third rail and replacement by overhead catenary
(ii) Installation of the new power supply
(iii) Re-signalling
(iv) Installation of communication systems
(v)   Staff training to drive and maintain the vehicles and to control the system
(vi) Station refurbishment and re-equipping

The existence of the live third rail was a major stumbling block. Whilst the power was on, access was so severely restricted for safety reasons as to virtually prohibit any work being carried out. Whilst the power was off BR could run no trains. Scott Hellewell, Metrolink's Operations Director, recalls that in April 1989, whilst he was still working with the Passenger Transport Executive attempts were made to persuade BR to substitute diesel multiple units (dmus) onto the line. This would have given contractors considerable access – under BR supervision and under the protection of its linesmen – up to twelve months before the final closure date of August 1991.

British Rail were not able to do this, being at the time desperately short of dmus as a result of protracted delivery dates on its class 158 Sprinter units and unreliability of earlier Pacers. Life-expired units were having to continue in daily use and no spare stock was available. Thoughts even turned to loco-hauled operation but lack of run-round facilities prevented any progress here.

It was necessary to accept that only very limited access would be available until the class 504 electric units were withdrawn. By July 1991 when the line south of Crumpsall was handed over to the contractors, thus allowing the O&MC to become operational, the majority of the work carried out had been of a preparatory nature. Work on the stations included the construction of access ramps, installation of cabling and communication channels and the installation of lifts at Heaton Park and Besses o'th Barn.

The third rail was protected by a wooden trough which prevented leaves lodging on its top surface – a lesson not learnt elsewhere! The pick up shoe can be seen mounted on the bogie sideframe.

British Rail's semaphore signals had to be replaced by colour lights, some fully automatic, others operated from the Control room at Queens Road.

Bowker Vale, clearly showing how the platform edge has been extended to give a nominal 75mm gap to allow easy entry for wheelchairs and push chairs. This work could not be carried out until the shut-down period began.

During the night the erection of gantries for the overhead wiring began, using a special works train based at Queens Road. After complete withdrawal of the BR service, work was able to begin in earnest on the whole line.

The preparatory work was taken through to completion and the big job – the inspection of the bridges – began. This latter task had not been possible until the contractors had full possession of the line. Many of these structures were some 140 years old and thorough inspection of the decking and brickwork was essential.

Access to the working areas was difficult and Balfour Beatty and GEC both resorted to the use of Unimogs (specially designed purpose-built Mercedes Benz road/rail vehicles) and other specially adapted lorries fitted with metal wheels to transport men and materials to their place of work. Metrolink had only its SPV (Special Purpose Vehicle) diesel locomotive and, to expedite work, hired diesel shunter locomotives and wagons from the East Lancashire Railway. The movement of these locomotives and wagons was accomplished by use of the access track to the Bury Electric Motive Power Depot.

Some work, such as installation of signalling equipment here being undertaken by operatives from GASL, (a GEC company) could be carried out whilst trains were running, though under the supervision of a BR linesman as seen here with his flags. All overhead work was carried out by Balfour Beatty as main sub-contractor to GEC. Stringing the overhead wire obviously required complete possession of the line. Note the modified Ford Cargo lorry, adapted for rail use.

These diesel locomotives are privately owned but their owners work for Metrolink in various capacities. Since they would be the drivers when the locos were in use, a conflict of priorities often arose when deciding which of their roles was more important! If they were in the workshops, no work could be carried out on the line when the presence of a locomotive was required. If they were out on the line the staffing levels in the workshops were depleted at a time when all available hands were needed. This was just one more situation to tax those endeavouring to make up lost time with inadequate resources.

One area which posed problems of a different nature concerned tunnels. There are four tunnels on the Bury line, at Manchester Road (Bury), Whitefield, Heaton Park and at Collyhurst. The need to provide overhead wiring for the LRVs meant that clearances, particularly in Collyhurst Tunnel, were severely restricted. Computer simulation modelling was used by W. S. Atkins who were responsible for checking and ensuring the accuracy of the alignment. Although the end result was extremely tight no problems were experienced during trials or, later, in service.

North of Crumpsall conversion work continued to be carried out at night – to the considerable annoyance of local residents – and on Sundays when there was traditionally no service on the line. This work included the laying of communication troughs and erection of the masts to support the catenary. Accordingly a concrete-mixing and mast-erecting train was stabled at the O&MC, being hauled up the line by a BR class 31 diesel for each working session. During this period the line remained the property of BR with the contractors having access for necessary work only.

Metrolink's electricity supply is separate from that of BR with power being taken direct from Norweb at 11Kv ac and fed to the system through eleven sub-stations. As the necessary cabling and equipment was installed sub-stations began to appear on or adjacent to the platforms during 1991. Five of these sub-stations supply the Bury line, being situated at Bury, Radcliffe, Prestwich, Woodlands Road and Victoria.

Relatively little work was to be carried out on the stations, other than Victoria which will be considered separately. The Bury Interchange was comparatively new, having been opened in 1980. It already incorporated lift and escalator facilities, thus giving access for mobility impaired people, having been designed as a manned station to receive crew-operated trains.

One aspect which gave cause for concern related to the escalator at Bury and resulted in the Interchange becoming a staffed station – the only one – for some time after operation began. The Railway Inspectorate was unhappy with the time it would take to hand operate the escalator in an emergency and it was agreed to provide trained Metrolink personnel to perform this task until modifications had been carried out by the manufacturer. The opportunity was taken to share this responsibility with the supervision of Hagside crossing, thus relieving some of the monotony of that job.

Along the line varying amounts of work were needed to bring other

(Upper) A curious feature of the operation is the lack of provision for a road based heavy-duty recovery vehicle – or, more sensibly, a road/rail vehicle capable of travelling on or off the rails. Recovery of a failed LRV from the street section will be dependent on the use of another LRV until the arrival of the SPV from Queens Road or wherever it might be at the time. The contractors used a variety of road/rail vehicles during the constructional period, one of which is shown here, but they were not of types suitable for LRV recovery. In April 1992 GMML purchased a road/rail Land Rover with rail conversion wheels to allow movement of staff and materials on the railway sections.
(Lower) The specially-equipped works train photographed at Queens Road.

Forlorn and forgotten – Radcliffe July 1991.

stations within reach of everyone. Ramps and/or lifts were provided where necessary but the wholesale refurbishment which had been intended – and was needed – became a casualty of budget pruning.

As it was necessary to keep within government cash limits some items had to be trimmed or removed from the scheme before the DBOM contract was let. The station refurbishment scheme for both the Bury and Altrincham lines was drastically reduced to cover only what was essential and some £900,000 was taken out of the programme by this action. Some of the work which was done on the stations was carried out before shut down with the rest being completed between August 1991 and the eventual opening date in April 1992. It was unfortunate that the new signs, ticket machines and other equipment thus clashed with the old careworn infrastructure, spoiling the effect which the new and imaginative corporate image was intended to convey. Such was GMML's concern about the condition of some stations, however, that it spent £100,000 of its own money in a quick 'lick-and-a-wipe' at Whitefield, Heaton Park, Bowker Vale and Crumpsall stations. At the latter two, GMML drivers formed themselves into two *ad-hoc* painting gangs – such is the 'team-spirit' in Metrolink. At Radcliffe and Prestwich more substantial refurbishment was required particularly to the subways.

During Summer 1991, an external factor increased the intense pressure on GMML, the Executive and sub-contractors alike. A major exhibition – Light Rail '91 – was to be held at the G-Mex Exhibition Centre in November 1991 in conjunction with a conference at the former Midland Hotel. Naturally it was everyone's wish that the system should be operational for that date but this would not be possible.

The combination of factors which would prevent operation beginning before April 1992 began to come together in the Summer of 1991 when the delivery of the first of the LRVs was delayed due to French traffic laws prohibiting the passage of outsize loads during the month of August – something apparently not foreseen by the British contractors.

In immediate terms this meant that there was no opportunity to examine, test, evaluate, commission or use for training any of the 26 LRVs. Number 1001, the first to arrive, reached Queens Road on 29th August 1991 and was off-loaded the following day. It was to be the sole representative of the fleet for several weeks.

Clearly any operation on the Bury line was now a good many weeks away since staff could not be trained to drive or maintain the LRVs. Also the signalling and communication package needed to be commissioned to enable the system to be controlled from Queens Road, as detailed in a later chapter.

Further problems now began to surface. It had been apparent to even the most casual observer that whilst the Bury line was performing quite reliably under BR's auspices it had scarcely been the recipient of much non-essential attention. Even whilst BR was still operating the line, weeds stood knee high between the rails and in the ballast alongside the track in many places.

A specialist consultant's report prepared by Gower Associates and commissioned by the GMA Consortium before the DBOM contract was signed had highlighted the need for considerable work on the line but this was either under-estimated or its significance partially misunderstood.

Whilst the line remained under its ownership the responsibility for safe operation remained with BR who discharged this responsibility in full. The line operated safely as a conventional 'heavy' rail system.

When it passed to GMML however, for light rail operation the line was examined on the day following cessation of BR operation and it was then apparent that much more work would be needed than had been allowed for.

CRASWELL PLATFORM MIRRORS – CHOSEN FOR MANCHESTER'S NEW

METROLINK

Providing a contribution to safety by permitting rearward visibility down the length of the train from the driver's seated position.

Used by main line and light rail systems in many parts of the world.

Available in a wide range of sizes, optionally in vandal resistant housings.

craswell scientific Ltd
MIRROR TECHNOLOGY

Unit 11 Orchard Trading Estate
Toddington, Glos. UK GL54 5EB
Tel: 0242 621534   Fax: 0242 621529

The Railway Inspector, present at the examination, clearly saw reason for concern because under his terms of reference the line would have to be examined to be passed as a brand new railway once the conversion work was complete. Several weeks were lost at this stage.

Here it is important to recognise what had happened on the Tyne & Wear Metro in similar circumstances. British Rail's trains are built to heavy rail specification, and can therefore accept more punishment from the track, especially where rail is not continuously welded. More lightly built LRVs, with their lighter bogies, cannot take this. Tyne & Wear was obliged to make expensive modifications to the vehicles' bogies after frame fractures resulted from running over track which was suitable for heavy rail but not for light rail operation.

Paul Neal, Metrolink's Operations Manager, had first hand experience of the Tyne & Wear system, and GMML were thus fully aware of these implications and the need to take preventive action. This included replacing several kilometres of rail and spot re-sleepering with over 1,950 new sleepers, in addition to removing the luxuriant weed growth which in some places was indicating that the ballast drainage also needed attention.

Furthermore it was necessary to carry out work on some of the 140-year old bridges in the approach to Victoria Station, in addition to repairs to the waterproofing of the Besses o'th Barn bridge which carries the line over the M62 motorway. It was necessary to completely remove all trackwork from the bridge for this repair. This modern bridge will need regular attention before its eventual replacement.

At Victoria Station a different situation existed. The design aspect of the DBOM Contract has been mentioned already, but where Metrolink and BR

Stations built on a curve require platform-based mirrors to allow the driver to be able to see the doors on the LRVs. One such example is seen at Radcliffe, and the mirrors, designed by Craswell, are positioned such that from the driver's cab the whole LRV can be seen.

Work progressing at Victoria Station before withdrawal of the British Rail service. The supporting columns for the roof have been exposed prior to being encased in a protective concrete box. In the background shuttering is in position ready to create the 'Berlin Wall'.

Metrolink's platform 'A' forms part of the main concourse at Victoria Station. LRVs load here for Bury and leave the station via the sharp curve seen in the illustration. This is the changeover point from street mode to segregated mode where drivers deactivate the circuits which control those functions needed for street operation, including the quieter horn, automatic step function for multiple operation, signal and point actuation.

came together the problems were considerable. During the Metrolink design period BR had had cause to review its safety procedures. The signalling fault resulting in the collision at Clapham, and the fire at Kings Cross Underground Station focused attention on passenger safety and in particular how outside agencies might jeopardise that safety. Metrolink had effectively become one of those outside agencies.

BR were concerned to secure adequate protection and needed to see the final designs for any part of the scheme which would impinge on its operations or property before it would grant possession for work to begin.

At Victoria reinforced concrete structures to protect the supporting roof pillars, and to prevent any LRV from mounting and crossing its platform and fouling the BR tracks were stipulated – and so the 'Berlin Wall' came into being. This additional and unexpected work resulted in extra costs and extension of timescale since the work required was considerable.

Even the more straightforward work at Victoria was not inconsiderable. A new island platform had to be constructed, with rail access created through the train shed wall leading to Corporation Street. A further platform was created at the entry to the station, together with passenger access to both platforms, including a pedestrian level crossing of one track. This arrangement was necessary to allow flexibility of operation. Metrolink's tracks and signalling had to be separated and isolated from their BR equivalents, and a siding with headshunt and crossover laid, again to allow flexibility of operation.

It also took a long time to resolve the location of the station equipment – with many abortive solutions being developed. Furthermore the City Planners had legitimate concerns about the aesthetics and finishes at Victoria Station Equipment Room and the treatment of 'the hole in the wall'. This situation was to be repeated at G-Mex.

On the platforms, ticket-vending machines, telephone kiosks, public address equipment and train information displays were installed, matching the equipment on other stations along the line, although, as would be expected, to a very much higher standard as befits a city interchange station.

The net result of the additional and unforeseen extra work here and elsewhere was that the Executive agreed an extension of the contract by 20 weeks and the opening date, as mentioned, was put back 20 weeks. On Monday 6th April, at 6.00am, amid scenes of enthusiasm and relief, Metrolink LRVs began to operate between Bury and Manchester.

At 06.00 on Monday 6th April 1992 the first revenue-earning LRVs entered service – here ,1004 breaks the tape at 05.50 as it enters Bury Interchange from Queens Road.

During the training period, and until operation through the city began, LRVs entered Victoria Station on the line leading to platform 'B', the same one they used to go back out to Bury or Queens Road.

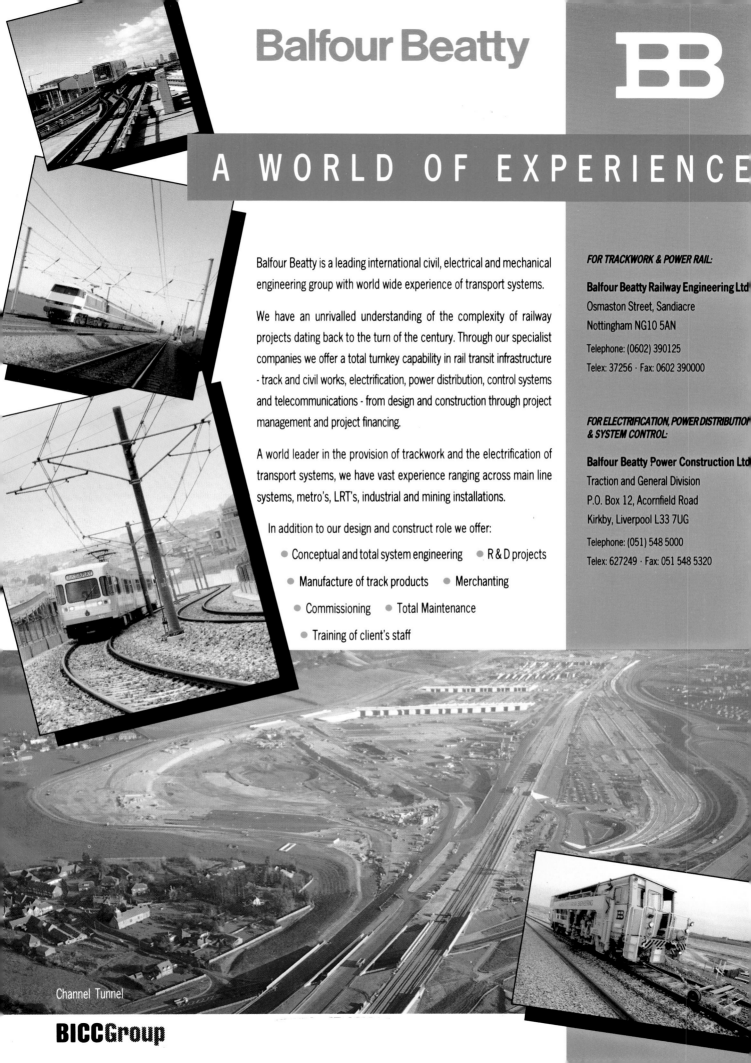

Balfour Beatty

BB

A WORLD OF EXPERIENCE

Balfour Beatty is a leading international civil, electrical and mechanical engineering group with world wide experience of transport systems.

We have an unrivalled understanding of the complexity of railway projects dating back to the turn of the century. Through our specialist companies we offer a total turnkey capability in rail transit infrastructure - track and civil works, electrification, power distribution, control systems and telecommunications - from design and construction through project management and project financing.

A world leader in the provision of trackwork and the electrification of transport systems, we have vast experience ranging across main line systems, metro's, LRT's, industrial and mining installations.

In addition to our design and construct role we offer:

- Conceptual and total system engineering
- R & D projects
- Manufacture of track products
- Merchanting
- Commissioning
- Total Maintenance
- Training of client's staff

FOR TRACKWORK & POWER RAIL:

Balfour Beatty Railway Engineering Ltd
Osmaston Street, Sandiacre
Nottingham NG10 5AN

Telephone: (0602) 390125

Telex: 37256 · Fax: 0602 390000

FOR ELECTRIFICATION, POWER DISTRIBUTION & SYSTEM CONTROL:

Balfour Beatty Power Construction Ltd
Traction and General Division
P.O. Box 12, Acornfield Road
Kirkby, Liverpool L33 7UG

Telephone: (051) 548 5000

Telex: 627249 · Fax: 051 548 5320

Channel Tunnel

BICCGroup

During the Study Visits (see Chapter 3) members had been impressed by the way in which Light Rail blended unobtrusively into the towns and cities which they examined. Careful and strategic siting of poles minimised their visual impact whilst the attention to detail created an environmentally friendly and attractive system. Unfortunately this has not yet been achieved on some sections of the City Centre lines where the Design, Build, Operate & Maintain contract came into play.

The contract provided for overhead to be strung at specified heights, to be capable of being used by pantographs and to supply the necessary energy, at 750 volts dc, to power the vehicles. Design and aesthetics were the contractor's sole responsibility, and the result is now only too plain to see. A proliferation of poles of a type standard on heavy railways have spoiled the appearance of parts of the streets. Despite the Parliamentary powers included in the 1988 Act, *"The Executive may affix brackets, cables, wires and other apparatus required for the purpose of operating the light rapid transit system to any building or structure ...,"* very few span wires were able to be used because of difficulties with individual buildings.

Removal of some unecessary poles will reduce the problem but comparison with modern continental systems demonstrates that in this, as in other areas, UK manufacturers have much to learn if LRT is to be readily accepted in British cities. European and American schemes have, in contrast, had the benefit of very substantial expenditure to ensure that environmental aspects are not overlooked.

Deja vu! Almost everywhere they dug it seemed that the contractors found rails from the original tramway system.

St. Peter's Square, April 1992. Here the LRV's quiet passage through to Piccadilly or Altrincham can be appreciated by those with time to relax in the gardens.

Amongst the people seconded to the Passenger Transport Executive from the various consultants to monitor the construction work were David Rumney (right) of Mott MacDonald and Conor Mc Guinness of CIE. Both became familiar figures in the city centre, being regularly seen in the streets inspecting progress on the system, as seen here in Piccadilly. Conor McGuinness returned to Ireland in March 1992, whilst David Rumney remains with the Executive at the time of writing.

Where the Royal Fine Arts Commission's advice has been taken, in the matter of the finish to the G-Mex ramp and bowstring bridge for instance, the result is outstanding – except for the poles – and together with St. Peter's Square forms the most attractive section of the street tramway.

A significant aspect of the city centre construction concerned the underground public utilities: sewers, gas, water and hydraulic pipes, electricity and telephone cables, all of which would be affected by the route of the track. Work to the value of £7 million has been carried out on diversion and strengthening of these services which was programmed and co-ordinated by a series of consultation groups representing the Executive, the Highway and Planning Authorities, the Police and the statutory undertakers. Monitoring and liaison was the responsibility of Mott MacDonald acting as consultant to the Executive, and David Rumney was seconded to the Executive to perform this task. These groups were set up in February 1988 and relocation work commenced in March 1989, enabling key areas to be released for track bed construction in accordance with the main construction programme.

To avoid future costly and disruptive repair works to the pipes and cables of the statutory undertakers beneath the on-street track sections of Metrolink, it was decided to strengthen or renew all services which crossed the track for a distance of one metre on each side. It is of interest to note here that the provision of the Tramways Act of 1870 remains in force which defines the area of road which is the responsibility of the tramway operator as the width of the track plus eighteen inches on each side of the track. Some longitudinal services have been rerouted clear of the tracks and several side-entry manhole chambers have been created to allow access to existing sewers. Carrying out these works as a direct contract by the Executive with the statutory undertakers enabled the trackwork within the city centre to progress with minimum disruption. The bulk of this work was completed before the main contract began in December 1989.

With particular relevance to the city centre an important factor of both construction and operation of Metrolink is traffic management. Manchester City Council dedicated areas of highway on the route to the sole use of the light rail vehicles. By a judicious adjustment of traffic flows on various streets, and by highway improvements, the traffic flow has been maintained after the opening of Metrolink. During the construction phase a Traffic Management Group representing all interested parties met weekly to discuss temporary solutions to traffic problems in the city centre produced by the work being carried out at the time. Once decisions had been reached, the Executive informed the press to alert motorists and users of all affected premises and fulfilled legal requirements with regard to paying for inclusion of road traffic orders in the local press. .

With the installation of traffic management, work was able to commence on the track laying. The sub-contract for the city centre track laying was awarded to Balfour Beatty Railway Engineering Ltd.

The average depth of the foundation for the rails is approximately 0.5m. below the existing road surface. The first operation was to break out the existing roadway and excavate the underlying road construction. During this operation the original tramway rails were often exposed and, after burning or cutting, were removed to make way for the new foundation. The excavation was bottomed-out and a thin layer of blinding concrete placed to form a clean working surface.

Steel reinforcing mesh was next placed on top of the blinding and spaced with concrete blocks to provide top and bottom mats of reinforcement. The steel mesh not only provides structural support for the overlying track but also acts as a conductor drawing off stray current induced by the movement of the light rail vehicles above.

Capcis March Ltd, a company within Manchester University and retained by the Executive, advised on all matters relating to current leakage which can, of course, cause electrolytic action with underground pipes.

Next came the construction of the concrete track bed and an on-going development process resulted in improved techniques and designs being adopted as the contract progressed. In their design for the GMA Consortium W. S. Atkins & Partners had considered the aspects of noise and vibration in the street section to be crucial to the success or failure of the system. Accordingly Roger Hull, Atkins' Project Manager, incorporated polymer fixing of the rails into his design. Although the concept was not new, its use on such a large scale was. It was also new to the UK. Tie bars, the traditional means of holding the track to the correct gauge, were dispensed with, except in points and crossings.

Manchester was to prove a difficult location for this type of construction. The original material took great exception to Manchester's high humidity, and despite the erection of temporary tents and attempts at reducing the humidity it was eventually necessary to change to a different manufacturer of polymer. This problem was to delay the street section quite considerably and also led to a further complication. Because the polymer is extremely expensive – estimates put its cost at around £1m – ways of reducing the amount needed were investigated. Originally a hollow box section extrusion some 135mm x 35mm was attached to the web of the rail with the intention of pressure filling it with cementatious grout. This would provide a continuous concrete strip along the length of the street rail, increasing the dead weight and thereby assisting in reducing vibration. It would also considerably reduce the amount of polymer required.

Interestingly, differences of opinion as to the purpose of this hollow box were apparent even amongst those responsible for its installation. Suffice to say that if it *was* pressure grout filled, the concept failed in the execution. The City Engineers found the box to be at least partially empty when they investigated the collapse of the road surface under the weight of passing buses in Mosley Street. In a long-running saga the road surface was cut and re-cut as channels were excavated alongside the rail and filled with a variety of materials. As late as January 1992 this remedial work was still being carried out.

A modified system substituted a round pipe at the foot of the rail, with a metal retaining 'wall' standing parallel to the rail but some 60mm away from it. This space was then filled to road surface level leaving a strip of different texture to show how the problem had been resolved, if indeed it had, for in April 1992 the surface again broke up in Lower Mosley Street.

The need to use continuous welded rail (cwr) to ensure smooth running has been referred to relative to the Bury line (see previous chapter). In the City centre cwr was required not only to eliminate the 'hammer blow' effect between wheels and rail joints, but also to eliminate the noise produced by wheels passing over such joints. Since each LRV has six axles the noise would have been considerable.

The solution is, of course, to weld the rails together but whilst this can be done off-site with railway rail, grooved tramway (girder) rail has to be welded *in-situ*. Here the contractors used the Thermit process, as old in concept as electric tramways themselves.

After the rails have been positioned, prepared and cleaned, they are set with a 26mm gap between the rail ends and the appropriate prefabricated sand moulds are placed in position. A crucible (as seen in the illustration) holding the powder – a controlled mixture of aluminium powder, iron oxides and alloying elements – is placed directly above the gap and, after the rail has been

Balloon Street showing the metal mesh incorporated into the track construction.

Plastic tents were erected over the track whilst the initial polymer was being used but the material was still susceptible to moisture.

The girder type tramway rail as used in the city section was manufactured in Luxembourg. Produced to Ri59 it incorporates a groove 42mm wide and has a projected life of 15 years – the duration of the initial franchise. Note the round pipe and retaining wall referred to in the text.

Thermit welding of the rails, joining them end-to-end, always fascinated passers by.

pre-heated, the mixture is ignited. Passers-by usually stop to see the firework display, and to watch molten steel flowing through the mould at some 2500°c.

Once the metal starts to cool the excess is chiselled off the rail head using a hydraulic weld shear or similar tool, leaving a projection to be ground and filed when everything is cold. The resultant join gives a smooth, quiet ride which will require very little maintenance over the years. This latter point is clearly important since the rails are buried in the road and cannot easily be examined below rail head level.

Banks of underground ducts are positioned alongside the trackbed foundation, within the swept path, to take the signalling and power cables. At least 21 channels are available of which Metrolink at present uses six, and the City Engineer's Department uses one for traffic light control which is linked to a computer in the Executive's headquarters in Magnum House, Portland Street. There is thus ample provision for any future cables for other purposes which may be expected to provide a source of revenue from rental charges.

Communication and draw pits are positioned every 50m. along the track and have, wherever possible, been sited outside the swept path of the rail vehicles. Signal cabling links the system with the O&MC at Queens Road.

Alongside the track, cabinets house the electrical equipment which picks up impulses from approaching LRVs and sends the appropriate command to the point motors where a change of direction is required. The wires buried between the tracks pick up the tram's presence and this information is fed into equipment in the cabinets.

Infilling with surface macadam reinstated the road surface where it is to be used by both Metrolink and road vehicles. The city centre section includes varying degrees of segregation, from street running with other traffic to private right of way, with intermediate categories of partial segregation where the alignment is shared with local buses or local access traffic. The fully-segregated section is paved, using buff coloured blocks to mark the swept path of the LRVs.

City centre construction work included highway improvements which

One of Manchester's most notable 19th century buildings is the City Art Gallery on Mosley Street. This picture may be compared with that on page 64 which shares the same location with an open-topped tramcar in the early years of the century. In this view, the Art Gallery overlooks the scene as track construction continues on 16th October 1990. The method of construction can be clearly seen with some rails placed in the concrete channels prior to the pouring of the fixing polymer. It was at first thought by the City Planning Department that Mosley Street was too vital a thoroughfare to be closed permanently to non-bus traffic. At the time this photograph was taken, it had already been closed for some considerable time due to delays in the construction work. This fact conditioned motorists to finding alternative routes and so formed an unintentional part of the traffic management schemes when ultimately Mosley Street was permanently closed to non-bus traffic. One of the reasons for the work taking so long was the impossibility of dealing with Mosley Street in one operation because of the need to leave York Street, Charlotte Street, Nicholas Street and Princess Street open for cross traffic. First, the preliminary work (digging up the road and re-locating the underground services) and then the reinstatement of the road surfaces and creation of the track bed, had to be carried out in three separate sections. In this view, the laying of the concrete track bed can be seen with ready-mixed concrete being poured into the timber shuttering at the Nicholas Street intersection. Further up Mosley Street, the Charlotte Street intersection awaits its turn. In the foreground, the rails have been delivered and are waiting to be positioned.

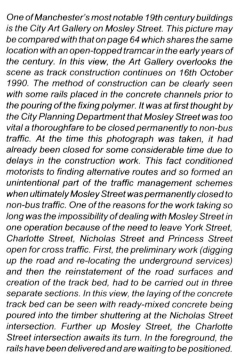

During 1991 there seemed to be no end to the work in the streets. The junction of Mosley Street and Parker Street in Piccadilly was a major problem as the preparatory work for the delta junction took place. Aytoun Street awaited the installation of the crossover, below left, whilst the reinstatement of the road surface in Piccadilly was a long drawn out affair partly because of the need to retain right of way for the buses.

This view of St. Peter's Square illustrates the trackside furniture and from the right can be seen the station sign, a timetable and plan, the backs of two ticket-vending machines, cabinets housing electrical equipment, the shelter and two telephone kiosks. The use of Portland Stone at this location produces a bright and clean effect of quality, sympathetic to one of the City's central squares bounded by the Edwardian Midland Hotel of terracotta and brick, the impressive circular Central Library and the Town Hall Extension. The City's Cenotaph stands in the memorial garden, on the left of this view, the site of the former St. Peter's Church, and this demanded considerable care in the design of the Metrolink station. The additional cost of the more expensive materials illustrates that tasteful design can be achieved when additional funding can be obtained.

Aytoun Street could not be reinstated until the crossover had been installed. Here the readymix concrete is pumped into the track foundation.

were carried out under separate contract between the Executive and Consortium member John Mowlem & Company PLC. These improvements consisted largely of road widening and alteration of junction layouts.

The construction of six stations or platforms was required on the city centre section, excluding the Victoria and Piccadilly interchanges. The city centre stations are of the side platform type except for Piccadilly Gardens which is of the island platform type. G-Mex station has staggered platforms facilitating passenger movements between BR's Deansgate station (formerly Knott Mill) and the G-Mex Exhibition Hall. St. Peter's Square has traditional parallel platforms. Mosley Street, Market Street and High Street stations consist of a single platform serving one direction only for reasons of available space. All stations are long enough to accommodate twin car sets.

Major requirements of the design of the city centre stations were that they should be as unobtrusive as possible and ensure maximum accessibility for everybody. To meet the first-mentioned requirement, these stations have not been provided with buildings, and passenger shelters are of a pleasing design making the maximum use of glass. Station equipment is sited in the basements of adjacent buildings. To be as accessible as possible for people in wheelchairs or pushing prams or pushchairs the platforms are provided with a raised section at one end, approached by ramps, to provide level access to certain doors of the light rail vehicle. The remaining area of the platform provides access to the vehicle by the use of automatically-operated retractable steps incorporated within the design of the vehicle. Platforms are generally two metres wide and the two levels of platform are connected by a ramp at a nominal 1:20 gradient. Platform height is 915mm above rail level at the high level and 450mm at the low level. The two platforms in St. Peter's Square are finished in white Portland stone, complementing the Central Reference Library and the Cenotaph. All others have red pavior blocks.

The on-street stations or 'profiled platforms' are thought to pioneer the availability in the UK of the same public passenger transport to both mobility impaired and other people.

The tracks are constructed 150mm below street level at the city centre platforms thus reducing the low platform height to about 300mm above pavement level. Each platform carries a large station name sign with GMML's 'M' logo, and incorporates a central information area including ticket vending machines, route maps, travel information, and a closed-circuit television scanner together with public address and passenger communication equipment.

The distinctive and attractive shelters are supplied by the French company J. C. Deceaux. To meet the requirements for unobtrusiveness (referred to above) accomodation for waiting passengers is minimal. The shelters will be maintained, cleaned and repaired under contract. Each station will be cleaned daily and the shelters will be cleaned every ten days.

The street section from the city centre makes its connection with the Cornbrook viaduct via a major construction project involving a new steel bridge sited between a concrete ramp on the city side and a concrete viaduct on the Altrincham side and a new station with two island platforms at G-Mex.

The steel bowstring arch bridge crossing Great Bridgewater Street has been designed to reflect its surroundings. The diamond shape of the roof lights of the G-Mex building has been repeated in the arch of the bridge and the square section of the box arch has been turned on its side to present a diamond shape. This bridge, like others on the system, is painted in Metrolink's striking and attractive aquamarine colour scheme.

The abutments are designed in a manner similar to the pilasters of the G-Mex viaduct. The pourable polymer system has been used for securing the rails on the bridge. This reduces noise which is specially important on bridges of this design and especially so at this location with the G-Mex Exhibition Hall and forthcoming Hallé Concert Hall located immediately adjacent on either side.

To ensure that the project would blend with the existing brick structures it was a requirement of the contract that the surfaces should present a brick appearance. To this end brick cladding was applied subsequent to the casting. In addition to traditional bricklaying large pre-formed concrete panels, incorporating the necessary brickwork, were produced by C. V. Buchan, an AMEC subsidiary. The end result is extremely attractive and few would realise how the effect has been achieved in the arched panels.

This major construction project was carefully devised to be sympathetic in design with the Victorian brick structure of the original Central Station. It complements the listed building, and the design of both the ramp and the bowstring arch bridge was approved by the Royal Fine Arts Commission. Manufacture and assembly of the bridge was carried out by the Belgian company Victor Buyck of Ghent as sub-contractor to Mowlem.

High Street Station, adjacent to Debenham's store, showing the gradual slope giving easy access to the high level section of the platform. Work on this station was delayed by the need to cap a well which was discovered during construction work in the cellar of an adjacent building where station equipment was being installed.

Number 1002 'Manchester Arndale Voyager', sponsored by P&O, heads for Victoria. Photograph by John Fox, courtesy Manchester Evening News.

To complete the G-Mex ramp twenty-six pre-formed concrete panels were produced by C. V. Buchan, 13 Spandrel arched units weighing 22 tonnes each and 13 parapet units weighing 11 tonnes each. The panels were cast horizontally face down, allowing all the bricks to be placed and secured onto a preformed grid, followed by the perimeter formwork and then the reinforcement. After all the checking was complete the concrete was poured.

Before and after. The reinforced concrete structure was a drab and ugly affair, but the brick facing and panels transformed the whole appearance. Until operation to Altrincham began all LRVs were checked at the signal near the head of the ramp, thus considerably increasing the chances of their being seen by passing motorists, pedestrians or bus passengers and unintentionally helping to assist in the Metrolink awareness campaign which GMML were conducting.

A major difference between the Altrincham line and the other two sections of Phase 1 – the Bury line and the City Centre – was the greater freedom of action for the contractors. Unlike the Bury line which was needed for movement of LRVs between the O&MC and the former Bury MPD for remedial work, modifications and commissioning, followed by on-line commissioning trials and driver training, and the City with its pressures of traffic and pedestrian movements and safety provisions, the Altrincham line was self-contained and the contractors could work largely undisturbed. Only where BR trains ran on adjacent tracks was there any need to accommodate third parties. Thus, although there were major works to be completed, and despite some problems with access at G-Mex and Cornbrook which were resolved, matters proceeded relatively smoothly.

In the first phase of Metrolink the conversion of the line from Altrincham Interchange to Manchester was the section which required the least change as far as the track and method of current collection was concerned. The track, which included a greater amount of continuously-welded rail, was in much better condition than that on the Bury line and the catenary system was already *in situ* and compatible with light rail transit.

An early complication was that part of the Altrincham line carried diesel multiple units on the BR route between Manchester and Chester. However, from May 1989 these services were diverted to use a former passenger line still in use by freight trains between Altrincham and Stockport.

The Altrincham line required ten main areas of work before LRVs could begin to operate over the line and into the City centre –

Overhead masts and wires, together with new trackwork were required on the Cornbrook Viaduct section.

(i)   The construction of G-Mex station and access from Lower Mosley Street (the latter dealt with in Chapter 12).

(ii)   The complete refurbishment of that part of Cornbrook Viaduct to be used by the LRVs.

(iii)   An underpass at Cornbrook Junction.

(iv)   Alterations to trackwork layouts in connection with single-line working.

(v)   The creation of a turnback siding immediately south of Timperley station.

(vi)   Installation of the new power supply.

(vii)   Re-signalling.

(viii) Installation of communication systems.

(ix)   Station refurbishment and re-equipping.

(x)   The reconstruction and underpinning of bridge number A22 at Barford Bridge over the River Mersey.

The construction of a new station at G-Mex, with individual platforms located on part of the site previously used for car parking, was straightforward. Unfortunately the vast amount of materials needed to be stored in this area greatly reduced the amount of space available for cars, with loss of revenue for the owners. As a result, it became necessary to use mobile cranes standing in Albion Street to lift into position equipment needed for the control room located at the end of the new viaduct when access could not be obtained otherwise.

Arrangement of single track layout between Timperley and Altrincham.

BR TO CHESTER

ALTRINCHAM

PEDESTRIAN FOOTBRIDGE

CONNECTION TO BR NETWORK

NAVIGATION ROAD LEVEL CROSSING

NAVIGATION ROAD

DEANSGATE LANE LEVEL CROSSING

BR TO STOCKPORT

TIMPERLEY

METROLINK TO MANCHESTER AND BURY

Cornbrook viaduct was originally built between 1876 and 1878 as part of the Midland Railway, and carried two lines into the former Central Station. Despite its name, this station, like the others in Manchester, was on the edge of the city centre. The approach was increased by a further three lines in the 1890s when a new viaduct was constructed to the northern side of the railway leading into the Great Northern Railway's goods station. From 1969 the Cornbrook viaduct was disused with little or no maintenance work being subsequently carried out. As a result the metal sections had become corroded and the brickwork had decayed. The GMA Group carried out an extensive repair programme including the replacement of one metal-deck bridge. This viaduct is unusual in that it divides into two independent structures at which point Metrolink uses the southern portion.

The new underpass at Cornbrook was necessary to separate the BR line from Manchester Piccadilly and Oxford Road to Warrington, powered by overhead line at 25Kv ac, from the 750v dc Metrolink line. Metrolink passes under the BR line and the design work allows for the proposed extension to Salford Quays and Trafford Park to be constructed without further major structural work at this point. This underpass was the one major constructional project which was not carried out by members of the GMA Consortium. The work was carried out by Shand Civil Engineering Contractors on behalf BR with a contract value of £6 million.

Between Deansgate Lane level crossing and Navigation Road there is insufficient room for a four track layout, ideally needed where Metrolink LRVs, and BR trains running between Stockport and Altrincham, run side-by-side. The solution was to make this stretch of the line – some 500m – bi-directional whereby BR would run its passenger and freight services in both directions over the east track and Metrolink LRVs would run in both directions over the west track. This required separation of the two lines and new points and crossings were installed (see diagram).

Once the Altrincham line had been connected to the rest of the Metrolink system, via the Cornbrook Underpass, the all-important gauging trial was able to take place to ensure that all platform, and other structures gave the necessary clearance. The test was carried out by LRV 1007, seen here at Brooklands being hauled by the SPV. The overhead wire was not energised at this time.

The platforms at G-Mex station are staggered to allow pedestrian access to the covered walkway leading to the BR Deansgate Station. The top photograph shows the southbound platform, normally used for passengers travelling on the Altrincham line, but seen during the period when Bury trains terminated at G-Mex. The ticket vending machine is shown to good advantage. John Fox photo courtesy Manchester Evening News.

Furniture at G-Mex station harmonises with the Castlefield redevelopment scheme – the centre picture shows one of the passenger shelters whilst the lower photograph shows the twin telephone kiosks common to all Metrolink city station platforms.

The Cornbrook Viaduct forms an impressive backdrop to an Altrincham bound LRV.

Car 1007 snaking off the viaduct section prior to passing under the BR line at Cornbrook Underpass. This project was handled by Shand Civil Engineering Contractors for British Rail.

The single-track section, with two level crossings, is clearly a potential source of delay, to Metrolink, British Rail and motorists alike, when at rush hours LRVs will be operating every five minutes in each direction. Control of the crossing gates remains with BR, introducing a further complication for Metrolink. To give some flexibility of operation by allowing LRVs to be turned back at Timperley, a turnback siding was created south of Timperley station.

Driver training for the Altrincham line began on Thursday 7th May, with LRVs operating between G-Mex and Timperley pending RI approval to operate through to Altrincham. The vehicles reversed at G-Mex by crossing the bowstring bridge and then changing lines by use of the crossover there.

Unfortunately the new equipment in the BR signal box, including Radio communication with LRV drivers as used throughout the Metrolink system, had not been commissioned in time to be mastered by BR staff before the Inspecting Officer of Railways visited Altrincham on 14th May 1992 and a further inspection was necessary before trial running could begin.

Installation of the new power supply was made easier by the existence of the catenary masts. New overhead wire of heavier gauge, as needed for the 750v dc system, replaced the former 25Kv ac wiring. Between Deansgate Junction and Navigation Road the overhead wires were removed, though this work was carried out by BR. There are five sub-stations on the Altrincham line at Altrincham, Timperley, Dane Road, Trafford Bar, and G-Mex.

Re-signalling of the line was carried out in similar manner to the work on the Bury line, save that there were no semaphores to replace. Whilst this work was being done the communication systems were also installed.

Refurbishment work on stations was restricted in similar manner to the Bury line, and for the same reason, to reduce costs. Buildings no longer required have been closed and boarded up, whilst J. C. Decaux shelters have been installed on the platforms. The latter failed to pass the IOR's inspection on 14th May and remedial work to increase headroom and strengthen the structures had to be carried out.

Improved access has been provided at all stations with ramps or lifts. Only at Timperley was it found necessary to provide lifts to both platforms. All stations now have Metrolink signs, ticket vending machines, closed circuit television, and public address systems as fitted on the Bury line.

An additional major item of expenditure, which the GMA Consortium had to absorb, was the underpinning and strengthening of the railway bridge which carries the line over the River Mersey at Barford Bridge. Some £0.5m was spent on bringing this bridge to a satisfactory condition.

Following withdrawal of BR electric trains between Manchester and Altrincham, these services now terminate at Deansgate station. The lack of a crossover at that station and its location on one of the busiest sections of BR line in Greater Manchester makes it necessary for them to travel beyond Castlefield to reverse. For a few weeks they ran into Trafford Park but once the existing line had been severed at Cornbrook Junction a stub end was created, allowing access to the crossover east of the junction, where they now reverse.

Plans are being developed for a station at White City on the Liverpool line to replace this arrangement.

Facing page, top to bottom.

A long standing anomaly was rectified when the station at Old Trafford, seen here, was renamed Trafford Bar. This allowed the former Warwick Road to become Old Trafford – the logical name for the station used by sports fans travelling to and from cricket and football matches.
Navigation Road level crossing seen during Autumn 1991, after the track layout had been modified. BR electric trains used the right hand track in both directions at that time.
Passengers waiting for the Manchester via Stockport-bound Sprinter watch the Altrincham bound Metrolink LRV clearing the level crossing at Navigation Road.

The physical connection between Metrolink (the left hand tracks) and British Rail (the right hand tracks) can be seen in this photograph taken from the footbridge outside Altrincham Station. Although it will not normally be required it has been used to allow access for a class 47 diesel locomotive hired to clear the rail head of surface rust which was causing signal detection problems after the shut-down period.

One of the fundamental requirements of the Metrolink scheme was the provision of interchange facilities at Piccadilly station, allowing Inter-City and suburban passengers to have easy access to and from the LRVs, *en route* to the City centre or Victoria station.

The construction of Piccadilly station, whereby the later extensions to the train shed are built on a metal raft supported by cast iron columns, leaves a substantial area below the station 'floor' track level. In years gone by this area, the Undercroft, had been used for trans-shipment of goods; latterly it had become a car park with some storage facilities in less accessible areas.

Because Metrolink's LRVs would enter at street level, crossing London Road in the process, the Undercroft provided the ideal location for the interchange station. Access to the Undercroft was seen as being simply achieved by cutting through the retaining wall in London Road, and creating a reinforced concrete structure to form the entrance.

From the new station's platforms, lift and escalator facilities could be provided, using a mezzanine floor to allow passengers to be turned through 90°, and giving access to the main line station concourse above – adjacent to the entrance to platforms 7-14. The escalator would be the only new one throughout Phase 1 of Metrolink.

One island platform was to have been provided for the LRVs, followed by a curve leading into a headshunt to allow storage facilities for two LRVs whilst also forming the track leading out of Piccadilly station to any future eastward extensions of proposed later phases to Glossop, Marple, Oldham and Rochdale. This headshunt was located in a tunnel which passes diagonally beneath the original parts of the station, and formerly carried a road known as Ashton Street.

New access had to be provided to the Undercroft and here again a high standard of finish has been achieved. The Central Manchester Development Corporation are to be congratulated on their assistance in this area.

One of the main supporting girders at Piccadilliy Station, seen in the new mezzanine area, after grit blasting and repainting. Columns 3ft. in diameter support the 4ft. 6in. girders giving an indication of the scale of loading. Each column supports a dead load of around 200 tons.

Preparatory work including track base construction and shuttering for the platforms and walls is seen below. The supporting columns are seen in full before the mezzanine floor was created. The right hand illustration shows the platform end, with pedestrian access via steps or ramp from the Fairfield Street entrance.

Whilst it was obvious that considerable work would be necessary no major problems were foreseen and the project was designed and costed by the Consortium and approved in principle by the Passenger Transport Executive and British Rail, subject to the consortia satisfying BR about the adequacy of their proposed derailment and collision barriers, and fire protection arrangements, to meet the loads produced by their particular vehicle.

Problems referred to earlier in this volume then began to surface. The contract allowed for the consortium to have 'possession' of the Undercroft, in order to begin work, on 30th April 1990. However, before they could have 'possession' BR had to be completely satisfied with the GMA designs and until it was could not grant access for work to begin. The designs already included vehicle-restraint measures but BR could not accept them until both the fire and collision characteristics of the LRV, which was still being designed, had been evaluated. The alternative would have been to have designed to BR's standard loadings for Heavy Rail which were considered by all parties, including the IOR, to be inappropriate for Light Rail. As it turned out, when the LRV loads were finally calculated, the figures were little different from those applicable to Heavy Rail, principally due to the design of the Firema vehicle, necessary to meet the tight design timescales, which resulted in a vehicle some 9 tons heavier than that envisaged by the Executive in its Reference Specification.

Central to BR's requirements was the need for full protection of its infrastructure, and in particular the iron columns supporting the whole station above. Two scenarios were envisaged by BR; firstly a runaway LRV crossing London Road at speed, derailing and colliding with one of these columns, damaging it and putting the whole structure at risk; secondly, a fire within the Metrolink station, causing the columns to be at risk from cracking when cooled down rapidly by water used to extinguish the fire.

When the design loads were applied to the original design it became apparent that the thickness of protection required around the columns in the

The Undercroft required considerable work to convert it to an Interchange Station and considerable expense to then provide a finish compatible with a station intended to be the gateway to the City.

Escalators and steps lead up to the concourse of the main line station – there are also lifts. Below, fitters check out the Ticket Vending Machines as the platform nears completion. Lower left is the view from Shepley Street with Piccadilly Station tower in the background whilst lower right can be seen the concrete box which is portrayed on the previous page during construction.

John C. Berry, formerly Project Manager (Manchester) with British Rail was seconded to the Passenger Transport Executive from Transmark in February 1988 to become the Executive's Principal Project Engineer.

Entrance to and exit from the Undercroft is protected by traffic lights where the LRVs cross London Road. The twin portals for the separate platforms can be seen, with an inbound vehicle about to cross the bus lane in the immediate foreground. Above the access portals work continues rebuilding the stone parapet.

centre of the island platform was such that there would be insufficient width remaining to accommodate two platform faces and a stairway. These conclusions finally emerged at the beginning of September 1990 and GMPTE's Principal Project Engineer, John Berry, vividly remembers emerging from a final meeting at the Department of Transport's offices in London realising that notes of the meeting would need to be supplemented by a plan of the alternative suggestions that had emerged. "I needed to get a plan to the consortium's design consultants quickly, so I sat in the September sunshine on a bench on the Embankment, opposite the Houses of Parliament, and re-drew the concept sketch using the top of my briefcase as a drawing board!" Within less than a week, this had been translated into a working engineering drawing and the race against time to secure BR's approval to all the details of a brand new scheme began. This was to take almost four months with a start on site finally being allowed on 5th January 1991.

The eventual solution was the creation of an enormous concrete box within the Undercroft, encasing the area used by the LRVs and also encasing each and every adjacent pillar. Mowlem, a major company in civil engineering by any standards, regards this as its biggest-ever reinforced concrete contract. Project Manager Jim McDermott quotes a figure of 6,000 cu m of concrete used in this area – a vast amount by any reckoning. The original design would have required only 700 cu m of concrete.

An additional six months were necessary to achieve what was required and were added to this part of the DBOM contract.

The cost implications and extension of timescale were considerable. Indeed, at one stage in 1990 the whole Interchange scheme was at risk and the Executive began to face the awesome prospect of LRVs terminating on the other side of London Road, in the derelict area between Aytoun Street and London Road itself.

Additional costs in the region of £2.5m were foreseen, and discussions with Government Ministers were frequent, long and earnest.

A £1.2m contribution from the Central Manchester Development Corporation helped considerably and was used to give the concrete box a finish appropriate to Manchester's principal station interchange. John Glestor, CMDC's Managing Director, regards the money as a sound investment in the process of upgrading that part of the city which falls within his area of responsibility.

Inside the station a combination of tiling terrazzo and vandal resistant wallboarding has transformed the otherwise drab finish whilst outside, the entrance has been brick clad, following the pattern set at G-Mex. A seasonal touch was provided by Mowlem when a tree, with coloured lights, appeared above the entrance to mark Christmas 1991.

After causing substantial delay and having major cost implication, Piccadilly Station in the Undercroft will provide a fitting entrance point to the City and the Metrolink system.

Metrolink cars are electrically powered, drawing their current from overhead wires as shown. The contract to design the power supply system and to distribute it was awarded to GEC Alsthom Transportation Projects Ltd of Stafford which in turn sub-contracted the work to Balfour Beatty Power Construction Ltd.

It was originally envisaged that a line voltage of 750 volts dc would be used on the street-running section where cars run at lower speeds. The more economical 1500 volt dc supply would have been used on the two former railway sections, where speeds of up to 50 mile/h will be achieved.

One of the main advantages of this situation would have been the ability to provide lighter section overhead on the railway sections and also to reduce the number of sub-stations to around five, whereas by using only 750v as many as 18 would have been required to provide sufficient power to allow twin unit operation throughout the system.

Design work and computer simulation with predicted traffic patterns and loadings showed that such a system was feasible. Because one of the braking systems fitted to the LRVs uses regenerative braking however, where the motors act as dynamos and feed current back into the system as they slow down, the energy saving would be reduced if the system had been split into three separately fed sections. This factor, and the need to plan ahead for future extensions which would also involve street running finally led to the decision to standardise on 750 volts throughout the system. The vehicle's equipment was thus simplified and there was a saving in equipment costs in the sub-stations.

Power is supplied by Norweb at either 11kV or 6.6kV depending on availability in different areas of the city. As shown in the accompanying diagram ten sub-stations then convert this supply to the 750v dc required to power the cars, and also provide power to change the electrically operated and heated points, the various control systems and the backup battery systems. The Queens Road Operation & Maintenance Centre has its own sub-station.

It was also originally envisaged that the LRVs would work coupled together 'in-multiple', when operational requirements or emergency situations warranted it, whilst still using only one driver. Unfortunately in the ever-present need for economies the system had to be built for single, as opposed to multiple unit operation, although the articulated units are able to operate in pairs, using the Dellner couplers fitted throughout the fleet.

When the trials took place early in 1992 it quickly became apparent that the sub-stations would not be able to cope with the loads imposed by double-units – some 2,500 amps are needed for each twin car set. Whilst there is sufficient power for one twin unit to operate in any one section, the operational implications are incompatible with reliable operation and Metrolink will only operate single cars for the foreseeable future. The operational and training aspects of this situation are discussed in Chapters 17 and 18.

All sub-stations have space for the additional power supply equipment and the whole power system has been designed to take account of possible failures and also equipment being taken out of service for maintenance.

The need to provide power for an intensive service of cars drawing some 1250 amps – 2500 amps in twin configuration – requires a substantial volume

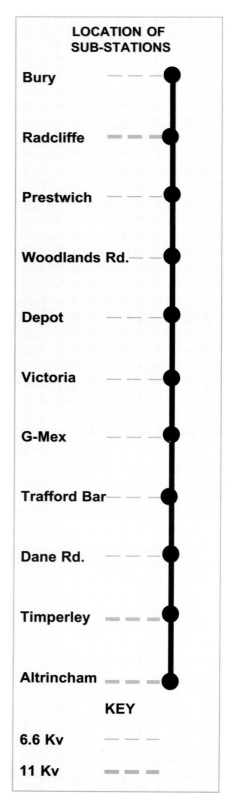

LOCATION OF
SUB-STATIONS

Bury

Radcliffe

Prestwich

Woodlands Rd.

Depot

Victoria

G-Mex

Trafford Bar

Dane Rd.

Timperley

Altrincham

KEY

6.6 Kv

11 Kv

Section isolators, located on top of appropriate poles, require rods to allow operation from ground level. Padlocks prevent unauthorised use. The associated wiring is also clearly visible.

The traction poles are secured by bolts set in concrete. In many cases the resiting of underground services had effectively eliminated the space required for the pole location – one unfortunate by product of the otherwise very effective advance works. Certain poles, marked with a green band and the letter 'E' (as seen on the second, fifth and seventh poles) indicate the presence of a trackside negative point for use in emergency. After the overhead line has been switched off a safety short-circuiting cable will be applied, connecting the overhead wire to this negative return, and ensuring that the line cannot be re-energised whilst fire or other emergency services are working adjacent to the track.

of copper to carry the current and two wires have been needed to meet loading specification. (A third wire would be necessary in the City Centre before unrestricted multiple operation could begin.)

On street the twin overhead wire is, in the main, supported by traction poles. The use of pantographs on the LRVs requires the overhead to be strung over the track, unlike systems using trolley poles where the overhead wire can be some distance to the side of the track.

The inability to provide suitable fixing points on buildings in some streets has been due to their modern construction whereby no suitably strong fixing points are available or, it is believed, an unacceptably high charge has been required by property owners for the right to provide fixing points.

Less satisfactory is the situation regarding the section breakers perched on top of some poles. The contractors expected to place these in trackside cabinets, a traditional location acceptable to the IOR. The City planners had other ideas, however, and would not accept such cabinets, hence the eventual positioning. Since all the point control equipment is in trackside cabinets, as seen in St. Peter's Square and outside Lewis's, for example, the planners' attitude is difficult for the lay man to understand.

In the City return current is designed to find its way back to the sub-station without leakage thanks to the construction of the track base and also the insulation of the street sections by bonding the rails in a plastic polymer. This had become a crucial aspect of construction following problems with stray current from the Tyne & Wear Metro which were first noticed at Newcastle University. Major Holden affirmed the efficiency of the earth return in Manchester in Chapter 10. Insulation on the railway sections is achieved in the conventional way by means of wooden sleepers and stone ballast.

During the conversion of the Bury Line theft of the copper bonds linking the non-welded rails became a frequent hazard. Despite the obvious need to weld these bonds to the rails they were merely attached by nuts and bolts. To make matters easier for both parties the thieves often left the stainless nuts and bolts behind! The arrival of Metrolink's police detachment – and visits to likely outlets for the bonds – eventually brought this to an end.

One major aspect which has given rise for concern is the ability of the system as built to cope with the projected operational flexibility. GMML, as operator, based its training programme and operational timetable on the strategic use of twin cars as previously mentioned. Its whole policy was structured accordingly and it came as a major blow when, in January 1992, any thoughts of twin operation had to be deferred. This aspect will have to be addressed and remedied as passenger loadings rise to meet expectations.

Notwithstanding this GEC Alsthom is confident that the system will be capable of coping with the present and future requirements of Metrolink including the use of additional cars. When the system is extended partially or to its maximum potential there will be a need for an additional sub-station to serve the City Centre – this will be located in the Undercroft.

The specially-designed and purpose-built Metrolink vehicles have been constructed by the Firema Consortium in Italy. Firema offered the best overall package in a competitive tender.

Each vehicle consists of two similar cars connected by an articulation unit supported by the centre bogie. By this means the 29-metre long vehicle can meet the design specification to negotiate a minimum radius of 25 metres, necessary for some of the sharp curves in the city, particularly those into and out of Market Street and High Street.

Because the cars will have to cope with two different boarding situations – on-street and from the existing railway station platforms – much thought was given to the best and most appropriate design. A further very important requirement was to provide access for disabled persons in wheelchairs, and also for passengers with children in pushchairs or with heavy luggage.

Whilst a low-floor design would have made provision for entry from the street easy for everyone, the existence of the 18 railway stations precluded this. As already recorded it was finally decided to construct small stations in the city streets at key locations, and to arrange for a section of these station platforms to be at the same height as the railway station platforms.

Because the height, degree of slope and general appearance of the on-street station platforms was recognised as being critical if the objectives of maximum access and aesthetic appeal were to be achieved, a mock-up was constructed and exhibited during the Autumn of 1988 in the then disused Birchfields Road bus depot. Almost four decades previously the city's last tram had made its last journey into this same depot.

In order to assist everyone involved in the project it was subsequently arranged that a prototype body shell would be delivered to Manchester in March 1990. It was set against a profiled platform to a modified design proposed by GEC Alsthom and housed in one of the arches under the main line railway into Piccadilly station. This allowed detailed examination of many aspects of the car's design to be made and also provided a useful forum for discussion with the many interested groups of people who needed or wanted to see the vehicle.

The availability of this prototype also helped in other ways. The interior of the cars has been designed in consultation with Metrolink's future passengers, some 2000 of whom visited the prototype during the several open days when it was available to everyone for inspection and comment. Following these most useful events many minor modifications were made in the light of points raised, though the car building programme was delayed in the process. Perhaps the Consortium had been too accessible. The seats were a particularly sensitive issue and caused the longest delay to completion of the bodies.

Design of the cars

The basis of the design features a steel underframe upon which is mounted the welded steel body. The wooden floor has an abrasion-resistant rubber covering. Each half of the LRV has fixed seats for 39 passengers and two fold-down seats, together with a further four in the articulation, as shown.

The design life of the cars is 30 years, allowing for major overhaul after

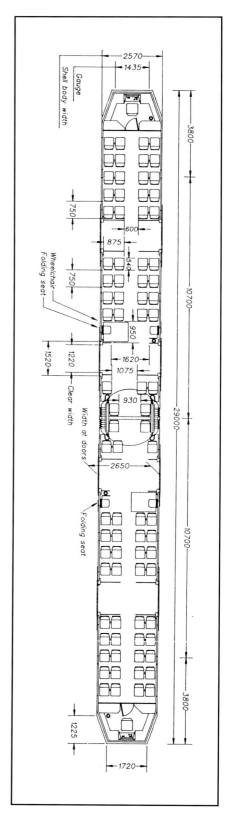

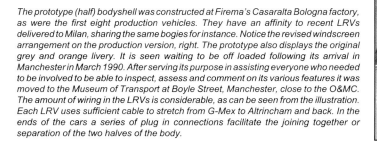

The prototype (half) bodyshell was constructed at Firema's Casaralta Bologna factory, as were the first eight production vehicles. They have an affinity to recent LRVs delivered to Milan, sharing the same bogies for instance. Notice the revised windscreen arrangement on the production version, right. The prototype also displays the original grey and orange livery. It is seen waiting to be off loaded following its arrival in Manchester in March 1990. After serving its purpose in assisting everyone who needed to be involved to be able to inspect, assess and comment on its various features it was moved to the Museum of Transport at Boyle Street, Manchester, close to the O&MC. The amount of wiring in the LRVs is considerable, as can be seen from the illustration. Each LRV uses sufficient cable to stretch from G-Mex to Altrincham and back. In the ends of the cars a series of plug in connections facilitate the joining together or separation of the two halves of the body.

LRV for Manchester Metrolink

publiespo

Articulated Light Rail Vehicle Firema type T 68,
for the GMA Group - Manchester Metrolink
- Total capacity 201 passengers
- 2 areas for wheelchairs
- Access from low and high level platforms
- Propulsion equipment GTO Chopper
- Maximum speed 80 km/h

FIREMA - quality, experience, technology

FIREMA Consortium
Viale Edison, 120
20099 Sesto S. Giovanni (Milano) - Italy
Tel. (39) 02 2494396 - Fax (39) 02 26225380

FIREMA

every ten years. Routine servicing will be carried out every 7 days and will take 5 hours. Each articulated set has cost slightly less than £1m which compares very favourably with the German-built LRVs ordered for Sheffield, for example, which will cost over £1.4m each. Albeit the latter cars are more sophisticated than the Metrolink units.

Power is taken from the overhead line via a roof-mounted pantograph manufactured by Brecknell Willis of Chard, Somerset. The pantograph is spring-loaded to maintain contact with the overhead wire and does not need turning at termini of course.

One half of the still-to-be completed first LRV makes the historic roll-out at Firema's Casaralta factory in July 1991. Hauled by cable connected to a fork lift truck the unit was taken from the assembly hall, via the factory's huge twin-tracked traverser, and positioned with the centre bogie on the electrically operated turntable where rotation to correspond to 25m radius curves allowed clearances to be verified.

The LRV is mounted on three bogies, the outer pair each being powered by two 105kw motors, whilst the central non-powered one supports the turntable connecting the two halves of the body via a flexible concertina gangway. Braking is incorporated on all three bogies. The 48 ton LRVs are designed to accelerate on the flat at a rate of 1.3m/s^2 when fully laden. This rapid acceleration will assist in maintaining schedules and reducing time lost in any delays to a minimum. Top speed of the LRVs will be 80km/h (50 mile/h) on the railway sections and 48km/h (30 mile/h) on street. Normal braking gives a deceleration rate of up to 1.3m/s^2 whilst in an emergency the cars will decelerate at an impressive 2.6m/s^2, stopping in their own length from 50km/h (30 mile/h). This emergency braking is achieved by the use of six magnetic track brakes which each apply a force of 60kN directly to the rail. Their power comes from the vehicle's batteries thus ensuring that the LRVs can be stopped in emergency even in the event of a total power failure. Emergency braking is automatically enacted in the event of an LRV passing a signal at danger, by the driver releasing the Traction and Braking Controller or striking the red emergency stop button in the centre of the control panel.

Table showing the impressive braking performance of the LRVs, courtesy GEC.

Air suspension ensures comfortable riding and the bodies incorporate insulation to reduce noise intrusion. The bodyshell interiors are sprayed with a sound-deadening material after priming and then most of the inside panelling is further insulated with fibreglass mat in sealed foil bags.

The vehicles incorporate thermostatically-controlled heating and fan-assisted ventilation, with fluorescent lighting and ventilation ducts recessed into the ceiling.

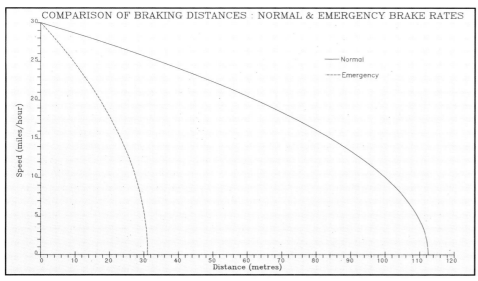

COMPARISON OF BRAKING DISTANCES : NORMAL & EMERGENCY BRAKE RATES

— Normal
---- Emergency

Speed (miles/hour)

Distance (metres)

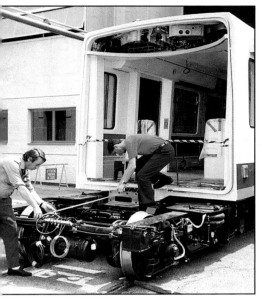

Checking clearances on the articulation bogie.

The emergency release, located above the doors.

Emergency call point for disabled passengers.

Hopper-type opening sections are fitted at the top of the main saloon windows. Two emergency communication panels are provided in each vehicle, mounted on the bulkhead door leading to the driver's compartment, and by this means contact can be made with the driver. Use of this call point also automatically alerts Control. There are additional communication points located adjacent to the fold down seats where wheelchairs are carried. Opening and closing of the doors is under the driver's control but the opening of individual doors is initiated by passengers pressing a button. This also activates the retractable step if it is required. Red emergency handles located above the doors allow emergency release by passengers. The nominal capacity of each articulated car is 201, of whom 86 are seated (4 in fold-down seats). In high-peak conditions 270 can be carried at a density of 6 m^2 sq. Research using existing traffic loadings together with projected traffic patterns enables Metrolink's planners to predict that no passenger should have to stand for more than 15 minutes outside the city centre on any journey. Should these figures be exceeded the Passenger Transport Executive, which, as owner, will monitor the system, will require changes to be made or impose penalties. It is a part of the philosophy that passengers should be able to travel standing in the vehicle, if need be, rather than standing at the station waiting for an LRV running to a less frequent timetable.

Both the interior and exterior of the cars have been designed to give a modern attractive appearance, and yet also to be capable of being easily kept clean and serviced. Externally the LRVs are finished in an attractive livery of pale grey and dark grey with aquamarine relief bearing the Metrolink logo, fleetname and number. Advertising will be carried in the form of sponsorship for individual units. Design Consultants were involved in this aspect of the cars' design. Fitch RS devised the Metrolink corporate identity and colour whilst Design Triangle developed the livery for the vehicle and the overall styling both inside and out. Modern materials reduce maintenance to a minimum and also meet stringent safety regulations. An automatic car washing plant at Queen's Road is used to wash every car once every 24 hours and Metrolink's management is determined that the fleet will attract passengers by its clean appearance. The large windows will allow excellent vision for passengers although, unfortunately, not being double glazed they very quickly steam up on wet days.

Construction of the cars

Although the body construction of the vehicles was carried out in Italy, some 60% of the LRV's content came from the UK. Thus traction and control equipment, cable, windows and windscreens, drivers seats, doors, braking equipment, pantographs and other items needed to be sent to the various factories as construction proceeded. GEC Alsthom, responsible for the supply of the LRVs, were fortunate in having in Manchester an international forwarding company with facilities and offices throughout Europe, but specifically at Chiasso on the Swiss/Italian border. Danzas provided a storage facility which allowed the various sub-contractors to forward their goods for onward transmission. The responsibility for ensuring that items went out in the correct sequence rested with Danzas. Their articulated 'piggy-back' trailers left Manchester every week and were transferred from road to rail at Dunkirk. The consignments were then taken by rail to the Agent's depot at Chiasso. Over 950 crates weighing some 352 tonnes were despatched in this way taking on average three days to reach their appropriate factory destination.

All five factories in the Firema Consortium, which was formed in 1980, have been involved in the work which has been co-ordinated and monitored by project engineers from Firema and GECA working together. The five factories are located at Bologna, Cittadella, two in Caserta, and Padua. GECA, in addition to its on-site representative Brian Middleton, the Assistant Project Manager, also had a team of its electrical specialists at each factory.

The underframe and body construction, fitting out, wiring and completion of the vehicles was divided amongst the other four factories as follows. All underframes were built at Casaralta, Bologna, where the first eight production vehicles were also assembled and fitted out. Cabs, bodysides and the articulation units were built at Fiore, Caserta, and seven vehicles were

Although the two halves of each articulated unit appear virtually identical from the ground, the external differences between the 'A' and 'B' sections are obvious here. The pantograph, which is raised by means of air pressure is seen extended to reach the wire at a height of some 6m. Also mounted on the 'A' half of the unit is the lightning arrester – designed to protect the equipment from surges of current – together with the brake resistors and the supporting arms for the articulation unit. These resemble an X in the photograph. The articulation has to cope with horizontal and vertical movement, on curves and gradients, and also with twisting movements where super-elevated curves are located on gradients, as at Cornbrook Underpass. Photograph by John Fox courtesy Manchester Evening News.

finished there. Roofs and the bodyshells were built at Casertane, Caserta (where the prototype had been produced), and seven vehicles were finished there. Four vehicles were completed at Cittadella.

There was thus a considerable amount of movement of partially completed components between factories in the early stages of construction but handling the contract in this manner enabled a greater number of vehicles to be in-build at one time, and was crucial to meet the very tight deadlines.

The bogies for all the 26 cars, plus a spare set to cover maintenance requirements, were constructed and assembled at Officine OMS in Padua. Similar to bogies supplied by Firema for operation in Milan they incorporate amongst other items wheelsets and axles from Germany and motors from GECA's factory in Preston.

Number 1001, the first vehicle to be completed, was not ready until July 1991, and was despatched by road – after a trial run to ensure it could leave the factory as one complete unit – on 23rd of that month. Its journey was not uneventful. Italian and French police held it up during peak holiday times and when it finally arrived on British soil it demolished one of the escorting BMW police cars whilst ably demonstrating the extreme manoeuvrability of its purpose-built trailer. It was the only car delivered as a complete unit.

Following arrival at Queens Road on 29th August the delicate and difficult job of unloading took place next day. A gently sloping ramp had been constructed and brought over on the towing vehicle. The complete vehicle was rolled off the low loading trailer, down the ramp and coupled, via the Dellner coupling, to the Metrolink SPV diesel locomotive. It was then moved into the workshops for commissioning by GECA staff before being handed over to GMML for staff training to begin.

Brian Middleton, GEC's Assistant Project Engineer, with Aldo Agosto, Firema's Project Engineer, inside a partially completed bodyshell at the Casaralta factory in July 1991.

Operation of the LRVs

The LRVs are designed to be operated by one person and driving can be performed from either end. The driver has a separate cab which houses all the controls to start and stop the car, operate the door circuits, control the lights and trafficators, activate heating and ventilation, communicate with passengers or Control at the O&MC at Queen's Road and so on. A deep windscreen and long side windows, all heated, give excellent visibility from the driver's cab and there are also large self-retracting pneumatically-operated mirrors fitted to the outside of the car. These mirrors are electrically heated and are adjustable from the cab.

Driving the car is achieved by use of the Traction and Braking Controller or 'joystick' handle which reverts to full brake mode when released. Pushing the handle forward initiates acceleration through the micro-processor-controlled chopper equipment which takes the place of traditional resistance-based control equipment. In its 'centre' position the handle allows the vehicle to coast without drawing power. The on-board electronic control systems will monitor the car's performance even whilst it is coasting. Pulling the handle back initiates the braking routines. A twist-action requires

*The complete articulated LRV, together with the tractor unit carrying the off-loading ramp, made an impressive sight moving along the motorways at around 45 mile/h. The computer controlled axles on the trailer made manoeuvring seem very simple but Zambetti's driver was clearly well versed in the art of moving long vehicles as anyone watching the off-loading and who saw him line up the vehicle precisely to the rail head from a distance of some 200ft, and from **behind** the trailer, will testify.*

After the delays and other problems encountered in transporting the first unit as a complete assembly, it was decided to bring all subsequent bodies in two halves. A special gantry was erected at Queens Road to facilitate unloading of the bodies directly onto their bogies. On one never-to-be forgotten morning six lorries waited to off-load causing access problems of some magnitude for staff and other contractors. On this occasion the seventh – missing – lorry had the vehicles' bogies!

the driver to maintain a constant force otherwise an immediate full emergency brake application will be made. This is the universally used 'dead man's handle' system which ensures safety of passengers in the event of the driver being taken ill or otherwise incapacitated, a principle which has been in existence since the advent of electric railways.

Braking is effected by a combination of regenerative and rheostatic action, combined with pneumatically operated disc and magnetic track brakes for maximum effect and safety. The precise levels of braking applied from each system are automatically adjusted by the Davies and Metcalfe equipment, to prevent wheel slip on acceleration or wheel slide on braking. There is also driver-operated sanding equipment.

The vehicle's computerised control system will first ascertain whether regenerative braking is possible (dependent on another vehicle being able to use the regenerated current). Any increase in line voltage following regenerative braking will be detected by the on-board monitoring equipment and the excess current will be dissipated through the roof-mounted resistors. The second stage of deceleration uses rheostatic braking, followed by air-operated disc braking via the discs fitted to all axles. The magnetic track brake is not controlled by the normal braking software but is automatically applied in emergency conditions as already explained. A spring applied parking brake completes the equipment.

At the beginning of each journey the driver will program the car's route into the console in the driving cab so that all the necessary points will be automatically set in the correct position. The selection and operation of points is handled by a device fitted to the LRV which actuates a transponder set into the road surface ahead of the change mechanism. By this means the points will be changed as the car approaches them and pedestrians will have moved out of the way. It is, of course, the driver's responsibility to check at all times that the lineside points indicator shows the expected direction, and that the points lie correctly.

The shape of things to come – multiple operation in Lower Mosley Street, during trials. When passenger loadings require this level of capacity Metrolink will have achieved the planners' objectives. Let us hope we shall soon see this goal reached.

The driver's controls are conveniently situated around the centrally mounted Chapman's seat. Prominent in this view is the control joystick (Traction and Braking Controller) with the in-built horn button, to the left of the control console. An ignition key can be seen to the left of the TBC. It has three positions, Off/Shunt/ Normal. In shunt mode the LRVs are limited to a maximum speed of 12 mile/h. This function can be used in the depot area for instance. Normal mode is used in service operation. The console has a speedometer (left) radio (centre) air vent and air pressure gauge (right) with digital clock above. The prominent red button above the radio activates the emergency stop. The microphone allows the driver to announce stops and to communicate, where necessary, with passengers. The telephone provides a direct link to the Control Centre. Extreme right is the key pad to allow route setting to be programmed. Other switches control the raising and lowering of the pantograph, flange lubrication (where fitted), heating and ventilation, wipers and screen washers, lighting and traffic indicator circuits, hazard lights, de-icing, sanding, brake application for starting on gradients, mirror controls and so on. Opening and closing of the doors is controlled from switches located to the driver's left and right as appropriate. The lever to change from segregated to street running is located on the right, below the key pad, and has three positions – Segregated (rail running), Street running without step operation and Street with steps. Operation of the steps will only be necessary when multiple operation begins and provision is included for automatic coupling and un-coupling from the console. A fault system display can be seen at the extreme left of the illustration. Photograph by John Fox courtesy Manchester Evening News.

To allow maximum flexibility in operation and productivity, the LRVs were designed to be operated 'in multiple'. By this means one driver would be able to control two (or in emergency up to four) units and the whole operation, including coupling up, could be performed automatically by means of the Dellner auto-coupler fitted to the ends of all LRVs. As recorded in the previous chapter this will now be more restrictive than originally planned due to limitations of power supply.

Access to the cars is through the wide sliding doors, and handrails and stanchions are provided for passengers' convenience. Because the vehicles will have to accommodate two different levels for passenger access, retractable steps are incorporated below each doorway. These steps will extend automatically as required on the trailing vehicles if or when the cars are able to operate in multiple. On-street, the leading vehicle will stop alongside the high ramp for level access.

On the vehicles two areas adjacent to the centre doors have been specially set aside for wheelchairs and a further two for passengers' luggage. Fold-down seats are provided in these areas which, as previously stated, also have two communication points. To assist those in wheelchairs the appropriate areas of the existing railway station platforms have been specially marked to ensure that they enter by the correct doorway. This is important for those wishing to alight in the city centre where only part of the on-street station is at the LRV floor height.

Tickets will not be sold on the cars, thus leaving the driver free to concentrate on the task of driving. Every station has a minimum of two ticket vending machines and it is the passenger's responsibility to see that he or she has a ticket before boarding. Tickets are of a paper type and there is no provision for cancellation by passengers when they board. On-vehicle checking will be carried out by a team of Customer Service Inspectors.

Commissioning

The first unit, number 1001, was used for 'Type Testing' to satisfy the Railway Inspector as to its suitability, and also to prove that it met the contractual obligations. This took some three months during which time the vehicle was fitted with instruments to allow setting up and monitoring of braking, acceleration, power consumption, software performance and so on.

Whilst this was in hand the remainder of the fleet was being delivered. Numbers 1002-1026 were delivered as separate halves, greatly easing transport logistics, and were assembled at the O&MC.

Each LRV was then put through a routine taking some 14 days on average, which first allowed for completion of build (installing signalling and radio equipment and other items which could not be tested in Italy). Next came a series of modifications needed to enhance performance or to correct deficiencies which became apparent as cars completed trial running and their suspension 'bedded-in'. A thorough basic check followed to ensure that all components had been correctly reconnected following reassembly.

The LRV was then ready for power testing, initially a static operation, followed by low speed movement in the depot area before full speed trials took place on the Bury line. After all testing was successfully completed the

Access for the mobility impaired. Metrolink has provided the first form of non-dedicated public transport that is accessible to people in wheelchairs. Station platforms are designed to have level access with a 75mm gap between the vehicle and the edge of the platform, thus facilitating easy access. During the settling in period, suspension of some of the units needed to be adjusted to achieve level entry. This view illustrates the situation encountered when suspension heights have not been adjusted to harmonise the vehicle floor with the platform.

By contrast when the alignment has been correctly adjusted access could not be bettered. New or improved access at many stations, including the provision of gently sloped ramps, and/or lifts, makes travel by Metrolink easier than any other form of public or private transport. This will undoubtedly prove to be a growth area as more people discover how easy travel – and especially shopping – has become. Note the two fold-down seats, one each side of the saloon, and the grab rail with integral low-level communication point for persons in wheelchairs. One of the push buttons to open the sliding doors can be seen to the right. Overall the impression inside the car is light, airy and attractive. Photograph by John Fox courtesy Manchester Evening News.

*Car 1009, **CIS 125 SPECIAL**, shows the positioning of the decals on sponsored cars and the reason for the change in location of the fleet numbers.*

cars were handed over to GMML. As the programme progressed in Italy Firema were able to carry out a full 'works test' on the final sixteen LRVs, under GECA supervision, but lack of full scale track facilities in any of their factories limited this to minimal movement.

Shortly after arrival 1001 was sent by road to Metro-Cammell for modification to the cross members in the articulation unit. Numbers 1002 onwards were modified during construction at Firema's factories.

A number of items requiring adjustment or modification came to light as trial running began. These ranged from software enhancement to optimise braking and acceleration performance, through suspension levelling to achieve correct platform alignment, to modification of the door runners to cure a friction problem which caused a small number of embarrassing failures in the first few weeks of operation.

The modifications requiring to be done to each of the 26 LRVs were sufficient to create a bewildering number of permutations since, clearly, not every car could be dealt with at once. At one point all 26 were 'unique' making training of engineering and operational staff extremely difficult. One particular difficulty in this period was the inability to couple up and move certain cars when one unit failed and another was sent to rescue it.

An unfortunate situation arose when the first vehicles were put through the car wash and turned out not to be watertight. Firema very quickly sent a team to reglaze the cars to rectify this embarrassing fault. More routine matters have required a continuous Firema presence on-site, some three or more persons normally being resident at Queens Road.

Livery and Passenger Information

The livery change from the prototype illustrated on page 105 clearly improved the cars' appearance. An early decision to seek sponsorship for the vehicles resulted in the fleet numbers being repositioned on the side of the cars rather than under the cab side windows, as seen in the illustrations.

Sponsored cars carry a variety of promotional items ranging from roof boards, through interior decals printed to railway style name panels under the cab side windows. System maps are carried on the saloon coving.

Number 1007 inaugurated operation in the City Centre, fitted with a circular plate carrying the coat-of-arms of the City of Manchester, as applied to the original trams. As already mentioned, 1007 was the fleet number carried by the last tram to run through Manchester, on 10th January 1949.

PASSENGER VEHICLE DETAILS

Overall length 29m   Overall width 2.65m   Overall height 3.36m
2 power bogies each fitted with 2x105kW traction motors.
Centre bogie unpowered, all bogies 2.065m wheelbase
Gross weight 63.1 tonnes (48 tonnes unladen).
Axle load 11 tonnes (motored) 9.5 tonnes (trailing).
Track gauge: standard – 1435mm   Wheel diameter 740mm (new).
Seating capacity 82+4 pull-down. Standing 122 at 4 per m². 2 wheelchair spaces.
Maximum speed 80km/h. Maximum gradient 6.5%. Minimum curve radius
25m. Contact wire height 3.8m minimum, 7.01m maximum

Fleet No.	Where Built	Delivery to UK	Handover to GMML	Sponsor
1001	Casaralta	28.08.91	6.04.92	
1002	Casaralta	16.10.92	6.04.92	Arndale Centre
1003	Casaralta	5.11.91	6.04.92	Co-op Bank
1004	Casaralta	27.11.91	6.04.92	
1005	Casaralta	4.12.91	6.04.92	
1006	Casaralta	29.12.91	6.04.92	
1007	Fiore	4.12.91	6.04.92	
1008	Cittadella	28.12.91	6.04.92	
1009	Casaralta	12.01.92	6.04.92	C.I.S.
1010	Casaralta	12.01.92	6.04.92	
1011	Casertane	20.12.91	6.04.92	
1012	Fiore	24.01.92	6.04.92	
1013	Cittadella	30.01.92	6.04.92	
1014	Casertane	30.01.92	TBA	
1015	Casertane	27.03.92	TBA	
1016	Fiore	13.02.92	06.04.92	
1017	Casertane	18.02.92	27.04.92	
1018	Cittadella	28.02.92	27.04.92	
1019	Casertane	06.03.92	27.04.92	
1020	Fiore	23.02.92	06.04.92	
1021	Casertane	05.03.92	27.04.92	
1022	Fiore	05.03.92	27.04.92	
1023	Casertane	18.03.92	11.05.92	
1024	Cittadella	02.04.92	22.05.92	
1025	Fiore	22.03.92	26.05.92	
1026	Fiore	09.04.92	26.05.92	

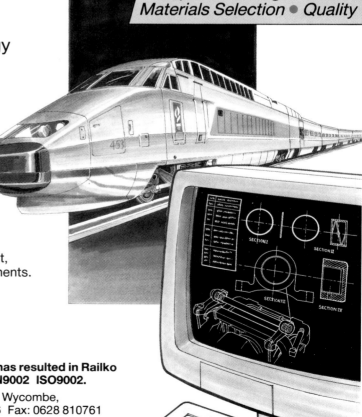

The method of creating Greater Manchester Metro Ltd (GMML) was almost certainly unique in public transport in the United Kingdom. Although GMML was the Contractor, and as such responsible to the Passenger Transport Executive for the implementation of the DBOM Contract, its small team had first of all to recruit staff to build up the organisation which would be required to perform the multitude of tasks needed to operate a street-running light railway expected to carry 10 million passengers per year.

Both in the GMA's bid and in the analysis prepared the total size of the workforce to operate Stage I of Metrolink was about 160 people made up as follows:

Management & Administration		20
Operations staff	- Drivers	60
	- CSIs	20
	- Controllers	20
Engineering		40
		160

This team had to be built up before commercial service could start. It was, therefore, a key element in the pre-operational budget. It followed that staff had to be recruited as late as possible giving due allowance for training. It also meant that the recruitment and training of staff had to go hand-in-hand with the delivery and commissioning of equipment including, most importantly, rolling stock and suitable lengths of line to use for both commissioning and training.

The first directors were Eric Black, Scott Hellewell and Don Kenny. At the beginning of 1990, Eric Black joined the organisation as Chief Executive, being seconded from GEC. Eric Black brought with him experience of Mass Transit construction and operation in Hong Kong and also experience of rail vehicle construction at Metro Cammell where he had been Director and General Manager of Projects.

Scott Hellewell had moved back to Manchester in 1988 to become the Passenger Transport Executive's nominee to spearhead the new company which would operate the system. A former GMPTE officer, he had returned to Manchester from South Yorkshire PTE where he had been Director of Operations. As the LRT scheme progressed Scott Hellewell was to take a major role and when the Tenders were accepted and Contracts let he moved to Queens Road to be on hand as work began. His position as Operations Director also incorporates responsibility for engineering matters.

The appointment of Don Kenny, seconded from Mowlem, completed the members of the Directorate. Don Kenny had previously been Commercial Director at London City Airport and joined Metrolink as its Commercial Director.

The Directors established a number of principles relating to personnel and training. These included:

1.   All staff would be salaried and with the same employment conditions.

Prime Minister John Major's ride – and spell at the controls – in a Metrolink car during the 1992 pre-election run-up, seemed to put the seal of approval on Light Rail. Eric Black (seen left), then Chief Executive of GMML, and Dr Keith Lloyd (centre), GMML Chairman, explained some of the finer points to Mr Major when he returned to the saloon. Alas, in June 1992, Treasury officials put Light Rail onto the back-burner with their announcement of non-availability of funding during 1992 for the West Midlands Centro project.

2. All staff would be on individual salaries and subject to an annual performance review.

3. Basic hours of work would be related to a 37.5 hour week, expressed as a 150 hour month.

4. All maintenance, other than rolling stock, would be sub-contracted. The Company would concentrate on the management and marketing of operations.

5. All Operations Department staff (ie operations and engineering) would be required to pass out as Drivers for driving trains in public service. Once so passed they would have to drive eight hours per month, in traffic, to keep up their expertise. This recognised that driving was to be a basic skill.

6. Operating staff would be fully trained by the Company, irrespective of their background.

7. Only qualified Engineering staff would be taken on and then given specific training relating to the specialist/unique equipment used by the Company.

8. There would be no Personnel or Industrial Relations Department, rather each manager would be responsible for his/her own personnel/staff matters.

9. There would be no Training Department – in spite of the enormous training workload – since this was likely to disappear after 18/24 months. The initial intake of staff at each level of each discipline would train subsequent recruits – 'the trainees would become the trainers'.

10. A Recruitment Officer would be taken on with a short term contract and be responsible for managing the whole process to the requirements of the individual managers.

11. All staff would pass through the same Induction Course so that, irrespective of background they would become 'Metrolink people'.

Subsequently two things happened to change staff numbers, one temporary and one permanent. In the spring of 1991 it was decided to phase in the SCADA system (see Chapter 19) over a period up to October 1992. This meant that a number of functions would require manual operation rather than using the SCADA system. The continued local operation of Hagside Crossing was a case in point. This required approximately 20 additional Temporary Operations Staff to be employed.

When tenders were sought for maintenance of the signals, permanent way, ticket vending machines etc, it was found that to obtain the response times necessary for an operating railway meant the contractors employing full-time dedicated staff. It was therefore cheaper for GMML to employ the staff direct themselves, cutting out the sub-contractors profit mark-ups and improving supervision. Thus the permanent establishment was increased by about 20 people.

Following the appointment of the directors, together with Miss Hilary Taylor to look after administration, the next requirement was to recruit qualified and experienced operating and engineering staff. Engineering Management Selection were retained by GMML to do this. Barry Scott, the Senior Partner, was well versed in the requirement of the railway industry, albeit mainly on the engineering side. Job and man specifications were prepared by the Operations Director and by a series of interviews short-lists of three people were drawn up for the key posts of Engineering Manager and Operations Manager.

It was logical that the initial appointees would have experience of the London Docklands Light Railway and also the Tyne & Wear Metro, since these two systems represent the only comparable UK operation, and also that British Rail could be expected to provide applicants with engineering and signalling experience. Thus Jim Harries and Paul Neal joined GMML in mid 1990. Jim Harries had previously been with British Rail and latterly been Engineering Manager then Terminal Manager at the Freightliner Terminal in Trafford Park Manchester. Paul Neal had worked with London Transport, Docklands Light Railway and joined Metrolink from Tyne & Wear Metro. Immediately these two set out devising the structure and staffing requirements of their respective sections – Engineering and Operations. The guidelines for this had already been established by the Directors when developing the pre-operational budget. However, within overall limits of staff numbers and budget they had considerable freedom.

Engineering Management Selection (EMS) were again used for the recruitment of the Engineering staff, but recruitment priorities had first to be established. Since Jim Harries was a Mechanical and Electrics Engineer it would have been logical to appoint a Civil Engineer first. That would also have been in line with railway custom – and practice. However, there were two critical areas that the Company had to 'get hold of' – rolling stock and signalling. Rolling stock was self-evident with the design of the depot progressing rapidly followed by its construction. There was the need to have an operational input to the LRVs themselves. Signal & Telecommunication system design was also moving forward and the technical and operational requirements needed progressing together. Furthermore, S & T engineers are a rare breed, much in demand, so priority was given to the recruitment of the Depot Manager and Signal Engineer. Nick Donovan and Mike Aitchison joined in the autumn of 1990, both from British Rail.

On the Operations side EMS was again retained to assess potential candidates, but a number of people had already expressed interest in joining Metrolink. After competitive interviews, Andy Morris and John McGuiness joined as Operations Assistant and Commercial Assistant respectively.

As previously indicated, it had been decided to appoint a Recruitment Officer. Don Kenny took this matter in hand since he had used this approach successfully in London City Airport. Thus it was that GMML came upon Elwyn Roberts. Elwyn had spent his working life in the personnel side of engineering industries related to the mining industry and industrial gases and had recently been made redundant.

Much of the credit for the quality of Metrolink staff must go to Elwyn Roberts and Barry Scott, for both very quickly identified with the Company and understood exactly its requirements and the qualities being sought.

Whilst all this was going on the construction of the railway – Design and Build – was proceeding apace. The GMA Consortium, which itself had set up the Operating company which held the Contract with the Executive was building (or sub-contracting) the various segments but GMML's team faced a mammoth task. Meanwhile, the Company's Operations Centre was being built by Fairclough Engineering as sub-contractor to GMA.

As 1990 progressed the structure of the Operations Department developed. On the Operational side there were to be three grades of staff: Drivers, Customer Service Inspectors and Controllers. Whilst Scott Hellewell and Paul Neal were in overall charge, Andy Morris took charge of the requirements for Drivers and Controllers and John McGuiness did the same for the Customer Service Inspectors. On the Engineering side, whilst Scott Hellewell and Jim Harries were in overall control, Nick Donovan progressed the staffing levels and organisation for the workshop and rolling stock

Don Kenny spent three years as the Commercial Director and Company Secretary of London City Airport Ltd where he was involved with the airport's pre-operational launch, together with its first two years of trading activity, before being seconded to GMML by John Mowlem & Co PLC. A qualified accountant, he has been employed by the Mowlem Group of companies since 1980 and has filled a number of positions, mainly financial, in a variety of locations ranging from Australia to the Middle and Far East.

As Commercial Director and Company Secretary Don Kenny's principal concern is to make sure that GMML is profitable. "It will never be a hugely profitable concern, but by good commercial use of the system's revenue potential through sponsorship and advertising, and the carefully-balanced fare structure, we shall generate the maximum possible return."

Metrolink management June 1992. Left to right:-
Paul Neal (Operations Manager)
Fred Roberts (Civil Engineer)
Nick Donovan (Depot Engineer)
Margaret Hyde (Marketing Executive)
Jim Harries (Engineering Manager)
Fred Fitter (Electrical Engineer)
Steve Auty (Assistant Civil Engineer)
Amanda Palmer (Company Accountant)
Steve Hyde (S & T Assistant)
Hilary Taylor (Administration Manager)
Don Kenny (Commercial Director and Company Secretary)
Nick Philips (Revenue Systems Assistant)
John McGuiness (Commercial Assistant)
Scott Hellewell (Operations Director)
Andy Morris (Operations Assistant)

Chelvin Hibbert (Chief Executive) and Mike Aitchison (S & T Engineer) were not on site when this photograph was taken.

maintenance with Mike Aitchison doing likewise in the S & T side. Jim Harries also had himself to progress both the civil and electrical engineering requirements.

The job of all these early appointees was to select the staff to build up the sections which had been established. However, at the same time these managers were busy checking plans and specifications as well as attending numerous meetings within the GMML/GMA structure and with other bodies such as the Passenger Transport Executive, BR and the City. By February 1991 it had been possible to draft a major advertisement for Operations and Engineering staff covering approximately 140 posts. The Directors were fortunate in being able to select from a wide range of applicants – over 9,000 persons applied for the first 140 jobs. The choice of suitable staff was not made easier by the huge number of applicants. The question of how to select from such a huge response became paramount and proved to be a mammoth task. Of the 5,600 completed application forms received John McGuiness personally checked 1400. Elwyn Roberts checked 1800 Driver and 1000 Storekeeper applicants, Andy Morris the 600 Controllers whilst the Engineering Managers checked the rest. Elwyn Roberts conducted all the first interviews for LRV drivers. He then set up the administration arrangements.

Following discussions with GM Buses Ltd (GMBL), GMML decided to carry out a two-stage interviewing process after which all candidates would go for a medical. GMBL carried out these medicals on behalf of GMML. They consisted of the usual PSV Medical augmented with the railway eyesight tests.

Training

Whilst the Company's training policy had been established earlier, considerable thought went into the training requirements particularly as it became clear that the majority of the staff were unlikely to come from a transport, let alone railway background. Furthermore the re-introduction of street-running and the scepticism in some quarters of the private sector's involvement meant that training was of paramount importance.

Some training could clearly be given in-house. Every person joining the Company goes through an induction course at Queens Road and the Directors of the Company are actively involved in these courses to ensure that staff are aware of the exacting standards required of them in order to promote Metrolink to the travelling public. In a competitive environment Metrolink is determined not to be found wanting in customer relations and levels of service.

Training for the operation of the system required the expertise available only from a tramway or light rail operator. Accordingly, discussions took place with Blackpool Transport Services Ltd, operator of the sole remaining UK tramway system using modern vehicles, but GMMŁ's requirements clearly could not be met. Training needed to be carried out on a system using Centralised Control, with automatic signalling and modern communication systems between Drivers and Control, since that was how Metrolink was to operate. Blackpool does not operate that way, nor could it train GMML staff during the summer when all its resources are fully committed to operating its own system.

There had been thoughts of sending the first Metrolink LRV to Blackpool as a logical part of any such training programme but in the event the Blackpool tramway's clearances would not have been sufficient for the long articulated vehicles (its track radii were too sharp) and, interestingly, there was insufficient electricity to power the car whilst normal operation was in force.

Through Scott Hellewell's involvements in the International Union of Public Transport (UITP) a number of operators were considered as being able to offer training experience appropriate to Metrolink's requirements. Whilst CIE with its DART system had given assistance to both the Passenger Transport Executive and the GMA Group, it lacks the all-important street running experience. Toronto and Tuen Mun had obvious relevance – without any linguistic problems – but time and cost ruled them out. Zurich, Hanover and Brussels were also considered and whilst the former has many attractions it was felt that logistics were against it. Consequently USTRA (Hanover) and TRANSURB (Brussels) were invited to submit costed proposals for training approximately 32 Metrolink staff – principally Controllers, Drivers

Training in Brussels was wide-ranging and thorough and, in addition to spending time learning to control the system, the first eight trainees also gained first-hand driving experience of the problems which beset on-street light rail operation. Despite its modern, fast-running vehicles Brussels has many sections of traditional street tramway which play havoc with rosters and timetables. This picture, taken specially for us by STIB, shows an all-too-typical rush hour scene with motor cars choking the tram tracks. Metrolink will not have this problem thanks to carefully planned traffic management which, in the main, allows only buses to share the short stretch of on-street tramway in Manchester.

and Vehicle Technicians. The Brussels package using the STIB facilities was the most cost-effective. Paul Neal went to the Brussels Tramway Training School, taking part in a training programme organised by TRANSURB, the training division of STIB (Societe des Transports Intercommunaux de Bruxelles). He was followed by Andy Morris and the first eight Metrolink trainees. These eight undertook a course including being trained to drive Brussels trams in service. Following a successful completion of their course in April 1991 they returned to Manchester to continue the programme by training their subordinates.

For several months it was necessary to continue theoretical training in Manchester. Paul Gijselings, Assistant Traffic Manager from STIB, spent six months in a training role at Queens Road but neither he nor his trainees had any opportunity to gain hands-on experience since no LRVs had been completed and neither of the railway lines was available to GMML's staff.

Engineering, signalling and other specialist staff were sent to the relevant manufacturers for training, and many visits were made to other systems in Europe to gain detailed knowledge. Experience gained on some of these visits was to reap considerable benefit, often more than covering the cost of the visit in immediate savings, in addition to longer term advantage. Because of the high calibre and wide experience of staff employed and the need for faster response times than contractors would offer it now became apparent that it would be both possible and economically sensible to perform certain functions in the Company's own workshops which would otherwise have been contracted out. This led to the recruitment of a small additional number of employees.

Paul Gijselings, right, talking about trams and pop music on the opening of the Bury line service.

Not until September 1991 did the first LRV enter the O&MC building at Queens Road, and then it was required for checking out and commissioning by GEC staff since Firema have no dedicated test track facility capable of putting a 48 ton LRV through its paces at speeds up to 50-mile/h.

Whilst engineering and operating staff were being trained, the Company continued to recruit and train other members of the organisation who would be responsible for its administration and day-to-day running. By the end of 1991 there were 198 employed at Queens Road.

Twenty-four drivers were trained in Brussels during the autumn of 1991 – they were converted to driving Metrolink LRVs by two Controllers who were seconded to Driver Instructor duties. Amanda Best and Chris Owen were then responsible to Andy Morris for the training of all subsequent drivers. Part of this training involved route familiarisation on the four sections (Bury line, Victoria-G-Mex, Altrincham line, Piccadilly Gardens-Undercroft) and they also drove LRVs for the various trials required as the system progressed. Amanda's most famous trainee to date is Prime Minister John Major who rode from Victoria to Bury on 24th February 1992, taking the controls between Bowker Vale and Prestwich.

Whilst Operating and Engineering divisions were expanding and consolidating there were many specific tasks they were able to undertake. Engineering staff assisted GEC personnel in carrying out the programme of modifications and commissioning of the LRVs whilst at the same time being taught how to service and maintain the vehicles.

Prime Minister John Major about to learn the finer points of driving from Amanda Best. On leaving the vehicle at Bury the PM observed "it was the most expensive train set he had ever played with".

The question of security on the system next arose. It was decided to engage a detachment of police – 29 in all – from the Greater Manchester force, and they now have their own Police Station facilities within the O&MC.

The short timescale achieved in creating the system imposed pressure throughout the whole training period and great credit is due to all concerned that so much was achieved in such short time. Out of a total workforce of some 198 persons only 28 could be said to have had any previous relevant experience in public transport.

Jeff Done, Deputy Project Manager for the GMA Group and Chief Project Manager for GECA TPL, has been involved with Metrolink since May 1988. He started his career with GEC as a graduate apprentice, moved to the Erection Department and then spent two years in South Africa commissioning the first micro-processor electric locomotives on SATS. During this period he gained a wide variety of experience in electric motive power, including the production of a prototype trolley bus and the testing of locomotive performance on the Sishen – Saldanha iron ore railway Jeff returned to Project Engineering working on tenders and projects. These included the BR class 319 dual-voltage multiple-units, Tuen Mun Light Rail and the London Docklands Upgrading. He recalls the tremendous thrill he experienced when the first LRV went through Piccadilly Gardens, and he could see the benefits to the City which Metrolink was creating. As he says, "it's not often you get the chance to build something so significant in your own home town, and it will always be here as a perpetual reminder." Recognising that "not everything has been wonderful" Jeff is pleased that they have been able to show that despite its difficulties DBOM can work. "The timescale has been the problem – it has been much more demanding than the technology."

Never a dull moment for Jim McDermott, Mowlem's Project Manager, as a phone call interrupts his photo call! Jim started on the Metrolink project in October 1989 having gained invaluable experience on the construction of the London Docklands Light Railway. Working as a Sub-Agent on the Island Gardens section he remembers that "every element of railway construction came into my section". His observation that "one of the biggest problems is never knowing until the very last moment the scale of the works" sums up much of Metrolink's challenge for him. After thirteen years with Mowlem he states their philosophy very simply – "we expect to leave people as friends" and wishes to place on record that "the PTE and Manchester City Council have been superb. Very Positive. And it isn't always that way!" He will not easily forget Castlefield – from the car reprocessors to the non-existent rivet heads on the viaducts when the paint was removed! At its peak the Metrolink project has employed some 1,000 men and 100 staff. Jim McDermott will always remember it as "Hellish. The hardest three years of my life – and I wouldn't have missed it for the world!".

David Horn, Fairclough's Regional Manager and a member of the GMA team, is used to pioneering projects. An oil refinery in Baghdad, power station in Bahrain, road building in Kurdistan, the Kielder Dam project in Northumberland, the Whitefield to Windy Hill section of the M62 – all are part of his pedigree. His three years with Metrolink have been most interesting and he sees how the DBOM contract has ensured that all the contractors have pulled together to meet the contractual deadlines. David recalls how the choice of an infill site caused problems for foundations of the workshops, requiring considerable piling, and reflects that the planners' requirements resulting in the pagoda roof will make future extension of the headquarters building more difficult. He is looking forward to working in Metrolink House for the next few months, dealing with maintenance contracts. "After spending a lot of time on motorways he sees light rail as a relatively cheap solution to cities' transport problems".

Operation

Chapter 18

The gauging trial described in the text, taking place on 15th September 1991.

The contractual specification requires a ten minute service to be provided from Bury to Piccadilly and from Altrincham to Piccadilly from 0600 until 2400 Monday-to-Saturday. At peak periods on Mondays-to-Fridays another ten minute service has to be provided from Bury to Altrincham and vice versa. Thus throughout the day there is a ten minute service into the city and a five minute service in peak periods. On Sundays and Bank Holidays a fifteen minute service is to be provided from Bury and Altrincham into Piccadilly. It is interesting to note that this service is approximately double that operated previously by BR under Section 20 arrangements for which the Passenger Transport Executive was paying about £3m per annum. The Metrolink service is provided entirely out of the farebox.

In addition to these basic service parameters there are some 'quality of service' requirements to be met also. Outside the city centre no passenger should have to stand for more than fifteen minutes. The maximum number of standing passengers should not exceed the nominal capacity of an LRV during the peak period, but may exceed it by up to 30% in the peak quarter hour. Since the nominal capacity of each LRV is 206 (86 seated and 120 standing) each peak period train should not carry more than 206 passengers. At this level the density of standees is approximately $4/m^2$, which is typical of rapid transit systems generally. For the peak quarter hour about 270 passengers can be carried; this equates to approximately $6/m^2$, again in-line with elsewhere. There is, of course, no legal maximum as to the number of passengers that may be carried on an LRV. If GMML does not operate 98% of the service – as measured in place-kilometres – there are financial penalties to be paid every 28 days. This tough service specification is far more exacting than that of any other operator, bus or train, let alone light rail. These requirements also preceeded such recent ideas as BR's Passengers Charter.

How the service is provided – the timetable, pattern of workings, transition from peak-to-off-peak etc – is a matter for GMML as is the make-up of the trains. Likewise the fares to be charged and the marketing strategies to be adopted are entirely a matter for the Company – these are dealt with later. Clearly with a minimum frequency stipulated in the contract and the minimum capacity of each train being the capacity of a single LRV (206 passengers) it is essential that GMML adopts commercial strategies to ensure each train at least breaks even and preferably makes a profit. The Company has little room for manoeuvre apart from efficient scheduling and rostering and careful planning of peak/off-peak transitions and suchlike.

The Executive's original concept was to operate a basic service Bury-Piccadilly-Altrincham-Piccadilly-Bury every ten minutes throughout the day Monday-to-Saturday. This would have been advertised as two separate services, since passengers cannot be carried into the headshunt at Piccadilly. A shuttle service was proposed for operation between Whitefield and Timperley and vice versa during the peaks. The peak vehicle requirement (PVR) for this service, would have been 31 which, with spares would have given an initial fleet of 37 LRVs. This allowed for a measure of double unit trains on peak workings. Whilst this might at first sight appear generous, it has to be remembered that the 10 minute BR service on the Bury line was provided with six coach trains each seating 500, during the height of the peak.

Since the LRV fleet was the biggest single cost of any item in the bid it will not come as a surprise that considerable ingenuity was adopted by the different consortia bidding for the job to reduce the number of cars each considered to be the minimum sufficient to operate the service. GMA's proposal was to adopt a Bury-Piccadilly-Altrincham-Piccadilly-Bury pattern but of single LRV trains, throughout the day, six days per week. Their 'shuttle' service became a through service of single LRV trains operating between Bury and Altrincham and vice versa. This was also said to remove the need for any turnback facilities at Whitefield. (Timperley had to be provided in case of problems on the BR section south of Timperley.) In the event GMA were persuaded to leave the Whitefield turnback facility.

The service pattern is determined by the running times and the need to achieve efficient LRV workings. Initial work took on the Executive's proposed pattern (hardly surprising since Scott Hellewell had done the work originally!) of Bury-Piccadilly-Altrincham-Piccadilly-Bury. Whilst running times in the segregated services could be calculated fairly reliably it was very difficult to assess realistic running times through the city centre. They were, of course, calculated scientifically having regard to the usual parameters but the problem arose in trying to assess clear runs (or otherwise) through the 15 traffic-light controlled junctions. With certain combinations of running time it was more efficient to operate the Bury and Altrincham lines as separate services. A major disadvantage of this was the problem created for driver relief. Furthermore it would have been difficult to perform vehicle changeovers. In the event the interworking of the two services has proved not only the most efficient, but also practicable method having regard to turnround facilities at the three termini, operation of the Delta junction and the single line section through Navigation Road – some achievement!

It had always been intended to introduce Metrolink in phases from north to south. Bury-Victoria was always to have been the first section. The next section could have been from Victoria either to G-Mex or Piccadilly. In the event the redesign of Piccadilly Station Undercroft caused delay (referred to elsewhere) so that the second section extended the Bury line service from Victoria to G-Mex. This had the added benefit of simplifying city centre operation by deferring the operation of the Delta junction. The third phase was to extend from G-Mex to either Timperley or Altrincham. This clearly

Scott Hellewell began his career in transport as a Civil Engineer with British Rail, becoming Section Manager for Bradford. Three years as County Transportation Planning Officer for the West Riding County Council were followed by his appointment as Chief Planning Officer with Selnec, later GMT. A former Vice President of the CIT and Fellow of the BIM he is also a personal member of the UITP, serving as one of the two British representatives on the International Light Rail Committee. He observes, with typical enthusiasm, that he is "thrilled to bits that at long last Greater Manchester has got the embryo of a public transport system which sets it up for the next century. The investment will pay off over many years irrespective of National transport policies". Photograph by John Fox courtesy Manchester Evening News.

would be influenced by BR over the section south of Timperley. GMML's preference was to open in one move to Altrincham, since this was clearly the traffic objective, and to enable a more effective training package to be developed. This arrangement was finally adopted.

Before going into the actual calendar dates achieved and some of the problems encountered, it is worth reflecting on the challenges facing GMML. Before a commercial service can be operated the whole of the fixed infrastructure must have been approved by the Inspecting Officer of Railways. The operator must also show that he is competent to run a passenger service, including handling a number of emergencies both singly and in combination. Once sufficient drivers have been trained to provide a service it is necessary to start 'Trial Running'. This is to operate the full public timetable, but without actually carrying any passengers. It is during this period that the emergencies are simulated. Some of these exercises involve the Emergency Services – Police, Fire and Ambulance. Furthermore, drivers must also be available to assist in carrying out test runs for GMA, and for training/route learning on other sections of the line.

It had been intended to introduce Metrolink as a ten minute service throughout the day operating twin-coupled LRV trains in the peak and single LRVs off-peak. This would have been easier to operate from the single platform (B) at Victoria and, requiring less drivers, could have been introduced sooner. However, power supply limitations meant that this was not practical and hence it was decided to introduce a basic twelve minute service throughout the day, doubling to a six minute service in the peak periods. This six/twelve minute pattern was maintained throughout the phased commercial operation. Likewise, with the agreement of the Executive, the decision was made not to run a Sunday service initially. This enabled much needed remedial work to be carried out on the track.

The phased introduction of commercial service was always subject to factors outside the control of its operator. Whilst staff recruitment had begun, on schedule as planned, in April 1991, lack of vehicles and equipment prevented certain key areas of training being carried out. (see Chapter 17)

Once the first vehicles had been commissioned and handed over to GMML for test running, operation was able to begin. On 30th September 1991 cars began to run between Woodlands Road and Queens Road, then between Crumpsall and Queens Road, the first section to be electrified, and there was relief that, at last, things were moving.

After the complete closure of the Bury line on 17th August 1991 the removal of third rail and erection of overhead made it possible to carry out test running through to Bury. This began on 12th December 1991, with the first car running into Victoria Station on 17th December 1991. Next followed a period of trial running, with driver training proceeding in parallel into the city centre. It had been hoped to begin commercial service on 23rd March 1992 but GMML decided that it needed another two weeks to fully familiarise all staff with the complete operating situation. Finally, on Friday 3rd April, the Railway Inspector gave his approval for commercial operation to begin on Monday 6th April.

During the pre-operational period GMML commercial staff were finalising the fare structure. The precise level was a balance between fares pitched too high, which would obviously deter passengers, and too low which would result in minimal profit – or even an operating loss. As a commercial venture, operating without subsidy, Metrolink has to be profitable. GMML kept its options open until the last possible moment, announcing its fare structure on 30th March 1992. This subject is dealt with in more detail later.

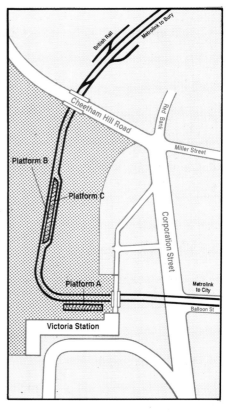

Victoria Station platform arrangements for Metrolink.

Chelvin Hibbert, GMML's Chief Executive presented the first passenger through the City with a bottle of champagne. The recipient, Ray Dunning, is the nephew of the driver of the last Manchester tram but is better known as the archivist and Operations Manager of the Heaton Park Museum Tramway. Chelvin commented that "Whilst today is undoubtedly a milestone in Manchester's transport development, Metrolink will neither be performing its true function, either as a mass people mover and congestion reducer, nor operating as a commercially attractive undertaking, until we are operating the extensions which must be built onto this spine."

Concious of the need to recapture former rail passengers lost to buses – either rail replacement or otherwise – a passenger awareness campaign was maintained throughout the shut-down period on the Bury line, with season-tickets being offered as prizes in return for completion of questionnaires designed to assist GMML in gauging passengers' needs.

The first morning of commercial operation, Monday 6th April, was cold and wet but when the first vehicles left Manchester and Bury simultaneously at 06.00 hours, despite the heavy rain they were given a rousing send off by staff, enthusiasts and the public alike. A 12-minute off-peak (09.30-16.30) 6-minute peak (07.30-09.30 & 16.30-18.30) service was operated Monday to Saturday. (As previously stated the contract requires 7-day operation with 10-minute and 5-minute frequency.) Although there were some teething troubles, the extended period of training could be seen to have been worthwhile. Metrolink staff were on hand at the stations and on the vehicles throughout the day for the first few weeks to assist passengers and answer their queries.

Initially all vehicles came into Victoria Station via the Aspin Lane crossover, thus entering platform "B" where they terminated. The frequency of service and driver training runs was such as to cause premature signs of rail wear on this sharp crossover which will normally be used only in emergency. Platform "C" remained unused, but allowed cars through to the City section for trials, testing, and driver training. On return from the City section the LRVs were held in the siding outside Victoria Station as seen in the photograph on page 58.

The next milestone was City Centre operation and a press call at Victoria Station at 05.15 on 27th April 1992 was well attended – no one wanted to miss this day! With a great sense of occasion LRV 1007 dutifully fitted with a circular metal plate carrying the Manchester City Arms, borrowed from the Heaton Park Museum Tramway, performed the tape breaking ceremony.

A change of platform usage took place once the City section was opened. It was no longer necessary for cars to cross into Platform "B", ready to reverse to return to Bury. The sequence was now that cars from Bury stopped at Platform "C" to unload and load, and then moved out to proceed to G-Mex. Cars returning from G-Mex stopped at the concourse platform "A", unloaded and loaded, and then left for Bury without stopping at platform "B" which is now only used at the end of the peak period to allow cars to reverse and return to Queens Road, although it is available should short workings be introduced or should it be needed in emergency.

Once again everything went reasonably smoothly though the occasional power failure, sticking doors or failed LRV made good press material – bad news always being preferable to good news unfortunately.

At the end of May 1992 GMML was able to report that 12,000 passengers per day were being carried and that 96% of its services were operating, albeit on the temporary reduced 6 minute/12 minute frequency and were within 2 minutes of their scheduled time. The operating performance is as already stated subject to continual monitoring by the Passenger Transport Executive and substantial penalties will be enforced if the very high level of service laid down in the Contract is not maintained.

When the Contract had been prepared the operation of a competing commercial bus service run by GM Buses was almost certainly not anticipated. The effects of this service in the first few months of operation were to reduce peak loadings on the LRVs – due to some extent to the lower fares on the express bus service – whilst Metrolink's off-peak loadings were higher than anticipated, often due to parents with push chairs and prams using the easy-access LRVs for shopping trips in the city centre. Clearly, though, the cost of travel was paramount in people's minds with journey time being less important.

Ticket and Fare Policy

The fare tariff for Metrolink is based upon a division of the 26 stations along its route between Bury and Altrincham via Manchester city centre into seven distinct zones lettered A to G. Each zone contains three stops, except for the city zone which has eight. Fares depend upon the number of zones entered. Passengers can thus travel anywhere within the city zone (between Victoria Station and G-Mex) for the minimum standard fare.

It was decided at an early stage that, like most LRT systems, tickets must be purchased before passengers board the vehicle. Drivers, being segregated in their cabins, are not concerned with tickets. Customer Service Inspectors board cars to check tickets, and passengers riding with an incorrect or no ticket are subject to a 'Standard Fare' immediate penalty. The inspectors also carry out other duties relating to passenger care and information.

Tickets are produced by the Henry Booth Division of Bemrose UK Ltd. Cash tickets are issued from Thorn EMI Electronics ticket vending machines (TVMs) of which there are at least two at every station or platform, painted in the Metrolink highlighted colour of aquamarine. Twenty four buttons provide passengers with the facility to book to any station on the system at various types of fare, and also to approximately 120 British Rail stations within the Greater Manchester area. The destinations covered by the TVMs are shown on the Metrolink journey planners located near to each TVM. Pressing just two buttons causes the amount of the fare to be displayed and the ticket is issued upon insertion of the appropriate coinage. All coins of 5p and above are accepted and the TVMs also issue change.

The various types of ticket available from TVMs cover standard single and return fares, half single and return, and concessionary fares. Signs on each machine indicate who is eligible to purchase each type of ticket and at what time of day. Children under five travel free and those under sixteen pay half fare. Pensioners and disabled persons pay half fare until 9.30am after which time they may travel any distance on the system for a flat rate concessionary fare of 25p. Outside peak hours all return tickets are automatically discounted to reflect a cheap day return fare.

Thus each fare for a Metrolink destination is based upon the number of zones entered, the type of ticket required and the time of day, whereupon the computer built into each TVM calculates and displays the correct fare accordingly. In addition Metrolink Period Passes for unlimited travel are available as weekly, monthly, quarterly and annual tickets which can be purchased from certain Post Offices, BR stations, Passenger Transport Executive bus stations and other selected outlets.

The Board of Greater Manchester Metro Ltd, as already stated, determines its own fares policy without any influence from the Passenger Transport Authority and Executive. Being an independent company, GMML must aim to make a profit. Unlike local commuter rail lines (including the former Bury and Altrincham services

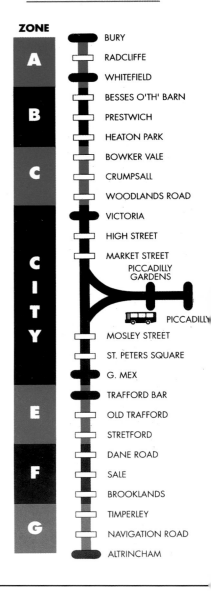

METROLINK ZONES

ZONE	
A	BURY
	RADCLIFFE
	WHITEFIELD
B	BESSES O'TH' BARN
	PRESTWICH
	HEATON PARK
C	BOWKER VALE
	CRUMPSALL
	WOODLANDS ROAD
	VICTORIA
CITY	HIGH STREET
	MARKET STREET
	PICCADILLY GARDENS
	PICCADILLY
	MOSLEY STREET
	ST. PETERS SQUARE
	G. MEX
E	TRAFFORD BAR
	OLD TRAFFORD
	STRETFORD
F	DANE ROAD
	SALE
	BROOKLANDS
G	TIMPERLEY
	NAVIGATION ROAD
	ALTRINCHAM

One of three special commemorative tickets produced by students of Bury College to allow all day travel – see page 130

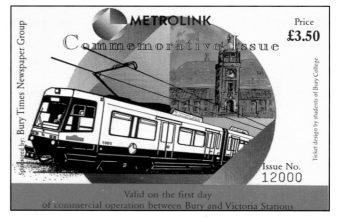

More than just the ticket.

*B*y supplying Manchester Metrolink with their Automatic Fare Collection Systems, including Ticket Vending Machines complete with a Computer Data Link, to the Central System Network, we are supporting Britain's latest Light Railway Project with proven sophisticated technology.

Our track record shows we're capable of keeping people on the move anywhere, a fact which will prove of great benefit to Metrolink and the people of Manchester.

THORN
Transit Systems International
Wookey Hole Road Wells
Somerset BA5 1AA England
Tel: +44 (0) 749 672081
Fax: +44 (0) 749 679363

THORN
Transit Systems
International

operated by BR) Metrolink will receive no subsidy from the Authority. Even the payment for revenue lost from concessionary fares is calculated so as to leave GMML no better or worse off as a result of taking part in the concessionary scheme. A balance has to be achieved between the need to maximise revenue and the avoidance of dissuading patronage thereby reducing revenue.

Using the journey between Bury and Manchester Victoria as an example, the Metrolink fare commenced at 15% more than the final BR fare. But BR fares increased during the shut-down period thus reducing the differential to an estimated 6%. Bus fares, including GM Buses competing express bus service between Bury and Manchester, will cost even less than the equivalent BR fare, but it is invidious to compare the two modes of travel. Metrolink provides a fast, comfortable service avoiding the delays of traffic congestion and running directly to eight destinations in the city centre. In a deregulated environment the passenger has a choice and as an inducement GM Buses normally uses its newest buses on its competing service. Metrolink journey times, however, must necessarily be faster than either the bus or the former BR train.

Metrolink staff were on hand to assist passengers as each section opened.

In his Editorial of May 1991, the Editor of *Modern Tramway* stated his belief that the service would attract so many new public transport users that at times there would be undercapacity on the system through lack of vehicles. The remedy proposed in Manchester, he believed, would be to regulate passenger numbers on the system by charging premium fares. The effect of competition (with its cheaper fares) has happened at the outset; future progress is awaited with interest to see whether the popularity of the system will grow to the extent that the rolling stock will prove insufficient, and if it does, how the situation will be remedied. Present form suggests that transit will indeed be rapid and worth the modest premium on the cheaper modes of travel.

Once the automatic ticket machines, produced by Thorn-EMI, were available a campaign was started to educate the travelling public in their use. The first such exercise was combined with the display of LRV 1002 at the Light Rail '91 Exhibition held at the G-Mex Exhibition Centre in November 1991. Subsequently a display was arranged in the Arndale shopping centre where members of staff were in attendance with ticket machines and interested members of the public were encouraged to operate the machines to receive souvenir nil-value tickets. The exhibition included also a platform and shelter and promotional literature was available. Staff members were also available at Victoria Station shortly before the commencement of operation, and afterwards, to familiarise the public with the ticket machines and to hand out promotional leaflets, season ticket wallets and miniature route plans.

Souvenir tickets were also produced to be valid on the first day of commercial operation of each section. Priced at £3.50 they offered unlimited travel and were much appreciated by enthusiasts and others wishing to photograph and ride on the new system.

Meanwhile the replacement bus services continued with GM Buses placing its newest buses on the Bury to Manchester Victoria route. Shortly before the Metrolink service commenced, GM Buses registered an express bus service between Bury and Manchester to provide an alternative and competing service from the outset. While GM Buses was a member of the operating consortium, its reasoning was that if it did not register such a service, a competitor might well do so.

Driver Training and Route Familiarisation

The training of drivers has been discussed in the previous chapter, and since all initial training took place on the Bury line, route familiarisation occurred simultaneously. Subsequently all drivers were given route familiarisation on the City section, including the use of a training video. This phase of their training including street signalling, driving with other traffic and amongst pedestrians, using the street stations and some limited use of coupled cars.

Driver training on the Altrincham line had been scheduled to begin on the same day that City Centre operation began but there was still work to be done, particularly with signalling, and not until 7th May did training begin, initially to Timperley. As recorded elsewhere not everything went to plan on the inspection of 14th May, when car 1021 ran through to Altrincham. A subsequent visit on Tuesday 19th May was to prove satisfactory, with the BR signalmen then showing their mastery of the new technology. During the training period, and despite the unusually dry weather, rust forming on the surface of the running rails caused track circuit and vehicle location problems for the Control Centre. It was decided to employ one of BR's class 47 diesel locomotives to polish the rail heads by running to and fro along the tracks and this took place during May. (There are two places where access to the main BR system can be used in emergency, and with BR's permission. On the Altrincham line there is a connection between Navigation Road and Altrincham, see page 96, whilst on the Bury line there is a connection alongside Metrolink's stabling point at Victoria East).

Trial running to Altrincham began on 8th June, and one week later, on 15th June commercial operation began, with cars running through from Bury at 12 minute intervals, augmented to six minutes in the peak. Training continued, with additional cars interspersed between service vehicles during the day, whilst at night the engineers worked with the IOR, Kit Holden, to test and prove the signalling and point operation over the Delta junction giving access to Piccadilly Gardens.

Another milestone was reached on Wednesday June 17th when the first LRV (a coupled-set) made its way into the Undercroft in the early hours of the morning. Everything proceeded satisfactorily and driver training/trial running began the following week, although last minute adjustments to signals and point detectors took several days to conclude. Once training began the remedial work to street paving on this section was also carried out – causing frustration to both drivers and paviors through poor timing.

The driver training and familiarisation over the Delta junction was crucial. The interface with the numerous buses entering and leaving Parker Street Bus Station, and in so doing crossing the Delta junction, means that extreme care will be necessary to ensure that the 'man line' from High Street to St. Peter's Square does not become blocked by LRVs stuck on the Delta junction whilst attempting to enter or leave Piccadilly Gardens Station.

The Delta junction will eventually determine the capacity of the system since all vehicles will be scheduled to pass over it whether travelling from Bury to Piccadilly, Bury to Altrincham, Altrincham to Piccadilly or Altrincham to Bury. LRVs coming into Piccadilly Gardens from St. Peter's Square via Mosley Street have precedence over those coming from Market Street. The emergency cross-over located in Aytoun Street was used during the training period when access to the Undercroft could not be obtained.

Finally the last section to the Undercroft was scheduled to be put into commercial service early in July, just a matter of days before Her Majesty Queen Elizabeth II opened the system on 17th July 1992.

British Steel Track Products, together with their railway engineering subsidiary Grant Lyon Eagre, can offer a complete package – including design, rail supply, construction, installation and maintenance of track, switches and crossings, using specialised rail borne equipment, such as tampers and ballast regulators.

British Steel Track Products meets the highest national and international standards on main line, LRT, and metro systems around the world.

Recent projects include the London Docklands scheme, Tyneside, Merseyside and Manchester.

Our wide ranging experience, in depth resources and engineering expertise all help to contribute to our capability of being able to deliver the goods to an exacting specification and schedule.

British Steel Track Products,
Moss Bay, Derwent Howe, Workington,
Cumbria CA14 5AE

Tel: 0900 64321
Fax: 0900 64800

Grant Lyon Eagre,
Scotter Road, Scunthorpe,
South Humberside DN15 8EF

Tel: 0724 862131
Fax: 0724 280262

"Homeward bound". Photograph by John Fox courtesy Manchester Evening News

Metrolink's impressive headquarters, where its offices, control centre, maintenance and workshop building, car washing plant, storage sidings and other allied facilities are located, forms an £8m four hectare brand-new purpose-built complex.

The scheme was handled by Consortium member AMEC through its Fairclough Civil Engineering subsidiary. Fairclough was thus responsible for the initial levelling of the site, subsequent erection of buildings and landscaping to meet the planner's requirements.

The location of the O&MC was decided after consideration of the possible use of the former Bury Motive Power depot at Buckley Wells, from where the BR electric trains operated. This idea was ruled out for several reasons, including its distance away from the centre of the Metrolink system (present and proposed future extended system), the unsuitability and poor state of the buildings and also, not least, the need for contractors to start work creating the complex some 12-18 months before the Buckley Wells site would have been vacated. As already recorded the former MPD was used by GEC and Firema, after BR had moved out, for commissioning and remedial work on the LRVs before they were handed over to GMML.

The Queens Road site is adjacent to the Intermediate Ring Road, thus giving good access for GMML staff, visitors contractors, and the Italian contractor Zambetti who delivered all the car bodies and their bogies. Vehicular and pedestrian entry to the complex is through a security barrier at the gate house situated at the top of the sloping access road which leads directly to the administration block. A staff halt has been constructed to give rail access to the site from Metrolink's LRVs.

The Operations & Maintenance Centre at Queens Road. Cars enter through the washer, lower left, and are stabled as shown. The workshop and offices are located in the large, central, building whilst Administration and Control are to be found in the pagoda roofed buildings right of centre. Note the two half LRV bodies waiting to be assembled. The Metrolink Bury-Manchester line uses the viaducts seen in course of refurbishment whilst below is the Oldham and Rochdale line. This would form one of the proposed Metrolink extensions. Photograph by John Fox courtesy Manchester Evening News.

The hydraulic wheel press in the workshops.

The wheel lathe referred to in the text.

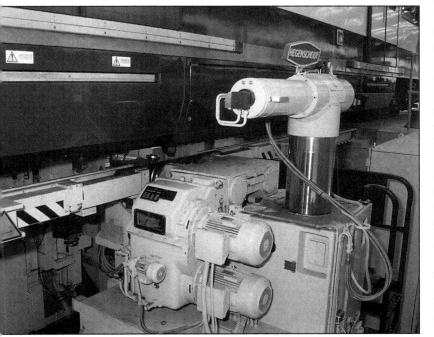

Additional buildings have been erected as the needs of the centre have developed, replacing in some cases Portakabins or temporary storage facilities. A Police Station has been created adjacent to the main office complex. Power for the O&MC is provided from an on-site sub-station.

Administration is centred on the two-storey prefabricated office block where, in addition to the Directors' offices, those of senior management, public relations, and the appropriate secretarial facilities are also to be found. On the ground floor a central reception area leads to a canteen on the one side and to locker rooms and toilets on the other. Control, the nerve centre, is also located on the ground floor.

MAINTENANCE

All maintenance is handled here and the 'M' of the DBOM contract was subcontracted from WS Atkins to Brown & Root who designed, equipped and commissioned the workshop complex to be capable of maintaining the present, or an enlarged future fleet of LRVs. Trackwork and overhead was handled by Balfour Beatty.

Maintenance facilities for most of the company's activities are handled from this complex, including signalling, telecommunications and permanent way work. The servicing and repair of the LRVs naturally forms the most obvious aspect of the complex but only cars undergoing maintenance or repair will normally be found inside the workshops since stabling is accomplished on the tracks outside the building as shown in the aerial view on the facing page.

The facilities provided for servicing the LRVs are located within the three-road workshop. Only one road is fitted with overhead line equipment; this also has a large pit area in which is usually kept an electrically-driven lifting pad to assist in the replacement of components from the vehicles. This road is normally used for servicing and examining vehicles. The other two roads are available for body lifting using the co-ordinated set of body jacks. An eight tonne travelling overhead crane also serves these two roads. At one end of the centre road is the wheel lathe used for re-profiling car tyres without the need to remove axles (or bogies) from the vehicles. All wheels in each LRV must be maintained at the same nominal diameter otherwise wheel slip may occur which would upset the traction control and slip detection equipment. A hydraulic wheel press is available in the workshop for the fitting of new steel tyres to the resilient wheels, a task which requires a pressure of over 1600 psi (80 bar). Cars lifted for bogie overhaul may not receive the same ones back as an overhauled float (spare) set will be used to keep cars in service with the least time off the road. Cars are moved on the unpowered roads by electric capstan and ropes similar to those at the old car sheds at Buckley Wells, Bury.

A work area equipped with machine tools such as a lathe, saw and drill, is used for repair purposes. Stores for components, staff offices, toilets and locker facilities are also provided in the building.

The first vehicle to arrive at the Maintenance Centre was the Special Purpose Vehicle (SPV) which will be used to recover failed LRVs. It can also be used to haul a flat wagon when track maintenance is taking place, and has a hydraulic lifting arm to enable work to be carried out on the overhead line equipment. It had a somewhat chequered beginning to its early Metrolink career.

The large open area below one of the three tracks allows easy access and movement of equipment and components, thus enabling maintenance to be carried out efficiently.

General view of the Control Room as seen through the booking-in window. Prominent in the foreground is the police desk; to the left is the Senior Controller's desk; beyond, the PEC (Passenger Emergency Call) station is in use. Twelve VDU screens from the various stations can be seen at the high level, whilst below the two duty Controllers are sitting at the two work stations. Four high resolution screens display signal and point aspects and LRV locations, as explained in the text. Low level lighting in this area aids viewing of the various monitors – the photographer's flash gives an artificially light appearance to the room.

CONTROL

Metrolink Control is designed to operate a fully-automatic railway which is expected to run without the need for intervention until outside factors introduce delays, or vehicle failures occur. Human intervention is then necessary to regulate the service back to timetable. Scott Hellewell based the concept on the Toronto Transit System, though he had also examined Amsterdam and Zurich's control systems which operate similarly. The relatively straightforward nature of the Metrolink route lends itself to automatic control of this nature.

GEC – through its various divisions – has been responsible for supplying and installing the whole of the signalling (segregated and on-street), communications and control, and power supply.

The method of controlling the railway was conceived (and accepted by the Consortium at Tender stage) as being capable of operation by one person. This has turned out not to be the case and all parties now see that this was an under-estimation. Practical experience has dictated that three persons will normally be required to adequately staff the Control Centre, as explained below. The Inspecting Officer of Railways also recognised the need to spread the work load, and to meet his requirements it was agreed that a second work station should be installed in Control before operation in the City and to Altrincham began.

The heart of the Metrolink system is thus its sophisticated computer-based Control Centre. All vehicle movements are planned and monitored from here and all service revisions are instituted and implemented by the duty Control staff. They monitor the system through Visual Display Unit (VDU) screens which display signal and point aspects together with vehicle locations.

There are two computer systems in use, SIGNET which handles all signalling functions, power and vehicle position displays, and SCADA (Supervisory Control And Data Acquisition). The latter is being used for the first time in Great Britain and is being commissioned in stages.

The Control Centre is manned every day throughout the year on a 3-shift basis giving 24-hour cover. The duty Senior Controller has total overall responsibility for the safe operation of the system. Two Controllers, responsible to the Senior Controller, man the two work stations which maintain contact with all vehicle movements and allow direct 2-way voice communication with drivers by radio. All operational staff book on and off through Control and at busy times, or in the event of an incident, it may be necessary to call in assistance. A 'spare' driver, for instance, may be brought in to use the public address system to keep passengers informed of reasons for delay and estimated arrival times of next trains. This facility is one which most improves passenger perception of the organisation at times where the service is subject to fluctuation or delay.

It is appropriate to mention here that the work carried out to achieve Control's main function, keeping an even interval service operating, may not even be recognised by passengers. The judicious turning back of a car to maintain the normal frequency elsewhere may not be obvious to most passengers if Control are on top of their job, although the knock-on effects in terms of driver's relief for meal breaks and so on can become quite complicated.

Staff duty rosters are known well in advance but there may be a need to revise them on an *ad-hoc* basis in the light of such operational requirements. Control has to ensure that drivers are available for all trains and must also liaise closely with engineering to check that all LRVs are cleaned daily and that maintenance schedules are kept.

When vehicles have to be changed over for any reason it is Control's responsibility to ensure that this has the minimum adverse effect on the service. It will then be necessary to up-date the information stored in the work station(s) relative to which vehicle is actually taking up which duty, driven by whom, and which radio codes are to be used for driver contact. This is one area which required there to be more than a single Controller since once a situation has arisen to upset the smooth running of the service several things will need to be done simultaneously to prevent a further deterioration. If the situation is an emergency, such as an on-street accident, then it can be appreciated that the number of functions requiring attention escalate extremely quickly. Meanwhile the routine aspects such as booking staff on and off, arranging meal reliefs, responding to passenger emergency calls and so on must also continue.

There is never a substitute for experience, and yet experience can only be gained when incidents occur. As previously recounted, there had been staged 'incidents' during the training period but no amount of practice ever equates to the real thing. Recognising this GMML decided to engage the services of a fully experienced Controller to 'sit in' and observe – and where necessary advise – on techniques and solutions to problems, thus greatly assisting the Control team in the early and most demanding period on the railway. Alf Maile was brought out of retirement to perform this task and his assistance has been invaluable. Alf has had 30 years with London Transport, followed by spells in Singapore, Hong Kong & Docklands with London Transport International, and worked a split shift system at Queens Road for several months before returning to retirement once more.

Daily management meetings monitor the previous day's performance. At present most of the necessary data is extracted manually but once the SCADA computer system is fully operational – expected to occur in Autumn 1992 – all such management analysis data will be provided automatically, greatly assisting efficiency.

SIGNALLING THE RAILWAY

The capacity of the railway, and therefore its ability to maintain its timetable and in so doing comply with its contractual obligations, depends absolutely on the signalling of the system. This aspect has been the responsibility of GEC Alsthom Signalling Ltd (GASL) of Borehamwood, Hertfordshire, the sub-contractor to GMA for the design, manufacture, supply and installation of a new train control and signalling system for Metrolink. Functions affecting signals, vehicles and power distribution are controlled by the SIGNET central computer system. The system includes four high resolution colour VDUs complete with keyboard and trackerball which allows the whole Metrolink operation to be monitored and controlled from the Operations Centre.

The Controller has a colour map of the system shown on one of the

GEC Alsthom Signalling engineers at work – above setting up a signal at the end of the railway section at G–Mex, inbound; below checking signalling circuits and traffic light responses with an "LRV simulator".

Keith Williams, left, looked after Metrolink matters on behalf of the City Engineer's Department whilst Mick Noone was responsible for work on the traffic lights and crossings in the City where the LRVs interface with road traffic through the UTC Computer in Magnum House.

Dick Carr, seconded to the Passenger Transport Executive from Mott McDonald, became the 'clerk of works' and grew to know every inch of the city section from G-Mex to Victoria and through to Piccadilly. It was his responsibility to monitor the ground works being carried out by all the contractors. Track and overhead matters were the responsibility of John Berry and David Rumney.

workstation VDUs, from which each vehicle's progress can be observed. There are also detailed maps showing the Altrincham line, the Bury line and the City Centre section with the boundaries at the G-Mex Centre, Victoria and Piccadilly stations, where the street running section commences and different driving rules apply. Trains automatically identify their positions on a diagram on the screen, thus enabling the Controller to observe the whole operation at a glance.

On the segregated, former railway sections, Metrolink is fully signalled by a two-aspect automatic system which incorporates the latest proven Solid State Interlocking (SSI) technology. The Controller sets the routes for all train movements in the interlocking areas and can switch certain parts of the system into a limited automatic working mode to ease his workload. Automatic track-circuit block working is used between interlocking sites. A station warning board is positioned at braking distance before each station in the segregated section, and Yellow/Green aspect repeater signals are used where the sighting of the normal Red/Green signal is restricted. An automatic train stop system stops any train which may attempt to pass a signal at red.

The Altrincham and Bury lines have been signalled so that vehicles can be turned at G-Mex and Victoria Stations, enabling each line to operate a shuttle service should the City Centre section be blocked. The signalling system allows for vehicles to be stabled in sidings at Timperley and Victoria Station as well as the platforms at Bury and Altrincham, the headshunt at Piccadilly Undercroft and at the depot. The depot has two leads which will provide alternative entrances/exits to improve operating flexibility. Both leads into the depot are signalled but there is no signalling in the depot itself. Vehicles moving under power in the depot complex use 'shunt' mode on their console, limiting them to 12mile/h. All movements in the depot area are authorised by Control via the radio system.

There is a single line section between Timperley and Navigation Road and provision has been made to turn vehicles at Timperley. There are emergency-worked ground frames at Whitefield, Crumpsall and Old Trafford providing trailing crossovers for use in emergency which are operated by the driver in conjunction with instructions from Control. The two level crossings in the single line section on the Altrincham line are under the control and safe operation of the BR signal box at Deansgate Lane, near Navigation Road. The level crossing at Hagside on the Bury line will, in due course, be operated remotely from Queens Road with CCTV supervision but can be operated locally in the interim and in cases of emergency.

Patience rewarded ! Deansgate Lane level crossing with one of BR's Sprinters heading away from the camera, bound for Stockport and Manchester, at the point where the two single line sections diverge. The BR line separates into two tracks as can be seen, whilst the separation of the Metrolink tracks is out of sight behind the LRV which is heading for Altrincham.

In the City Centre, from G-Mex to Victoria or Piccadilly, the LRV's are driven 'on sight', but are controlled at road junctions by a set of dedicated signals. These signals are overseen by the city's Urban Traffic Control (UTC) system at the Passenger Transport Executive's headquarters in Piccadilly. This system, set up by GMC, monitors traffic signals throughout the urban area and can be used to adjust the traffic signal programmes to cope with delays or any special needs arising from events within its area.

Communication between LRV's and the UTC and its traffic signals is done via the Vehicle Recognition System (VRS), each vehicle having two transmitter coils mounted under the centre bogie, this central location giving an accurate indication of the LRV's position in the road. Signals from the transmitter are received by detector loops in the roadway. Four types of detector are used, TRTS (Train Ready to Start), AD (Advanced Detector), SD (Stop Detector) and CD (Cancel Detector), though each can perform more than one at a time.

Once detected by the loop, the data is passed to the new traffic signal equipment at each junction involving LRT operation. There are 15 traffic light controlled junctions in the City Centre at five of which Metrolink has priority. Following initial operating experience, however, priority is being given at a further three junctions.

The passage of the LRV through the junction is recorded by the Cancel Detector which 'tells' the signal controller that any remaining all-red period of the signals after the 'proceed' and 'amber' periods may be cancelled to prevent delays to traffic.

Detectors are linked to trackside VRS units which are connected by optical fibres, running in the cable troughs in the track formation, to the Control Centre at Queens Road. The VRS also gives service and route information keyed in by the driver at the start of a journey, sending this to Control as well as to any facing pointwork via its trackside VRS.

The question of what type of signals should be used for Light Rail Vehicles was discussed by a Light Rail Transit street running working party made up of representatives of the Railway Inspectorate, the Department of Transport, and traffic signal engineers from Manchester and Sheffield as explained in Chapter 10. The design had to be compatible physically and electrically with standard British traffic signals. To add a further red/amber/green head to existing signals would have produced an unnecessary clutter of signals. It is also essential that signals should not cause confusion to drivers of normal road vehicles. Even with a distinctive symbol or shape, the use of coloured signals would be potentially confusing, particularly since LRV signals are not familiar to road vehicle drivers.

The preferred solution is a signal quite unlike a normal road traffic signal. White bar symbols are used as LRV signals in several European systems. The Metrolink design uses a white horizontal bar meaning 'stop' and a white vertical bar meaning 'proceed', incorporated into a single signal aspect of 300mm diameter. The vertical bar can be changed to one at 45 degrees to indicate 'proceed left' or 'proceed right'.

The points in Piccadilly Gardens are automatically set for each vehicle, depending on a route code entered by the driver at the start of each journey into the vehicle's electronic recognition system. Points indicators in the street enable the drivers to check, together with observing the point blades, that the points are set correctly. It is a safety feature of the system that the City Centre points only move just before an LRV reaches them by which time pedestrians will have stepped out of the way of the LRV and the point blades. All points have provision for heating in icy weather.

The signalling system is covered by a backup or protected power supply. In emergencies, the driver or operating staff can hand-crank point machines. A key switch on the traffic light controller at each junction can be operated in an emergency to request a phase for the LRV.

There is an emergency crossover at G-Mex which is worked from Metrolink Control. A spring-loaded emergency crossover is also provided in Aytoun Street, enabling vehicles to turn short of Piccadilly Station. The scissors crossover, headshunt and siding at Piccadilly, whilst normally set for automatic operation, can also be worked from Control.

MONITORING THE RAILWAY

With some 500 departures per operating day, monitoring of the railway must be done on a 'by exception' basis. It is therefore assumed that trains are running to time or within pre-determined tolerances unless a Controller observes that they are not, or a Driver, Controller or Customer Services Inspector out-on-the-line reports some occurrence or out-of-course running.

Monitoring services also includes dealing with emergencies. These may be mishaps on the Metrolink system, or may be external, such as a fire in the City Centre. The Metrolink Police detachment have a desk in the Control Room and there are direct 'hot' lines to both the Greater Manchester Police and Greater Manchester Fire Brigade Control Rooms. There is also a direct line to BR's Deansgate Junction signalling centre, because it controls Metrolink between there and Altrincham. Two emergency buttons – the 'red mushrooms' – located on the Senior Controller's desk allow instant cut-off of power to the depot or City sections of the system should this be necessary.

The two work stations from which the two Controllers monitor the system. The small screen is displaying radio data and the Controller nearest the camera is in contact with an LRV driver. Beyond his colleague is the power display diagram.

Although GMML do not display a passenger timetable – with a fixed short interval frequency there is no need – there is a working timetable for use by train controllers. Each vehicle is allocated a Train Description Code as it leaves the O&MC, ranging from 01 to 18 (or more if more LRVs are in service). This code is not related to its fleet (or vehicle) number, but identifies the vehicle in relation to the working timetable. A letter indicating the vehicle's destination follows the initial two digits (Altrincham; Bury; Victoria; Queen's Road; G-Mex; Piccadilly) followed by a final number between 0 and 9. Thus the first train leaving Queen's

Road for Bury will always be 01B1, changing to 01A1 as it leaves Bury for Altrincham, and so on.

This description is keyed into and displayed by the VDU monitors and moves from section to section on the various screens as the car progresses along its route. The data is fed into the system from the vehicles and signals as journeys are made. In the City section wires carried in plastic ducts buried beneath the road surface take the place of the familiar concrete troughs which run alongside the railway sections.

Further identification is carried by the uniquely coded radios fitted to the LRVs. Each car carries two radios (one in each cab) enabling direct voice contact to be maintained between the Controller(s) and Drivers. This can be selective: just to one vehicle; by zone – ie all vehicles on the Bury line; or to all vehicles on the system.

The radio monitor is programmed to hold, and then, in response to the Controller keying in the appropriate radio code, to display, the vehicle number, train description code and driver's name. It is thus important for the Controller to know from which end a car is being driven when attempting to reach the driver! Contact can also be made with some 30 mobile radios carried by staff or fitted in road vehicles.

The Metrolink communications system consists of three sub-systems: telephony, closed circuit television (CCTV) and low speed data transmission. The telecommunications system is based on a cable network connecting all three sections of Metrolink to the control centre at Queens Road. The band width required for CCTV dictates that an optical fibre cable is used for the network. All the controlling equipment for the telecommunications system is to be found on the control centre console. Twelve colour screens linked to the closed circuit television cameras located at all stations and other key locations allow constant monitoring of the situation on the system. A separate monitor is used to deal with Passenger Emergency Calls (PECs) whereby the Controller is able to respond to the call whilst observing the situation through the appropriate on-station CCTV. Certain CCTV cameras can be remotely controlled to allow them to 'zoom in' to the particular area needing investigation.

The telephony sub-system consists of a digital private automatic branch exchange (PABX) with a standby power arrangement for telephone communication throughout the system. Each platform is provided with a telephone extension for employee use. There is direct telephone communication from the O&MC to level crossings, police, fire and ambulance services, and a two-way communication system from the lifts to the O&MC.

A large illuminated panel displays the power situation, for which Control is also responsible, enabling any faults to be immediately identified and appropriate action initiated.

Further panels show the rolling stock situation, identifying cars available for service from information supplied by the workshop staff, and, separately, the location of every car currently within the O&MC to enable drivers to locate their vehicles when taking up their duty.

A further, dedicated, monitor displays the status of all the Ticket Vending Machines (TVMs). In addition to routine malfunctions these machines incorporate 'Molest Alarms' which alert Control if they are tampered with. Cash from these machines is collected and accounted for by Securicor and is not, therefore, GMML's direct responsibility.

In introducing a new concept such as Metrolink it was considered to be important to have a visual identity which would act as a memory trigger to the public and be synonymous with a high level of service. The basic elements of this identity were determined as symbol, colour and typeface. Fitch Design Associates was engaged to create a corporate identity, taking account of these elements, embracing livery, signing, typestyle and stationery.

At the heart of the Metrolink house style is the Metrolink symbol based on an abstract version of the capital letter 'M'. It is initially intended that it should be used with the logotype as a signature until it becomes sufficiently established to be used alone. The letter 'M' is placed in a circle, inclined to the right at an angle of 45 degrees with shading gradually decreasing from dark grey to silver within the 'M', contrasting with complementary shading from silver to dark grey within the background circle. The logotype is a unique form of capital lettering which has been specifically drawn to unite the word 'Metrolink'. Symbol and logotype are to be combined in a number of 'signatures' to suit the spaces available on signs, etc.

The Metrolink colours have been carefully chosen to convey an impression of quality and refinement. The colours are dark grey, light grey, silver and aquamarine. The latter is used sparingly as a highlight, and silver is used only on the symbol. Basic livery is light grey and dark grey, with dark grey used for the lettering of the logotype. Two typefaces have been chosen for applications other than the Metrolink logotype. The Frutiger family of type is intended for headlines, bold headings and emphasis, and all other print is from the Sabon family.

Station signs

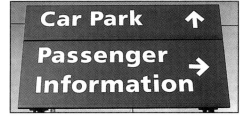

Station signing is based on a modular system comprising the Metrolink identity, the station name and an optional digital clock. Standard panels on the station walls enclose a route map, a safety zone emergency unit and a staff helpline concealed behind the route map. Additional spacing panels are fitted as necessary. Signs are in Frutiger bold typeface in upper and lower case, in white on a dark grey background with a highlight strip in aquamarine. Where it is necessary to give directions to a number of destinations, information relating to travel takes priority at the top. Capital letter height is 120mm for platform identifying signs and 90mm for directional signs.

Route maps are in two forms, horizontal for use inside vehicles and vertical for use on station platforms. Ease and speed of reference have determined the design, and where possible symbols have been used to keep the information simple, including the standard British rail, bus and parking symbols. Frutiger bold typeface is used for the maps which continue the colour scheme with aquamarine as a highlight and to identify the central section of the line.

The station information system is designed to be immediately clear to the passenger and at the same time to present a corporate identity which will become increasingly familiar to the travelling public.

Communications Media

In addition to publicity material generated by the Executive and GMML, Metrolink's prospective customers were kept well informed of progress by the local newspapers, radio and television with newspapers and local radio carrying the bulk of this regular advice. Live television coverage was supplemented by various feature programmes, a documentary entitled 'Travelling Light', and also a BBC three-part programme.

The 'heavyweight' newspapers printed longer articles from time to time during the construction period.

Tony Young, the Executive's Operational Planning Manager, had a regular fortnightly session on Monday afternoons in which he was interviewed by Natalie Anglesey on BBC's Greater Manchester Radio. He also appeared regularly on the independent Piccadilly Radio. Both radio stations broadcast a series of interviews with officials of GMML and the Executive whilst Metrolink news and updating on television appeared on BBC's 'North West Tonight' and the independent 'Granada Tonight', both broadcast at 6.30pm and often featuring Metrolink at precisely the same moment!

A regular weekly traffic news update containing news of Metrolink works affecting motorists through diversions or road closures, compiled on behalf of the Executive by David Rumney and Geoff Brierley, appeared in the 'Manchester Evening News' every Monday. Councillors Joe Clarke and Jack Flanagan featured regularly in the local press to keep Metrolink and the Executive's viewpoint in the public eye. Directors of the Executive and GMML have also appeared frequently on television both to keep the public informed and to maintain Metrolink's high profile. Less helpful were some of the letters in the local press!

A crucial contribution to the success of the City Centre operation was the work carried out by the Passenger Transport Authority and Executive in keeping local businesses informed of progress and warning them of forthcoming street closures. Geoff Brierley (left) was given the responsibility for the liaison work and is seen here in Piccadilly with David Brown, Chairman of the Manchester Chamber of Trade. There was close co-operation between the Authority, the Executive and both the Chamber of Trade and Chamber of Commerce, and the liaison work was absolutely crucial in retaining the goodwill of the city businesses.

Tony Young at his regular broadcast spot on BBC's Greater Manchester Radio with presenter Natalie Anglesey. He reported Metrolink progress and advised of road closures and city centre changes. This formed one of many valuable public relations exercises and helped to keep the public informed of the reasons for inconveniences as well as maintaining a high profile for the Metrolink system.

During the early days of the system's development talks were given to a wide variety of organisations including local societies, Womens Institutes and gatherings of Civil, Mechanical and Electrical Engineers.

The Executive also developed an extensive programme of visits to schools throughout Greater Manchester which proved extremely popular. The Metrolink project was adopted as an option for GCSE. This work was undertaken by Jane Nearney who is now the Executive's Press and Public Affairs Manager, and Geoff Brierley.

As work on the system progressed the Executive acted as host to visiting delegations from around the world – keen to see how Manchester had achieved the breakthrough and also interested to know how the DBOM contract was working. On a more local level there were regular meetings with bus operators to appraise them of forthcoming changes in bus stop positions, or closures of Parker Street Bus Station, in an on-going scheme to assist passengers and drivers and to keep traffic flowing through the City.

The communications media recognise Metrolink as a newsworthy system and have contributed greatly to making the name a household word throughout the Greater Manchester area.

Traffic signs

On the return of rail vehicles to urban streets the Department of Transport devised new types of traffic signs for use where trams (as the Department designates LRVs) and other traffic combine and intersect. In its literature the Department acknowledges that the first new system is in Manchester, but in recognising the interest in light rapid transit around the country it realised that it was necessary to legislate for and publish standard signs applicable to any light rail scheme. Manchester's new traffic signs and signals for Metrolink were in position by the end of 1991 and are in accordance with the relevant Railway Inspectorate requirements and Department of Transport specifications.

Illustrated overleaf are the new Light Rail Transit signs together with the Department's explanations and comments.

TRAM ONLY SIGNS

The sign above means that no vehicles other than trams should pass the sign. It is an offence to do so. It is similar to the sign for bus only facilities, and is used where only trams are allowed to enter a particular street, for instance one that is one way except for trams. The sign below shows a two way tram lane in a one way street.

SIGNS FOR TRAM DRIVERS

Black and white diamond-shaped signs give instructions to tram drivers - other vehicles should ignore these signs.

LEVEL CROSSINGS

This sign means that drivers of other vehicles must give way to trams at a level crossing without barriers or gates. Where trams run separated from other traffic, crossings of roads will be treated in a similar way to railway level crossings. At some there may be barriers, at others just "Give Way" signs. Remember that trams may approach the crossing from either direction.

NEVER STOP PARTIALLY OR WHOLLY
ON A TRAM CROSSING.

Further information may be obtained from:

Department of Transport
Traffic Signs Branch
2 Marsham Street
London SW1P 3EB

THE DEPARTMENT OF TRANSPORT   PRINT by The PRINT FACTORY Ltd, LONDON   T/INF/207
AUGUST 1991

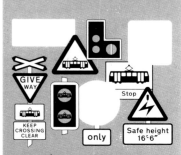

A GUIDE FOR DRIVERS AND PEDESTRIANS

Light Rapid Transit Systems (called "trams" in this leaflet) are returning to British streets. The first new system is in Manchester.

New types of sign have been devised for use where trams and other traffic mix.

This leaflet from the Department of Transport explains what these look like.

WARNING SIGNS

This sign warns you where tram tracks cross a road or pavement. Trams will often run along the same streets as other traffic, or through pedestrian areas, without being separated off. Drivers of other vehicles should give trams priority where it is safe to do so. The trams' running area will be bounded by a broken white line. Drivers should not park or wait wholly or partially within this area. If you need to cross the line, look out for approaching trams. In pedestrian zones, a change in the surface level may be used to show where the tram runs.

This sign reminds you to watch out for trams at a crossing point. It is used at places where pedestrians cross regularly. It will say "LOOK LEFT" or "LOOK RIGHT" where trams only come from one direction. Where there are no barriers, pedestrians may cross the tram tracks anywhere. REMEMBER THAT TRAMS MAY APPROACH FROM EITHER DIRECTION.

WARNING SIGNALS FOR PEDESTRIANS

When these lights flash, it means that a tram is approaching. It is used with the "TRAMWAY LOOK BOTH WAYS" sign at places where cyclists or pedestrians regularly have to cross tram tracks, and there is limited visibility. The lights will start to flash alternately about 10 seconds before a tram arrives. DO NOT BEGIN TO CROSS THE TRACKS WHILE THE LIGHTS ARE FLASHING. TRAMS APPROACH QUICKLY AND QUIETLY.

TRAM STOP

This sign will be used to indicate a tram stop. Drivers of other vehicles should not stop or wait at a tram stop.

TRAFFIC LIGHT SIGNALS

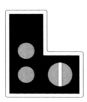

The signal mounted on the right above allows tram drivers to proceed through the junction although other traffic is stopped by the red light. Where trams run along the street, light signals giving them instructions at junctions will often be mounted alongside ordinary traffic light signals. The instructions to trams may not be the same as to other vehicles.

OVERHEAD WIRES

This sign shows the safe height available under tram wires and electric cables. Be particularly careful if anything you are transporting sticks out above the roof of your vehicle.

Chapter 21 | Future Plans

The completion of the first phase of Metrolink is, of course, merely the end of the beginning. What has been achieved must be seen as what it is, the re-introduction of light rail into a major United Kingdom conurbation, against enormous odds and with great potential for the future.

The case for Metrolink, the trials and tribulations of funding and building the system together with some of the problems encountered on the way and how they were successfully handled, have been recorded throughout this book. The project has set records – it has taken less than ten years from concept to completion. The complex building contract took only 30 months despite the complexities of the city centre, and great ingenuity was deployed in achieving this. What matters now, however, is what happens next.

Metrolink's future cannot be in doubt. The vast amount of time spent evaluating the scheme, and the enhanced economic benefits following bus deregulation have produced the assurance that Metrolink is a system which meets many transport objectives. It is the Passenger Transport Authority and Executive, however, who will have to consider where next to build Metrolink. The key to that once again will be funding.

It is already clear from Phase 1 that future extensions of Metrolink are unlikely to be funded totally commercially. The amount of private sector funding obtained from the concession payment – effectively a capitalisation of future profits for operating the system – has been a relatively small proportion of the total cost of the system. Although there may be a contribution to future phases in this form, the vast majority of funding will have to come from conventional sources. However, with an imaginative approach to future funding mechanisms it is hoped that the private sector may have a significant if not decisive role in winning Government approval for future extensions.

This will require the Authority and Executive to develop future extensions to Metrolink which can be judged against the criteria which the Government now uses for Section 56 grants. In effect the cost of the scheme will have to be met by a combination of reductions in traffic congestion and accident costs, savings in capital expenditure on keeping the existing rail network going, topped up where possible by capital contributions from the private sector. If extensions are serving areas with development potential there is an important opportunity to get such contributions from developers. It will, however, need a buoyant economy and property market for these to be forthcoming.

The methods used to justify grants for extensions to Metrolink and other light rail systems are, of course, different from those used to justify roads. Chris Mulligan, the Executive's Director General, considering Metrolink's future in an interview with one of the authors wished for "a level playing field when comparisons are made between benefits from investment in road construction and those accruing from introduction of light rail". Given such a situation he sees how much easier it would be to justify development upgrading and improvement of the rail network – both heavy and light.

Clearly the next move lies with the Government. We must hope that as it sees Metrolink – and soon Sheffield Supertram – taking traffic from the roads, and reducing pollution and congestion it will be encouraged and will look more favourably towards investment in light rail. It has already agreed to contribute towards an extensive monitoring exercise of Metrolink's impact which is being carried out jointly with the Passenger Transport Executive.

Even before the question of extensions is considered, the day may dawn when the capacity of the existing system is insufficient for the Bury and Altrincham lines. Perhaps we should recall two of the points from the study visit to Nantes in 1985 – "the (French) Government is committed to light rail" ... "a further 20 articulated vehicles are to be ordered to reduce the peak time headway". The question of who would finance any additional vehicles for the existing lines is one which has not yet been considered.

The Passenger Transport Executive has already got powers to extend Metrolink to a number of areas and these are outlined in Chapter 4. It, however, sees Metrolink as something much more than a means of updating and improving conventional rail lines and giving town and city centre access. It can be a vital tool in the development of many areas of Greater Manchester. By combining its street running and off-street capabilities the possibilities for Metrolink extensions throughout the County are considerable.

Areas which may have potential include serving the East Manchester development areas and the Olympic Site, with a possible extension towards Tameside; another possibility is extending through the Hulme development in the direction of Wythenshawe and possibly creating a second link to Manchester Airport. This is in addition to the lines which are already identified as potential Metrolink extensions in the original rail study.

"We must work to create Metrolink, not just as a two-line system, but as the core, together with conventional rail, of a reliable countywide backbone to the public transport network. We can do this by taking advantage of its strengths including high frequencies, fast journey times, and above all in a deregulated environment, predictability", said Bill Tyson.

Meanwhile, let us wish Metrolink every possible success in the future.

Jack Flanagan, Chris Mulligan and Roger Hall raise their hats to the achievement as car 1002 stands outside G-Mex at the Light Rail '91 Exhibition in November 1991.

Metrolink added considerably to the workload of the Executive's PR Department, not least in making arrangements for the Official Opening by Her Majesty Queen Elizabeth II. Here Jane Nearney and Tony Young accompany an official party on one of the many trips organised during Spring 1992.

Service of Dedication

To celebrate Metrolink, and in thanksgiving for the achievement of the opening of the first phase, a non-denominational service was held in St. Ann's Church, Manchester, the Parish Church of the city centre, on 17th June 1992.

Over fifty people attended the service representing the Passenger Transport Executive, GMML, many of the contractors, the Consultative Users Group and members of the general public.

An introduction by the Rector (Canon Michael Arundel) was followed by hymns old ("He who would valiant be 'gainst all disaster.") and new ("God of concrete, God of steel."), and contributions from people

who had been associated with the project and those who may use it. These included Tony Young of the Passenger Transport Executive, Scott Hellewell of GMML, David Holt of the LRTA, Albert Walmsley from St. Clare, Blackley, Brenda Triggance-Clarke representing the mobility impaired and the co-authors of this volume.

All the contributors felt the desire to give thanks for the safe and satisfactory opening of the system, whilst remembering with sorrow the one person who lost his life during the construction. David Holt remembered many friends of Metrolink who did not live to see it completed including   David Graham,

Terence Goulding, Maurice Marshall, Cliff Taylor, Stanley Swift, Ian Davidson and Anthony Gavin. He also remarked that Metrolink has shown the way forward for the City – not only in transport but also for shops and businesses.

In many ways the most telling observation came from Brenda who was "so glad that there would in future be no need to have to book 24-48 hours in advance before being able to go out".

Prayers in the form of a litany were led by the Revd. Tim Baynes, Industrial Chaplain and organiser of the service, and the Revd.   Eric Ogden led the Thanksgiving. The service ended with the Blessing.

A PASSION FOR JUDAISM

A Festscrift

Essays in honour of Tony Bayfield

edited by

Jonathan Romain

The movement for
REFORM JUDAISM

Copyright © 2011

Movement for Reform Judaism and the Authors

ISBN: 13 978-0-947884-22-2

Cover design by Benedict Romain

First published in 2011 by

The Movement for Reform Judaism

The Sternberg Centre, 80 East End Road, London N3 2SY

www.reformjudaism.org.uk

Published and bound in Great Britain by
DSPrint, Enfield

CONTENTS

3

PREFACE

I was enthralled. I was in my first year at Leo Baeck College, training to be a rabbi, and the class on Jewish education was being led by Rabbi Tony Bayfield. He was speaking about the time when he was a teenager at South West Essex Reform Synagogue and how he had been mesmerised by its then rabbi, Alan Miller. Tony's face lit up as he recounted the sermons he had heard about Prophetic Judaism, and how Jewish ethics had to take precedence over rituals, dogmas or convenience if ever there was a clash between them. He made me feel as if I was the teenager listening directly to Miller himself and I experienced a surge of religious enlightenment that was to stay with me the rest of my life and guide my own subsequent career. That moment exemplified both Tony's own passion for Judaism and his ability to pass on that enthusiasm.

This admiration for Tony is shared by countless others in the Movement for Reform Judaism, and especially by its rabbis. Hence this *Festscrift* in his honour by those with whom he worked closely for many years both as professional leader and as rabbinic colleague. Moreover, while other books have been dedicated to leading figures in former decades – such as Rabbi Werner van der Zyl (*Reform Judaism*) and to Rabbi Ignaz Maybaum *(A Genuine Search)* – this is the very first *Festscrift* in 170 years of Reform Judaism in Britain.

It is also significant that when the idea was mooted, I expected that I would have to expend much effort persuading frantically busy rabbis to find time to write in-depth essays. In fact, the opposite was true : there was an avalanche of offers. Moreover, the quality of the contributions, be it in terms of scholarship or insights, is another compliment to him. We, the rabbis of the Movement, present this *Festscrift* as a salute to the many years he has devoted to the cause of Reform Judaism.

A pleasing incidental aspect of the book is that it has allowed members of the Assembly of Reform Rabbis UK to bring into the open their academic research in a way that Sabbath sermons and articles in the synagogue newsletter do not permit. Those congregants who are surprised at the expertise or chosen topic of 'their rabbi' should look again at the person they thought they knew.

The essays are arranged in alphabetical order of the author's surname, with the exception of the one directly on Tony, which is placed at the very beginning, as befits a *Festschrift*. In the vast majority of cases, they have been specially written for this book. As each one was written by a different person, readers will note that there is a wide variety of styles in the book. Differences will also be apparent in the systems of transliteration used and the formatting of footnotes. It was decided not to impose a rigid uniformity of style, and so the variations reflect the preferences of the individuals concerned.

My thanks go to all the contributors who responded so enthusiastically and who rushed to meet the tight deadline. This is the fourth book in four years that the Assembly has produced and indicates the wealth of talent it contains. I am also appreciative of Rabbi Amanda Golby and Raymond Goldman for their help in proof-reading the final manuscript.

Jonathan Romain
June 2011

COLIN EIMER

Colin Eimer, born 1945, studied Geography at the London School of Economics, then Leo Baeck College. Rabbi, Union Libérale Israélite, Paris (1971-1974); Bushey & Radlett Reform Synagogue (1974-1977); Sha'arei Tsedek North London Reform Synagogue (1977-). Director, Vocational Training at Leo Baeck College (1980-1995); Lecturer in Hebrew Grammar (1975-2006.)

Tony Bayfield - in a MANNA of Speaking

How do you write an appreciation of somebody without sliding, on the one hand, into obituary – Tony is, after all, very much alive; or, on the other hand, into hagiography – while Tony is definitely special, he's equally definitely not saintly!

Born in 1946 in Ilford, he went from local Grammar School to Cambridge to study law. He and his future wife, Linda, were already an 'item' from Summer Camp days and journeyed up and down between London and Cambridge to be with each other. They married in 1969 and their very special relationship was only cut short by Linda's so-untimely death in 2003. They were blessed with three children, each of whom followed their parents in one way or another: Lucy became a teacher; Daniel a lawyer and Miriam a rabbi. Tony chose rabbinic training at Leo Baeck College rather than a doctorate in criminology (so maybe not such a major career shift?....) From 1972-1982 he was rabbi of the North-West Surrey Reform Synagogue in Weybridge. The skills, talents, concern, creativity, compassion which have been his hallmarks throughout his career were already in evidence then. Amongst the skills that Linda developed in Weybridge was a bit of shadchanut (match-making); the outcome being that I married a woman from their community.

Tony and I met as students at the Leo Baeck College and our rabbinic paths have intertwined for almost 50 years. We have shared jokes, ideas and books, as well as the joys and pleasures of being rabbinic professionals.

By 1980, the Reform Synagogues of Great Britain was in something of a doldrum of direction and leadership. One of Tony's mentors, Rabbi Dow

7

Marmur, brought together some rabbis and communal leaders in an informal Think Tank to look at how things might be moved forward. While not in overt opposition to the formal RSGB leadership, it was so implicitly. Tony was part of that group. We talked about many things: expanding and professionalising the Leo Baeck College; developing a Progressive Jewish Day School; 'flexing our Reform muscles' vis-à-vis a traditional Jewish world moving ever to the right; a merger of the Reform and Liberal movements which, sadly and not for want of trying on both sides, never came to fruition. In 1981, the Manor House in Finchley, North London, came on the market and was acquired by a consortium of the Reform Synagogues of Great Britain, the Leo Baeck College, (what became) Akiva School and the New North London Synagogue. It became increasingly clear that Tony had the qualities needed to develop the venture and he was appointed director of the Manor House Trust. (1)

From the outset, he conceived of the site as a Jewish Community Centre, saw Jewish life and culture in its broadest frame and developed a particular vision of what it was to be a Progressive Jew in the world.

Part of that vision was to create opportunities for interfaith dialogue and he soon established a Jewish-Christian dialogue group at the Sternberg Centre. In 1992, in the introduction for a book on that group, he described what the Centre had become and paints a picture showing how he had translated vision into practice:

> It is a broadly-based Jewish intellectual, educational and cultural centre, a place of meeting, outreach and interface. It contains a museum of Anglo-Jewish social history, a cultural society which mounts art exhibitions and musical recitals, a bookshop, a library, a cafeteria which is the base for an educational programme for young people with learning difficulties. It houses a Jewish educational agency which services the needs of synagogues and their Sunday schools; an organisation reaching out to students at university; a programme of training for volunteer carers who visit the sick, comfort the bereaved and assist the elderly in Jewish communities nationwide. The Centre has a series of social clubs – for people in their twenties and for single, divorced and widowed people of all ages – and a 'chavurah' project which supports and promotes alternative, less-formal modes of Jewish association. There are initiatives in the field of medical ethics, business ethics – and even a biblical garden. In the midst of all this activity, interfaith work has always stood out. (2)

Tony was appointed Chief Executive of the (now renamed) Reform Movement in 1994. By then, it had gained in numbers, profile, stature and position in Anglo-Jewry, in no small measure due to his work and influence since 1982.

Tony and I co-chaired the Assembly of Rabbis of the Reform Movement in 1981-1983, and jointly organised a memorable rabbis' visit to Lebanon in the aftermath of the Lebanon War of 1982. We spent many years jointly interviewing prospective rabbinic candidates for the Leo Baeck College, who invariably came into the room having heard terrible things about us. We, however, simply could not understand how two 'pussy-cats' might have been so badly maligned! Tony was closely involved with the College throughout his time at the Sternberg Centre: as teacher; as ideologue arguing for greater theological content and professionalism in the course; as inspiration and confidant for so many rabbis both during their training and subsequently; and, obviously, as representative of one of the Progressive Movements supporting the College.

Theology has always been one of his passions, and, in particular, serious, contemporary Progressive Jewish theology. The Manor House Group mentioned above also led to many other interfaith ventures – not just Jewish-Christian – as well as attempts to build connections within the disparate parts of Anglo-Jewry. One of only three Jews honoured by Lambeth Palace with an Honorary Doctor of Divinity in 2006, he was honoured in the 2011 New Year's Honours list with a CBE. Earlier this year he retired as Chief Executive of the Reform Movement and plans to devote time to lecturing, writing and public representation.

Tony is an excellent preacher. For many years he has been the guest preacher on Erev Rosh Hashanah in my community. Invariably he begins with where he's been on holiday that summer and we wait with baited breath to see how he turns travelogue into theology, how personal experience shifts into something broader and deeper.

Two of his drawbacks can be spoken of publicly. Firstly, his support for West Ham Football Club (he lists 'suffering with West Ham' under 'hobbies' in his Who's Who entry. Not for nothing do many think the club is actually called 'West Ham Nil.') Secondly, he bears a passing physical resemblance to the English comedian, Ronnie Corbett, and a more-than-passing resemblance to that comedian's propensity for awful and laboured puns!

Tony launched a quarterly journal soon after starting at the Manor House. Called MANNA, unsurprisingly, one of his puns but as with many of them, conveying a deeper meaning and message. His idea of '2020 Vision' for the Reform Movement was similarly inspired.

Tony brings passion to whatever he does. He has produced formal theology (3) but reading through 27 years of MANNA editorials gives some 'handle' on those passions, on what has motivated him over these years. In the first editorial he stated MANNA's purpose:

> [It] has just one creed – that all party lines must be crossed and transgressed. The religious and the secular, the radical and the conservative, the orthodox and liberal – all shall have a place within these columns. (4)

That first editorial was entitled 'Pluralism,' and the ethos expressed in that one has seldom been far from the surface in all subsequent 109 editorials.

Nearly 15 years later, his frustration with what he calls the 'hegemony of the fundamentalists' is almost tangible:

> Jewish neuroses – the obsession in Anglo-Jewry with authenticity; the tendency to define Judaism is terms of kashrut and Sabbath observance; we have failed to move beyond the profound sense of victimhood bestowed on us by the Shoah. Why is it that groups and religious organisations who parade a theology of the "there's been a tragedy, check your mezuzah" variety are held in such respect? Most probably it is the impact of fundamentalism and neurotic behaviour brought on by past Jewish experiences. That is why two communal initiatives are so important – the first is JCoSS(5) ; the second is Responsability(6) ...Let us welcome the first signs that our community is rising above its neuroses and voicing its frustration with the seductive hegemony of the fundamentalists. *Expressing a credible theology; uniting around values by which we can live and find meaning and purpose; working with others to repair the world; and seeking to be a blessing even when others are not a blessing to us – that is mainstream Judaism.* [my italics.](7)

By their nature, editorials are often responses to ephemeral, passing issues of the moment, though even there he couches his words in more-lasting formulations. He writes on Kurt Waldheim's election as President of

10

Austria(8), the Guinness Trial(9), the first Gulf War(10), the European Code of Conduct on the Arms Trade(11), two 'no-nonsense' editorials on the Hugo Gryn affair(12); the new millennium:

> It is just possible that this millennium date which is only marginal to Jewish life and consciousness may nevertheless prove to be a convenient date from which to record that the Jewish people, both in its land and in the Diaspora, began to move out from the shadow of self-absorption and self-defence and began to recover its vocation and mission. To be a blessing, to provide humanity with a vision, to remind humanity that each of us is created *b'tzelem Elohim*, in the image of God. (13)

As MANNA was developing, there was much talk in the Jewish community about demography: declining numbers, 'survival' and 'continuity.' What could be done, he asks, about such widespread social trends? He laments the reception given to would-be converts, and how the possibility of having their converted status called into question by "some dyspeptic Beit Din or other is monstrous." He doesn't dismiss the 'usual suspects' cited by Jewish communal leaders to 'explain' the decline in Jewish numbers: materialism and the decline of the Jewish family through divorce and intermarriage. But he sees it as an incomplete, even complacent, narrative:

> Are those the things killing Anglo-Jewry or is it our sadly-deserved image as hide-bound, boring, shallow, intolerant and parochial?" He calls for a speedy "change in both image and reality, to produce a Judaism which is vital, compelling, profound, tolerant and open-minded. (14)

Given that 'organising principle', it is hardly surprising that another key theme running through the editorials should be a reaction against fundamentalism, wherever it manifested itself.

In the 1990s it seemed that a way might have been found for all converts, whatever their 'entry point' into Judaism, to be accepted throughout the Jewish world. (15) The specific issue to which he is responding is less-important than what he says about fundamentalism(16)

The tragedy of Ne'eman is that a mind set that was once thought to be antiquated lunacy has now become a dominant trend within Orthodoxy.... The tragedy is underlined by the blind hatred and destructive power of the rhetoric of rejection. The tragedy is compounded by the power of a minority to terrify others within the Orthodox world into fearful acquiescence.......even at this 11th hour, it is hard to believe that medieval rhetoric coupled with threats of repudiation could really hold sway over the leaders of our community. Could British Jewry not set an example to the world and muster the courage and leadership to remove the question mark from Sacks' "One People?"(17)

Another part of Tony's theology evident from his editorials was his attitude to what has been called 'civil religion,'(18) exemplified in its Jewish frame, for example, in the writing of American sociologist Jonathan Woocher. (19) Civil religion is 'Judaism lite,' 'religion without theology,' 'Judaism without God.'

The Sternberg Centre is a religious institution. It may explore Judaism through culture, forge links with Israel, hold seminars on topical issues, train community carers but it houses the headquarters of a movement of synagogues and a rabbinic training college. And it has a rabbi as Director. Its central purpose is religious. ... Everything that we stand for flows from our commitment to God. (20)

And out of that he developed the supplements that provided a platform for an emerging Progressive Jewish theology. One of the most-important of those appeared 3 years later as *Progressive Judaism: a collective theological essay and discussion paper* which he described as "incontrovertibly theistic, distinctly liberal and authentically Jewish. It is intended as a lead not a creed, as a document to be discussed rather than affirmed."(21)

During Tony's Jewishly-formative years, one of the watchwords of the Progressive Jewish world was 'prophetic Judaism' which understood the obligation to work for the improvement of society as an integral part of Jewish life. Today it is called tikkun olam. It had always been part of Jewish teaching but its voice had become muted in the pulpits of traditional synagogues. Ritual matters – kashrut, Sabbath observance and the like - seemed to have displaced ethical and moral concerns. An early editorial reflected this:

The official Jewish community can be seen as obsessed with formality – committees, internal politics, group survival. These are the priestly rituals of our days. The official community – Orthodox and Reform – keeps a low ethical profile. It often suggests that there is no particular Jewish view on the great contemporary moral issues and is rendered speechless when, in fact, there is more than one Jewish view. This leaves us with a fringe community, often not seen in synagogues, still less frequently at committee meetings. It is frustrated by the limited horizons of the establishment, and demonstrates about women's rights and the nuclear issue. So it appears that the passionate and radical ethicist has no place in formal Judaism....We are a community obsessed with ritual rather than moral rectitude. The obsession is more than merely quaint. It is suffocating. (22)

This thinking was an ongoing concern in much of his work in Outreach both within and beyond the Jewish world:

It is now more than ever essential that Judaism return to its prophetic model and challenge power and the abuse of power at every turn, saying 'this cannot be right,' 'this cannot be justified.' 'This' being poverty and homelessness. 'This' being terrorism with its claim to possess the Truth and its utter lack of respect for human life. (23)

In the mid-1980s, the Church of England issued its Faith in the City report on social problems in inner cities. Immanuel Jakobovits, Chief Rabbi at that time, argued that immigrant Jews had improved their lot by dint of hard work and application and so, by implication, should the poor and disadvantaged of our time. A MANNA editorial responded:

Rabbi Jakobovits gives a conservative interpretation of Jewish tradition, especially when he comments on contemporary ethical and social issues. His is not the definitive view of Judaism or Anglo-Jewry on abortion, artificial insemination, women in Jewish life, inner cities. (24)

Israel was seldom far from editorial concern and increasingly so into the new century. The background to much of the 'lifetime' of MANNA was the Oslo Peace Process, two Intifadas, Gulf Wars and a post-Zionist view of

Israel. Editorials became increasingly emboldened in the face of the impasse in arriving at a two-State solution. In a "Dear Mr Sharon" editorial to the Israeli Prime Minister, Tony wrote:

> Present policies are not working. They offer neither leadership nor hope, neither vision nor strategy, only growing hatred, rising bloodshed and deepening despair. I know that the terrorism perpetrated by suicide bombers is despicable and intolerable but it cannot be eliminated by military action......Declare a Peace Conference. Bring everybody involved. Lock the doors and not let them out until a settlement – the only settlement that is conceivable – has been reached. So that this year the festival of freedom, so recently and so inhumanly disfigured – freedom from violence, fear, oppression and suffering for all in Israel/Palestine – can be realised speedily and in our days. (25)

It is not easy to be Chief Executive of a body like the Reform Synagogues of Great Britain, pushed and pulled by many contributing constituents and leaders, just one organisation among many 'competing' for adherents in an essentially numerically static Anglo-Jewish world. Inevitably, there will be dimensions of the work where you are little more than an 'apparatchik,' in the worst sense of the word. It goes with the territory. Tony seems to have dealt gladly with fools and 'kept his cool' in the face of large and sometimes prickly egos, both lay and rabbinic.

What we see in his editorials is an ability to demonstrate the broader context of pluralism, arguing not simply for a bigger 'market share' but as a matter of justice and correctness. Tony has managed to do all this for nearly 30 years with integrity, decency and *mentschlichkeit*. (26)

1. It became the Sternberg Centre for Judaism in 1984.
2. Bayfield, A *Dialogue with a Difference* (SCM London 1992) p.viii. Not mentioned, because not relevant in the context, were the activities of the original four Manor House Trust organisations.
3. Bayfield, A, *God's Demands and Israel's Needs* (RSGB 1981); *Sinai, Law and Responsible Autonomy* (RSGB 1993)
4. Manna No 1, Autumn 1983
5. The Jewish Community's only cross-communal Secondary School, opened in 2009
6. A Social Action initiative
7. *Manna* No 97, Autumn 2007
8. ibid. No 12, Summer 1986
9. ibid. No 29, August 1990
10. ibid. No 31, Spring 1991
11. ibid. No 60, Summer 1998
12. ibid. No 53, Autumn 1996 and No 55, Spring 1997
13. ibid. Manna No 66, Winter 2000
14. ibid. Manna No 2, Winter 1984
15. The Ne'eman Commission, chaired by Ya'akov Ne'eman, a minister in the Israel Cabinet. Ultimately it floundered on the Israeli Chief Rabbinate's refusal to accept the findings.
16. *Manna* No 59, Spring 1998
17. A reference to Jonathan Sacks' book *One People?* (1993) subtitled, significantly in this context, *Tradition, Modernity and **Jewish unity*** (my emphasis)
18. The phrase was first coined by Jean-Jacques Rousseau. Robert Bellah, the American sociologist, developed it in 'Civil Religion in America' in *Daedelus*, Vol 96, No 1, Winter 1967.
19. Woocher, Jonathan 'Sacred Survival: American Jewry's Civil Religion' in *Judaism* Vol 34, No 2 Spring 1985
20. *Manna* No 16, Summer 1987
21. ibid. No 27, Spring 1990
22. ibid. No 3, Spring 1984
23. ibid. No 73, Autumn 2001
24. ibid. No 11, Spring 1986
25. ibid. No 75, Spring 2002
26. Yiddish word combining a sense of humanity, integrity, decency and humility.

MIRIAM BERGER

Miriam Berger received *s'micha* in 2006 and took the role of Associate Rabbi and then Principal Rabbi at Finchley Reform Synagogue. The Rabbinate is no quick career path but having grown up in a rabbinic home and read Theology in Bristol she knew from a young age it was her vocation.

I am my Father's Daughter

In the early 1980s the BBC made a documentary focusing on a day in the life of a rabbi as a way of teaching the general public about Judaism. The documentary focused heavily on the rabbi's family and how Jewish life permeated every element of the family's fabric. It was no surprise that I remember this documentary so well as "From Where I Stand" featured Rabbi Tony Bayfield and his three year old daughter and as it was my television starring debut, I became its most avid viewer watching our recording daily. Yet it is less surprising that when making a documentary about Judaism, the rabbi's family become such a focus. Throughout Jewish history the values, practices and formation of the Jewish people have been articulated through the image of the Jewish family. Not just the images of the Genesis families through the generations but throughout both *halachic* and *aggadic* texts.

Many Jewish communities are accused of being too family focused, catering for the family when those who do not fit into that traditional model are left on the periphery looking in and feeling excluded. As a congregational rabbi, I struggle with these accusations, trying to make everyone feel welcomed in and trying to avoid falling into the trap of catering only for those who live within a particular image of what a family set up looks like. Many of our entry points to congregational life are still centred around the family, such as weddings, the education of children and *bnei mitzvah*. But whilst the community must ensure they can preserve those traditional entry points, many more are created to encourage entry and re-entry into congregational life whenever it is the right time for the individual, not when it has been conventional for the community in its past.

Judaism cannot be encapsulated into any single model to describe it because it is a living, breathing entity which is going to be different for every person who grapples with it. For some it is ritual without belief, for others spirituality without a need for physical actions, for some an intellectual discourse, and for others a framework for striving towards social justice and *tikkun olam* (the repairing of the world). Yet as I came to write this essay in honour of my dad at the point of his retirement and as I wanted, along with my colleagues, to mark the work that he has done for the Reform Jewish community in Britain, I could not help but pull together some of the interesting ways that the model of the family is used to teach the fundamental values of Judaism. Judaism is something I have been living and breathing since day one, and one of the primary reasons I went into the rabbinate was because of the place that community took in our family life. There were no boundaries between the two concepts: community is and always was part and parcel of our lives. Yet this is more of a fundamentally Jewish concept than I ever understood. What underpins the Jewish community are values set out by using the model of the Jewish family.

Throughout the book of Genesis the desire for each couple to procreate is a fundamental motif traced through the chapters. This is not simply a personal longing, this is not the expression of a couple wanting the fulfilment of children or even a son and heir but rather part of the covenant established with each generation. The covenant is not one which brings personal gain in one's own lifetime but is one constantly promoting the benefits it will bring to the generations to come. (1) The section of Deuteronomy used as the traditional second paragraph of the Shema moves between the use of the plural, indicating collective responsibility and the singular identifying the personal experience. As it asserts our role and God's role within the covenantal relationship its conclusion states, "Then you and your children may live long on the land that God promised to give your ancestors as long as there is a sky over the earth." (2) The very essence of the longevity of the covenantal relationship, the very essence of the nationhood of Israel relies on that which is passed on through the generations.

Marc Brettler understands the end of the *kedushah* within the *Amidah* when we are reminded of the imperative, for all generations to tell of God's greatness that, "this statement functions also as a summary for all three of the first blessings, as it refers to God's greatness, the theme of the first and second blessings, and His holiness separating this off as a unit within the Amidah." (3) The concept of *l'dor v'dor*, from generation to generation clearly underpins the values of Judaism. One cannot state anything about God or our

17

belief without asserting the imperative for this to be understood throughout the generations and thus begin to explain why the concept of family is so central to Jewish life.

Nationhood, belief, covenant yet also responsibility to create a functional, ethical society are wrapped up in notions of the family unit. The Talmud divides the large number of Torah ordained *mitzvot* into two types: civil laws which focus on ethical, social, and moral issues designed to regulate behaviour of one person towards another (*ben adam le-chavero*); and religious or ritual laws, which dictate how man should relate to God, (*ben adam le-Makom*)(4). Nahum Sarna a 20th century biblical scholar, suggested that these two types of *mitzvot* should not be seen separately because there is an indiscriminate commingling and interweaving of cultic ritual and moral imperatives. Their observance helps form the relationship between man and God, and their fulfillment will allow us to be "holy people" to God. We can trace from the narratives, such as the stories of the inappropriate sexual exploits of Noah's family (5) or Lot's daughters (6) through to the holiness code of Leviticus (7) that preserving the integrity of the family provides the stable foundations from which Judaism grows. Examples such as the Daughters of Zelophechad (8) enable us to see case law working to develop the intricacies of Jewish law, again using the model of one family, one example on which through debate we build structures.

The family however cannot be seen in isolation, as each family unit forms the basis for community. We are told in the Exodus narrative how the paschal lamb must be consumed the night before the redemption from Egypt. The rules are very poignant, "In the tenth day of this month they shall take to them every man a lamb, according to their fathers' houses, a lamb for a household; and if the household be too little for a lamb, then shall he and his neighbour next unto his house take one according to the number of the souls; according to every man's eating you shall make your count for the lamb." (9) This image complemented all of our family *sedarim* as our family grew to fill our dining-room and beyond, including within our number all those close to us whose own number seemed depleted through the usual tribulations of life and whose annual place at the seder table could soon enough not be distinguished from blood relatives. Though these days *sedarim* are over-catered and extra numbers are rarely used to ensure that there are no leftovers and that everything is consumed within that night - as was the imperative of the paschal lamb, the image of that night before the Exodus reminds us how a community becomes as powerful as the sum of its parts and provides a model of extended family to ensure the whole Jewish community feels part of a

18

whole in a nurturing way. When our narrative moves us to settling the land we are a group of tribes, each tribe descended from one of Jacob's sons. We may move into the language of tribes but what is a tribe if not an extended family and it is that tribal mentality, the single degree of separation which keeps the Jewish community feeling like a family however blessed it is with numbers and will continue to do so were we to become as numerous as the stars in the sky or grains of sand on the shore as was promised. (10)

The triumvirate of leadership model which is established after the Exodus not only relies on the family unit but also promotes the unique roles for each family member within the collective. Moses is singled out by God as the leader of the Jewish people to be joined by Aaron first in a complimentary position but soon to carve out his own role in the Priesthood. *Shirat Hayam*, the song of the sea, hints at Miriam's leadership among the women and the *midrashim* around her death (11) and the implications that the community lacked water (12) at that time provides the peg on which to hook the rabbinic tradition of the well that followed Israel in the wilderness and dried up when Miriam died gives her the reputation for being the nurturing leadership within the triumvirate. Genesis is riddled with the sibling rivalry narratives of Isaac and Ishmael, Jacob and Esau and Joseph and his brothers, yet even among Aaron, Miriam and Moses we can see that the sibling rivalry motif continues to exist. "Miriam and Aaron spoke against Moses because of the Cushite woman whom he had married" (13) but this time God intervenes and reprimands Aaron and Miriam. The dysfunctional family is a motif that is equally important. Rabbi Tony Bayfield uses the metaphor of the relationship between siblings and that of a parent towards his children to explain the multiple covenant theory of the Abrahamic faiths.

> Is not all true love founded on mutual respect and valuing, on the equality implicit in each knowing for certain that the other will be accepted for themselves? And does not the love between siblings provide a unique bond for working together in partnership? And does the good parent not avoid favoritism, valuing each sibling for who they are, providing them with the inner security to be both humble and confirming, and binding each in a covenant of love forever. (14)

Rabbi Bayfield took the dysfunctional out of the families of the Genesis story and made sense of the individualistic and different relationships. Children may squabble, they may posture for position in the family but a parent has an infinite amount of love to share between their children equally.

19

Personalities make up families and different paths are going to be chosen and going to be right for different people. These concepts have to be woven into our readings. As Jews it is easy to read the story of Abraham passing on his covenantal relationship with God down to Isaac without giving enough significance to what can be dismissed as the tying up of a loose end, or can be embraced as the establishment of a new branch of the covenant. "And God heard the voice of the lad; and the angel of God called to Hagar out of heaven, and said to her: 'What is the matter, Hagar? Fear not; for God has heard the voice of the lad where he is. Arise, lift up the lad, and hold him fast by the hand; for I will make him a great nation." (15)

The model of family life does not simply portray a microcosm of the Jewish world but it also allows us to see how the Jewish world interacts with Christianity and Islam through this same window of family life framing a microcosm of the world. Family is not portrayed as perfect, nor as something that is easy, but by framing Judaism and the other Abrahamic faiths through the metaphor of family we can build our tolerance from a place of love and feel blessed with all we have or realise the importance of working to create what we need.

I am often reminded (teased) about a contribution that was made to the first UJS/Limmud Shabbat Book, *The Seventh Day*. In it a tale of a 10 year old, homesick rabbi's daughter is told as an introduction to a piece about the significance of blessing one's children around the Friday night dinner table. Rabbi Bayfield went on to write,

> Our family Friday night has been the heart of the week and the cornerstone of our family for as long as I can remember. Don't run away with the idea that it has always resembled those idealised posters and book illustrations of Jewish education – full of beatific smiles, love and peace. For years we never managed to get through from the blessing of the children to the serving of the first course without a tantrum, squabble or successful wind up. I have been trying for 25 years to achieve the halakhically correct silence between the completion of the blessing over bread (*motzi*) and the eating of the challah, but to no avail. Nevertheless, the magic weaves its spell and kabbalat Shabbat speaks to us of love and family ties – and of God. (16)

The essay goes on to talk about the ritual of blessing one's children but the significance of this piece is not the personal humiliation, nor the painting of

20

the average Jewish family Friday night dining experience but rather his concluding words, "Re-reading this piece I am struck by the sentimentality. But, then, sentiment has an important place in religion. Love, pride, memories and hopes have a central place in Jewish and family life. They are all contained in that ritual of blessing." (17)

Jewish family life has indeed been the blessing passed on to me in my life and one which I sincerely hope to pass on to my children with the same purely positive connotations. It is sentimental, but it is also the model which has preserved the religion through the generations. Rabbi Bayfield through his life and through his work maintained this Jewish tradition of using the family as a model for the teaching, living and perpetuation of Judaism. As the recipient of this lesson on so many fronts I learnt the most important concept from him. However we define family, whether the rabbi's family life as portrayed in "From Where I Stand" or the individual who walks into the community and gets brought into its heart, this model of each generation becoming an even stronger link in the chain of Jewish tradition, uses the family to sustain it and preserve it. We attempt to recreate it on a bigger scale in our communities to ensure everyone has access to this model of Judaism through communal meals, *sedarim* and inter-generational activities and relationships. We know that Judaism depends on it. Love, pride, memories and hope is not something that simply exists on a sentimental level in family life it is what enables each of us to take from the past, ritualise it in the present and ensure it is passed on for the future.

1. Genesis 17:7
2. Deuteronomy 11:21
3. Ed. Rabbi Lawrence A Hoffman, *My People's Prayer Book*, Jewish Lights Publishing, Vermont 1998, Vol. 2 p.87
4. Yoma 85b
5. Genesis 9:22
6. Genesis 19
7. Leviticus 17-19
8. Numbers 27
9. Exodus 12:3-4
10. Genesis 22:17
11. Numbers 20;1
12. Numbers 20:2
13. Numbers 12:1
14. Tony Bayfield et al, *He kissed Him and They Wept*, SCM Press London 2001, p.39
15. Genesis 21:17-18
16. UJS/Limmud, *The Seventh Day*, Great Britain, 1997, p.34
17. ibid, p.35

LIONEL BLUE

Lionel Blue was rabbi of the Settlement and Middlesex New Synagogues before becoming European Director of the World Union for Progressive Judaism, then Convener of the Reform Beth Din. He is well known for his religious broadcasts on radio and television. He has received the OBE and the Templeton Prize.

Remembering the Second World War and the Holocaust

Shivering with cold during the Second World War, evacuated from London, I took refuge in semi-heated public libraries till closing time, reading everything and anything.

That's how I stumbled across this sentence by Nietzsche the German philosopher who fascinated Hitler. 'Don't gaze too long into the abyss' he wrote 'lest the abyss gaze into you.' I knew what he meant. The horror of the Holocaust, its sadism, its madness had gazed into me even before the war though I lived in safe England which actually didn't feel that safe. I remember anti-Semitic insults daubed on Jewish streets. 'Perish Judah!' scrawled on synagogues and my father planning my route home from school through Jewish streets so I didn't get roughed up.

The horror intensified as the refugees from the Nazis arrived in London's poor Jewish East End, each with a more terrifying tale to tell. That was when my nightmares began. And that is why seventy years later I still cannot bring myself to visit Auschwitz, Belsen and Birkenau or watch Anne Frank on TV. I was so sure Britain would be invaded and I'd also end up in a gas chamber - there were worse ways too!

The first things the Holocaust collapsed were my comforting childhood beliefs. So many prayers must have been said in the trucks to the camps. How many had been answered in any way I could understand - so why pray? And where was God in that increasing horror? Was he sleeping, dozing, drunk, or just couldn't be bothered? So I gave up this useless god and

23

marched with the reds instead.

The Holocaust also made me cynical about religious establishments. Every army good bad and murderous in the last World War had received a blessing, every horrific regime a religious legitimation. Since they couldn't even spot evil in front of their noses, I washed my hands of them.

The abyss also collapsed my belief in myself. A fascist band came marching down the street. My mother thrust me into a doorway to protect me. I remember secretly wanting to join them and play a fascist drum myself. I was fed up with being a persecuted Jew. I wanted to be on the winning side for a change. Perhaps there was a bit of a Nazi in me. Perhaps there's a bit in most of us. It's safer to acknowledge it.

The abyss Nietzsche talked about questioned me ever more closely. Later on the question began to take this form: 'What would you have done', it said, 'if the Nazis had only shot gypsies, tortured gays and imprisoned liberals, but had left Jews alone and you were a rabbi in Berlin? Would you have sacrificed your career or would you have looked the other way.' I don't know but sometimes I still torture myself with guilt for a situation I never had to face, thank God!

After the war I had to cross into Germany a country I'd always avoided because it was a Jewish charnel house, the abyss I feared. But there a strange thing happened. The abyss seemed to turn inside out, a common experience when we ask God's help to confront our fears. I even began to see little lights of self sacrifice and love shine in it, the more touching because they came from ordinary people I met as I hitchhiked across the ruins of the Third Reich.

A woman returned to her Berlin flat in 1943. 'Get out, get out ' whispered the concierge, the Gestapo have come'. The woman tore off her Jewish badge and walked the streets in despair, finally knocking on the door of a school friend of long ago. The friend gasped, but didn't telephone the police but a bureau for bombed out people to get her a new Aryan identity. That was the price of friendship in those times.

And there was the man in the train who asked me to reunite him with his daughter. When the synagogues were torched in 1938 he'd tried to put out the flames. A friend warned him to make his peace with the Party for the sake of his wife and children. So he'd joined the Party and now his daughter wouldn't speak to him.' Tell her how bad it was at that time' he said urgently 'she might believe you,' which I did. Would I have risked my family to put out the flames?

In a gay bar I listen to stories of hidden friends saved from torture in that dark time. Would I have walked on the other side?

I remember Rabbi Leo Baeck who in September 1939 hurried back to Germany after leading a group of children to safety in England. His duty lay with his shattered congregation.

I remember a Jewish doctor urging an elderly patient to vote in the new democratic election. 'Frau Dr.', he said, 'I only voted once before and look at the suffering I caused, especially to you who has been so good to me. I am too stupid to vote.'

And there was the pastor who issued baptismal certificates to delay deportation and the gentile wives of Jewish husbands who demonstrated outside Gestapo offices.

Here are some lessons I learnt from my visit to Germany. Some of the angry questions I hurled at God boomeranged back at me. Why had He not taken a hand in that terrible time? Because we human beings are the only hands He has to redeem this world.

I learnt from the Holocaust to beware of unpurified nationalism. Love your country and your culture but don't try to love your own more by loving others less. That way lies murder whether it's the Balkans, the Holy Land, Northern Ireland, the Congo, wherever.

I no longer cared if God was all powerful or all anything. It was enough to watch His goodness at work transfiguring people. As I returned to England the words of Nietzsche were replaced by the words of the agnostic Roman Emperor Marcus Aurelius whom I'd also bumped into in those wartime libraries : 'I've known the nature of the good' he wrote and saw that it was beautiful. I've known the nature of evil and saw it was ugly.' I can only add, 'And me too!'

My unofficial saints helped me take my first small step out of my prison of anger and hate. Their lights were my guiding stars.

This first appeared as a sermon at St Martins in the Fields, London.

BARBARA BORTS

Barbara Borts is currently the rabbi of Newcastle Reform Synagogue. This article is abstracted from her PhD work through the University of Durham, on the music of the Reform movement in the UK. She is a singer and a violinist, and is studying privately to become a cantor.

The Early Reform World – What They Sang

Much has been written about the history of the origins of the Reform movement in the UK, but little about its musical heritage. This article attempts to uncover the earliest musical history and sources of the Associated British Synagogues, the first federation of Reform synagogues in the UK. This is a work-in-progress, the first parts of an ongoing detective story, and, as such, will be a snapshot of what I have been able to uncover by the beginning of March 2011.

As is well-known, West London Synagogue [hereafter known as WLS] was the first of the Reform synagogues in the UK, founded in 1840 as a break-away from the Spanish-Portuguese Bevis Marks Synagogue, although also including some Ashkenazi families. WLS established early on the choral tradition for which it is still known: at first, an all-male choir, and later a mixed -voice choir were formed. The organ was installed in 1859. That music was important in the culture of WLS is evident by the appointment of Charles Kensington Salaman (1814 – 1901), an eminent Anglo-Jewish composer and musician, as the Director of Music, and Charles Verrinder a renowned non-Jewish organist as the accompanist. Between 1861 and 1892, Salaman and Verrinder collaborated on six volumes of music.

The music was a mix of English music with some Sephardic elements in it, reflecting their origins, and included music by the above-mentioned Salaman and Verrinder, as well as by Naumbourg and Sulzer, two *hazzanim* from France and Germany, respectively, and Mombach, German-born, but who spent his career in England. It is clear that the earliest music of this first

26

synagogue derived in the main from Jewish composers, but the arrangements were often in the hands of the non-Jewish organists.

What relationship did it bear to the music of its parent synagogue, Bevis Marks? Chazzan and current musical director Eliot Alderman writes:

> Unfortunately my congregation has kept poor records of its own history, never mind that of other synagogues, and in fact I have tried to contact people at WLS a couple of times to see if they can shed any light on the Spanish & Portuguese musical history itself! As far as Verrinder goes, many of the pieces he arranged are bastardized forms of Spanish & Portuguese chants (e.g. Sabbath Psalm 92, Great Kaddish), probably due to his unfamiliarity with Oriental rhythmic patterns and modal characteristics. I think we can be fairly sure that many of those pieces were in fact sung in their pure Spanish & Portuguese form in the early WLS. They were definitely not sung in harmony by the Spanish & Portuguese choir of the time, because our choir arrangements for these items are in fact adaptations of Verrinder's using the original form of the melody.

> On the other hand, there are a few items in Verrinder's works (the more obviously Western-sounding ones) which are still sung today in very similar forms at the S&P, such as the Yigdal melodies for regular Shabbatot and Festivals, so it may well be that Verrinder's arrangements actually represent an older/more "authentic" form of those melodies than is currently sung in the S&P synagogues. Nonetheless, I find it relatively likely that there were a few Ashkenazi tunes sung at that time in the WLS, because those Ashkenazim would have found the S&P style totally alien to them...? But this is pure speculation on my part.

West London Synagogue also produced hymnals; I have a copy of the 1938 edition. It is interesting to examine its contents. Of the thirty-four pieces published in the hymnal, twenty-five are English hymns of which only nine are in Hebrew. The music can be described as follows: music by classical music composers, three of which are English Psalm arrangements, and one of which is an adaptation of *mah tovu*; Christian hymns rendered in English, some set to Psalms; some 'cross-overs' – traditional Jewish melodies set to English texts; various Jewish composers music set to English texts, two of which are settings of Psalms and one of which is a translation of Hebrew text; and Hebrew texts with music by both Jewish and non-Jewish composers.

Although the 'how' and 'what' of the music at WLS has been examined, the 'why' of music needs further research. It is clear that the WLS tradition is one of beautiful music, decorum and order, its choral tradition possibly influenced by both the strong choral tradition here in the UK and "...the general 'movement for better music' manifest in...churches throughout mid-Victorian Britain."

It is instructive to compare the WLS Hymnal of 1938 with that of the American Reform movement version, the Union Hymal, first published in 1897, and revised in the 1930s. One might have imagined that a 'songbook' intended for a congregation would somehow convey the meaning of the music to be sung and its place in the worship service. However, the WLS Hymnal lacks both this type of preface, and as well, has no editorial attribution, except for noting that four of the pieces were used with the permission of the Union Hymnal.

The much larger Union Hymnal was intended for a movement, not one synagogue, and was published under the auspices of the American Reform professional body of rabbis known as the CCAR, or Central Conference of American Rabbis, with the music provided by the American Society of Cantors. The Union Hymnal includes music by classical music composers; a small number of pieces composed by non-Jews, including a couple of hymns; and a vast number of pieces composed by Jewish composers, *hazzanim* or otherwise identified as consciously Jewish.

We are missing any kind of preface or statement of reflection on the purpose and nature of the music used in the early UK Reform movement, but here, in the USA Reform hymnal, the Committee on Synagog [sic] Music set out their mission. In fact, it is indicative of the sense of mission that they begin with such a statement altogether. This edition, a revision of an earlier iteration, was bolstered by Jewish content. The editors wrote that this revision should "ring true to the Jewish spirit" and "be as Jewish as possible".

> The Committee on Revision was actuated by a desire to produce a hymn book which would stimulate congregational singing, inspire Jewish devotion, revive the value of Jewish melody...lean heavily where possible on Jewish motifs...and encourage in the religious schools a love for Jewish poetry and song...and finally contribute to the field of hymnology a publication which would be essentially Jewish in color, spirit and purpose... Even a superficial glance through the contents of this volume indicates how many of the hymns

are based upon traditional melodies. But...the needs and tastes of our congregations are not one, but many. A number of old and new hymns have been included which are in the general tone, but which are not specifically Jewish.

It is significant that the American Reform movement was more reflective about the place of music in its services because this project was directed and led by cantors, and because of the relative differences in the approach to the place of music in the service. However, in omitting to include a preface, WLS omitted to share the process of deciding upon their music, and one can only conjecture. More work needs to be done on this aspect of the musical life of the burgeoning UK movement.

The musical heritage of the subsequent five original synagogues has been subject to far less study and attention. The second synagogue, Manchester Reform Synagogue, was founded in Manchester, in 1856. According to Rabbi Selvin Goldberg, music may have played an early role in the split from the Orthodox synagogue:

> ...in 1840... the first shots in the battle which culminated in the creation of the Manchester Congregation of British Jews were fired. In that year schism occurred. One reason among others was that some members were anxious to have an organ in the synagogue...it appears...that the history - in fact, the existence - of the Manchester Congregation of British Jews was involved with the knotty problem of religious music.

In 1858 they held their first service with choir and organ, and used the prayer book of the WLS, but seemingly they did not use its music. According to Goldberg, they turned to "...the freshly liberated community of Hamburg for inspiration. Much of the music was copied from that Reform Synagogue, but one item was taken from Vienna, whose synagogue used the Sabbath Psalm set to music by Schubert...." According to musicologist Abraham Zvi Idelsohn, Hamburg music was composed almost entirely by Christian musicians, was sung by a boys' choir, accompanied by organ, and was overseen by a Portuguese musician to help them to "abolish all ugliness of medievalism" in their music.

Bradford Congregation was the third of the original synagogues, founded in 1873/4. I have yet to find out much about its musical history prior to the 1940s. In the late 40s and into the 50s, Rudi Leavor and Ruth Sterne remember that the music they sang was mainly Lewandowski, brought over in two volumes by Rabbi L. Gerhard Graf. Rudi recalls that they were in possession of the six WLS volumes of music, but he does not know how they got there, nor does he remember how much of that music they actually incorporated into their service.

The fourth of the synagogues, the Settlement Synagogue, was founded in 1919 by Basil and Rose Henriques, and in 1929 created its own prayer book, a thin volume called The Prayer Book of the St. George's Settlement Synagogue, which contained both prayers and hymns. According to members Kitty Taylor and Les Gilbert, at first the services tended to be rather anglicised, but over the years, more Hebrew was introduced. Unlike WLS, where the first choristers were male, Rose Henriques, the main force behind the music, formed a choir from the girls at the club and accompanied them on the organ. They came to use for their music two sources, the *Voice of Prayer and Praise*, (known as 'the blue book') which was published by the United Synagogue, and thus, was a collection of music used in Orthodox synagogues, and a hymn from the prayer book, which would be in English. Although it is unclear what music they sang at their incipience, by the time of the establishment of the Association of Synagogues in the 40s, according to Kitty Taylor, the music sung was mainly in Hebrew, with hymns in English. They referred to their in-house songbooks as *schmattes*, because they were hand-written on cloth. This particular book was used mainly for festivals, and included both music from 'the blue book' and Lady Henriques's own words, mainly in English, set to transcriptions of classical music pieces.   Kitty recalls, "We were in an invidious position because we were the only synagogue affiliated to both movements, [Liberal and Reform], so those on the far left were quite happy with all the English hymns and as we moved to the right religiously, we were asking for more Hebrew in our music. Eventually the majority of English hymns died out, although the Henriques themselves moved to the left with the liberals." It seemed to Kitty that, "There was very little time for anything Hebrew, because there were so many English hymns."

People recall that quite a number of the hymns were attributed to Lady Henriques, but, when pressed, could not be certain that she had actually written them. It was also mentioned that she set these words to classical music melodies, a favourite being Beethoven. In examining the prayer book, it is clear that many of these were borrowed from elsewhere, but how they got there, it would be difficult to say.

This synagogue is truly anomalous in its musical heritage, which seems to be a reflection of its original members, who, unlike most of the other Reform synagogues, were drawn from the Eastern European, not the Western European, world, and were thus heirs of a different liturgical music tradition. As the Settlement was also part of a 'project' designed to anglicize the Eastern European Jews, this could explain the mixture of 'traditional' East European melodies such as one would find in the 'blue book' and the Anglo (and German) Reform traditions of hymns in the vernacular.

Sadly. Glasgow Reform Synagogue, which was founded in 1933, has not had the benefit of a synagogue historian, so uncovering their musical tradition is proving to be difficult. Two older members are slowly attempting to remember and record the music of the earlier days, and I must await their work.

The sixth of the original six synagogues was North Western Reform Synagogue, also founded in 1933. In the beginning, the synagogue used the music of WLS, but in 1943, Rabbi Dr Van der Zyl, a German rabbi, came to Alyth. Van der Zyl was himself a trained *hazzan* and, like Rabbi Graf, brought to Alyth the music of the German Reform world, namely, Lewandowski.

By the time the six synagogues banded together and formed the Association of British Synagogues in 1942, the music used by these synagogues varied by synagogue and was drawn from many different sources, both Christian and Jewish, English and German, with some Sephardi music and perhaps a negligible amount from Eastern Europe. There was, as yet, little analysis of the nature and function of music in liturgy. This kind of thoughtful process, and the beginnings of a more unified musical tradition, was to come later.

I want to thank all of those who shared their memories with me. It is very important to preserve these memories before it is too late.

DANNY BURKEMAN

Danny Burkeman is one of the Rabbis at West London Synagogue. He was ordained at the Hebrew Union College-Jewish Institute of Religion in Los Angeles, California, and completed a Masters in Jewish-Christian Relations at Cambridge.

The Evolving Place of Jerusalem in the Fourteenth Benediction of the *Amidah*

The Importance of Jerusalem

> *Ten measures of beauty descended to the world: nine were taken by Jerusalem and one by the rest of the world*
> *(Talmud Kiddushin 49b)*

Jerusalem is a unique city; no other city can claim a religious connection to Jews, Christians and Muslims. Jerusalem is not simply a terrestrial city located in the Middle East; it is also the holy city where humanity encounters the divine. For Jews, Jerusalem is the city in which the Temple once stood, the dwelling place of God. This is David's capital, the city which was promised to the people as their birthright in Genesis, and the place which God will ultimately rebuild and return them to. Following the destruction of the Temple in 70 CE, the city and the Temple Mount acquired newfound significance. 'The rabbis now insisted that all the key events of salvation had taken place on Mount Zion ...finally the Messiah would proclaim the New Age from Zion [Jerusalem] and redeem the world' (Armstrong 1996:169). It was for an ingathering of the exile to a rebuilt Jerusalem that Jews have been praying since the city's destruction.

The Fourteenth Benediction of the *Amidah*

The *amidah* is the central prayer within Jewish liturgy. As Reuven Hammer wrote: 'The Sages called it *ha-tefilla* – the Prayer – almost as if there were no other' (Hammer 1994:156). It is also known as the *shemona esrai*, meaning 'eighteen', named for the number of benedictions which the prayer contains, although in its current form it is made up of nineteen benedictions. Ismar Elbogen claims that the additional benediction is the fifteenth, which refers to the Messiah and the descendants of the House of David. Elbogen notes that in the Palestinian tradition the fourteenth benediction about the rebuilding of Jerusalem, ends 'God of David, Builder of Jerusalem'. In the Babylonian version the two themes are separated with the fourteenth benediction about Jerusalem and the fifteenth about the Davidic line and the Messiah (see Elbogen 1993:34-5)(1).

It is the fourteenth benediction which calls for the restoration of Jerusalem, and for this request to have been included, it is evident that it must have been written in its final form after the destruction of the Temple (2). Louis Finkelstein contrasts the various forms of the passage found in Palestinian and Babylonian sources; as a result of this he concludes 'that the prayer for Jerusalem was not part of the original Amidah' (Finkelstein 1925-6:35); he claims that it was initially 'introduced in Palestine at a very early time, but not accepted in Babylonia' (ibid.:34).

The traditional fourteenth benediction is:

> Return to Jerusalem your city in compassion and dwell in
> its midst as You promised You would, and rebuild it soon
> in our day into an eternal structure, and quickly establish
> David's throne within it. Blessed are You, Adonai, who
> rebuilds Jerusalem

> (Hoffman 1998:141-2)

It is possible to distinguish four separate requests before arriving at the final benediction. The initial petition states: 'Return to Jerusalem your city in compassion'. This echoes the words of the first chapter of Zechariah. God instructs Zechariah to tell the people: 'Turn back to me – says the Lord of Hosts – and I will turn back to you' (Zechariah 1:3). Following this, Jerusalem's sorry state is considered, although it ends on an optimistic note as God states: 'I mercifully return to Jerusalem' (Zechariah 1:16). The *amidah* calls upon God to once again fulfil the words of Zechariah; after the Babylonian exile, God returned to Jerusalem, the initial request is for a repeat performance.

Earlier in the *amidah* God's quality of mercy is mentioned, with God praised: 'who resurrects the dead in great mercy'. The resurrection of the dead is an eschatological expectation, almost impossible to conceive. It is only possible as a result of God's great mercy. Similarly for the Jewish people, God's return to Jerusalem, and all it entails, has eschatological significance which can only come from God. In considering God's mercy (*rhm*), 'The Biblical conception of compassion is the feeling of the parent for the child' (Kohler 1904:201)(3). A parent's love is enduring and it is as though the Jewish people are the children who are appealing to God's parental love for the rebuilding of Jerusalem, regardless of whether they deserve special treatment.

The second request builds upon the first by asking God to 'dwell in its [Jerusalem's] midst as You promised You would'. Once again there is an echo of Zechariah as he said: 'Shout for joy, Fair Zion! For lo, I come; and I will dwell in your midst' (Zechariah 2:14). This promise was made at the time of Zechariah, when the Jews were returning to Palestine from Babylon; in the *amidah* it is taken as a promise which is still binding upon God. The passage does not overtly mention the rebuilding of the Temple, and therefore suggests that the sanctity of Jerusalem is inherent in the place, not just because of the structures which were built there.

Together these two petitions can be read as a double assertion. God is called upon to 'return to Jerusalem' and to 'dwell in it'. God is requested to do this *berachamim* 'in mercy', and if that is not sufficient, because *dibarta* 'as You said'(4). The people's behaviour will not be the motivation for God's return to Jerusalem, rather it will be as a result of God's mercy and God's promise; it is solely in the power of God, and so the only avenue open to the people is prayer.

The third and fourth clauses may also be read together, with the dual request of rebuilding Jerusalem into an eternal structure and establishing David's throne there. In this call for God to build the city, the Temple is conspicuous by its absence. However, it is worth noting that the two words used: *uvaneh* and *beyamenu* generally appear in the liturgy in specific relation to the building of the *beit hamikdash* 'the Temple'(5). The language therefore includes echoes of the Temple within Jerusalem's rebuilding. The *amidah* proposes a new set of circumstances for the rebuilt Jerusalem. In the *TaNaCh* it is clear that humans were responsible for building Jerusalem, and specifically the Temple; in the prayer the focus has shifted with the petition to God to undertake the task of being the builder.

In the final clause, prior to the closing benediction, the focus is on the throne of David. This throne is initially referred to in the *TaNaCh* in the context of the transference of the monarchy from Saul to David (2 Samuel 13:10). On one level this can be read as a call to restore the kingship, symbolic of Jewish national sovereignty in general. However, the deeper significance is the belief that the line of David will ultimately lead to the Messiah. As Jeremiah prophesied: 'I will raise up a true branch of David's line. He shall reign as king and shall prosper, and he shall do what is just and right in the land' (Jeremiah 23:5); The eschatological significance of the Messiah, who will come at the end of days, is linked with Jerusalem as the inheritor of David's throne, and the one who will initiate the building of the next Temple.

Despite eschatology being concerned with the end of days, in this benediction there is an urgency to the request. The building is requested: *bekarov* 'soon' and *beyamenu* 'in our days', and in connection to David's throne the request is for it to be established *meherah* 'quickly'. The prayer seeks to move God to act swiftly, regardless of whether the people's behaviour has changed in such a way as to warrant the change in circumstances.

The paragraph finishes with a blessing, 'Blessed are You, Adonai, who rebuilds Jerusalem'. Hoffman has translated it as 'rebuilds Jerusalem', however it would be equally accurate to translate it as 'builder of Jerusalem'. This designation *boneh yerushalayim* only appears once in the *TaNaCh*, 'The Lord rebuilds Jerusalem; He gathers in the exiles of Israel' (Psalms 147:2). God's building of Jerusalem is accompanied by the ingathering of the exiles, placing it as one of the events of the Jewish people's redemption. This offers a further eschatological element to the benediction.

In the Reform *Siddur*, Forms of Prayer, the fourteenth benediction reads:

> Turn in mercy to Jerusalem and may Your presence dwell   within it. Rebuild it as You have prophesied, then it shall indeed be called 'city of righteousness, faithful city'. Help us establish it as a place worthy of prayer for all peoples. Blessed are You God, who builds Jerusalem
>
> (MRJ 2008:81)

The opening clause is the same as in the traditional liturgy, but the message and request is then altered significantly, before concluding with the same blessing. God is still called on to dwell within the city, but in this alternative vision of Jerusalem there is no reference to 'David's throne', and therefore the implicit incorporation of the aspiration for the Messiah and a Third Temple.

However, this alternative vision of Jerusalem is still drawn directly from the *TaNaCh* and from God's promise. In this prayer, the promise draws on Isaiah 1:26; 'I will restore your magistrates as of old and your counsellors as at the beginning. After that you shall be called city of righteousness, faithful city'. The idea of righteousness relates to the root *tzedek*, which also means justice. By using these words from the Prophet Isaiah the Reform *Siddur* ensures that the vision of Jerusalem emanates from *TaNaCh*, but it also presents a vision which focuses on the value of justice and faithfulness, without focusing on the specifically Jewish elements which may be called for in a rebuilding. This is a development from the previous edition of Forms of Prayer (1977), which had simply dropped the reference to God's prior promise from the fourteenth benediction. The new form of the benediction allows for the maintenance of the traditional language with a new vision of the Jerusalem of God's promise.

This image of Jerusalem as a 'city of righteousness' is further developed in the benediction with the aspiration for the city to be 'a place worthy of prayer for all peoples'. This idea can also be found in the writings of Isaiah, who states: 'For My House shall be called a house of prayer for all peoples' (Isaiah 56:7). It is worth asking why the Reform liturgy did not use the language of Isaiah to describe their Jerusalem aspirations, avoiding the words *beit tefilati* 'house of my prayer'. Isaiah 56:7 is part of a consideration of other peoples coming to accept God and keeping the Jewish commandments(6). By referring to Jerusalem as 'a place worthy of prayer for all peoples' Isaiah's vision is altered. The different wording is crucial for the Reform vision of Jerusalem as a centre for all peoples regardless of how they come to God; suggesting the inclusion of the other monotheistic religions who view Jerusalem as holy.

Here too the Reform liturgy has changed from the previous edition of Forms of Prayer which made reference to *mechon tefillah* 'a centre of prayer' (RSGB 1977:236-7). The word *mechon* 'centre' was used in connection to the Temple, when it states: 'I have now built for You a stately House, a place where You may dwell forever' (I Kings 8:13). In the 1977 liturgy there was an altered vision of the Temple, in 2008 the idea of a specific structure is removed, so that the request is simply for Jerusalem to be *mekom tefillah* 'a place of prayer'. The passage maintains an eschatological expectation for a rebuilt Jerusalem, but this is a Jerusalem which will be open to all religions, and not only to the Jews; this is a vision of Jerusalem which God *dibarta* 'spoken' or 'promised', but it is not the traditional vision of the fourteenth benediction, it is a vision drawing on the words of Isaiah. In the Liberal

Siddur, the prayer is changed to read:

> Let Your presence dwell in Jerusalem, and Zion be filled
> with justice and righteousness. May peace be in her gates
> and quietness in the hearts of her inhabitants. Let Your
> Teaching go forth from Zion, Your word from Jerusalem.
> We praise You, O God, Builder of Jerusalem
>
> (ULPS 1995:57-8)

As was the case in the Reform liturgy the references to David's throne is removed, but so is the reference to the promise from God. There is a new vision for Jerusalem, with the Temple absent. Although it begins with God's presence dwelling in the city, the focus then shifts to the nature of Jerusalem, a city which will be characterised by justice, righteousness, peace and quiet. The use of these values may be a critique of the contemporary Jerusalem which does not possess them, and therefore requires a prayer requesting them, effectively calling for a new type of Jerusalem. When considering Jerusalem's history as a city disputed by Jews, Christians and Muslims, it is clear that there has rarely been peace and quiet within her gates. Her inhabitants have often been persecuted, with a complete absence of justice and righteousness (7). This reference to 'her inhabitants' is intended to be all encompassing, including all of the people living in Jerusalem: Jews, Christians and Muslims.

The Liberal liturgy only mentions the idea of building Jerusalem with the final blessing which concludes the benediction. Preceding this is a reference to Isaiah's eschatological vision for Jerusalem: 'For instruction [Torah] shall come forth from Zion, The word of the Lord from Jerusalem' (Isaiah 2:3). What is significant is that instead of referring to *torah*, the liturgy speaks of *toratecha*, this can be translated as 'Your Torah' or 'Your teaching' (8). The Liberal liturgy moves away from the particularity of Torah, which is God's Jewish teaching to state 'Your teaching'. This broadens the idea from being particularly Jewish to incorporate other religious teachings which have emerged from the holy city. As with the Reform liturgy, there is an attempt to move to a more universal, inter-religious Jerusalem.

What Can we Learn ?

The differences between the traditional fourteenth benediction, and the examples found in the Reform and Liberal liturgies reveal the evolution in the way in which Judaism has related to the city of Jerusalem. The traditional liturgy is fixated on a Jerusalem which corresponds to the ancient Jewish eschatological hopes for the rebuilding of the Temple and the re-establishment of the Davidic line as rulers of the city. This vision of the Jewish Jerusalem fails to recognise the connections developed by Christians, Muslims and others to the city in the years following the destruction of the Second Temple.

All three examples of the fourteenth benediction conclude with the blessing of God as 'the builder of Jerusalem', in all cases there is a sense in which the city of Jerusalem remains unredeemed and requires the intervention of God to help the city to realise her full potential. The major contrast is the way in which both the Reform and Liberal liturgies seek to find a way to reconcile the Jewish vision of Jerusalem alongside the bonds felt by other religious groups. Both the Reform and Liberal liturgies utilise the words of Isaiah to present a more pluralist vision of the rebuilt Jerusalem. The city which is being prayed for is one which is still steeped in the words of the *TaNaCh*, but it is also a city which will be open to all her inhabitants, regardless of religious affiliation. The vision of Jerusalem as a city open to all and at peace may, especially in our current context, be viewed as an eschatological vision for the holy city.

The universal eschatological vision of the Reform and Liberal liturgies is not without precedent, as the *aleinu* presents a vision for all humanity coming together before God.

> And all humanity shall speak out in Your name, and all the
> wicked of the earth shall turn to You. Then all who inhabit
> this world shall meet in understanding and shall know that
> to You alone each one shall submit, and pledge themselves
> in every tongue
>
> (MRJ 2008:311)(9)

This prayer includes no mention of God's kingdom being based in Jerusalem or the development of the city into a capital for all peoples. The universal eschatological vision is therefore not new; the Reform and Liberal development is that Jerusalem has been advanced to become a central component of this future universal vision within the *amidah*. The fourteenth benediction of the *amidah* therefore offers an important insight into the way that the streams of Judaism relate to the city, and what they aspire to as their eschatological vision of the end of time.

38

1. The Babylonian tradition generally developed into the accepted Jewish liturgy.
2. For more on the history of the fourteenth benediction and its influences see Kohler 1924:403-5.
3. The Jewish Encyclopedia translates the Hebrew root רחם as compassion.
4. The literal translation is 'You said', although Hoffman chooses: 'You promised'.
5. One example in the *shacharit* service is: 'May it be thy will, O Lord our God and God of our fathers, that the temple be speedily rebuilt in our days' (Singer 1984:56).
6. The text mentions specifically: 'All who keep the Sabbath and do not profane it, And who hold fast to My covenant' (Isaiah 56:6).
7. Karen Armstrong's *A History of Jerusalem* includes within it an account of the city's history and the various conflicts and persecutions which have occurred (see Armstrong 1996).
8. The word *torah* comes from a root meaning teaching, and maintains that meaning, although it has also been developed into a specific noun referring to the Torah (the Five Books of Moses), which God gave to Moses at Sinai.
9. The translation is taken from *Forms of Prayer*, however, the Hebrew text is the same in the 'traditional', Reform and Liberal liturgies.

Bibliography

- Armstrong, Karen (1996) *A History of Jerusalem: One City, Three Faiths*. London: Harper Collins Publishers.
- Elbogen, Ismar (1993) *Jewish Liturgy, A Comprehensive History*. Philadelphia: The Jewish Publication Society.
- Finkelstein, Louis (1925-6) The Development of the Amidah. In *The Jewish Quarterly Review, volume 16* (pp.1-43). Philadelphia: The Jewish Publication Society Press.
- Hammer, Reuven (1994) *Entering Jewish Prayer*. New York: Schocken Books.
- Hoffman, Lawrence A. (Ed.), (1998) *My People's Prayer Book: Volume 2 – The Amidah*. Vermont: Jewish Lights Publishing.
- Kohler, Kaufman and Hirsch, Emil (1904) Compassion. In I. Singer (Ed.) *The Jewish Encyclopedia* (vol. 4, pp. 201-2). New York: Funk and Wagnalls Company.
- Movement for Reform Judaism (MRJ) (2008) *Forms of Prayer*. London: MRJ
- Reform Synagogue of Great Britain (RSGB) (1977). *Forms of Prayer for Jewish Worship: Volume One, Daily, Sabbath and Occasional Prayers*. Oxford: Oxford University Press.
- Singer, S. (1984). *The Authorised Daily Prayer Book of the United Hebrew Congregations of the British Commonwealth of Nations*. London: Eyre and Spottiswoode Limited.
- Union of Liberal and Progressive Synagogues (ULPS) (1995) *Siddur Lev Chadash*. Hertford: Stephen Austin & Sons Ltd.

DOUGLAS CHARING

Douglas Charing is the Founder-Director of the Leeds-based Jewish Education Bureau, and the author of many popular school books on Judaism. He is also the Visiting Rabbi to the Southport Reform Synagogue and the Bradford Synagogue. He also lectures on the New Testament Through Jewish Eyes.

Paul - Apostle to the Gentiles or Apostate to the Jews ?

For centuries, Paul has been considered by most Christians as a former Jew whose conversion to Christianity allowed the new religion to grow and divorce itself from its parent, Judaism. For almost all Jews, and some liberal Christians, Paul became a Jew-hater who could be considered as the real founder of Christianity. Most Jews have come to terms with regard to Jesus, in that he was a loyal Jew until the day of his death. There have been countless books written by Jewish scholars who have depicted Jesus in very positive ways.

Jewish scholars, however, have not shown the same attitude towards Paul. Such books as Claude Montefiore's *Judaism and St. Paul* (1914), Joseph Klausner's *From Jesus to Paul* (1942) and Samuel Sandmel's *The Genius of Paul* (1970) show some affection for Paul, but he is still seen as an apostate who probably had scant knowledge of rabbinic Judaism. In short, the enigmatic apostle is either revered or reviled, whereas Jesus is usually seen as attractive and appealing. Nearly all Jewish writers proudly proclaim the Jewishness of Jesus, but equally deny the Jewishness of Paul. Half the New Testament is about Paul, including seven letters written by him, yet, despite this relative abundance of material, there is no detailed reconstruction of his life. Reliable information about Paul is sketchy and only a tenuous biography is possible.

In his own time, Paul had many critics, including some of the disciples who felt that he was trying to hijack the Jesus movement and even make it gentile. The Ebionites were believers in Jesus the Messiah but rejected any belief in him as a deity. They recounted disparaging stories about Paul and imputed to him unworthy motives. To them, Paul was a villainous Jew

41

with a passion for dominion. In later centuries Jewish writers have mainly negative views on Paul. 'What Paul says about Peter tells us more about Paul than about Peter', argued Spinoza. 'No one misunderstood Judaism more profoundly than Paul', wrote Claude Montefiore. 'Paul transformed Jesus into a 'metaphysical entity'', claimed Samuel Hirsch.

How Jewish was Paul ? He says of himself : 'I progressed in Judaism far beyond many Jewish students of my time, for none was more keenly enthusiastic than I to master the traditional lore of my ancestors' (1). Elsewhere he is reported to have said : 'I lived according to the most precise expression of our common faith - a Pharisee' (2). He also stated that he studied under Gamaliel (3), although Frederick Grant believes that Paul 'shows very few traces of rabbinic influence or training'(4), a view shared by almost all Jewish scholars.

Yet Paul quotes from Scriptures, especially Isaiah (some 65 times) and Psalms (some 42 times). Moreover, some of his so-called Christian theology can also be found in rabbinic literature, as will be seen shortly. Marcus Borg and John Dominic Crossan see Paul (like Jesus) as 'working within Judaism. Neither intended that a new religion would emerge in his wake' (5). When in Galatians, Paul speaks about his 'former life in Judaism' (or in the Jews' religion), the Greek could be better translated as 'earlier life', which makes it sound far less anti-Judaism (6).

We now turn our attention to some key areas of so-called Pauline theology. The first is Paul's attitude to the Torah. In most translations Torah is translated as 'law'. The highly respected liberal Christian scholar of the early 20th century, R. Travers Herford, accuses Paul of perpetuating the mischievous error of translating Torah as law (7). The Greek word used is *nomos*, sometimes 'law' or capitalized as 'Law'. Some scholars argue that when Paul uses the word 'law', he is not always refering to the Torah, but to Roman law, and that Paul held the Torah in the same high esteem as did the Pharisees and other learned Jews. Some of the so-called negative views on Torah and its observance was not directed towards Jewish observance but towards Gentiles following much of the Torah. Paul always treats Jewish sacred texts with great reverence and respect, and frequently sees them as a source of divine authority. He teaches that 'the Jews are entrusted with the oracles of God' (8). It is true that Paul also writes,' the letter kills, but the spirit gives life' (9), but then in a similar vein, the Palestinian Talmud states that 'to act according to the strict letter of the law is not the way of the hasidim' (10). Paul never speaks against Jewish observance of the Torah, but he often speaks strongly against Gentile observance.

The second area centres around Paul's attitude to Jesus. As a follower of Jesus he naturally recognises his messiahship, but as a loyal Jew maintains a clear distinction between Jesus and God, and thus Paul could not have either invented or acknowledged the divinity of Jesus, with regard to the Trinity. Sometimes Paul's Messiah Jesus is almost semi-divine. In this he is in good company with Akiba who was rebuked by Rabbi Jose, the Galilean for "profaning the Divine Presence" 'by teaching that the Messiah occupies a throne alongside of God' (11). The word 'Lord' occurs over two hundred times in Pauline writings. 'Christ', the most common term, is used some two hundred and fifty times. 'Son of God', found in Pauline epistles is used just fifteen times. Unique to Paul's writings is the term 'Christ Jesus'. Again, none of these terms reflect divinity, although later Christianity did regard them in this way.

The third area is vital to traditional Christian theology, although more connected to the Protestant than the Roman Catholic tradition. Since Martin Luther, Judaism has been described as salvation through works (i.e. the Torah), whilst superior Christianity is a system of salvation through faith. This has stood at the core of Protestant Christianity for centuries.

Did Paul actually teach justification through faith in Jesus? Again, it is all in the translation. The Greek, *pistis iesou*, has always been translated as 'faith in Jesus', yet it is grammatically awkward to do so. Many modern scholars now prefer to translate 'faith of Jesus', so justification through faith in Jesus should probably be read and understood as justification through the faithfulness of Jesus. Marcus Borg and John Dominic Crossan advise getting

> Paul and his letter to the Romans out of the sixteenth century polemical Reformation world and back into the first-century imperial Roman world. It is incorrect and begets misunderstanding to read Paul for what he was not : a Lutheran Protestant criticizing Roman Catholicism or, worse still, a Christian criticizing Judaism. It is correct and avoids misunderstanding to read him for what he was : a Christian Jew within covenantal Judaism criticizing Roman imperialism (12).

There is one disturbing passage in Paul's writings, namely First Thessalonians. He makes a vicious censure of the Jews by accusing them of killing both Jesus and the prophets (13).

Assuming this passage to be authentic, scholars are generally agreed

43

that Paul does not intend to slander the entire Jewish community, since he often makes clear that he considers himself and the other apostles fully Jewish. This charge against the Jews has reverberated down throughout history in the most terrifying and often unexamined manner. Even the Q'uran in many suras picks it up mindlessly and repeatedly, as in, for example, 2:61, 3:21, 4:155.

'With all Paul's faults, with all the injuries his Christology has wrought, we have more reason to be grateful to him than we have cause for censure. As Jews, we are indebted to him for spreading the ethics of Judaism among a Gentile world...for showing us how, by the removal of obsolete, meaningless and repellant ceremonies, rites, and observances, Judaism, pure and simple, might be made a world-conquering religion', wrote American Reform Rabbi Joseph Krauskopf. In a similar vein, Isaac Meyer Wise, the founder of American Reform Judaism added : 'All Jews of all ages hoped and expected that the kingdom of heaven would encompass all nations and tongues; but Paul undertook to realize this hope, this is his title to greatness'. So Paul was not the first Christian, neither was he the founder of Christianity, but he should be fondly remembered as a loyal Jew who spread Christianity. It probably was not his intention for his Judaism for the Gentiles to become a separate and independent body. He would probably have also been surprised that his letters were collected together and given a place in the Greek Christian Scriptures. It would be wrong to see him as a Jew who abandoned the faith of his fathers. So, as Jews, we should see Paul not as an apostate, but as a loyal Jew whose vision earned him the title of apostle to the Gentiles.

(1) Gal. 1:14
(2) Acts 26:5
(3) Acts 22:3
(4) Frederick C Grant : *Ancient Judaism and The New Testament* Oliver and Boyd,1959
(5) *The First Paul* SPCK,2009
(6) Gal.1:13
(7) *The Pharisees* Allen and Unwin,1924
(8) Rom. 3:2
(9) 2 Corr. 3:6
(10) Terumot, 8:4
(11) Hagigah, 14a.
(12) *The First Paul*
(13) 1 Thess. 2:14-16

HOWARD COOPER

Howard Cooper is a rabbinic graduate of the Leo Baeck College, a psychoanalytic psychotherapist in private practice and an author. He is Director of Spiritual Development at Finchley Reform Synagogue and blogs on rabbinic and other themes at www.howardcoopersblog.blogspot.com

"It Has Never Ceased..."

A Midrashic Reflection on the Shofar in the Light of Martin Buber's Reading of *v'lo yasaf* in Deuteronomy 5:19 (1)

> For a liberal Jew like myself, the revelatory experience of Sinai described in the Bible is both real and powerful...the documents which describe, transmit and flow from the event [are]... reality tamed as myth; encounter transmitted through human beings and human agency.
> (Tony Bayfield, Sinai, Law & Responsible Autonomy, RSGB, 1993)

No-one knew what was happening. The old man had gone, up the mountain, up into the clouds. Someone said it would make no difference, he'd always had his head in the clouds. We were a sceptical people, even then. And time has not mellowed us. Neither time nor history. If anything we have become even more stiff-necked, because of our history and over time, more cynical about leaders who think they have the answers, think they have a hotline to holiness, a route-map to the promised land.

Nowadays, don't we always know better, we chosen people? We know how to cover the angles, we know which way is up, nobody can outwit us, nothing can surprise us, we've seen it all before. Who needs the Law laid down from on high when, with our *yiddishe* kop, we know so much already?

45

But on *this* day (2), no-one knew what was happening. He'd disappeared, up into the mountain, to meet old El himself, or newer gods, or trim his beard and think his lofty thoughts, or - who knows? – just to get away from us unruly rabble. Six hundred thousand of us, they said – but, *nu*, who's counting? We're storytellers, no? Mythographers, with license to tell it as we want, embroider here and there, true to the imagination - not like those number-crunching Levite accountants, pestering the old man with their worries about a desert journey without relief or benefits that anyone could see. About one thing though, we were sure: nothing good would come of this. The sun smote us by day, the moon chilled us by night, and death sung lullabies of Egypt in our ear.

The rumours began as soon as he'd gone, flashing through the camp like lightning, yet illuminating nothing except our fears: his heart was weak and he'd gone off like a wounded goat to die...he wanted to enslave us yet again, to a different god... he'd left in a huff after quarrelling with his brother...he'd been killed by the riffraff who'd joined our great escape...we had stories aplenty, but as usual we knew nothing.

The boldest amongst us predicted something else - 'a moment of destiny', the scribes insisted, 'when the future will be revealed'. That was too glib for me, too pious: how could a nation's fate be transformed through words alone, words narrated from on high by some unseen author(ity) dictating how things have to be? And we must live the story to the end of days? What *chutzpah* we possess to tell the tale that way, that we alone were called *bayom ha-ze*, and claimed for ever more. But so it turned out - though at the time we only glimpsed the script in shadow, as if through a glass, darkly.

Though what remains in the mind's eye is, above all, the weather. We'd left in a hurry, remember, in the springtime - overcoats discarded and umbrellas not yet invented - and here we were, six weeks out of Egypt, in the desert, high summer, and there was thunder and lightning and torrents of rain as if Shaddai himself was storming the heavens and then from out of nowhere a whirling and rumbling in our ears like the grinding of a titanic battle and on the third day trembling storms of dust, clouds of dust and sand, thick clouds of sand and smoke, in your eyes so they could not see, in your mouth so you dared not speak, in your ears so you couldn't hear yourself think, dust ascending as in a flaming furnace, the earth shuddering beneath our feet, our world afire, tumult in our hearts, and from all around a sound, reverberating, a sound pounding us, bonding us, a sound finding us, founding us...

But wait, we are not ready for that...

46

We who were left at the foot of the mountain - a great multitude of disparate souls yet bound together as if one family - for us, heaven assaulting our senses, there was a single desire, overwhelming, monomaniacal, all-consuming: survival. How to protect ourselves from the quaking storm of the flaming furnace of unendurable heat? How to resist the looming mountain - seemingly alive and inescapable - held over our heads as if to crush us with its awesome gravity? How to endure the unendurable? The people waited, cowering, submissive, while the unbearable went on unbearably - as it does – the people waiting for something else to happen: waiting for death, or revelation, or someone to appear from offstage and - *deus ex machina*, as it were – restore some hope to our bewildered hearts.

Where was Moses? When would he return? Would he, indeed, ever return? It was then that we realised how much we needed him. We were lost without him. Lost in the desert of course - some said we were at Sinai, others said Horeb, while a few refused to give the place a name at all, for we could have been anywhere – but also lost in another, graver sense. We were lost psychologically - a word we did not even know then, but have grown familiar with since, during the long journey away from there to distant lands and cooler climes.

On that day we needed our leader more than we'd ever realised. But if we're honest, we can see how we've always needed a leader to follow, to obey, to tell us what to do, to take away the unbearable responsibility of personal decision. In this, we chosen people are no different from the rest. Moses or Mao, Vladimir Ilyich or Golda or Adolf, in our hearts we crave a leader, strong and with vision, man or woman, someone who will protect us and inspire us, give us a sense of purpose and belonging. In all of us there is still the child, vulnerable, defenceless, who looks outside for help, for salvation, for security and answers. We were well-named in our saga - 'the *children* of Israel'. That's us, still emotional orphans, still looking outside ourselves for someone to tell us how to live. But on that day he had gone - up the mountain, into the clouds.

It may be hard now, looking back, to appreciate what his shepherding had meant to us. You see, we owed him everything: firstly, naturally, our freedom; but more than that he was teaching us stuff, revealing new laws for new times, our very thoughts transformed at his bidding. Everything was *his* doing, *his* inspiration, *his* creation. Remember that he had come back to us, out of exile, and broken our bondage to the status quo by challenging the all-controlling god-like rulers of our land - in the name of freedom, and justice. The excitement of those days is impossible to convey. So long oppressed and now participating in what, even as it was happening, we knew was one of the great events in recorded time: the rise of a downtrodden people, a total break with a dishonourable past, and the promise - oh, so seductive - the promise of a new and enlightened society where a daily life of decency, compassion and comradeship would at last prevail. What a vision he had! Sheer inspiration. True, he could be frightening to behold – but he taught us how to live with one another in ways unenslaved by the past. No wonder some call him *Rabbenu*. We will never see his like again.

And the miracle of it is how, in different lands, in different ages, our story recurs: the myth humanity craves is re-created, the impulse towards justice and freedom keeps being renewed, as if it were an eternal spirit always alive within the human soul, a divine spark waiting to flare into being. The contemporaneity of the past: the vision of a society based on cooperation rather than competition.

But on *this* day, the first time, there was only the huddled masses, and the storm around us, and the fear of the storm to come, when all we had gained would be lost, when all we had dreamt would turn to nightmare, when all that had been promised would turn to dust in our mouths...

And then we heard it. Each man, each woman, each child, alone, heard that sound. 600,000 and more, together, we heard that sound that pierced us and stilled us and silenced the storm around us and the quaking within us.

We had never heard that sound before - and yet we knew it, as you know it still, as if its echo began as we drew breathe in the world, as if its echo came forth as the world itself came into being. It was a call, a summons - primeval, insistent, yearning - a cry from deep within time, hidden in our memories, there from the very beginning, before the beginning, waiting to be heard, a sound primitive and immediate, breaking through our shabby defences like the tide sweeping away a child's proud castle of sand, wave after wave, stripping us bare, hollowing us out, hallowing us into peoplehood.

The sound of the shofar - though we only learnt its name later on, when we tamed its call and used it to proclaim our new moons and holy days, or rally the troops, to go into war, to shake our enemies to the foundations. A sound like no other sound. An unearthly sound. A terrible, forlorn sound, wrenching the heart out of us, wrenching the heart back into us, it went on and on, reverberating inside our skulls, beating against our eyes, forcing them to open, to open and see that this moment was destined to go on for as long as time endures, so that in every place this sound was heard, in every community the shofar sounded, it was but an echo, a memory, of that first time, at Sinai -

or wherever - when God spoke in a 'voice', in a sound, in the shofar revelation of the word, the voice of the sound of the silence within the soundlessness of being, the sound of eternity silently vocalising the Eternal One - 'I AM, Eternal, divine...' - God's still small voice whispering ceaselessly within each human being: hear, return, remember, pay attention - this is the purpose of your life, your origin, your destiny. This is your Torah. I plant it within you.

Words strain, crack, and sometimes break, under the burden, under the tension - birds cease to sing, oxen no longer bellow, the sea is calmed, no angels' wings disturb the ether, the world slips, slides into silence, not even the sound of holy hymning on high is heard, words perish, decay with imprecision, will not stay in place, will not stay still.

But the shofar reaches back, underneath words, defying language - and moves us on, on to the end of time: for on that day, the day of judgment, the great shofar will sound, as it is written, for at the end of days the Messiah will be announced with the shofar. I will call to you, I was there at the beginning and I will be there at the end, *alpha* and *omega*, *aleph* and *tav*. I AM what I AM.

When you hear the shofar and you and the shofar are one, when you perceive the voice of the shofar, holding your breathe while the note lasts, you are hearing the end of time, which is also the beginning of time, for the end and the beginning are One, *echad*. And all is always now. There is no before and no after (3).

The shofar's call is the most ancient sound that humanity still hears. It elides time. It comes to shake our certainties, to unsettle our complacency, our too-comfortable understandings, our easy answers, our lazy presumptions. Farewell to surefootedness.

That first time when we heard it we realised that the legend was true. We'd thought the whole thing a myth, a folk-tale to soothe the pain of our exile. But now, as the shofar-voice thundered within us, we recalled the story we had heard so many times, that our father Abraham had refused to sacrifice his son, his future, our future, on the altar of ideology, on the altar of what he thought his God had told him. Our father Abraham had seen that ram caught by its horns in the thicket: at that very place - oh, divine coincidence - where his future was bound; and had thus ensured our survival by substituting the animal for his son. Continuity through adaptation. And preserving the future by shifting from literalism to symbol. A holy moment, that paradigm shift in human thinking.

And legend had it that, lest no-one believe his story, Abraham had retrieved the ram's horn from the ashes of the sacrifice and had bequeathed it to his son, and thus to the generations to come - a grotesque family souvenir but preserving the memory of the day when faith won out over death. Yet whether it was faith in God or faith in himself, he never really resolved. And thus was bequeathed to us the question of whom to trust: the testing, commanding voice of 'God' - or the divine voice within. The horns of our dilemma.

And the horn itself, scorched and scarred, was passed down by Isaac to Jacob, who took it to Egypt and left it with Joseph, where it gathered dust and seemed to disappear within the bitterness of slavery, until this day when the mountain hovered over our frantic heads, threatening us with the extinction from which our forebear had been saved, as if a grim cycle was nearing completion...and then we heard it sound, this resounding horn of hope and history, penetrating our hearts with new life. For then we knew - we just knew - that we would never be sacrificed again. Total annihilation? Impossible.

We would survive, scarred by the memory of our encounter with the divine, carrying its message of liberation and hope into a world scared to receive it, scared because the voice seemed to promise so much, how could it ever be fulfilled? We have carried this sacred message of hope like a yoke around our necks – burdened by a revelation in which we also rejoice. It weighs us down, we try to shake ourselves free, but we are bound for life, bound to live in its shadow. Bondsmen yet again.

We received a vision in those days, incarnated in a text, the like of which has never been seen since. It was a challenge to perfection, of a sort, a utopian dream of a society ordered under the rule of God, where human beings would overcome their egotism and vanity, their greed, their pettiness, their inability to see beyond the next milestone, and would create communities bounded in trust. And the crown of this vision was the Jubilee year, the climax of a fifty year cycle, a time when the land itself would rest, when property sold would revert to its original owners, and when those who were enslaved would receive their liberty.

The Torah - God's dream for us, and the embodiment of our dream of God - puts it with simplicity, with directness: 'Sound the shofar...and proclaim freedom on earth for all its inhabitants' (4). This idealism has never been surpassed - and never realised. The shofar would announce the beginning of this extraordinary experiment in human community: the earth is God's property which has been made available for all of us; it is not to be exploited for the enrichment of some to the detriment of others. And as servants of God we should not remain enslaved to any other human being or social system. The necessity for the periodic redistribution of wealth and the essential equality and dignity of each human being: this was our vision, revealed when the shofar calls.

The memory of God's ultimatum causes us no rest. The unattainable vision of that shofar-sound has reverberated through the prophetic books, and echoes inside Western consciousness until this very day. That corrosive pressure to surpass ourselves, to ensure that the prophetic passion for justice and the absence of oppression is not only an ideal but is transformed into action here and now - where else have we heard this shofar call to revolutionary change? Do we not hear it in the messianic dreaming of Marx, of Trotsky, of Ernst Bloch and Rosa Luxemburg, that clarion call for human beings to transcend their limitations, their common, instinctual behaviour, to end their mutual exploitation and create society anew?

Some calculate at 80% the proportion of Jews in the ideological development of messianic socialism and communism. For this vision generations have died. In its name falsehood and oppression spread over a good portion of the earth. But the dream remains magnetic. The shofar-dream still summons us to renounce selfishness, worldly excess and unbridled individualism, and subsume our personal being into that larger vision of community.

It is said that at Sinai, God's voice split into seventy voices and seventy languages, so that all the nations should hear and understand: a universal message. And it spoke to each of us who was there - and were we not all there? - in our own private language, intimate and knowing, searching us through and through, claiming us for itself, inscribing within us an indelible, searing hopefulness about what we might become. A terrible and blessed burden, that memory, that hope.

1. Martin Buber, *Ten Rungs: Hasidic Sayings*, (Schocken Books, New York, 1962/1970), p.60
2. Exodus 19:1
3. Cf. Pesachim 6b : *eyn mukdam u-me'uhar ba-Torah*
4. Leviticus 25: 9f

PAUL FREEDMAN

Paul Freedman is Principal Rabbi of Radlett & Bushey Reform Synagogue. He has a particular interest in liturgy, focusing on a theological *piyyut* for his rabbinic thesis, and served on the Editorial Board of the current Reform *siddur*. He is married to Vanessa and father of Joshua and Katie.

Reforms of Prayer:
Evolution of British Reform Liturgy

Seder Ha-T'fillot or 'Forms of Prayer' (2008) is in fact the eighth edition of this volume, the first having been published in 1841 as the prayerbook of the West London Synagogue, as were the four subsequent editions. The sixth edition, however, states on its frontispiece that it was "edited for the use of their own and allied congregations by the ministers of the West London Synagogue of British Jews". The seventh edition of the prayerbook was described in its preface by Rabbi Hugo Gryn as "no longer that of the West London Synagogue but...to serve the Reform Synagogues of Great Britain, happily a growing movement of like-minded congregations."

This study focuses on the development of 'Forms of Prayer' from one edition to the next. This is not to pretend that each edition is unaffected by other prayerbooks but we should recognise the considerable extent to which it is influenced by its predecessor. Even if almost fifty years pass between the publication of one edition and the next, still only a week separates the two Sabbaths on which subsequent editions are used in a congregation. As loud as the voices calling for prayerbook reform, are those resisting change and expressing contentment with the existing liturgy. The emphasis is less on the detail of individual prayers but on the overall content, style and structure of the 'Daily, Sabbath and Occasional' volume.

Published within a year of the establishment of the West London Synagogue of British Jews, the main purpose was the "abridgement and deletion of the prayers that aroused the most opposition."[1] Its full contents were: weekday services, *birkat ha-mazon*, night prayers, *erev shabbat* service and *kiddush*, *shabbat* morning and afternoon services, an evening service for after *shabbat*, *rosh chodesh* services including *musaf*, *chanukkah* and *purim* services, prayers for journeys, for surviving danger, for childbirth and for the sick, a death-bed confession, a special *birkat ha-mazon* for mourners, and the counting of the *omer*. According to Petuchowski, in producing a new prayerbook, "the editors not only sought to reduce the sheer bulk of the accumulated liturgical material of the Tradition, and to unify the Ashkenazi and the Sephardi rites. They also had a theological axe to grind." He suggests that British Reform Judaism at that time exhibited "very little of the radicalism which characterized its German and American counterparts. But it was decidedly opposed to Rabbinic Judaism."[2]

The aims were to make prayer intelligible and to remove those prayers which do not express sentiments of "a pure and elevating character," or that are "deficient in devotional tendency." The service was shortened further since the editors also held that a "service should be confined within such a period of time as to afford ground for the expectation that, from the beginning to the end, it may be able to command the constant, unwearied, and devout attention of the congregation."

One of the ways in which the service is shortened is that some of the psalms of *psukei d'zimra* are assigned for reading on a specific day of the week or *shabbat* in the month. This also introduces variety into services and avoids completely excising some of the psalms from the liturgy. When compared to other liturgies (progressive or not) there are a number of features worthy of note. The rubrics in the *kedushah* indicate that it was read aloud (antiphonally by the 'minister' and the 'congregation'). There is no rubric to suggest that the *amidah* was read individually and in silence before this communal reading. Any reference to angels, even indirect, has been removed. Unusually, the *kedushah* is also included in the *amidah* of the weekday evening service.

The tenth paragraph of the weekday *amidah* is a petition for the ingathering of the exiles. Of this paragraph Petuchowski[3] writes that "no Reform prayerbook [in 1972] includes petitions for the liquidation of the Diaspora and the assembling of all Jews of the world in Palestine", except for two that he cites. Nevertheless, the first edition of Forms of Prayer retains a traditional (Sephardi) text: "Gather us speedily together from the four corners of the earth unto our own land."

The twelfth paragraph of the weekday *amidah* is the 'benediction against sectarians'. Historically, "no benediction has undergone as many textual variations as this one."[4] In the first edition it is simply absent.

The *shabbat musaf* has been reduced to an (unrepeated) abbreviated *amidah*. Occupying just over a page, the layout and page headers suggest that it is considered part of the *shabbat* morning service. Despite being shortened, it still retains its references to temple sacrifices, asking that God "conduct us with joy to our own land, and plant us in our own territories; that we may there, in thy presence, perform the offerings incumbent upon us."

The *aleinu* is both shortened and amended. The negative comparison with other peoples has become the positive (though still particularist) "who has chosen us from amongst all people, and hath given us his Law." The counterbalancing universalist second paragraph, (*al kein*) as an Ashkenazi tradition, is absent. Finally, as part of a quasi-Karaitic tendency to "shun Rabbinic formulations"[5], it is interesting to note that the *kaddish* appears only in Hebrew, never in Aramaic.

The order of the second edition, published fifteen years later is broadly similar to the first. New sections are introduced for circumcision, naming a girl, and a prayer to be said by the minister on the *shabbat* after a funeral. The rubrics describing how the *kedushah* is read have gone, though the text itself is unchanged. It now also appears in the *erev shabbat amidah*.

The third edition appeared in 1870 and differs very little from the second apart from introducing a 'table of references to some of the special services' and clearer rubrics throughout. *Shabbat musaf* is explicitly titled and listed in the table of contents, though its text is otherwise unchanged. The fourth edition was published just twelve years later in 1882 and, though the table of references has been moved to the back of the volume, is little more than a reprint of the third.

Sixteen years after the fourth edition, the fifth edition was published. There are a few small but apparently ideological changes in this edition and these have been implemented so that the page numbering still mostly corresponds to that in the fourth edition. A small change in the rubric at the beginning of the *shabbat* morning service has the effect of considerably shortening the *birchot ha-shachar* section. More significantly, a prayer that had appeared in place of the *korbanot* study section of *birchot ha-shachar* and at the start of the *minchah* services in all four earlier editions, has been removed. The *musaf* service is retained, but the paragraph specifically referring to the ingathering of the exiles for the purpose of reinstituting sacrifices is omitted. A new element in this edition is a service for the day of 'confirmation'.

The first five editions of Forms of Prayer had been published at fairly regular intervals and, radical as the first edition had been, each following edition remained under the influence of its first editor, Reverend David

Marks. The sixth edition, however, was published in 1931 after a gap of thirty-three years and some two decades after Marks' death. This edition was noticeably different in both structure and content. The editors intended the prayerbook for "our own and allied congregations," presumably recognising the wider use of the fifth edition that it replaced. They sought "to meet the needs of the present age, by modifying and omitting where this has been deemed advisable, by reintroducing some ancient prayers, and by adding others entirely new."

The sixth edition, unusually, starts with the *shabbat* services, presumably reflecting the main use of the prayerbook in synagogue. Unlike the fifth edition, it also includes a marriage service, funeral service, memorial service, consecration of a tombstone, prayer for visiting a grave and a 'service upon admission to the Jewish faith'. There is also a sizeable section of prayers for use in the home, including one for the dedication of a new home. More than half of the volume forms a psalm anthology. The volume ends with 'a closing prayer' which is, in fact, the second paragraph of the *aleinu* that had not appeared in any previous edition.

The *shabbat* services are the only services that appear in full. All other services rely on navigating the book as outlined in the extensive 'table of reference'. The services offer variety through use of the psalm anthology but also a choice of six new prayers in the *shabbat* morning service and six more 'prayers for silent devotion'.

The *kedushah* continues to appear in evening as well as morning services. In the 'prayer for use in the daily service' (in fact the *emtzayyot* of the *amidah*) seven of the traditional thirteen blessings are absent. *Musaf* has been entirely removed from the prayerbook as has the established substituted phrase in the *aleinu*, "who has chosen us from amongst all people, and hath given us his Law." The second paragraph of *aleinu* is included as a closing prayer at the end of the prayerbook and *kaddish* still appears only in Hebrew.

Although the next edition did not appear for another forty-six years, a supplement to the sixth edition was produced in 1952. It is noteworthy for a number of reasons. It was edited by the ministers of the Association of Synagogues in Great Britain and although it contains only evening services it appears to reflect changes in common liturgical practice that had emerged over the preceding twenty years.

The supplement also contains a 'close of Sabbath' service that now includes *havdalah*, a memorial service and a short psalm anthology. The *amidah* is the same as that for weekday evenings in the sixth edition, except that the *kedushah* has gone again. The text of the first paragraph of *aleinu* is as in the sixth edition but is now immediately followed by the second paragraph. In a break with over a century of British Reform tradition, the Aramaic text of *kaddish* is included as an option after the Hebrew. The preface to the 1965 edition of the festival *machzor* acknowledges that "the Aramaic version of the Kaddish [is] now in use in almost all our Synagogues."

The seventh edition is more different from its predecessors than any other edition before it. From its inception, it took eleven years, "an inordinately long time,"[6] to produce, the main reason being that it was "produced by a committee." This committee of rabbis was chaired by Rabbi Hugo Gryn. According to the editors, Rabbis Lionel Blue and Jonathan Magonet, "the difference between the last edition of the Forms of Prayer in 1930 and the present one is a measure of the tragedies and triumphs of the years between."

The volume starts with a selection of preparatory readings and then *shabbat* services for evening, morning and afternoon, as well as a comprehensive selection from *Pirkei Avot*. The daily services follow, as well as new services for Holocaust Memorial and Israel Independence Day. Other innovations are a few pages of blessings for various occasions, a *bar-mitzvah* and *bat-mitzvah* prayer, prayers for an anniversary, before an operation, during dangerous illness, on behalf of the dangerously ill, for committee meetings, interfaith meetings, and a *yahrzeit*.

Recognising that "until recently piety flowed from the home to the synagogue" but that "today the reverse is often true," the editors included a sizeable section of home services, including a 'Sabbath Eve Home Service' and fuller 'Thanksgiving after Meals' as well as prayers for children. Furthermore, a selection of *z'mirot* is included as part of the Friday night service. As well as a revised Psalm anthology, there is a short song anthology and an impressive study anthology of readings where "you can find extracts from the Talmud of course, but you will find, for example, Kafka rubbing shoulders with a Hassidic Rabbi, and excerpts from Anne Frank's diary side by side with passages from the *Shulchan Aruch*."[7] The volume ends with a glossary and then a short section of notes on use of the prayerbook.

As did its predecessors, the seventh edition offers alternatives in the *shabbat* services, however this concept is extended to six themed introductory sections of the *shabbat* morning service that come together at the *amidah*. The *kedushah* still appears (as an option) in the *erev shabbat amidah*. Two longer forms of the *kedushah* now appear in various morning and afternoon *amidot* and these contain previously-excised indirect references to angels.

The daily *amidah* has a full nineteen blessings, though a number have been reformed in the Hebrew as well as in translation. The tenth paragraph, traditionally 'ingathering of the exiles', has become a broader petition for redemption, though the paragraph cleverly opens with the traditional wording. In the twelfth paragraph, the traditional prayer against 'slanderers' has become one against 'slander'.

Musaf, removed for the first time in the previous edition, remains absent. *Aleinu* appears with its second paragraph as in the supplement to the sixth edition, however the wording of the first paragraph has Marks' substitution restored as in the first five editions, but now translated "who has chosen us from all peoples by giving us His Torah." In the main services, the *kaddish* is now only in Aramaic. The Hebrew *kaddish* is printed later in the prayerbook, as is the *kaddish d'rabbanan* in Aramaic. The seventh edition also differs from all of its predecessors in its use of modern idiom. "People felt very strongly about the 'Thee' and 'Thou' question,"[8] but in the end it was felt that using modern idiom came "much closer to the Hebrew intention and the immediacy and intimacy of the Hebrew language."

In general, the seventh edition was (perhaps with the exception of the first edition) the most radical, yet at the same time "it is one of the most traditional Prayer Books that the Reform movement has ever produced."[9] It includes new material but reintroduces traditional structures and prayers that had previously been removed.

Similarly, the eighth edition is now also considered to be at the same time more radical and more traditional than all its predecessors. It contains a plethora of new material, as well as gender inclusive language (in common with the 1995 festival *machzor*) and transliteration. In a return to the order of the fifth edition, the daily services precede those for *shabbat*. Yet more of the traditional liturgy (particularly Ashkenazi) is included and selections within this fuller framework are left to the individual (congregation). *Musaf*, with a new subversive central paragraph, is restored in both an abbreviated and longer form. Sadly, the historical curiosity of Hebrew *kaddish* did not survive. All in all, however, the latest edition has more in common with its immediate predecessor than with the six editions before.

Over the last century and a half, the liturgy of the British Reform movement has evolved sometimes slowly and sometimes more noticeably. References to the ingathering of the exiles, reinstitution of sacrifices, angels, resurrection of the dead, and certain particularistic formulations have, either by removing, changing or just interpretatively translating the Hebrew, increasingly been avoided. An early trend towards making those reforms that had not been made in the first edition (for example, removing 'offensive' paragraphs of the *amidah*) is balanced by a later return to 'traditional' forms. By the seventh edition, the daily *amidah* again had nineteen blessings and the Aramaic *kaddish* was given primacy.

The editor of the first edition tended towards shortening the service rather than adapting the liturgy on ideological or theological grounds. As the content of Forms of Prayer has been increasingly reformed according to modern sensibilities, at the same time the services have also grown longer. Generally, the opportunity for variety in services has increased, partly for its own sake, but also as a way of including more of the traditional liturgy (and some new material) in the *siddur*.

Prayerbooks are not written in isolation. Whatever other influences there may be, of the age in which the prayerbook is produced, it is evident that each edition draws heavily on the one that precedes it. Only the editor of the first edition had any real freedom from this legacy. In producing a subsequent edition, there is an inevitable tension between preserving the current liturgy and changing it, or even reflecting changes in practice that have already occurred. Where changes are made, these might be innovations to meet the spiritual needs of today's (and indeed tomorrow's) generation or the reintroduction of traditional prayers to provide some continuity with an earlier (Ashkenazi, Sephardi or original Reform) heritage. As congregations become accustomed to the 'new' edition and the differences from its predecessor, it is clear that this eighth edition will, in years to come, have a considerable influence on the ninth.

[1] I. Elbogen, *Jewish Liturgy – A Comprehensive History*, JPS (1993), p.320

[2] J. Petuchowski, *New Trends in the Liturgy of British Reform Judaism* in *Judaism*, 15 (Fall 1966), p.492

[3] Supplementary material written by J. Petuchowski for the Hebrew edition of Elbogen's *Der jüdische Gottesdienst in seiner gesichtlichen Entwicklung* in I. Elbogen, *Jewish Liturgy – A Comprehensive History*, p.332

[4] I. Elbogen, p.45

[5] J. Petuchowski, *New Trends in the Liturgy of British Reform Judaism*, p.492
[6] H. Gryn in J.Rose, *The Birth of a Book*, in *Living Judaism*, (Summer 1976), p.8
[7] L. Blue in J.Rose, *The Birth of a Book*, p.4
[8] H. Gryn in J.Rose, *The Birth of a Book*, p.7
[9] L. Blue in J.Rose, *The Birth of a Book*, p.4

Forms of Prayer

Marks, D.W. (Ed.), *Forms of Prayer – I Daily and Sabbath Prayers*, J.Wertheimer & Co. (1841)
Marks, D.W. & Löwy, A. (Eds.), *Forms of Prayer – I Daily and Sabbath Prayers*, 2nd Edition, Wertheimer and Co. (1856)
Ministers of the West London Synagogue (Eds.), *Forms of Prayer – I Daily and Sabbath Prayers*, 3rd Edition, Wertheimer, Lea and Co. (1870)
Marks, D.W. & Löwy, A. (Eds.), *Forms of Prayer – I Daily and Sabbath Prayers*, 4th Edition, Wertheimer, Lea and Co. (1882)
Ministers of the West London Synagogue (Eds.), *Forms of Prayer – I Daily and Sabbath Prayers*, 5th Edition, Wertheimer, Lea and Co. (1898)
Ministers of the West London Synagogue (Eds.), *Forms of Prayer – I Daily, Sabbath and Occasional Prayers*, 6th Edition, OUP (1931)
ASGB, *Forms of Prayer for Jewish Worship – Evening Prayers*, 1st supplement to volume 1, OUP (1952)
RSGB, *Order of Service – II Prayers for the Pilgrim Festivals*, Polak & van Gennep (1965)
RSGB, *Forms of Prayer for Jewish Worship – I Daily, Sabbath and Occasional Prayers*, 7th Edition, OUP (1977)
RSGB, *Forms of Prayer for Jewish Worship – II Prayers for the Pilgrim Festivals*, Cambridge University Press (1995)
MRJ, *Seder Ha-t'fillot – Forms of Prayer – I Daily Sabbath and Occasional Prayers*, Jongbloed (2008)

HELEN FREEMAN

Helen Freeman trained originally as a speech therapist. She then went on to qualify as a rabbi, being ordained by the Leo Baeck College in 1990. She is currently at the West London Synagogue, working particularly in pastoral care and its development. She has also qualified as a Jungian analyst.

A Jewish Response to Serious Illness

Towards the end of 2003 my twin sister phoned me from Australia. "It seems we have a genetic condition, you need to go to the doctor', she said. After searching the internet, because we are blessed with something very rare, I went to my GP, who sent me to a consultant at Guys Hospital, who eventually diagnosed me with ductal carcinoma in situ.

Suddenly, instead of visiting people in hospital, rushing around between different wards, I was the patient, feeling vulnerable and scared, having to make big decisions about the best treatment. But, even with the news that the best possible treatment for the underlying condition was a double mastectomy and reconstruction, I had to consider the options. The Talmud says: 'the world continues in its accustomed fashion'(1). I continued working in my congregation, all the while taking time to have genetic counselling and meet the surgeons who would carry out the procedure.

As the new year began, I gave a sermon about my favourite rabbi Nahum Ish Gamzu. He gained this odd name because when challenges and distressing situations hit him , he would always say: *gam zu l'tovah* – 'this too is for the good'. (2) Oddly, in common with other people with serious conditions, I felt that the diagnosis was a blessing in disguise, a call to take my health more seriously, to try and eat a healthier diet, to appreciate a walk in the woods with my dog, a chance to appreciate the beauty of God's creation. The Talmud says that 'Three things restore a person's good spirits, beautiful sounds, sights and smells'(3). When one is contemplating a serious operation followed by many weeks of convalescence, the natural world is extremely healing and allows one to come to terms with the diagnosis. Together with my husband, who was in synagogue for Shabbat services the day of my operation, we made the decision that I would like to be on the healing prayer list, a public acknowledgement of the seriousness of the surgery, but also a very reassuring feeling that we were surrounded by the prayers of the community at a very difficult time. One of the sources of the healing prayer used in our synagogues, praised for its brevity, is the prayer of Moses on behalf of his sister Miriam. She has been turned white with the skin disease *tza'ra'at* as a punishment for initiating gossip about Moses marrying a Cushite woman. Moses, full of concern for his sister, who saved him as a child by her intervention with the Egyptian princess says *el na, r'fa na la* – 'oh God please heal her.'(4). This five word prayer is seen as an ideal form of prayer, heartfelt and not overlong, it just expresses the supplicant's need for God's help.

More than that, the whole incident can be seen as an example of God's sense of humour. Miriam and Aaron had been gossiping about Moses marrying a Cushite woman. Though the midrash find a way to say that this is a reference to his wife Zipporah because Cushite (Ethiopian) is the same as *y'fat mar'eh* – 'good looking' in the system known as Gematria (5), it is more likely that the gossip was due to the fact that she was black, and God, as it were, gave Miriam a visual lesson that if being white was so superior, she was going to be whiter than white because of the skin disease *tza'ra'at*. This example of humour in the Torah always makes me smile, though finding humour in illness is sometimes a struggle, and sometimes it is a rather black sense of humour.

After my own operation, I was given a morphine pump to use when I was in pain, and it was so effective that I really never suffered, and sailed through it, or so I thought. When I breezily said I was doing SO well that it was fine to go onto lesser medication, I had a salutary shock and had to smile at my own lack of experience of being a patient and my hastiness in assuming that I was doing better than I really was.

When I first went down to the hospital cafeteria, I realised for the first time the vulnerability of being a patient, the fear of being knocked into by someone who was in a rush, as I always had been when I was visiting. In Jewish tradition, the commandment of *bikkur cholim* – 'the visiting of the sick' is taken extremely seriously. Most synagogues have a group of volunteers who will visit other members of the congregation or shop for them when they are sick. The Talmud says: Rabbi Acha bar Chanina said: 'Whoever visits a sick person takes away one sixtieth part of his suffering.'(6) But it is important to know how that visit should take place, how to be sensitive to the sick person, not to visit too soon, not to stay too long, not to overwhelm someone who is not long out of surgery.

For our own congregation, we have a wonderful group of volunteers for whom I had done a study session on *bikkur cholim* many years before I knew quite how personally relevant it would be for me. For this I used the 16th century code of Jewish law, the Shulchan Aruch. There it goes into great and practical detail about how exactly one should approach a person trying to recover from serious illness. The very first law says that 'it is a *mitzvah* – a commanded action to visit the sick, families and friends straight away and those more distant after three days, but if the sick put pressure on them they too can go straight away' (7).

Having had personal experience of a family member who was tired to the point of exhaustion by a well meaning friend who visited her and sat for a long time eating her grapes and chatting, I was particularly impressed by another halachah which obligates Jewish visitors of the sick to be much more respectful and aware of the needs of the person in the bed. 'Even an older person should visit a younger one, even several times in a day, even someone of his own age, and one who does even more than this is truly to be praised *as long as he doesn't unduly pressure the person*' (8).

I tried very hard to be a good patient, but for someone whose perception of herself is as active and involved, being passive, sore and unable to sleep very well was extremely frustrating. By chance, my operation was in St Thomas' Hospital on the south bank of the River Thames. So when I couldn't sleep in the early days, with drains inserted for the fluids that build up, I never had to call a nurse, because just there, on the other side of the Thames was Big Ben. I knew, to the last minute what the time was, all through those difficult early nights. Sometimes I prayed, sometimes I cursed, sometimes I just tossed and turned. What I wish I had known then, for the grumpy sleepless sick person, was that there is a great deal written, stories and meditations, all from a Jewish perspective that would have been a great relief during sleepless nights.

One of the most interesting rabbinic approaches to healing liturgy was that of Rabbi Nachman of Bratzlav. In the Jewish world he is probably best known for his saying: 'All the world is a very narrow bridge, the most important thing is not to be afraid. It is not surprising then to learn that Rabbi Nachman was something of a depressive and would sometimes disappear for days at a time (to the enormous frustration of his disciples, I am sure). Perhaps the narrowness of the world bridge sometimes became a bit too much for him and he needed to be alone. He knew about having dark and difficult times in one's life and designated ten of the psalms as 'healing psalms.' For instance

Psalm 16 which begins: 'protect me God, for in You I take shelter.' When one is buffeted by endless examinations and intrusions and an uncomfortable feeling that one's body is not one's own, then to feel the comfort of God being always there is a very healing experience.

One of the most difficult things about engaging with serious illness from a Jewish point of view is that it is profoundly disempowering, at least in the early stages. People who are dynamic professionals or busy and active parents, or young people who never thought illness would come their way are suddenly put into the position of dependency. You have to wait for the specialist's diagnosis, if you have a lumpectomy then you are absolutely reliant upon the lab to let you know the results.

Whether the disorder be physical or psychological, almost all sufferers go through the stage of anger, resentment, even bitterness, when the question they want to ask is 'Why me, why was I given this path through life?'. It comes from a world view that sees nothing worthwhile in suffering, which is to be avoided if it all possible, and fought against if one is destined to struggle with serious illness. That sort of positivistic approach to life can become quite a challenge to those that do suffer with serious health disorders. The worst thing is that unreal and unkind attitude that blames the patient for their attitude or life style that might have led to the disorder. That is well expressed by the American scholar Robert Crawford who comments that `health is the language of a class that, even as it disintegrates, continues to believe in its self-making salvation. Health practice lends itself to a logic of survival: individuals must do what they can to protect themselves from harm`. The problem with that attitude is that rather than being empowering, it creates a climate in which the sick person is at fault for their sickness (9).

Sickness in itself can be an isolating experience. Debilitating treatment makes a person too tired to cope well with the company of others, depressive illness makes an individual withdraw from society, anxiety disorders make the presence of other people too intrusive to endure.

And yet, the most healing aspect of the Jewish approach to illness is that it underlines time and again that the Jew exists in community and cannot heal himself, however knowledgeable and pious he might be. This fact, that redemption from suffering comes from the presence of sympathetic others is addressed in a section of the Talmud in tractate Berachot, dealing with blessings and whether suffering can ever be a good thing. Berachot 5a explains in the name of Rabbah or possibly Rav Hisda that if suffering comes upon a person they should look at their deeds and whether they have wasted time when they should have been studying Torah. If neither of these examinations give a clue as to the reason for the suffering, then they must surely be *yissurin shel ahavah* – 'chastisements of love'. This concept is justified with a proof text from Proverbs that says `The one whom the Eternal loves He reproves, like a father the son in whom he delights` (10). In the discussion that follows as to what qualifies suffering to be *yissurin shel ahavah*, one of the points that is made is the importance of *da`at* – 'knowledge' of the purpose of what is going on. This we might describe in modern times as a conscious awareness of the meaning of the suffering. This is extremely difficult to achieve, but points towards the significance of talking therapies in the treatment of depression and other psychological disorders. Once the suffering has meaning, it can begin to feel purposive.

But Berachot 5b shows us that even rabbis struggle to deal with pain and suffering and need supportive help to get them through difficult times :

> Rabbi Chiyya bar Abba became ill. Rabbi Yochanan came to see him. He said to him: "Are your sufferings pleasurable to you?' He said to him: 'Neither they nor their reward'. He said to him: 'Give me your hand'. He gave him his hand and he lifted him up. Rabbi Yochanan became ill. Rabbi Chanina came to see him. He said to him: 'Are your sufferings pleasurable to you?'. He said to him: 'Neither they nor their reward'. He said to him: 'Give me your hand'. He gave him his hand and he lifted him up. Why? Shouldn't Rabbi Yochanan lift himself up? It is said: 'The prisoner cannot free himself from prison.'

Up to this point in the section it is relatively unproblematic, it seems to emphasise that pain and suffering are never welcome, even by the most pious and learned, but the way to cope with them is to be involved with the community and have one's colleagues and friends available to avoid sinking into the sort of depression that often comes from suffering that seems to be meaningless.

One of the difficulties with people suffering serious illness is their sense that the kind individual fulfilling the commandment of *bikkur cholim* – 'visiting the sick', is unable to empathise with their fear and their pain, in effect can't really understand on a deep level at all. This is approached in a very striking way by the next visitor as the story continues in Berachot 5b:

> Rabbi Elazar became sick. Rabbi Yochanan came to see him. He saw that he was lying in darkness. Rabbi Yochanan uncovered his arm and light fell from it. He saw that Rabbi Elazar was crying. He said to

him: `Why are you crying? If you are crying because of the Torah that you did not learn fully, have we not learned: `It makes no difference whether you have learned a great deal of Torah or a small amount, as long as your heart is directed towards heaven`? Or it may be because of the lack of sustenance because you had so little money; well not every man merits two tables. If it is because you didn't have many children or any in fact, see, here is the bone of my tenth son'. He said to him: `I am crying on account of this beauty that will waste in the dust'. He said to him : 'Ah, for certain that is what you are crying for'. So the two of them cried. Either way he said to him : 'Are your sufferings pleasurable to you?' He said to him : ' Neither they not their reward'. Then he said to him: `Give me your hand. He gave him his hand and he lifted him up'.

It is important to understand a little of Rabbi Yochanan's background, he was associated with profound suffering. According to one tradition his father died during his mother's pregnancy and his mother in giving birth, so he was born an orphan. (11) As if that was not enough, he had lost ten sons and carried the finger bone of the tenth in his pocket, to show as it were that he was utterly realistic about suffering (12). Whilst Rabbi Yochanan`s method of communicating his own experience of pain is a little odd for modern taste, his story teaches us the importance of authenticity in dealing with serious illness. He cries when he is upset, he is fearful of death, he is absolutely able to be present for his friend and colleague and so is able to help him through his illness.

Reflecting on Rabbi Yochanan`s part in the story, its perhaps not surprising to note that virtually every author who is writing about Jewish healing in the modern world has his or her own experience of suffering or bereavement. That experience gives modern Jews the same sense of speaking from deep knowledge that gives authenticity to their writing or rituals

In my own community we have instigated healing services on a regular basis. They include much music, some produced by young musicians in the congregation, a chance to light a candle and take something beautiful away, a small stone or other remembrance. The group constantly changes, has few regular congregants, but is a healing space. We have learned that healing is not the same as cure and that true healing might allow a person a peaceful end to their life. The story of Rabbi Yochanan and his colleagues teaches us above all the need to accompany people in their journeys through illness so that they find meaning and community in a time of fear and pain.

1) Talmud Avodah Zarah 54b
2) Talmud Ta'anit 21a
3) Talmud Berachot 57b
4) Numbers 12:13
5) Midrash Tanchuma Tzav 13
6) Talmud Nedarim 39b
7) Shulchan Aruch, Yoreh Deah, Hilchot Bikkur Cholim, 235:1
8) Shulchan Aruch, Yoreh Deah, Hilchot Bikkur Cholim, 235:3
9) quoted in Cutter (ed) 2011 page 219
10) Proverbs 3:12
11) Kiddushin 31a
12) Quoted in the name of Rabbi Nissim of Girondei in Cutter
    (ed) 2011 page 111

Bibliography

William Cutter (ed) *Midrash Medicine: Healing Body and Soul in the Jewish Interpretative Tradition* , Woodstock, Vt, Jewish Lights 2011
Douglas J Kohn (ed) *Life, Faith and Cancer: Jewish Journeys Through Diagnosis, Treatment and Recovery*, New York, URJ Press 2008

AMANDA GOLBY

Amanda Golby was ordained in 1988, and
has mostly served congregations outside of
London. Prior to that, she indexed the
Jewish Chronicle for the years 1896-1900.
She has a particular interst in how the
Jewish calendar can help those who are ill,
bereaved or carers.

Jewish Healing and
the Spirituality of Time

 I am delighted to be contributing to this collection to mark Tony's
retirement as Head of the Movement for Reform Judaism. We have known
each other personally and professionally for very many years, and, of course, I
also have very special memories of Linda, *zichronah livrachah*. My
experience of illness has had a much happier outcome, and, I feel that Tony
and Linda, and now Tony, and I might have different approaches to illness
and healing as part of our Jewish lives, but I am grateful to be able to use this
forum to share some of my ongoing thoughts and interest in this matter.

 For a variety of reasons, there have been major changes within the
Jewish world over the last 30/40 years. These have come about for many
reasons, and I can only look now at one small aspect. When Tony was at the
Leo Baeck College, there was probably very little talk, if any, about
'spirituality', and probably none about 'healing'. Both have become 'buzz
words' of our time, though I admit to having great difficulty with each, or
rather acknowledge that both can be interpreted in a multiplicity of ways. In
the words of Rabbi Dr Arthur Green:

> 'ruchaniyyut is 'spirituality' in Hebrew. It derives from the word
> 'ruach' which means both 'wind' and 'spirit', and was seen by the
> ancients as mysterious. ...'ruach' goes back as far as Genesis 1:2...
> But abstractions like 'ruchaniyyut' are not part of the biblical way of
> thinking, and it is no surprise that this word does not appear in
> Hebrew until the Middle Ages... The term is most widely used in
> Hasidism...There it is mostly a value statement. A person should
> devote his or her life to 'ruchaniyyut'...This refers to such spiritual

things as study, prayer and good deeds, as opposed to 'gashmiyyut', which would mean acquisition of wealthy, bodily pleasures and other 'worldly' concerns....'. (1)

I have a concern with the word 'spirituality' when it is somehow 'hijacked' to apply only to one type of service, approach to God and prayer, often stressing special singing and, perhaps, meditation. I do not wish to be misunderstood. That is very valid, very helpful to many people, but I would perhaps welcome a more pluralistic approach. There are those who find it within more concrete ways as well, as Green says, 'in prayer, study and good deeds'. For myself my 'spirituality', though I find the word difficult, comes from the relationship that I strive to have with living in relationship to the Jewish calendar. This does not mean, just, observing the festivals, but the centrality of Shabbat, the marking of Rosh Chodesh, the links between the festivals, such as the journey from Pesach to Shavuot, travelling through Elul, and there are other examples. Of course, this is my 'ideal'. Some years, some seasons, work better than others, for a whole range of very human reasons.

In addition to what I term 'the spirituality of time', with regard to the traditional Jewish day, week, month, year, I have also developed, because of my own experiences, because of that which I have encountered with others, learned from others, a sense of the possibilities of the healing which the Jewish calendar, Jewish time, can bring.

I first became aware of this, several years ago, when I came out of hospital, facing considerable uncertainty, on the day before Pesach. While I obviously knew the date, I was not feeling very well, and just pleased to be home, and not very bothered by not having a Seder. Someone, however, might have been worried that this might be a major problem for me, because my Irish Catholic surgeon said to me, (and I doubt he would have come out with it on his own), that he knew it was going to be Passover, but he regretted I would not be able to take part in any of the rituals this year. It was interesting. I was not nearly as upset about this as some of my congregants were, on my behalf. And I think it was because Seder was, for many them, even for those most involved with Jewish life, one of the few very important Jewish occasions of the year, and to have missed it would have left them truly deprived. I was disappointed, but knew there was much else Jewishly within me to sustain me.

On the night itself I read from the Haggadah, and listened to a tape of some of the prayers and songs, and had an experience at least as important as any that I have had before or since at a Seder. I had an abundance of bitter herbs and tears, and felt anything but free. However, as I sat alone, and read and listened, I truly understood that I did have a real freedom as to how I dealt with the difficulties, the uncertainties that lay ahead. That did not require me to be a saint, certainly that would not be very Jewish. I could legitimately have down days, times of feeling emotionally and physically low, certain things were totally out of my control, but I did have a freedom as to how I dealt with those things which were within my control. That was truly 'liberating', a very powerful Pesach experience, which has laid the foundations for much which is now of the greatest importance to me.

Both that year and the next, I found myself back in hospital over Succot and Simchat Torah, on both occasions with serious infections. By the time that I was again able to attend a Simchat Torah service, I was very much looking forward to it. Yet I found myself having a difficult experience with one of the passages in the Reform Movement's Machzor. It is the passage that we read before Hallel on that day, and I'm sure in my pre-illness life, I would have read it with much enthusiasm, knowing that it expressed a wholeness with regard to the calendar to which I aspired. I was aware that, of course, the Medzibozher Rebbe, on whose words it was based, would not have imagined an egalitarian congregation, but I would have had no problem with interpreting it in that way. However, suddenly that which promised so much, seemed so very exclusive:

> The festivals in Tishri teach us to serve God with all our being. On Rosh Hashanah, which is the day for Remembrance, we served God with our minds, which were full of memories. On Yom Kippur we worshipped God with our heart, because fasting strains the heart. On Succot, as we held the Etrog and Lulav, we used our hands in God's service. And now, on SimchatTorah, let us praise God with our feet, as we process with joy around our synagogue dancing with our Torah scrolls. (2)

I found myself very challenged by this. What about those who can no longer remember, or whose memories are so very painful, that Rosh Hashanah is truly difficult? What about those who are unable to fast? What about those who are unable to use their hands or feet? What about those who are looking after them?

We are reasonably good in providing physical access for those who need it, though not good enough. We may be good about helping those whose mobility is restricted, we try to help with those whose hearing is limited, but can we think of someone who has never heard the sounds of the Shofar, and should we not try to let them at least feel its vibrations. I was very aware of the challenges when each year in Southport I led a Seder at a Home then under the auspices of the Jewish Blind Society. There were those who could no longer see, those who had never been able to see. We need to be conscious of these needs.

If the word 'spririituality' has entered, or at least, re-entered our vocabulary, then the word 'healing' has re-entered it even more recently, and again with variety of interpretations, none right for everyone, but hopefully, there is a right way for all those who seek 'healing', within a Jewish context. Clearly healing has always existed within our tradition, and a very helpful account is given by Dr Laura Praglin in an essay 'The Jewish healing tradition in historical perspective' (3). Jewish sources deal with both physical and emotional healing, and I never cease to be impressed at the real understanding in the traditional Mi Sheberach for healing, brought to a far greater community over recent years by Debbie Friedman z'l. It is so important to acknowledge that a complete healing, a whole healing, requires both the physical and emotional elements.

Yet there are some who find this prayer difficult, and indeed have trouble with the second paragraph of the Amidah, when we speak of God as *rofeh hacholim*, healer of the sick. We could discuss at length about our inability to understand, the seeming unfairness of random suffering, disability, premature death, whether from illness or accident, all subjects which Tony has considered at length, and will, I hope, continue to do so, and yet I think it is essential to differentiate between 'healing' and 'cure'. Much has been written about this, and I share with you words from Rabbi Nancy Flam, a pioneer in the work of Jewish healing. 'Jewish tradition has long recognized that there are two components of health: the body and the spirit. The Mi Sheberach prayer, traditionally recited for someone who is ill, asks God for *refuah shleima*, a complete healing, and then specifies two aspects, *refuat hanefesh*, healing of the soul/spirit/whole person and *refuat haguf*, cure of the body. To cure the body means to wipe out the tumor, clear up the infection, or regain mobility. To heal the spirit involves creating a pathway to sensing wholeness, depth, mystery, purpose and peace. Cure may occur without healing, and healing without cure. Pastoral caregivers and family members of seriously ill people know that sometimes lives and relationships are healed even when there is no possibility of physical cure; in fact, serious illness often motivates people to seek healing of the spirit'. (4)

While the cycle of the Jewish year is of the greatest importance to me, I am aware of how difficult it can be at different times for so many. While I wrote above of my abilities to transform the Seder, the Pesach experience, this is not possible for everyone. One can transform festivals, but not usually when one is in the midst of the experience. The Seder is never very easy, unless one is part of a rare family grouping where all seem to want the same things. There are ideals, there is reality. For many it is a very difficult time. For many it is a time of remembering, perhaps not coming out of Egypt, but family members who are no longer there. It is a time which may highlight loneliness for many. There are, I believe, ways of transforming festivals, and growing from them, using them as a route to 'healing', if not cure, but it takes much work, and perhaps requires many people having a greater understanding of the deeper significance of Chagim than they have had.

It is clearly difficult to experience a Seder knowing that one is very ill, that perhaps it is the last one. It is, of course, also difficult for the carers, the bereaved... I know that however much joy Tony gets from Sedarim with the generations, there is also the sadness that Linda is not there to share it, to 'shep nachas', with the family that meant so much to her. And, for many, it seems that a festival is accompanied by a Yahrzeit, so there are more poignant memories. Some communities here have started to hold an 'Empty Chair Seder', Rabbi Helen Freeman and I attended one in New York three years ago, when we were there to research our shared and separate aspects of Jewish healing, and while it needs a certain amount of adjustment for use 'this side of the pond', has great potential to be helpful to some. As with everything else in life, in Judaism, and certainly within a Judaism that values pluralism, it is not a 'one size fits all'.

The Jewish Healing Center of New York produces a journal, 'The Outstretched Arm', which deals with many aspects of healing, and importantly linking healing with all the Chagim. There are important teachings about, for example, the appropriate four questions, the symbolism of Matzah, the plagues.... It is only possible to touch briefly on this here. Rabbi Simcha Weintraub, the outstanding director of the Center, who has contributed so much to this important work, wrote an article in the early days in 1992, an article 'The Haggadah and Healing', focusing on the significance and ways of interpreting the plagues and the three key symbols of *pesach*, *matzah* and *maror*. He writes:

> The Haggadah recommends that "in every generation, each individual should feel as though he or she had actually been released from

Egypt". This sentence empowers those have struggled with illness to rethink the three symbols through the prism of illness and recovery. Relate the many aspects... of these intensely personal experiences to the national story of slavery and freedom. Do you feel that you are still enslaved? In what ways have you been set free? If you had to name three actual physical symbols to parallel those of the Seder, what would they be? What encapsulates both your confinement and your delivery? What embodies your suffering and bitterness? As you articulate aspects of your odyssey with illness, treatment and recovery, try to relate them to the Exodus story and the liberation of the Hebrew slaves. How was their experience like yours? What emotional, psychological and spiritual processes did they have to undergo that reflect your own? Your midrash-your personal interpretation based on your particular experience-links your history to that of the eternal narrative. It is a unique one that adds to the meaning of Passover for all assembled. "In every generation" means nothing if not here and now, and "every individual" implies all those gathered at your table, and their most profound experiences. (5)

To derive maximum meaning from festivals, from the Jewish calendar, as a source of healing, we need to help people to have the greatest possible understanding of the Jewish calendar, and that requires on-going work at many levels. Too often, sadly, we do not get beyond the basics. But, I believe there is great potential. While I am focusing here on Pesach, the whole Jewish year, is full of significance, and I am also indebted to the work of Rabbi Amy Eilberg, another pioneer in the world of Jewish healing. Ideally, for everyone, Pesach is more than the Seder, and, perhaps, even more ideally, the journey continues through the period of the Omer, to Shavuot. This again brings many possibilities for healing, but is probably much more complicated to convey than the significance of the Seder, the most widely-observed celebration of the Jewish year. Always, though, we have the 'special', and the 'ordinary', and it is the 'everyday', and the weeks of the Omer are almost that, that have the greatest potential to be transformative. It is those we need to work at to enable us to experience the special 'differently'. In the words of Rabbi Eilberg:

Shavuot arrives after a long lesson in waiting, in patience, in process. Among the many meanings of the period of the counting of the Omer...is the sense that revelation- guidance, wisdom, truth-does not

72

come to us readily, not even as a necessary result of a new experience of freedom. Just as our ancestors endured a long period of wandering in the desert before revelation came, we, too, must, like it or not, cultivate patience, and sometimes take long journeys through deserts of pain, confusion and disorientation, before wisdom will present itself. The ritual of counting encourages us to pay respectful attention to the process that brings us from freedom to revelation…Revelation means that the Divine communicates with us - collectively, as a people, and as individuals. Of course, the process of listening for the voice of the Divine in the midst of the din of life, or the terrors of illness, is not always easy. And the ancient sources of Torah often require significant translation before we can recognize their applicability to our own life struggles. But Shavu'ot promises us that Torah is a reservoir of endless wisdom from which we may drink at any time of our lives. (6).

Tony, I hope a long and healthy retirement will enable you to contribute to the reservoir of Torah, and that a deepening of our understanding of the possibilities of Jewish healing will, similarly, add to it.

(1) Green, Rabbi Dr Arthur: 'Ruhaniyyut, in Matlins, Stuart M, (editor): *The Jewish Lights Spirituality Handbook: a guide to understanding, exploring and living a spiritual life*, Vermont, Jewish Lights, 2001 pp3-4.
(2) *Forms of Prayer for Jewish Worship: volume 2, Prayers for the Pilgrim Festivals*, London, R.S.G.B., 1995, page 222
(3) Praglin, Laura J: 'The Jewish healing tradition in historical perspective', in Person, Hara E (editor): *The Mitzvah of Healing: an anthology of essays, Jewish texts, personal stories, meditations and rituals*: New York, Women of Reform Judaism, 2003, pp1-15
(4) Flam, Rabbi Nancy: 'The Jewish way of healing' in Person, Hara E, as above, pp16-22
(5) Weintraub, Rabbi Simcha, 'The Haggadah and Healing': in *The Outstretched Arm*, journal of the Jewish Healing Center, New York, volume 1, No. 2 Spring 1992
(6) Eilberg, Rabbi Amy: 'Cycle of Jewish Time and Healing', Keynote talk at National Center for Jewish Healing Conference, November 10th 2003

MARK GOLDSMITH

Mark Goldsmith has served North Western Reform Synagogue (Alyth) since 2006. He wrote his Rabbinic Thesis at Leo Baeck College in 1996 on "The Jewish Law of Sale". Tony Bayfield introduced him to studying Jewish business ethics. Since then Mark has been a teacher and organiser in this field.

What Matters is the Human Cost – the Thrust of Jewish Business Ethics

The typical pattern of a Middle Eastern Shuq or market is for most of the tradespeople selling similar goods to set up their stalls near to each other. Typically in a traditional market there will be say a dyers section, a spice sellers section, a butchers section and a fruit and vegetable sellers' section. The street names in many of the older British towns and cities often retain the history of a time when this was the case in Northern Europe too, including streets in the City of London such as Poultry, Cornhill and Fish Street Hill.

How was a vegetable seller, for example, to make a living in such a set up when they are trading next to many other vegetable sellers?   Often children would be sent to the market to buy produce for home. They would go to the stall from which their family customarily bought. But suppose that one vegetable seller comes up with a clever technique to bring the children to buy from his stall. He starts giving out tasty roasted corn and nuts to children who choose to bring their parents' business to him – a time honoured technique still very much used to market to children.

The vegetable sellers in the alley where this kind of business is done might go to complain to the authorities in charge of the market, that one vegetable seller is gaining unfair advantage and stealing their business. However, according to the Mishnah and Talmud if this market were under the supervision of Jewish law, the entrepreneurial vegetable seller would be able to continue to use his techniques of sales promotion. Though one Rabbinic authority, Rabbi Judah, is recorded in the Mishnah (1) as saying that the practice of give-aways to entice people to buy should be banned, the majority of Sages say that not only is the practice permitted but also that all the sellers

74

are equally able to use the practice – "Because he [this stall holder] can say to him [another stall holder], 'I give away nuts; you give away plums.'" (2)

A similar question is asked in the same place in the Mishnah and Talumd of the permissibility of price competition between traders in the same products. Whilst Rabbi Judah would see this practice banned and a fixed price set, the majority of Sages support price competition because they feel that it is necessary in order for a healthy market to exist which serves the interests of suppliers and buyers alike.

This is also the case for traders who might wish to restrict competition from new traders in their town. As long as the new trader pays his taxes and does not constitute a new environmental hazard, such as a leather tanner opening for the first time in an area of town which does not currently suffer from the odours that such a business would create, other traders cannot restrict his entry into the trade of the town (3).

From these and similar texts, it might appear that the primary aim of Jewish business law is to create a free market where the new entrants are just as able to thrive as those who have traded for a long time and where consumers have a choice of product and price offerings. It is certainly an important aspect of the field. Possibly the free market is especially necessary for Jews for historical reasons, as Jews both out of choice and out of compulsion have always been a mobile people, shown even today by our worldwide distribution. It is necessary for a displaced Jew to be able to make a living wherever they may settle.

However, above the free market aim comes a higher level aim of Jewish business law. This is to ensure that when we are in economic relationship with each other we treat each other with humanity and consideration. This aim has its foundation in the Torah texts which begin the development of Jewish business law. Wages must be paid right away to a daily hired labourer so that they are able to sustain themselves and their family (4). The legislation which begins in the Torah as governing leaseholds of land, but is in later Jewish texts interpreted as requiring a cap to be put on profits from sale or buying, says that "if you sell anything to your neighbour or buy anything from your neighbour's hand you shall not wrong one another" (5). This makes the obligation to treat your trading partner with consideration mutual. When collecting on a loan made to another person a creditor may not enter the home of his debtor but must grant the debtor the dignity to pay him by choice (6). These are only three examples of many which have their basis in creating an equal and humane relationship between all parties in trade.

Maimonides extends from this principle a general rule for the behaviour of a *Talmid Chacham* – a person who truly understands the core of Judaism. "All the transactions of the *Talmid Chacham* must be honest and done with integrity. His no should be no and his yes yes. In financial matters, he must be strict with himself but lenient with others. He pays the purchase money immediately… If others are legally indebted to him, he grants them an extension to pay, is forgiving, and lends graciously. He does not interfere with the business of his neighbours, and never acts harshly towards anybody." (7)

Jewish business law does not allow a person to gain an unfair or unjust advantage. One may not create personal economic advantage by stopping another person from trading effectively. The specific sin of *genevat da'at* was interpreted from the Torah as a subcategory of stealing. This literally means "stealing the mind" and a classic example in given in the Shulchan Aruch: "It is forbidden to cheat people in buying and selling and to defraud them [*lignov da'atam* - to steal their minds]. For example, one is required to point out flaws in an article being sold to a buyer. So it is forbidden to sell the meat of an animal with is not suitable to be considered *kasher* as though it were slaughtered in a *kasher* fashion, even to a non-Jew [who is not obliged to eat meat which is *kasher*]" (8). Among the issues here is that the person buying is, without their knowledge, being given something of lesser value than they have a right to think that it is, hence value is being stolen from them, no less an offence than taking money directly from the person.

The influence of business on the world in which all Jews live is especially great in our time. In 2010, of the world's top 100 economies 42 were corporations and 58 were countries. The world's largest business, Wal-Mart is the world's 26th largest economy, its turnover being the same size as Sweden's GDP, and Royal Dutch Shell and Exxon-Mobil are the next largest. They are respectively the world's 34th and 35th largest economies, the size of South Africa or Thailand (9). Businesses of this size are controlled by relatively few people and their actions are inevitably driven by a combination of their own moral codes as well as the economic needs of the businesses. Even one of the strongest advocates of free enterprise, Milton Friedman, wrote that business managers are responsible for conducting the business in accordance with the desires of shareholders "which generally will be to make as much money as possible while conforming to the basic rules of the society, both those embodied in law and those embodied in ethical custom." (10).

Rabbi Jonathan Sacks notes that in a world where business is of such scale "…we must ask: Does it enhance human dignity? Does it create self-respect? Does it encourage creativity? Does it allow everyone to participate in the material blessings of the created world? Does it protect the vulnerable and help those in need to escape the trap of need? Does it ensure that no one lacks the means for a dignified existence? Do those who succeed share their blessings with those who have less? Does the economic system strengthen the bonds of human solidarity? .....These are the questions we must ask of global capitalism if we are to exercise responsibility." (11)

Jewish business law aims to do so in many areas. Though this is not an exhaustive list, these examples cover a large scope of the Jewish business law that remains within the ethical arena today and add to a general requirement to deal in good faith.

Selling must be done in an open way. This means that a seller and a buyer should only consider a sale to be valid if both parties are fully aware of the value of goods or services at the time of sale. So for example a buyer who regularly buys cars for scrap needs to point out to a seller if he is buying for driving as the car will have a different value. Similarly if a seller knows that a car is not safely driveable it is his responsibility to point this out to the buyer and not to leave it to the buyer to find out.

Pricing should not be exploitative. Thus in a time of shortage it is not allowed in Jewish law to hoard necessities in order to make additional profit. The classic texts on this issues use a prophetic text as their basis from Amos: Concerning those who hoard fruit, lend money on usury, reduce the measures and raise prices exploitatively, Scripture speaks of them when it says: 'When will the new moon be gone, that we may sell grain? And the Sabbath, that we may set forth corn? Making the *ephah* small, and the shekel great, and falsifying the balances of deceit." And [concerning these] it is [further] written in Scripture, "The Eternal has sworn by the pride of Jacob: Surely I will never forget any of their works." (12) A free market in necessities which causes distress to the poor is not acceptable. Meanwhile in the same text it is seen as perfectly permissible to hoard spices and other luxuries in expectation of better prices in the future as this will not cause oppressive distress.

The classic interpretation of wronging another person in trade is where there is a large disparity between the offer price of an object and its market price – unless the buyer is aware of this and agrees to it. Jewish business law allows a disparity of up to one sixth of the total price (13) which enables a trader to make money from selling goods in high demand – but will not allow him more than that unless the buyer expressly agrees to be overcharged, perhaps because this is a luxury item in shortage. Importantly the legislation also applies to buyers who know or subsequently find out that they are paying a sixth or more less than the market price. It means that a person cannot make extreme amounts of money from their trading partner's ignorance. Thus a person who knows that an old bottle of wine is potentially worth £1000 on the open market cannot then buy it from another person for £100 without sharing this knowledge with the seller. They are then put on an equal footing.

Jewish business law asks that a trading partner takes responsibility for their actions. This includes in the giving of advice or the creation of situations which might cause an offence to take place. Thus the Mishnah rules on a number of situations where a buyer is by their actions encouraging a seller to do the wrong thing. "It is not right to buy either wool or milk or kids from the shepherds, nor wood nor fruits from those who are in charge of fruits. It is however permitted to buy from house-wives woollen goods in Judea, flaxen goods in Galilee or calves in Sharon, but in all these cases, if it was stipulated by them that the goods are to be hidden, it is forbidden [to buy them]."(14) Essentially a buyer should consider if they are potentially enabling a person to steal from their employer or if they have suspicions about the way in which goods are being sold before they enter into transactions which might be fraudulent. The principle behind this is expressed elsewhere in the Talmud, "Said Abaye to R. Joseph: Why should you want us to penalise the purchaser [of contraband items]? Let us penalise the vendor! — He replied. It is not the mouse that is the thief but the hole." (15)

Rabbi Asher Meir adds further examples of human care in Jewish business law (16). Debtors are accorded a great degree of protection in the Torah. Creditors may not charge interest, all debts are annulled on a seven year cycle and items taken in pledge which are basic necessities must be returned. These protections would have meant that a destitute borrower would remain able to borrow without entering into an inescapable cycle of debt and to return to some dignity. When, by the times of the Mishnah, this legislation created a situation whereby creditors would not lend close to the seventh year of the cycle, the *prozbul* (the legal formula amelioratinging it) meant that the lender sold the debt to the court. Therefore rather than one person, the creditor, having power for ever over the debtor, it was the entire community, represented by the court, to which they were responsible, thus preserving the debtor's dignity as an equal person. In the past few centuries the interest prohibition has been circumvented by the *heter iska*, recasting interest payments as profit payments to a silent partner and expressing the relationship of borrower to lender as being equal partners in a business deal.

A number of times in Torah, law concerning business relationships is within a context which ends with the words "I am your Eternal God who brought you out of the land of Egypt." This phrase indicates the paradigmatic experience for the Jewish people of the inhumanity of slavery and oppression, redeemed by God. Three examples of this juxtaposition are the requirement to forego interest on loans, the requirement to have a blue thread in *tzitzit* (the fringes on a prayer shawl) and the requirement to have accurate weights and measures (17). In each case a Talmudic texts suggests, it would be possible for a trader to cheat another person without them realising – God's interest in what we do in business means however that the trader's inhumanity will not be overlooked! "It is I who will exact vengeance from him who ascribes his money to a Gentile and lends it to an Israelite on interest, or who steeps his weights in salt [thus increasing their weight before he goes to buy at the market], or who [attaches to his garment for sale threads dyed with] vegetable [indigo] blue and maintains that it is [real and rarer] blue [derived from molluscs]." (18)

Jewish business law, studied by Jews today as an ethical guide, encourages us to be effective business people. We are encouraged to trade freely and successfully, making a good living. Above this we are encouraged to trade fairly with equal consideration for those with whom we trade. We should not exploit each other and should ensure that our trading partners have the information that they need to make good business decisions. Judaism always keeps us in relationship with others, religiously, socially and in business – putting God's recognition of what we do as our final guarantor of fair play.

1. Mishnah, Bava Metzia 4:12
2. Talmud, Bava Metzia 60a
3. Shulchan Aruch, Choshen Mishpat 156:5-7
4. Leviticus 19:13
5. Leviticus 25:14
6. Deuteronomy 24:10-11
7. Maimonides, Mishneh Torah, Hilchot De'ot 5:13
8. Shulchan Aruch, Choshen Mishpat 228:6
9. World Bank 2010
10. Milton Friedman (1970) quoted in Pava, Moses L., *Business Ethics - A Jewish Perspective* New York: Yeshiva University Press, 1997, p. 148
11. Sacks, Jonathan, *The Dignity of Difference* London: Continuum, 2002, p. 89
12. Babylonian Talmud, Bava Batra 90b quoting Amos 8:5 and 7
13. Mishnah Bava Metzia 4:3
14. Mishnah Bava Kama 10:9
15. Talmud Gittin 45a
16. Meir, Asher, *Globalisation and the Jewish Question* Jerusalem, 2007 pp. 4-8
17. Leviticus 25:36-38, Numbers 15:38,41, Leviticus 19:36
18. Talmud, Bava Metzia 61b

MICHAEL HILTON

Michael Hilton is Rabbi of Kol Chai Hatch End Jewish Community. He is the author of The Christian Effect on Jewish Life (1994). He serves on the Executive Committee of Harrow Inter-Faith Council and has recently completed an MA thesis on the History of the Bar Mitzvah ceremony.

Why Face East ?

I go to the home of a mourner to conduct a service during the *shiva*, the days of mourning after a funeral. "Which direction is East?" I gently enquire, looking round the spacious living room, with its gallery of copies of old masters. After a hurried consultation, the answer comes back, with a sweeping gesture which takes in apparently the full length of the wall: "This way, rabbi." I gaze at the wall, and a copy of Manet's *Olympia* gazes straight back at me; Olympia looks equally unconcerned about her nudity and my embarrassment. Thinking on my feet, I wheel around 90% to the right, facing south towards the garden. "Evening service, page 30," I call out, "and we'll be facing this way."

Embedded in this story are three customs about the correct orientation for Jewish prayer. Firstly, in Ashkenazi Europe the prevailing tradition has been to face East, even in places where that is not directly towards Jerusalem; secondly, the orientation does not need to be carried out with great precision; and thirdly, the correct direction can be overruled by other considerations, such as not praying towards an image or an inappropriate picture. All of these three customs are well documented in the history of this topic.

For ancient cultures, the direction East, towards the rising sun, had a particular fascination. The English word "orientation" comes from the Latin word *oriens* ("East"), from the root *orior* meaning to rise or get up. In Biblical Hebrew the word *kedem* means both "East" (Genesis 13:14) and "in front" (Psalm 139:5). It also indicates an earlier time, "before" (Lamentations 5:21), perhaps reflecting the tradition that human history began at the Garden of Eden, which was in the East (Genesis 2:8, though interpreted by Rashi to

81

mean that the garden was in the eastern part of Eden). Genesis describes the Garden of Eden as being the source of four rivers, two of which have been identified with the Tigris and Euphrates. Medieval maps were normally drawn with the East at the top (1). But the children of Abraham do not worship the sun, so the tabernacle in the desert was pitched with the entrance towards the east (Numbers 2:2) and the ark towards the west, and the Temples in Jerusalem followed the same orientation, so that those in the courtyards standing facing towards the Holy of Holies would have been facing West. Only the impious would face East:

> And he brought me into the inner court of the House of Adonai, and behold, at the door of the Temple of Adonai, between the porch and altar, were about 25 men with their backs towards the Temple of Adonai, and their faces towards the east, and they worshipped eastwards to the sun.
>
> (Ezekiel 8:16)

Ezekiel describes this as a terrible desecration of the Temple, facing East and bowing down to the sun.

In late antiquity, in the Talmudic tradition, we find those who still objected to facing East for prayer:

> Rav Sheshet held: the presence of God is everywhere, because he used to say to his attendant; set me in any direction except towards the east. This was not because the presence of God is not there, but because the *minim* teach it. But Rabbi Abbahu said: The presence of God is in the west.
>
> (Babylonian Talmud, Babba Batra 25a)

Rav Sheshet (who lived around 300 CE) was blind, hence the need for his attendant to position him correctly for prayer. This suggests that those who could see would use the sun or known landmarks to position themselves. Who were the *minim*, the heretics, who taught that the presence of God is in the East? Sun worshippers? Perhaps. But they could also have been Christians. It has been the prevailing custom for Churches to be built facing East, and this is documented from the second century onwards. Tertullian describes this as "facing the light" and Gregory of Nyssa reasoned that the Orient was the original home of humanity (2). Rav Sheshet's debating partner here, Rabbi Abbahu, is frequently mentioned as disputing with *minim*, and Rav Sheshet

82

himself may have been familiar with parts of the Christian scriptures, as is evidenced by his saying to an opponent, "Aren't you from Pumbedita, where they draw an elephant through the eye of a needle?" (Babylonian Talmud, Babba Metzia 38b, cf Matthew 19:24).

Here and in all the texts about the direction of prayer, there is a specific prayer being referred to, the *amidah*, also known simply as the *tefilah* ("prayer"). It has been the custom in many synagogues since ancient times for the seating to be arranged so that the congregation face in various directions, but will stand and turn towards the ark for the *amidah*. Most commonly, where there is a central *bimah*, seats are arranged in three sides round it, to enable worshippers to look towards the reader and in particular, to be able to follow clearly the scriptural readings from the *bimah*. So the whole discussion about correct orientation technically only applies to the one central prayer of each service. The Talmudic text continues with some different opinions:

> Rav Yitzchak said: He who wishes to become wise should turn to the south while praying, and he who wishes to become rich should turn to the north. Rabbi Joshua ben Levi said that he should always turn to the south, for by obtaining wisdom he will obtain wealth. But was it not Rabbi Joshua ben Levi who said that the presence of God is in the West? One should turn sideways (Rashi: to the south)
> (Babylonian Talmud, Babba Batra 25b)

This suggests that it was the subjective needs of the worshipper which were the decisive factor, not the location of Jerusalem, the sun, or indeed anything in the world outside. But this whole section in Babba Batra seems to be contradicted by another discussion in Berachot 30a, a text based on Tosefta Megillah 3.16 (Hebrew) 3.14 (Neusner):

> Those who are outside the Land of Israel turn towards the Land of Israel, as Scripture states (2 Chron 6:38) "And pray toward their land.. the city which you have chosen and the house which I have built." Those who in the Land of Israel turn toward Jerusalem, as Scripture states (2 Chron 6:34) "And they pray to you toward this city which you have chosen and the house which I have built for your name." Those who in Jerusalem turn towards the Temple, as Scripture states (2 Chron 6:32) "When he comes and prays towards this House." Those who are in the Temple turn towards the Chamber of the Holy of Holies and pray, as Scripture states (I Kings 8:30) "When they pray

towards this place." It turns out that those standing in the north face south, those in the south face north, those in the east face west, and those in the west face east. Thus all Israel turn out to be praying towards one place.

This text creates a verbal picture of Jews standing in circles around the world, each facing towards the boundary of the next circle. In the innermost circle stand those in the Temple. This ruling derives in turn from a passage in Daniel, where he prays before being thrown into the lions' den:

> Although Daniel knew that the document had been signed, he continued to go to his house, which had windows in its upper room open towards Jerusalem, and to get down on his knees three times a day to pray to his God and praise him, just as he had done previously.
> (Daniel 6.10 (6.11 in the Aramaic))

When the codifiers of late medieval and early modern times were writing their rule books, they were well aware of the two passages from the Talmud (Berachot and Babba Batra) which appear to give totally different rulings. One approach was to treat the Berachot texts as definitive, and to rule that one should pray towards the land of Israel. But others tried to reconcile the two, resulting in some strange rulings such as this one:

> This means that he faces east, but he turns sideways towards the south if he wishes to become wise or towards the north if he wishes to become rich.
> (Beit Yosef Orach Chayyim 94)

Were these various instructions followed in practice? Because we have evidence from the archeology of ancient synagogues, we can attempt something unusual in the history of Jewish practice - we can try to compare the evidence from the texts with what really happened in public prayer. The Temple at Elephantine in Egypt (fifth century BCE) was built facing Jerusalem. But the archeological evidence from early synagogues is conflicting, and the confusion is compounded by ongoing scholarly debates about whether many remains from first-century Israel were synagogues or not. The earliest building now thought to be a synagogue has been excavated on the Greek island of Delos. It dates from the second century BCE, and has a niche low down in the northern wall in which a Torah scroll, lying horizontally, could have been kept. But the position of the niche tells us nothing about which way the congregation might have faced while praying, since it was simply a storage place, not a fixed Ark. That came much later.

The excavated synagogue at Capernaum in Galilee, which is perhaps the building mentioned in Luke 4, has a north-south orientation, with the entrance towards the south. It would thus appear to be facing away from Jerusalem. It is possible, however, that the congregation would turn and face the entrance for prayer. The remarkable synagogue at Dura Europos, covered with frescoes illustrating biblical scenes, was very liberal in its use of images, and seems to be representative of a kind of Hellenistic Judaism which does not survive. Yet it was precise in its orientation, with a niche, looking just like the *mihrab* in a mosque, in the Western wall facing Jerusalem.

Archeological evidence from Islamic countries shows that most synagogues across the Sephardi world were built facing towards the land of Israel. But this was not the case in Ashkenazi Europe, where the prevailing custom has been for synagogues to face East regardless of location, even in places such as Poland or Ukraine. So the Shulchan Aruch (1564) rules:

> If he is praying facing one of the other directions, he should turn sideways so that his face is towards the land of Israel if abroad.
> (Shulchan Aruch Orach Chayyim 94.2)

Adding the ruling for Ashkenazi Jewry, Moses Isserles (Krakow,1520 - 1572) comments:

> We turn our faces to the east, because we are settled to the west of the land of Israel, and consequently our faces are towards the land (Tur and Semag). But we do not make the position of the Ark or the direction of prayer correspond exactly to the place of sunrise, because this is the way of the Minim.

Isserles writes as if he was ignorant of geography. It was quite correct for the *Tur*, Jacob ben Asher (1269-1343), writing in Spain, to state that Israel was to the East. It was perhaps a little stranger for Moses of Coucy (thirteenth century) writing the *Semag* in France. But Isserles lived in Poland. It is possible that notions of geography followed the textual tradition, so that Israel was still thought to be vaguely towards the East even in Eastern Europe. It is equally possible that many towns were built on an East-West axis, with the main churches facing East, and Jewish communities wanted to blend in with their surroundings, and were reluctant to place their public buildings at odd angles. It is interesting to see how Isserles adds a qualification to the prevailing custom, lest Jews should be thought to be imitating a Christian practice.

There are other sources which support this strong European Ashkenazi tradition of an East-West orientation for a synagogue. The orientation towards the Temple has an underlying idea of entering the presence of God. "Build me a sanctuary, and I will dwell among them" (Exodus 25:8) "Thus said Adonai of Hosts: I have returned to Zion and will dwell in Jerusalem" (Zechariah 8.3) Abba Binyamin, in Berachot 5b, states that he placed his bed north-south. The Talmud gives two reasons for this, firstly, that this guarantees male children, and secondly that it would prevent his wife from having a miscarriage. The Tosafot comments that this is about the correct orientation for sex, and the reason is that 'the presence of God is situated East-West'. Other texts explain that this is because the Temple was built on an East-West axis. For example, Sefer Ha-Chinuch 254 (following Berachot 61b) states:

> It is forbidden for a man to relieve oneself, or to sleep, in a position between east and west, because the holy place was at the west.

It is the presence of God which is the important factor for prayer. The ultimate purpose is not to face the land or the Temple as an end in itself, but to imagine that when praying the *Amidah*, we move into God's presence. Facing East from Europe was considered good enough.

Jews praying at the Western Wall in Jerusalem also face due East, towards the wall, rather than north-east, towards the supposed site of the Temple itself. The wall is a retaining wall, built by Herod to extend the platform above it on which the Temple stood. It had no religious significance when it was built, and has only had a special sanctity since the eighteenth century (3). Today, prayer at the wall has become a central expression of Jewish identity, though a few voices are raised against the practice. Nobody questions the precise orientation of worshippers at the wall. But at other times and places Jews have persisted in questioning established practice, and the more pious Ashkenazim expressed concern about which way to face when visiting a synagogue which quite obviously faces in the wrong direction. Should you face towards the Eastern wall like everyone else, or get out your compass and turn towards Jerusalem? In order to solve this problem, the following ancient text was found to be useful:

> If he was riding on a donkey he should dismount to say the Amidah. If he cannot dismount he should turn his face; and if he cannot turn his face he should direct his heart towards the Holy of Holies

> (Mishnah Berakhot 4.5)

With this in mind, the *Arukh Ha-Shulchan* of Yechiel Michel Epstein (1829-1908) rules that the various opinions in the Talmud are not really in disagreement. There may be various reasons for facing in other directions, but one's heart should always be inclined towards Jerusalem. Therefore, he adds, one can understand the custom of Eastern European Jewry to build their synagogues towards the east, as it is sufficient to face in the general direction of the land of Israel, and to direct one's heart towards Jerusalem.

Similarly, modern rulings have accepted that the congregation may need to face in a different direction where a synagogue has been constructed within an existing building, or where the site does not easily permit the traditional orientation. This makes sense. Judaism is essentially a practical religion, and does not demand that one walk around with a compass all day. Jerusalem and the land are invisible from abroad, so even when the synagogue faces the right way, it is still an orientation of the heart which is the essence of the idea.

The correct orientation has also been a feature of Jewish cemeteries. The prevailing custom is to bury with the feet facing Jerusalem or towards the East. But as with synagogues, there are many exceptions to the general rule. The orientation of graves in Qumran on a north-south axis has been interpreted as showing that the community there wanted to demonstrate their opposition to the priestly class in Jerusalem (4). In the ancient world as today, religious decision making could not be separated from the politics of the time.

So what is the meaning of facing East? Unlike Muslims, who pray towards a city and a building which remain at the centre of their faith, Jews pray towards a Temple which has not been in existence for nearly 2000 years. For many centuries, the direction of prayer suggested a deep sense of nostalgia, a longing to return. But with the arrival of the modern state of Israel, the orientation has taken on a new significance. The texts make clear that Jews pray not just towards the Temple, not just towards the Jerusalem, but from abroad towards the land. Thus it was that this became the only religious practice mentioned in *HaTikvah*, Israel's national anthem "With eyes turned toward the East, looking toward Zion."

It is problematic that the anthem is written only from the perspective of Ashkenazi Jewry. Yet its singing directs the hearts of Jews around the world, wherever they may be, to the land of Israel and Jerusalem. Why face East? Today we must add Zionism to the traditional reasons. Facing the land shows solidarity with Jews around the world, who turn to the same place, and shows the longing for the land which has ever been part of our tradition. Synagogues which depart from the traditional orientation sometime do so to demonstrate that Zionism is not central to them. For many years, the Liberal Jewish Synagogue in St John's Wood, London, had two sanctuaries which faced in opposite directions.

Jews remain a religious group anchored to a particular place and to festivals which mark the seasons of the year. Christianity retained the link with the seasons, but did not retain the idea of praying towards a particular place. Islam, on the other hand, has a particular geographical centre for prayer, but broke the link with the seasons. In this respect as in many others, Judaism can be considered the most worldly of the three Abrahamic faiths, the most anchored in the concerns of this life and of this world.

1. BL Gordon, "Sacred Directions, Orientation, and the Top of the Map," *History of Religions*, 10.3 (1971), 211-227.
2. *Catholic Encyclopedia*, "Orientation of Churches."
3. Simon Goldhill, *Jerusalem: City of Longing*, 2008, 73 - 81.
4. J. Zias, "The Cemeteries of Qumran and Celibacy: Confusion Laid to Rest," *Dead Sea Discoveries 7*, (2000), 220-253.

DEBORAH KAHN-HARRIS

Deborah Kahn-Harris lectures in Bible at Leo Baeck College and works congregationally at Sha'arei Tsedek North London Reform Synagogue. She served as the Teaching Fellow in Judaism at the School of Oriental and African Studies from 2008-2009 and has just been appointed Principal of the Leo Baeck College.

Who Are We: An Exploration of Voice in Lamentations 5: 19-22[i]

Lamentations 5 presents an interesting contrast from the rest of the book. Whereas chapters 1-4 are all alphabetic acrostics likely written in the *qinah* metre (a three plus two rhythm of stresses) and often in the first person singular, chapter 5 differs in all these respects. It is not an alphabetic acrostic nor written in the *qinah* metre. Critically, it is not written in the first person singular, but rather in the voice of the first person plural. To whom does this voice belong ? Additionally, as verses 19-22 comprise the end of both chapter 5 and the work as a whole, I will address myself particularly to these verses and the ways in which voice functions within them.

Chapter 5 is widely regarded as a 'communal lament'. Most scholars consistently note the importance of the 'communal' or 'choral' voice, but virtually none explore what the use of this communal voice might mean in the context of Lamentations.[ii] Why employ this voice in the book's final chapter? Who is included and excluded by the use of the first person plural? Who is or who defines the community here? Ought the reader include themselves in the communal voice? What has happened to the individual voices of the previous chapters? Is God's voice part of the communal? What difference does it make if the first person plural is automatically defined as the communal?

In Lanahan's "The Speaking Voice in the Book of Lamentations", he addresses the issue of the "choral voice":

> The chorus is not simply the reporter, the city, the veteran, and the bourgeois speaking together; the chorus has its own character,

subsuming each individual *peona* in an act of prayer which transcends the viewpoints and the inadequacies which the poet perceived and expressed through the first four chapters.[iii]

Lanahan analyses Lamentations 5, describing it as 'a prayer to God to express its [the chorus's] need for relief'.[iv] Curiously, although Lanahan is writing about voice, he does not explore why this prayer should have been written in the 'choral voice' rather than in another individual voice.[v] He writes of the 'chorus' transcending the limited perspectives of the individual voices, but he does not examine the ways in which this 'chorus' might achieve such transcendence and what else may or may not be implied by or extrapolated from the use of the first person plural.

Chapter 5 begins with the voice of the first person plural never attempting to define to whom that voice (or voices) belongs, never overtly rooting itself in any of the other voices of Lamentations. Although the first usage of the first person plural appears in the middle of chapter 3, the use of 'we' there is completely different – clearly a device of the male speaking voice of chapter 3 – and no compelling evidence exists to suggest that the two should be identified as the same speaker(s).

A more interesting comparison is the 'we' of chapter 4. In verses 17-20 the 'we' voice is introduced, but is resolutely not the voice of chapter 3. This 'we' has more in common with the 'we' of chapter 5 – the 'we' is more challenging to identify and less clear in its purpose. Re'emi suggests that this shift of voice is reflective of the author's participation in the events recounted.[vi] Berlin posits that the shift of voice may represent "the speaker's move from being an objective observer to being a member of the Judean community."[vii] Provan, however, concludes that 'we' here is simply the people of Zion, though without any attempt to describe who those people might encompass.[viii]

Returning to chapter 5, to whom might the 'we' voice belong? To an amalgam of the other voices contained in the book of Lamentations? To undefined others who have yet to speak in Lamentations? To survivors living in Jerusalem or exiles in Babylon? To a sort of Greek chorus not yet identified? To the generations of readers? No way exists of knowing to whom the voice belongs definitively, precisely because at one level the use of the first person plural form from beginning to end in chapter 5 with no other identifying markers, has the effect of anonymizing the voice. The first person plural here is both everyone and no one at all.

The consistent identification of the first person plural voice as the communal voice is problematic. The use of the term 'communal' already ascribes a decision by the exegete about to whom the voice belongs. Who the exegete believes the community to have been may well colour the ways in which s/he interprets this chapter. 'Communal' may also colour the ways in which the reader understands this chapter. The use of the term 'communal' has had the effect of turning the 'we' into a sort of collective. Even I am using the singular 'voice' as opposed to reflecting the plurality inherent in the first person plural and using 'voices'. In framing chapter 5 as a communal lament, exegetes have masked the plurality of the 'we'; they have effectively rendered it singular, even if the intention is collective.

Additionally, the term 'communal' erases any sense of the anonymity in this voice, the ways in which whoever authored this text has been able to give voice to their own concerns while remaining secretive about to whom the voice belongs. Authorship then becomes an issue of contention. Unlike the previous chapters where an editorial voice creeps into the text, in chapter 5 nothing so overt occurs. If, however, Lamentations were the product of a school/group of authors, like the Temple singers, the first person plural might make more sense. Chapter 5's first person plural would reflect the plurality of the authorial voice, a direct personification in the text of the Temple singers or some other form of collective authorship. Could the plurality of chapter 5 reflect a genuine plurality in authorship of the text and what would it mean if it did?

The use of the first person plural presents yet more vexing problems. Who is included and who is excluded in this voice? Could women have been part of this plural voice? Given the lack of gender differentiation in the first person plural of Biblical Hebrew, no way exists to tell whether women are intentionally included or excluded. In "The Mark of Gender" Monique Wittig describes the problem of pronouns as markers of gender and, crucially, in the sense 'that they represent persons'.[ix] She writes,

> …although they [pronouns] are instrumental in activating the notion of gender, they pass unnoticed. … pronouns mark the opposition of gender only in the third person and are not gender bearers, per se, in the other persons. Thus, it is as though gender does not affect them, is not part of their structure, but only a detail in their associated forms. But, in reality, as soon as there is a locutor in discourse, as soon as there is an 'I,' gender manifests itself. There is a kind of suspension of

grammatical form. A direct interpellation of the locator occurs. The locutor is called upon in person.[x]

And who the locutor is in Lamentations 5 is the question at hand. From a semantic standpoint Lamentations clearly contains the female voice of Zion in earlier chapters, which could mean that part of the plural voice in chapter 5 belongs to women. As Wittig points out,

> One knows that, in French, with *je* ('I'), one must mark the gender as soon as one uses it in relation to past participle and adjectives. In English, where the same kind of obligation does not exist, a locutor, when a sociological woman, must in one way or another, that is, with a certain number of clauses, make her sex public.[xi]

The problem for the first person of biblical Hebrew is similar to English in that neither the perfect nor the imperfect marks the gender. Like French an adjective would mark gender, but adjectives in relation to the first person plural would only be grammatically feminine if the entire group speaking were feminine, the masculine being employed both for groups solely comprised of men and for mixed groups. Therefore, if the first person plural of Lamentations 5 does contain the voice of women as part of a mixed group, the reader must be attuned to other signals that enable the sociological woman to 'make her sex public'.

What would these signals be? If the first person plural of chapter 5 were the collective voice of the Temple singers, we might posit that women may not have been included and, moreover, that the collective was a highly limited entity, deriving from an elite social group.[xii] Yet it remains impossible to prove conclusively whether women should or should not be considered part of the plural voice of Lamentations 5.

For the post-modern reader, another key question must be to what extent is the reader meant to identity with the 'we' of Lamentations 5. To what extent am I, the reader, the exegete, contained within this voice? How does imagining myself as part of this voice influence my reading of the text? For Dobbs-Allsopp the 'we' voice of chapters 3, 4 and 5 is linked precisely because he understands this voice to co-opt the reader purposefully, rendering the readers as the 'third embodiment of suffering' in Lamentations.[xiii] Dobbs-Allsopp understands that:

This final rendition of suffering again travels over the same geography of pain as was traversed earlier. The difference is that this time it is explicitly the reader's pain and the reader's suffering, which makes all the difference. The screams and atrocities and protests that these poems figure are thus coercively superimposed on the reader so that they are felt and understood and experienced and finally voiced as the reader's own.[xiv]

For me, chapter 5 feels naturally like a space to which I might belong. I find reading this anonymous 'we' and not making some assumption about my own inclusion challenging. Particularly in verses 19-22 I am co-opted by the 'we' voice. In these final lines of both the chapter and the book, the subject shifts from a description of the horrors that have befallen the people to a plea to God, a small petitionary prayer that seems torn between hope and despair. The tone changes in verse 19; the enumeration of tragedies ceases and is replaced with a declaration of God's eternal enthronement. Verses 20-22 then reveal overpowering tension between the eternally enthroned God and God's unending abandonment of the people. As a rabbi, I find reading a prayer without looking for myself within it impossible.

The use of Lamentations 5: 21 in the Jewish liturgy encourages an even closer connection for me to this text. I cannot read this verse without hearing the liturgy ringing in my ears. Lamentations 5: 21 appears as the final line at the close of the Torah service and also on Yom Kippur during the *shema kolienu*. When I sing these words, I do so as prayer, as a line of liturgy emanating from my own lips, my own desire to communicate with God. I automatically include myself in the plural voice, which I hear as the voice of myself and my community (and often literally as the 'choral' voice).

Reading the book of Lamentations in the synagogue on Tisha B'Av further reinforces the sense of inclusion that I, as a reader, feel. The destruction of the Temple is not a distant past to which modern Jews have no connection, but rather, an event we should consider as though it happened to us. Reading Lamentations at Tisha B'Av becomes a personal reference point, heavily influenced by the possibility inherent in the text of reading one's own self into the first person plural of chapter 5.

And so what happens if these final verses of Lamentations are imagined as a multi-vocal plurality rather than a monolithic whole? As a partial response to that question, I have composed a contemporary midrash as a modern, feminist rejoinder to the biblical text. In my midrash I offer one possible reading of Lamentations 5: 21-22:

Zion said: 'Return us, Eternal One, to You' but the Man-who-has-known-affliction hastily added: 'But we shall surely return'. And together: 'Renew our days as in ancient times.' But Zion in her sorrow grew anxious: 'For if you have utterly despised us, have been exceedingly wroth against us,' and the Man-who-has-known-affliction was struck down, just at that moment; thus the rabbis added: 'Return us, Eternal One, to You and we shall return, renew our days as in ancient times.'

Here I imagine verses 21-22 as a dialogue. First, the use of *nashuva* struck me. In this construction the verb is used rarely in the Bible. Where it refers to return to God, it appears only three times – here, Hosea 6:1 and Lamentations 3:40. In both Lamentations 3 and Hosea 6 the verb is spoken by a man calling forcefully to the people to return to God. Therefore, I have placed *nashuva* in the mouth of a male voice. Returning to the beginning of the verse, I realised that parallelism was not at work – *hashivenu*, though employing the same root, appeals for something different. *Hashivenu* as the causative plea is not a call to the people to return, but rather a call to God to enable return. I heard within that plea the voice of anger and despair – You caused these traumas, God; therefore, You are responsible for ensuring our return is possible. That voice is surely Zion, who angrily and desperately recalls her anguish in Lamentations 1-2. So *hashivenu* became her voice; *nashuva* became the voice of the Man of Lam 3; and the desire for a return to ancient times, a shared voice. When next the despair returns, I could not hear the Man of Lamentations 3 anymore; he is persistently the hopeful voice of Lamentations. The anguish and hopelessness of the final verse must be the final words of Zion. But why did the Man not reply? Perhaps because despite his hope, he was no longer physically able to. So who is left to reply, to counter the terrifying possibility that the final verse may true? Only those who no longer reside in the text are left to reply and according to ancient Jewish tradition that reply comes in the repetition of the penultimate verse. In all public recitations of Lamentations in the Jewish community, the penultimate verse of the book is repeated at the end.[xv] We do not end on words of reproach according to the rabbis, so with their words, their voices, I ended my midrash – making it simultaneously the voices of antiquity and my modern voice. Whose voice does my midrash really represent in the end? Whose theology does it secretly reveal?

These three voices – the voice of Zion, the Man and the post-biblical community – become the voices which I hear in Lamentations. Are these the actual voices of Lamentations 5 or are there others? Is our voice in the text? From Rabbi Tony Bayfield, my teacher, mentor and colleague, I have learned that our own life experiences are a rich source of theology, our voices are as fundamental to Judaism as any others. Here I have imagined what happens when we combine those voices – the voices of the ancient and the modern – when we meld them together to cross time and space to create a theology of our own.

1. A version of this essay was originally delivered at the Jewish-Christian Bible Week at Haus Ohrbeck, Germany in 2009.
2. Mintz discusses the use of the first person plural in ch. 3, but only in passing regarding ch. 5. Dobbs-Allsopp briefly explores the first person plural in chs. 3-5.
3. Lanahan, pg. 48. The reporter, the city, the veteran and the bourgeois are Lanahan's shorthand for the voices in Lam 1-4.
4. Ibid, pg. 49.
5. Provan, pg. 125: "In Greek and Latin mss., the fifth poem bears the title 'A prayer' or 'a prayer of the prophet Jeremiah'…; also Berlin, pp. 114, 116; Hillers, pg. 155; Dobbs-Allsopp, 2002, pg. 140; Re'emi, pg. 127.
6. Re'emi, pg. 123.
7. Berlin, pg. 112. Also see Provan, pg. 120.
8. Provan, pg. 121.
9. Wittig, pg. 78.
10. Ibid, pg. 79. Wittig writes regarding French and English pronouns. In relation to Biblical Hebrew grammar her points need slight alteration since both second and third person pronouns are bearers of gender, but her point remains true for the first person.
11. Ibid.
12. The Temple singers appear to be derived from or related to the Levites (Neh 11:22), making them socially elite within Israelite society. See Renkema, pp. 52-53 for a fuller description of the Temple singers. Ezra 2:41 and Nehemiah 7:44 identify the Temple singers as *bnei yosef*, normally translated as 'the sons of Asaph', but might equally mean 'the children of Asaph. In the context of these passages, which are a list of those who came out of exile in Babylon, the assumption must be that only men are discussed. I Chr 25:2-7 contains a more complete genealogy of the sons of Asaph: "God gave Heman fourteen sons and three daughters; all

these were under the charge of their father for the singing in the House of the Lord...", implying that Heman's three daughters were among the Temple singers. These women were still socially elite and under the charge of a patriarch, but they represent the possibility that women numbered among the Temple singers during the period of the Chronicler (a period substantially later than the composition of Lamentations). Even this discussion itself substantiates the main point that determining whether or not women are to be included when the biblical text employs the plural is exceedingly difficult.

13. Dobbs-Allsopp, pg. 34-35.
14. Ibid.
15. According to Rashi to Lam 5: 23 (The text that Rashi comments from already knows this tradition; hence, Lam 5: 23 is the repetition of Lam 5: 21.) : 'In order that one does not conclude with words of reproof it is necessary to repeat the previous verse again and thus with Isaiah, Twelve [Minor Prophets] and Ecclesiastes'. The tradition of repeating v. 21 predates Rashi; though, the tradition does not appear in the Talmud.

Bibliography

Berlin, A. 2002 *Lamentations: A Commentary*, Old Testament Library Series, Louisville: Westminster John Knox Press.

Dobbs-Allsopp, F.W. 2002 *Lamentations*, Interpretation Bible Series, Louisville: John Knox Press.

Hillers, D. R. 1984 *Lamentations*, Anchor Bible Series, Garden City, New York: Doubleday and Company, Inc.

Lanahan, W. March 1974 "The Speaking Voice in the Book of Lamentations", *Journal of Biblical Literature 93*.

Mintz, A. January 1982 "The Rhetoric of Lamentations and the Representations of Catastrophe", *Prooftexts*, Vol. 2, No. 1, pp. 1-17

Provan, I. W. 1991 *Lamentations*, New Century Bible Commentary Series, Grand Rapids: William B. Eerdmans.

Re'emi, S. P. 1984 *God's People in Crisis: A Commentary on the Book of Lamentations*, International Theological Commentary Series, Edinburgh: The Handsel Press Ltd.

Wittig, M. 1992 "The Mark of Gender", *The Straight Mind and Other Essays*, New York: Harvester Wheatsheaf, pp. 76-89.

JOSH LEVY

Josh Levy is a rabbi at Alyth where he oversees the conversion programme. The treatment of conversion in rabbinic literature is an area of particular interest, having written his rabbinic thesis on the minor tractate *Gerim*. He believes that Reform conversion reflects the authentic Palestinian tradition of openness and welcome.

Are Reform Converts Real Converts?

British Reform Conversion and Halachah

The title is, of course, deliberately provocative. The legitimacy of Reform conversions is not really the question. The product of a Reform conversion is recognised as a convert ex post facto by the majority of world Jewry. Those who argue otherwise do so from a position in which Jewish practice is judged against a standard set by Orthodox *poskim*, and in their hands alone is the authority to decide who is inside and who is outside the Jewish community. This is not our position. Nor is it tenable for the future of world Jewry.

Nonetheless, it is instructive to consider our practices in the light of halachic discourse, if only to establish those areas in which we position ourselves in tension with Orthodox halachah and why. In the area of conversion, this is an especially complex question, with disagreement as to what constitutes normative halachah. Within early halachic literature there are multiple models of conversion, not all of which are compatible with one another. Moreover, the halachah of conversion has continued to adapt, and in some places been radically transformed, even since the medieval period. In analysing the relationship between Reform conversion and halachah, it is therefore not sufficient to cite a particular position as 'normative halachah'. Instead it is necessary to identify strands within conversion literature and to examine how Reform conversions are placed within these strands.

Discourse in the halachah of conversion can be divided into two broad areas. The first is the **ritual process of conversion** – what are the required components in any transformative ritual? The second area, more subjective, is the **judgements made by a status-conferring authority** concerning the motivation and commitment of the potential convert. These two areas correspond to two different paradigms of conversion in halachic discourse, with differing views of how to judge the legitimacy of a conversion process. Though there are differences between Reform practice and Orthodox halachah in the first area, our conversions broadly contain the same core elements. In the second area there is far greater divergence, reflecting the enormous disparity between Orthodox and Progressive views of a meaningful Jewish life.

The ritual process of conversion
The core elements of the ritual process of conversion are found in two baraitot in Tractate Yevamot of the Babylonian Talmud. In Yevamot 46a we find a Tannaitic dispute as to the essential steps for conversion which ends with the statement:

> The Sages say: one who immersed but did not circumcise or circumcised but did not immerse is not a convert until he circumcises and immerses.

The requirement for both circumcision and immersion is codified in post-Talmudic material, for example in Maimonides' Mishneh Torah (1).

The two core elements of circumcision and immersion are also found in a further baraita in Yevamot 47a-b (2) which gives the template of the rabbinic conversion procedure. This baraita, which is presented without substantive variation in the great medieval codes, has been subject to detailed analysis by a number of scholars (3). The baraita adds two further elements to the conversion ritual, examination and instruction. The examination of a prospective convert consists of a defined question (What do you see that you come to be converted? Do you not know that the Jewish people at this time are pained, oppressed, harassed and torn, and that afflictions come upon them?) and response (I know and am unworthy). The process of instruction in the baraita is complex. It consists of making known a selection of commandments, with specific reference to agricultural gifts to the poor, instruction in the punishment for transgression of commandments, especially the laws of forbidden fats and of Shabbat, and discussion of the reward for observing the commandments. Importantly, the baraita maintains that "we do not overwhelm him, nor are we too detailed with him", before moving on to circumcision and immersion.

In later halachah these additional aspects of examination and instruction are understood to represent a more substantial process of enquiry as to motivation and a requirement for acceptance of the Torah. However, in the baraita, the examination and instruction process appears to be primarily of a ritual function. It does not require assent other than the set response to examination, and an obscure reference after instruction, that *kibel* – he accepts. As the Israeli scholars Avi Sagi and Zvi Zohar have suggested, the cognitive component within this model of conversion is minimal. Rather, in this model, and indeed in most Talmudic sources, "giyyur [is understood] as a ritual process focused upon the body of the proselyte... such a model is not grounded in cognitive commitment." (4) The model of conversion in Yevamot does not address motivation, nor does it require an explicit acceptance of Torah, but instruction in a limited selection of mitzvot.

The model of conversion process found within Yevamot therefore presents four ritual elements, all of which are found within a British Reform conversion: examination; a process of instruction; circumcision; ritual immersion. Of these, the physical requirements of circumcision and immersion are the key elements in transformation of identity, and both are required of our candidates for conversion. Immersion for conversion did fall out of use in British Reform during the twentieth century, but was reintroduced in 1980 following "a broad consensus in the Assembly of Rabbis that the procedure for conversion should, wherever possible, be in conformity with traditional practice" (5). Circumcision for conversion has never fallen out of practice in British Reform Judaism. According to a resolution of the Central Conference of American Rabbis in 1892, a Reform rabbi in America *may* perform conversions "without any initiatory rite, ceremony, or observance whatever"(6). This is not our practice.

Conversion without circumcision

Reform conversion may differ in regard to the core physical requirements presented in Yevamot where a candidate presents with factors demanding special consideration. Most significantly, conversion is allowed without circumcision where medical complications make circumcision impossible.

This is counter to the position of normative Orthodox halachah, which finds itself caught in an unfortunate catch-22, expressed well by the Orthodox writer Maurice Lamm:

The rabbis hold that jeopardizing a gentile's life for the sake of converting to Judaism is not only against Jewish law it is also a desecration of God's name... On the other hand, the Rabbis were not given the right to set aside circumcision, regardless of circumstances. Therefore this candidate may not be accepted (7).

This is the position also of the Conservative and Masorti movements whose responsum on the subject quotes a number of Orthodox halachic authorities before concluding that:

If a man has a serious medical threat to life or health which cannot later be resolved in his life, then he should be advised that acceptance into the Jewish faith through Halachic conversion is impossible for him, and that he be encouraged to follow the seven Noachide Laws and be considered among the "righteous gentiles" of the world. (8)

The Reform decision not to adhere to strict Orthodox halachic practice in this case does not reflect a lack of commitment to circumcision as a core component of conversion, but rather reflects a difference in understanding of what constitutes appropriate application of Jewish law. Primarily, this is the belief that strict law should be balanced by *rachmanut* - compassion. To preclude someone who wholeheartedly wishes to become a part of the Jewish people and to come under the protection of the *Shechinah* on the basis of complications in physical or mental health is to place the strict application of Jewish law over the Jewish demand for mercy and compassion. Furthermore, the demands of equality - that we are all created *B'tzelem Elohim*, in the image of God – make it discriminatory to preclude someone from Jewish identity on the basis of physical or mental health conditions.

Modern halachic discussion about this problem has come to contain uncomfortably extreme symbolic language. Excessive importance is now attached to the foreskin as a source of impurity and of gentile identity. This suggests, for example, that the removal of the foreskin removes the 'abomination of gentilehood' (9) without which Jewishness cannot be attained or that the foreskin is inherently impure, and therefore lack of circumcision is an obstacle to the efficacy of ritual immersion for conversion. These positions are not ones which can carry any weight in modern progressive Jewish discourse. The fundamental issue is whether circumcision can ever be set aside in order to accommodate someone whose physical or mental health makes it too dangerous to proceed. Orthodox Halachah says no. British Reform Judaism says yes.

The judgements made by a Beit Din

The second broad area within the halachah of conversion concerns judgements made by a Beit Din. This area includes aspects of Orthodox Halachah such as the definition of an authoritative court and the recent halachah of retroactive annulment of conversions. These reflect a different model of conversion to that presented above, one in which conversion is not primarily a ritual process but a cognitive process. Legitimacy of conversion is determined not by process but by the motivation and commitment of the potential proselyte. This area represents the greatest divergence between Reform practice and Orthodox halachah, not because Reform Judaism sees conversion as a non-cognitive process, but because of the different understanding of what constitutes a legitimate Jewish life.

Motivation for conversion

One of the most common critiques of Reform conversion is that it is a conversion of convenience for those with inappropriate motivation. Such criticisms fail to recognise the diversity within halachic literature on the relevance of motivation to conversion. Within mainstream halachic discourse it is possible to find three distinct positions:

An extreme strict position, in which anyone found to have converted for any reason other than the 'sake of Heaven' is not a legitimate convert. This position has recently come to the fore in ultra-Orthodox halachah, especially in Israel. A possible source for this position can be found in the minor tractate Gerim 1:3, which states: "Anyone who does not convert for the sake of heaven is not a convert".

An extreme lenient position, in which motivation is not a relevant factor for conversion. Those known to be of ulterior motivation are still to be welcomed and recognised as converts. This is sometimes, erroneously, presented as the position of British Reform conversions. Even if this were the case, it would be well grounded in halachic material. It is the implied position of Yevamot, in which, as we noted above, motivation is not brought as a factor. It is also consistent with the position of Rav that:

> The halachah is that [those converting with a motive other than the sake of Heaven] are legitimate converts. We do not push them away in the way that we push away converts at the beginning, but we accept

them. And they require a cordial reception. Perhaps they [will come to] have converted for the sake of the Name (10).

A middle position in which motivation is relevant at the time of conversion but converts later discovered to be of inappropriate motivation are still converts. This was normative halachah for most authorities in the medieval period (11). Within this position, there is a division between those authorities who maintain that the existence of any 'ulterior motive' precludes a Beit Din from allowing conversion, and others who maintain that a dual motivation that includes both an 'ulterior motive' and the desire to convert for the sake of Heaven is considered legitimate.

My observation of current British Reform practice is that it is the latter position that best reflects the practice of our Beit Din. Potential converts coming to our Beit Din are questioned about their motivation. A candidate who was converting solely and openly for an ulterior reason, with no personal relationship with Jewish practice and identity would not be allowed by their sponsoring rabbi to come before a Beit Din. Of course, as some Orthodox authorities have also observed, it is very unlikely in the modern world that, without coercion, someone without a level of personal engagement would come forward for conversion at all. It might therefore be reasonable to make a presumption of 'conversion for the sake of Heaven'. The nineteenth century Salonikan authority, Rabbi Samuel Matalon wrote, for example, of the conversion of a woman in a relationship with a Jewish man:

> There is no concern here that her *giyyur* is motivated by her interest to marry him, as she is already living in his house, and they behave as a couple, and she lacks for nothing. What might then be her further gain if she were to convert, if not that her intention is 'for the sake of Heaven'? (12)

Acceptance of the mitzvot

Perhaps the fundamental question in the discussion of motivation for conversion is the definition of conversion for the 'sake of Heaven'. Within Orthodox halachah, this is inextricably linked with the idea of *kabbalat mitzvot* - the acceptance of the commandments. This requirement is presented most clearly in a baraita in the Tosefta, Demai 5:2, which is also repeated in the Babylonian Talmud, Bechorot 30b:

A proselyte who took upon himself all matters of Torah excepting one thing, they don't accept him. Rabbi Jose son of Rabbi Judah says: even [excepting] a small matter enacted by the scribes.

Acceptance of the mitzvot has become the defining feature of Orthodox conversion. Maurice Lamm writes: "The entire conversion process hinges on this one theme - committing one's life to keeping the tradition", continuing, "If a convert... rejects the practice of a specific mitzvah... he disqualifies himself as a credible candidate for conversion" (13).

Within Orthodox conversion, *kabbalat mitzvot* is not merely a ritual requirement, but for most authorities, also requires sincere intent to keep the mitzvot. In effect, *kabbalat mitzvot* has become the primary evidence for legitimate motivation for conversion. When taken with an extreme strict position on motivation, by which those who convert without appropriate motivation are not to be recognised as converts, this has become the halachic justification for retroactive annulment of conversions (14). Failure to keep mitzvot in later life is taken to be evidence of a lack of sincerity at the time of conversion, thereby invalidating the conversion process.

Kabbalat mitzvot is the requirement at which Reform practice diverges most clearly from Orthodox halachah. Reform conversion does not require acceptance of the yoke of the commandments. It does require a comprehensive process of instruction in how to live a Jewish life, consistent with the model in Yevamot. It also includes an expectation that Jewish practice will be an enduring part of a convert's life after conversion, something which we might consider to be a *de facto* acceptance of the *concept* of Jewish obligation. However, there is no requirement to commit to specific aspects of Jewish law. Any requirement of *kabbalat mitzvot* would be incompatible with a number of key aspects of Reform Jewish ideology:

1. That there are certain mitzvot that we no longer recognise as binding or indeed as ethically acceptable.

2. That we are committed to responsible personal autonomy. This is incompatible with a demand on an individual to commit to certain practices.

3. That we are committed to individual growth and change, recognising that an individual's life may change, and their relationship with Judaism may change with it.

4. That we are committed to equality. Recognising that many born-Jews do not commit to Jewish practice, in all denominational movements, we can not ask more of those who choose to join us than we do of ourselves.

In this aspect, there is no question that Reform conversion practice is not in line with Orthodox halachah. Nor could it be and still reflect our understanding of Jewish life and practice.

Are Reform converts real converts ?

This essay has provided a brief survey of a number of strands in the halachah of conversion. We have seen that the ritual process of conversion in the British Reform movement would, without question, be recognisable as a Jewish conversion to the Talmudic sage. The core elements of the rabbinic conversion are found in our practice. Where we deviate here from Orthodox, and Conservative, practice we do so out of a commitment to a Law that does not discriminate and cause pain but is applied in a way which shows compassion for the needs of the individual. We have also seen that our perspective on legitimate motivation for conversion is not incompatible with perspectives found within mainstream halachic discourse. It is only on the question of *Kabbalat Mitzvot*, which is fundamentally incompatible with Reform ideology and our understanding of a legitimate Jewish life, that Reform practice diverges spectacularly from modern Orthodox halachah.

However, the most fundamental difference between the Reform approach to conversion and that of Orthodox halachah is not one that we have addressed. We actively welcome converts. We recognise that they add a great deal to our communities. We reject mainly Babylonian traditions that regard them with suspicion, which lead to the building of high walls topped with halachic barbed wire to keep them out. We are heirs to a Palestinian tradition (15) which is comfortable with those who attach themselves to the Jewish community and believes them to be special – for us and for God. In truth, it matters not if our converts are considered 'real converts' by others. They are ours, and they are *gerei tzedek* – converts of righteousness.

1. Mishneh Torah, Issurei Biah 13:4
2. A variant source of this baraita exists in the minor tractate Gerim 1:1
3. The best published examples are Shaye J D Cohen, *The Beginnings of Jewishness*, University of California Press, 1999: chapter 7; Avi Sagi and Zvi Zohar, *Transforming Identity*, The Kogod Library of Judaic Studies, 2007: chapter 7.
4. Sagi and Zohar, 2007: p116
5. Assembly of Rabbis leaflet on Tevilah, 1992
6. For a discussion of this resolution and its aftermath, see Richard Rosenthal, Without Milah and Tevilah in Walter Jacob and Moshe Zemer, *Conversion to Judaism in Jewish Law*, Rodef Shalom Press, 1994.
7. Maurice Lamm, *Becoming a Jew*, New York, 1991: p217
8. Kassel Abelson and David J. Fine, editors, *Responsa: 1991-2000*, The Committee on Jewish Law and Standards of the Conservative Movement: p132-136
9. Quoted in Sagi and Zohar, 2007: p283
10. Yerushalmi Kiddushin 4:1
11. See, for example, Mishneh Torah Issurei Biah 13:14. As is widely acknowledged, Maimonides contradicts his own ruling on ulterior motivation in one of his responsa.
12. quoted in Sagi and Zohar, 2007: p41
13. Lamm, 1991: p209, 211
14. A good example of this is the 1983 responsum of the Israeli ultra-Orthodox rabbi Yosef Shalom Eliyashav
15. See, for example, Numbers Rabbah chapter 8.

JONATHAN MAGONET

Jonathan Magonet, former Principal of Leo Baeck College (1985-2005) and now Emeritus Professor of Bible, is editor of *Seder Ha-t'fillot, Forms of Prayer* (8th Edition) of the Movement for Reform Judaism, and of the journal European Judaism. He is regularly engaged in interfaith dialogue with Christians and Muslims.

Sixty-Five Years of Progressive Judaism in Europe

It is both a pleasure and a privilege to contribute to this Festschrift honouring Tony Bayfield. He has been one of the leading theological thinkers in the UK Reform movement, helping it identify its ideological and spiritual position. A similar task remains to be done in the broader European scene, particularly as the various progressive movements across the Continent gain in numbers, self-confidence, authority and responsibility.

In 1946 in London was held the first post-war conference of the World Union for Progressive Judaism. Rabbi Dr Leo Baeck, already in his seventies, gave the Presidential address. He said:

> Since the last conference of our World Union a terrible ordeal has swept over the Jewish people and over humanity....We must never forget what we have lost and whom we have lost. (1)

But rather than dwelling on the past, Dr Baeck looked towards the future. He spoke of two kinds of Judaism. The first he characterized as a 'little Judaism', one that concerned itself primarily with the building of congregational life. He pointed out that:

> The Congregation is the living germ-cell of Jewish life. Judaism cannot live without the Jewish Congregation; but the Congregation is not the ultimate purpose; it is not an end in itself. It is there for the

sake of Judaism, for the sake of the great Jewish whole; in that only has it its true life. That must never be forgotten. (2)

Alongside this 'little Judaism' he urged commitment to a 'greater Judaism':

Judaism must not stand aside, when the great problems of humanity, which are reborn in every new epoch, struggle in the minds of men to gain expression, battle in the societies of mankind to find their way. We must not, as Jews, deny ourselves to the problems of the time, nor hide ourselves, as Jews, in face of them; they must not be something that goes on outside our Judaism, in another sphere. We are Jews also for the sake of humanity; we should be there, quite especially in this world after the war; we have our questions to raise and have to give our answer. To rouse the conscience of humanity could here be our best title-deed. (3)

Baeck concluded by speaking of two things that were essential for this new period. The first was Jewish learning, and the need to re-establish it after so many 'treasure houses of the mind were demolished or scattered' (4). But the other aspect was the universal task:

We believe in the dawn of light, in the dawn of our light. We should begin again, take up again what was interrupted. We shall ourselves grow stronger in giving to others; 'the Ark of the Covenant will bear those who bear it.'We shall see clearer in showing others. We shall gain the wider outlook in striving to guide others. (5)

Three years later, in 1949, the World Union for Progressive Judaism Conference again took place in London. In his Presidential Address, Dr Baeck with true prophetic insight introduced another element of significance for the Jewish future:

And now Islam, too, has again moved into the close neighbourhood, the inescapable proximity of the Jewish spirit; once more, as in a great period of the Middle Ages, the two are regarding each other. Today they are almost compelled to face each other, not only in the sphere of policy, but also in the sphere of religion; there is the great hope, maybe one turning to some remote future – but mankind lives also on remote hopes – that thus they will behold each other and then meet each other on joint roads, in joint tasks, in joint confidence in the future. There is the great hope that Judaism can thus become the builder of a bridge, the 'pontifex' between East and West. (6)

Baeck's distinction between 'little Judaism' and 'greater Judaism' raises many challenges. On the whole the past sixty-five years have seen the main emphasis within Jewish life on the former. Particularly in continental Europe Jewish communities have struggled to rebuild their infrastructure with the focus primarily on internal communal, welfare and social needs.

Dr. Baeck had spoken of the need for Jewish learning and to replace the destroyed 'treasure houses of the mind'. Though the idea of creating a seminary in England to replace those that had been destroyed by the Nazis was already mooted in the early 1940s, it was only in 1956 that what was to be called the Jewish Theological College of London was opened. Dr. Baeck died shortly after, and the College was renamed Leo Baeck College in his honour. Ten years after its creation there was already beginning to emerge a new sense of purpose for the progressive Jewish communities in the UK and Continental Europe, but a purpose not confined to immediate Jewish concerns alone.

1966 saw the creation of the journal *European Judaism*, edited by Dr. Ignaz Maybaum, describing itself as *A Journal for the New Europe*. The editorial board was made up of younger rabbis associated with the College and the Reform and Liberal movements in the UK. The first editorial included a prediction about the future that would only be realized thirty years later:

> No account of world Jewry today can ignore the Jews of the Soviet Union. Even if the dream of the Eurocrats of a 'Comecon' embracing countries east of the Iron Curtain is slow in materializing, future political events could suddenly re-unite the Jews of Russia with their brethren in Europe. A strong and independent European Jewry can hope to see itself as the natural link between world Jewry and a slowly emancipated Russian Jewish community. (7)

In looking for a role for European Jewry between the two great centres of Jewish life, Israel and the United States, the editorial tried to define its situation and potential:

> European Judaism faces a unique task, basically imposed by neither political power nor affluence, but by the need to help the Jew play his

part creatively in a unifying Europe, while at the same time acting as a guardian of the Europe of the past. The Jew can become the exponent of all that is best in regionalism in the midst of the new supra-nationalism....

Influences from the two most powerful Jewries, the United States and Israel will continue to intersect in Europe. A European community confident in its own Judaism, and its unique position, will not be adversely influenced by such cross-currents. It will look towards both the New World and the new State for material, intellectual and religious strength, but on the basis of independence; our own seminaries, our own religious, cultural and secular institutions, our own energies concentrated on re-building European Judaism as a distinctive religious force. ..... For there can be no successor to the great European Jewish heritage except a reborn European Judaism itself.

One of the first graduates of the Leo Baeck College was Rabbi Lionel Blue. In 1964 he was appointed Religious Director of the European Board of the World Union for Progressive Judaism. His task involved helping develop the various emerging Progressive Jewish communities in Europe and it was my privilege to accompany him from time to time as Chairman of the Youth Section of the World Union. Part of our task was to find potential candidates to study for the rabbinate at Leo Baeck College. This led to a number of conferences, the first in the Anne Frank House in Amsterdam in 1964.

Writing in the first issue of *European Judaism* Lionel Blue echoes the concerns of Dr. Baeck, but from his own particular perspective:

Survival cannot be synthetic, but a by-product of purpose. Since the war major efforts have gone into rebuilding synagogues. This is the bread and butter of every Jewish organization. Hardly anyone, however, has concerned himself with what should be said inside the synagogues. As a result the young people do not attend them. The décor is contemporary, but the sermons are not.

What can the Jew give? Much more than he usually thinks. He does not, though, naturally ask this question. The nineteenth century posed a different problem – what could modern Europe give the Jew? Citizenship, liberalism, higher education, were fought for and achieved. Few considered the question in reverse. This is the key question, and I give a personal and tentative answer.

Jews have become European before the unity of Europe has been established. No other group received so much from the nineteenth century European enlightenment, and no other group is so dependent on its success for its own survival. Nationalism, authoritarianism and irrationalism, whether on the left or the right, have had as their most obvious enemy the Jewish, bourgeois, liberal culture of central and western Europe. The surviving Jewish communities can either opt out of the struggle, or give a lead to a European unity which goes deeper than tariff and tax changes. (8)

Insofar as there was a reaction to the appearance of the journal and its perception of a new European Jewry, it was sceptical. Such 'prophetic' understanding of a Jewish role was far ahead of its time. The members of the editorial board of the journal represented a young generation of Progressive rabbis, some with refugee childhoods, who were very much in the vanguard of a postwar quest for a new kind of Jewish identity. Students from Leo Baeck College, under the auspices of the Youth Section of the World Union for Progressive Judaism, organized the first international Jewish student conference since the war in Berlin in 1965. In 1969 I became involved in what was to become the Annual Jewish-Christian Bible Week, in Bendorf, now transferred to Haus Ohrbeck, Osnabrueck. Lionel Blue himself became one of the pioneers of Jewish-Christian-Muslim dialogue through conferences that began in the mid sixties at the Evangelische Akademie in Berlin with Pastor Winfried Maechler. Writing in 1975 in *European Judaism*, in an issue devoted to the three religious traditions, Rabbi Blue could reflect on the results of several years experience in this work as founder and vice-chairman of the Standing Conference of Jews, Christians and Muslims in Europe (JCM). He noted the ignorance of Islam amongst Jews as one of the first obstacles to be addressed, but also the challenges ahead once the familiar Jewish-Christian dialogue had to accommodate a new partner:

The pattern of Jewish-Christian dialogue is now known. It has progressed from compliments to honesty, and since Vatican II the two religious groups encounter each other not to continue more sophisticated forms of mediaeval disputations, but to learn from each other and, if necessary, borrow from each other. The needs of

European society after the holocaust have forced the dialogue to deepen....

> The religious terminology of Europe has a Christian basis....Although Jews have little understanding of such terms as the Trinity or the Incarnation, they do know when they do not know, and though puzzled treat these terms with a cautious respect. Muslims are missionary, and need to learn the rules and the dialectic of western European religious discussion, and the assimilation has already been half done for them by Jews.... (9)

Rabbi Blue includes a perception that has turned out to be prophetic:

> Looking to the future though, its (Islam's) basic simplicity, and the possibilities which lie within it, could produce a far greater missionary success in Europe than its religious rivals would credit. (10)

He notes the problems of such a trialogue because of the Middle East conflict, but concludes:

> The importance of the European context is that it makes such learning [about one another] both necessary and possible. In the Middle East the groups confront each other, and in America one element is completely missing. Here they all exist, and the external situation forces them into dialogue and trialogue, if only because they are too weak to do without it. (11)

The willingness to come to Germany on the part of a younger generation of rabbinic students and rabbis, and to interact positively with German Christians and later Muslims, became one of the tangible expressions of this attempt to express a 'greater Judaism', to offer a Jewish voice to a changing Europe. (12)

Nevertheless, we must jump forward more than twenty years before the broader view of a Jewish role and purpose within a new Europe became a central issue for discussion and debate. At another Conference of the European Board of the World Union for Progressive Judaism, in Munich in 1997, the first on this scale to be held in Germany since the war, Dr. Diana Pinto spoke about 'The New Jewish Europe: Challenges and

111

Responsibilities'. She noted that even to talk of a 'new Jewish Europe' almost amounts to heresy for some, particularly in the United States and Israel:

> In this view, European Jewry died at Auschwitz and, in the process, Europe became the equivalent of post-expulsion Spain, a closed chapter with respect to Jewish life. The Jews still left in Europe today are seen at best as a struggling remnant when not as a 'vanishing Diaspora', their ranks far too thin, their religious and cultural identity far too weak to generate any meaningful Jewish presence. (13)

While acknowledging these concerns Dr Pinto points to four factors that have radically changed the situation:

> 1) the fall of the Berlin Wall, marking the end of the Cold War divide and inaugurating the opening up of the European continent to the values of democratic pluralism and human rights; 2) the intensification of Christian-Jewish dialogue, culminating in the Vatican recognition of the State of Israel and in the acknowledgement of the role of the Churches in the anti-Semitism that led to the Holocaust; 3) the political and cultural transformation of the Holocaust itself, from a source of private Jewish grief to the motor of new national and European self-understanding with its correlate, the creation of an ever more vibrant Jewish space; 4) and finally (for better or for worse), the transformation of Israel into a fully responsible international actor, accountable for its deeds with respect to the central criteria of democracy and human rights. (14)

Dr Pinto goes on to indicate some of the ways in which the particularities of the Jewish situation can offer something to European society as a whole:

> Jews in Europe have another role to play in the strengthening of pluralist democracy in Europe. As the inheritors of a religious tradition which, since time immemorial, has always sought to conjugate a specific identity with universality principles, Jews must pursue this task even today. They are better equipped than most groups in the art of preserving their specificity while also militating for universal rights and values....

It goes without saying that Jews in Europe are in the front line in the combat against anti-Semitism, but they should also be in the front line with respect to the equivalent combat against racism, xenophobia and the hatred of all 'others'....Such an awareness should condition Jewish positions with respect to Europe's treatment of refugees, asylum seekers, and immigrants. Jews, especially in the West, cannot behave as though they had always been traditionally-rooted citizens of their respective countries, as though the Holocaust had never taken place. (15)

A decade after that paper the mood seems to be less optimistic. There are concerns that anti-Semitism is on the rise, both inherent forms within European society and in reaction to conflict in the Middle East. A recent study by Nick Lambert (16) points to continuing anxieties amongst the older generation of Jewish communal leadership about the process of integration and ways in which Jews may once again be excluded in a newly emerging European 'superstate'. A more positive possibility is seen in the younger generation by Alberto Senderey, the JDC, Director of Community Development, Europe, because they are more open to change and more flexible about the nature of their Jewish identity:

Europe is undergoing a process of integration where borders between the West and East are getting more and more diffusive. In this accelerating changing scenario, Jews build their Jewish identity according to a 'cut and paste' model, enriching themselves from diversity. (17)

Sixty years after Leo Baeck's distinction between a 'little Judaism' and a 'greater Judaism', we face the same choice, or rather the need to consider both aspects of Jewish life in Europe. Undoubtedly we have focused on the rebuilding of communities and infrastructure needed after the war. Nevertheless with regard the 'greater Judaism', that has all-too-often been left to individuals with a sense of mission who happen to be Jews, but who are often outside of any formal Jewish framework. Our focus is very much inward, and local.

Since I have introduced something of my own history into this talk, let me end with a personal anecdote. In 1977 I co-edited with Rabbi Lionel Blue the 7th edition of 'Forms of Prayer', the Sabbath and Daily prayerbook of the UK Reform movement. As a last minute decision we included a number of woodcuts of European synagogues, most of which had been destroyed during the Shoah. It was a form of remembering what was lost in that destruction. In 2008 the Movement published the new 8th edition (18). We debated whether or not to include the same pictures of synagogues and in the end decided not to put them in the main body of the book, but they can be found in the end covers as a reminder. We agreed instead that the new illustrations should be based on Hebrew calligraphy, and invited artists from the different Jewish communities that had been re-built or newly created since the end of the war. We were fortunate to find artists from Belgium, France, Germany, Holland, Russia, Spain and Switzerland as well as the UK, Israel and the USA. It is a small gesture to acknowledge a new reality. But perhaps it also expresses a hope about an even greater development that lies before us.

1. Quoted from John D Rayner 'The Seventy-fifth Anniversary of the World Union for Progressive Judaism' *European Judaism* 35,1 Spring 2002 144-150, 147-148.
2. Leo Baeck 'The Task of Progressive Judaism in the Post-War World' Proceedings of the Annual Conference of the World Union for Progressive Judaism, July 28th, 1946, 53-60, p 56.
3. Ibid p 56.
4. Dr. Baeck's appeal for a renewal of Jewish learning has been answered in part in recent decades. The Abraham Geiger Kolleg, Potsdam and the Levisson Instituut, Amsterdam have followed the Leo Baeck College, London and the short lived Institut International d'Etudes Hebraiques, Paris, in ordaining progressive rabbis. The phenomenal success of Limmud throughout Europe and beyond, in some ways modelled on the Frankfurt Lehrhaus, reflects a hunger to learn and teach, while programmes like Paedeia in Sweden and a variety of university courses on Jewish studies raise the academic level.
5. Ibid p 58.
6. 1949 Sixth Conference, held in London [World Union for Progressive Judaism] In Memoriam Leo Baeck (Issued by the World Union for Progressive Judaism, London – undated pamphlet) p 42.

7. Editorial *European Judaism* Vol 1, no 1 (Summer 1966) 2. During the final years of the Soviet Union students and graduates of Leo Baeck College regularly visited Refuseniks. One result of this intimate contact was the decision by the College to seek out, train and send back young men and women to become rabbis in the newly emerging post-Soviet societies.

8. Lionel Blue 'The Other Europe' *European Judaism* Vol 1, no 1 (Summer 1966) 30-34, 33.

9. Lionel Blue 'The New Paradigm of Europe' *European Judaism* Vol 9, no 1 (Winter 1974/5) 2-5, 2,3.

10. Ibid 4.

11. Ibid 5.

12. The annual Jewish-Christian-Muslim International Student conference (JCM) has now existed for more than 36 years. Throughout that time attendance at least once during their five years' training has been a requirement for all students on the rabbinic programme at Leo Baeck College. This has helped develop a broader interfaith understanding amongst generations of progressive rabbis in Europe.

13. Diana Pinto 'The New Jewish Europe: Challenges and Responsibilities' *European Judaism* Vol 31, no 2 (Autumn 1998) 3-15, 4.

14. Ibid 5.

15. Ibid 12-13.

16. Nick Lambert *Europe and the Jews in the Twenty-First Century* (Vallentine Mitchell, London 2007). See also his article 'In Hiding: The Jews of Europe' *European Judaism* Vol 40, no 2 (Autumn 2007) 71-74.

17. Alberto Senderey '"Communities and Jewish Communities in Europe", Transcript of first Plenary of the Third General Assembly of European Jewry, Budapest 20-23 May 2004' *European Judaism* Vol 38, no 2 (Autumn 2005) 99-114, 114.

18. *Seder Ha-t'fillot (Forms of Prayer: Daily, Sabbath and Occasional Prayers)* 8th Edition (The Movement for Reform Judaism, London 2008.

CHARLES MIDDLEBURGH

Charles Middleburgh is Hon. Director of Studies at Leo Baeck College where he has taught since 1984, and a graduate of University College London. He also serves the Progressive Jewish Celts of Ireland and Wales, and is an occasional lecturer at the Irish School of Ecumenics, Trinity College, Dublin.

The Pernicious Primate

Towards the end of the prayer entitled *Ribbon Kol HaOlamim*, Sovereign of all worlds, is a small phrase which states, '*u-motar ha-adam min ha-be-heymah ayin ...*'. In the latest version of *Forms of Prayer* (1) it is translated – 'even our superiority over the animals amounts to nothing'; in the Liberal *Siddur Lev Chadash* (2) – 'our superiority over other animals amounts to little'; in the Conservative Rabbinical Assembly's *Siddur Sim Shalom* (3) the text is translated 'human pre-eminence over beasts is an illusion'; in *My People's Prayer Book* vol.5 (4) edited by Rabbi Lawrence A. Hoffman we find 'man barely rises above beast'; the 'Birnbaum' *siddur* (5) has 'man is not far above beast'; and the 'Sacks' *siddur* (6)'the pre-eminence of man over the animals is nothing'.

Comparison of these renditions shows considerable commonality but only two, it seems to me, have it exactly right – the versions of *Siddur Lev Chadash* (for which I must put my hand up and admit that I fought to have the word 'other' inserted, even though it has no Hebrew equivalent in the phrase in the prayer) and *Siddur Sim Shalom*, both of which unequivocally seek to put human beings in their proper place. So what <u>is</u> our proper place?

Our religious tradition tells us unambiguously, starting with the book of Genesis 1.27-30, that we are the crown of Creation: not only are we created in the image of the Deity but said Deity then gives everything else that has been created into our hands for our specific use. If that isn't going to give mankind a superiority complex then nothing will! And Judaism is far from the only one of the major religions that promotes human superiority over the natural world; indeed compared to the heights (or depths, depending on your point of view) that Christianity, thanks to St. Thomas Aquinas himself inspired by Aristotle (7), takes it, <u>we</u> have a reasonably good track record.

Mainstream religion, invented by man, hardly surprisingly takes such a view, indeed it would be strange for it to be otherwise. Though a wonderful antidote to this shared delusion may be found in *The Circumference of Home*, by the writer and traveller Kurt Hoelting who states (8):

> I think that basically everything is sacred and that our job is to align ourselves with this truth by figuring out what is most sacred and working from there. A smart primate that weighs 150 pounds and has a bad habit of fouling its own nest is a poor candidate, to my way of thinking, for the honor of most sacred creation in the universe. I don't care how many titles it has behind its name.

And so say I.

But other forms of religious belief, be they those of native peoples or those which believed in goddesses rather than male deities (created in their maker's image), take the very different view that there is a deep practical and spiritual connectivity between the human and animal worlds, and between human beings and animals. The authors of *The Myth of the Goddess*, Jules Cashford and Anne Baring, write that in Palaeolithic times '...animals must have been seen as the embodiment of divine power, the gift of life to the tribe' and commenting on the great Palaeolithic cave paintings of France and Spain they add (9):

> Were the animals experienced as the generative powers of the Goddess, which guaranteed the continuation of life? It is likely that they were already regarded as diverse expressions of the all-encompassing reality of the Great Mother Goddess, who was carved outside the caves, which held inside, on their womb-like walls, images of the bewildering variety of forms to which she had given birth.

Sadly for the world, however, and particularly the natural world, religions invented by men insisted on the superiority of their creation and, as even the briefest survey of human history bloodily demonstrates, threatened by the existence of anything that disagreed with their own conception, eradicated it with single-minded brutality, suspending their own teachings about compassion and respect without a backward glance.

How much was lost and how much the animal world suffered as a result. Thus a harmful pattern was set by religious tradition which continues in both religious and secular cultures into the 21st century, in spite of the fact that science has clarified matters beyond reasonable doubt.

In his fascinating book *Your Inner Fish* (10), Dr Neil Shubin, Chair of the Department of Anatomy at the University of Chicago and a leading palaeontologist, uses the latest genetic and paleontological research to demonstrate the multiplicity of connections between homo sapiens and other forms of life along the evolutionary journey, and particularly the way in which analyses of such things as the human ear or eye prove our own evolutionary process. As he says of the eye (11):

> When you look into eyes, forget about romance, creation and the windows into the soul. With their molecules, genes and tissues derived from microbes, jellyfish, worms, and flies, you see an entire menagerie.

Jerry A. Coyne, Professor of Ecology and Evolution at Chicago University and another champion of Darwin, has written passionately about the importance of knowing our place in his splendid book *Why Evolution is True* (12).

Coyne commences with a hefty side-swipe at those throwbacks to the primordial gloop who espouse the arrant nonsense of 'creationism' or so-called 'intelligent design' and the ways in which they seek to use judicial process to change the teaching of children by putting their own weird ideas on a par with the truths of science. Darwinism may not be perfect, but, as the judge in the last significant trial on this issue (Dover, Penn. 2005) opined (13):

> To be sure, Darwin's theory of evolution is imperfect. However, the fact that scientific theory cannot yet render an explanation on every point should not be used as a pretext to thrust an untestable alternative hypothesis grounded in religion into the science classroom to misrepresent well-established scientific propositions.

In a book that is an absolute tour de force, Coyne writes a chapter entitled What About Us?' in which he considers the development of hominids, and particularly focuses on the way the evolutionary tree that ultimately led to us about one million years ago divided. This knowledge should help us to ground ourselves more realistically and discourage us from indulging in the fantasies we have, inspired by many religious teachings, that we are a species apart.

Another significant reminder of human limitations should be the extraordinary capabilities of birds and mammals which our relatively enlarged brains have helped us replicate mechanically but which we can never hope to copy in our actual bodies, at least not yet and not for several million years, if ever.

Consider the human eye, one of the wonders of our bodies, granting us a faculty which we all prize. Yet compared to the eye of a peregrine falcon it is nothing! In *The Peregrine*, J.A. Baker writes (14):

> The eyes of a peregrine falcon weigh one ounce each; they are larger and heavier than human eyes. If our eyes were in the same proportion to our bodies as the peregrine's are to his, a twelve stone man would have eyes three inches across, weighing four pounds. The whole retina of a hawk's eye records a resolution of distant objects that is twice as acute as a human's ... this means that a hawk, endlessly scanning the landscape with small abrupt turns of its head, will pick up any point of movement; by focussing upon it he can immediately make it flare up into a larger, clearer view.

Or consider the human ear, and the range of sound that it can pick up; yet we cannot hear what a bat hears, or communicate over miles via ultrasound like elephants or whales. Consider the human voice, the vehicle of speech which transforms human communication and so much more besides, think of Luciano Pavarotti or Joan Sutherland, and then ponder the fact that the Common Skylark's song contains thirty-six separate notes per second. If that doesn't make you feel humble nothing will!

When Alfred, Lord Tennyson used the phrase 'nature red in tooth and claw' (15) he was indulging in a classic anthropomorphisation of the natural world, where animals killing other animals for food was deemed by some Victorians to be 'cruel'; yet though we may find the sight of a cheetah bringing down an impala, or a lion pride killing a wildebeest hard to watch, they are doing it for an explicit purpose, to feed their young.

The animal kingdom has not yet thrown up a Genghis Khan, a Hitler, a Stalin or a Mao, men with the gratuitous death of millions on their record, or perpetrated the wanton and callous cruelties and indignities that groups of people, and individuals, inflict on others, often in the name of God or religion. Walt Whitman was on to something when he wrote in 'Song of Myself' (16):

I think I could turn and live with the animals
.... they are so placid and self-contained,
I stand and look at them long and long.
They do not sweat and whine about their condition,
They do not lie awake in the dark and weep for their sins,
They do not make me sick discussing their duty to God,
Not one is dissatisfied...not one is demented with the
    mania of owning things,
Not one kneels to his kind that lived thousands of years
    ago,
Not one is respectable or unhappy over the whole earth.

I have always felt that it is only when human beings allow themselves to experience the natural world not as a breed apart but as organic with it that we truly realise not only our own nature but how much there is to share. Henry Beston, in his classic of nature writing *The Outermost House*, puts it very well (17):

Whatever attitude to human existence you fashion for yourself, know that it is valid only if it be the shadow of an attitude to Nature. A human life, so often likened to a spectacle upon a stage, is more justly a ritual. The ancient values of dignity, beauty and poetry which sustain it are of Nature's inspiration; they are born of the mystery and beauty of the world.

And elsewhere in the same book Beston states even more powerfully (18):

We need another and a wiser and perhaps a more mystical concept of animals Remote from universal nature and living by complicated artifice, man in civilisation surveys the creature through the glass of his knowledge and sees thereby a feather magnified and the whole image in distortion. We patronize them for their incompleteness, for their tragic fate of having taken form so far below ourselves. And therein we err, and greatly err. For the animal shall not be measured by man.

In a world older and more complete than ours they move finished and complete, gifted with extensions of the senses we have lost or never attained, living by voices we shall never hear. They are not brethren, they are not underlings; they are other nations, caught with ourselves in the net of life and fellow prisoners of the splendour and travail of the earth.

For those bound by the teachings of religious tradition to put themselves on a par with, let alone see themselves as in some ways inferior to other parts of the natural world, is anathema, but I find such pretensions so ludicrous, so in defiance of obvious truths, so counter-intuitive to what science has taught us over the last 200 years, as to be beneath the effort of trying to convince them otherwise.

Ultimately, when all is said and done, we would do well to remember that, pace Aristotle, Galen, Avicenna, Maimonides, Ibn Khaldun, Erasmus, Shakespeare, Goethe, Pope, Milton, Mill, Mann, Monteverdi, Bach, Beethoven, Michelangelo, Raphael, Rembrandt, Monet, Chagall, Einstein, Berlin, Hawking, Berners-Lee, and my ultimate hero, Charles Darwin himself, we are just primates, and pretty pernicious ones at that, and it is high time we knew our place!

1. *Forms of Prayer* Movement for Reform Judaism (London 2008) p.168
2. *Siddur Lev Chadash* Liberal Judaism (London 1995) p.123
3. *Siddur Sim Shalom* The United Synagogue of America (New York 1985) p.13
4. *Birkhot HaShachar* (Jewish Lights Publishing, Woodstock, Vermont 2001) p.157
5. *My People's Prayer Book*: Vol. 5 (Hebrew Publishing Company, New York 1949) p.24
6. *Authorised Daily Prayer Book of the United Hebrew Congregations of the Commonwealth*: 4th edition, edited with a new translation by Chief Rabbi Sir Jonathan Sacks (Collins, London 2006) p.23
7. 'There is no sin in using a thing for the purpose for which it is. Now the order of things is such that the imperfect are for the perfect ... it is not unlawful if man uses plants for the good of animals, and animals for the good of man, as the Philosopher states.' *The Summa Theologica*: part 1, question 64:1, edited and translated by the English Dominican Fathers (Benziger Bos., New York 1918)
8. Hoelting, Kurt *The Circumference of Home* (Da Capo Press, Cambridge, Mass. 2009) p.140
9. Baring, Anne and Cashford, Jules *The Myth of the Goddess: Evolution of an Image*, (Viking Arkana, London 1991) p.27, p.39 and elsewhere
10. Shubin, Neil *Your Inner Fish* : A journey into the 3.5 billion year history of the human body (Allen Lane, London 2001)
11. Ibid. p. 157
12. Coyne, Jerry A. *Why Evolution is True* (Oxford University Press 2009)
13. Ibid. p.xi
14. Baker, J.A. *The Peregrine*, (nyrb, New York 1967) p.35
15. Lord Tennyson, Alfred 'In Memoriam A.H.H.', 1850, Canto 56
16. Whitman, Walt 'Song of Myself' (Shambhala Centaur Editions, Boston and London 1998) p.54
17. Beston, Henry *The Outermost House: A Year of Life on the Great Beach of Cape Cod* (An Owl Book, New York 1928) p.218
18. Ibid. p.24f.

JEFFREY NEWMAN

Jeffrey Newman read Philosophy and Psychology at Oxford. Inspired by Rabbi Lionel Blue's religious 'passion for justice', he studied at Leo Baeck College and is now, forty years later, Emeritus Rabbi of Finchley Reform Synagogue. He and his wife, Bracha, have three children and one grandchild.

Shoah or Churban?

Reflections occasioned by Pierre Bouretz *Witnesses for the Future* (1)

The popular Japanese novelist, Haruki Murakami, provides a clue to the entrancing plot of his Kafka on the Shore with a particularly apt quote – placed for the reader at a somewhat unexpected moment - from Henri Bergson:

> The pure present is an ungraspable advance of the past devouring the future. In truth all sensation is already memory. (2)

Murakami's work is built upon the Second World War, particularly the devastations of Hiroshima and Nagasaki, and the effect of collective trauma upon the individual and society. The Anglo-Jewish community has similarly struggled through a period of apparent consolidation and normalisation following the Holocaust and the birth pangs of the State of Israel. It is perhaps not surprising that, on the whole, the Jewish world appears largely oblivious of wider global concerns. Though rabbis certainly give topical sermons and may make references, for example, to miracles at Chanukah in relationship to world oil shortages, there is little mainstream Jewish involvement in the critical issues which are likely to effect the future for our children and our children's children – whether climate change, shortage of resources, over-population or biodiversity and the disappearance of species.

But Judaism is nothing if it does not dream of the future and find ways to realise those dreams. The task laid upon Abraham 'to be a blessing to humanity'(3) remains the central call of the Jewish people and this is not a dream in the sense of some vague, vacuous hope – Torah, oral and written, is filled with the details as to how the present can be repaired. Such is *tikkun olam* and we lose sight of it at our peril. But there is a promise: 'The doctrine of the Messiah who will be sent by God to redeem Israel and usher in a new era in which all mankind will worship the true God is one of Judaism's most distinctive teachings.'(4)

To help us, Pierre Bouretz has written an extraordinary book *Witnesses for the Future*, a rich *kol bo* of nine twentieth century, originally German, Jewish thinkers. Bouretz (1958 -) is Director of a French Higher Education Social Sciences Academy and a Jewish scholar of repute. The book is beautifully translated and easy to read and his comment upon Scholem is true of his own work: its strength is that 'it manages at one and the same time to block out vast structures in broad outline and to fill in miniatures'. (5)

Leo Strauss once suggested, perhaps optimistically: 'No one can be both a philosopher and a theologian...but every one of us can and should be either one or the other, the philosopher open to the challenge of theology, or a theologian open to the challenge of philosophy.' (6) Bouretz provides us with both the materials and pointers to find our own way through the thickets but there is no avoiding the complexities. Understanding here demands struggle but the work is lightened by fascinating details. An example occurs in the Introduction and gives a taste of what follows:

> There is a page in Kafka's journals that reveals, even better than the "Letter to His Father," the private feelings shaping a historical consciousness. He has just heard the prayer that ends the meal after a circumcision, and notices that, with the exception of two grandfathers, no one understands the meaning of the words. "I saw Western European Judaism before me in a transition whose end is clearly unpredictable and about which those most closely affected are unconcerned." That note is dated 24 December 1911. In reading Scholem's autobiography, we discover that he, on the very same day, attended a family Christmas ritual for the last time, a ceremony that for him had become a palinode: thereafter he would leave his parents' home for that evening. For him it was the fact that a portrait of Theodore Herzl had been placed at the foot of the Christmas tree that brought on the crisis. (7)

The confusions of Jewish life and thought and the events of the century that were to unfold form the background context which shapes the writers. They, Bouretz explains, are:

> Jewish thinkers, born during the time of the disenchantment of the world, of the "death of God," and the destruction of reason [who] in a sense, [they] saved German idealism...chiefly because they remained metaphysicians. It is true that each expressed this in his own fashion: classical in Cohen, and reflected in the history of philosophy in Strauss; reconstructed for Rosenzweig, Levinas and Jonas; wrenched apart for a Benjamin who would find in Bloch a kind of surviving brother who had revived hope; gracefully by way of Buber's empathy with his mystical object; austere in Scholem, who at times pretends to be no more than a detached historian. (8)

These are the nine writers and the liveliness of the book lies partly in the richness of their conversations and interchanges. In fact, the relationships and the details of their lives are so evocative - the fact that Heschel taught Buber modern Hebrew (9), for example, or how moved Scholem was by finding Kafka's picture on S.H. Bergman's piano on his arrival in Jerusalem (10) - that we may be tempted to relegate their ideas to secondary consideration. Bouretz does not do this. Instead, he scrutinizes, through close examination of one or more areas of each writer's work:

> ...an idea sometimes perceived as the only one to survive the decline of the Tradition, but sufficiently malleable to be interpreted for different ends: that of a messianism that delineates, on the horizon, a consummation of history, or announces its apocalyptic interruption, suggesting a continuous perfection of the world or at least its progressive repair. (11)

How do we think of the time of the Messiah? This is a central question and the past is made present here as the writers look back in order to make sense of their own times. The way of looking is pivotal:

> Know that there is a twofold way of looking at all worlds. The one reveals their exteriority, that is to say, general laws of the world in terms of their external form. The other reveals the inner being of the worlds, that is to say the essence of human souls. (12)

125

The key issues turn out to be 'language,' 'time' and 'evil' (as well as 'Zionism and Israel'.) As early as 1918, (that is, well before Heidegger's major 1927 work on *Being and Time,*) Scholem wrote in his Diary some *Remarks on Judaism and Time*, first quoting Hermann Cohen, in words that echo those of Bergson but without the passion and entirely missing the key Jewish component of memory:

> Being is not immobilised in the present, but it is in suspense
> beyond the present. Present and future are united in that Being
> that is God.

Scholem then, probably influenced by his discussions with Benjamin, refers to Exodus 3:14,

> The true Name of God is also the *I* of time. This means that the basis,
> but also the complement, of all empirical time is the divine, the
> eternal present; thus God will be what he was in all the generations.
> He continues, What does the biblical expression "in all the days"
> mean? The fact that the kingdom of God that "will be" is already
> present and that the messianic kingdom is the "present of history."
> (13)

Scholem appears to suggest here that the germ of messianic times is present at every moment. But how does this concept survive the destruction of European Jewry? Bloch's work is unexpectedly helpful. He, too, breaks with the tradition (begun by Calvin and continued by Mendelssohn,) of translating the Name of God as, 'I am the Being who is eternal,' and chooses instead the words of Buber and Rosenzweig: '"I shall be who I shall be" – that is, not a substance identical with itself but 'the solidarity of God with the human experience of time, against the backdrop of an unpredictability of the future.' (14) This enables Bloch to re-read Job in an original way. Basing his interpretation on Job 19: 25-27, initially on the phrase 'I know that my redeemer lives,' Bloch points out that Job and God do not speak the same language: the God of the Creation is answering one who calls in the name of the God of the Covenant. Bloch points to the derivation of 'redeemer' from the root meaning of *goel*: blood avenger! Bouretz comments, '[Bloch] solemnly calls upon God...against God... Messianism is here made manifest, in all the strength of its antithesis to the given world.' (15) In the idea of a world born of a divine contraction (*tzimtzum*), Bloch sees the indication that messianism is older than belief in the Messiah: 'Instead of the glory of the alpha or morning of creation, the wishful space of the end or day of deliverance presses forward.... no religion has passed through so many layers of sublimation, even of utopianization of its god.' (16) Bloch here rejects "theodicies of non-responsibility" – the multiplicity of figures elaborated to explain the experience of evil - by finding, at one and the same time, "a language in which to accuse" and "a light to nourish his rebellious hope." (17)

This sensitive reading of *goel* demonstrates the importance of examining language in detail. The meaning of 'messianism' and associated words and concepts changes through history, which leads directly to the sharp warning that Scholem gave on the use of Hebrew in Palestine as the vernacular and the potential descent to the abyss: 'if we...resuscitate the language of the ancient books so that it can reveal itself anew to [the Volapuks], must then not the religious violence of this language one day break out against those who speak it?' (18) Of course, at another level entirely, mystics like Abulafia penetrating below the level of words, listen to the individual letters and their combinations so that the 'plucking of each is compared to a finely tuned string and becomes music.' (19).

Jews, of course, are great music lovers, not least amongst them Rabbi Tony Bayfield, who has found in it sustaining energies and would probably agree with Schopenhauer's observation of 'its unrivaled capacity for listening to being'. Bloch, too, hears hints in music of the coming of the Messiah and Bouretz, drawing upon him, writes:

> To Nietzsche, music was of all forms of culture the one that comes last, bringing to one epoch the language of the one preceding it before disappearing. Handel, bringing to the ear the best of Luther, Mozart musically evoking the courtly style of Lous XIV, or Beethoven externalizing an eighteenth century "of vague elation, ruined ideals and fleeting joys": so many indications in [Bloch's] view that music "comes too late" when it frees what the world of yore contained in a muted mode. (20) Bloch even suggests:

> > clairvoyance is long extinguished but should not, however, a clairaudience, a new kind of seeing from within, be imminent, which, now that the visible world has become too weak to hold the spirit, will call forth the audible world, the refuge of the light, the primacy of the inner flame instead of the former primacy of seeing, if ever the hour to speak in music comes?' (21)

Clearly we have in Bouretz almost limitless resources to study how twentieth century Jewish thinkers both dealt with the issues they confronted and were able to think towards a future, philosophically and theologically.

Now, the divine unity upon which Jewish thinking is dependent, which it exemplifies and out of which the messianic strain arises, calls us as we look towards the future, to act in righteousness and justice in meeting the needs of our times and so bring about the coming of the Messiah. So are we taught by the Prophets, who passed judgment on their times, criticising false values in the Name of the oneness of the true God. If part of Rabbi Tony Bayfield's unique contribution has been educational as the way to enhance Judaism's self-understanding, another has been inter-faith work, both learning from other traditions, and teaching our understanding and experience, so that, as Rosenzweig explained, the Star can radiate outwards. Murakami's work, for example, won The Jerusalem Prize in 2009 and Steven Johnson chooses to use Benjamin's *Angel of History* as the prologue to his tale of how a doctor and a clergyman, working together, discovered in the 1840s that cholera was a water-borne disease, leading to its potential eradication. (22) The Angel hovers, looking back but irresistibly blown forward by the storm from Paradise. 'Where a chain of events appears to us, he sees one single catastrophe which keeps piling wreckage and hurls it in front of his feet... What we call progress is this storm.' (23)

Each of the nine teachers was in continual dialogue with the great philosophers and theologians of the age: Kant and Hegel in particular, but also Nietzsche and, of course, Heidegger. In the 'global village' in which we now live where the speed, the ubiquity of communication and developing paradigms of thought, (including the necessity to hear the voice of women, (24)) forces us to recognise the unity of humanity and all life, we, too must engage with great teachers from other traditions who will challenge us to make sense of the situation in which we find ourselves and respond adequately.

We may turn, for example, to the Latin American 'liberation' theologian, Leonardo Boff, who drawing on new understanding that has emerged in our time (25), writes:

> A sustainable way of life is humankind's new ethical and cultural dream. It entails another way of conceiving the common feature of Earth and humankind and, accordingly, it demands a true revolution in hearts and minds, values and habits, forms of production and relationship with nature. It entails understanding that "Humanity is

part of a vast evolving universe" and that "Earth, our home, is alive"; it also entails living "the spirit of human solidarity and kinship with all life," and assuming responsibility for the present and future well-being of the human family and the larger living world," taking care to use the scarce goods of nature rationally so as not to do harm to natural capital or to future generations who also have a right to a good quality of life and minimally just institutions, "being more, not having more" and living "with reverence for the mystery of being, gratitude for the gift of life and humility regarding the human place in nature." (26)

In 1981, Rabbi Bayfield chose to entitle his guide for young people, Churban (27) basing himself on the teaching of Rabbi Maybaum that 'the churban has the messianic power of achieving progress.' (28) Maybaum's messianism did not include a return to Israel, while Scholem and Buber thought that it was only 'over there' that the Jewish people could 'revive,' (29) (though Buber himself quickly became critical of Zionist leadership.) The current apparently intransigent situation of Israel will, no doubt, be just one area which Tony will consider as he continues his work to realise the vision: 'Let ours be a time remembered for the awakening of a new reverence for life, the firm resolve to achieve sustainability, the quickening of the struggle for justice and peace, and the joyful celebration of life.' (30)

1. Published by John Hopkins Baltimore 2010) The title is taken from a letter from Benjamin to Scholem, page 7
2. H. Bergson *Matter and Memory* quoted by Murakami, H. *Kafka on the Shore* (Penguin 2005) page 294
3. Genesis 12:3
4. Jacobs, L. *A Jewish Theology* (DLT, London 1973) page 292
5. Bouretz page 350.The text is fully referenced and citations can be found on notes to the page.
6. ibid.page 14
7. ibid page 3
8. ibid page 6
9. ibid page 359
10. ibid page 225. Kafka's influence is constantly present.
11. ibid page 6
12. ibid page 429, probably from Safed kabbalists.
13. ibid page 238
14. ibid page 469. On page 864 note 169, Bouretz comments: 'This translation could claim the authority of Rashi, who draws on the Talmud (Berakhot 9b) to explain: "I will be with them in that trial as I will be with them in their subjugation other empires".'
15. ibid page 466 The passage from Bloch that Bouretz quotes is, he notes, missing from the English translation
16. ibid page 468. Pages 469-70 deal with the conflict between responsibility and hope exemplified by Jonas and Bloch. Bouretz quotes Levinas, 'Monotheism surpasses and subsumes atheism, but it is impossible for those who have not reached the age of doubt, loneliness and revolt,' and suggests this could not be better illustrated than by Bloch page 475
17. Levinas comments (Bouretz op. cit. pages 472-3) that Bloch's exceptional daring here resides in the effort to place the presentiment of a victory over death at the exact point where philosophy begins: astonishment. This follows Plato who suggests that philosophy begins in wonder.
18. ibid page 344 in a 1926 letter from Palestine to Rosenzweig. The Volapuks speak an artificially constructed language.
19. ibid page 262
20. ibid page 450. Schopenhauer, Bouretz notes, hears it the other way round: music heralds or ushers in the age.
21. ibid page 451

22. Johnson, S. *The Ghost Map* (Penguin 2007) Johnson is a systems thinker, a specialist on internet development.
23. Bouretz op. cit. page 215
24. Bouretz comments Arendt was excluded as being "marginal as a 'witness for the future,' though exemplary from the point of view of a thinking of 'dark days' (a phrase she borrowed from Brecht)." Note 15 page 722. Perhaps, however, her thought remains too challenging.
25. Particularly that of James Lovelock, the *Gaia* theory, that Earth is a living system.
26. Boff, L. The Ethics of Care in Corcoran, P.B. and Wohlpart, A.J. *A Voice for Earth* (Georgia UP, Athens and London 2008.) Quotes are from the Earth Charter www.earthcharter.org
27. Bayfield, A. *Churban* (Michael Goulston Educational Foundation, London 1981)
28. Maybaum, I. *The Face of God after Auschwitz* (Polak and van Gennep, Amsterdam, 1965) In contrast to *churban, shoah* suggests destruction without hope.
29. Bouretz op. cit. Page 163 Rosenzweig says that Scholem wrote to him that the Judaism of the Diaspora 'was in a state of the clinically dead'
30. The sentence that completes the Earth Charter, contributed by Rabbi Awraham Soetendorp.

MARCIA PLUMB

Marcia Plumb is the director of Neshamah, directs the spiritual formation programme at Leo Baeck College, is the Rabbi for Akiva School, and one of the rabbis at Sha'arei Tsedek North London Reform Synagogue. She has written on spirituality issues and is a spiritual counsellor for individuals and families.

Isn't Spirituality Only for Adults?
The Importance of Spirituality for Children (and Grandchildren!)

For Tony who loves theology, the search for meaning, and his grandchildren (not in that order)
And for Linda who loved all children, including the child in herself

Many people think that the inner life of the spirit is too complex for children to grasp. The role of the Divine in history and the mystery behind creation is hard enough for adults to imagine, and therefore is not relevant to children. Other adults are sure that children are too absorbed by computer games to be mesmerized in awe by the beatings of a butterfly wing.

Anecdotal evidence and scientific studies prove otherwise. Adult cynicism has not yet arrived in children so they are great believers in a God with whom they can converse. Children accept wonder as a natural part of the world in which they live. Children can watch worms crawl and bees flit for hours. They are mesmerized by the natural world.

One Year 8 child said: ' Sometimes, when I play with my dwarf hamsters I wonder how anything so small and delicate could be made or even live. I have been told about a big bang which created the world but how could that create such a delicate thing so I don't believe that. I often think how things could become from nothing…into the skills we have today. Also how will it end? And what was here before us? All these unanswerable questions keep me in awe and wonder.'

Another Year 8 child said, 'When I got a new telescope I was curiously looking at the stars and I was thinking about how far away they were from earth because most of them were only pin-pricks in the night....Also the Milky Way is small compared with the other galaxies. I was wondering how long space did actually go on for. Did it go on for infinity, what happens when it finally runs out? Or is space round, if you travelled forever, would you eventually hit earth again?'

A Year 10 child wondered: I have had a spiritual experience. I thought if God made us who made God? And I have often wondered if I am really here or not, and when I die whether I will just not exist or will I exist spiritually.'

These children are asking existential questions about their futures and the future of creation. They assume that there is an eternal force that exists outside of themselves. They have a deep sense of spirituality.

What do we mean by the elusive term 'spiritual'? Here are a few definitions of spirituality.

1. It is a view that life is of great value. One defines one's relations to others in a manner that expresses concerns about oneself and others. Humanists might define this as simply ethical, but a spiritual person might base one's life and one's behaviour on the belief that all life is precious and that life itself is a gift from God. If one believes that, then one has no choice but to be hopeful, and loving to others.

2. The National Curriculum Council's document describes spiritual development as having to do with: 'relationships with other people, and for believers, with God. It has to do with the universal search for individual identity—with our responses to challenging experiences, such as death, suffering, beauty, and encounters with good and evil. It has to do with the search for meaning and purpose in life and for values by which to live.' ('Spiritual and Moral Development: A Discussion paper', 1993)

3. David Kibble describes spirituality as 'A lifelong process of encountering, reflecting on, responding to and developing insight from what, through experience, one perceives to be the transpersonal, transcendent, mystical or numinous. It does not necessarily involve the concept of God.' (David Kibble, Spiritual Development, *Spiritual Experience and Spiritual Education*)

Children have a variety of ways of expressing their innate spirituality, wonder and appreciation of the world around them. Their spiritual characteristics are not static. Rather they develop over time. (Lerner, *Making*

Humans Human:Spirituality and the Promotion of Positive Youth Development)

Ofsted has found that pupils may display evidence of personal responses to questions about the purpose of life, and to the experience of e.g. beauty and love or pain and suffering. (OFSTED, 1994) Pupils also display a capacity for reflection and curiousity and a sense of awe and wonder; an ability to discuss beliefs; having relationships that are open; valuing imagination, inspiration and contemplation; and asking questions about meaning and purpose. (OFSTED, 1993).

We know that children have spiritual experiences. Those who take a child's spiritual journey seriously have a wealth of knowledge from which to draw to help us develop a child's inner life. There have been many studies done that help us promote a child's spiritual well-being. These studies prove that a spiritually sensitive child will be a better citizen in society as a well as a high achieving student. Here are some examples of studies done on the affect of spirituality on a young person's development.

1. In adolescence, spirituality is significant for the healthy, positive development of a person's sense of self...'. We believe that spirituality may foster an integrated moral and civic identity within a young person and lead the individual along a path to becoming an adult contributing to self, family, community and civil society...Data suggests that the process of exemplary positive development among youth - a process we label as 'thriving' - involves both the direct effects of spirituality on positive development and the mediation of religiosity between spirituality and thriving.' (Koenig and Lawson)

2. Spirituality is the transcendent virtue that is coupled with the behaviours reflecting an integrated moral and civic identity. Erikson proposed that when young people identify with ideologies and histories of faith-based institutions, 'identities can be placed within a social-historical framework that connect youth to traditions and communities that transcend the immediate moment, thereby providing young people with a sense of continuity and coherence with the past, present and future.' (Erikson, 1959)

3. A child or adolescent feels relatedness not only towards the parents and extrafamilial others, but also toward God. Relatedness to God (King, Lynch and Ryan, 1989) or how safe and loved by God an individual feels, as well as how loving one feels toward God, may also influence personality development in youth. A more positive, warm, supporting relationship with God should facilitate autonomy in the child and lead to more internalized beliefs about God; the child will be more likely to engage in religious

behaviour because he enjoys it and feels it is important in her life. In adults, anxious attachment to God is related to neuroticism and negative affect, suggesting that personality and one's relationship to God are linked. (Rowatt and Kirkpatrick, 2002). (Kneezel, Teresa, and Emmons, Robert, *Personality and Spiritual Development*)

4. Studies suggest a connection that links spirituality to civic engagement outside organised religion. Transcendent experiences help shape ideological beliefs of young people, which may orient them toward community service work.

5. In a cross-sectional sample of several hundred diverse urban youth, a study found that religiously active adolescents who had high levels of social capital (measured by indicators of social interaction, trust and shared vision) had higher levels of moral functioning. This moral functioning was provided by their spiritual values.

6. Studies show that students most likely to succeed are affected by educational models that include spirituality and religiosity, which lead to thriving (as opposed to only traditional religiosity, which focuses largely on specific rules and guidelines offered by a particular faith community).

When children encounter the ideas of scientific proof, astronomy and Darwinian theory, they begin to question God's role in the shaping of the universe and in history. They become rooted in fact rather than faith. As they get older, children can lose the ability to see God around them, through nature or as a presence who walks with them. They begin to want proof. 'Is God real?', they ask. 'If God were real, God would make me fly.' (Year 4-5 students) In late primary and secondary schools, children need a bridge between the 'magic' of childhood belief and science so they don't lose faith entirely. Faith based education needs to provide opportunities for children to make a connection between their need for proof and their need for mystery. Theologians and scientists know that there need be no contradiction between science and faith, but children need to be led across what can seem to be a rationality chasm.

What can faith educational settings and educators do to provide this bridge?
• Provide opportunities for students to share, reflect on and evaluate:
 o Their own and others' feelings of awe and wonder
 o Their own and others numinous experiences or experiences of
  the transcendent
 o Matters of personal concern
 o Their own and others' religious experiences

o Their beliefs and feelings about God (or something beyond or within themselves)
• Encourage pupils to use and develop their imagination in regards to spirituality
• Encourage pupils to help others, especially the young, the old and the disadvantaged, in order to maintain their sense of wonder and gratitude, as well as develop their moral functioning.

Hope, love, compassion, trust, gratitude and seeing each individual, including the self, as an image of God, is important for living a life that is healthy and well-grounded. Children who inculcate these spiritual perspectives of themselves and the world will contribute to the community and society, achieve well academically, and will feel safe in the world. By bringing an explicitly spiritual dimension to our educational processes and curricula, our schools and faith communities will help shape the next generation to be spiritually and morally sound.

Erikson, E.H. (1959). Identity and the Life-cycle. *Psychological Issues*, I, 18-164

Kibble, D.G. (1978) *Moral Education in a secular School* Bramcote: Grove books.

King, K.M., Lynch, J.H., and Ryan, R.M. (1989). *The relatedness to God scale*. Unpublished manuscript, University of Rochester, Rochester NY.

Kneezel, Teresa, and Emmons, Robert. *Personality and Spiritual Development*. Spirituality and Human Development: Exploring Connections.

Koenig, H.G. and Lawson, D.M. (2004). *Faith in the future: Health care, aging, and the role of religion*. Philidelphia: Templeton Foundation Press.

Lerner, Richard *On Making Humans Human: Spirituality and the Promotion of Positive Youth Development*

OFSTED (1993) *Handbook for the Inspection of Schools*. London: HMSO.

OFSTED (1994) *Spiritual, Moral, Social and Cultural Development*. London: HMSO

Rowatt, W.C and Kirkpatrick, L.A. (2002). Two dimensions of attachment to God and their relationship to affect, religiosity, and personality constructs. *Journal for the Scientific Study of Religion* 41, 637-651.

DANNY RICH

Danny Rich JP is the Chief Executive of Liberal Judaism, having previously served as Rabbi to Kingston Liberal Synagogue, Surrey for nearly two decades. He serves as a hospital and prison chaplain, and as a magistrate. He recently undertook a year's course in Islam at the Woolf Institute in Cambridge.

Muslim Perceptions of 'the Other'

The founder of Islam, the Prophet Muhammad, was born in the last quarter of the sixth century CE in the town of Mecca where, in addition to the native settled and nomadic pagan Arabs, he was to encounter Jews, Christians and Sabaeans. In his lifetime Muhammad created the basis of the third of the world's great monotheistic religions, and his life and work was to inspire a vast empire, and to lay the foundations for a way of living which today 'reportedly one fifth of humanity' consider their own.

A way of living is not created in a vacuum, and both responds to, and is a response to, the prevailing religious, political, economic and social situation in which it develops. In forging a new identity, Islam had to decide what it was like and what it was unlike; how much was it a continuum of what had gone before and how much was it radical; who was to be 'inside' as a part of the new community and who were its enemies; who was 'the Other' and what, if any would be 'the Other's' relationship with the new creation.

This essay will seek to explore how the concept of 'the Other' developed in early Islamic thought, by examining the oldest available pair of Islamic texts, the Qur'an and the Medina Charter. In the verses from the Qur'an, it will examine the tension between the universal and the particular and the changing categories of 'the Other', and ask why they might have developed. In the Medina Charter, it will look particularly at the role of the Jews, and finally this essay will conclude with comment upon the relevance of a critical assessment of Muslim perceptions of 'the Other' for inter faith dialogue today.

The most well known 'universal' Qur'anic sentiments are contained in the second sura, *al baqarah* 213:

The people were one community; then Allah sent forth the Prophets, good tidings to bear and warning, and He revealed therewith the Book with the truth, that He might decide among the people touching their differences…Allah guides whom He will to a straight path.

This is preceded by 62:

Lo! Those who believe and those who are Jews and Christians and Sabaeans, whoever believes in Allah and the Last Day and does right, surely their reward is with their Lord, and there shall no fear come upon them and neither shall they grieve.

In spite of the twin dangers of translation (for every translation is an interpretation) and selecting verses out of their context of the whole, when these two passages are combined with the Qur'anic statement in 2:256 – 'There is no compulsion in religion' - it is clear that in this section of the Qur'an 'the Other' is certainly not without value, at least to be tolerated, and indeed has merit, perhaps akin to that of Muslims. It is possible to suggest that the existence of 'the Other' is part of the Divine purpose in that any 'difference' of belief and any required correcting is in the gift of Allah. It reminds one of the thirteenth verse of the forty ninth *sura al hujurat*

O mankind! Lo! We have created you from a single male and female, and have made you nations and tribes that you may know each other. Lo! The noblest of you, in the sight of Allah, is the best in conduct

In spite of these universal statements the Qur'an contains their opposite too. In the ninth *sura al tawba* 29 it is written

Fight against those who do not believe in God or in the Last Day of Judgement who do not forbid what God and the Prophet have forbidden or practice the true religion among those who have been given the Book, until they pay the poll tax from their hand and are humiliated

and again in the third *sura al Imran* 85:

And who seeks a religion other than Islam it will not be accepted from him, and he will be one of the losers in the Hereafter

138

Although it remains outside the scope of this essay, traditional and modern scholars of text criticism and students of the Qur'an have a number of schools of hermeneutics and methods of accommodating textual problems including, for example, seeming contradiction, or apparent repetition. Peters (2003, p.194), for example, reminds the reader that one verse may be abrogated by another if the latter is considered to be later in chronology.

Nevertheless the extent to which a tradition includes or excludes 'the Other' does not deny the necessity to define oneself in contrast to neighbours or rivals. The Qur'an uses four general terms: *muminun*: believers, *muslimun*: submitters, *mushrikin*: associators, and *kafirun*: deniers to describe the types of people its author encountered in seventh century Arabian society. In a specific sense it describes Jews and Christians as *ahl al-kitab*: People of the Book, and elsewhere Jews and Christians are mentioned as such severally or jointly, and on three occasions (2:62; 5:69; and 22:17) the Sabaeans are listed with Jews and Christians.

The target of these terms is not always clear, such that Esack (1997, p.148) concludes that the terms are used 'interchangeably'. This is truer when seeking to define who of 'the Other' is included. For example, were Jews and Christians before the revelations to Muhammad and even in seventh century Arabia *muslimun*? In a long passage in *sura al baqarah* 130-136 the historical Jew (that is Abraham and his descendants) are *muslimun* but there is ambiguity about whether the contemporary Jewish community would be considered likewise.

> When the Lord said unto him (Abraham): Surrender! He Said: I have surrendered to the Lord of the Worlds. And they say: be Jews or Christians, then you will be rightly guided. Say: Nay, but the religion of Abraham, The upright, and he was not of the idolators…

There is perhaps a little less ambiguity when it comes to defining which of 'the Other' is excluded. The Qur'an clearly identifies two types of other: the *mushrikin* and the *ahl al-kitab*. *Mushrikin* invariably refers to pagan Arabs, particularly in Mecca, who opposed Muhammad's early attempts to bring monotheism to the existing powerful elite. There were at the time a number of pagan tribes, centred around the *ka'aba* (Bloom and Blair 2002, p.27). The cult was tied up with political and economic power too (particularly the payment of annual and other revenues to the 'keepers' of the ancient idols), and whilst Jews and Christians appear not to have been part of the controlling elite in Mecca and were, therefore, unaffected by

Muhammad's revelatory monotheism, a challenge to the religious pagan cult had wider implications for its adherents. Muhammad's first attempt to explain his revelation took place in Mecca where his target audience seems to be those ethnically closest to him, these Arab pagans. Mecca was on the caravan route and these pagans were familiar with Jews and Christians. In his declaration of clear monotheism Muhammad was ideologically closer to his Jewish and Christian neighbours than to his initial target audience (Rogerson 2003, pg 140), and many of the Qur'anic verses which speak positively of the People of the Book may reflect an early strategy in which he hoped that the Jews and Christians would certainly support his efforts to convert pagans to monotheism and might themselves perceive Islam as the completion or perfection of their own faiths.

If there appears to be consistency about the Qur'an's attitude to *mushrikin* there seems a shift in Muhammad's relationship with *ahl al-kitab*. Their identity is not in doubt. There were well-established Jewish and Christian communities in the region, and Medina 'was a leading Jewish community in ancient Arabia'. (Roth 1972, vol 11: column 1211). There is some doubt about exactly who the Sabaeans were but they are evidently a minority community.

This paper has demonstrated (see, for example, above 2: 62 and 213) the general positive approach of the Qur'an to *ahl al-kitab*. It is made more specific in the fifth *sura al ma'idah* where both marriage with Jewish and Christian women and the consummation of food prepared according to Jewish and Christian religious rites is permitted.

> This day are good things made lawful to you. The food of the People of the Book is lawful for you, and your food is lawful for them. And so are the virtuous women of the believers and the virtuous women among the People of the Book lawful to you when you give them their marriage portions...

This contrasts sharply with the strong condemnation of marriage with *mushrik* women declared in Qur'an 2:221, and forces one to ask whether it is theology alone which promotes such hostility. After all, there are Qur'anic verses which infer that both Jews and Christians have, at least, incompatible or incomplete theology. The discussion of the Christian doctrine of the Trinity (see *sura al ma'idah* 73) and a number of verses (see, for example, 5:70 and 78) which talk of the *bani yisrael* The Children of Israel (early generations of Jews) indicate that, in spite of theological difference(s), the *ahl al-kitab* are

140

insiders in some sense but still 'the Other' whereas the *mushrikin* are 'the Other' who represent a threat which implicitly is about more than theology, and can only be political and economic in nature.

The biography of Muhammad tells us that in the face of hostility from the pagan Meccan Arab tribes who sought to kill him (Ramadan 2007, p.78), Muhammad was forced to flee to Medina where he drew up the Medina Charter in c622 CE. The document governed relations with the powerful Jewish tribes of the town but in its opening preamble it indicates that those (Jewish) tribes who are in alliance with Muslims will form part of the new nation (*umma*) with a charter of rights and protections, on the one hand, and responsibilities on the other.

The Jews were promised not only equal treatment, but freedom to practice their religion and physical protection for both themselves and their allies. In return the Jewish tribes were obligated to a process of mutual consultation and aid and to bear the appropriate share of military costs, and they were expected to be loyal to the emerging Muslim nation in Medina, presumably in the event of hostilities with the pagan Arab Meccan tribes who had driven the first Muslims out of their territory. Armstrong (2002, pp.16-17) suggests that 'Muhammad had been greatly excited by the prospect of working closely with the Jewish tribes' but was disappointed when they refused to acknowledge his prophetship and then by their subsequent political treachery.

Muhammad's success in Medina was to be replicated less than a decade later following the Battle of Badr at which he overcame the tribes of Mecca who conceded ideologically, politically and economically. Relations with the Jews deteriorated too, and although, there is evidence that the Jewish community in the main remained loyal to its own style of monotheism, Muhammad seems to have feared their political disloyalty. There are a number of Qur'anic verses which speak of 'some Jews' or 'a Jew' committing an offence but the early relationship of Muhammad with the Jewish tribes of Medina and the region was to end in slaughter when Muhammad became fearful that the Jews had undermined the new *umma* from within by seeking alliances with their previous neighbours, the pagan Arab tribes. (Ayoub 2006, p. 24).

The success of Islam and its establishment as a political entity brought new challenges including how to treat 'the Other'. The Qur'an itself shows that changing political circumstances altered the perception of 'the (Jewish) Other'. In terms of 'the Other' in Islamic history, Pratt (2005, p.121) proposes three paradigms: the originating paradigm (Qur'an and Medina), the historico-legal paradigm (*dhimmi*) and the contemporary paradigm (neo anti-Semitic). Whether or not one might draw the paradigms in exactly the same manner, there is little doubt that the very fact that the earliest Islamic texts, the Qur'an and the Medina Charter, show a developing perception of 'the Other' which is rooted in political necessity, gives Jews and Muslims (and others) the possibility of revisiting historical perceptions which may be far removed from the original intent of the founder of Islam. If this is so, it may be possible that Jews and Muslims and others may 'reclaim their traditions from murderous sectarianism and return to the compassion which is at the core of their faith' (Chittister 2006, p.x)

Bibliography

Ammah, Rabiatu. *Dhimmis in Islam*: A Review. Birmingham: CSIC, 1996

Armstrong, Karen. *Islam: A Short History*. New York: Random House, 2002

Ayoub, Mahmoud M. *Islam: Faith and History*. Oxford: One World, 2004

Bloom, Jonathan, and Sheila Blair. *Islam: A Thousand Years of Faith and Power*. New Haven: Yale University Press, 2002

Chittister, Joan with Murshid Saadi Shakur Chishti and Rabbi Arthur Waskow. *The Tent of Abraham: Stories of Hope and Peace for Jews, Christians and Muslims*. Boston: Beacon Press, 2006

Esack, Farid. Qur'an, *Liberalism and Pluralism*. Oxford: One World, 1997

Hewer, C T R. *Understanding Islam: The First Ten Steps*. London: SCM, 2006

Johns, Anthony H., and Abdullah Saeed. 'Nurehdish Madjid and the interpretation of the Qur'an: religious pluralism and tolerance'. In *Modern Muslim Intellectuals and the Qur'an*. Edited by Suha Taji-Farouki. Oxford: University Press, 2004, pp 67-96

Nasr, Seyyed Hussein. *Ideals and Realities of Islam*. Islamic Texts Society: Cambridge, 2001

Peters, F E. Islam: *A Guide for Jews and Christians*. Princeton: University Press, 2003

Peters, F E. *The Children of Abraham: Judaism, Christianity and Islam*. Princeton: University Press, 2004

Pickthall, M M. *The Meaning of the Glorious Qur'an: Explanatory Translation*. Bellsville: Amana, 1996

Pratt, Douglas. *The Challenge of Islam: Encounters in Inter Faith Dialogue*. Aldershot: Ashgate, 2005

Ramadan, Tariq. *The Messenger: The Meanings of the Life of Muhammad*. London: Penguin, 2007

Rogerson, Barnaby. *The Prophet Muhammad: A Biography*. London: Abacus, 2003

Roth, Cecil. *Encylopedia Judaica*. Jerusalem: Keter, 1972

Royal Aal al-Bayt Institute for Islamic Thought. *An Open Letter and Call from Muslim Leaders*. Royal Aal al-Bayt Institute for Islamic Thought: Jordan 2007

Sachedina, Abdulaziz. 'The Qur'an and other religions'. *In The Cambridge Companion to the Qur'an*. Edited by Jane Dammen McAuliffe. Cambridge: University Press, 2006, pp 291-309

JONATHAN ROMAIN

Jonathan Romain is rabbi of Maidenhead Synagogue. He writes for *The Times*, *Guardian* and *Jewish Chronicle* and appears on radio and television. This is the eleventh book he has written or edited. He received the MBE for his work with mixed-faith couples. He is chaplain to the Jewish Police Association.

Religion and the Media

I suspect it is true to say that God's spokespeople are experiencing mixed fortunes in the media stakes at the moment.

It is ironic that those who blazed an early trail in the communications industry and were responsible for brilliant innovations such as the two tablets of stone and the Gospels, along with powerful parables and mesmerising sermons, are now finding it hard to make their voice heard. Ask most people who is the most famous cleric in Britain and there is a very good chance that they will come up with the Vicar of Dibley. Even those who realise she is a fictional character will struggle to name a real one. This may in part be an indictment of real vicars not being able to make their mark nationally, but it is not helped by the insistence of producers to use secular figures to front religious programmes – such as Roger Bolton on *Sunday* or Melvyn Bragg in *Faith in Our Times* - rather than trust a minister to be engaging and challenging. Normally a scientist presents a science programme and an historian introduces a history series, so why are not religious professionals allowed the same opportunity ?

Moreover, look at the scheduling timetable and you will find religious broadcasting banished to the very early hours of the morning or the very late slot, with the clear assumption that if you are at all interested in religious issues you must also be an insomniac. Equally annoying is the habit of putting on religious programmes on Sunday mornings when those most likely to appreciate them cannot do so as that is precisely the time when they are at church. Can you imagine the outcry if *Blue Peter* was shown whilst children were at school?

144

There is also a propensity to assume that the best way to tackle faith is through humour. A disproportionate number of religious programmes are comedies – *Rev*, *Vicar of Dibley*, *Father Ted*, *All Gas and Gaiters*. Humour is certainly a powerful tool that many a preacher employs, but usually in order to illustrate a serious point, not to fill up the slot. To be fair, amid these frustrations, there is also much to praise about the media's religious output. There have been some excellent productions - from the everlasting *Songs of Praise*, to short series such as *Friends Who Disagree* in which exponents of different faiths who respect each other examine the issues that divide them. Ernie Rae's *Beyond Belief* is another example of excellence. *Monastery* needs a mention too. Even the *Vicar of Dibley* had its merits, because, despite a few hiccups, Geraldine is depicted as a warm, caring human being and a minister one can trust - a definite advance from the buffoonery of Father Ted or Derek Nimmo's limp handshake of a character. In fact, Geraldine was sufficiently credible to help front the Make Poverty History campaign. Personally I would not have minded a parallel series by the same script-writers on 'The Rabbi of Dibley'.

Of course, there is always the backdrop of figures about falling church attendance or shrinking synagogue membership which may give the impression that religion today is on the wane, and therefore deserves less coverage. Not true. The growth in new religious movements, the high number of conversions from one faith to another, and the yearning for New Age spirituality indicate that religion is not declining, but it is changing. The big questions still remain: who am I? What is the purpose of life? Why do things often seem to go wrong? What will happen to me in the next world? The challenge for mainstream faiths is to answer such concerns clearly and coherently, and if the public do not come to the pulpit, then for clerics, the media is the best way of us reaching them. It would be a great mistake for faith leaders to retreat from mainstream broadcasting and seek solace in the religious channels that are more common in the United States. We are commanded to stay in the public arena. I am sure it says somewhere in the Bible 'Thou shalt not abandon the average viewer, nor his son, nor his daughter, nor his live-in partner and her children".

The onus, though, is on faith leaders to give a message that is worth hearing. We cannot expect the media to do our job for us and cannot expect broadcasters to push the faith on-air that we are failing to sell outside the studios. Likewise, we cannot blame them entirely when the stories they do cover do not come out in the way we want. We have to take half of the blame : for not briefing properly and for not getting our view over in a sympathetic or dynamic way. We have to recognise that if we want the media to be involved in our stories, it is part of our task to make their life easier. Let me suggest three ways in particular. First, it means accepting that there is no special pleading for religion - if we want coverage we have to earn it, through stories that are newsworthy and of genuine interest to the wider public. A press release on a new interpretation of a verse in the Gospel of St John that could dramatically advance biblical scholarship, may be wonderful for those who devised it but is of little relevance to anyone else. However, a release on why there are strong religious reasons for legalising brothels, or what faith has to say about the possible discovery of intelligent life in space, may well deserve column inches or radio time.

Second, it also means accepting that religion does not have a deferential place - our stories have to stand up to the same journalistic criteria as all other types - and reporters who are rigorous about analysing political or economic news will rightly apply the same standards to faith matters. That includes pushing aside bluff, hypocrisy or double-speak. In turn we should not resent such attempts or regard it as the media being 'out to get us', but view it as a natural part of investigative journalism. If our stories do not stand up to scrutiny, then we should not put them out in the first place. By way of example, Chief Rabbi Jonathan Sacks was very embarrassed when he was lambasted in 1997 by both the Jewish and non-Jewish press after it came to light that he had written a private letter attacking the much admired and recently deceased Reform rabbi Hugo Gryn. Sacks had not only described Gryn as 'among those who destroy the faith', but had done so shortly before he was due to speak in praise of him at his memorial service. It was a religious own-goal that deserved to be exposed. He was being duplicitous and got found out. He has since apologised and moved to establish better relations with Reform synagogues.

Third, it also means framing our stories in a way that is comprehensible - given the level of ignorance about religious detail either among some journalists or in the audience for whom they are catering. For instance, in a talk I delivered a few years ago I mentioned The Last Supper and was asked whether that meant the final meal before a nuclear war ! I have long given up referring to the bread and wine which Jews have on the Sabbath eve as being akin to the Eucharist. It was obvious that people totally missed the analogy, and they either did not understand the reference or thought I was referring to a pop group, confusing it with the Eurythmics.

The reality is, though, that however hard we try, it is often difficult for a religious voice to be heard in the general media. On one level it is because of the competition from so many other areas - such as politics, sport, and celebrity gossip - but there are also inherent media characteristics which are diametrically opposed to religious values. For instance, the media tends to concentrate on bad news - disasters, wars, skullduggery. Its key words are 'scandal' and 'horror'. In complete contrast, religion veers much more to good news : how people comfort or help each other. The word 'religion' comes from the verb 'religio', which has the root meaning of 'to bind together'. Our key words are 'enriching' and 'healing'. There is a major disparity of focus between the media and religion.

Another problem is that the central religious value is to love your neighbour as yourself, and not to throw stones at others, whereas the media thrives on confrontation and condemnation. It means that when the media does want a religious opinion, it instinctively goes for the most extreme - so as to provide sharp counterpoint - and therefore does us a double disservice : not only ignoring the moderate majority because we are not controversial enough, but also stereotyping religion as the preserve of the prejudiced. Even when vicars and rabbis who do not rant and rave get on air, there are serious problems to overcome : the seven deadly media sins of Confidentiality - Prostitution - Energy - Hard Calls - Hurting Friends - Conscience - and Personal Exposure.

Confidentiality : over time you come to know your colleagues pretty well, and I am sitting on some wonderful stories of clerical impropriety which would guarantee me a front page scoop in *The Sun* and even a demure mention in *The Times*. But I have to live with myself the next day, and also be able to have relationships with those around me based on trust and respect. I have a real dilemma coming up soon. I am writing a history of my congregation in Maidenhead. It will prove a good read for those living locally but frankly will not be of interest to anyone outside the area. However, if I include a chapter entitled "Scandals", which would reveal some extraordinarily colourful stories to which I am privy, it would make the *News of the World* look tame by comparison and boost my sales hugely. Of course I would change the names of those involved, but would it not still be breach of trust, putting marketing and Mammon ahead of communal harmony ?

This leads to the second danger : Prostitution. There is a thin dividing line between helping the producers and editors package your message in a way that you feel is not quite you, but which they insist 'gets it across much better' - between that and acting in a way that becomes so alien that you are prostituting yourself and end up paying too heavy a price. An instance of crossing that threshold was agreeing to be on the *Kilroy* television programme

147

several years ago. It was on a serious subject : mixed-faith marriages, an issue in which I specialise, but it was reduced to vying physically for the microphone, with no real debate and just shouting slogans. When they asked me back some months later on another topic, I said 'no thanks'. One media rape was enough.

Conversely, just on the right side of the thin line between publicity and parody, between sticking to my message and selling out to someone else's, there was a very successful children's TV programme featuring cardboard characters Zig and Zag. One day I was asked to appear on the programme to explain what it was like being a rabbi and what the job involves. I cannot describe how silly it felt bending down and talking to two pieces of painted cardboard one metre high, but as I found out afterwards from the countless parents who had watched with their children, it reached a surprisingly large audience and got across the essence of Judaism in a simple but effective way. Boundaries – it is not always easy to tell where they lie.

Dilemma number three is Energy and the extent to which it is invested. If you are doing a project you think worthwhile, how much energy do you expend promoting it ? It is very time-consuming sending out press releases, trying to persuade editors it is a new issue that has not been covered before, that it is a human interest story, that it is substantial enough for them to include; so often it is tempting to say 'this is all wasting time I could better use in the project itself'. But then that means you fail to share the good news, abrogate the airwaves and newspaper columns to items that you consider of comparatively little value. People inside the media often do not appreciate how difficult it is for those outside to make their voice heard.

A fourth dilemma is Hard Calls and whether to go public in the first place. As one of the spokespeople for the Movement for Reform Judaism, I come across issues where we ought to speak out, but which I know will be misinterpreted or give offence. For instance, homosexuality : we are clear that being gay is not a sin or a perversion, but a natural state for those concerned; they were created homosexual by God, should not be subject to any discrimination, and their sexuality should not be a public issue at all. But saying that does upset some people, including more conservative members within our own ranks, and it would be much safer staying quiet and concentrating on more acceptable issues - but would it be religious ? Do we have a duty not to shy away from the media when it will lead to unpopularity ? My answer is a resounding 'yes', but I am aware that being right does not stop one being vilified, while it may sometimes set one's cause back to go public too soon or too frequently.

The same applies with the fifth dilemma : Hurting Friends. I had great respect for the commitment of former Cardinal Cormac Murphy O'Connor to inter-faith relations. But that meant it was difficult being asked to go on ITN News to criticise him for something he said on an entirely different subject which many Jews found disturbing, when he compared the level of abortions that occurred being akin to the Holocaust. Do you say to yourself, 'look, he is a friend, turn a blind eye and in a few days the news will have moved on to something else'. Or do you think : 'if someone else had said that, there would be no question of a robust public response, so why give the Cardinal special favours ?' In the end I did go into the studios, and although I was careful to criticise his policy, not him personally, of course the announcer slid them together with "meanwhile the Cardinal has been attacked by Rabbi Jonathan Romain"....and the message I gave got distorted.

This is connected with dilemma six : Conscience. What do you do when you feel that you disagree with something to which the rest of your faith group adheres ? Because you are in the media, where you have the know-how and access to intervene, do you speak up and risk opprobrium, or toe the party line but feel deeply dishonest? I have had that struggle on some issues that many other rabbis support but I do not - one was the government proposal to introduce Holocaust Memorial Day, which I thought was the wrong name and should be broadened beyond a specifically Jewish experience to include all who suffer from prejudice and persecution - and be called instead Victims Day or Tolerance Day, but not Holocaust Day. It was a minority position among rabbis – but I have access to the media – and balancing conscience and consensus is an awesome responsibility.

The seventh media challenge - Personal Exposure – arises from the fact that, when working with religious programmes, you very often meet fascinating people from other faiths. It gets you thinking : 'well, they are so strong in their faith and it makes a lot of sense in many ways....maybe my version is not the only path, or even the best of many, just one of many'. It makes you less absolute, more relative....and while you can be genuinely enriched by the interfaith contact, it can also undermine some of the certainties you once had... (which you might think is for the good anyway) but it can be a scary experience when you first encounter it. It can also mean that when you then go back to your own faith community you are not quite so at home as before with the other people there and the more limited horizons they have. It can be very painful encountering what previously was familiar to you but now appears as prejudice. One result is that there is in this country a middle group evolving inbetween those of faith and those of no faith : an

149

interfaith community in which a remarkable cross-fertilisation of ideas and experiences is occuring, and those in the religious media are often in the very midst of it.

Amid all of these challenges and dilemmas, my one Golden Rule for media survival is 'remember your roots'. It is illustrated best by the ladder in Jacob's dream which stretched from earth to heaven (Genesis 28.12). Religious figures may achieve dizzying heights through the media, and reach out to mass audiences, but their ladder has to be resting solidly on personal integrity and core beliefs, otherwise it will lack firm foundations and will eventually topple over. So, from this side of the microphone, it means aiming high but never forgetting the religious values that sustain us.

This first appeared in Owen Gower and Jolyon Mitchell (eds), Religion and the News, Aldershot: Ashgate, 2011 and is reprinted with their kind permission

SYLVIA ROTHSCHILD

Sylvia Rothschild grew up in Bradford, the third Reform synagogue in England. A graduate of Manchester University, she was ordained by Leo Baeck College in 1987 and was minister of Bromley Synagogue till 2002. Married with three children she works in a job-share rabbinate with Sybil Sheridan at Wimbledon Synagogue.

British Women Rabbis:
the First Forty Years

Forty years after Jackie Tabick began to train for the rabbinate it is surely time to evaluate the generation of women pioneering this role.

This will not be an academic analysis, but an overview and flavour of the experiences of the women who were in the frontline. A way to check against the views of Lily Montagu who, in a sermon preached at the Liberal Jewish Synagogue in 1956, said "There is little doubt that if women are prepared to recognise that their ministry must depend on the development of their full intellectual powers, as well as those of heart and spirit, they will before long see their services eagerly accepted by congregations. Why not?" (1)

For Lily Montagu women would be welcomed alongside men in the congregational rabbinate once they understood they were to be openly scholarly and rational, and not hide behind softer 'feminine' skills of empathy or relationship building. Once women would "come out" so to speak as intelligent, then the world of the community rabbinate would be open to them, the congregations enthusiastic – even impatient – to employ them. This rather places the onus for acceptance onto the women rabbis. It surely also reflects the time of the birth of the highly ideological Liberal movement.

The lived experience of women rabbis has resonances with Montagu's thinking, but is different. One of the themes from all the women rabbis I contacted was the importance of study for them, the value and confidence gained from being able to rest securely on a foundation of intellectual competence. For the earlier women rabbis there was added pressure to being seen to be intellectually skilled. This was expressed in statements such as "your reputation in the community was only as good as your last sermon", and they spoke also of the weighty feeling of being responsible each for the other – a mistake or absence of knowledge in one woman rabbi/student was seen as applicable to all the women, so they laboured long and hard not to let each other down.

And yet, while study and textual competence were clearly drivers in the formation of women rabbis, more even than their male counterparts, something else became clear very early on. Women were rabbis in a different way, they were interested in building relationships rather than imposing authority; they flattened hierarchies and saw themselves as facilitators rather than using authoritarian modes of behaviour. This is clearly described on behalf of all her colleagues by one rabbi thus "I think my rabbinate is very relational based. I build community through building relationships which I think is a more feminine leadership style but it works for me and I don't think there is anything inferior to that model than the more detached, masculine, pedestal model of rabbinate." (2) Another wrote: "I got all of the counselling type issues but am not sure if this was about my gender or because I was trained and interested and he (the male senior rabbi) wasn't" (3).

Almost all colleagues commented on being seen as more accessible than their male colleagues – some referred to women from the orthodox synagogues coming to talk to them because they would rather have spoken to a woman, others talk of the honour of quite intimate moments of spiritual encounter with congregants where, in the words of one "I can't be sure, but believe the fact that I was a woman rabbi made it easier for this young man... He hadn't gone to my more senior male colleague; he came to me" (4). Certainly comments from many congregants demonstrate they see women rabbis as accessible and open in a way that male rabbis are not perceived to be, and that this is about both gender and style. Research in the USA has shown that women rabbis – like women leaders in other fields - use a more collaborative style, with emphasis on co-operation and communication rather than leadership from the front, and hierarchical structure. Studies among American women rabbis also found that many of them wish to remain in the congregation where they have developed emotional links with the community, rather than move to larger communities as their more career-conscious male colleagues have done.

This difference in leadership style, with its attendant accessibility and dismantling of structures leads to unfortunate assumptions on the part of congregants. In the words of one colleague speaking for all women rabbis: "I get treated to the ordinary range of offensive behaviour to which women rabbis are subjected: the uninvited touching and kissing, which I first experienced as a student rabbi; being sidelined in a gathering of mostly male clerics; people telling me, in voices expressing surprise, how well I have done! And on occasion, when I have introduced myself as a rabbi I have been corrected and called *rebbitzin*. It's humiliating and unacceptable of course." (5) Others commented "Sometimes a male chair cast himself as paterfamilias who knows best." (6) Or the typical experience of a student rabbi who was told on Yom Kippur 'It is nice to have something nice to look at on the *bimah*' (7). The sexually loaded comments continue through the stories from the earliest rabbis to the latest – of being asked when they last went to the *mikveh* before reading Torah; of being kissed with the accompanying comment and leer "I've never kissed a rabbi before"; of remarks about the length of hem or depth of neckline; of being asked to wear a gown so as not to look female on the *bimah*, or even of being told that the crossing of legs on the *bimah* was distracting – said to three women rabbis. (6)

The sexuality of women in the rabbinate is a repeated theme: setting aside for a moment the issue of lesbian rabbis, women rabbis have been seen as either threatening to the norm or else disappointing their congregation by taking time out to have babies. One colleague was told that it was "OK for her to have two children but if she had a third, the synagogue couldn't be expected to put up with the disruption". (8) One was given good support with the first child, but accused of lying to the community when announcing her second pregnancy. They believed she would have only one child. (6) Several colleagues who had children while in post found that relationships changed from having been extremely supportive of person and pregnancy, to hostile once the baby came. Negative reactions included congregants asking the new rabbinic mother "how can you be a parent to us if you are being a parent to that" (9); or on negotiating a place at the synagogue nursery, being told "I shouldn't take advantage of the synagogue, I was abusing my position. When I said I had been involved from the nursery's inception she said 'well it is not as if the nursery needs him, the rabbi's child won't bring any special benefit and it is oversubscribed'"(6). Another early colleague described her contract: "I had no pregnancy clause in my contract. When I mentioned it, it was suggested I take 'sick leave'. When my son was born, I worked up to his birth, took five weeks off and returned for Rosh Hashanah. My mother sat through Yom Kippur in the synagogue kitchen with him, a runner informed me when he needed feeding and a rota of lay leaders took over while I fed him. Looking back now it seems absolutely crazy.... At the time I was determined to prove that my having a baby was not going to affect my work with the congregation at all."(6) Another wrote: "there was no model for women rabbis and maternity leave and the synagogue didn't seem to think of it, so I took off ten weeks. I just thought you had the baby and went back to work. Looking back I feel I was stupid and rather naive." (6)

Most of the earlier women rabbis who had children worked right up to the week the baby was due, and were back within a few weeks, rather than have motherhood used as a reason for them not to be seen as doing their job fully and properly. One rabbi even worked through an ectopic pregnancy "as it was High Holy Days and I didn't want to let anyone down". (6) All cannot now understand why they did what they did, describing it as crazy behaviour and contributing to exhaustion and depression, yet the impetus not to be seen as female and therefore weak or unprofessional was extraordinarily powerful, and of course taking time out for women's things might impact on colleagues. This view had some basis in reality for some were told that while they had interviewed best for a job they were not chosen as they might get pregnant and take leave. (6)

To avoid problems, some colleagues described either choosing not to work with other women of child bearing age or else not applying for pulpits. The anxiety of women rabbis is well told in this story : "As a young rabbi aged thirty, green as you like, eager to please, I was horrified to find I was pregnant having signed my contract and begun work. I felt terrible and wanted to protect them from any pregnant female rubbish so I wrote a wonderful sermon about Rebekah's pregnancy, and told the community that my pregnancy would be different, I would be strong and it would be straightforward and I wouldn't let them down. However I fainted and gave it sitting down. How ludicrous! I was intent on being as unfemale as I could be". (10)

The picture isn't all bleak - some communities have been very supportive of maternal rabbis: one moved some evening meetings to the rabbi's home so she didn't have to be out every night; two gave generous maternity benefits above statutory maternity pay; one waited until a rabbi had given birth and spent three months with her baby before she came to work for them; even communities where unhelpful remarks were made, tended to also have extremely kind congregants, although even they misunderstood, as in this story. "The funniest thing that happened was one Shabbat morning I came in and led the torah breakfast, and then the kids' service, and got down to the main service in time to read torah and give the sermon. Afterwards, at Kiddush, a woman came over and said, 'I don't know how you manage to do everything with two young children, no wonder you had to come so late to shul!' (11)

Women rabbis with children have generally not worked full time or tended to work in rabbinic teams as associates with specific time boundaries or functions in the community. Of the forty-six women ordained as rabbis by Leo Baeck College (hereafter referred to as LBC) and working in England, only four have been working full-time as the sole rabbi in their community when their children were born and continued to work as such. Four were full-time associate rabbis in communities, of whom three now work full-time as their children are growing/grown. Three have been working in part-time posts for the bulk of their children's lives, and four are working but not in the congregational rabbinate. Two with children before training continue to work, one part-time and one fulltime. The numbers tell a story that one cannot explore here, but the older generation tell of their salary covering childcare and food only, of the exhaustion of juggling commitments to synagogue and family, of having to keep going so as "not to let the others down". Another said "I was always having to prove – mainly to the women in the congregation – that I could do the job just as well with a baby as before, and was therefore worth keeping on". Any time taken off for children's illness etc – though legitimate – was guiltily repaid with extra work by many of the rabbis I spoke to. Regina Jonas is on record as saying that a woman could be either a mother or a rabbi but not both, and even argued that a female rabbi should remain single in order to exemplify the ideal of *tzniut* – dignified restraint. (12) While I think she points to the difficulty of the situation, many women rabbis with children would not agree with her, and indeed have spent much of their rabbinate disproving her point – albeit sometimes at great personal cost. Curiously only one rabbi said that having children caused her to change career plans.

For other women, maternity was not the issue. Being single brought its own problems in terms of developing intimate relationships – the same issues as those for men, of whether to date within the community or not, whether to keep the partner secret or not. However unlike male rabbis, few women reported having been offered shidduchim within the community. And for other rabbis, sexual orientation was the dominant theme – one wrote "It is quite hard for me to disentangle my experience as woman from my experience as lesbian". (13) Moreover, training for the rabbinate as a gay person was traumatic for both men and women students. At LBC the first openly gay students were both women who began studying in 1983, whereas the first openly gay men entered the college over a decade later.

Gaining a first job after ordination was another shared experience for many of the women. LBC had agreed to take women students on the understanding that while it could offer *semicha* to the right candidates, it could not guarantee that such candidates would get jobs. Earlier women students recall signing a document accepting this position. though men were not expected to do so. The general theme in the earlier days was that the men were offered pulpits quite early in their final year and the women then interviewed (or not) for the rest. One rabbi interviewing for a post in a synagogue with a previous woman rabbi was told "they didn't want another woman" because a woman worked in a nearby synagogue and the officers felt that they would have an advantage if they could find a man to fit their post.

Sadly, while both progressive movements profess full gender equality as a philosophical stance, this is not always true in the behaviour of their synagogues. One woman commented "in my year there were four UK graduates, two men and two women. The men had jobs by around January, the other woman and I applied for every job and finally got something just before graduation. I probably got my pulpit because there were only women applicants! (6) One woman in the UK started her own – very successful – community, but most women contented themselves with a jigsaw puzzle of part time jobs. Very few in the earlier days found a full-time pulpit, and even today they remain a small minority. For the class of 2009 comprising 2 men and 6 women, both men found jobs as full-time associate rabbis in large congregations, one woman took a full-time position in a small community, two women found associate posts (one full and one part time) two had no formal congregational position a year after ordination and were putting together portfolio positions, one had a part time congregation. (14)

Most women have been happy with their career patterns, though some would rather have had single full-time positions rather than portfolio careers. One rabbi however specifically wrote to say she was delighted with two part-time communities making up one full-time post, and would not have it any other way (15). However it is good to note that the large flagship synagogues of both movements are currently headed by a woman senior rabbi. All the women took pains to say how much they enjoyed the rabbinate as a fulfilling and enjoyable profession which stretched their hearts and minds and was endlessly fascinating and diverse. Women have brought so much to the rabbinate – different models of working, different relationships to texts, and - belatedly – different attitudes to boundaries and new ways of time management so that having children is no longer thought of as problematic but as an enriching part of the rabbinate.

There has clearly been progress and an increasing recognition that the movements must accept responsibility for ensuring that women and men are equally respected and chosen as rabbis in communities. Women are also no longer behaving as if their gender should be a problem for communities, which is certainly more healthy for the women involved. One recent graduate wrote "When I first mentioned the rabbinate, women rabbis only ever warned me about glass ceilings and discrimination, even telling me to qualify as a teacher first so I would have something to fall back on. This has certainly not been my reality. I do however realise that with a baby on the way I am about to enter a new chapter in my life and in my rabbinate, and I will have to start making compromises that I have never had to make before. However every career driven woman who becomes a mum must find herself in this situation and I see no difference in the situation I am in to those of a doctor or lawyer except I am my own boss, have very flexible working hours and live two minutes from the synagogue and therefore think in some ways it is easier for me" (17) which is certainly a change from the views and experience of her older colleagues. Pleasingly another recent graduate wrote "I just love doing what I'm doing - the relationships and learning are eternally rewarding. I feel very grateful to all the women before me who mean it wasn't a question in my mind that I could be a rabbi! (18)

Women rabbis have indeed developed their full intellectual powers, and not deserted those skills of heart and spirit, as suggested by Lily Montagu. They have also gained in confidence as they have seen colleagues find different ways of being in the rabbinate, and no longer feel the need to prove themselves in the way the earlier generation did. However it is not yet certain that their services are eagerly accepted by all the congregations in the movements and there is a way to go before full equality in the pulpit is normalised. And so we find that we ask the question that Lily Montagu asked all those years ago – full equality in the rabbinate "Why not?"

(1) Lily Montagu in Ellen Umansky *Lily Montagu Sermons, Addresses, Letters and Prayers* Edwin Mellen Press 1985 p184)
(2) Rabbi Miriam Berger
(3) Rabbi Helen Freeman
(4) Rabbi Janet Burden
(5) Rabbi Elizabeth Tikvah Sarah
(6) Reported by a colleague in correspondence with the author
(7) Rabbi Debbie Young Somers
(8) Reported by two colleagues with different numbers of children cited
(9) Rabbi Sylvia Rothschild
(10) Rabbi Rebecca Quassim Birk
(11) Rabbi Jackie Tabick
(12) Elisa Klapek, *Fraulein Rabbiner Jonas* p11
(13) Rabbi Elizabeth Tikvah Sarah
(14) http://news.reformjudaism.org.uk/press-releases/eight-new-rabbis.html RJ website
(15) Rabbi Janet Burden
(16) Rabbi Rachel Montagu
(17) Rabbi Miriam Berger
(18) Rabbi Debbie Young Somers

MARC SAPERSTEIN

Marc Saperstein became Principal of
Leo Baeck College in July 2006, after
having held prestigious positions at three
American Universities. He is author of
six books and more than 50 articles on
various aspects of Jewish history,
literature and thought, with a special
emphasis on the history of Jewish
preaching.

Rabbinic Leadership in Time of Crisis

Rabbi Isaac Aboab II (1433–1493)

Modern historians have tended to denigrate the leaders of Spanish
Jewry during its last generation on the Iberian peninsula. Except for
Abravanel, this fateful period is usually presented as one of intellectual
mediocrity, a generation that produced no shining stars in any field of Jewish
cultural endeavor. The present article will focus on one of the most important
of these leaders, Isaac Aboab II, to evaluate the validity of this portrayal.

Aboab's stature as one of the most important Talmudists in the
generation of the expulsion is attested by many. Himself one of the
outstanding disciples of Isaac Canponton, his own disciples included Jacob
Berab, Joseph Fasi, Moses Danon, and Abraham Zacuto. Joseph Karo's
maggid singles out Aboab's *yeshivah* as pre-eminent in the recent past,
promising Karo that "your academy will be even greater than that of My
chosen one, Isaac Aboab;" Levi ibn Habib, rabbi of Jerusalem, described
Aboab as "the greatest of his generation." (1) Aboab's commentary on *Orah
Hayyim* of the *Arba'ah Turim* was an important source for Karo, who refers in
his own commentary to a question disputed in the Aboab yeshivah. He also
wrote a commentary on *Yoreh De'ah* and Novellae on Tractates Betsah,
Ketubot and Kiddushin. (2)

In addition, we are told that he wrote responsa in the "thousands and
myriads: he made them proliferate, but we do not know who will gather
them." (3) Two of these responsa were published at Livorno in the mid-
eighteenth century (at the end of *Shiv'ah 'Einayim*). Both deal with a trustee

159

who sold the portion of a house belonging to orphans, who challenged the validity of the sale when they reached maturity. Aboab shows considerable independence in his decision, writing,

> The Talmudic statement [Gittin 52a] that trustees may not sell real estate applied to their time, when real estate was the basis of their livelihood, and their primary responsibility pertained to it. Today, however, when our livelihood is based primarily on moveable property, which is better than real estate in every respect, and it is well known in our time that there is no work more demeaning than [that involving] real estate [cf. Yebamot 63a], we should change the law in accordance with the place and the time. . . . In this position of mine, I do not rely on anyone else, for I have not found it in any other decisor. However, together with my other arguments, this is what the law should be. (4)

Even assuming that such independence of legal reasoning was relatively unusual in his work, if the actual number of his responsa was anywhere near 1000, the loss of such a substantial corpus has deprived us of what would undoubtedly be a major resource for Spanish Jewish life in its final generation.

Aboab's interests and talents were considerably broader than the world of the Talmud and Jewish law. His Biblical commentary—a supercommentary on Rashi and Ramban—enters fully into the arena of Biblical exegesis. (5) One could not prove from this work that the author was a distinguished halakhic authority at all, nor could one document a solid grounding in either philosophy or Kabbalah. It shows little in the way of an intellectual agenda, other than to guide the reader through some of the problems in the classic commentaries of the two masters. More than anything else, it gives the impression of Torah study "for its own sake."

Particularly important for our purposes are Aboab's sermons. (6) To be sure, the evidence of his preaching is less than ideal. Most of the material preserved in the book published as *Nehar Pishon* is a summary, apparently written by the preacher's son from his father's notes and from notes taken by disciples, and not a full transcript of anything that was said (7). Unlike the sermons of Aboab's younger contemporary Joseph Garçon (8), these sermons are not identified by date or place of delivery, only by the Torah lesson, life cycle, or holiday occasion. Nevertheless, we get from these texts clear evidence that Aboab took preaching as a serious responsibility, reflecting on the techniques and conventions of the art, occasionally preaching twice on the same Sabbath (at Shaharit and Minhah services), delivering wedding sermons and eulogies as well as the expected sermons for Shabbat ha-Gadol and the Sabbath of Repentance. (9)

Some of these sermons seem to be intended for the broadest kind of audience. Consider the following passage, in which Aboab is discussing the actions of Jacob's sons following the rape of Dinah:

> It is human nature that when people quarrel, whether over words or deeds, and come for reconciliation between themselves, if they are truly sincere, they will say, "Even though this and that occurred between us, and such and such happened, it makes no difference." If the reconciliation is insincere, they say, "Never mention what happened again," while the aggrieved party holds on to his anger and bides his time until an opportunity comes for revenge. So it was with the sons of Jacob. They calculated to themselves how it would be possible to take vengeance against Shechem. When Shechem and his father Hamor came to ask for Dinah, they said, "Even though you have done this shameful thing to our sister, we will overlook this insult and give her to you in marriage, provided that you circumcise every male." That is why they believed them. And this is the meaning of the verse, The sons of Jacob answered Shechem and his father Hamor with guile (Gen. 34:13). What was the guile? That they said, that he defiled their sister Dinah (ibid.) [implying sincere reconciliation], and subsequently killed them. (10)

Here we have an insight of some psychological depth, expressed in a form that any listener can understand and identify with, used to explain a problematic verse. It is a preaching style intended to endear the preacher with a popular audience.

On the other hand, a few of the printed sermons seem to have been addressed to rather sophisticated and learned audiences. The level of philosophical material in some of these sermons can be quite high. Elsewhere I have published a passage in which Aboab cites Thomas Aquinas's Commentary on Aristotle's *Metaphysics*, in which Aquinas identifies a problem in Ibn Rushd's commentary. (11) According to Steinschneider, this work by Thomas was translated into Hebrew by Abraham Nahmias, apparently in 1490 in the city of Ocaña. If so, it appears that Aboab, who lived in Guadalajara not far from Ocaña (12), acquired the translation, studied at least part of it, and incorporated a section of it into his sermon between the completion of the translation in 1490 and his death in 1493. The entire passage seems more characteristic of a lecture at the University of Paris than the conclusion of a sermon by a Spanish Talmudist, a rather amazing clue to the expectations of at least one kind of Jewish audience and the intellectual breadth of an important rabbi.

More significant than the mere citation of these authors is the way they are used. Occasionally, Aboab will refer to an extreme philosophical idea that cannot be accepted. He argues against the "philosophizers" (probably referring to Gersonides) who deny God's knowledge of particulars (13), and refers with disdain to "the destroyers of our religion" who teach that after death the soul will be unified with the active intellect or with God" and thereby lose its individual identity. (14) For the most part, however, Aristotle and other philosophers are cited by Aboab (and the other Spanish preachers whose works we know) not in order to refute them, or to contrast their teachings with those of Torah. On the contrary, they are usually cited as established truths, self-evident principles, universally accepted doctrines that can be used as building blocks for subsequent assertions. (15)

Where there is an apparent contradiction between the Torah and philosophical truth, Aboab often sets out to resolve it. "It is said that this Torah lesson about the creation of the world is contradicted by principles derived from reason and logical demonstration; therefore we will speak at greater length in order to show that the subject of the *parashah* agrees with the intellect and science."(16) He realizes that material in the Torah that appears to contradict reason—for example the use of anthropomorphic and anthropopathic language about God—may make it more difficult for thinking Jews to believe, and that these problems must be addressed and resolved in philosophical terms. (17)

Also noteworthy is his use of philosophical tools, particularly drawn from philology and logic, to solve exegetical problems. Noting the redundancy of an extra verb "to be" at the end of Leviticus 27:10, Aboab begins, "To resolve this puzzle, you should know that there are two terms in the language of the Christians that the translators did not know how to render properly until recently. The first is in their language *ente* and in ours it is *nimtsa*; the second in their language is *essentia* and in ours *heyot*. In addition, you should know that things that exist (*nimtsa'im*) can exist in reality or in the imagination." (18) This distinction enables the preacher to explain both the strange wording of the verse and a statement of Maimonides about it.

Philosophy influences not just the content but also the modes of thought and forms of argumentation in some of Aboab's sermons. Like other contemporary preachers, he will occasionally resort to the use of syllogisms to set forth his argument, a homiletical technique about which Hayyim ibn Musa had complained decades earlier. (19) This was a mode of thinking that many Jews apparently found convincing, and that could be readily followed in an oral discourse. Clearly a new manner of Jewish preaching, it reveals the influence of Aristotle's works on logic that had recently been translated into Hebrew. Like other Jewish preachers of his age, Aboab also used in his sermons the form of the "disputed question," one of the characteristic modes of medieval scholastic discourse, a striking innovation in Jewish homiletics. Aboab employs the disputed question form in discussing repentance, a particularly problematic doctrine in the generation of the Expulsion, investigating in one sermon "whether repentance is efficacious" and in another "whether repentance is a root of the Torah." (20) This scholastic form of argumentation also seems to have had a genuine appeal for many Jewish listeners, and Aboab shows how it was accommodated naturally into Spanish Jewish preaching.

Aboab was not averse to discussing Kabbalistic material in his sermons. The limited evidence for the use of Zoharic quotations and Kabbalistic doctrines in public preaching at this time has led some scholars to conclude that with rare exceptions Kabbalah was not incorporated into sermons before the late sixteenth century. (21) Aboab provides another example indicating that this generalization may reflect the paucity of the sources rather than the realities of pulpit discourse. Thus he cites the *Midrash ha-Ne'elam* on Genesis 4:12 (Cain's punishment) and on Leviticus 4:22 (the sin of the *nasi*), summarizes Kabbalistic interpretations of Genesis 32:26 (the wounding of Jacob) and Numbers 12:3 (Moses" humility), presents a Kabbalistic understanding of the sefirotic significance of repentance and a Kabbalistic explanation of why the new month is not mentioned on Rosh Hashanah. (22) There is no indication that the discussion of such material from the pulpit is in any way daring. It is rather a way of enriching the preacher's presentation.

Despite the rather theoretical nature of the material cited thus far, Aboab was by no means oblivious to problems of social import. His awareness of tensions between Christians and Jews is reflected in several passages. "The Gentiles vilify us and say, "You have no share in the world to come,"" a remark that appears to cause special hurt. (23) They want us baptized. (24) Predictably, Aboab found little to praise in the Christian religion, conceding that they shared with Jews the goal of worshipping the true God, but insisting that "they err in the means and paths they take, making light darkness and darkness light." (25) At the same time, Jews should be careful to avoid behavior that might engender Christian contempt for Judaism. "Since we live among the Gentiles, we must be careful in speaking with them that your 'Yes' means *yes* and your 'No,' *no*, careful not to trick them or to do them any injustice or wrong, for this is how our Torah and our God are forgotten in their speech." (26)

He was not afraid to speak out about social justice among Jews. Discussing the problem of loans to the poor in the context of the Biblical legislation (Deut. 15:7-9), he makes a specific contemporary application:

> This problem pertaining to loans has arisen many times, especially where I live. Because the Torah forbids the taking of interest when a loan is given to a Jew, no one wants to lend to him. Since the impoverished Jew cannot get an interest-bearing loan as a Gentile can, he cannot find the money he needs, and he dies of hunger. Thus the commandment turns into a transgression. I am tempted to say that it should be considered a greater sin for someone to refuse to make the loan than it is for someone to make the loan and take interest, for in the first case there is danger and in the second there is not. . . . I have dwelt at length on this because I see wretched Jews crying out and not being answered, because of our sins, in this time of dearth. (27)

This is a rather extraordinary passage. Jewish ethical and homiletical literature is filled with denunciations by moralists of businessmen who fail to observe properly the prohibitions against loans on interest; rabbis frequently emphasize the seriousness of these laws and urge that Jews consult with competent authorities who will keep them from improper loans. (28) Rarely do we find a leading rabbinic figure saying, in effect, that the transgressions entailed in taking interest are less serious than depriving the poor of what they need to survive. This statement bespeaks a leader of considerable conscience and courage.

In short, the works of Aboab, and especially his sermons, provide evidence of a rabbi who could draw on all the intellectual resources of contemporary Jewish culture—halakhic expertise, Biblical study, philosophy, Kabbalah, and social consciousness—and bring them together in communicating with his people. But what about the great historical issues of the day? Here we are likely to be disappointed. As is characteristic of the genre, what we find is general and allusive rather than concrete and specific. The assertion that the present generation, "because of our sins," cannot see God's providence as the generation of Moses did (29) may well fit the dark months of 1492, but it is too commonplace a sentiment to have historical value.

A parable cited from Midrash Tehillim describes "A father and son were walking on a road. The son, tired and weak, asked the father if they were far from the city [their destination] or near it. The father said, "Remember this sign: when you see a cemetery, that will indicate that we are near the city. . . ." Thus when we see calamities draw near, it is a sign of the coming of the Messiah." This has been cited by historians as an example of an immediate response to the Expulsion, and indeed it may be. But the messianic dimension is almost entirely absent in these sermons. If the passage is indeed authentic and not a later interpolation, it may be nothing more than a conventional response to sorrow. (30)

There are also references to martyrdom. In one sermon, Aboab says, "The soul that does not cleave to its body does not feel it when they separate it from that body, for it is cleaving to God. That is why man has been compared to an upside-down tree with its roots above. One should therefore cleave to God, cleave to one's true root, and then he will not feel it even when they take his life." (31) This appears to express the tradition that the martyr feels no pain despite the tortures of execution, a tradition known in this generation from the somewhat later "Megillat Amraphel." (32) Yet in a different passage the preacher seems to be clarifying his position and repudiating the radical claim:

> This is like someone who accepts death as a martyr. There is no doubt that he will feel distress at the time he is being put to death, for the body is affected by it. But insofar as he imagines that by this death he attains true communion [with God], his mind will rejoice. (33)

Without information about the date or circumstances of delivery, it is impossible to be certain what resonance these passages about martyrdom would have had among the listeners who heard them. They indicate, however, that the experience of the martyr was being addressed as an actual issue at a time when Jews could witness the burning of those relaxed into the arms of the secular powers.

Was the vision of a man like Isaac Aboab inadequate to the great historic challenges of his age? His extant writings provide little clear evidence of a profound mind or a charismatic personality. (34) He did not have the stature of Samuel ibn Nagrela or Moses Maimonides, who could both dominate their specific environment and produce work of enduring value. These writings do, however, suggest a leader of considerable talent - rooted in Spain yet capable of leaving it as an old man and preparing the groundwork for accommodation elsewhere (35); expert in the traditional Talmudic literature but fascinated by philosophy and open to the teachings of Kabbalah; capable of communicating to Jews who lacked more than a rudimentary Jewish education and to the most sophisticated intellectuals; passionate about both the nuances of halakhic interpretation and the large issues of social responsibility. How many others, who are little more than names to us or whose names we do not even know, were leaders of similar calibre gracing the Spanish Jewish communities during their final decades? That is a question to which historians may never be able to give a fully adequate response.

ENDNOTES:

Because of constraints regarding space, the endnotes, which include not only the identification of sources but further substantive information, could not be included in this publication. The text of this article, with complete endnotes, will be accessible on the Leo Baeck College Website:
(http://lbc.reformjudaism.org.uk/Sermons-Papers/sermons-a-papers.html)

SYBIL SHERIDAN

Sybil Sheridan, ordained at Leo Baeck College in 1981, is one half of the rabbinic job-share at Wimbledon and District Synagogue with Rabbi Sylvia Rothschild. She wrote *Stories from the Jewish World*, edited *Hear Our Voice*, co-edited *Taking up the Timbrel* and has contributed to numerous books and journals.

A Belief in Angels

How We View Angels Today

Shalom Aleichem mal'achei hasharet...
Peace be upon you, ministering angels... (1)

So begins one of the most popular of the Sabbath evening Hymns. We welcome the angels, invite them to come into our house to bless us, and let them take their leave. The hymn is associated with a passage of the Talmud:

> It was taught, R. Jose son of R. Judah said: Two ministering angels accompany man on the eve of the Sabbath from the synagogue to his home, one good and one evil. When he arrives home and finds the lamp burning, the table laid and the bed covered with a spread, the good angel exclaims, 'May it be so on another Sabbath,' and the evil angel unwillingly responds 'amen'. But if not, the evil angel exclaims, 'May it be so on another Sabbath,' and the good angel unwillingly responds, 'amen'. (2)

The tale remains popular despite its non-PC assumptions - Rabbi Ellen Frankel celebrates the story with her children :

> Whether out of pride or dread, our children were always glad that our Sabbath table looked so festive and the food smelled so appetizing, even if delay challenged their patience to wait for the *Motsi* [the blessing over bread at the start of the meal] For them, the Angels

featured in *Shalom Aleichem* were harbingers of redemption in a very tangible way. (3)

Do people really believe today, that angels accompany them on their way home from synagogue? Or is it simply a story to tell the children, to keep them engaged? On consulting colleagues and congregation, I found some took it literally, others metaphorically, others, simply enjoyed the tune. Elliot Dorff writes,

> I understand angels as a personification of life's experiences, so I do not worry about justifying their existence as real beings. At the same time, I am appreciative of the sheer beauty of angel talk. As embodied creatures we understand concrete things more than abstractions. Given Jewish belief in an unembodied God beyond all representations, angel talk provides a graphic and emotionally potent way to conceptualise God at work in the world. (4)

Or in the words of an eight year old I consulted, 'Angels are little bits of *Ha-Shem* that are found in the world'.

One rabbi responded:

> I think one has to remember the original meaning of *Mal'ach*, as messenger. If one does this, then so many things can be considered as God's messengers i.e. wind, rain, peace of mind, and the latter will give meaning to 'angels' in the prayer. My therapist, whose name is Angela, is very religious but is not a member of any official movement, is a firm believer in angels and we have long discussions on the subject. As a matter of interest, my late wife was a firm believer in angels and used to tell me that she often saw her guardian angel at the check-out in Tesco. He was a very handsome man! (5)

When *Shalom Aleichem* first appeared, it was criticized by rabbinical authorities. The phrase 'Bless me with peace' violates the injunction not to invoke blessing of anyone but God. and while the angels might be doing God's bidding by acting as ciphers through which the human can speak to God, this too is problematic. Judaism claims no intermediaries in the dialogue between God and humanity. Nevertheless *Shalom Aleichem* was kept in our liturgy by popular demand.

The disjunction between rabbinic reservation and lay acceptance is illustrated in a *Selichot piyyut* that is equally theologically suspect:

> Angels of mercy, usher in (our petition for mercy) before the Lord of mercy. Angels of prayer, cause our prayers to be heard before Him who hears prayer. Angels of supplication, cause our supplications to be heard before Him who listens to supplication. Angels of tears, bring in our tears before the King, who is reconciled by tears. Intercede for us and multiply prayer and entreaty before the King, the most high God.... (6)

Rabbi Abraham Rosenfeld, describes what was a rabbinic dislike, then grudging acceptance of this prayer:

> Many a commentator abstained from translating this prayer, objecting to the idea of praying to angels....most commentators agree that prayer is a Jacob's Ladder joining earth to heaven.... Various symbols have been read into the imagery of the ladder and the angels upon it. One view is that it represents the vehicle by which one's prayers ascend to heaven and through which salvation descends from heaven. (7)

That they must ascend to heaven before descending (8) puts angels back in the earthly realm.

> We understand that ordinary people are messengers of the Most High. They go about their tasks in holy anonymity, often even unknown to themselves. Yet, if they had not been there, if they had not said what they said, or did what they did, it would not be the way it is now. We would not be the way we are now. Never forget that you, too, yourself may be a messenger.... (9)

Many British Rabbis share this view:

> Angels...simply refer to fellow humans who can be (or who can be used as) instruments of a message or as forces for good; certainly there are people who can have that function today, but that then veers more towards being a lammed vavnik [the myth that the world is sustained by thirty six *lammed vav* righteous individuals in the world at any one time.] (10)

The writer goes on to suggest that this is a more believable concept, but would suggest a great many more than thirty six are operating in the world. The *piyyut* talks of multiplicities of angels, and there is evidence in our hymn of many more than the two angels mentioned. The Talmud itself states 'There is not a stalk of grass that has not its angel in heaven.'

Associating *Shalom Aleichem* with the Talmudic passage reduces the many angels to two - a good angel and a bad. They correspond to the contradictory forces that guide our nature, the *yetzer ha-tov* and *yetzer ha-ra* - inclinations to good and evil. Angels become part of our psyche.

In the Kedushat ha-Shem in the Amidah (11), however, angels are uncompromisingly supernatural. In it, we quote '*Kadosh kadosh kadosh*' - holy, holy, holy - of the vision of Isaiah:

> In the year that King Uzziah died I saw my Lord sitting upon a throne, high and lifted up, and his train filled the temple. *Seraphim* stood above it: they had six wings. Each had six wings; with two they covered their face, and with two they covered their feet, and with two they flew.
> One cried to another, and said, 'Holy, holy, holy, is the Eternal God of hosts; the whole earth is full of his glory. (12)

Seraphim are not *mal'achim*. There is nothing remotely human about them, they belong to another world - one that also includes *keruvim* and *ophanim* (13) - creatures conjured up in dreams and visions. Their function too is different - they praise God.

> The Rabbis believed in angels the way we believe in a conscience - that is, they use projective language while we use introjective language. They saw God without, while we like to see God within. The goal for many moderns is to go 'deep down inside ourselves' or to 'get in touch with ourselves.' In antiquity the same thing was expressed by the desire to go out of ourselves and to join the realm of the angelic host. (14)

The desire to join the angelic host is expressed in the choreography. The supplicant should close their eyes, look heavenward and rise on their toes three times - each one higher than the last. This is said to be in imitation of the *seraphim*, whose faces are covered by wings and who 'hover' around the throne of glory. Since Isaiah 6 describes *Seraphim* as only having one foot -

we are imitating a 'hopping' motion when we rise on our toes. However, many today identify the movement with an aspiration not to be like *seraphim* but to 'get closer to God.' - or to become 'the best we can possibly be'.

Hoffman's idea of projective and introjective thought as dividing us from the ancients, is taken up by Rabbi Rami Shapiro:

> When we speak about the deepest levels of human insight we tend to speak in myth and metaphor. When myths speak of outward journeys, they are usually talking about inner ones. When they speak of gods and angels being separate from ourselves, they are actually referring to aspects of ourselves. Myth arose at a time in human development when all inner experience was projected outward to make it accessible to human investigation... (15)

Yet a number of my consultees were quite comfortable with the idea of heavenly realms beyond our knowledge and comprehension. The novels of Philip Pullman, deftly capture the beliefs of our age. They describe a world devoid of God but full of parallel universes that teem with thousands of other beings. Given this scenario, when we raise ourselves on our toes the desire really is to be like the angelic *Seraphim*. Angels, who do not sin, who have no complications in their lives, who exist only to sing. (16) Of course there are other views:

> Being a scientist, I usually explain that 'angel', rather like 'messenger of God', is an old, pre-scientific, code word for what nowadays are more specifically referred to as either laws of physics or natural phenomena, such as gravity, electricity or magnetism. In ancient times there was no understanding of the scientific reasons for natural phenomena, so people thought that God sent an angel, or messenger, who caused some particular effect. Nowadays we might think about matters in a different way, because of our different education. (17)

Rationality does not, for many people, 'hit the spot.'

> Fairies are to angels as an old man is to God. Since I don't shy away from talking about God even though people often think of an old man, I similarly don't shy talking about "divine messengers."... I would find it hard to say the *Kedushah* if I didn't think I were joining in the praise already being sung. All metaphor, of course, but very important. (18)

One rabbi recalls,

> Was it not Rosenzweig, who said,"I know seas don't part and donkeys don't talk. But once a year, on *Shabbat Shira* (when we read of the parting of the sea) and *Sidrat Balak* (the story of Bilaam's Ass), I'm prepared to accept that they do" (19)

Another writes:

> Can't we hold on to rational and non-rational truth at the same time? It's a bit like dreams, real and unreal, but with a meaning that language and concrete thought can't deal in...I think that one can have a relationship with angels as story figures, as elements of midrashic theology for instance, without believing they are really all flying around or walking around waiting to do my will. That is, they are real to me as expressions of theological inquiry, but not at all real, if you see what I mean. (20)

A third prayer gives another view of angels. The night prayer known as *Beshem ha-Shem*:

> In the name of the Eternal God of Israel, may Micha'el be at my right hand, Gabri'el at my left, in front of me Uri'el, behind me Rapha'el and above my head, Shechinat El. (21)

The prayer is based on a Midrash which describes each angel, and where they were positioned around the Throne of Glory. (22) Their names are explained in the Midrash also. Michael – from the Hebrew *mi ca-el*? - 'Who is like God?' - from Exodus 15:11. Gabriel takes his name from the Hebrew *gavar* - 'might of God' - with the proof text being the passage from I Chronicles 5:2: 'For Judah prevailed over his brothers'. Uriel - the light of God does not occur in Tanakh, though he becomes associated with the wisdom contained in the Holy books. 'Arise, shine for your light has come,' it says in Isaiah 60:1. Raphael is the angel of healing the proof text being from Numbers 12:13 and Miriam's leprosy where Moses cries 'God, please, heal her now.'
In the book of Exodus, God promises,

> And I will send an angel before you; and I will drive out the Canaanite, the Amorite, and the Hittite, and the Perizzite, the Hivite, and the Jebusites. (23)

We have the picture of angels flanking the sides of the camp of Israel; moving along with the tribes in their formation. They are there to protect against attack, and to go with the people into battle as they secure their land. These angels are war-like creatures - they make up the army of the 'Eternal' they are the Hosts at His command - the cohorts and legions. While Israel fights its enemies below with four angels in attendance, the rest of God's angels do battle against the forces of darkness above. In our night-time prayer, their function is to guard. Michael has his sword drawn as it were; the four angels surround the bed are ready to fend off anything that could possibly attack us in the darkness.

But the text does not call the named beings angels per se, and the names themselves derive from attributes of God. Presiding over the four, is *Shechinat El*, the Presence of God. At once the representative of the Godhead to whom the angels must answer, but also, because of the linguistic similarities with the named angels, something ambiguous. In Kabbalah, the *Shechinah* is part of the Godhead. Presumably too, then *Micha-el*, *Gavri-el* *Uri-el* and *Rapha-el* are parts of God too. '..Little bits of *Ha-Shem* that are found in the world.'

Of the three passages chosen from our prayerbook, logic would dictate that this last, in the 21st Century would be the least likely to persist. It is not part of the fixed requirements for prayer, - just a pious wish against the evil spirits of the night. Said to children when small, the lovely comforting feeling of being tucked up in bed, with reassuring presences to counter the terrors of the dark, these children continue to recite the prayer as a talisman as they grow up, reciting it to their children in turn.

Many described feeling the presence of such guardian angels. A fleeting touch between sleeping and waking, or at moments during serious illness. One woman, a Holocaust survivor, who spent most of the war years hiding in different European countries under different assumed names confessed in later life to having had an abortion during those troubled years. As she lay dying she saw coming towards her a little girl with a young man who she recognized as her guardian angel who had kept her baby safe all those years just as he had protected her during the Shoah. (24) Others speak of talking to a nurse and coming to some sort of revelation, or recognition, or realisation that changes their perspective and enables them to return to life, or meet death with equanimity. Some will claim that nurse to be the angel, others that the angel was there with them at the time. So guardian angels, both protect against and accompany towards the end of life. The guardian angels that have been introduced to them when very young in that 'little death'- as sleep is called in rabbinic literature.

> In the context of, say, *keriat shema al hamitah*, [the night time shema] I can speak of Gavriel, Azziel etc. It's what I feel when reciting *Hashkivenu* that bit about 'causing us to lie down in peace.' Ever since I had kids, I remember that lovely moment of tucking them in at night, putting the duvet over them and shaping it around the contour of their body, to hold them, to keep them safe. So for me, *hashkivenu* will always be the "God-as- parent-tucking-us-in-at-night" prayer. But in other contexts I really don't like the suggestion that God is parent, we are children, because I believe it infantilises our relationship with God. (25)

> Donald Winnicott (British psycho-analyst) taught about "transitional objects", such as baby's favourite toy or special bit of blanket. This transitional object mediates between the baby and the world. It is not an 'objective' experience, but nor is it totally 'subjective'. This object is at one and the same time a representation of the baby's self interacting with the outer world, and also a representative of some especially benign aspects of the outer world, in particular of Mummy and/or Daddy. So it can be thrown out of the cot, representing baby's wish to get out of the cot, and then baby needs it back in the cot for its own security. The transitional object simultaneously represents mummy, or the outside world in a good way. So baby can be left by actual Mummy and Daddy as long as it has its comforting object with it. I think angels are something like that, mediating between us and God. (26)

Is there a difference between the views of my colleagues and those held by their congregation some of whom, it seems, accept literally the notion of angels? Going into a bookshop, one finds maybe half a shelf of books on religion - and two or more shelves on angelology. Angels have been divorced from God and now have a life of their own. Writing this talk excited a surprising amount of attention from people asking if they could hear it, or demanding copies of it to send to people they thought it might 'help'. What is it about angels that fulfil a need un-met by our traditional notions of God? There are angel cards - a sort of theological tarot - illustrated cards with a word or phrase on them designed for reflection or meditation. At least one Reform Rabbi is making use of them in their counseling sessions.

So, rabbis, be aware. Just as our predecessors' objections to *Shalom Aleichem* were swept away on a tide of popular demand, our rationalising of the angels appearing in our liturgy may ultimately prove equally irrelevant. We may struggle today with concepts of God, but angels continue to have a fond and firm hold on our imagination.

1. *Seder ha-Tefillot: Forms of Prayer* London 2008 page 104
2. Shabbat 119b
3. Shabbat at Home; *My People's Prayer Book* Ed Laurence Hoffman Jewish Lights Woodstock 2004 p70
4. Ibid
5. Sidney Kay
6. Piyyut by Rav Amram: Abraham Rosenfeld *Selichot for the whole year* p21
7. Ibid
8. Genesis 28:12
9. Laurence Hoffman in *Mishkan Tefillah* New York 2007 p142
10. Jonathan Romain
11. Seder ha-Tefillot p226
12. Isaiah 6:1-3
13. Ezekiel 10
14. Laurence Hoffman *My People's Prayer Book* the Amidah p9
15. Rami Shapiro *The Angelic Way* NY 2000 p12
16. cf. Psalm 148.
17. Ron Berry
18. Neil Amswych
19. Colin Eimer
20. Shulamit Ambalu
21. Seder Ha-Tefillot p 443
22. Bamidbar Rabba II: 10
23. Exodus 33:2
24. Related by Sylvia Rothschild
25. Rabbi Colin Eimer
26. Rabbi Danny Smith

MICHAEL SHIRE

Michael Shire serves as Vice-Principal and Director of the Department of Jewish Education at the Leo Baeck College. He lectures at the College and elsewhere on Jewish Religious Leadership and Transformational Learning. He is a graduate of Hebrew Union College, University College, London and Leo Baeck College.

Religious Education: A Theological Approach

Rabbi Dr. Tony Bayfield has been my teacher for over 20 years. It was an article that he wrote about Developmental Psychology and Jewish Education (Bayfield 1979) that first sparked my interest in Faith Development as a new field at the nexus of Developmental Psychology and Theology. In many ways, in this chapter on the theology of childhood, I have drawn upon and extended Rabbi Bayfield's lifelong interest in religious education. I have been privileged to work with him in contributing to the development of Progressive Jewish Education in the United Kingdom.

A recent approach to understanding the religious views of children and childhood has been prevalent in Christianity through Catholic teachings on Catechesis and Christian doctrines of theological education (Groome 1980, Moran 1983). Questions that such theologians ask are: What is God saying to us in the existence of childhood, in the necessity that life must begin with childhood and that all peoples must enter into a time of formation and education? To whom do children belong and who should determine their future and growth?

Childhood is therefore seen not to be merely a stage to pass through as the developmentalists would have it, but rather a state of being profoundly spiritual 'a part of our being before God' (Shier-Jones 2007, p.xii). Theologians of childhood believe that there needs to be a fuller understanding of this state of being and how religion can contribute to the way childhood is shaped and formed. Here there is a distinction to be made between children and childhood. Very little theological speculation, especially in Judaism, has

176

been done on the nature of childhood though thought has been given in the tradition to the moral and spiritual status of the child. However Judaism's rabbinic and philosophical tradition does portray the purposes of childhood.

The Blessings of Children and the Blessings Children Bestow

Children are considered a great gift in Judaism. Parents who produce children are considered to be blessed and there are many and varied customs and ceremonies to introduce a child into the Jewish community. While classical Judaism does not have an abundant theoretical literature about the nature of childhood itself, it is through rituals, legal traditions and interpretative literature that we learn what Judaism teaches about the spirit of the child. Childhood itself is an important state of being in Judaism signified both by the cherished status of children in the classical literature and by the child-parent relationship that epitomizes the way in which the human-Divine relationship is understood. Just as children are received as a blessing, they, in turn, bless their own parents as well as the larger community as indicated in the concept of *Zechut banim* –through the merits of the children, the parents deserve honour.

Judaism understands that the spiritual life of children is expressed through study of Torah (understood as all of Jewish learning), by participation in the ritual and prayer life of the community (*avoda*) and in righteous action and acts of lovingkindness (*gemilut hasadim*). The mission of the child is to glorify the name of God on earth: 'You shall be to me a kingdom of Priests' is understood literally in that every child is considered to be a predestined priest to be prepared to serve God and complete the work of creation. The distinct nature of the spirituality of children in Judaism is therefore expressed as a purity of nature and a potential for the highest aspiration of holiness and goodness. Treasured and cherished, Judaism values children and childhood as perhaps the most pure form of being created in God's image (*b'zelem elohim*). A classic passage from the *Midrash* illuminates the incomparable status of the child in the very act of God's revelation:

> When God was about to give the Torah to Israel, he asked them, will you accept my Torah? And they answered, we will. God said, give me surety that you will fulfill its ordinances. They said let Abraham, Isaac and Jacob be our pledges. God answered, but the patriarchs themselves need sureties.....Then Israel said, our children shall be our sureties. God said such as these pledges I will indeed accept. Straight away the Israelites brought their wives with their children, even

infants at the breast, even babes yet unborn. And God gave them power of speech even to those yet in the womb. He said to them, I am about to give your parents the Torah, will you pledge yourselves that they will fulfill it.. They said, we pledge ourselves. Then God rehearsed command after command and to each in succession the children promised obedience. (Tanhuma Vayiggash 5:1)

The Talmud states that childhood is a garland of roses, while the prophet Malachi calls children 'the seed of God' (Malachai 2:15). One rabbi states that the very breath of children is free of sin (Shabbat 119a) while the Jerusalem Talmud pronounces, "Better are the late fruits we ate in our childhood than the peaches we ate in our old age." (J.Talmud Peah 87:4). Children are regarded as the hope for the future in that they have been entrusted to parents as a Divine gift.

There are said to be three partners in the creation of a child; mother, father and God according to Ecclesiastes Rabbah 5. Children are therefore a component of God's creation and not exclusive to the parents who bear and raise them. Before birth the tradition postulates a pre-birth existence whereby the unborn soul struggles with the notion of being born against its will. It says, 'up to now I have been holy and pure; do not bring me into contact with what is common and unclean!' Two angels are said to take the unborn soul and show him the glory of the righteous who dwell there and the sufferings of the sinner. The unborn soul wants to remain pure and cherished, yet the soul knows that it must adapt to the human world of trial and struggle to fulfill God's purpose.

What then is the theological purpose of children in the scheme of creation? A famous story from the rabbinic tradition seeks to affirm the purity of God's realm while acknowledging the task of humanity in being growing and learning creatures: New born children are contrasted with angels and lowly beasts of the field:

On the second day of creation, God created the angels with their innate goodness. Then God created beasts with animal instincts not knowing right or wrong. Since God was unhappy with these extremes, God created humanity who would combine characteristics of both angel and beast in order to have free will to follow his good or evil inclination. In order for free will to be truly exercised, the child is made to forget all that he or she has learned as an unborn soul. Before it enters the world, an angel strikes it on the upper lip and all

178

knowledge and wisdom disappear. The ridge in the upper lip is the result of this stroke. (Niddah 30b)

From investigation of attitudes in the *Midrash* based on biblical narratives of the childhood experiences of Joseph, Samuel and David, we can see emerge a state of childhood being treasured for a special role. Childhood is seen as a condition of purity and deep spiritual connection especially through awe and wonder of God's creation and Divine purpose. Biblical stories about children demonstrate their ability to see what others cannot as in Joseph's dreams or Samuel's call in the Temple. Childhood is a state treasured in the young and one to be fostered even into adulthood. Invoking the prophet Elijah, harbinger of the Messiah, at a boy's circumcision demonstrates that each newborn has the potential to change the world and bring it to completion and perfection. The sublime notion of harmony and perfection as described by the prophet Isaiah incorporates a young child playing with a wolf and lamb, leopard and goat and lion and calf at the end of days.

There is no single picture of childhood in Judaism and the promotion of childhood to an elevated status in the *aggadic* (narrative) literature is counter indicated by the *halachic* (legal) treatment of children as minors. Minors do not have obligation or responsibility in contrast to adults. Halachaic restrictions are placed on what children can be obliged to do ritually and are treated differently within Jewish law and practice from adults, particularly in regard to obligations in the public domain. However there is a strong understanding that the purpose of childhood is to carry out the Commandments and learn to enter the world of duty and religious obligation.

Ritual and Moral Obligations of the Child

Judaism's view of learning is not just a means to train children but to educate them to be engaged in a higher purpose. Thus, the Hebrew word for education is *hinukh* – dedication or commitment. Knowledge of Torah does not necessarily lead to commitment or engagement. Rather, living a life of religious sensibility with a duty to others is the determinant of the pious Jew. For Judaism, education ultimately is essentially an ethical activity. Studying, practising and celebrating Torah is what leads to spiritual renewal and commitment to God's moral purpose for all. The Jewish notion of education is not instrumental in that it seeks to achieve something extrinsic to the learner, rather it is spiritual in that it offers God's vision of goodness for all (Alexander, 2004). Children learning and studying therefore are elevated to the highest connotation and their teachers are perceived as the very guardians of the world in which they live and a security against evil:

> Yuda Nesiah sent Rabbi Hisda, Rabbi Assi and Rabbi Ammi to traverse the cities of the land of Israel in order to appoint Bible and Mishnah teachers. They came to a city and they found no teacher of Bible or Mishnah. They said; bring us to the guardians of the city. So they brought them to the senators of the town. They said, 'are these the guardians of the town? They are the destroyers of the town'. Who then, they said, are the guardians of the town? They said the teachers of Bible and Mishnah, as it is said; Unless God guards the city, its watchmen stay awake in vain (Psalm 127:1)

Maimonides viewed the child as unaware of the knowledge of good and evil so that parents are given a fundamental obligation to instill the values which will lead her to choose well while the child is yet young. Therefore the child cannot fulfill the Commandments for which they have no sense of their moral rightness. These early years are precisely to set children on the right moral path of life based on knowledge of the unique nature of the child and their innate qualities and character. Tradition then holds that only at the time of Bar Mitzvah does the 'moral inclination' – *yetzer hatov* enter the soul (Ecclestiastes Rabbah 69). Now the adolescent is able to make a positive choice in carrying out the Commandments and becomes obligated to a greater or lesser extent depending on gender. The spiritual elements of the soul are now in place to carry out the Jewish task of learning and living as an adult.

Studying and Learning as Quintessential Childhood Practices

The vital role of learning in fulfilling the purpose of childhood and finally entering the adult world is richly described in Jewish literature. The elaborate ceremonies developed from early rabbinic times continue to this very day with influence from all the cultures and countries in which Jews have lived. The traditional approach to learning was to start with the study of Leviticus and its sacrificial order. The rationale for this priority was that just as sacrifices are pure so are children...'therefore let the pure learn about the pure' (Leviticus Rabbah 7:3). Children are seen as pure of heart and mind and therefore regarded as potential for ultimate service to God through the Priesthood. This is echoed in the story of Samuel who is indentured to the High Priest in the Temple by Hannah, his mother, in thanksgiving for his long awaited birth. His innocence as a child is emphasized in God's call to him in the Temple being the only one who can hear God's voice. Only a child's receptivity has the ability to perceive God's presence and respond to a call for duty and lifetime service. Samuel as he grows and develops becomes the paradigm for the child's potential as Priest and Prophet teaching others through wisdom and moral conscience.

The emphasis on the individual child and their singular inner life is reflected in the work of Jewish educator and humanitarian Janusz Korczak. Putting himself in the position of the child, he writes revealingly:

> Our language is limited and hesitant (so it seems to you) for it is not completely grammatical. Because of this it seems to you that our thinking is confused and our feelings shallow. Our beliefs are naive for they are not based on bookish learning and the world is so wide. ..we live as a nation of dwarves vanquished by giants, by priests who derive their coercive power from the occult. We are an abused class, which you would keep alive in exchange for tiny concessions and very little effort. We are very very complex creatures – taciturn, suspicious and close lipped and the scholar's glass and eye will tell you nothing if you do not believe in us and sympathise with us. (Korczak 1968).

In this the educator must get to know the child fully, understand his spirit and unique world and acknowledge his right to respect and love. Each child carries his own particular world within him, his own needs and wishes, hopes and dreams. The educator is obliged to respect this unique world while helping each child to discover the beauty and the sublime that he carries within him. Korczak was well aware of getting to know the child: her great sensitivity, how easily she is impressed, and how quick she is to anger, love, hate, cry, admire. The child's heart is open to the world creating her own personal world from these impressions. Korczak's view was that childhood is not a period preparatory to life but an essential and integral part of life itself which cannot be measured by its usefulness for adulthood but is absolutely valued for itself.

Childhood as Symbolic of God's Relationship with the Jewish People

Even though the People of Israel are often depicted as failing in their duty to fulfill God's mission, nevertheless their status as child to a Divine parent is never questioned. This concept emphasizes the unconditional love of parents to children. As children are the fulfillment of their parents' hopes, so

Israel is the crowning glory of God's creation. When Rabbi Akiva living under Roman occupation in Judea describes man's belovedness by virtue of being created in the image of God, he emphasizes the nature of the child-Divine relationship.

> Beloved is Man for he was created in the image of God. Beloved are the people of Israel for they are called the children of God. Beloved are the People of Israel for a precious tool was given to them with which the world was created. (Mishnah Avot 3:14)

Within humanity as a whole, the Jewish people occupy a special position as the 'children of God'. This love for children is enduring and eternal. Even when children cease to behave, they are still their parents' sons and daughters. Similarly Israel's special position is one that does not change according to Israel's behavior.

Jewish Education needs to balance opportunities for spiritual experience with our expectations of children and value their natural fascination and enquiry. We should not only listen to the child and their spiritual experiences but listen for them. As we begin to hear their spiritual narrative, some will be unsettling. Not all spiritual issues are positive and we have to recognize that the boundaries between spiritual and religious will be blurred. There will be regular probing questions about the nature of life. This searching is an expression of their spirituality and a search for identity. We have to encourage children on their philosophical quest but words cannot fully express a spiritual experience suggesting that play, creativity, music are essential elements of a spiritual education. Rather than encouraging children to become adults, we should value them as being children.

The emphasis should not be on teaching children correct or orthodox doctrine about God. Rather the emphasis should be on enriching children's vocabulary and through conversation developing images and concepts which will enable children to grapple at their own level with the issues and experiences involved in God-talk. (Hull 1990, p. 15)

The varying Jewish conceptions of childhood encompass a purity of the child with a powerful potential to grow in wisdom and goodness. Judaism understands childhood to be both formative and lifelong, and indeed a paradigm for the holiness and moral purpose of life itself and symbolic of the human-Divine relationship itself.

Bibliography

Alexander, H. (2004). *Spirituality and Ethics in Education*. Brighton: Sussex Academic Press.

Bayfield, A.M. (1979). Religious Education: Towards a New Approach in Dow Marmur, *A Genuine Search*, RSGB 1979.

Groome, T. (1980). *Christian religious education*. San Francisco: Harper and Row

Hull, J. (1990) God Talk in Young Children in *University of Birmingham Papers in Religious Education*

Korczak, J. (1968) The Educational Teaching of Janusz Korczak in *Zvi Kurweil*, Tel Aviv, Culture and Education.

Moran, G. (1983). *Religious education development*. Minneapolis, MN: Winston Press.

Shier-Jones, A. (2007). *Children of God*. Peterborough: Epworth.

Shire, M. J. (1987). Faith Development and Jewish Education. In *Compass*. New York: UAHC.

Shire, M. J. (1998, Winter). Enhancing Religiosity in Jewish Education. *CCAR Journal: A Reform Jewish Quarterly*

Shire, M. J. (2003). Educating the Spirit. In S. Blumberg & R. Goodman (Eds.), *Teaching about God and Spirituality*. Denver, CO: ARE.

Shire, M. J. (2006). Learning to be Righteous: A Jewish Theology of Childhood. In K. M. Yust, et al. (Eds.), *Nurturing child and adolescent spirituality*. Langham: Rowman and Littlefield.

REUVEN SILVERMAN

Reuven Silverman has served Manchester Reform Synagogue since 1977, has lectured at Manchester University in Modern Hebrew, Modern Jewish Thought and in Psychotherapy, and has a counselling practice. His PhD was on 'The Jewish Reception of Spinoza' and he published *Baruch Spinoza: Outcast Jew, Universal Sage* in 1995.

Jewish Physicians of the Soul

Psychology and religion have traditionally been considered to be poles apart. As a rabbi who practises counselling, I avoid taking on congregants as clients because of the relationship complications that may arise from dual roles. There is nevertheless a growing interest among psychotherapists in how spirituality might be directed towards healing and wholeness. Boundaries are opening to allow for cross-fertilization in areas where humanists and the religious can learn from each other.

The enormous contribution of Jews to psychology is generally in inverse proportion to their Jewish identification. Freud, whilst he rejected religion as an 'obsessional neurosis,' did associate himself culturally with Jewish institutions and claims have been made for his Jewish influences. (1) Abraham Maslow, whilst wholly secular, openly related to teachings of prophetic Judaism. (2) Roberto Assagioli, who established Psychosynthesis, was also a founder of the Italian Progressive Judaism movement. (3) Two of the most overt exponents of Jewish teachings, who are my subjects here, are Erich Fromm and Viktor Frankl. Together their works provide a fertile field for studying the advantages and limitations of combining Judaism with psychology.

Erich Fromm (1900-1980) was a post-Freudian psychoanalyst and social psychologist of extraordinary popularity world-wide. Born in Frankfurt of Orthodox Jewish parents, he had both a classical Jewish and a general education and hoped to make Talmud study his life's work. (4) In the 1920s

184

he was involved with Buber and Rosenzweig in establishing the Frankfurt Lehrhaus. It is not clear what distanced him from Judaism but the First World War profoundly affected him, turning him away from all that divided humanity. He nevertheless maintained his Jewish identity. His PhD was on Jewish Law from a sociological perspective. Later he turned to psychoanalysis and when Hitler came to power he left Germany and continued as a practising and academic analyst in the United States. A critic of Freud, he blended Freudian categories with Marxism, restoring the spiritual insights avoided by both. Always close to his Jewish roots, he devoted an entire book, *You Shall Be As Gods*, to a study of Bible and Halachah. His best-seller *The Art of Loving* has been called a 'modern midrash'. (5) Regarding himself as an 'atheistic-mystic', Fromm was widely eclectic in his use of religious and philosophical wisdom with the aim of teaching how the transformation of society depends upon personal character training.

A cornerstone of Fromm's theory of self-development is the Golden Rule of the Torah, 'love your neighbour as yourself'. In his interpretation, self-love is a prerequisite for love of neighbour. You cannot love your neighbour adequately if you love yourself inadequately. For Fromm this opposes a general tendency in Western thought to equate self-love with selfishness and in Freudian psychology with narcissism. He holds that in fact the opposite is true. Fromm adopts Spinoza's view that self-esteem is a virtue, the primary aim of which is to preserve one's existence by realising one's inherent potentialities. (6) He accepts Spinoza's division of self-esteem into two categories. The first is love of being esteemed by others. This is 'inadequate knowledge' or imagination, causing competition for recognition, and potential conflict. Contrasted with this is the self-esteem derived from knowledge of your own effectiveness, or of being the cause of other people's joy, according to Spinoza. For Fromm it is the basis of being or becoming a 'productive character'.

Productive love is opposed to possessiveness and dependency. It is unconditional and characterised by care, responsibility, respect and knowledge. Fromm cites the Hebrew term *rachamim* meaning compassion, connoting God's love for man and man's love for his neighbour. From a root meaning 'womb', it indicates a mother's unconditional love for her child. (7)

The productive character expressing this love is the antithesis of the authoritarian character ubiquitous in every society and epitomized by Nazism. The individual's productive self-love is suppressed by the authoritarian character, subordinated to obedience to the leader. Adam and Eve's disobedience and the Building of the Tower of Babel are given by Fromm as examples of disobedience against an authoritarian God, hence the beginnings of an autonomous ethic in the Bible. The omniscient God knew that Adam would rebel. The rebellion becomes a metaphor for man's individuation, his growth to selfhood.

The Eden story is Fromm's paradigm for psychological evolution. It implies a stage of complete harmony of man with nature. The attainment of reason, symbolized by the eating of the forbidden fruit, broke that harmony. The first act of disobedience, as well as of freedom and independence, it brought infinite potential for both growth and suffering. The story warns against regression to the prehistoric stage. Fromm calls this, in Freudian language, a tendency towards 'incestuous symbiosis', a fixation to mother earth, a dependency upon blood and soil, race and clannishness. Emergence from Eden is psychologically symbolic of the journey from birth to maturity, leaving the womb to live independently and creatively with the potential to develop in the widest possible human sphere. Paradoxically people are afraid of this freedom and avoid it. (8)

Whilst Fromm's jargon may nowadays be distracting, his belief that religion and psychotherapy are complementary remains a live challenge. Character change is possible and necessary in both disciplines. (9) The psychological basis for the love of God for Fromm is also the need to overcome separateness, alienation of man from himself, from others and from nature. The process of psychoanalysis, which for Fromm included self-analysis, using for example meditation for getting in touch with the unconscious, dissociated parts of oneself, is closely related to the mystical experience of being at one with the All. Fromm finds descriptions of this kind of religious experience in Spinoza, Meister Eckhardt, Zen Buddhism, and the Burning Bush story in Exodus where God is identified to Moses as 'Ehyeh', pure Being. By this, he counters the narrow Freudian conception of religion as dependence on a protecting and punishing Father with the mystical and not necessarily theist experience of unification with all being. In social terms Fromm thought that the post-Freudian purpose of psychoanalysis was not the discovery of unconscious conflicts for 'social adjustment' but all that flows from an awareness of being at one with the All: wonder and concern for truth, integrity and ethics. (10) The human being as image of God is infinite and not a 'thing' or a market commodity; this is modern idolatry. (11) Fromm, the non-theist, sees the concept of God as liberating people from their slavery to the demands of space and time.

With the intriguing blend of anthropological detachment and Jewish pride that runs through Fromm's writings, he describes the Shabbat in glowing terms as an institution which restores harmony in society and between man and nature. (12) Psychologically, the day liberates people from dependency on things, freeing them from the realm of having into the realm of being. Even some minutiae of Shabbat observance which Fromm had given up, such as not carrying articles in the street, had value in transforming one from the 'having' to the 'being' mode.

Fromm was exceptional in his use of Jewish and other religious and philosophical sources. He has been criticized by some for secularizing, for example by ignoring the divine commandment element in the Golden Rule, the inadequacy of self-love and the need for transcendence. (13) Others have reproached him for preaching. What is undeniable is that his writings provide a valuable psychological commentary to Jewish sources and applies those insights, coupled with a fervour derived from the Hebrew prophets, to social improvement.

Viktor Frankl (1905-1997), shared a similar background with Erich Fromm. A Viennese psychiatrist, his concentration camp experiences led him to develop Logotherapy, the therapy of meaning. Survival, he found, depended not merely on the daily struggle to stay alive, but on a sense of purpose including belief in the future. In his experience, the prisoner who lost his faith in the future also lost his spiritual hold; he let himself decline and became subject to mental and physical decay.

Frankl departed from current thinking about motivation which accepted Maslow's hierarchy of needs. Frankl had seen people whose every physical need had been denied them survive whilst others succumbed. The distinguishing factor between them was whether or not they had a sense of meaning or purpose in their life. Meaning begins with self but transcends one's self-centredness.

Frankl's career began in 1930 treating suicidal patients. In 1938 he was in charge of Neurology at the Rothschild Hospital, the only Jewish hospital in Vienna. He declined the offer of a visa to America when Hitler rose to power, refusing to abandon his family or his patients.

He was deported to Theresienstadt and Auschwitz. At Theresienstadt he worked with Leo Baeck and Regina Jonas, the first woman rabbi in Europe, whom he gave the job of counselling new arrivals. Frankl lost his parents and his first wife in the camps. The earliest significant event was when he had to surrender his clothes on arrival. He had to give up a manuscript for a book which was in his pocket. In exchange he received the rags of an inmate who had been sent to the gas chamber. In the coat pocket he found a page torn from a prayer book containing the *Shemah*. He took this as a challenge to live his thoughts instead of merely putting them on paper. Frankl saw that sometimes the worst conditions bring out the best in human nature. He was convinced that whilst physical freedom might be denied, oppression could not rob one of the inner freedom of courage and dignity. He believed in facing challenges and fears. He took up mountaineering although he was afraid of climbing, and because he had a fear of flying, at age 67 he qualified as a pilot. This was consistent with his therapeutic method which he called 'paradoxical intention'. It is recognised as an effective way of countering phobias and anxieties by deliberately intending to feel them rather than fight them, hence to transcend them.

The premise of Logotherapy is that what gives our lives meaning is not in relation to ourselves alone but to people and events outside ourselves. We need to have aims towards which we are constantly striving. Such aims cannot just be of vague self-improvement as a long-term goal. They inhere rather in choices and decisions which are made from hour to hour and from moment to moment. They involve accomplishing concrete, personal demands, specific tasks. By forgetting oneself and fulfilling these, one fulfils oneself. Whilst this may bear echoes of the concept of mitzvah, it is essentially secular, responding to existential issues. The therapist's role is to help people find meaning in their existence. Frankl adds a spiritual dimension. In common with Fromm, who is also in a sense existentialist, he presents a critique of Freud, replacing the Freudian super-ego concept with conscience, the roots of which are in the 'spiritual unconscious'.

The method Frankl proposed for discovering meaning was through getting in touch with the unconscious layers of the self. Meaning, however, flows from action rather than reflection. Conscience, or 'the ethical instinct' shows the way. In addition, love and art are rooted in the 'spiritual unconscious.' Conscience is revealed in the analysis of dreams. Analogous to Freud's 'libido' which is repressed into the unconscious and re-emerges in dreams, is what Frankl calls the 'religio'. Even in highly irreligious people, religiousness is latent. Repression of religiousness leads to neurosis. A similar idea is found in Jung, but whereas Jung taught that each individual receives a spiritual heritage from an impersonal pool of images shared universally since prehistory, Frankl maintains that unconscious religiousness stems from the personal centre of each individual, relating to the 'unconscious God', latent in everyone but transcending the self. It is not clear to what extent Frankl's God-concept is a projection of self.

Frankl sometimes used the religious faith of his patients to help them to find meaning within their suffering. One example he gives illustrates for me a major stumbling block when mixing psychotherapy with religion. A rabbi from Eastern Europe had lost his wife and children in Auschwitz. He remarried but his second wife was sterile. The rabbi was in despair that there would be no-one to say kaddish for him after his death. Frankl asked him whether he did not hope to see his children again in heaven. The rabbi broke down in tears and said that his children, since they died as innocent martyrs, would thus be worthy of the highest place in heaven whereas he as an old sinful man could not expect to be assigned the same place.

Frankl responded: "Is it not conceivable, Rabbi, that precisely this was the meaning of your surviving your children: that you may be purified through these years of suffering, so that finally you, too, though not innocent like your children, may become worthy of joining them in heaven? Is it not written in the Psalms that God preserves all your tears? (Ps. 56:8) So perhaps none of your sufferings were in vain."(14)

Frankl, in my view, is out of line here with most humanistic psychotherapy practice in the directive and doctrinaire way in which he introduces religious teachings into the therapeutic dialogue. He speaks as if he shared his patient's strong faith. Whether he did or not is immaterial. He drew on the man's own spiritual resources. His own contribution was a suggestion that his suffering had a meaning. The intention was to give him a will to hold on to the meaning. It probably would have worked, since Frankl, in his notion of purification, was implicitly invoking the rabbinical teaching of *yissurim shel ahavah* (chastisements of love – from God). What it failed to achieve, which a more Socratic approach might have yielded, was to allow the sufferer to find his own meaning.

The essential principle which drives his therapy, in my view, cannot be faulted. Meaning may take an infinite number of forms, but is best expressed in terms of action or what Frankl calls 'responsibleness' to another person. What sustained him through the tortures of the enforced labour in Auschwitz was the image of his wife. He did not know if she was still alive but wrote "had I known then that my wife was dead, I think I would still have given myself, undisturbed by that knowledge, to the contemplation of her image, and that my mental conversation with her would have been just as vivid and just as satisfying. 'Set me as a seal upon thy heart, love is as strong as death.' " (15) It is the sense of meaning in his relationship which is operative here, confirmed by the verse from Song of Songs; psychological support not dependent on spirituality or vice versa, but the two working in tandem.

Relationship was also the core of Frankl's theological position. It need not be expressed exclusively as an I-Thou. It can also be an internal dialogue, between an ego and an alter ego. In Frankl's words: "God is the partner of our most intimate soliloquies."(16)

In sum, the works of Fromm and Frankl exemplify psychology informed, although not exclusively, by their Judaism. Both are often quoted in Jewish religious literature, including Progressive prayer anthologies. Fromm, in his humanist reaction to Freud, returned to Judaism, as part of a humanist re-valuing of religion. Frankl, as eclectic as Fromm, came closer to a conventional religious commitment, to the point where occasionally it could be intrusive. Both found that their concepts of self-transcendence were confirmed by 'religious' and specifically Jewish teaching.

Whilst they both dealt with key existential issues of isolation, meaninglessness, death and freedom, Frankl's focus was close to cognitive-behavioural methods of working with them, whereas Fromm's analytical approach was concerned, somewhat idealistically, with character training. Both strongly emphasized ethics and conscience with spiritual overtones but without a religious agenda.

Fromm used his experience of Nazism as a means of describing to the world how a wide range of character traits, such as narcissism, incestuous obsession with nation and land, and possessiveness may become massively destructive, frequently echoing the Hebrew prophets against modern forms of idolatry. Frankl drew on his concentration camp experiences to help people seek meaning in suffering.

In their enthusiastic engagement with issues of faith, both of them, Fromm the non-theist paradoxically more than Frankl the theist, show how an alliance of psychology and Judaism can provide bridges from the secular to the spiritual.

1. Robert, M., *From Oedipus to Moses: Freud's Jewish Identity*, London, Routledge 1977
2. Hoffman, E. *The Right to be Human: A Biography of Abraham Maslow*, New York: McGraw-Hill, 1999.
3. Firman, J and Gill, F., *Psychosynthesis, A Psychology of the Spirit*, New York, State University Press 2002, p.14
4. Funk, R., *Erich Fromm, His Life and Ideas*, New York, Continuum, 2000, p. 8f
5. Hausdorff, D., *Erich Fromm* New York, Twayne, 1972, p.103 quoting Rabbi Jacob Petuchowski
6. Fromm, E., *Man For Himself*, New York, Routledge & Kegan Paul, 1971, p.134f
7. Fromm, E., *The Art of Loving* New York: Harper and Row, 1956, pp. 49ff.
8. Fromm, E., *Man For Himself*, p. 149 cf. Fromm, E., *The Fear of Freedom*, London, Routledge & Kegan Paul, 1960 pp. 27-28
9. Fromm, E., *The Art of Listening* (posthumously published) London, Constable 1994
10. Fromm, E., *Psychoanalysis and Religion*, Yale, 1950, p.115-116 cf. Fromm, E., *You Shall Be As Gods*, New York, Rinehart & Winston, 1966 pp. 26-28
11. Fromm, E., *The Sane Society*, London, Routledge & Kegan Paul, 1959, p.122
12. Fromm, E., *To Have or To Be*, London, Abacus, 1979, p.56-57
13. Cooper, H. *Soul Searching: Studies in Judaism and Psychotherapy*, London SCM 1988, pp. xx-xxi
14. Frankl, V., *Man's Search For Meaning*, Washington Square Press, 1985, p.95
15. Ibid. p. 141
16. Frankl, V., *Man's Search For Ultimate Meaning*, New York, Basic Books, 2000, p.151

From a public lecture : 'Contributions of Jews to Psychology', University of Manchester Centre for Jewish Studies, March 9, 1999

DANIEL SMITH

Daniel Smith is Senior Minister of Edgware & District Reform Synagogue, and is a past chairman of the Assembly of Reform Rabbis. He was founding chairman of The Raphael Centre – a Jewish Counselling Service, and tutor in Pastoral Care and Community Skills at Leo Baeck Rabbinic College

Pharisees and the Continuity of Judaism

The rabbis saw themselves as the heirs of the Pharisee sages who were the successors of the men of the 'Great Assembly', and had a direct line of authority going back to Moses. (1) The Pharisees tried to emulate the example of Ezra the Scribe, who "had set his heart to study the Law of the Lord, and to do it, and to teach the statutes and ordinances in Israel" (Ezra 7.10). These three verbs, 'to study', 'to do' and 'to teach' sum up three of the ideals of the Pharisees, although the hierarchy of these three activities was a matter of debate. (2)

The Pharisees also followed the example of Ezra in holding public readings of the Torah. They introduced wider circles to the study of the Law, encouraging and enabling perceptive laymen to devote themselves to Torah study. (3) Maccoby points out that every Sabbath and festival service included an element of instruction, namely readings from the Bible. Members of the congregation would participate in leading services and reading Torah. (4)

Many Israelites were not able to understand Hebrew, so the Pharisees introduced the custom of accompanying readings with translations into Aramaic, the vernacular of the time. These practices valued education and encouraged 'democratisation,' and are crucial elements in the long-term survival and success of Pharisaism.

The Pharisees emerged as a distinct group about 160 BCE, shortly after the Hasmonean revolt. The term 'Pharisees,' (*perushim*) may mean 'those set apart' by keeping stricter purity laws, or it may refer to those who belong to a ritual table-sharing fellowship. (5)

Neusner describes the origins of the Pharisees who started as a political party active in the reign of John Hyrcanus and Alexander Janneus, but temporarily dropped out of the picture after Alexandra Salome. (6) He suggests that Hillel (1st century BCE.) was the leader who transformed Pharisaism from a political party with active political concerns to a religious sect following more quietistic pietist paths. (7)

Up to the destruction of the temple in 70 CE, the Pharisees were an identifiable group within the Jewish community. The Pharisee authority of that time was Rabban Yochanan ben Zakkai, and his disciples have been described as the last generation of the Pharisees. (8) The title 'Rabbi' became common for the generations that came after Yochanan.

In Yochanan's time there were a number of groups competing for Jewish allegiance including the Pharisees, Sadducees, Essenes and Zealots. Other sects, such as the Christians, also claimed that they were the true inheritors of Biblical Judaism. This essay focuses on the traits of Pharisaism that ensured that subsequent Jewish generations would follow Rabbinic Judaism, and trace their connection to Biblical Judaism through the Pharisee sages and their teachings.

Although the year 70 CE is generally seen as the crucial changeover date from Pharisaic to Rabbinic Judaism, it may have taken generations before the impact came to be understood, and centuries before Rabbinic Judaism became established as mainstream 'normative' Judaism. (9)

There are three major primary sources on the Pharisees, namely the Gospels, Josephus and the rabbinic writings. All these sources reflect the interests of their authors, the context in which they live, and the audience for which they wrote.

The Gospels extol the aims of Jesus and Paul in opposition to those of the Pharisees. The modern scholar, Steve Mason, comments on the attention paid to the problem of the Pharisees by Christian theologians and biblical scholars: "In the past, as is well known, such investigators were predisposed to regard Pharisaism as a foil for emerging Christianity". (10)

Saldarini makes the criticism: "Earlier studies by Christians suffered from the tendency to read the polemical accounts of the Pharisees, scribes and Sadducees in the New Testament as history and then use it to interpret the rabbinic sources, a tendency which still persists in some New Testament scholarship". (11)

Maccoby questions the authenticity of some New Testament passages, particularly those that have Jesus arguing with the Pharisees concerning the Sabbath. He sees this as a case where Jesus is in fact supporting a Pharisee argument against what was then the Sadducee position. The Pharisee sages themselves had made the case that the law to preserve life was paramount above the law to keep the Sabbath. (12)

Josephus (c 37-100 CE) had been a Jewish commander in the rebellion against Rome in 66 CE. Captured by the Romans, he spent his later years in Rome under the patronage of Roman emperors, compiling his histories of the Jewish people for a Roman audience. He presents the Pharisees as if they are one of a number of philosophical schools of thought. The Pharisees are said to have rational arguments and lenient legal positions, and are presented as being most popular among the people.

Josephus describes Pharisee leniency when a king wished to have a certain offender killed, but the Pharisees said that the miscreant should be punished by flogging and not by death. Josephus comments that in general the Pharisees tend not to be severe in punishment. (13)

According to Josephus, the Pharisees are renowned as wise men who are most able and authoritative in interpreting the law. Pharisees believe that God or fate controls everything, yet the decision whether to do right or wrong rests mainly with humanity. The Sadducees, on the other hand, deny the power of fate altogether, holding that each has total free choice to decide which moral direction to take. The Sadducees reject the notion of reward and punishment in the after-life, while the Pharisees have faith in the continuity of the soul. Pharisees are generally friendly to each other and have good peaceful relations with the general public, while the Sadducees quarrel with everyone, even with each other. (14)

Josephus describes the Sadducees as being harsh in judgement, and adds that they had influence with the rich but were not favoured by the general public who gave their support to the Pharisees. (15)

In comparison with the Essenes, Pharisee legal interpretations were also more lenient and flexible. For example, the Essenes wanted all Jerusalem to have strict purity laws, whereas the Pharisees limited these laws to the Temple precincts. Joachim Schaper writes: "The Essene concept was much stricter, probably caused by the urge to err on the side of caution rather than run the risk of violating divine prescripts. The Pharisees took a different stance. They were open to the insight that Law had to be adjusted to the living-conditions of the people". (16)

When considering the classical rabbinic texts about Pharisees, it is clear that these writings were for internal Jewish consumption rather than an attempt to influence a wider non-Jewish audience. According to Neusner, "The rabbinic traditions about the Pharisees as a whole may be characterized as self-centred, the internal records of a party concerning its own life, its own laws, and its own partisan conflicts". (17)

The Pharisees held that along with the written law of the Torah, Moses and his successors also had an oral tradition of interpretation. Their oral interpretations had the authority of tradition combined with the flexibility of contextual contemporary understanding.

Schaper comments: "The teaching of halakha (Jewish law) at times had to be innovative to keep up with the pace of social and economic change and the new living conditions it created. It is the Pharisees' great and most important merit to have risen to that particular challenge". (18)

The Pharisees made Judaism flexible and able to react to changing circumstances. By means of oral law the Pharisees enabled the Bible to become applicable in every situation. The tradition of oral transmission had the further advantage that it gave authority to a group of interpreters (namely the Pharisees themselves) who held the keys to unlock the power and vibrancy of Torah. This authority was dynamic and creative, and allowed for a variety of new possible interpretations to be expressed, and for their case to be argued in the court of reason. The people who held moral authority and religious power were no longer the aristocracy or the priests or the wealthy, but those who were learned in the law and had the skill to interpret the law with wisdom.

For example, the Pharisees interpreted the biblical passage which calls for the punishment of "an eye for an eye" (Exodus 21:24). They insisted that the passage should not be taken literally, but should be understood as a demand for financial compensation. Similarly the Pharisees created so many caveats and cautions concerning capital punishment, that they effectively abolished the possibility of enacting the death penalty within Judaism. Another important areas of Pharisee reform was in enhancing the status and rights of women, especially in the area of marriage and divorce law. (19)

Rabbinic writings include a vast number of debates, respectfully recording a variety of different opinions argued by different Pharisee authorities. The respect shown to differing positions is proof that a variety of views can be respectable and possible. Pharisaism managed to avoid a static, fixed structure of thought, but venerated the learning of the sages and their ability to argue their case.

The Pharisees' commitment to education was a very significant factor in their popularity and in their ability to ensure the continuity of Judaism. Prestige came from knowledge and not from birth or ancestry. The Pharisees said: "A learned bastard takes precedence over an ignorant High Priest." (Mishnah Horayot 3:8).

The Pharisees were the first group in history to introduce compulsory universal education regardless of rank or wealth, although their understanding of universal education was to make learning accessible to all males. Shimon ben Shetach established schools in Jerusalem and surrounding districts, and ruled that parents had to send their children to them. (Palestinian Talmud Ketubot 8: 11, 32c) In time this practice was extended throughout Israel. The Talmud ordained that teachers of young children should be appointed in each district and each town, and that children should enter school at the age of six or seven. The Talmud includes discussions about methods of teaching, rules for size of classroom (each teacher should have only 25 pupils), regular times for teaching, proper sanitary arrangements for schools, avoidance of excessive punishment, and how to make learning interesting and stimulating. (20)

Beyond the commitment to childhood learning, there was a system of further education for those who had the ability to take on rabbinic studies. It was effectively a university system. Progress depended on merit and ability rather than on wealth or breeding. Hillel and Akiva, two of the greatest authorities, were role models of students who grew up in great poverty and became the greatest authorities of their generations.

Pharisees were inclusive, and wanted to bring in many participants, whereas a commitment to the hereditary caste system had limited Sadducee expansion. Hillel presented a Pharisaism that was accepting of converts, and was also willing to engage with non-Jewish 'Fearers of God.'

The Pharisees created a literate society in which tradition and culture could be accessible to all. This commitment to education and literacy may have been the most significant factor helping Rabbinic Judaism survive and flourish over many centuries.

The Pharisees found a way to observe strict religious practice while maintaining a worldly occupation. In contrast, the Essenes were too ascetic, esoteric, intense and unworldly to appeal to the mass of the population. The Essenes did have some influence on the Pharisees and possibly on early Christianity, but they did not have much influence on politics in their time. (21)

At the other extreme, the Zealots had an emotional nationalistic appeal. They had political power for a short period of time, but were too violent and inflexible, and ultimately proved self-destructive as well as harmful to other Jews.

The Jerusalem Temple had been the centre of cultic practice and the centre of Sadducee activity. When the temple was destroyed in 70 CE, the Sadducees lost their power base, their *raison d'être*, and having little further relevance they disappeared from Jewish history.

In the centuries before the temple was destroyed, the Pharisees changed the way that the Jewish community gathered and worshipped. Before the temple was lost, they had developed institutions that could maintain communal Jewish life. They created congregations that gathered in synagogues, with regular daily, Sabbath, and festival services that took place at the same times that the priests would offer daily, Sabbath, and festival sacrifices in the temple. It was almost as if the Pharisees had been preparing for the loss of the temple, so as to ensure the survival of Jewish life even without its erstwhile central institution.

The Pharisees had already begun the process, later developed by rabbinic Judaism, of having Jewish communal practice centred in synagogues which were lay-led institutions that did not rely on priests or even on buildings. All they required was the gathering of at least ten adult males in order to have a fully functioning service. Synagogues were essentially democratic institutions that allowed those who were more able or more motivated to take leading roles in organisation and worship.

The Pharisees also emphasised the importance of Jewish home-life, and the rabbis further developed their practice of bringing aspects of temple ritual into every Jewish household. On Sabbaths and festivals, the family dining table became an altar with candles. Every person could make blessings over meals where they shared bread and wine. In the Jewish home, every parent could act as a priest, giving the Priestly Blessing to the children. The Sabbath evening home service has been one of the strongest emotive experiences that helped Jews keep their identity. Ahad Ha'am, the 19th century essayist, observed "More than Israel has kept the Sabbath, the Sabbath has kept Israel".

The Pharisees also developed the personal religious life of individuals. This meant that when Jews lost control of their government and their land, and when they had almost no political or military power, they still could practice great religious devotion in the limited areas of authority that remained to them. People could be observant Jews in the way they dressed (e.g. with fringed garments that were not made of diverse materials), and in the way they ate (keeping kosher regulations). People could serve God in the way they conducted their personal, marital and family life, in the way they conducted trade or business, and in the way they kept Sabbath. The Pharisees

197

developed a liturgy with daily prayers and blessings that enabled people to sustain a close and meaningful relationship with a caring God who was intimately involved with the details of individuals' lives.

The concept of 'intention' was of particular importance in the Pharisees' reformulation of the biblical heritage as they challenged a priestly worldview that was more behaviouristic. (22) Intention and motive were essential factors in Pharisaic religious life, particularly in the area of prayer. The effect was to further democratise religion. It set the stage for later kabbalistic theories which were subsequently developed in Chassidic thought, where impoverished Jewish peasants who lacked any worldly influence or political power, could nevertheless have significant impact on the universe by having appropriate intentions in their prayers and meditations.

The Pharisees gave Rabbinic Judaism the tools to develop a model of how to be religious without power. Ordinary people could be religiously observant despite hardship and oppression.

Rabbinic Judaism was a system that worked for centuries; and even great persecution could not crush it. It might be argued that the greatest threat to Rabbinic Judaism came not from oppression but from freedom. When the ghetto walls were broken down, Rabbinic Judaism stopped being as effective as it had been through all the centuries since the loss of the Temple. The European enlightenment brought about the emancipation of the Jews who became free to travel, trade, and participate in the life and politics of nations. Rabbinic Judaism had much to say about personal, family and communal life, but had little to do with international politics, military power, global finance and contemporary culture. Significant numbers of Jews stopped following the laws of Rabbinic Judaism.

Jews are now struggling to respond to the two great events of the 20th century. Post-Holocaust Judaism experienced a crisis as profound as that following the destruction of the temple, and rabbinic theology has yet to find a clear and meaningful response. Secondly, rabbinic leaders in modern Israel have not always found adequate moral responses to the problems faced by a state that exercises national, political and military power. Modern times may now require a reforming movement that would be as revolutionary and effective as the Pharisaic movement of 2000 years ago, so that Judaism can rejuvenate itself and be revitalised and relevant in new times and changing conditions.

1. Saldarini, Anthony J, Pharisees, *Scribes and Saducees in Palestinian Society*. Edinburgh, 1989, p. 8: "It is very likely that the pre -70 Pharisees contributed to the emergence of the post -70 rabbis". See also Schaper, Joachim, "The Pharisees", in William Horbury, W. D. Davies and John Sturdy (eds.), The Cambridge History of Judaism, vol. 3: *The early Roman Period*. Cambridge, 1999, p. 402; Pirkei Avot, 1.1.
2. e.g. Simon ben Gamliel's statement in Pirkei Avot 1.17.
3. Schaper, p. 404.
4. Maccoby, Hyam, *Judaism in the First Century*, Sheldon Press, London 1989 p. 70.
5. ibid, p. 40.
6. Neusner, Jacob *The Rabbinic Traditions about the Pharisees before 70*. (part 3 Conclusions) E J Brill Leiden, 1971 p. 305.
7. Neusner, pp. 305-306.
8. Podro, J. *The Last Pharisee: the life and time of Rabbi Joshua ben Hananyah*, Valentine Mitchell, London 1969.
9. Stemberger, Gunter, *Introduction to the Talmud and Midrash*. Edinburgh, 1996, p. 5.
10. Mason, Steve, *Flavius Josephus on the Pharisees* E J Brill, Leiden 1991 p. 5.
11. Saldarini, p. 7.
12. Compare John, 7.3 to Mekhilkta on Exodus 31:13, both of which argue that when the health of the body is in danger, one may abrogate the Sabbath.
13. Josephus: *Antiquities*, Book 13, 10:6.
14. Josephus, *The Jewish War* Book 2, 8:14.
15. Josephus, *Antiquities*, Book 13, 10:6.
16. Schaper, p. 408.
17. Neusner, p. 304.
18. Schaper, p. 409.
19. Maccoby, p. 56.
20. e.g. Baba Batra, 21a.
21. Graetz, Heinrich. *History of the Jews*, vol. 2: *From the Reign of Hyrcanus (135CE)*. JPS, Philadelphia, 1898, p .30..
22. Eilberg-Shwartz, Howard, *The Human Will in Judaism: The Mishnah's Philosophy of Intention*, Brown Judaic Studies, 103, Atlanta, Georgia, 1986

JACQUELINE TABICK

Jacqueline Tabick received *s'micha* from Leo Baeck College in 1975 and worked at West London Synagogue till 1998. She is presently the rabbi of North West Surrey Synagogue in Weybridge. She chairs the World Congress of Faiths and is a member of the executive of the Interfaith Network.

Your People Shall Be My People...Why?[i]

...One day we were just sitting there having a meal, and Guy was sitting there very thoughtful, it must have been a Shabbat evening. The kids had taken the dishes to the kitchen. I said, "Are you thinking about conversion?"

I don't know where it came from. Before then I had never mentioned it, it was fourteen years of marriage, it had never been an issue, I had never asked him to, I had never expected him to, just come along with me to the fun services that was all, so we are a family, the children feel that we are doing this as a family. That to me was the only really important thing. And he agreed.

"How on earth did you know"? He asked.

"I don't know, I can read you and I had a funny feeling."

He said "Yes actually I have been thinking about it for quite some time".

I just shrugged my shoulders and said, "O.K. it would be wonderful if you did"[ii]

What makes people decide to become Jewish? Guy had known his wife for several years before marriage, had been married to her for fourteen years, had Jewish children, and then suddenly, it seems, decided to change his religious identity. What questions, needs, dreams, challenges in his life took him to this moment?'

200

Such questions led me to undertake research into those who had converted to Judaism, under the auspices of the Movement for Reform Judaism, 1952-2002.

Candidates presenting themselves for conversion have to submit an application to the Reform Beit Din. In a randomly selected collection of 512 applications, the reasons presented by the candidates were content analysed. The proportions of these different motives can be seen in Table 1 given below.

Do note that this table records how often candidates chose to mention these specific categories. They were not presented with any form of checklist from which to choose which motives they might wish to mention, therefore, the fact that a motive was not recorded does not mean that a candidate does not in fact support such a feeling, it was just not mentioned by them, maybe because they felt other motives were more important, or because they had just not remembered that particular reason when completing the form. Most candidates mentioned several motives on their application forms.

Table 1.1 The Proportions of the Motivational Themes Identified in the Applications to the Beit Din.

Themes	Number	% Who mentioned this item
Interest in learning about Judaism	50	11
Motivation arising from contact with Jews.		
(i) Wish to establish a Jewish home, admiring Jewish family life	134	30
(ii) Pressure from partner or partner's family	9	2
(iii) Enjoyment of partner's family's way of life		
(iv) Desire to bring up children in a religiously united family.	77	17

(v) Involvement with a Jewish partner sparked conversion	224	50
	257	57
Previous connections with Judaism		
(1) Jewish father or other family connections		
	68	15
(ii) Friends or work associates		
(iii) Connections to Israel	120	27
(iv) Interest in the holocaust	44	10
	25	5
1. Motive: Spiritual or religious interest		
(i) Identification with Jewish moral values		
(ii) Enjoyment of festivals, rituals	36	8
(iii) Loss of previous faith	85	19
(iv) Identification with Judaism,	86	19
(v) Enjoyment of community	198	44
(vi) Enjoyment of Culture	73	16
	24	5
2. Previous rejection by Orthodox Beit Din	26	5

Source: Application Forms

It must be remembered that there are bound to be some difficulties interpreting this data as the candidates knew that their form would be presented to the Beit Din. This knowledge may have resulted in them under-reporting any pressure to convert placed upon them by their Jewish partners and under-playing the family motives for conversion which are deemed unacceptable in Jewish tradition.

The information on these forms together with a series of interviews with converts informed the creation of a survey that was distributed to Reform synagogues and posted to known individuals who no longer saw themselves as Jews. There were 366 respondents to the survey. Tables 2 and 3 illustrate the responses of the respondents to the questions concerned with initial reasons for conversion. They were presented with ten possible motives for conversion, as listed below, and were asked to rate the levels of importance of each of the items when they decided to convert.

Table 2 Reasons for deciding to convert

	Very important or important	Slightly important or not at all important.	
	Percentage	Percentage	No.
I felt that I needed to find a more meaningful faith	46%	54%	308
I had a Jewish partner and I wished to respond to his/her wish that I convert	55%	45%	236
I had a Jewish partner and I wished to respond to his/her *family's* wish that I convert	17%	73%	208
I was attracted to the religious, ethical and/or spiritual aspects of Judaism	71%	29%	336
I was attracted by the warmth I saw in Jewish life	67%	33%	331

I have Jewish family roots that I wished to affirm	52%	48%	94
I already felt Jewish to some extent and I wanted to develop this	38%	62%	318
I mixed a lot in Jewish circles and this caused me to think about conversion	27%	73%	315
I felt close to the Land and the people of Israel	28%	72%	314
I had a Jewish partner and felt that conversion would enhance our future life as a family.	89%	11%	289

Source: Survey

Figure 3 Reasons for deciding to convert in descending order of salience.

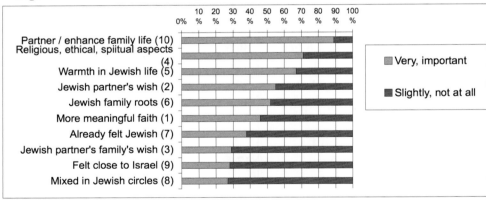

Source: Survey

These ten items were entered into a factor analysis and three underlying dimensions were revealed which together account for 59% of the variance. The underlying factor constructs can be thought of as:

1. Degree of intrinsic motivation to become Jewish.
2. Level of family pressure
3. Strength of the desire for family unity

Factor 1 The most salient dimension seems to be the degree to which **intrinsic motivation**, both ethnic and religious, played a part in the decision to convert. In examining this area, the analysis pointed to the following variables as the ones that loaded highest on this factor:

- I already felt Jewish to some extent and wanted to develop this
- I felt close to the Land and people of Israel
- I mixed a lot in Jewish circles and this caused me to think
about conversion

and, to a lesser extent,
- I was attracted to the warmth I saw in Jewish homes
- I was attracted to the religious, ethical and/or spiritual aspects of Judaism.
- I felt I needed to find a more meaningful faith
- I have Jewish family roots that I wish to affirm

Rambo talks of the various changes in religious affiliation that may take place through conversion. [iii]:

it will mean a radical shifting of gears that can take the spiritually lackadaisical to a new level of intensive concern, commitment and involvement.

One of the extraordinary journeys found in the qualitative data tells of a man in his 50s, married to a non-Jewish woman, who in 2002 explained [iv]

...there have been three constants running through my life
1. From my earliest childhood I have believed in the God of Abraham, Isaac and Jacob.
2. I have always had close association with Jewish friends.
3. I have struggled to reconcile what I was taught as a Christian with my understanding of the Bible.

In particular, over the last 10 years I have been drawn to

explore what I could only describe as 'feeling Jewish.' I unsuccessfully started to trace my genealogy to find any Jewish relatives. I have taken part in five charity bike rides in Israel where I felt a tremendous affinity with the land and I started to explore the Jewish roots of Christianity.

At Church, my spirituality always leaned towards the Old Testament, as I knew it. I could not fathom from the Christian teachings how God could suddenly forgo the previous 2000 years of Jewish practice and start up what was basically a new religion where the church replaced Israel. I looked at Messianic Judaism, which just confused me, as it seemed neither one thing or the other...

This was conversion *lishma*, for its own sake and in recent years, this motivation has increased. Indeed, sometimes, both partners in a couple will present themselves as candidates *lishma*. As did Mr and Mrs ... who were in their 30s with a baby son. They wrote,

...We have found ourselves and God in Judaism. Having done so we have no alternative but to become Jews and live God's law and commandments as given through Moses, bringing up our son ... to love Judaism as we do... (v)

Factor 2 reflects the strength of the **pressure** exerted by the Jewish Partner and his/her family. Two variables load onto this factor:

- I had a Jewish partner and wanted to respond to her/his wish that I convert and
- I had a Jewish partner and wanted to respond to his/her family's wish that I convert.

Factor 3 seems to reflect the level of their **desire to create a Jewish family** exemplified by items such as:

- I had a Jewish partner and felt that conversion would enhance our future life as a family and to a much lesser extent, but still reflecting this theme,
- I was attracted to the warmth I saw in Jewish life.

206

The most salient reason for conversion that is given by the respondents was that the convert had met a Jewish partner and wished to raise their family in a home united by religion. Thus in 1958, a woman of 30 stated [vi]

> ...To be fully harmonious in all aspects of my faith life with my husband and hopefully to have a family who will be totally united...

Or in 2000, a woman wrote[vii]

> ...I have known my husband for some 10 years now and over the years have witnessed the traditional Jewish festivals and how they bring unity between the families. I am currently pregnant and wish for my family to have a single identity...

However, though this might have been a preliminary reason, it does not mean that it was the only motive for conversion. This is seen in a statement from a 22 year old in 1966 [viii]

> ...it would be honest to admit that my first reason for intended conversion is to marry my Jewish fiancé. However since studying Judaism and having observed the ceremony I have become increasingly interested in it and feel that it is the religion which I would be happy for me and my children to follow...

The family motive can even be continued beyond death. A really poignant letter appears in the files from 1946. It describes the tragic circumstances surrounding a widow, 26 years old who was, as she put it, 'not particularly brought up in the Church of England'. She met and married a Jewish Canadian man. In 1944 she was delivered of twins who died, then her husband was killed in action a few months later. She wanted to join her mother-in-law in Toronto once she was Jewish. She wrote:

> ...As you say I do not know Judaism, I only know my beloved husband is a Jew. I love him, not only the man but for all he stood for, his ideals, his way of living...perhaps it is this that is making me want to take the Jewish religion, but I do not think so, there is something deeper than this, something that I cannot explain. God is the maker of all mankind. He made me and I feel has caused me to live for a

207

reason. I have been near death many times, but always He spared my life...God gave my dear husband to me and He has now taken him away. For a while I knew bitterness...but now I try to understand and believe that God knows best and that all these things are for a purpose. Perhaps I shall find the answer in the taking of the Jewish faith...

It was felt important to understand more fully the factor reflecting the strength of the pressure of the Jewish partner or family. Therefore a further factor analysis was carried out employing other questions reflecting this issue. This also revealed three underlying dimensions.

1. A general strength of family support.

The variables which loaded highest on this factor were:

- Late family support

- The Family respected me for becoming Jewish

- They did not think the conversion would make me a real Jew

- The family helped me learn about being Jewish

- They treated me just like any other Jewish relative and did not

    make an issue of my conversion

- The family had no contact with the couple

2. A more religiously orientated strength of support perceived as coming from the partner

The variables which loaded highest on this second factor were

- He/she still doesn't recognise me as a real Jew

- He/she resented my enthusiasm and knowledge

- He/she saw the conversion as something we had to get through but was not really interested in the religious aspects

- He/she became more involved in Judaism when I converted and this interest has continued ever since.

3. The strength of personal desire on the part of the proselyte, to satisfy expectations

In this last factor, the variables which loaded the highest were just three

- I had a Jewish partner and wanted to respond to his/her wish

that I convert

- I had a Jewish partner and wanted to respond to his/her

family's wish that I convert

- Did the Jewish family apply any pressure on you to convert to

Judaism now that the relationship was established?

These three dimensions account for 46% of the variance

It is important to note that the converts understood the support/pressure being projected upon them by their Jewish partner or family in very interesting ways. The factors are highly predictable from the items that were included in the analysis but the fact that the support of the family was seen in very general terms while the support of the partner is seen more in terms of perceived engagement in the religious elements of the process is worthy of note. What this says is that as far as the converts were concerned, the level of general encouragement of the family/partner is different from the level of true interest in the religious elements of the process. The family/partner might be supportive, but not really interested in the religious development of the convert and vice versa.

As far as many of the partners were concerned, ethnic and communal links with family and heritage were seen as more important than what some converts understood as religious reasons. Thus a woman commented that while [ix]

> ...My Jewish husband is not particularly interested in attending regularly but goes to the important festivals and friends' bar mitzvahs.... I am glad I converted to Judaism.... It seemed a small thing to do to please my husband and my family...

There were also some positive comments regarding their partner's religious interest. One respondent mentioned that she had converted because [x] 'There was a death in my partner's family (his younger brother) and he became more religious which affected his view of life/religion.' Another commented that she had become Jewish because of the [xi]

> ...continuing support of a partner. I could see the passion he had for his religion and felt it would be harder for him to stop being Jewish than for me to become Jewish...

The second factor analysis confirms the complexity involved when it comes to unravelling the balance between what is perceived by the proselyte as aggressive pressure to convert and what is welcomed by other converts as active support.

It seems from the qualitative evidence that this support/pressure can range from just a gentle expression of a mere desire, or hint, or maybe even just a hope that conversion will take place to the opposite extreme, namely threats or a level of emotional blackmail that the conversion <u>must</u> take place.

One comment from the survey comes from a woman who converted in her early 20s who wrote[xii], 'I felt great pressure from my husband's family that I would be unacceptable as a wife if I didn't convert.' Another woman, who converted in her mid 30s when already married to a Jew, commented,[xiii]

> ... I met with great hostility from my husband's father - less so his mother - and a lot of pressure to convert for THEIR sake. I resisted this because I felt that my own Catholic observant parents could put forward an equally strong reason for my husband to convert.

Just maybe, positive religious support by a convert's partner was regarded as too obvious a component of their relationship to comment upon, which may explain the relative dearth of positive examples even though from the statistics it is clear that such support was indeed enjoyed by the majority.

From the research, it would seem that there is a strong element of instrumental reasons for conversion: people wishing to give the children a religiously united home and marriage in a synagogue to one's Jewish partner, but that also, especially from older converts, singles or those married to non-Jews, and these groups have increased in the last 10-15 years, intrinsic reasons have a high degree of potency.

In addition, even when the instrumental motivation is present, maybe even prominent, such conversions can often be expected to be accompanied and transformed by more intrinsic motivational factors.

(i) Material taken from work in progress on a complete study of proselytes 1952-2002
(ii) Interview.
(iii) Rambo, Lewis *Understanding Conversion* Yale University 1998 p.2
(iv) Application 824
(v) Application 650
(vi) Application 441
(vii) Application 798
(viii) Application 262
(ix) Survey 119
(x) Survey 10
(xi) Survey 34
(xii) Survey 37
(xiii) Survey 185

LARRY TABICK

Larry Tabick was born in Brooklyn, NY. He has a B.A. from the George Washington University and an M.A. from the University of Toronto. He is a graduate of the Leo Baeck College and serves Shir Hayim – Hampstead Reform. He and his wife Jackie have three children.

That Extra Soul

My involvement in the process of editing the latest edition of our movement's *siddur* concentrated my mind (pun intended!) on a subject that has fascinated me since I discovered Kabbalah in the deep recesses of the library of the University of Toronto. That subject is the kavvanot, the kabbalistic meditations designed to accompany the traditional prayers and rituals of Judaism.

The notion of *kavvanot* first arose among the earliest named kabbalists in Provence and was apparently understood by them as a revelation granted to them by the prophet Elijah. (1) Over the course of the succeeding centuries, the *kavvanot* grew in number and complexity, reaching a climax in the teachings of the Ari, R. Isaac Luria (1534-1572), and even more intricacy in those of R. Shalom Sharabi, the Yemenite kabbalist (1720-1777). The Hasidic movement initiated by the Ba'al Shem Tov, was ambiguous about the *kavvanot*, revering them on the one hand, but rarely encouraging their use on the other. They have played no part in the Reform movement, at least not until fairly recently. (2)

Nowadays, the Kabbalah, once hardly spoken of outside of very small select groups, seems to be everywhere. This proliferation has brought many consequences. One is that teachers often impart Kabbalah as if it were separate from Judaism. Conversely, there are many Jewish teachers for whom Kabbalah is still foreign, not to say, alien. In attempting to convey some simple *kavvanot*, I am trying in a small way to bridge the gap between kabbalistic theory and Jewish practice.

Space constraints preclude a full exposition of the concept of ten *sefirot* here, BUT it should be borne in mind that the *sefirot* may be approached in three ways: they may be thought of as 1) aspects of God's personality, as it were, 2) as a chain of being between the unknowable God (*ayn sof*, the Infinite) and the created universe, and 3) as present in all that exists. In particular, they can be 'mapped out' on the human body, with the uppermost triad corresponding to the crown of the head and the lobes of the brain, the second three the two arms and the trunk, and the third as the legs and the genitals. The last *sefirah* can represent the way we present to the outside world. Here is a useful chart of the *sefirot* as a tree with roots above and branches below:

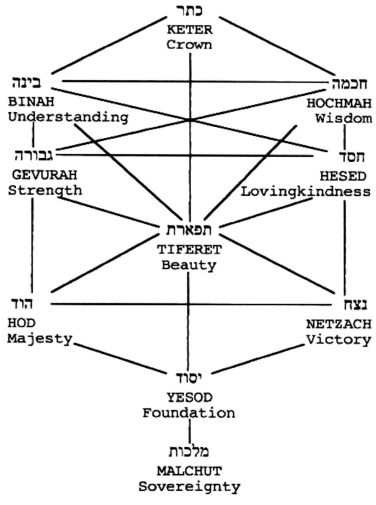

Lecha Dodi: **The Shabbat Bride**

The Sabbath of course is different, special, a day set apart, when many of our normal activities are put aside in favour of rest, contemplation and study. Services are longer than on weekdays, with additional items to make this day unique in the week. Its arrival and departure are also marked by distinctive rituals of inauguration and disengagement.

The Shabbat evening service includes a unit of psalms and songs prior to the Barechu, the call to community prayer and start of the "official" service consisting of the *Shema* and its blessings, the *'Amidah*, and concluding prayers. This introductory unit is known as *Kabbalat Shabbat*, Receiving the Sabbath, and reached its current shape among the Kabbalists of Safed in the sixteenth century. In its most usual form, it consists of Psalms 95-99 and 24, the kabbalistic hymn *Lecha Dodi* by R. Shlomo Alkabetz, plus Psalms 92 and 93. The six opening psalms represent the six working days just gone by. *Lecha Dodi* is an extended song welcoming the Shabbat as a Queen and a Bride, and as such is the key transitional point of the unit, while Psalms 92 and 93 represent the Shabbat itself. (Psalm 92 is the only psalm designated as "a song to sing for the Sabbath day" [verse 1])

In effect, this is already a meditation. As we sing or recite the six opening psalms, we may rehearse in our minds the key events of the last six days, and set them aside, along with all the issues they raised, so that we can focus on the healing power of the Shabbat just beginning. *Lecha Dodi* is that beginning. Imagine the Shabbat herself as a Queen or a Bride entering the synagogue and entering your heart. To suggest this, many synagogue communities have the custom of standing at the last verse and bowing towards the door as they sing. But there is more.

Lecha Dodi is a song of multi-layered imagery; we view this through the prism of the chorus: 'Come, my friend, to greet the bride, to welcome the Shabbat eve.' First there is the social level: we encourage each other ('my friend') to accept the Sabbath upon ourselves. Then there is the national level: the Bride is *Keneset Yisra'el*, the Community of Israel seen as an idealised social entity. (Verses 3-4 & 6-8 in particular emphasise the messianic redemption of the people.) Finally, there is the kabbalistic level: *Malchut* ('the bride'), the tenth *sefirah* is the *Shechinah*, the feminine Presence of God, coming to meet *Tif'eret*, her husband, ('my friend'). The redemption of the Jewish people from their historic exile is paralleled and accompanied on the spiritual plane by the redemption of the *Shechinah* from her exile in the physical world. *Lecha Dodi* is our song of welcome to a temporary foretaste of the Messianic Age. (3) This redemption can be achieved in the here and now, at least temporarily. (4).

Kabbalat Shabbat: The Extra Soul x3

But there is another way of approaching the Shabbat evening service that is also based on kabbalistic precedents. The Talmud tells us(5) that every Jew gains an extra soul with the onset of Shabbat, and that this extra soul departs at the close of the holy day. (6) Kabbalists (in common with ancient and medieval philosophers) usually speak of three levels of the soul - the *nefesh*, *ruach* and n*eshamah*. In considering the Talmudic doctrine of the extra soul that is unique to Shabbat, they came to the view that we gain an extra soul (or soul-increment) at each of these three levels. The question then is, at what points do these arrive?

In the Zoharic literature, the question is answered in several ways. In one place,(7) we are told that the extra *neshamah* arrives at the prayer *Hashkivenu* ("Cause us, our Parent, to lie down in peace") in the *Ma'ariv* service for *Erev Shabbat*, but this is largely a re-statement of the Talmudic teaching of a single extra soul. In another place,(8) it is taught that extra *nefesh* arrives at *'Atah kiddashta* (4th paragraph of Evening *'Amidah*), the extra *neshamah* at *Nishmat kol chai* (in morning service), and the extra *ruach* at *'Atah 'echad* (4th paragraph of Afternoon *'Amidah*). In either event, this has the effect of spreading the arrival of the different soul increments over the whole of Shabbat.

R. Hayyim Vital (1542-1620), the student and disseminator of the teachings of the Ari, answered the question in this way:

> On *Erev Shabbat*, one should concentrate on receiving the extra *nefesh* when Shabbat arrives, the [extra] *ruach* at the *Barechu* (Bless the Eternal…), and the [extra] *neshamah* at *ufros* ('and spread over us the shelter of Your peace'). (9)

This brings the arrival of the various extra souls entirely into the Friday evening service, which makes more sense to me. The phrase 'when Shabbat arrives' is a bit unclear here, but the *Barechu* is the call to community prayer, the start of the formal service, when we leave behind the *Kabbalat Shabbat* section, and enter the *Shema'* and its blessings. Ufros is a phrase from the *Hashkivenu* prayer mentioned in the Zohar. Like the *Barechu*, *Hashkivenu* forms a boundary, in this case between the *Shema'* and its blessings and the *'Amidah*, and, strictly speaking, is part of neither.

Alexander Süsskind of Grodno further developed Vital's notions in the eighteenth century. In his discussion of the service for the start of Shabbat he says:

> *Bo'i veshalom* ('Come in peace....') [the final verse of *Lecha Dodi*]: A person should say this verse with an exceedingly mighty joy, for during this verse a person receives the extra *nefesh* associated with the evening of the holy Sabbath...

> *Barechu*: Before answering 'Blessed is the Eternal Whom we are called to bless [forever and ever],' one should concentrate on drawing to oneself the additional, extra *ruach*, and concentrate one's thoughts with these words: Behold, I am drawing to myself, and to all Israel, the additional, extra *ruach* associated with the evening of the holy Sabbath.

> *Hashkivenu*. [At the words] 'And spread over us the shelter of Your peace' and again at the words 'Who spreads the shelter of peace over us...' one should draw to and receive upon oneself the additional, extra *neshamah* associated with the Sabbath eve.... And at 'and over all this people Israel' one should intend to draw the extra *neshamah* to all Israel. (10)

For meditation purposes, I decided to take Süsskind's ideas in conjunction with a teaching I found in Isaiah Horowitz' <u>Shnei Luchot HaBrit</u> ("The Two Tablets of the Covenant"). In this text, he locates each of the three souls in different parts of the body, and offers an useful mnemonic device to help us remember them.

> The levels of the *nefesh*, *ruach* and *neshamah*... [reside, in reverse order, in] the brain (*Moach*), heart (*Lev*) [and] liver (*Kaved*), [the opening letters of] which together spell *MeLeCH* ('king'). (11)

These identifications provide a method of focusing your thought on particular parts of the body ('head, heart and guts') as the three key points of the *Erev Shabbat* service outlined by Süsskind are reached. (Additionally, the reference to *melech* reminds us that our souls represent the divine Sovereign within our bodies as well as our souls.) Thus, at the last verse of *Lecha Dodi*, I imagine an extra, supplemental *nefesh* entering my liver. At the *Barechu*, I think about the extra *ruach* entering my heart, and at *Hashkivenu*, the extra

216

neshamah entering my brain. Thus:

Soul level	Definition	Powers	Site	Entry point
nefesh	vital force	sustenance, growth, the senses, sex	liver	last verse of *Lecha Dodi*
ruach	will	control of body, emotional drive	heart	*Barechu*
neshamah	intellect	thought	brain	*Hashkivenu*

Four Services

Ordinary weekdays are characterized by three services: *Ma'ariv*, *Shacharit* and *Minchah*. Like most holy days, Shabbat has four renditions of the *'Amidah*, three that correspond to the daily services, plus *Musaf* (the 'Additional Service'). How may this configuration of services be used for meditation?

Rabbi Meir ibn Gabbai, a popular medieval kabbalistic writer, made the following suggestion:

[In the Shabbat Afternoon Service] we pray 'You are one and Your name is one.' This represents the completion of the prayers, for then all the 'luminaries' [= *sefirot*] have been united through the mystery of the four services. For the evening prayer ('*Arvit*) [for Shabbat] is for the All-inclusive Bride (*kalah ha-k'lulah* [= Malchut]) to be betrothed to the Bridegroom [= *Tif'eret*].   [In] the morning service (*Shacharit*) [we pray] 'Moses rejoices' -
a mystical reference that the Bridegroom rejoices with 'the gift of his portion' who has ascended to be joined with him, and he includes his arms [= *Hesed* & *Gevurah*]. The Additional Service mystically refers to the Righteous One (*tzaddik*) [= *Yesod*] of the universe, including both pillars, Yachin and Boaz [= *Netzach* & *Hod*] upon which the 'house' [= the sefirotic tree] rests. Thus the seven levels bring about sweetening [being] mystically united, and so God is one and God's name one. (12)

Ibn Gabbai's symbolic language requires interpretation. Unlike other days, when the central blessings of each rendition of the 'Amidah are the same, on Shabbat they are different. Each has its own flavour and feeling, and ibn Gabbai has assigned sefirotic connections to them. He takes as his starting point God's oneness as mentioned in the 'Amidah for the Shabbat Afternoon Service; this is the culmination of Shabbat, the moment when all the *sefirot* have been joined together, the instant when blessings for the coming week have been assured. Meditations for the other services are leading to this pinnacle of divine unity. Thus, the service on Friday evening emphasises the *Shechinah*, *Malchut*, the holy bride, in union with her husband *Tif'eret*, as we have seen, but this is merely the inauguration of the process of bringing all ten *sefirot* together. *Tif'eret*, along with *Hesed* and *Gevurah*, are brought into play at *Shacharit*; *Yesod*, along with *Netzach* and *Hod* at *Musaf*. And although he doesn't say so explicitly, it would appear that these seven lower *sefirot* are to be brought into unity with the upper triad, *Keter*, *Hochmah* and *Binah*, at *Shabbat Minchah*.

Thus, we arrive at the following list:
Ma'ariv – Malchut
Shacharit – Tif'eret, with Hesed & Gevurah
Musaf – Yesod, with Netzach & Hod
Minchah – Keter, with Hochmah & Binah.

Havdalah: When Shabbat Goes

When I started to consider the departure of the extra soul-increments, I wondered whether they are thought of as simply going when Shabbat ends, or whether they gradually dissipated, like the power in a battery. As we have seen, the Talmud says that the extra soul departs with *havdalah*, but this view was not universal. The Zohar(13) follows the Talmud, but Hayyim Vital did not. He took a gradualist approach, stating that it is only the highest level (the additional *neshamah* of the *neshamah* [=*yechidah* (14)]), which departs at end of Shabbat. The additional *neshamah*, he said, goes on Sunday evening, the additional *ruach* on Monday evening, the additional *nefesh* on Tuesday evening. (15)

Personally, I prefer the Talmudic/Zoharic notion that the extra soul-increments leave us at the end of the Sabbath, perhaps with *havdalah*, the ceremony of separation that formally brings the holy day to a close. *Havdalah* consists of four parts: a series of introductory verses plus three blessings, for wine, for spices and for light (spoken over a plaited candle). It seemed to me

218

that these three correspond to the three soul levels.

Wine symbolises our physical nature, because it has both taste and smell; therefore, as we say a blessing over wine at *havdalah*, we can focus once more on our *nefesh*, the aspect of our soul that animates our body, on the state and position of our body and its parts, and on our physical sensations and needs.

The spices, of course, have *reiach*, smell, which reminds us of our *ruach*, the soul that drives us. Smelling the spices may put us in mind of the emotional rest we have experienced over Shabbat, that has allowed us to be re-invigorated to face the stresses and strains of the week that lies ahead.

The light of the plaited candle represents the light of the intellect, the mind, as it brings consciousness to bear on ever-wider aspects of our lives, and the fact that we extinguish the flame at the end of *havdalah* suggests that the light of consciousness is easily forgotten in the struggles of the six working days.

Yet, though *havdalah* marks the departure of the Shabbat and the three extra soul-increments, their influence remains with us as a residual effect, as Vital suggests, bringing illumination into our working lives too. Consciousness of our body, emotions, and mind is something we can achieve for occasional moments during the week, and our experience of rest and the higher awareness that last Shabbat brought us will sustain us until the Day of Rest returns again in six days' time. More than that, the wine, spices and candle may serve as sensual 'aids' to help us get through the week, as reminders that our three soul-levels, though diminished, have not disappeared and that spiritual insight is possible even in stressful work and home situations. (16)

Specific *kavvanot* exist for virtually all traditional blessings and prayers, and one could spend a lifetime studying and practising them. Those I have offered here are merely a taster. Research would reveal many more, and meditation could allow you to create your own. The effort will be repaid many times over.

1. Gershom Scholem, <u>Origins of the Kabbalah</u> (Philadelphia: Jewish Publication Society, 1987), pp. 243-247.
2. I have in my possession, for example, a pamphlet entitled 'An Arrangement of Prayers for Sabbath Morning' prepared by Rabbi Herbert Weiner in 1995 for his Reform community in Maplewood, New Jersey. This text includes kabbalistic *kavvanot*.
3. See *Berachot* 57b.
4. This is a common interpretation. See for example the following: 'I have seen in the [kabbalistic] books a brief explanation of this, and this is it: "My beloved" (*Dodi*) is the Holy One, blessed be He [= *Tif'eret*], and we are praying for the wondrous end-time when He will comfort the *Shechinah*, known as a "bride".' Alexander Süsskind (died 1794) <u>Yesod VeShoresh Ha'Avodah</u> (Jerusalem, 1978), p.164.
5. *Betzah* 16a & *Ta'anit* 27b.
6. This is not always the view taken by the kabbalistic tradition, as we shall see below.
7. I, 48a.
8. <u>Tiqqunei HaZohar</u> ("The Repairs of the Zohar"), (ed. by Reuven Margoliot) (Jerusalem: Mossad HaRav Kook, 1948), *Tiqqun* 18, p. 34a.
9. Hayyim Vital (1542-1620), <u>Peri 'Etz Hayyim</u> ("The Fruit of the Tree of Life") (Jerusalem, 1980), p.382.
10. Alexander Süsskind <u>Yesod VeShoresh Ha'Avodah</u>, pp. 164,166.
11. Isaiah HaLevi Horowitz (c.1570-1626), <u>Shnei Luchot HaBrit</u> ('The Two Tablets of the Covenant') (reprint of 1863 ed.; Jerusalem: 1975), *Bet Yisra'el*, v. I, p. 7d. English translation in Isaiah HaLevi Horowitz, <u>The Generations of Adam</u> (trans. Miles Krassen) (New York: Paulist Press, 1996), p. 116.
12. Meir ibn Gabbai (1480–after 1540), <u>Tola'at Ya'akov</u> ('O Worm, Jacob' [Isaiah 14:14]) (Jerusalem, 1996), p. 92.
13. III, 35b.
14. A soul level which only a few attain.
15. Hayyim Vital, <u>Peri 'Etz Hayyim</u>, p. 381.
16. I am grateful to Chani Smith for this last suggestion.

ALEXANDRA WRIGHT

Alexandra Wright is the Senior Rabbi of The Liberal Jewish Synagogue, St John's Wood, London. She received *s'mikhah* (ordination) from Leo Baeck College in 1986 where Rabbi Bayfield was her tutor while she was a student.

Quantum Theology

'We each exist for but a short time and in that time explore but a small part of the whole Universe. But humans are a curious species. We wonder, we seek answers. Living in this vast world that is by turns kind and cruel, and gazing at the immense heavens above, people have always asked a multitude of questions: How can we understand the world in which we find ourselves? How does the Universe behave? What is the nature of reality? Where did all this come from? Did the Universe need a creator? Most of us do not spend most of our time worrying about these questions, but almost all of us worry about them some of the time' (Stephen Hawking, extract from The Grand Design, 2010, published in Eureka in The Times, September, 2010).

As much as these words belong to the field of scientific speculation, Hawking's questions also belong to the realm of religious thought, touching on many of the themes that lie at the heart of theology: the transience and fragility of human life, the immensity of the universe and the minuteness of our own corner of that universe, good and evil, the meaning of life and the origins of the universe.

What is most significant about Hawking's words is his acknowledgement that such questions have eternal value. Is it not true, that in each generation we return to those fundamental uncertainties, in order to try and find our own way of answering them and so find our own meanings in the world? Is Hawking any different from the author of the book of Job, from Plato or the Rabbis, from Kepler, Newton or Einstein? In one hundred years' time, or in five hundred, if we are still an animate species, will not those same questions remain, their answers informed by the times in which our descendants live?

Such questions arise, not only from our contemplation of the physical world, but from something intangible, incorporeal, almost mystical, something that lies beyond or very deep within ourselves. Hawking's hermeneutic, his reading or interpretation of the world, emerges from his own discipline of science, and, as he points out, questions about the history of the universe or the nature of its existence have always provoked new theories or models from Plato and Newton, to modern quantum theories. But such developments are surely not unique to the history of science. Every generation of scholars and religious thinkers has also produced their own theories and models, coloured by their own beliefs and by the influences of the outside world. So, if classical physics assumes that the Universe has a single, well-defined history, classical biblical or rabbinic theology makes a similar kind of assumption, couched in theological terms – that God has created the universe and continues to guide that universe and be concerned and involved in the lives of human beings, urging them towards a common goal of redemption at some unspecified future time. Both arguments accept that the universe operates according to certain laws and that one can make certain predictions about the future course of events. The classical model is based on an acceptance of fundamental truths, yet with hindsight, acknowledges that it does not possess all of the truth as we know it now, and probably less of the truth as we will know it in the future.

If quantum theories, today, explain the universe, not in terms of a single definite history, but by studying the behaviour of the 'subatomic' particles which make up the objects in our universe, then post-modern interpretations of religion, emerging after the failure of modern Enlightenment methods to determine definitive meanings, have delivered a similar twist to their scientific counterparts. Quantum theories in physics demonstrate, that while it is possible to predict to the minutest statistical average how the universe will evolve, it is still not possible to define particles as single realities, because – and I'm sure physicists will put me right if I have misunderstood this – these particles might exist and move simultaneously in different places and different universes. At the centre of 'quantum theology' (if I can coin a phrase) lie our sacred 'texts', the particles that make up our religion: the traditional texts of Bible, midrash, liturgy, Jewish law, philosophy and belief, but also history and culture, community and social action. Just as Hawking and others are finding new ways of reading and interpreting the universe, so post-modern scholars and interpreters, are finding new theories and techniques for studying religion, history and culture. They are arguing that there is no single and correct interpretation, rather an array, a 'multiverse' choice of approaches that lead to a huge assortment of interpretations and a recognition that there is no one correct, definitive understanding of Judaism – our culture, our beliefs, our identity and history are complex and multi-layered.

I think that is probably where the analogy must end. Rabbis with virtually no scientific background should probably not venture too far into the field of science, quantum mechanics or M-theory. But is it significant that Hawking's 'definitive answer' to the question of whether there is an ultimate theory of the universe, lies in this M-theory? Isn't it rather strange that Hawking himself tells us that the 'M' might stand for 'master', 'miracle' or 'mystery', or even all three: three words of great interest to any religious thinker who grapples with the notion of God's 'mastery' or power, whose cultural and religious myths are composed of stories of miracles, and who, inevitably in contemplation of human existence, must acknowledge the great mysteries of life and death.

And yet Hawking's embrace of a theory that ostensibly answers the questions about the origins, the behaviour and our place in the universe, has nothing to do with God, miracles or even mysteries. It is not necessary to invoke God,' he says, 'to light the blue touch paper and set the Universe going.'

Despite the poetic epic of creation that stands at the beginning of the Torah, a record of how the authors of the Torah interpreted their world, few of us would disagree with Darwinism or with Hawking's notion of 'spontaneous creation'. Even if God does not provide an efficient explanation for the Big Bang, and even if it isn't necessary for us to 'use' our belief in God to defend the notion of 'Intelligent Design' in the way that creationists do, does that mean that God must be redundant to us, a casualty of the theological recession?

Can we not still believe in God and name Him as Creator? Can we not acknowledge that God just might be the First Cause of all effects, eternally existent, even before the origins of the universe? When we address God as 'Sovereign of the universe, whose word brings on the evening…whose understanding changes times and seasons…' do not our prayers still have meaning and resonance for each one of us, otherwise why are we here? Are we not affirming a historic faith that connects us with generations that have gone before us and the generations of the future? When we praise God who delivered us from Egyptian slavery, who bound us to the covenant at Mount Sinai, are we not acknowledging that we are part of a people, whose foundational text of the Exodus from Egypt has taught us what it means for a

223

people to be oppressed and the importance of freedom? When we beseech God to pardon our sins on Yom Kippur, to sweep away our transgressions, is it not because we seek a moral and spiritual re-alignment in our relationships with others and with the deepest part of ourselves, that some people call God?

Science may be able to explain the existence of thousands upon thousands of universes and to deliver a complete theory of the universe, but how does it change what we do or what we believe? Will its results prevent us from contemplating our place in the world? Will it stop us from appreciating with wonder the intricate design and beauty of the universe? Will it disconnect us from the sense that we are part of one creation, bound together by our common humanity? Will it stop us from celebrating together the festivals of our ancient tradition or studying the history of our people and its culture? Will it prevent us from gathering together in a house of mourning to bring comfort to grieving friends or relatives? Or wondering at the miracle of new birth? The laws of the physical universe might explain the flap of the butterfly's wings, the movement of tectonic plates, or analyse your dog's consciousness, but they do not address the inexplicable, the mysterious, the uncertainties of human and natural life.

Scientific explanation does not deal with the more tentative, spiritual questions that address meaning, that search for interpretation of events or demand patience and resilience in the face of uncertainty or suffering. It does not address the question that lies at the heart of a living religion such as Judaism: what is our role in life? How do we measure the strength of the human spirit? How can we overcome our own selfishness and share this planet and its massive resources in ways that are more equal and that acknowledge the existence of others who are not like ourselves?

On one of the most beautiful days of a walk in Scotland one summer's holiday, I arrived at a place one can scarcely even call a village, Spittal of Glenshee. As you begin the long descent from the Highlands, miles of moorland, covered in purple heather, a strange looking structure comes into focus. It is a one-storey building, its exterior walls made out of logs, making it look like one of those mid-west saloon bars you see in old cowboy movies. This, however, is the Spitall of Glenshee Hotel, one of the ugliest buildings I have ever come across, situated in one of the most beautiful places in Scotland. Crossing the threshold of the hotel, a notice informs you that there has been the constant presence of an inn on the site since 961 AD, that it has burnt down at least 15 times and that the hotel's insurers have calculated the next time it will burn down will be in 2029. A reassuring thought for guests!

This, perhaps, is how science deals with the uncertainties in life, dealing out statistical averages to predict the future. But as Ionesco once said: 'You can only predict things after they have happened.'

Only religion, and religion in the best possible sense, balances those classical beliefs – that there is a God, that God is compassionate and just and concerned with all animate life and with the earth and its blessings - on the one hand, with risk and uncertainty, on the other.

The strength of a good religion, such as progressive Judaism, lies in its willingness to be sensitive and open to science, for it is indispensable to our understanding of the universe and is providing some of the answers to questions that have long eluded us – including questions about once incurable diseases. But can science explain the structure of human consciousness? Can it interpret and give meaning to our brief life in the world? We may wonder at the immensity of the heavens, and science may help us understand its structure, but do we become better individuals because of that? Is not science, at times, more likely to invent even more sophisticated weaponry, so that we can kill each other? Can science teach us to be kinder, more understanding individuals? In great humility, I would suggest that how we are with each other belongs to the province of religion in its broadest sense, not a religion of arrogance and fundamentalist avowal, but of great sensitivity, such as our own Jewish faith, that helps us to manage the anxieties of living with uncertainty, but that prompts us gently to explore an unseen and infinitely mysterious God.

This first appeared as a sermon delivered on Kol Nidre 5771 (2010) at the Liberal Jewish Synagogue, London

Other available publications from the Movement for Reform Judaism

FORMS OF PRAYER

Daily and Sabbath Siddur

Pilgrim Festivals Machzor
(Pesach, Shavuot Sukkot, Simchat Torah)

High Holydays Machzor
(Days of Awe : Rosh Hashanah and Yom Kippur)

BOOKS

Faith and Practice - A Guide to Reform Judaism Today
by Rabbi Dr Jonathan Romain

God, Doubt and Dawkins - Reform Rabbis respond to *The God Delusion*
edited by Rabbi Dr Jonathan Romain

Great Reform Lives – Rabbis who dared to differ
edited by Rabbi Dr Jonathan Romain

Really Useful Prayers – What to say when you don't know what to say
edited by Rabbi Dr Jonathan Romain

Tradition and Change - A History of Reform Judaism in Britain 1840-1995
by Anne J Kershen and Rabbi Dr Jonathan Romain

Werner van der Zyl - Master Builder

A Collection of Essays about his Life and Work

'RESPONSA' SERIES

Bar Mitzvah and Bat Mitzvah - A Reform Perspective

by Rabbi Dr. Michael Hilton

D-I-Y Rituals - A Guide To Creating Your Own Jewish Rituals

by Rabbi Laura Janner-Klausner

I'm Jewish, My Partner Isn't   by Rabbi Dr. Jonathan Romain

Kashrut for Pesach   by Rabbi Dr. Michael Hilton

Marriage   by Rabbi Rachel Montagu

Mixed Faith Burials   by Rabbi Dr. Jonathan Romain

What is Reform Judaism?   by Rabbi Tony Bayfield

For orders details, contact the Movement for Reform Judaism,

The Sternberg Centre, 80 Eastend Road, London N3 2SY

0208-349-4731   www.reformjudaism.org.uk

SENTINELS
of the
WEAR

The River Wear Watch

A History of Sunderland's River Police and Fireboats

by
Neil W. Mearns

This book is dedicated to the memories of the officers and men of the River Wear Watch and to the countless persons whose lives have been lost within the Port of Sunderland throughout the years.

First published in 1998 by Neil W. Mearns, c/o Fulwell Post Office, 48 Sea Road, Fulwell, Sunderland, England, SR6 9BX, from which address copies of this book can be obtained.

British Library Cataloguing in Publication Data.

A catalogue record for this book is available from the British Library.

ISBN 0 9533377 0 7

Printed by Studio Print, Admiral Chaloner House, Belmangate, Guisborough, Cleveland, England, TS14 7AD; Tel. 01287 610710.

Contents

Foreword

by David Mellish, Q.P.M.
Acting Chief Constable of Northumbria Police

Northumbria Police was formed in 1974 by an amalgamation of Northumberland Constabulary and part of Durham Constabulary. Both organisations were, in their turn, the product of earlier amalgamations of a number of individual police forces, each with its own unique culture and traditions.

When Sunderland Borough Police took over responsibility for policing on the River Wear in 1961, it inherited from the River Wear Watch a tradition of policing on the river which is still maintained today by officers of our Marine Unit. In common with those other now defunct police forces, the River Wear Watch donated some of the threads from which the fabric of our modern organisation is woven.

This meticulously researched publication focuses on one chapter in the story of our evolution as a police force. It provides a fascinating insight into the way things were. It will, I am sure, be of value to local historians and students of policing; but it should also be of immense interest to police officers past and present who, like me, are eager to find out more about the origins of policing in the Northeast.

The quality of this book is testament to the dedication of its author, Neil Mearns, who has devoted countless hours of his own time to its preparation during thirteen long years of research. I commend its contents to you.

Acknowledgements

The author wishes to extend his grateful thanks to the following individuals and organisations for their invaluable assistance in providing information and access to research and photographic material, without which this book could not have been completed:

Tyne and Wear Archives Service; Sunderland Museum (Tyne and Wear Museums); City of Sunderland Central Library (Local Studies Section); Imperial War Museum; National Museum of Science and Industry; National Maritime Museum; Northeast Press Ltd., Sunderland Echo; Port of Sunderland Authority; Northumbria Police Marine Unit; John Yearnshire, Sunderland; Station Officer J. T. Bryce, Tyne and Wear Metropolitan Fire Brigade; Martin Routledge, Sunderland Museum; Dennis Barker, South Hylton, Sunderland; Andrew Calder, Red House, Sunderland; Nigel Green, formerly of the Sunderland Echo; Mr. E. Frost, Doxford Park, Sunderland; the late Mr. W. H. Dodsworth, ex-constable, River Wear Watch; the late Mr. R. M. Swan, ex-constable, River Wear Watch; Billy Bell, Hendon, Sunderland; Mr. L. G. Britton, Northumberland; Mr. and Mrs. A. B. Rodenby, Leicestershire; Mr. J. T. Oliver, Sunderland; Mr. H. Appleyard, Billingham; Mr. J. Brownhill, Sheffield; Mr. G. F. Spink, Grimsby; Mrs. J. Watson, Washington; Mrs. S. A. Freeman, Whitley Bay; Mr. S. A. Robinson, Sandton, South Africa; and Mr. D. Laythorpe, Sunderland.

References

The following documents and publications have been used as sources of reference:

Records of the River Wear Watch Commissioners (Tyne and Wear Archives Service Accession No. 746); Marine Policing Records (Northumbria Police Marine Unit); Local Newspapers (1831 - 1997); Various Acts of Parliament (1810 - 1987); Port of Sunderland Handbooks; 'Lloyds Register of Ships'; 'Mercantile Navy List and Maritime Directory'; 'Back on the Borough Beat' by John Yearnshire (1987); 'Sunderland Fire Brigade' by J. T. Bryce (1993); 'Sunderland - River, Town & People' edited by E. Milburn and Stuart T. Miller (1988); 'History of Durham' by William Fordyce (1857); 'Where Ships are Born' by J. W. Smith and T. S. Holden (1946); 'Coastguard' by William Webb (1976); 'Crimes of Yesteryear' by Nigel Green (1990); 'Local Records or Historical Register of Remarkable Events'; 'Local Historians Table Book'; 'Engineering'; 'The Fireman'; 'Fire and Water'; 'Police Review' and 'The Victoria Cross'.

In addition, sincere thanks are due to the former Chief Constable of Northumbria Police, Sir Stanley Bailey, C.B.E., Q.P.M., D.L. for granting permission to publish this book and to research and quote archive records of the River Wear Watch; also to David Mellish, O.B.E., Q.P.M., Acting Chief Constable of Northumbria Police, who retired in April, 1998, for kindly agreeing to write the foreword. The author also wishes to extend his gratitude to Mrs. E. P. Cairns and Mr. P. M. Old for their help in proof reading the manuscript; and to Mr. Ian Mearns for his assistance with the preparation of maps of the River Wear and Docks. Finally, the author wishes to record his appreciation for all the support, advice and assistance provided by his wife, Maureen during the preparation of this book.

List of Illustrations

19. Memorial card produced following the deaths of Sergeant John Hasker and P.C. Jonathan Dryden, who lost their lives on 4th November, 1895 whilst engaged at the scene of a fire at Joshua Wilson and Sons' warehouse in the East End of Sunderland. *Sunderland Museum (Tyne and Wear Museums).*

20. The great destruction brought about as the result of the Havelock House fire which broke out on 18th July, 1898 is clearly evident as firefighters dampen down the ruins. *Northeast Press Ltd., Sunderland Echo.*

21. The *Fire King*, built in 1906 by Henry Scarr of Hessle-on-Humber, pictured off Manor Quay between 1906 and 1913. Inspector Lakin is standing on the starboard side, second from the stern. *Sunderland Museum (Tyne and Wear Museums).*

22. The second *Fire Queen*, launched in 1885 by S. P. Austin and Sons, together with the *Fire King*, engaged in combating an esparto grass fire on board *S.S. Ella Sayer* at East Quay, Hendon Dock on 7th March, 1907. *Sunderland Museum (Tyne and Wear Museums).*

23. The third *Fire Queen*, constructed in 1911, also by Henry Scarr, poses in the River Wear near J. L. Thompson and Sons Ltd. during the early years of her career. *Sunderland Museum (Tyne and Wear Museums).*

24. John William Arthur Rochford *(1869 - 1952)*, who held the position as Inspector of the River Wear Watch from 1913 until his retirement in 1949, then aged eighty. *Author's collection.*

25. Captain George Butchart *(1843 - 1916)*, a highly respected local maritime figure and ardent member of the River Wear Watch Commission from 1890 until his death. *Author's collection.*

26. The collier, *S.S. Corcrag (ex-Hornsey)*, *(built 1898 / 1,803 g.r.t.)* pictured under way during the period 1920 - 1924. On 10th November, 1918, whilst lying at buoys in the River Wear near to Thornhill Quay, a serious fire which had broken out on board, threatening engulf the ship's magazine, was heroically dealt with by members of the Watch. *National Maritime Museum.*

27a. A 12 pounder brass shell casing, from on board *S.S. Hornsey*, which was retained as a souvenir by Inspector Rochford. *Author's collection.*

27b. Markings on the base of the shell casing. Note the year of manufacturer - 1917. *Author's collection.*

28. Five brave men *(left to right)*: Inspector John William Arthur Rochford, Sergeant George William Jennings, P.C. Herbert Adams, Sergeant William Jackson and P.C. William Nichols Steel are pictured outside Shire Hall, Durham on 7th May, 1920 after receiving their Kings Medals for Gallantry from the Earl of Durham as a result of their actions on board *S.S. Hornsey* on 10th November, 1918. *Author's collection.*

29. John Caffrey, V.C. *(1891 - 1953)*, who originated from Birr, Kings County, Ireland and served as a constable with the Watch in 1919, before transferring to Sunderland Borough Police. *Author's collection.*

30. Viewed from the public stairs between S. P. Austin and Sons' shipyard and Scotia Quay are the River Station *Manual*, the *Fire Queen* and a Watch rowing boat. The approximate date of the photograph can be ascertained from the France Fenwick and Co. Ltd. collier, *Bearwood*, seen in the background, which was owned by that company between 1919 and 1927. *W. Bell collection.*

31. On parade at the Garrison Field, Gill Bridge Avenue, Sunderland, during the 1920's, members of the Watch are inspected by Superintendent Crawley and His Majesty's Inspector of Constabulary. *Author's collection.*

32. Watch personnel on board the *Fire Queen* during the 1920's. P.C. Jonathan Freeman is standing on the extreme left and Inspector Rochford is on the far right. *Author's collection.*

33. *Fire Queen* lies alongside the *Manual* in 1923. *Author's collection.*

34. John Edward Dawson *(1862 - 1942)*, who, as Chairman of the River Wear Commissioners, conducted a campaign of attrition against the Watch, after the passing of the River Wear Watch Act in 1923. *Author's collection.*

35. Firefighters engaged at the scene of a fire which broke out on 6th November, 1923, amongst thousands of pit props stored on the east side of Hendon Dock by George Horsley and Co. *Author's collection.*

36. *Fire King* engaged in pumping operations alongside the quay wall in Hendon Dock on 7th November, 1923. *Author's collection.*

37. Seventeen members of the Watch's establishment of twenty-two, pictured on 8th March, 1925: **Top row** *(left to right)*: Jonas S. Blakeston, George James Elstob, Alexander Knapp, George Thomas Tildon, Charles Peter Page and George William Jennings; **Centre row** *(left to right)*: John Mark Cartmer, unknown, John William Arthur Rochford, Robert F. Mustard and William Nichols Steel; **Bottom row** *(left to right)*: Gilbert J. Mellefont, *unknown*, Herbert Adams, Peter W. Atkinson, Thomas Swales and James Rich. *Author's collection.*

38. Motor launch, *Vigilante* which was acquired second-hand in 1928 and remained in service until 1933. Superintendent Ruddick is seated at the stern, with Inspector Rochford standing behind Constable Rich. *Author's collection.*

39. The *Fire Queen* makes a spectacular sight as she discharges five jets of water simultaneously at Claxheugh, South Hylton. *Northeast Press Ltd., Sunderland Echo.*

40. An aerial view of the lower reaches of the Wear during the 1930's. The River Station, *Fire Queen* and other Watch craft are the lower group of vessels which can be seen in the bottom right hand corner of the picture. *Sunderland Museum (Tyne and Wear Museums).*

41. A pre-1932 photograph of the River Station, *Manual* with steam launch, *Patrol* moored on her port side and the *Fire Queen* on her starboard. *Northeast Press Ltd., Sunderland Echo.*

42. River Police sergeant passing the time of day with a cyclist on the Low Street near Wylam Wharf. *Author's collection.*

43. John Thomas Burnop, who was elected as a River Wear Watch Commissioner in 1939 and also served as a shipowning representative on the River Wear Commission. *Author's collection.*

44. P.C. John Patterson who served as a constable with the Watch between 1932 and 1961. As an army reservist, he was the only Watch member to see active service during World War 2. *Author's collection.*

45. The scene at the junction of John Street and Borough Road on the morning of 10th April, 1941, as firefighters tackle the blaze at Binns' East side Departmental Store, destroyed during the previous night's air raid. For almost fifteen hours, the *Fire Queen* had pumped water half a mile, from the river to Mowbray Park lake, to feed pumps engaged at the incident. *Sunderland Museum (Tyne and Wear Museums).*

46. The collier, *S.S. Zealous* being pumped out by the *Fire Queen* at Hetton Quay on 5th June, 1942, after sustaining serious damage following the detonation of a delayed action bomb which had fallen into the river the previous night. *Sunderland Museum (Tyne and Wear Museums).*

47. A busy wartime scene on the Wear during the 1939 - 1945 conflict, looking north across the Wear from S. P. Austin and Sons' towards J. L. Thompson and Sons Ltd. Note the camouflage paintwork on the ship fitting out at Manor Quay and the barrage balloon aloft. *Northeast Press Ltd., Sunderland Echo.*

48. Alfred H. J. Brown, F.C.I.S., M.Inst.T., the General Manager and Clerk to the River Wear Commissioners, who also performed the duties of Clerk to the River Wear Watch Commissioners from 1946, until his death in 1957. *Author's collection.*

49. **S.S. Raloo** poses a major hazard to the navigation of the port, after sinking at North Quay buoys on 3rd February, 1946. *Northeast Press Ltd., Sunderland Echo.*

50. **S.S. Raloo** in trouble again, this time after running aground at North Sands in February, 1947. *Northeast Press Ltd., Sunderland Echo.*

51. Robert Cyril Thompson, C.B.E., who was elected to the River Wear Watch Commission in 1948. He had headed the British merchant shipbuilding mission to the U.S.A. and Canada in 1940 and 1941. *Author's collection.*

52. Plan of the dumb barge, **Pikes' No. 10** prior to her conversion as a floating headquarters for the Watch in 1949. *Author's collection.*

53. Senior police officers of the West German *Wasserschutzpolizei* accompanied by Superintendent Tait of the Borough Police during their visit to the River Wear Watch on 9th March, 1950. *Northeast Press Ltd., Sunderland Echo.*

54. The **Fire King**, lying at her moorings at the entrance to the Sea Lock in Hudson Dock during the late 1950's. The Dock Police Station can be seen in the top left corner of the picture. *Northeast Press Ltd., Sunderland Echo.*

55. Sergeant Ernest Stark, with a party of visiting students from the Police College, on board the **Fire Queen** during the 1950's. *Author's collection.*

56. River Police Constable dressed for maintenance duties on board the **Fire Queen** in the 1950's. Note the immaculate condition of the firefloat and launch moored alongside. *Author's collection.*

57. Members of the River Wear Watch are present at a memorial service held on board the paddle tug, **Eppleton Hall** on 12th February, 1951, for the four crew members of the steamtug, **Stag** who were lost a year previously when she capsized at sea. *Northeast Press Ltd., Sunderland Echo.*

58. The crew of motor launch, **Vigilant** observe attentively as tugs manoeuvre the newly launched stern portion of a ship towards the quayside. The occasion is either that of the launch, from John Crown and Sons Ltd., of the stern section of the Norwegian tanker, **Rondefjell** *(15,067 g.r.t.)*, during 1951, or of another Norwegian tanker, **Andwi** *(12,315 g.r.t.)*, in 1954. *Author's collection.*

59. A view of **Fire Queen** alongside River Station, **Pikes' No. 10**, in 1953. *Northeast Press Ltd., Sunderland Echo.*

60. In the cabin of the River Station, during 1953, Constable Richard Davison completes clerical work, watched by Constable Richard Swan *(left)* and Sergeant Thomas Hunter *(right)*. The occurrence book is also on the table. *Northeast Press Ltd., Sunderland Echo.*

61. Adjacent to Wearmouth Bridge, the six inch dry rising main is one of today's few existing reminders of the Watch. By this means, water was pumped from the river to street level by the **Fire Queen** during serious departmental store fires, at Binns in 1941, and at Joplings in 1954. *Author's collection.*

62. **Fire King** on John Crown and Sons' Strand Slipway on 12th May, 1955, undergoing what was to be her final overhaul. *Northeast Press Ltd., Sunderland Echo.*

63. Watched by a constable on board the **Fire Queen**, motor launch, **Patrol** leaves her moorings in 1959. The tugs, **Cleadon**, **Prestwick** and **Ryhope**, belonging to France, Fenwick Tyne & Wear Co. Ltd. provide an interesting background. *Northeast Press Ltd., Sunderland Echo.*

64. Walter Beattie Allan, a partner in Allan, Black & Co. and a director of the Albyn Line, who, on 28th October, 1959, was the last shipowner to be appointed to the River Wear Watch Commission. *Author's collection.*

65.   This 1959 photograph shows that the Wear was still a hive of activity with colliers undergoing repair at, what was by then, Austin and Pickersgill Ltd's Wear Dockyard and new ships fitting out on the north side of the river at Manor Quay. *Northeast Press Ltd., Sunderland Echo.*

66.   The firefloat, *Fire Queen* and motor launch, *Patrol* lie quietly alongside the River Station, ***Pikes' No. 10,*** in 1959. *Northeast Press Ltd., Sunderland Echo.*

67.   Ernest Alfred Stark, who was promoted to Inspector of the River Wear Watch on 30th May, 1957 and served in that capacity until dissolution in 1961. *Author's collection.*

68.   Sergeant 'No. 2' Thomas James Hunter, a member of the Watch between 1930 and 1961. *Author's collection.*

69.   P.C. William Henry Dodsworth, who served with the Watch from 1928 until 1961. *Author's collection.*

70.   Sergeant Robert F. Mustard on board the pristine ***Fire Queen***, together with an unknown gentleman. *Author's collection.*

71.   The entry in P.C. Dodsworth's note book concerning the recovery of an unidentified torso from the River Wear at Corporation Quay on 12th October, 1960. *Author's collection.*

72.   The River Wear Watch's 'Foul Anchor' cap badge. *Author's collection.*

73.   River Wear Watch Inspectors' cloth cap badge. *Author's collection.*

74.   River Wear Watch uniform button. *Author's collection.*

75.   River Wear Police whistle. *Author's collection.*

76.   Lying forlorn and forgotten in a corner of Hudson Dock, the ***Fire King*** and ***Fire Queen*** present a sorry sight in this 1962 picture as they await their fate. The superstructure of the ***Fire Queen*** has already been partially dismantled. *Northeast Press Ltd., Sunderland Echo.*

77.   Motor launch, ***Patrol***, pictured in May, 1962 in the service of Sunderland Borough Police River Section. Note her immaculate condition. *Northeast Press Ltd., Sunderland Echo.*

78.   Constables Malcolm Donkin and Albert Swinbank of the Borough Police River Section on board the ***Patrol***, in 1962, operating her new two-way v.h.f. wireless. *Northeast Press Ltd., Sunderland Echo.*

79.   Another view of the ***Patrol***, taken in 1964, showing the launch's white livery. *Northeast Press Ltd., Sunderland Echo.*

80.   Grim faced Borough firemen at the scene of the fatal fire on board ***M.V. Toronto City*** at Doxford's Quay on 30th October, 1966, when seven men lost their lives. *Northeast Press Ltd., Sunderland Echo.*

81.   Members of Sunderland Borough Fire Brigade tackling the blaze on board ***M.V. Landwade*** at T. W. Greenwell and Co. Ltd's quay on 15th April, 1967. The blackened superstructure where four persons died is evident. *Northeast Press Ltd., Sunderland Echo.*

82.   The Borough Brigade's new smoke extraction unit is used to good effect at a fire on board the West German collier, ***Hanngrid***, at Hudson Dock, also in April, 1967. *Northeast Press Ltd., Sunderland Echo.*

83.   Members of the Auxiliary Fire Service exercising with a Bikini Raft Unit on the River Wear in 1964. Normally, each craft carried a crew of two. *Northeast Press Ltd., Sunderland Echo.*

84.   A Northumbria Police diver working with lifting bags at Hudson Dock in 1981 following the sinking of Lawson-Batey Tugs Ltd's motor tug, ***Alnwick***. *L. G. Britton.*

85. Northumbria Police Marine Sub Division's Wear Station, North Dock, December, 1980. Police launches, *No. 4 (nearest camera)* and *No. 5* are moored to the pontoon in the corner of the dock, whilst a Watercraft launch is undergoing refurbishment on the quayside. Four U.S.U. vehicles can be seen inside the compound together with an assortment of portacabin accommodation. *Author's collection.*

86. Tyne and Wear Metropolitan Fire Brigade's fireboat, *Vedra*. *Tyne and Wear Metropolitan Fire Brigade.*

87. Members of the Northumbria Police Underwater Search Unit prepare their equipment before undertaking a search for two children thought to be missing near the Old North Pier in April, 1995. *Northeast Press Ltd., Sunderland Echo.*

88. A popular duty for Northumbria Marine officers is attendance at the Sunderland International Air Show, held annually off the coast of Seaburn. Here, police launch, *Northumbria* keeps spectator craft at a safe distance during the touchdown of a Catalena flying boat. *L. G. Britton.*

89. *M.V. Viking*, formerly the firefloat, *Fire King* pictured at Grimsby Marina with all sails fully rigged. *Author's collection.*

Introduction

On the northeast coast of England stands the historic seaport of Sunderland, through the midst of which flows the River Wear into the North Sea. It was this river upon which the growth and prosperity of the town for so long depended, the first authentic evidence of Sunderland as a place of maritime commerce being contained in a Charter granted by Bishop Pudsey to 'Weremouth' in 1154. The earliest reference to shipbuilding on the Wear dates from 1346 and in 1396 the exportation of coal from the river was first recorded. From being a comparatively small haven, the port subsequently developed, under the patronage of the River Wear Commissioners, into an important sea terminal chiefly exporting coal, but also handling an extensive volume and variety of other cargoes. In addition, the growth of shipbuilding and ancillary industries would earn Sunderland the proud distinction of being the largest shipbuilding town in the world.

Today, the Port of Sunderland presents but a shadow of its former self, with coal exports having ceased in 1986 and the death of the shipyards two years later. Now the river is filled with silent echoes of ghosts of the past, its fate beyond the control and comprehension of those whose lives evolved around it.

In spite of the gloom, strenuous efforts have been maintained by port managers to assure its survival as a commercial enterprise, with shipping and industrial activity still to be seen on the river and in the docks, although by no means on the same scale as once was common. Whilst having little relevance to the continuance of mercantile activity within the port, redevelopment of the riverside has taken place at various locations and increased waterborne leisure activities add a touch of colour and action to the harbour scene.

However, it was against a backdrop of the Wear's distinguished past that the River Wear Watch performed its duties. For over 121 years, through eras of sail, steam and diesel, during the transition from wooden to steel ships and throughout two world wars, its members carried out the role of policeman, fireman and salvor. Alas, as with so many other institutions in the port, the Watch is now consigned to history.

There is little doubt that the force held an unique position in the chronicles of British policing. Whilst many other docks and harbour forces have existed and still do, none have conformed exactly to the manner in which the Watch was organised and carried out its duties. Having been born by reason of the vested interests of local shipowners, the force soon became recognised as a valued public service.

That the Watch survived for so long is remarkable in itself. Even as its establishment was being proposed by local shipowners in 1839, vehement opposition was encountered from Sunderland Corporation which demanded the sole right of control. In spite of compromise being reached, the Commissioners who were subsequently vested with the management of the force frequently had to fend off further moves to usurp their powers.

Yet by the turn of this century, attitudes had changed, with the Commissioners having decided that their functions could best be performed either by the River Wear Commissioners or Corporation.

Accordingly, for over sixty years, frequent attempts were made to secure the transfer of the Watch to either body, all without success. In the end, with the Watch Commissioners unable to carry on any longer, the Corporation's intransigence forced the issue and the Watch was finally laid to rest in 1961.

This book seeks to chronicle the history of the Watch from establishment to dissolution and places emphasis upon many of the more notable occurrences to which its members were required to attend. Running parallel to this theme, are accounts of how the force was organised, managed and financed. Detailed descriptions of firefloats, launches and other craft used to perform its duties are included and many insights into the personalities associated with the Watch are provided. Also reflected are the close and sometimes difficult relationships with the Borough Police and Fire Services, the River Wear Commissioners and other agencies.

While the narrative primarily concerns the River Wear Watch, this is not quite the full story. Chapter 1 is devoted to the original River Watch which, under the auspices of Sunderland Improvement Commissioners, patrolled the river from 1810 until 1837.

Since the demise of the River Wear Watch in 1961, the manner in which police and firefighting services have been undertaken in the port has changed dramatically. The term 'river police' has been superseded by 'marine police', and whilst still having a prime responsibility for the protection of life and property, the modern day descendant of the old-time river policeman has a far wider range of duties to contend with, many of which would seem strange to his predecessor. The final chapter, therefore, briefly records the progression of policing and firefighting in the port since the Watch's dissolution.

Despite the change in fortunes for the Port of Sunderland, the requirement for an effective marine policing and firefighting capability is still of great importance and will remain so for as long as the Wear continues to flow into the sea.

As a footnote, during the twelve months preceding the completion of this book, no fewer than twelve persons have lost their lives in the waters of the River Wear at Sunderland in a variety of circumstances. A number have also been seriously injured and the lives of others placed at risk resulting from incidents which have sporadically occurred.

Chapter 1

THE SUNDERLAND IMPROVEMENT COMMISSION RIVER WATCH.

(1810 - 1837)

As a prelude to the story of the River Wear Watch, which was to commence its 121 years of existence in 1840, it is of significance to point out that the history of policing on the Wear can be traced back far earlier. In fact, for a period of twenty-seven years prior to its formation, a body of watchmen and night constables were employed on the river. Unfortunately, little of them is known.

ESTABLISHMENT OF ORIGINAL WATCH ON THE WEAR

On 1st May, 1810, an Act was passed by Parliament for *"Paving, Lighting, Watching, and Cleansing the Town of Sunderland, near the Sea, in the County of Durham, for removing the Market, for building a Town Hall or Market House, and for otherwise improving the said Town;* ***and for establishing a Watch on the River Wear."***

It should be explained at this stage that Sunderland had become the collective name for the townships of Sunderland, Bishopwearmouth, Bishopwearmouth Panns, Monkwearmouth and Monkwearmouth Shore. The first named had become a parish in its own right in 1719, whilst the remainder were sub divisions of the ancient parishes of Bishopwearmouth and Monkwearmouth. It would not be until 1837 that official unification of the townships would take place, when Sunderland's borough status was finally recognised in consequence of the Municipal Corporations Act of 1835.

The Improvement Act, therefore, related only to the Township or Parish of Sunderland, with other provisions being enacted in respect of the other townships.

One of the main reasons for the Act was to benefit public safety, resulting in a *"well-regulated Watch"* being established in the township and the formation of a River Watch on the Wear, between the Pier and Rectors' Gill at Bishopwearmouth.

To maintain and support the River Watch, a duty of one penny per ton was imposed upon all ships, except limestone vessels, trading to and from the port, this levy being collected at the time of the first voyage each year.

A body of commissioners was appointed under the Act to execute its provisions, with 150 being named therein for this purpose, with powers to appoint watchmen, fix their wages, erect watch-houses and to arm the force as they saw fit.

THE SUNDERLAND IMPROVEMENT ACT OF 1826

During the following years, the size and population of the township were subject to a great increase and it was found that the provisions of the 1810 Act were, in many respects, defective. As a result, the Sunderland Improvement Act of 1826 was passed for *"Paving, Lighting, Watching, Cleansing and improving the Town and Parish of Sunderland near the Sea, in the County of Durham, for removing the Market, and for otherwise improving the said Town."* This Act, which received Royal Assent on 26th May, 1826, repealed the previous Act of 1810, with the exception of clauses relating to the maintenance and establishment of a Watch on the River Wear.

Although the original River Watch was retained, the new Act introduced wider and more specific provisions relating to it, which were identical with those made for the regulation of the Town Watch.

The Commissioners were now authorised and required to appoint able-bodied watchmen and night constables within the town and also on that part of the River Wear, between the Pier on the east and Ayre's Quay (a short distance upriver from Rectors' Gill) on the west, and on its quays and shores during such periods of the year that they saw fit.

They were empowered to direct where the watchmen and night constables were to be stationed, the manner in which they were to be armed, how often they were to make their rounds, the limits of their rounds and their hours of duty. The Commissioners were also given authority to dispense with the services of such employees and to appoint others in their place. They were to provide 'proper places, boxes and coats, and watch houses' for their men and were to make any orders and regulations which they saw fit to preserve peace and order and an effective police within and for the safety of the inhabitants of the town and other persons employed or having property on the River Wear.

The watchmen and night constables, themselves, were to keep watch and ward within the town and on the river and were to apprehend all *"felons, malefactors, rogues, vagabonds, suspicious and disorderly persons, vagrants, thieves, night walkers, beggars and all disturbers of the public Peace"* and take them before a Justice of the Peace within twenty-four hours, or as soon after as convenient.

To discourage what was almost a national pastime of the era, a penalty of £5 could be imposed upon anyone overturning a cabin provided for the watchmen or constables. More often than not, these boxes were occupied when pushed over!

For failing to observe orders imposed by the Commissioners, Watch members were liable to forfeit forty shillings, and to dismissal, if the breach was deemed serious enough.

It was not uncommon for the watchmen and night constables of the time to resort to public houses whilst on duty. To counter this, a publican supplying them with liquor was liable to a fine of £5.

Members of the Watch did, however, enjoy the full range of powers afforded to any constable of the time and could receive compensation in the event of being wounded or disabled in the execution of their duty.

THE TALE OF THE CAPTAIN'S SUPPER

The manner in which certain individuals in the service of the River Watch sometimes carried out - or did not carry out - their duties is illustrated in the following extract which appeared in the Sunderland and Durham Gazette on 19th February, 1831:

"A few nights ago, we have been informed that the Captain of the River Watch was discovered in the embraces of Morpheus at an early hour of duty, a proof of the omnipotent power of the omniferous deity; his slavious vulgarity denominated a whistle, escaped from his cognizance - On the following evening owing to the fresh, the Boat under the command of this watchful guardian of property could not be used - the Watch was accordingly stationed on the shore, one of the men had been on patrol during the evening, on quitting which, he was appointed to watch for the remainder of the night, he begged that the drowsy Captain would allow him to go home for supper, but the worthy commander snorted the emphatic monosyllable, 'No' - Near the witching time of night, whilst going his rounds, he observed some material substance in a lime kiln - the hour was rather eerie but determined to bring his courage up to the sticking point he ventured forward, and - I beg pardon for inserting the fact, it was the worthy Captain whose portable larder appeared rather prominent - he seized the opportunity, pounced upon the Captain's viands, and supped most deliciously, while the worthy commander, dreaming of ships, boats, and river surveillance, unconsciously allowed the marauder to feast at his expense and to replace his conveyancer diminished of its savoury contents - Our Commissioners, we trust, will adopt such measures as shall keep this watchful guardian awake in the future."

CESSATION OF THE RIVER WATCH

On 14th November, 1837, following the passage of the Municipal Corporations Act of 1835, the Sunderland Borough Police Force was formed and from that date the powers of Sunderland Improvement Commissioners to maintain a river watch ceased. Almost two years would elapse before a police presence was again to be seen on the Wear.

Despite a well-established belief that bodies of old-fashioned watchmen were inefficient - often with good cause, much was learned from the experiences of the River Watch whilst under the control of the Sunderland Improvement Commissioners. Indeed, this was endorsed in the annual report of the Committee of the Sunderland Shipowners' Society which was read at the Society's annual general meeting on 17th August, 1840 when the opinion was expressed that the new River Wear Watch, due to come into being, *"would be attended to with the same success."*

Chapter 2

CONCEPTION OF THE RIVER WEAR WATCH.

(1839 - 1840)

SUNDERLAND AND THE RIVER WEAR

In 1839, when the story of the River Wear Watch began to unfold, Sunderland was a busy, fast growing and prosperous industrial town. It was the River Wear that provided the lifeblood of the town and upon which the prosperity of its inhabitants depended. The great number of shipyards (sixty-five in 1840) on the riverbanks and their great output had already earned Sunderland the reputation of being the most important merchant shipbuilding centre in the country. As well as shipbuilding, trade flourished, with hundreds of sailing ships belonging to the port. The staple trade was coal from the Durham Coalfield which was shipped from numerous points on the river.

Despite the boom, the whole range of social evils encountered in Victorian Britain existed in many districts of the town, particularly those in proximity to the river. Squalor, filth, disease, poverty, vice and crime were prevalent, and were to remain so for years to come.

Sunderland, at that time, was an infant borough. Local government had been very disorganised, with the provision of public services being in the hands of a multitude of boards of commissioners and surveyors. For a while, despite the passage of the Municipal Corporations Act, the situation only improved slightly as the newly created Sunderland Corporation was almost entirely concerned with the administration of local justice, together with the management of the Borough Police Force. It would not be until the passage of the Borough of Sunderland Act in 1851 that most local services would be brought beneath the Corporation's umbrella.

Owing to the dependence placed upon the river, it was natural that the main centres of population should evolve around it. This was particularly so with the East End of the town on the south side of the river (the area comprising the former township of Sunderland). Much of this area consisted of small, dingy, overcrowded housing packed together and intersected by passageways and alleys running down towards the river. Sanitary conditions were a breeding ground for disease and it had come as no surprise when Asiatic Cholera had broken out there in 1831, the first visitation of the disease to the British Isles. Thieves, beggars, vagrants, prostitutes and various other unsavoury characters also frequented the district, whilst scores of alehouses perpetuated drunkenness.

In spite of the gloom, the riverside presented itself as a hive of industry, with trades of every description normally found in a maritime town being carried on in proliferation. On Monkwearmouth Shore, on the north side of the river, a similar situation existed, although not on the same scale.

The opening of the North Dock, in 1837, by the Wearmouth Dock Company, had done little to reduce congestion in the river, resulting from the scores of sailing vessels that crowded the tideway. The River Wear Commissioners, originally formed in 1717 as the Commissioners of the River Wear, were responsible for the conservation of the river as far up as Biddick Ford, a distance of about nine miles from the sea, and although they had carried out many improvements to the harbour, much still remained to be done.

Such was the background, against which the shipowners of the town saw the need to protect their interests.

DISQUIET BY SHIPOWNERS OVER LACK OF RIVER WATCH

As stated previously, on 14th November, 1837, the Watch Committee of the Council for the Borough of Sunderland had appointed a police force for the Borough under the Municipal Corporations Act of 1835, upon which event the powers vested in the Sunderland Improvement Commissioners for maintaining and establishing a river watch had ceased. From that time, the Town Council had levied a Borough rate and maintained a police force throughout the Borough, with the exception of the River Wear. Despite many being rated to the Borough rate as inhabitant householders, the town's shipowners were also rated upon and paid almost £400 per annum on their shipping property, which was then rated as stock in trade.

By 1839, crime on the river had increased dramatically, with cargoes and other property on board the ships, lighters, keels and other craft using the port being at great risk from the criminal fraternity. In June of that year, the master of the brigantine, *Phoenix* of Stettin had been brutally murdered on board his vessel whilst in port.

In addition, vessels themselves were exposed to grave danger from fire and from the great floods and freshes that occasionally swept the river. Within a space of a few weeks, three serious shipboard fires had broken out.

Weary of lack of initiative by the Town Council and action by the Borough Police in protecting their property, the shipowners decided to take matters into their own hands. They considered that it would be greatly to their advantage if an efficient river police force, equipped with firefloats was to be formed.

FORMATION OF TEMPORARY PRIVATE WATCH BY SHIPOWNERS

On 29th August, a general meeting of the Sunderland Shipowners' Society, presided over by Caleb Wilson, was held in the Exchange Buildings in High Street East. The object of this meeting was to establish a proper and effective watch on the river to protect shipping during the approaching winter. This was only intended to be a temporary measure, pending an enabling act of parliament being obtained as an essential prelude to the creation of a permanent watch.

Thus, on 1st October, 1839, the duties of the Society's Private Watch, consisting of four men, commenced. The services of Sergeant Ralph Annison of the Borough Police, described as being one of their best men, were secured and he was appointed Captain in charge. To finance the venture, a rate of one ha'penny per net registered ton was levied upon shipping using the port, which was to be paid at the Customs House each time a vessel arrived in the river. Ships not registered at Sunderland were exempted from payment of these dues.

PROPOSED CREATION OF PERMANENT WATCH

The shipowners had now to go to Parliament to sanction the establishment of a permanent river watch. Little time was wasted, for on 12th October, 1839, notice of their intention to apply for such a bill was published. In essence, the Bill sought to vest in a body of commissioners, the power to levy rates upon all shipping entering the Port of Sunderland, for the purpose of maintaining a separate police force for the protection of shipping on the River Wear; for watching its quays and shores, and other parts of the Borough; and for providing and supporting floating fire engines.

OPPOSITION FROM THE TOWN COUNCIL

Little did the Shipowners' Society anticipate the opposition which would threaten their scheme. The Town Council met on 13th February, 1840 to discuss the matter and immediately sought to amend the proposed Bill. Whilst unanimous in agreement as to the necessity for the river to be policed, the Council opposed the Bill in principle as they saw it as a flagrant impingement upon their existing right as a corporation to control the police for the entire Borough. Moreover, it was apparent that one of the great principles of the Municipal Corporations Act, namely the vesting of the management of all municipal affairs in one elected body, was being undermined by the establishment of what was described as *"another irresponsible, self-elected and aristocratic commission."* It was therefore resolved to oppose the Bill, unless control of the proposed River Police Force was vested in the Corporation. A deputation, consisting of Aldermen Spoor, Kirk and White, together with Councillors Moore and Pratt, was duly appointed to wait upon the Committee of the Shipowners' Society to deliver the Council's ultimatum.

Although received with great courtesy, the deputation had their proposals rejected out of hand. It was now for the Town Council to initiate steps to oppose the Bill, which was to receive its first reading in the House of Commons on 26th February.

A Town Council meeting followed on 20th February. The meeting was an acrimonious affair, with Councillors Nicholson and Booth vehemently supporting the case of the shipowners in the face of determined opposition from the majority of those present. Besides the main objections, already stated, others were put forward by the Bill's opponents, of which Alderman Spoor and Councillor Moore were in the forefront.

With the presence of two sets of police in the town, it was feared that frequent collisions of authority would ensue between them. This was disputed by the shipowners, who cited examples of the police in the Port of London and at Liverpool Docks which operated independently of municipal authorities. There was considerable disquiet as to the shipowners' intention to police not only the river, but the quays, shores and other parts of the Borough. This, contended the shipowners, was necessary to enable their men to be able to assist their Borough counterparts. In any case, it was claimed by the Council, the quays and shores were already effectively watched by the Borough Police, although the necessity of possessing boats was conceded. Furthermore, the shipowners proposed to arm their men as they saw fit. "Would muskets be issued to quell disturbances?", councillors demanded to know.

The Private Watch, established during the previous October, was branded as ineffectual and treated with derision. With hardly a day passing without river thieves being brought before the magistrates by the Borough Police, could the shipowners give even one instance of their Watch having apprehended a single offender? They could not, but maintained that criminals were so afraid of their men that they did not dare attempt any depredations.

Then there was the question of the Commissioners, themselves. True, they were all men of honour and integrity, but would not always be there. Who knew how future shipowners might deploy an armed force at their disposal?

To finance their new force, the shipowners sought powers to levy dues, not only upon local shipping, but upon strangers too. It was feared, especially by the coalowners, that this would drive away trade from the port. The shipowners argued that such a tax would be reciprocal, as their ships were subject to various dues at other ports. Besides, strangers would benefit from the River Watch whilst visiting the Wear.

It was pointed out by the Council that, as the port's shipowners already paid their proportion of the Borough rate, they would be taxed twice for the maintenance of police forces should the Bill pass into law. This, the shipowners were prepared to endure. As they were prepared to pay for it, they asserted, it was only a matter of justice that they should be permitted to have control of their own police force. Furthermore, a considerable proportion of their number resided outside the Borough boundaries and did not, therefore, contribute towards the Borough rates. It was deemed proper and necessary that these persons, equally with others, should share the expenditure. This, however, could only be achieved by an act of parliament.

The question arose of the Corporation providing a river police force from the rates, under their own control. This would, no doubt, have contented the shipowners, but it became apparent that the Corporation did not have the means to do this and the shipowners would, despite not having control, be required to finance it themselves. This infuriated the shipowners who saw the situation as being "a dog in the manger story" - the Corporation would not police the river themselves, nor would they allow the shipowners to do so.

The shipowners were accused of seeking special privilege in demanding their own force. It was argued that they were no more entitled to such a force as were any of the manufacturing industries of the town.

Along with the provision of police, the Bill was also the means by which floating fire engines were to be obtained. If necessary, contended its opponents, such engines could be acquired and maintained by voluntary subscriptions without need for recourse to an act of parliament. In fact, during 1836, the Sunderland Shipowners' Society had carried out a feasibility study on the propriety of obtaining firefloats for the Wear and had inspected those then in operation on the River Thames. Nothing, however, had become of this.

Despite the intransigence of the Town Council, a compromise was suggested by Alderman Spoor which he thought might satisfy all the parties concerned. His proposition was for the shipowners to agree upon the number of men required for their Watch, be responsible for their selection and pay them from a separate fund, whilst the management and direction of the force would be vested in the Superintendent of the Borough Police. Although not acted upon at that time, this proposal was eventually to form the basis for a settlement in the dispute.

Although it was believed unlikely that the Government would sanction the Bill on its second reading, owing to its incompatibility with the Municipal Corporations Act, the Town Council resolved to petition against it as a safeguard. Accordingly, the petition, signed by the Mayor, Dr. Brown, on behalf of the Corporation, was duly presented to the House of Commons on 17th March by Andrew White, M.P.

A committee was also appointed by the Town Council to put into effect opposition to the Bill. It was thought wise that government advice be sought in the first instance and as a result, a deputation comprising Councillor Moore and the Town Clerk, Mr. Brunton, accompanied by the M.P.'s, Hedworth Lambton and Andrew White, met with the Secretary of State for the Home Office, Mr. Fox Maule in London on 19th March.

The deputation found Maule very sympathetic to their cause. He stated that he would object to any of the Commissioners named in the Bill, or subsequently elected, being responsible for the appointment of members of the River Police or having any control over them. He would also require the Bill to be altered, to vest with the Superintendent of the Borough Police the appointment of such number of river policemen as the Commissioners might require; and for the Superintendent, alone, to be responsible for the direction of the force, how and where they were to be stationed, and to have the power of their dismissal and replacement by others.

The Superintendent was to be in no way amenable to the Commissioners. In case they were dissatisfied with his conduct or had cause for complaint against him, the Commissioners were to have the power to refer his conduct to the Town Council, as a court of appeal, which would then consider the matter and make whatever directions it thought fit.

Unless the Bill was altered accordingly, insisted Mr. Maule, the Government would oppose it.

Incredibly, with the weight of the Government behind the Town Council, the Shipowners' Society still maintained its demand of having ultimate control over the new force and chose to pass the following resolutions at its committee meeting held on 7th April:

(1) "That a clause be inserted in the Bill to the effect that the Superintendent for the time being of the River Police shall be vested, under the Commissioners, with the same powers, and shall be subject to the same regulations and restrictions in respect to the River Police constables, as the Superintendent of the Borough Police is vested with under the Council in respect of the Borough Police constables under his command."

(2) "That in every case in which a complaint is made against the Superintendent of the River Police, for the time being, for misconduct in such office, such complaint shall be referred to six acting Commissioners, who with the Mayor, for the time being, shall constitute a court of appeal to settle and determine such complaint, and finally to adjudge thereon."

The following day, the Town Council met to discuss the report of their committee on the progress of affairs. With both parties remaining poles apart, it now appeared that the issue could only be resolved by Parliament. Hence, the Town Clerk travelled to London to oppose the Bill on behalf of the Council and to place amendments before the parliamentary committee.

COMPROMISE REACHED

On 13th April, the day before the Bill was fixed for its committee stage, the parties involved met in London for a last ditch attempt to resolve the predicament. Present at the meeting were Mr. Brunton, the Town Clerk, for the Corporation; Messrs. Nicholson and Ord, the Shipowners' Society's deputation; and Mr. John Pexall Kidson, secretary and solicitor for the Shipowners' Society. Also in attendance were the Members of Parliament for Sunderland, Alderman William Thompson and Andrew White, who both expressed their anxious desire that all differences should be amicably settled.

After considerable discussion, a compromise was at last agreed upon, whereby the basis of the amendments contemplated by Mr. Fox Maule were finally accepted by the shipowners.

PASSAGE OF THE RIVER WEAR WATCH ACT OF 1840

The Bill subsequently passed unopposed through committee and the River Wear Watch Act received its Royal Assent on 4th June, 1840. Whilst the Sunderland Shipowners' Society had finally realised its demands for a river police force, albeit not in the form that had originally been envisaged, the Council were satisfied that sole control had not been vested with the shipowners.

It now remained for the River Wear Watch Commissioners to carry out the provisions of their new Act.

Chapter 3

ESTABLISHMENT OF THE RIVER WEAR WATCH

(1840)

INAUGURAL MEETING OF THE RIVER WEAR WATCH COMMISSIONERS

The River Wear Watch, or River Wear Police, as the force was frequently referred to, was officially born on 1st September, 1840. On that day, a large gathering of local shipowners crowded into the commission room of the Exchange Buildings in High Street East, for the purpose of putting into effect the provisions of the River Wear Watch Act. Although additional and amending legislation would be introduced in later years, it was this Act upon which the foundations of the Watch were built and would stand throughout its subsequent history.

APPOINTMENT OF COMMISSIONERS

The pre-eminent task of this inaugural meeting was the appointment of River Wear Watch Commissioners, with forty-nine being appointed that day. The Act disqualified any person from acting as a Commissioner unless being the owner of shipping registered at the Port of Sunderland to the value of at least £1,000 and having residence in the Borough, or within seven miles of its boundaries. One hundred and sixty-five persons - thirty-three being shipowning members of the Town Council - were named in the Act as Commissioners, only sixty-three of whom were to qualify to act as such by virtue of qualification restrictions.

FUNCTIONS OF THE COMMISSION

The raison d'Ítre of the Commissioners was to establish, support and maintain a proper and effective Watch, or Police Force, on the River Wear at Sunderland, between the piers on the east and Deptford on the west, for the protection of shipping and cargoes from *"thieves, depredators, or other disorderly persons"* and from fire and other misfortunes. They were also to supply fire engines, boats and other vessels, together with necessary apparatus and equipment, watch-houses, clothing and arms.

Before taking office, each Commissioner was required to make a declaration before at least two others, to the effect that he complied with all the prescribed qualifications. A penalty of £50 could be imposed upon anyone acting as such whilst disqualified or not having made the declaration. Any act carried out by a Commissioner acting in such circumstances was, nevertheless, retrospectively deemed to be lawful. It was not permissible to act as a

Commissioner whilst holding any office for payment under the Act. It became practice, for example, for the treasurer to be appointed from the Commission and then having to relinquish his position on the board. It was acceptable, however, for a commissioner to act as a justice of the Peace, provided that he had no personal interest in any proceedings.

The Commission was required to hold a meeting each quarter with a quorum of five being mandatory for business to be conducted. A majority was required in all orders made, the chairman having the casting vote. For an order to be revoked or altered, it was necessary for a greater number of Commissioners to be present than attended the meeting at which the order was originally made. In addition, a committee meeting was convened each month to discuss routine matters and topics of specific importance, prior to their referral to the Commission, as a whole, for resolution.

The Commissioners were empowered to appoint officials to perform certain functions, namely those of treasurer, clerk and collector (or receiver) of dues. The office of clerk was a very important one and was for many years undertaken by practising solicitors, John Pexall Kidson being the initial holder of this post. Mr. Kidson was well known throughout the County of Durham and had succeeded George Stephenson as Town Clerk of Sunderland in 1838. The following year, jointly with his son, John (later to become the second Clerk to the Commissioners), he was appointed clerk to the Borough Justices and was to hold this office until his retirement in 1854.

ARMING OF THE WATCH

Whilst the River Wear Watch Act authorised the arming of the force, the types of weapon by which this was to be accomplished were not specified.

Cutlasses were certainly issued from 1866, following the upsurge of Fenianism, though whether they had been issued earlier and for how long, must remain a matter for conjecture. An array of such weapons, reputed to have once formed part of the Watch's equipment, is on private display in Sunderland Magistrates' Court building.

Truncheons, on the other hand, were routinely carried by the River Police, their not infrequent use in anger being well documented. A beautifully decorated example of a Victorian River Wear Police truncheon is exhibited at Sunderland Museum.

It is also known that a number of revolvers were stored in the Dock Police Station early in the Twentieth Century, the likelihood being that these were issued to certain member of the Watch during wartime.

SUPERINTENDENT OF THE WATCH

Sole control and management of the Watch were vested in the Superintendent of the Borough Police Force whose appointment as Superintendent of the Watch was an additional capacity. This was a particular requirement which had been insisted upon by the Home Office.

The Superintendent had all the powers, duties and responsibilities in relation to the River Police as he was endowed with in respect of the Borough Force. He was authorised, with the consent of his Commissioners, to appoint such numbers of able-bodied men as River Police constables as the Commissioners deemed necessary. He alone was empowered to invoke dismissal of constables for misconduct, although it was also lawful for two magistrates to dismiss a constable for negligence or being unfit for duty. Indeed, any constable convicted of neglecting his duty or for failing to observe rules and regulations was also liable to spend fourteen days in the House of Correction, or to be fined forty shillings. An early recipient of such punishment was a river policeman who was jailed for indecently assaulting a colleague. It is of interest to note that the Act stipulated that the Superintendent should be paid *"fair and reasonable"* remuneration, whilst constables were to be granted such wages *"as the Commissioners saw fit."*

In practice, close co-operation over the management of the Watch existed between the Superintendent and Commissioners, with much of the force's day-to-day running being delegated to the Inspector of the Watch and the Clerk to the Commissioners. This arrangement seemed to work well, without major disagreements becoming apparent. Whilst some Superintendents would become more involved than others in the internal affairs of the Watch, others were seen as more of a figurehead with the enforcement of discipline being their prime concern.

In case of dissatisfaction with the Superintendent, or with any aspect in which his duties were carried out in relation to the management, direction or control of the River Police, the Commissioners were permitted to refer any appeal, complaint or representation to the Town Council or Borough Justices for arbitration.

DUTIES OF RIVER POLICE CONSTABLES

Constables were required to keep a proper and effective watch upon all parts of the river under their jurisdiction during the whole or such periods of the year as the Commissioners deemed necessary. The Commissioners were empowered to fix and vary the establishment of men in the force and over the years there was to be a great deal of fluctuation in this respect. Under the Act the duties of constables were defined as: *"to preserve the Peace by day and night, to prevent felonies and misdemeanours, to apprehend offenders against the law, and to assist in saving and protecting shipping and other property on the river in cases of accident, distress or danger arising from freshes, or floods, fires and other casualties."*

Whilst saving and protecting shipping and other property on the river were laid down as part of River Police duties, it is curious that the protection of life was not specified. Perhaps this was an oversight on the part of the shipowners, whose main concern was the protection of their own interests, or perhaps it was assumed that the force would carry out this function - always regarded as the prime duty of a constable - in any event. Whatever the reason for the omission, saving life became a routine task, with hundreds of people owing their lives to the men of the Watch over the years.

Constables were to be sworn in the manner directed by the Municipal Corporations Act and as such, were to have all the powers and privileges of other constables similarly appointed in the country. By virtue of their office, all constables appointed under the River Wear Watch Act were empowered to act as such throughout the Borough of Sunderland and liable to be called upon to do so. The Act also clarified that the rights and powers of the Borough Police to act on the river or in the Port of Sunderland would be in no way affected, diminished or prejudiced by the creation of the Watch.

CONDITIONS OF SERVICE

To coincide with the formation of the Watch, a book entitled "Rules, Orders and Regulations, for the Guidance and Government of the River Wear Police Force" was published and issued to each of its members. The book - a copy of which survives in the Local Studies Section of Sunderland Central Library and gives an invaluable insight into the force - outlined the duties and responsibilities of each rank, organisation of the force, conditions of service, and sought to provide guidance on the powers of the police to deal with various offences (known as felonies and misdemeanours).

It was emphasised that the principal objects of the Watch were the prevention of crime and of loss and injury to vessels and property on the river. Officers and constables were exhorted to *"endeavour to distinguish themselves by such vigilance and activity as may render it extremely difficult for anyone to commit a crime within that portion of river under their charge,"* as the absence of crime would be considered *"the best proof of the efficiency of the Police."*

Conditions of service were strict, the men being required to devote the whole of their time to the police service and to appear always, even when not on duty, in full uniform. They were to consider themselves liable to be called upon at all times when off duty and would lay themselves open to immediate dismissal for unfitness, negligence or misconduct.

LEVY OF THE RIVER WEAR WATCH RATE

To finance the River Wear Watch, the Commissioners were empowered to levy a rate, not exceeding one penny per net registered ton, upon each vessel entering or leaving port on her first voyage each year. Unpaid dues were to be recoverable by seizure of ships' effects under a distress warrant issued by magistrates. With the approval of the Commissioners of H.M. Customs, shipping would not receive customs' clearance unless the River Wear Watch Rate had first been paid. Certain vessels, namely those belonging to the Royal Navy, or in the service of the Customs, Excise, Post Master General or the Ordnance received complete exemption from the payment of such dues.

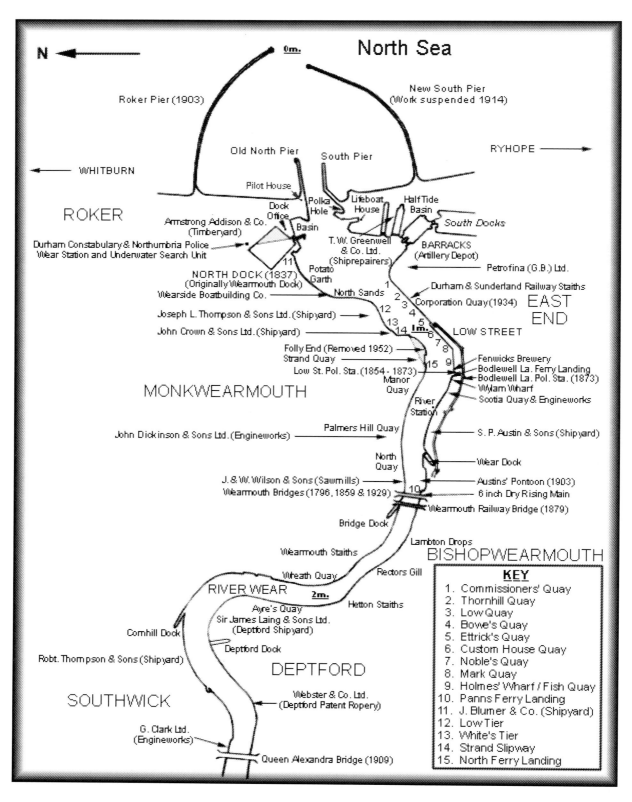

N

North Sea

Roker Pier (1903)

New South Pier
(Work suspended 1914)

RYHOPE ⟶

⟵ WHITBURN

Old North Pier   South Pier

Pilot House

ROKER

Dock
Office   Polka
Hole   Lifeboat
House   Half Tide
Basin

Armstrong Addison & Co.
(Timberyard)   Basin   South Docks

Durham Constabulary & Northumbria Police
Wear Station and Underwater Search Unit   T. W. Greenwell
& Co. Ltd.
(Shiprepairers)   BARRACKS
(Artillery Depot)

11   Petrofina (G.B.) Ltd.

Potato
Garth   1   Durham & Sunderland Railway Staiths

NORTH DOCK (1837)
(Originally Wearmouth Dock)   North Sands   2   Corporation Quay (1934)   **EAST
END**

Wearside Boatbuilding Co.   3

Joseph L. Thompson & Sons Ltd. (Shipyard) ⟶   12   4

13   5   LOW STREET

John Crown & Sons Ltd. (Shipyard) ⟶   14 **1m.**   6
7
8

Folly End (Removed 1952)   Fenwicks Brewery
Strand Quay ⟶   15   9   Bodlewell La. Ferry Landing
Low St. Pol. Sta. (1854 - 1873) ⟶   Bodlewell La. Pol. Sta. (1873)

MONKWEARMOUTH   Manor
Quay   Wylam Wharf
Scotia Quay & Engineworks

River
Station

John Dickinson & Sons Ltd. (Engineworks) ⟶   Palmers Hill Quay   S. P. Austin & Sons (Shipyard)

North
Quay   Wear Dock

J. & W. Wilson & Sons (Sawmills) ⟶   Austins' Pontoon (1903)
Wearmouth Bridges (1796, 1859 & 1929) ⟶   10   6 inch Dry Rising Main

Wearmouth Railway Bridge (1879)
Bridge Dock

Lambton Drops
BISHOPWEARMOUTH
Wearmouth Staiths

Wheath Quay   Rectors Gill

RIVER WEAR **2m.**

Ayre's Quay   Hetton Staiths
Sir James Laing & Sons Ltd.
(Deptford Shipyard)

Cornhill Dock

Deptford Dock

Robt. Thompson & Sons (Shipyard)   **DEPTFORD**

SOUTHWICK   Webster & Co. Ltd.
(Deptford Patent Ropery)

G. Clark Ltd.
(Engineworks)

Queen Alexandra Bridge (1909)

KEY
1. Commissioners' Quay
2. Thornhill Quay
3. Low Quay
4. Bowe's Quay
5. Ettrick's Quay
6. Custom House Quay
7. Noble's Quay
8. Mark Quay
9. Holmes' Wharf / Fish Quay
10. Panns Ferry Landing
11. J. Blumer & Co. (Shipyard)
12. Low Tier
13. White's Tier
14. Strand Slipway
15. North Ferry Landing

1a. Map of the River Wear from the Harbour mouth to Queen Alexandra Bridge.

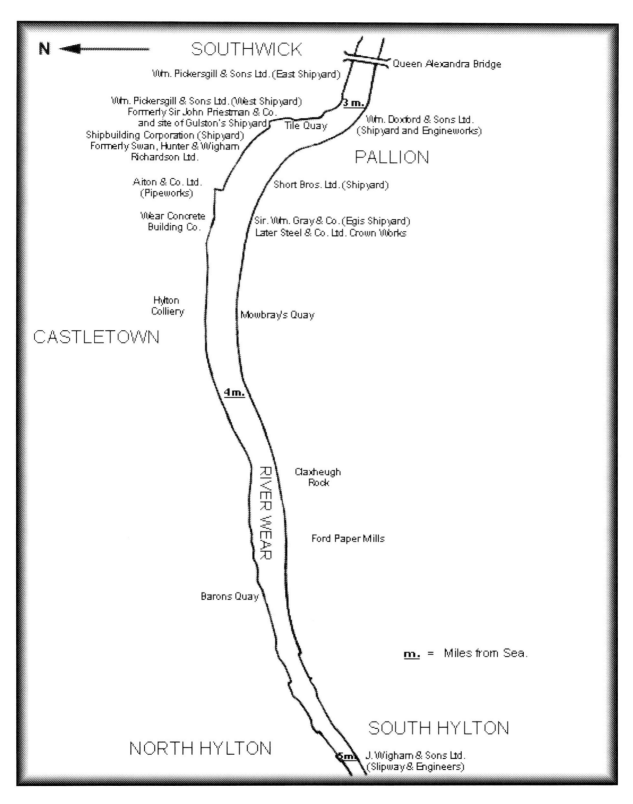

N ← SOUTHWICK

Queen Alexandra Bridge

Wm. Pickersgill & Sons Ltd. (East Shipyard)

Wm. Pickersgill & Sons Ltd. (West Shipyard)
Formerly Sir John Priestman & Co.
and site of Gulston's Shipyard

Shipbuilding Corporation (Shipyard)
Formerly Swan, Hunter & Wigham
Richardson Ltd.

3 m.

Tile Quay

Wm. Doxford & Sons Ltd.
(Shipyard and Engineworks)

PALLION

Aiton & Co. Ltd.
(Pipeworks)

Short Bros. Ltd. (Shipyard)

Wear Concrete
Building Co.

Sir. Wm. Gray & Co. (Egis Shipyard)
Later Steel & Co. Ltd. Crown Works

Hylton
Colliery

Mowbray's Quay

CASTLETOWN

4m.

RIVER WEAR

Claxheugh
Rock

Ford Paper Mills

Barons Quay

m. = Miles from Sea.

SOUTH HYLTON

NORTH HYLTON

5m. J. Wigham & Sons Ltd.
(Slipway & Engineers)

1b. Map of the River Wear from Queen Alexandra Bridge to Hylton.

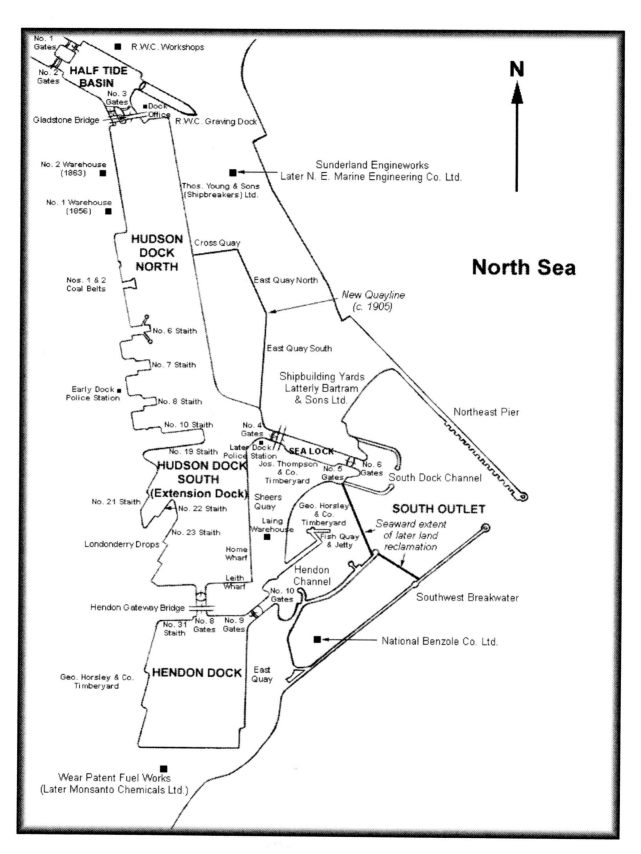

2. Plan of the South Docks, Sunderland, based upon their layout in 1895 with later additions.

3. Philip Laing *(1770 - 1854)*, shipbuilder and shipowner, who was one of the original River Wear Watch Commissioners appointed in 1840. *Author's collection.*

4. Sir James Laing *(1823 - 1901)*, one of Sunderland's most famous shipbuilders, who was elected to the River Wear Watch Commission in 1847. *Author's collection.*

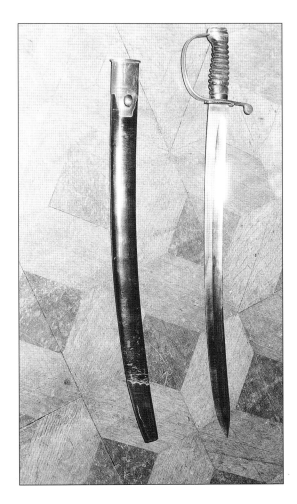

5. One of the cutlasses and sheaths which were issued to members of the Watch in 1866. *Author's collection.*

6. An array of River Wear Watch cutlasses which are on private display in Sunderland's Magistrates' Court building. *Author's collection.*

7. A beautifully decorated example of a truncheon issued to members of the Watch during the Victorian era. It is painted with the identification 'River Wear Police No. 1.' *Sunderland Museum (Tyne and Wear Museums).*

8. Bodlewell Lane Ferry Landing in 1870. Near the top of the stairs stood Low Street Police Station which was occupied by both River and Borough Forces between 1854 and 1873. The building was a converted house which had previously found use as a brothel. *Northeast Press Ltd., Sunderland Echo.*

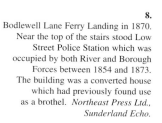

9. Bodlewell Lane Police Station, which opened on 10th February, 1873 and was shared by Sunderland Borough Police and the River Wear Watch until vacated by the latter on 13th May, 1925. *Author's collection.*

10.
A police constable in attendance at the tollbooth of Bodlewell Lane Ferry Landing towards the end of the 19th Century. *W. Bell collection.*

11. Edward Temperley Gourley who became a member of the Watch Commission in 1858. He was a prominent Sunderland shipowner who later became a Member of Parliament for Sunderland and received a knighthood. He was one of the seven original proprietors of the Sunderland Daily Echo which was first published in 1873. *Author's collection.*

12.
The original steam fireboat, *Fire Queen*, built by Merryweather and Sons of London in 1874 and which remained in service until 1886. *Author's collection.*

13. Members of the River Wear Watch pictured between 1875 and 1878. Inspector James Lakin is standing on the far left and Superintendent Joseph Stainsby is on the extreme right. *Author's collection.*

14. James Lakin *(1837 - 1913)*, who held the rank of Inspector in the River Wear Watch from 1875 until his tragic death in 1913. *Author's collection.*

15. A constable employed by the River Wear Commissioners making his rounds at North Dock, circa 1880. (From a painting by J. Carmichael). *Sunderland Museum (Tyne and Wear Museums).*

16. The busy scene off Sunderland Harbour on 10th February, 1888, during the raising of **S.S. *Pinnas***, when the ***Fire Queen*** played such an important role. *W. Bell collection.*

17. River and Borough policemen engaged during the aftermath of the Wear Patent Fuel Works fire at Hendon Dock on 28th July, 1891. *Sunderland Museum (Tyne and Wear Museums).*

18. Another view of the devastation caused by the great fire at Wear Patent Fuel Works in 1891. *Sunderland Museum (Tyne and Wear Museums).*

Sacred to the Memory

OF

Sergeant, JOHN HASKER, Aged 47, &

P. C. JONATHAN DRYDEN Aged 40.

WHO DIED ON DUTY, AT SUNDERLAND,

NOVEMBER 4TH. 1895.

Take warning by our sudden call,   For in our lives we little thought,
   That you for death prepare,   Our end had been so near,
For it will come you know not when,   All you that have a longer time,
   The manner, how, or where.   For Death Oh then prepare.

19. Memorial card produced following the deaths of Sergeant John Hasker and P.C. Jonathan Dryden, who lost their lives on 4th November, 1895 whilst engaged at the scene of a fire at Joshua Wilson and Sons' warehouse in the East End of Sunderland. *Sunderland Museum (Tyne and Wear Museums).*

20.
The great destruction brought about as the result of the Havelock House fire which broke out on 18th July, 1898 is clearly evident as firefighters dampen down the ruins. *Northeast Press Ltd., Sunderland Echo.*

21. The *Fire King*, built in 1906 by Henry Scarr of Hessle-on-Humber, pictured off Manor Quay between 1906 and 1913. Inspector Lakin is standing on the starboard side, second from the stern. *Sunderland Museum (Tyne and Wear Museums).*

22. The second *Fire Queen*, launched in 1885 by S. P. Austin and Sons, together with the *Fire King*, engaged in combating an esparto grass fire on board **S.S. *Ella Sayer*** at East Quay, Hendon Dock on 7th March, 1907. *Sunderland Museum (Tyne and Wear Museums).*

Chapter 4

THE EARLY YEARS

(1840 - 1859)

Following the controversy that had surrounded the creation of the River Wear Watch, it was with great satisfaction and some relief that the shipowners were now able to embark upon their venture.

APPOINTMENT OF SUPERINTENDENT BROWN

The appointment of Superintendent, catered for within the framework of the River Wear Watch Act, was placed in the hands of William Brown, then thirty-seven years of age, who had held the superintendency of Sunderland Borough Police since its formation in 1837. Having already served for eight years with the Metropolitan Police, Mr. Brown was to perform his duties during the formative years of the Watch with the same zeal and initiative that he had already demonstrated with the Borough Force.

RALPH ANNISON APPOINTED INSPECTOR

Ralph Annison, a former Borough Police sergeant and Captain of the Shipowners' Society's Private Watch, was appointed Inspector of the new River Force. As such, he was to be responsible for its day-to-day running. His drive and determination would prove largely responsible for its initial success.

CAPTAINS OF THE WATCH

Four captains, named Dixon, Metcalfe, Tinmouth and Jefferson, all being men of great character and resolve, were also appointed to supervise the men. The title 'Captain' was to be abolished in 1861 and substituted with the rank of 'Sergeant,' presumably to fall into line with other police forces of the day. Perhaps resentment from seafaring skippers, who did not appreciate their title being usurped in such manner, also played some part in forcing this change.

Following Annison's retirement in 1854, Captain Lancelot Jefferson was promoted to Inspector in his place.

BOATMEN

Until 1859, the establishment of constables - or boatmen, as they were originally called - varied with the time of year. During the winter months, vast numbers of sailing ships invariably laid up in port. To combat the increased risk of theft, fire and vessels being cast adrift in inclement conditions, additional men were therefore employed between the months of September and April (inclusive).

By 1849, besides the Superintendent and Inspector, the force consisted of four captains (at a weekly wage of £1) and seventeen boatmen (at a weekly wage of 18 shillings). From May to August, the number of boatmen was reduced to ten.

Often, prevailing circumstances persuaded the Commissioners to extend a period of employment or to employ numbers in excess of the norm. For instance, in 1845, they resolved to appoint an additional eight constables during the winter period and to place an additional boat on the river near Pallion. How they were able to do this is questionable as Pallion was outside the Watch's jurisdiction. These constables were then retained into the summer months in consequence of the large number of vessels fitting out with stores for America.

THE EVILS OF DRINK

As with many other police forces of the era, the evils of drink were often a great temptation for members of the Watch. With alehouses in proliferation along the riverside and liquor being freely available on board many ships, it is not surprising that cases of drunkenness amongst the force were commonplace.

Discipline was strict and sought to discourage the men from drinking on duty. It was expressly forbidden for a constable to enter a public house, unless in the immediate execution of his duty. Publicans were liable to be fined heavily for supplying intoxicants to policemen on duty or for allowing them to remain on their premises without good cause.

On commencing duty, constables were inspected by their captains to ensure sobriety, likewise upon concluding their tour. It was not uncommon, therefore, for fines and dismissals for drunkenness to be imposed with some regularity. Sometimes the Superintendent found it necessary to issue a written order to the whole force, warning of the dire consequences for personnel found to have been drinking on duty. In later years, it became known for repeat offenders to be offered one final chance by being given the opportunity to sign the pledge as an alternative to dismissal.

VESSELS ADRIFT

Despite initial problems associated with drinking, the force was generally highly successful in performing its duties. Many members were old sea dogs and as such were used to the discipline and harsh conditions accompanying their calling. Above all, they remained undaunted in the face of danger as was demonstrated upon countless occasions when, with a gale howling in their faces, they would board a ship adrift in mid-river and succeed in remooring her.

The prevalence of vessels slipping or breaking their moorings was of great concern to the River Wear Watch Commissioners, with no fewer than 332 such incidents being dealt with by River Police officers during the first ten years of the force's existence.

These occurrences frequently led to Watch Commissioners calling for greater attention to be paid to the mooring of ships. For instance, the report of the River Wear Watch Committee, published on 27th December, 1847, adverted to *"the very insufficient manner in which many vessels are moored, especially those which enter harbour in the evening or during the night, when it seems to be the most invariable custom of the pilot and crew to moor their vessel as quickly as possible without any regard being had to the same being properly effected, their only object being to get on shore as soon as they possibly can."*

THE GREAT ICE RUSH

A far more serious cause of ships being damaged and breaking adrift was the freshes and floods that periodically devastated the river and which tested the resourcefulness of the Watch to the limit.

The most notable of these events which began on the night of Sunday, 17th January, 1841 and continued well into the following morning, is regarded as the most destructive flood on record at Sunderland Harbour. This is what happened:

Following a long period of severe frost, a thaw came on and a great quantity of ice accumulated between Wearmouth Bridge and the ferry landing. Heavy rain began to fall on the Sunday evening, with some ships being driven from their moorings at Deptford and Pallion, but soon being made fast again.

About midnight, larger pieces of ice floated downriver which, meeting with obstructions, were driven over and under each other to form huge unwieldy masses, cemented together for a depth of several feet. The current was impeded so much that, around Pallion, the river level stood six feet higher than at Mark Quay in the East End. About 4 a.m., the inevitable occurred with the 'ice dam' yielding to the increasing pressure, resulting in a torrent of water and ice rushing downriver with irresistible force, carrying all before it.

Entire tiers of ships were torn away from their moorings at Lambton and Hetton Staiths and swept beneath Wearmouth Bridge, breaking their masts in the process and being dashed against vessels moored below. Further tiers were overwhelmed and thrown into a mass of wrecks extending the width of the river opposite to the Durham and Sunderland Railway Staiths.

The awesome sounds of rushing water, crashing of ice, shouting of men, shrieks of terrified apprentices and the breaking of masts, bulwarks and bowsprits echoed in the morning air.

Daybreak was to reveal the full extent of the catastrophe, the sight of which was likened to an enemy fleet following its defeat at the hands of Nelson or Napier. All around lay sunken and wrecked sailing vessels of every description. Amongst those suffering this fate were the *Pilgrim* of Lynn; the *Caroline Korff* of Altona; and the *Deux Amis*, a French vessel; together with the *Rosebud, Kirton, Seaflower* and *Queen Victoria*, all of Sunderland. Some had been driven to sea, including the *Era* of Rochester; the *Beatitude Lamb* of London; a French barque; and the *Jean, Gamma* and *Young*, all of Sunderland. Most were later picked up off the Durham coastline, many without crews, but others were never seen again. In addition, a vast quantity of valuable timber had been washed out to sea. Numerous coal staiths had been demolished or rendered unserviceable and quay walls had collapsed as mooring posts had been wrenched from their foundations. The River Wear Commissioners' valuable steamer, *Utility* was almost a wreck and the port's steamtug fleet had been decimated, amongst these being the *Safety, Hare, Earl of Durham, George and Ann* and *Neptune.* About thirty keels had been wrecked and the majority of the harbour boats and other small craft in the river annihilated. Fortunately, twenty-five vessels, about half of which were steamers, had sought timely refuge in Wearmouth Dock, thus preventing greater loss.

Many acts of courage were witnessed that fateful morning, not the least of which were attributable to the men of the River Wear Watch. Yet, with so much havoc having been caused, fatalities had been almost inevitable. Miraculously, only two lives were lost. One was that of a boy belonging to the *Richard*, who, in attempting to escape to another vessel, had drowned after falling into the river. The other life was lost on board the *Newby*, which had grounded near the North Pier. In doing so, her boom had swung over to leeward and carried away a young fitter named Davison. The remaining seven crewmen on board had taken refuge in the chains before being rescued by the manager and two watchmen of the Wearmouth Dock Company.

The following afternoon, with the assistance of the River Police and some of the steamers which had been sheltering in the dock, a passage was made through the blocked channel resulting in the ice, together with large quantities of timber and flotsam, drifting out to sea.

It took many months for most of the damage to be repaired and the river finally cleared of wreck. Total losses were estimated at over £91,000, an astronomical sum at that time. Although serious floods had occurred before and would do so again in the future, the disaster of 1841 would never be equalled.

PATROLLING THE RIVER

It is evident that during the early years of the Watch, life for a river policeman was often difficult and dangerous. Foot patrols were carried out on the quays and shores, whilst on the river, open rowing boats, offered no respite from the weather. Usually two boats, known as *Wear Police Galley No. 1* and *Wear Police Galley No. 2*, kept watch upon the tideway, these later being referred to as cobles. Officers were stationed at premises in Low Street, later moving to a nearby building which was shared with the Borough Police.

As well as their pay, the men were provided with free uniform. On appointment, each received a greatcoat, jacket, waistcoat, cape, hat, two pairs of trousers and two pairs of boots, this issue being repeated the following year with the exception of the greatcoat and cape. A white metal cap badge, depicting a foul anchor was adopted as the force's insignia.

THE SCOURGE OF FIRE

The frequency with which fires broke out on the river was a cause of grave disquiet to the shipowners and had been a prime reason for the establishment of the Watch. The Commissioners, having recognised the deficiencies of local parish brigades, sought to remedy the situation by equipping their force with the best means available to combat such outbreaks.

As some sixteen months would elapse before delivery of the Watch's first firefloat, improvisation and vigilance would prove to be the best tools in extinguishing fires. During their initial six months of existence, Watch patrols discovered and boarded three vessels ablaze on the river and subdued the flames using nothing more than buckets of water, thereby preventing serious damage from being occasioned.

Carelessness was the main cause of such fires. Often, apprentices would retire to their hammocks, leaving lights burning below, or coal trimmers, having finished their work for the day, would fail to extinguish candles in the holds of collier brigs.

FIRST FIREFLOAT ENTERS SERVICE

During December, 1841, the long awaited firefloat entered service. Known initially as the ***Wear Engine***, she had been constructed for the River Wear Watch Commission at a total cost of £779 18s.1d, being based upon a design then in use on the River Thames at London. The vessel was a large flat-bottomed keel fitted with a deckhouse and a huge manual pump, supplied by Tilley and Company. Having no propulsion of her own, the services of any available steamtug or other suitable craft had to be requisitioned to tow her to scenes of fires. Amongst the steamboats providing this service during the 1840's and 50's were the ***Atlas***, ***Jack Tar, Olive*** and the quaintly named ***Peep O'Day Boy***. Operated by up to seventy men, most of whom were volunteers paid at the hourly rate of one shilling, the pumps were worked by two long handles, stretching from bow to stern. These men would face each other and work the handles up and down with a steady rhythmic thud, by which means a great jet of water could be discharged.

It was not long before the new engine was called into action. On the morning of 18th December, 1841, the schooner, ***Susan*** of Guernsey, coal laden with Captain Askett in command, was proceeding south from the Tyne when it was discovered that a fire had broken out in her hold. Despite her crew's efforts in cutting open the deck and pouring in water, the fire kept increasing, although not actually breaking out into a flame. Eventually, two steamers took her in tow to Sunderland Harbour, where she grounded on the ebbing tide at the entrance to Wearmouth Dock.

The ***Wear Engine*** was brought alongside and played jets of water both above and below deck. In a very short time the fire was completely extinguished. Although the ***Susan's*** deck and beams, together with a quantity of cargo, had been badly damaged, the ship was saved and subsequently repaired.

The local press spoke highly of the new engine, stating *"It was highly satisfactory to witness the capabilities of the new fire engine brought into play, which was the first time it had been used, except in practice. Its operations were directed by Mr. Brown, the active and intelligent Superintendent of Police and Inspector Annison, to whom, and the officers under their direction, great credit was due for their promptitude and exertion."*

FIRES ASHORE

The benefits that could be derived by use of the floating engine in connection with fires on land were soon being appreciated and exploited to the full, as the following account illustrates:

About 7 p.m. on 10th April, 1842, smoke was seen issuing from the bakery and grocery premises of Mr. John Wolstenholme, situated at the junction of High Street and Silver Street in the East End of Sunderland. Initially, two fire engines from the town and one from the Barracks attended, together with large parties of police and soldiers. However, as the water company did not keep their pipes filled on a Sunday or during the night, no water was available with which to feed the engines. An effort was made to obtain water from the river but, as the tide was low and the access from the riverside was up a very steep bank or via flights of steps, it was found impossible to keep even one engine fed from that supply.

It was ultimately decided to have recourse to the floating engine which was kept in a central part of the harbour. As no steamer was in readiness for towing at that state of the tide, the engine had to be hauled manually, causing some delay, during which time the fire rapidly gained in strength. It was evident that the fire had taken hold of the whole of the first storey and was only being contained by the doors and shutters being kept closed to prevent the admission of air, but which also prevented the salvage of property inside.

After a short time, the fire burst through the downstairs shutters and windows with great ferocity and took hold upstairs. Adjacent premises were also placed in imminent danger. Residents above Mr. Wolstenholme's warehouse were lucky to escape with their lives after being trapped when the ground floor became enveloped in flames. One of them, a woman, jumped from a first floor window; another, an old man, was lowered down by a rope, whilst the remainder were rescued by ladder.

When the fire was at its height, it was feared that the entire building might collapse as the timber beams above the large shop windows and doors were being quickly consumed and the cast iron pillars supporting the beams were bending.

At this point, the water pipe from the floating engine arrived, having been laid from Low Street up the old Custom House Stairs into the High Street. It commenced operations with incredible effect, the Barracks' engine being simultaneously put to work using water supplied in buckets. In a short time the danger to surrounding property had greatly diminished as the strength of the flames decreased, but it was over an hour before the fire was brought fully under control. The use of the engines was discontinued about 9.30 p.m. but it was found necessary to resume their operation at intervals for a further hour until the fire was totally extinguished.

All the household furniture, together with the stock contained in the ground floor shop and warehouse were completely destroyed. Structural damage was so severe that the building later had to be demolished. Taking account of damage to nearby properties, losses were estimated at between £1,400 and £1,500. The fire was believed to have originated from the upstairs parlour fire that had been left burning whilst the occupants were at chapel.

It was of great note that the floating fire engine which had been specially obtained for the protection of shipping and for extinguishing fires in the immediate vicinity of the river could be made available for use in fighting fires some considerable distance away. In this instance, water pipes had been extended from the engine for a distance of 264 feet, at an elevation of 100 feet above river level. Even under those difficulties, water had been discharged with a force that no ordinary fire could withstand for any length of time.

For the services rendered by the **Wear Engine**, the Watch Commissioners claimed the sum of £10 from the insurers of the properties involved in the fire, thus creating a precedent. In years to come, the Commissioners' policy of requiring payment for the use of firefloats in connection with outbreaks of fire on shore would often provoke bitter controversy.

WEAR ENGINE 'B'.

About April, 1849, a second newly built firefloat, similar to the existing engine, entered the service of the River Wear Watch. Built at a cost of £800, she was acquired in anticipation of the need for an additional engine for the South Dock, which was due to open the following year. On being commissioned, the new engine was named **Wear Engine 'B'** and her older counterpart re-designated as **Wear Engine 'A'**.

GREAT FIRE AT NEWCASTLE AND GATESHEAD

On the morning of 6th October, 1854, a terrible fire and explosion occurred in manufactory and warehouse premises situated in Hillgate on the south bank of the River Tyne at Gateshead. As a result, flaming projectiles had been hurled across the river, causing a great conflagration in the Quayside area of Newcastle. Fires on both sides of the river raged unchecked, with great devastation and many casualties being occasioned. In desperation, the authorities communicated with neighbouring towns by means of electric telegraph, requesting urgent assistance.

Their call for help was at once heeded by the River Wear Watch Commissioners who despatched a body of constables to Newcastle on board **Wear Engine 'A'**. On her arrival, the floating engine, in conjunction with a similar vessel from Tyne Dock, South Shields, performed valuable service in helping to extinguish the raging inferno, before returning to the Wear on 11th October.

In a letter subsequently sent to the Watch Commission, the gratitude of the people of Newcastle was shown in the following terms:

"The Mayor of Newcastle desires to return his acknowledgements to the Commissioners of the River Wear Watch Act for the promptness with which their fire engine was despatched on the occurrence of the late fire.

The Mayor is sure that he only expresses the general sentiments of the Town when he adds that the powerful assistance thus afforded and the exemplary conduct of the men in charge, contributed most materially to the subduing of the fire."

INITIAL EFFECTS OF THE WATCH

The importance of the River Police's firefighting function can be gleaned from statistics published between 1840 and 1855, during which period they had been instrumental in extinguishing a total of 163 fires. Of these outbreaks, sixty-three were on board ships, sixty-nine on boats and thirty-one in shipbuilding yards or other premises.

Moreover, commencement of regular patrols was accompanied by a noticeable decrease in crime on the river, much of which concerned the theft of ships' stores and seamen's personal effects. Offenders, when caught, were usually dealt with summarily before the magistrates and upon conviction, could expect to spend a term in the House of Correction. Sometimes, in minor cases, the charge would be dismissed on condition that the perpetrator agreed to leave town forthwith. An interesting power, often exercised by the police, was the arrest of persons "failing to give a good account of themselves."

Occasionally, the mere presence of the Watch would have an immediate sobering effect upon guilty parties. For instance, in March, 1842, a report was received that a quantity of clothing, books and other items had been stolen from on board the brig, **Anthony and Ann**. Suspicion immediately fell upon the crew of the brig, **New Forest** of Lymington which was lying alongside. Whilst Inspector Annison and his men were conducting a search of the latter vessel, a seaman named William Lawrence fell from the fore topmast cross trees and was gravely injured. With Lawrence having drawn attention to himself in such a manner, a search was made of his hammock, in which was found concealed all the stolen property.

On investigating the case, the magistrates decided that the seaman's fall was attributable to his guilty conscience and fear upon seeing the police on board, and withdrew the charge owing to the severity of his injuries.

The Watch also proved highly effective in curtailing the practice of throwing ships' ballast into the river, an offence that had been extremely prevalent for many years, causing great hindrance to navigation in the port.

With the passage of Merchant Shipping Acts during the Nineteenth Century, the apprehension of errant seamen and apprentices for insubordination or desertion also became a frequently undertaken function.

PRESERVATION OF LIFE

Preservation of life from drowning was a duty performed by the Watch for which its members were accredited with little recognition despite having rescued no fewer than two hundred persons from the waters of the port during the force's first twenty years of existence.

The first life saved was that of a man who had fallen over the quay onto the foreshore and who, lying incapacitated, would have been drowned by the rising tide but for the vigilance of the River Police.

Early River Wear Watch Committee quarterly reports concerning the activities of the force relate numerous examples of such rescues.

An extract from the report of 4th May, 1842 states:

*"On 8th February, a boy who had fallen overboard from the ship **Ellen**, was saved by the police. On 3rd March, a man, who had leapt from the North Quay into the river with the intention of drowning himself, was prevented from carrying his intention into effect. On the night of 4th March, about 12 o'clock, two young boys were picked up between the piers, whilst drifting to sea in a boat without oars and who, but for their having been picked up by the police, would most probably have been lost. A lad also was saved on 21st March from drowning, having fallen out of a boat into the river."*

The following report, dated 9th November, 1842, provides details of further rescues:

"On 15th September, seven young men, who had upset the boat in which they were, were saved by the exertions of the police, but for whose presence, the probability is, that some of the parties would have been drowned. On the night of 23rd September, a man named John Thompson, who had leapt off the Bridge, was picked up in an insensible state by the police, by whom he was conveyed to the shore, and medical assistance procured, but in vain, as he only lingered a few hours. On the night of 25th September, a man named John Wilson, who had fallen overboard, was saved from drowning by the police."

Gratitude was sometimes the furthest thing from the minds of certain individuals pulled from the water by the River Police. At 3 a.m. on 16th January, 1847, for instance, Inspector Annison and his crew were on patrol in their coble when their attention was drawn to three men named Thomas Smith, Henry Lilly and Thomas Murray who were in a boat attempting to remove a chain from some moorings. Whilst doing so, their boat sank and the three had to be rescued by the police officers. Instead of offering their thanks, the men, who were somewhat the worse for drink, began jumping up and down in the police coble bottom. On being put ashore at North Sands, they then proceeded to assault the Inspector before making off. Warrants were issued for the arrest of all three, who were later brought before the magistrates and heavily fined.

HAZARDS OF WATERFRONT DUTY

The inherent dangers accompanying waterfront duties are well illustrated by the following three accounts of police officers who lost their lives during a five year period between 1849 and 1854:

DEATH OF P.C. NEWBY WILSON AT WYLAM WHARF

Early one morning in July, 1849, P.C. 10 Newby Wilson was making his rounds on Wylam Wharf off the Low Street in the East End of Sunderland when he became ill and fell over the quayside into the river. Although rescued, he died shortly afterwards.

DROWNING OF P.C. ROBERT HEIRD AT NORTH DOCK

The next fatality took place during the early hours of 19th October, 1852 and involved P.C. Robert Heird, again of the Watch, whose collar number was also '10' - a somewhat unlucky number at that time!

Shortly after 1 a.m., one of the Wearmouth Dock Company's watchmen had heard cries of distress emanating from the direction of the dock basin. Although the dockmaster had been called out, nothing untoward was found until around 7 a.m., when a policeman's hat was observed floating on the surface of the water. Grapnels were obtained and eventually the lifeless body of P.C. Heird was recovered. The watch on the unfortunate man's body had stopped at 1.10 a.m. - about the time when the shouts had been heard by the watchman. Inspection of the edge of the quay revealed an imprint of the sole of Heird's boot on a broken kerbstone.

At the subsequent inquest, a verdict of 'accidental death through the dilapidated state of the kerbstone' was returned, to which the Sunderland News and North of England Advertiser added its own sombre note:

"A public servant stumbles in the dead of night and meets a watery grave, unnoticed and unaided, through a cause that the slightest inspection might have prevented."

The entry by Inspector Annison in the River Wear Watch occurrence's book concerning the matter is rather brief, to say the least:

"Alarme was given that P.C. No. 10 Robert Heird had tumbled of the North Dock quay into the dock and was drowned. He was got out of the water and was taken to his mother's house in the Low Street, Sunderland."

DEATH OF BOROUGH P.C. GREY - WAS IT MURDER?

The third police officer to die unnaturally whilst on waterfront duty during this period was P.C. Edward Grey of the Sunderland Borough Police Force, who met his death in the most suspicious of circumstances in the East End of the town.

After working night shift, the officer had failed to parade off duty on the morning of Friday, 10th March, 1854. Despite an extensive search being undertaken by both the Borough and River Forces, it was not until the following night that the constable's body was discovered in the river near Noble's Quay by Captain Dixon of the River Wear Watch.

Although closely examined, the corpse revealed no marks of violence and it was supposed that, on a dark and stormy morning, Grey had stumbled and fallen into an unprotected part of the river. It was noted that his pocket watch had stopped at 5.17 a.m.

Nevertheless, enquiries were conducted in the Low Street area of the town where P.C. Grey had worked his beat. A local whore, Mary Ann Colvin, known as 'the flirt', soon provided information that threw the whole issue into a new light.

She told detectives that around 5 a.m. on the Friday morning, whilst speaking to a man whom she claimed not to know, at the foot of Spencer Lane, P.C. Grey had passed by and told them that they had better move on.

The man, about 5 feet 9 inches tall, dressed in a dark velvet cutaway coat, fustian trousers and a 'wide-awake' hat, and who appeared to be a quarryman, had not taken kindly to being spoken to by the officer. "There are too many bastards like you wearing blue coats," he had angrily declared, before storming off towards the ferryboat landing. After bidding Colvin "good morning," Grey had then continued his rounds, strolling off along the Low Street in the opposite direction to that of the man.

"But," said Colvin, "shortly afterwards, the man turned and began retracing his steps in the direction of those taken by P.C. Grey, as if to follow him." She had then lost sight of both men and returned home.

Despite an extensive investigation, the 'quarryman' was never traced. The verdict of the inquest jury was a noncommittal "found drowned," they being unable to decide how the officer had entered the river, due to lack of evidence.

Although now only a matter for conjecture, grave suspicions must remain that the man in the 'wide-awake' hat was in some way responsible for the death of P.C. Grey.

EXISTENCE OF WATCH COMMISSION UNDER THREAT

Throughout their early years, the River Wear Watch Commissioners did much to consolidate the position of the force, but always kept a wary eye for others who sought to remove them from their hard won office.

The first real threat to their authority came in 1847, following a long-standing dispute between Sunderland Corporation and Bishopwearmouth Improvement Commissioners as to which of the two bodies should exercise local authority functions in relation to public health and other services within the Parish of Bishopwearmouth. Two government surveying officers, J. J. Rawlinson and W. Hosking, duly investigated the rival claims and were agreed that the only way in which to deal with the problems of Sunderland as a whole, was to set up a single local authority endowed with the management of all local affairs and to wind up the miscellany of existing self-elected commissions. They opted for the Corporation as being the best suited to carry out these functions and saw no reason to exclude the Watch Commissioners from their recommendations.

Later that year, the Health of Towns Bill was introduced into Parliament by Lord Morpeth. If passed, the Bill would have transferred the powers of the Watch Commissioners to the Town Council of the Borough. The Watch Commissioners reacted with alarm, convening a special meeting on 17th June, when it was unanimously resolved to oppose the Bill by all possible means. The chairman of the meeting, E. B. Ord, together with the Clerk, Mr. Kidson, were instructed to proceed to London and to place before Lord Morpeth and the M.P's for the Borough, George Hudson and Andrew Barclay, the Commissioners' grave disapproval of the Bill's proposals. Whilst their endeavours ultimately contrived to secure the Watch's exclusion from the provisions of the Bill, it turned out to have been a pointless exercise as the Bill itself was withdrawn at the end of that parliamentary session.

Nevertheless, the problems of local government remained unresolved and the future of the Commissioners continued to be uncertain. In 1848, the Public Health Act was passed, in consequence of which, by the direction of the General Board of Health, Robert Rawlinson, one of the superintending inspectors appointed under the Act, visited Sunderland during December, 1849. His brief was to carry out a preliminary inquiry into the sanitary state of the town and to report to the Board of Health, in order that this body might judge the propriety of applying the Public Health Act to Sunderland. His wide ranging terms of reference included investigation of the sewerage, drainage, supply of water, burial grounds, paving, lighting and watching of the Borough.

The inquiry was held at Sunderland Police Court before numerous representatives of the Corporation, the various commissions in the town and other interested parties. A myriad of reports was read concerning all aspects of municipal services, included in which was a detailed report presented by Mr. Kidson, outlining the organisation and activities of the River Wear Watch.

Representatives of the Town Council, notably a Mr. Ranson, seized this opportunity to attempt to discredit the Watch Commissioners in the eyes of Mr. Rawlinson, hoping that he would be influenced, on making his final report, to recommend their absorption by the Corporation.

Despite the antagonism of the Watch Commissioners, Mr. Kidson received a letter from Rawlinson early in 1851, stating his proposed intention to report in favour of vesting their powers and funds in the Town Council.

A subcommittee was appointed to resist the report's proposals which, together with the 1847 report, was to form the basis of the Borough of Sunderland Act, 1851. By means of this Act, Sunderland Corporation finally became autonomous in almost all fields of local government.

Fortunately for the Commissioners, with little time to spare, they were once again able to bring pressure to bear within the right quarters and achieve the exclusion of the Watch from the provisions of the Act.

PROBLEMS WITH COLLECTION OF WATCH RATE

By levying the maximum permitted River Wear Watch Rate of one penny per net registered ton upon shipping, the Commissioners had been able to fund the purchase of their firefloats and place themselves in a sound financial position. By 1852, however, their viability had allowed dues to be reduced to one ha'penny per ton.

On the other hand, certain difficulties which had beset the collection of the rate were brought to a head during 1851. Dues were payable in respect of the first voyage, either inwards or outwards, made by a vessel each year, to the Receiving Offices of the Collector employed by the Commissioners. A visit by the River Police to any vessel which had failed to pay the Collector usually had the desired effect. It transpired that certain unauthorised persons had been taking advantage of the ignorance of some ships' captains, particularly foreigners, by purporting to be bona-fide collectors and charging dues for *every* voyage made. Large amounts of cash had been misappropriated in this manner and on discovering the extent of the fraud, the Commissioners took every step possible to bring the offenders to justice. That a new Collector, Mr. W. J. Smith (whose offices were at 54 Sans Street) was appointed in 1851, was perhaps more than coincidental.

Another problem associated with the collection of the rate around this time was the increasing number of masters who sought to evade payment altogether. Resultant prosecutions were accompanied by a salutary effect upon others, with few difficulties afterwards being experienced.

INCIDENTAL REMUNERATION

Incidental remuneration was derived by the Commissioners from a variety of sources. Valuable baulks of timber, belonging to shipbuilding yards lining the riverbanks, would often be found adrift and only returned upon payment of a percentage of their value.

Charges made for the use of firefloats in extinguishing land fires were also a useful source of income, as were salvage claims that were occasionally proceeded with when drifting vessels were remoored by the River Police. Such claims, however, were frowned upon by shipowners who were of the opinion that claims of this nature should not be pursued, as members of the Watch were merely carrying out their appointed duty in protecting shipping. In 1855, for instance, the River Wear Commissioners took a dim view of the first such claim made against them which, in this case, had arisen as a result of one of their floating cranes breaking its moorings. Although agreeable to the payment of reasonable compensation for services rendered, the R.W.C. refused outright to accede to the salvage demand which, in due course, the Watch Commissioners thought better of taking to court.

Another interesting means by which the Watch Commission sought to increase its bank balance - and its sphere of influence - was proposed at its quarterly meeting of 20th January, 1845, when the following resolution was passed:

"That in all cases where vessels shall be wrecked or stranded in the vicinity of the Port, the Superintendent of the River Wear Police do take and retain possession of such vessel and materials for the benefit of the parties concerned, provided the owners and crew are wishful to avail themselves of such aid and assistance, and to remunerate the persons employed therein."

It is not clear how often this service was provided, although it is known that conflict with local coastguardsmen did arise in subsequent years, when the protection of wrecks had become part of the latter's duties.

POLICING THE SOUTH DOCK

As mentioned earlier, South Dock - originally known as Sunderland Dock - was opened in 1850, having been constructed by the Sunderland Dock Company. It was essential to the development of trade in the port and was to form the basis for the eventual larger dock system on the south of the Wear. Ultimately, the dock would become known as Hudson Dock after the company chairman, the legendary 'Railway King', George Hudson who was also M.P. for the Borough.

The large number of vessels using the dock brought about new demands upon the resources of the River Wear Watch, not only for firefighting, but for general police work too. Although no formal arrangements existed with the Dock Company for policing its property, members of the Watch did carry out dock patrols directed primarily towards the protection of shipping, deriving their powers from their special act of parliament which empowered them to act as constables throughout the Borough of Sunderland.

In 1855, however, when the Sunderland Dock Act was passed for the purpose of authorising the Dock Company to carry out further works, to consolidate previous Acts and for other purposes, the status of the Watch was reinforced by Section 118, which officially extended its jurisdiction to the dock, as if this was part of the River Wear.

By the Wear Navigation and Sunderland Dock Act of 1859, ownership of the South Dock was transferred into the hands of the River Wear Commissioners, with the powers of the Watch to act therein being renewed. An interesting feature of this particular Act, which incorporated the Harbours, Docks and Piers Clauses Act of 1847, was that it also empowered the River Wear Commissioners to appoint their own special constables. Such constables were to be employed within the limits of the Commissioners' harbour, docks, piers and other premises and were to have jurisdiction within one mile thereof. Although during subsequent years the R.W.C. did employ constables from time to time, they did not operate a formally organised police force. In contrast, the forces of many other harbour and dock authorities throughout the country were, and still are, constituted under the provisions of the 1847 Act.

END OF EMPLOYMENT OF CONSTABLES ON SEASONAL BASIS

As mentioned earlier in this chapter, a number of constables were employed by the Watch on a seasonal basis until 1859. On 20th May of that year, the Watch Commissioners voted to terminate this arrangement and to establish the force on a permanent footing. In effect, the change meant that instead of employing twelve constables in summer and eighteen during the winter months, sixteen men would be retained all the year round at little additional expense. The Inspector and five captains continued to be engaged throughout the year.

The Commissioners also took this opportunity to establish a superannuation fund for members of the force. Such a fund, first mooted in 1851, had previously been considered impractical owing to the continual changes amongst the constables.

PAY OF THE RIVER POLICE

The pay of the River Police at this time compared most favourably with that of the Borough Force. The Watch Inspector received £100 4s. 10d per annum (including an allowance for accommodation), as opposed to a maximum of £78 received by Borough inspectors. Captains earned 25 shillings per week, three shillings more than Borough sergeants, whilst River constables were paid 21 shillings per week compared with town P.C's who received between 19 and 20 shillings.

Unfortunately, as the years passed, although endeavouring to do so, the River Wear Watch Commissioners were unable to maintain parity with Borough Police rates of pay for any prolonged period. Ultimately, this would result in numerous pay claims being submitted by their men.

RELATIONSHIP WITH THE BOROUGH POLICE

During the second half of the 1850's, following the appointment of Robert Gifford as Superintendent of the Watch and Borough Police in 1855, an interesting development arose with regard to the relationship of the two forces. Whilst constables employed by the Watch had jurisdiction throughout the town and were under the management and direction of the Superintendent of the Borough Police in his capacity as Superintendent of the Watch, they were not part of the Borough Force, nor would they ever be so. Although the Watch's regular duties were confined to the river, docks and nearby shores, its members were frequently called upon to assist the Borough Police in other parts of the town, apparently without comment by the Commissioners. The shared tenancy of Low Street Police Station often resulted in the River Police dealing with matters which were clearly the province of the town police. Assistance would be afforded in extinguishing fires which had broken out far away from the river and on occasions, the streets would even be patrolled by the Watch whilst their Borough counterparts were engaged in drill practice!

It would appear that Gifford, together with his successors, to varying degrees, considered the Watch to be at their disposal for use in the Borough as they saw fit. In doing so, however, they were almost certainly acting within their powers under the River Wear Watch Act. It seems strange that no opposition was voiced by the Commissioners, especially as the Borough Force was being supplemented at the expense of the shipowners, without a single penny being contributed by the Corporation.

Following the creation of Her Majesty's Inspectorate of Constabulary in 1856, the purpose of which was to visit and enquire into the state of efficiency of every county and borough force, the annual inspection of Sunderland Borough Police would also include a review of the River Police which could not be official in nature because of its non Home Office status.

By 1860, the River Wear Watch had become a well-respected organisation, established on a secure footing and performing a valuable service, not only to the shipowners, but to the port and town as a whole.

Chapter 5

THE ERA OF INSPECTOR NATHANIEL ALLAN

(1860 - 1875)

NATHANIEL ALLAN APPOINTED INSPECTOR

On 1st March, 1860, Nathaniel Allan was appointed as Inspector of the River Wear Watch, in place of Lancelot Jefferson who had been forced into premature retirement owing to serious illness. Having previously served with the Berwickshire, Edinburgh and Sunderland Police Forces, Allan was a man of great experience and came highly recommended for the post. However, as shall be seen later, his impulsive manner would lead to him having to justify his actions to the Watch Commissioners on more than one occasion and eventually to his downfall.

Allan had been a member of the Fire Extinguishing Department of Sunderland Borough Police since its establishment in 1855 by the Corporation Watch Committee, to undertake the role of firefighting previously carried out in a disorganised fashion by members of the force in conjunction with local parish engines.

The importance of the Watch in 1860 and the immense responsibility borne by Allan and his men, can be placed in perspective by reference to shipping returns for that year, when 11,971 vessels, having an aggregate of almost two million registered tons, were cleared from the Port of Sunderland. In addition, 112 ships were launched into its waters. On 22nd November, 1860, for example, 686 sailing vessels were berthed in the port, of which 365 were moored in the river, 313 in South Dock and 8 in North Dock. Moreover, these figures do not take into account steamships and other miscellaneous craft in port at that time.

REORGANISATION OF WATCH DUTIES BY SUPERINTENDENT STAINSBY

At the time of Allan's appointment, the Superintendent of the Watch was Joseph Stainsby who had held that position since 1858 when Robert Gifford had resigned. Stainsby, formerly of the North Riding Constabulary, was highly innovative, a strict disciplinarian and would devote much of his time to Watch affairs.

In 1864, he brought about a complete reorganisation of River Police duties, simultaneously issuing fresh orders for the conduct of the men.

Their newly defined duties were as follows:

DUTIES of INSPECTOR (with effect from 31st August, 1864):

To work an average of ten hours in each twenty-four.
To perform outside supervision three times per week between 10 p.m. and 6 a.m.
To occasionally attend relief at 6 a.m.
The remainder of duty to be performed for the good of the service.
Not to attend court unless required to do so.
Always to wear uniform whilst on duty.

DUTIES of SERGEANTS (with effect from 30th November, 1864):

DAY DUTY.

First Relief:

One sergeant on duty 6 a.m. - 9 a.m., 1 p.m. - 4 p.m., then 7 p.m. - 10 p.m.
To parade reliefs at 6 a.m. and 7 a.m.
All men on duty to be visited during the above periods.

Second Relief:

One sergeant on duty 9 a.m. - 2 p.m., then 2 p.m. - 6 p.m.
To parade reliefs at 9 a.m., 2 p.m. and 6 p.m.
All men on duty to be visited during the above periods.

NIGHT DUTY.

South Side:

One sergeant on duty 10 p.m. - 6 a.m.
All men on duty at South Dock and on the south side of the river as far up as Wearmouth Bridge to be visited during the above period.

North Side:

One sergeant on duty 10 p.m. - 6 a.m.
All men on duty from North Dock to Southwick on the north side of the river to be visited during the above period.

Detective:

One sergeant to be on duty in plain clothes.

DUTIES of CONSTABLES (with effect from 30th November, 1864):

Collectors:

Two on duty 9 a.m. - 12 noon, then 1 p.m. - 5 p.m., collecting Watch Rates.

South Entrance and Dock Fire Engine:

One on duty at South Entrance & Dock Fire Engine, two hours before until two hours after each high tide.

River Engine - Day Duty:

One on duty at River Fire Engine 6 a.m. - 6 p.m.

River Engine - Night Duty:

One on duty at River Fire Engine 6 p.m. - 6 a.m.

DAY DUTY:

River - First Relief:

Two on duty on river 6 a.m. - 9 a.m., then 2 p.m. - 6 p.m.
One of the above then on duty at North Dock and North Quay 7 p.m. - 10 p.m.
One of the above then on duty in plain clothes on Low Quay, Low Street and The Panns 7 p.m. - 10 p.m.

River - Second Relief:

Two on duty on river 9 a.m. - 2 p.m., then 6 p.m. - 10 p.m.

Docks - First Relief:

One on duty at South Docks 6 a.m. - 9 a.m., 2 p.m. - 6 p.m., then 7 p.m. - 10 p.m.

Docks - Second Relief:

One on duty at South Docks 9 a.m. - 2 p.m., then 6 p.m. - 10 p.m.

The man on first relief to go to the west side of the dock, and the man on second relief to go to the east side 7 p.m. - 10 p.m.

NIGHT DUTY.

Commencing on the River:

Two on duty on the river 10 p.m. - 12 midnight.
One of the above then on duty at North Dock 12 midnight - 4 a.m., then on duty on the river 4 a.m. - 6 a.m.
One of the above then on duty at North and Wreath Quays 12 midnight - 4 a.m., then on duty on the river 4 a.m. - 6 a.m.

Commencing at North Dock:

One on duty at North Dock 10 p.m. - 12 midnight, then on duty on river 12 midnight - 2 a.m., then on duty on east side of South Dock 2 a.m. - 6 a.m.

Commencing at North Quay:

One on duty at North and Wreath Quays 10 p.m. - 12 midnight, then on duty on river 12 midnight - 2 a.m., then on duty on west side of South Dock 2 a.m. - 6 a.m.

Commencing at South Dock - East Side:

One on duty at South Dock - east side 10 p.m. - 2 a.m., then on duty on river 2 a.m. - 4 a.m., then on duty at North Dock 4 a.m. - 6 a.m.

Commencing at South Dock - West Side:

One on duty at South Dock - west side 10 p.m. - 2 a.m., then on duty on river 2 a.m. - 4 a.m., then on duty at North and Wreath Quays 4 a.m. - 6 a.m.

Parade of Relief:

Every officer and constable will parade at the River Police Station ten minutes before the time appointed and report himself when going off duty.

The revised duties certainly provided a great deal of variety in the long working day and were, undoubtedly, intended to relieve boredom and to encourage the men to achieve a good working knowledge of all areas within the port. Nevertheless, one wonders, if at times, they knew whether they were coming or going.

RULES AND REGULATIONS

Some of the force orders introduced by Superintendent Stainsby also make curious reading:

"The constables must pay particular attention to orange peel put on the footpath, and take it off, and any person depositing it, their names and addresses must be obtained and reported forthwith."

"Members of the Force on sick leave are not allowed out after 6 p.m."

"The whole of the officers and constables are cautioned against pushing any person who may be in the act of committing any offence. They may caution anyone so offending and if the offence is persevered in they must take the person into custody using no more violence than is absolutely necessary for that purpose."

"When a prisoner is apprehended for a Felony, either with or without warrant, he must be distinctly told what he is charged with, but the constable is not on any account to endeavour to get or elicit any statement or confession from a prisoner. Nevertheless, he is not to caution a prisoner against incriminating himself by making any voluntary statement, but he is attentively to notice and make a memorandum where opportunity affords it of every expression a prisoner may make so that the ends of justice may not be frustrated, and the constable will have to be prepared to report any statement when required. taking care to use the exact words used by a prisoner."

"The Chief Constable, having had complaints made to him about some of the officers and men using profane language, he now cautions them against this disgraceful practice and trusts that there will be no need for further complaints."

"All prisoners are to be treated with as much gentleness as safety permits, and every appearance of familiarity with prisoners is to be avoided."

"Constables when giving their evidence should stand upright in a respectful attitude and give ready and distinct answers to the attorneys on both sides, bearing in mind that it is their duty to afford every information in their power whether for or against an accused party and before being called to give evidence in court, should refresh their memories from notes of the circumstances taken by them at the time of the apprehension. No constable is on any account to whisper, speak or interfere in any way with a witness whilst he is giving evidence."

"Smoking is forbidden inside any police building."

THE PAY OF THE RIVER POLICE

During the 1860's and 70's, the River Police frequently sought to increase their pay in line with that received by the Borough Police. The river men contended that, as their duties were more dangerous than those of their Borough counterparts, there should be an assimilation of the pay of both forces. Indeed for much of this period, members of the River Wear Watch received slightly higher wages than their Borough colleagues.

Whenever, the Borough Police received a pay award, it became usual for Watch personnel to make a counter claim to restore the differential. In spite of the Watch Commissioners' limited financial resources, they usually received such applications sympathetically as they fully appreciated the importance of the duties carried out by their men and held them in the highest regard.

In 1865, the following pay scale applied to Watch constables:

1st year	-	**20s. per week**
2nd & 3rd years	-	**21s. per week**
4th - 7th years	-	**22s. per week**
After 7 years	-	**23s. per week**

By comparison, Borough constables received the following:

On appointment	-	**18s. per week**
After 6 months	-	**19s. per week**
After 1 year	-	**20s. per week**
After 3 years	-	**21s. per week**
After 7 years	-	**22s. per week**

Dock gatemen, employed by the River Wear Commissioners at this time, received **18 shillings per week.**

By the end of 1871, River Wear Watch pay stood at:

Superintendent	-	**£100 per annum**
Inspector	-	**40s. per week**
Sub-Inspector	-	**29s. per week**
Detective Sergeant	-	**29s. per week**
Sergeant	-	**26s. per week**

Constables:
4th Class (on appointment)	-	21s.6d per week
3rd Class (after 6 months)	-	22s.6d per week
2nd Class (after 18 months)	-	23s.6d per week
1st Class (after 2 years)	-	24s.6d per week

Plus 9d per week boot allowance.

Further pay awards were granted in 1873 and 1874, when it was decided that only three classes for constables would exist in future. The members of the Watch had proposed that a merit class be introduced, as in the Borough Police, which enabled their constables to earn an additional 1s.6d over and above regular pay. The Commissioners felt that they could not agree to such a proposal as their force was small and all of the officers - many of whom were old servants - were generally good men.

STATISTICS OF WORK UNDERTAKEN, 1864/65

An indication of the volume of work undertaken by the River Wear Watch during this period is shown by the following return for the year ending 30th August, 1865 (the end of the Watch Commissioners' financial year):

Persons charged	-	*164*
Comprising of:		
Felony	-	*64*
Mercantile Marine Act	-	*52*
River and Dock Acts	-	*8*
Other offences	-	*40*
Lives saved	-	*11*
Fires extinguished	-	*8*
Ships found adrift and remoored	-	*11*
Value of property found adrift and restored to owners	-	*£787*

COLLECTION OF WATCH RATE BY R.W.C. AND THE POLICING OF SOUTH DOCK

In 1865, the office of Receiver (a term which had become synonymous with that of Collector) of Watch Dues became vacant on the resignation of Mr. W. J. Smith, this vacancy coinciding with a proposal by the Traffic Committee of the River Wear Commissioners that they should collect the dues on behalf of the Watch Commissioners. A recommendation, in 1861, for the collection of dues to be placed in the hands of H.M. Customs had not been proceeded with.

For some time, the R.W.C. had been concerned about the imperfect system of policing the South Dock and suggested that the two constables then engaged in connection with the collection of the Watch Rate would be better employed in watching the dock. In return, the R.W.C. would agree to collect the Watch Rate free of charge. Although the Watch

Commissioners felt that they could not legally appoint constables specifically to watch R.W.C. warehouses and other private property, they were unanimous that there was an absolute necessity to increase the establishment of their force to effectively watch the river and docks, primarily to safeguard shipping.

Accordingly, the Watch Commissioners agreed to accept the proposal and to provide extra policemen to patrol the dock, as far as this could legally be achieved. Apart from the two constables freed from collecting dues, the force was strengthened by the appointment of two additional constables and a sub-inspector. In addition, a new coble, suitable for use by one man, was purchased for the purpose of patrolling the dock by night. The R.W.C. also provided a station and lockup on the quay for the River Police. For many years the Dock Police Station was situated on the east side of Hudson Dock between Nos. 6 and 7 Drops.

SERIOUS INCIDENTS AND OCCURRENCES

The serious nature of incidents to which the River Wear Watch was frequently required to attend to, and the dangers faced by personnel whilst carrying out their duties, are illustrated by a number of notable occurrences which took place during the term of Inspector Allan's employment:

ATTEMPT TO BLOW UP STATIONARY ENGINE AT SOUTH DOCK

One night in April, 1861, whilst making his rounds at South Dock, the attention of Sergeant Tinmouth was directed towards unusual noises emanating from a stationary steam engine situated near one of the warehouses. Cautiously, he approached the engine and to his horror, realised that someone had attempted to sabotage its boiler by drawing the fire damper and fastening down the safety valve lever. At considerable personal risk and without thought for his own safety, the sergeant let off steam from the boiler, thus averting a serious explosion.

The River Wear Commissioners, who owned the engine, were so impressed by the conduct of the elderly sergeant that they rewarded him with the sum of two guineas - almost two weeks' wages. Despite the offer of a substantial reward, neither the reason for the attempt to wreck the engine, nor the identities of the perpetrators, were ever discovered.

MURDER OFF THE DURHAM COAST - A QUESTION OF JURISDICTION

On Wednesday, 2nd September, 1863, the River Wear Watch was concerned with a most unusual case of alleged murder which had been perpetrated off the Durham coastline.

During the previous night, the four crew members of a Hartlepool fishing smack, Matthew Williamson, Andrew Bogey, Robert Robson and Benjamin Robson, had shot their herring nets approximately seven miles east-southeast of Seaham Harbour, when suddenly, out of the blackness, they observed a ship bearing down on them from the south, about half a mile distant.

The ship was the French schooner, *Jeune Adeline*, crewed by four men and two boys, together with her master, Captain Jean Guiot, who was at the helm. Although it was a clear night and other fishing boats were in the area, Guiot had not seen the vessel ahead of him. Frantically, the fishermen stirred up their fire and sounded the fog horn in an effort to warn the schooner of their presence, but to no avail.

Without altering course, the French ship struck the smack on the stem, carrying away her bowsprit and cutting the swing rope by which she was riding. At first, the rope did not part and fearful that their boat would sink, three of the fishermen, Williamson, Bogey and Robert Robson jumped for their lives into the fore rigging of the *Jeune Adeline.*

By this time, the French crew, who previously had been nowhere to be seen, appeared on the port side of the ship and rained blows onto the heads of the men who were trying to climb on board. Williamson and Bogey were knocked back into their boat but climbed back again into the schooner's main chains. Robert Robson managed to retain his hold in the fore rigging, whilst the fourth man, Benjamin Robson, remained on board the smack in the hope of being picked up by one of the other boats fishing nearby.

One of the French crew who had been attempting to dislodge Robson from the rigging then caught sight of Williamson who, having his knee on the gunwales, was about to climb on deck. The Frenchman rushed towards Williamson and struck a fearful blow to his head with a wooden log, causing him to release his hold and tumble into the sea between the two vessels. The unfortunate fisherman immediately sank beneath the waves and was drowned.

Robert Robson succeeded in boarding the ship and made straight for the master, pleading with him to put the helm up and allow the ship to sail by the wind. Captain Guiot, stamping angrily on the deck, replied with a torrent of violent language in his native tongue and attempted to strike Robson.

Whether Robert Robson returned to his fishing boat or remained on board the schooner is not clear, but it is evident that information of the incident was communicated to the River Police at Sunderland. On arrival of the *Jeune Adeline* in the port, members of the River Wear Watch were waiting and took into custody her captain and entire crew on a charge of wilfully murdering Matthew Williamson.

The Frenchmen were subsequently brought before the magistrates at Sunderland Police Court and evidence surrounding the incident heard. The prosecution attempted to prove that all concerned were acting in unison by repelling the fishermen from their ship and as such, all were guilty of the offence. But, as the defence claimed, the defendants were probably unaware of the collision and were justified in preventing strangers from climbing on board. In reply, the prosecution contended that upon looking over the side, they would clearly have seen what had taken place. Evidence from the three surviving fishermen pointed to one of two of the *Jeune Adeline's* crewmen - either Lefevre F. Joseph or Eugene Jean - as having struck the fatal blow. Unfortunately none of the witnesses could identify which was the assailant.

The case against the captain, however, was weak. It was clear that he had remained aft at the helm whilst the fishermen had been endeavouring to climb on board and had taken no active part in preventing them from doing so. Nevertheless, if it could be determined that his crew were acting under his instructions, a charge of manslaughter might be substantiated against him.

Before anyone could be committed to stand trial, there remained a basic underlying issue to resolve; Did an English court have jurisdiction to try this particular case? The issue was that the unlawful act had been committed against a British subject, on board a vessel of French nationality, outside British territorial waters. The magistrates, themselves, felt that they had no jurisdiction in the matter, but wished to be sure as they were also of the opinion that a *prima facie* case existed against two of the crew, if not the captain too.

Accordingly, Guiot, Joseph and Jean were each remanded in custody, pending information being received from Crown law officers as to the jurisdiction question. The remainder of the crew, against whom insufficient evidence existed, were released.

Eventually, the Home Office confirmed the magistrates to be correct in their view that they had no authority to act in the case and the remaining prisoners were discharged into the custody of the French Consul, Monsieur Niboyet.

The French authorities, having given an undertaking to investigate the case, later tried the three defendants under French law. Nevertheless, to the consternation of the friends and relatives of the deceased, all were finally acquitted.

FIRE HOSE TURNED UPON CROWD DURING VISIT OF FRENCH FRIGATE, 'LA DANAE'

The courtesy visit to Sunderland by the French frigate, **La Danae**, late in 1864, was proclaimed as a great manifestation of the Anglo-French Alliance. Her arrival in the South Dock on 29th September was accompanied by considerable public interest, with little expense being spared in providing civic hospitality for her 380 officers and crew. During her stay, the frigate was regularly open to members of the public who flocked to the dock in their hundreds to view life on board the French man o'war.

An incident which occurred on one such occasion somewhat marred the visit, although fortunately there were no lasting repercussions.

On the afternoon of Sunday, 2nd October, 1864, many inhabitants of Sunderland and others from farther afield thronged the quayside, eager to go on board. Such were the numbers present that it was decided to remove the access gangway as the ship was crammed to capacity with visitors. Once this had been done, the mood of the crowd changed and they began surging towards the ship and the quay edge.

Supervising the crowds that day was Inspector Allan who became extremely concerned for their safety due to the danger of people being pushed over the edge of the quay or being crushed to death. With the air filled with the screams of women and children, the vastly outnumbered members of the Watch strove to control the crowd and pull children to safety.

Realising that the situation had become critical and that something drastic had to be done, Allan ordered the manual firefloat stationed nearby to be brought into action. Holding the nozzle of the hose himself, he instructed his men to commence pumping. On doing so, the Inspector directed a strong jet of dock water onto the mass of people, driving them away from the frigate and causing them to disperse. Thus the danger was alleviated.

Whilst those in the crowd whose position was the most perilous, although drenched, were most relieved to find safe refuge, others who did not appreciate the full extent of the actual danger began booing and jeering the police. Some pelted officers with missiles, whilst others threatened to seize Allan and thrown him into the dock.

Eventually, upon the arrival of Superintendent Stainsby, order was restored without loss of life or serious injury being occasioned.

Inevitably, complaints were made to the Watch Commissioners regarding Allan's conduct. As a result, meetings of the River Wear Watch Committee were held on 6th and 20th October, 1864, at which witnesses for and against Allan gave evidence.

Fortunately for the Inspector, the overwhelming weight of the evidence was in his favour. After some discussion - and with one dissension - the Commissioners, with what appears to have been a note of censure, passed the following resolution:

"That the Committee regret exceedingly that Inspector Allan deemed it necessary to use the fire engine in dispersing the crowd, but the Committee are of the opinion from the overwhelming evidence which has been given before them, that if he had not done so, a great loss of life would, in all probability, have taken place."

Whilst Inspector Allan's actions had been vindicated, he was to hold the unique distinction of being responsible for the only instance at Sunderland - and probably the country - whereby a firefloat was used to disperse a crowd.

THE HAZARDS OF CHOLERA

Occasionally, the River Police were exposed to the hazards of infectious diseases imported by foreign going ships. In such cases the River Wear Watch was often requested to remove an infected person from a vessel to a place of quarantine.

In one such case, during July, 1866, Inspector Allan and one of his men received orders to convey the captain of the barque, ***Amanda***, ashore from the anchorage in Sunderland Roads. The captain, who was seriously ill with cholera, was taken to the Cholera Hospital in the South Dock where he subsequently died.

Allegations concerning the medical care of the deceased led to an inquiry being conducted by the Port Sanitary Committee at which the Inspector was required to give evidence. Although Allan's conduct was found, on this occasion, to have been beyond reproach, the Watch Commissioners, unhappy about being mixed up in the affair, sought guidance as to their future responsibilities in such instances.

P.C. BENJAMIN WILTON DROWNED IN SOUTH DOCK

About 9.45 p.m. on Tuesday, 17th March, 1863, twenty-eight years old P.C. Benjamin Wilton, a member of the Watch for only twelve months, was patrolling the South Dock when, in the darkness, he tripped on a length of discarded chain and stumbled over the quay edge into the murky waters of the Tidal Basin. Struggling to keep afloat, his frantic cries for help went unheard before, weighted down by his waterlogged uniform, he sank and was drowned.

As soon as he was missed, a search was organised and the dock basin dragged. Shortly afterwards, worst fears were confirmed as a grappling iron hauled the lifeless body of the unfortunate constable to the surface. Ironically, it was Wilton's brother who made the grim discovery, although it is not recorded whether he was also a Watch member or merely assisting in the search.

The South Docks had claimed one more victim, leaving behind another widow and two fatherless children.

DEATH OF CONSTABLE WILLIAM HIRD

Yet another fatality involving a River Wear Watch officer occurred on the night of 29th November, 1866, when P.C. William Hird met his death at the South Dock extension whilst on duty near to Londonderry Drops. After missing his footing in the gloom, the officer had broken his neck after falling over the edge of the jetty into the dock below.

At the subsequent inquest, held before Coroner C. Maynard at the Bath Hotel, Moor Street, the River Wear Commissioners were severely criticised for alleged inadequacies in the provision of lighting and protection at the docks. One of the witnesses, Inspector Allan, stated that there was not a lamp within fifty yards of where P.C. Hird had been killed.

Although the jury initially recommended a verdict of 'accidental death,' this was not recorded owing to the dissension of one of its members who was of the opinion that death could not be accidental if it had been due to inadequate lighting and protection. In reply, Coroner Maynard advised the jury that, if they chose, they could bring in a verdict of 'manslaughter' against the River Wear Commissioners, whose responsibility the dock was.

After retiring once more to consider the implications, the jury decide to drop the word 'accidental' and returned a verdict *"That the deceased came to his death by falling over the quay in consequence of insufficient lighting and protection."*

In the light of this verdict, the Coroner stated his intention to write to the River Wear Commissioners and Board of Trade recommending urgent improvements to safety standards at the docks.

After seeking legal advice, P.C. Hird's widow claimed compensation from the River Wear Commissioners for the loss of her husband. The claim, however, was rejected by the R.W.C. Traffic Committee which considered that no liability could be attached to the R.W.C.

Determined not to let matters rest there, she then instigated civil proceedings which, to the dismay of many, were successfully defended by the R.W.C.

DANGER AT THE DOCKS

Despite the River Police's vigilance, drowning fatalities in the docks continued to be a frequent occurrence. Although improvements were periodically undertaken in the provision of lighting and safeguards, the docks always remained a dangerous place for anyone who ventured there, especially at night.

Besides performing rescues and dealing with drowning incidents, Watch personnel would often be called upon to attend the scenes of many horrific accidents which occurred on the quays, vessels and railways within the South Dock estate, frequently resulting from the lack of safety awareness and precautions.

An interesting advance, by means of which accident victims could be quickly transported to hospital from the docks and East End of the town, was the inauguration of a railway ambulance service by the North Eastern Railway Company in 1872. Between that year and 1888, 611 cases were conveyed to the Royal Infirmary, with an average journey time of only seven minutes.

CONFLICT WITH THE COASTGUARD

In 1856, control of the Coastguard Service had been transferred from the Board of Customs to the Admiralty, its primary functions then becoming the defence of the coasts and the provision of a reserve for the Royal Navy in time of war or emergency. Whilst still retaining some responsibility for the protection of the Revenue, this was a minor role in comparison with previous years. Other duties subsequently taken on included assistance to vessels in danger, taking charge of wrecks, the operation of life saving equipment and an active participation in the lifeboats being set up around the coast.

It would seem, however, that Coastguard in the Sunderland area took some of these latter responsibilities very seriously indeed and that by 1870, they had made themselves most unpopular by the manner in which they sometimes conducted themselves.

On the night of 17th February, 1870, the schooner, *Vision* of Lossiemouth, in attempting to enter the Wear with a cargo of pit props, struck the bar with considerable force. Despite the local lifeboat having been launched, coastguardsmen unsuccessfully attempted to fire a rocket line to the stricken vessel. Eventually the crew of the *Vision* were rescued by the lifeboat and landed on the beach together with their belongings, whereupon they were assisted by members of the River Police under Sub-Inspector Lakin and the Volunteer Life Brigade under Captain Wilson, who was also the deputy dockmaster.

Shortly afterwards another coastguardsman, arriving on the scene, unceremoniously pushed aside the police and brigade volunteers, telling them in no uncertain terms that they had no business to be there. Such was the man's conduct, that one of the police officers present threatened to place him under arrest for abusive behaviour. Nevertheless, Sub-Inspector Lakin, acting a most courteous and gentlemanly manner throughout and not wishing to come into personal conflict, allowed the coastguardsmen to take charge.

Fully aware that the conduct of one of its members had been nothing short of disgraceful, the Coastguard later tendered its most sincere apologies to River Police and Life Brigade, but not before the matter had been fully reported in the local press.

It was in the docks, however, that the conduct of the Coastguard was subject to the greatest complaint. Nightly, its members would hide beneath upturned boats or skulk in dark recesses on the dockside, before leaping out upon unsuspecting seafarers going about their lawful business.

In one incident, the officers of a steamer, having already been subjected to an examination by Customs officers in the presence of several coastguardsmen, were pounced upon by the very same Coastguard members and forced to submit to a humiliating search of their persons and belongings in the open air. The Customs officers, who were still nearby, protested vigorously on behalf of the seamen. As a result of this altercation, Lieutenant Hinvest of the Coastguard made a formal complaint of incivility and discourteous conduct to him as a gentleman against one of the Customs patrol. Despite a number of independent witnesses speaking in favour of the Customs officer and strongly against the Coastguard, the former was fined heavily and reduced in rank.

The River Police, learning of threats to throw coastguardsmen into the dock if they did not desist from their officious and insolent manner, were forced to show great vigilance and restraint to protect them.

ALLEGED MANSLAUGHTER AT SOUTH DOCK

A further incidence of unlawful killing was dealt with by the Watch in 1871, this time at the South Docks.

About 11.45 p.m. on Friday, 21st April, River P.C. Thomas Low was going about his duties on Hudson Dock when he was approached by a rather agitated Customs officer, named John Nicholson. "Come quickly, there's a man in the dock," he blurted out, whereupon the two men ran to the east side of the dock basin, abreast of the pumping house near Gladstone Bridge. On arriving there, P.C. Low found that James Cole, a dock watchman, had secured a long boat hook to the clothing of a man's body by which means he was suspending above the water. After jumping into a nearby coble, the officer rowed to the body and fastened a line around it. With some difficulty and with the assistance of others present, it was then hauled onto the quayside. Although P.C. Low saw no signs of life, several of those present felt there was a chance of saving the man and he was carried into an engine house and laid on the felt covered boilers, where every attempt was made to resuscitate him. Unfortunately, all efforts were in vain.

The deceased was a short, powerfully built man, aged around 37 years, with light brown hair and a 'chin-ender' beard. He was wearing yellow corduroy trousers, a jacket and a Crimean shirt. That he was not wearing a hat was later to assume some significance. On searching his clothing, the police took possession of a tobacco box, a pocket knife, 6s.31d in cash, and a book entitled "A sure way to find out the true religion." There was, however, nothing by which to identify him.

Enquiries by the River Police soon revealed that they were investigating a suspicious death. Both the watchman, Cole and the Customs officer, Nicholson, together with others who had been about the dock, reported that the deceased had been involved in a furious row on the quayside with another man who had been seen walking away from the place where the body was recovered.

Immediately, a search of the dock precincts was commenced to trace this person and within the hour, River Police Sergeant Richardson came across a man, named John McGowan, sleeping in the open air at the south end of the R.W.C. yard, about one hundred yards away from where the body had been recovered. On being awakened by the sergeant, McGowan, who was obviously under the influence of drink, became very abusive and was taken into custody. On the way to Low Street Police Station, he violently resisted the officer and it was only with great difficulty that he was taken there.

At the police station, McGowan made several statements incriminating himself. Inspector Allan, having noticed blood on the prisoner's hands, enquired where this had come from. "It's off that ---------- sod's snout," McGowan replied. A cap was also found in his pocket. On being asked about this, McGowan answered "It belongs to my mate."

The police felt that there was sufficient evidence to prefer a charge against McGowan and accordingly charged him with causing the death of the man found in the dock, to which the prisoner replied "I hope the bastard's dead," thus further incriminating himself.

McGowan was brought before the magistrates the following morning and claimed that he could not remember any of the previous night's events. He stated that he was a native of Carlisle and had only come to Sunderland the day before from Newcastle. The court was told that he was a blacksmith by trade and that he was also known by the name, Foster. At the end of a short hearing, the defendant was remanded in custody pending the outcome of the inquest which was to be held before Coroner Maynard on Monday, 24th April at the Market Hotel, Coronation Street.

The inquest was told that, despite many people having viewed the corpse, none had been able to identify it. Samuel Allum, landlord of the American Hotel had, however, recognised the deceased as having been on his premises during the evening of his death. Moreover, he had been in the company of the prisoner. Allum had turned both of them out on several occasions owing to their drunken behaviour and for quarrelling with soldiers in the bar.

After hearing evidence of the events which had taken place at the docks, the coroner adjourned the inquest for further witnesses to be called.

The inquest was resumed the following Monday, with evidence being heard from a surgeon, Dr. Evans who had performed the post-mortem examination upon the deceased. The doctor stated that, whilst the cause of death was undoubtedly drowning, he had found a large effusion of blood on the surface of the brain that could have only been caused by violence and which, in itself, was probably sufficient to cause death. In addition, several abrasions, which had apparently been caused before death, were present on the head. There was, however, no injury to the nose, which seemed to contradict McGowan's account of how blood came to be present on his hands. Dr. Evans was of the opinion that the head injuries had been caused by the head coming violently into contact with the ground on several occasions.

From the evidence of further witnesses and others previously heard at the opening of the inquest, it was clear that McGowan had been involved in a heated drunken argument with another man near to the place where the body had been found. Although none of these witnesses had actually seen blows being struck or the deceased entering the water, a pumping engine fireman named Robert Donville had heard what appeared to have been scuffling. Furthermore, Customs Officer Ralph Brown had heard one say "You're not going to put me in the dock, are you?"

In summing up, the Coroner said it seemed that there was some doubt whether any blows passed, or if the dead man had been knocked into the dock by a blow. Before the jury could return a manslaughter verdict, they must believe that McGowan had performed some act which caused the deceased to enter the water. If they thought it possible that the men separated after squabbling and never came to blows then they would return an open verdict. Likewise, if they considered that the evidence did not clearly show that the deceased got into the dock through the act of the prisoner, they would again return an open verdict.

After a lengthy deliberation, the jury returned a verdict of 'manslaughter' and McGowan was committed to stand trial at Durham Summer Assizes.

He was detained in custody until Monday, 10th July, 1871, when he appeared before Lord Chief Baron Kelly at the Assizes to face the charge against him. Proceedings were brief, with the judge pointing out that the deceased had died as the result of drowning and that there was no evidence to show how he had entered the water. The jury, therefore, had no option but to return a verdict of 'not guilty.' Little credence had been paid to McGowan's incriminating replies made shortly after his arrest, due to his inebriated state.

So it was that McGowan left the court a free man. As for the man with the 'chin-ender' beard, lying in an unmarked pauper's grave, his identity would never be known.

NEW POLICE STATION AT BODLEWELL LANE

In September, 1854 Sunderland Corporation had leased a house in Low Street near the ferry landing and converted it into a police station and lock up for use by both the Borough and River Forces. Even then the premises had been of ill repute, having previously been used as a common brothel house by local whores. For many years, the Low Street Police Station, as it was known, had been totally inadequate for the purpose for which it was intended. The building which contained two miserable cells, measuring six and thirteen feet square, had even been adversely commented upon by the Government Inspector of Police in his report of 1870.

Local newspapers frequently called attention to the state of the place which, in February, 1871, was condemned by the Sunderland Times as being *"a miserable hole and having a pestiferous atmosphere, being utterly unfit to contain a human being, even in the worst state of debauchery."*

The question of a replacement station had been before Sunderland Corporation for some time and in February, 1872, the foundation stone for the new building was laid at the western corner of Low Street and Bodlewell Lane by Mr. Robinson, chairman of the Corporation Sub Watch Committee.

The land upon which the building was to be constructed was the property of the Corporation Bridges and Ferries Committee. It had been felt by many that it would have been better utilised for commercial purposes and that an alternative site situated on the riverside to the east of Fenwick and Company's brewery, at the foot of Beehive Lane, would have been far more suitable for the purposes of the River Police. Indeed, this was true, as a clear view would have been afforded both up and downriver and it would have been possible to moor craft close by.

Completion of the station, which was opened without ceremony on 10th February, 1873, took one year. Occupancy was again shared between the Borough and River Forces, with the River Wear Watch Commissioners initially paying £60 per annum to the Corporation as rent for their use of the building which had been erected at a cost of around £2,200.

The premises were constructed of red brick with stone facings and consisted of four upper storeys, together with a basement, built on a site measuring 51 feet by 32 feet.

On the ground floor were situated the charge office and inspector's office, the entrance to the former being at the end of Bodlewell Lane. Behind these rooms was the heating room, to the rear of which were located two cells. At the back of these cells was a building housing the fire apparatus.

Extending over the charge room and inspector's office, on the first floor, was the River Wear Watch Commissioners' board room, measuring 24 feet by 15 feet. Behind this room, a tier of four cells was situated above the fire apparatus house. Compared with the cells in the previous building, those in the new station were spacious and had the capacity to accommodate up to fifty prisoners.

The second floor contained the River Wear Watch Inspector's apartments, comprising kitchen, parlour and three bedrooms.

On the top storey were situated a mess room and four bedrooms for eight constables, whom it was intended to barrack there.

Finally, the basement contained a large wash house, coal cellars and storerooms.

The dubious honour of being the first person to be locked up in the cells was bestowed upon a man named John Ragan, who was run in by P.C. Finlayson of the Borough Police at 4 p.m. on the day of opening, on a charge of being drunk and riotous.

ACQUISITION OF STEAM FIREFLOAT, 'FIRE QUEEN'

Up to the end of the 1860's, the two floating manual fire engines had performed sterling service on behalf of the River Wear Watch Commissioners. By 1869, however, they had become somewhat outdated with steam driven firefloats having become established elsewhere. It was generally felt that the Commissioners should keep up with technological developments and purchase such a craft to augment **Wear Engines 'A'** and **'B'**, the former of which was beginning to show signs of ageing.

In 1862, the Commissioners had almost been forced, prematurely, to replace **Wear Engine 'B'** which had been run into and sunk by the **Lorenzo** of New York in Hudson Dock on 19th October after the latter had broken adrift from Londonderry Drops during a severe gale. Although the float had been raised and repaired, it had been necessary to institute proceedings in the Admiralty Court to recover the cost of the damage.

The two manual engines operated by the Watch suffered from a number of disadvantages. Their requirement to be towed to the scenes of fires was expensive and vessels suitable to perform towage were not always readily available, resulting in potentially serious delays in arriving there, especially when the tide was low. In addition, they required a large number of volunteers to man their pumps, each volunteer being paid by the hour for his services. A steam firefloat would overcome all of these drawbacks and have the added benefit of being able to perform salvage duties, a task to which the manual engines were not suited.

Accordingly, at the quarterly meeting of the Commissioners held on 18th February, 1869, Superintendent Stainsby produced plans for a new firefloat to be worked by steam power and fitted with a screw propeller. The engines were to be supplied by the celebrated fire engine manufacturers, Shand Mason of London, whilst the iron hull - 30 feet in length - would be constructed in Sunderland by Wellington Ironworks.

Mr. Stainsby reported that there was a great necessity for a third firefloat as not all parts of Hendon Dock, opened the previous year, could be reached by the manual engine stationed in Hudson Dock (This could only be transferred between docks when the lock gates were open around high tide). He recommended that the manual engine stationed in the river be replaced by the new steam firefloat and relocated to Hudson Dock, and the manual in Hudson Dock be transferred to Hendon Dock.

Although a committee was appointed to oversee the acquisition of the new engine, the estimated cost of between £1,400 and £1,500 was regarded as prohibitive for the Commissioners who had only £826 in the bank at that time and the plans were shelved.

During the next few years, the question of purchasing a steam firefloat was raised at regular intervals. Although much discussion took place on the subject, nothing was done until the quarterly meeting held on 27th February, 1873.

The issue was introduced by Alderman Nicholson who pointed out the importance of procuring such an engine. It was explained by Mr. Hodgson that the Commission had been awaiting a favourable time to enter the market in the hope that prices would become cheaper. The Commissioners anticipated that they would have approximately £1,300 in hand by 31st August - the end of their financial year. The chairman, Alderman Reed, felt that the time had now arrived to seriously turn their attention to the proposal. Although the maximum rate of one penny per ton had been in force for some time to build up funds, the Commissioners would still be required to borrow money with which to make good the deficit in the estimated cost of around £2,000. After further discussion, it was resolved to call upon the Committee to consider the question again.

The Committee's report proved to be favourable and in 1874, the River Wear Watch Commission took delivery of their new firefloat. The vessel was named, *Fire Queen* and had been constructed by Merryweather and Sons of London at a cost of £2,189 0s.6d.

Built from iron, the float had a length of 40 feet, a 9 feet 6 inch beam and a depth of 4 feet 9 inches Her shallow draught of about 2 feet forward and 2 feet 6 inches aft, would prove most useful in tackling fires at low water. Propulsion was by means of a pair of independent vertical steam engines, each working a 28 inch screw propeller, giving a maximum speed of around 9 knots. Each engine was fitted with a cylinder of $5^3/_4$ inches diameter by 6 inch stroke.

The fire engine was of Merryweathers' 'Admiralty' pattern, so called on account of it having been adopted by the British, French and Prussian governments for dockyard service. Its steam cylinders each had a diameter of $8^7/_8$ inches with a 24 inch stroke, the pumps having the same stroke and a 6 inch bore.

At full power, the firefloat was capable of discharging 1,110 gallons per minute through an open hose, when used for pumping purposes. When in action as a fire engine, it was able to pump water through a $1^7/_8$ inch jet over a horizontal distance of 300 feet and could discharge up to twelve jets simultaneously.

The boiler was of Merryweather and Field's patent and fitted with what were commonly known as 'Field' tubes, there being 426 such tubes in all. It was arranged to drive both the fire engine and propelling engines at the same time, if required. Steam could be raised from cold water to a pressure of 100 pounds per square inch within ten minutes of lighting the boiler.

Following acceptance trials, the *Fire Queen* entered service and was stationed on the river opposite Potts' shipyard.

The Watch Commissioners could be justifiably proud of their new acquisition. The vessel was a compact and neat craft, her general lines having the appearance of a graceful yacht. Her twin engines gave excellent manoeuvrability amongst shipping in the congested port. Moreover, her pumps were able to deliver more than four times the volume of water per hour than the manual engines were capable of.

The Commissioners were seen to be completely fulfilling their obligation to protect shipping, with the *Fire Queen* soon being in great demand, particularly for fires on shore in proximity to the river, as the Borough Police Fire Department did not yet possess a steam fire engine. It was decided to charge owners of riverside properties the sum of twelve guineas for the first hour in which the *Fire Queen* was engaged, and ten guineas for each subsequent hour. In addition to salvaging sinking vessels, the firefloat was also to be utilised for filling ships to test for leaks.

Amongst the first fires attended by the new steamer were serious outbreaks at G. S. Gulston's shipyard at Southwick on 2nd November, 1874 and on board the barque, *Jane Cargill* at Potts' shipyard ten days later. Reports indicate that this outbreak had been subdued with great rapidity and had it not been for the presence of the *Fire Queen*, the vessel would have been burned down to her water line.

CHARLES KIDSON APPOINTED AS CLERK TO THE RIVER WEAR WATCH COMMISSIONERS

In May, 1874, after long and faithful service, John Kidson tendered his resignation as Clerk to the Commissioners. He was succeeded in the post by his son, Charles Kidson.

UNTIMELY RESIGNATION OF INSPECTOR ALLAN

Inspector Nathaniel Allan's career with the River Wear Watch came to an abrupt end late in 1875, following his involvement in a most controversial incident at South Docks, again with a 'French connection'.

On 11th October, the French barque, *Julie* of Le Havre was lying in the Half-Tide Basin having been lengthened in No. 2 Graving Dock by the workforce of Richard Iliff, a local shipbuilder and repairer who had originally built the 506 gross tons vessel in 1870 in partnership with a Mr. Mounsey.

A dispute had arisen concerning the rights of possession of the ship between Mr. Iliff and the French authorities. As a result, the French vice-consul, stationed in the town, sought to have the vessel removed from Iliff's custody. In order to do so, the vice-consul, accompanied by a solicitor and the French captain who had brought the vessel into port, procured the assistance of the River Police.

Consequently, Inspector Allan, together with these three men, boarded the barque and ordered Iliff's men to go ashore. They refused to do so and sent for Iliff who, upon his arrival, demanded to know under whose authority the Inspector was acting. Curtly, Allan told Iliff not to teach him his duty and pointed to the vice-consul, who produced the old register of the ship from his pocket. Allan, touching Iliff on the arm, instructed him to vacate the ship together with his men. Iliff refused, whereupon Allan said "Such an intimation should be enough for any gentleman." Iliff responded, saying "Nothing shall move me from this vessel except a force superior to my own." "So be it," retorted Allan who then left the ship.

Within the hour, Allan returned with a body of about forty Borough and River policemen. Iliff was lifted bodily over the side of the ship and unceremoniously dumped on the quay. He again managed to get back on board, once more to be subjected to the same treatment.

His employees were powerless to resist the overwhelming force of the police and eventually quit the vessel.

The River Police then took charge of the *Julie* and moved her into Hudson Dock, where two constables remained on board, day and night.

Iliff immediately lodged a strong complaint over his treatment at the hands of the police. On looking into the matter, the River Wear Watch Commissioners were of the opinion that their Inspector had acted outside the scope of his duties and ordered that the barque be returned to the shipbuilder.

Still furious, Iliff persisted with his complaint and on 18th November, 1875, the Commissioners considered the issue at their quarterly meeting. Both Allan and Iliff were subjected to a lengthy examination before the Commission, consisting of Messrs. W. Nicholson (presiding), F. Ritson, G. W. Hudson, R. Humble, C. Hodgson, G. C. Pecket, G. Foreman, I. Whitfield and M. Weiner.

Despite maintaining that he had acted in good faith on the advice of the solicitor who accompanied him on board the *Julie*, Allan was forced to tender his resignation, with only Weiner having spoken in his favour. Allan, doubtlessly feeling betrayed by his Commissioners, was a bitterly disappointed man. He subsequently accepted an appointment with the North Eastern Railway Company, although in what capacity is not known.

Although having lost an ardent servant, the Watch Commissioners had in his replacement a man who was to become one of the most highly respected officers ever to wear the uniform of the Watch, namely James Lakin.

Chapter 6

THE WATCH UNDER INSPECTOR JAMES LAKIN

(1875 - 1899)

APPOINTMENT OF INSPECTOR JAMES LAKIN

Following the enforced resignation of Nathaniel Allan, the natural choice for his successor lay in James Lakin, then Sub-Inspector of the Watch, whose appointment as Inspector was confirmed on 30th December, 1875.

Lakin was a native of Swainby, a village close to the Cleveland Hills in the North Riding of Yorkshire, where his father had farmed land and acted as manager for some neighbouring lime kilns. As a youth, Lakin had been employed as a clerk to a Leeds barrister, before joining the North Riding Constabulary. In 1865, having served for a short period in that force, he moved to Sunderland where, at the age of only twenty-eight, he was appointed deputy to Inspector Allan.

His promotion highlighted the high esteem in which he was held by both the River Wear Watch Commissioners and Superintendent Stainsby. He was to become one of the most revered characters ever connected with the River Wear.

SUPERINTENDENTS OF THE WATCH

In May, 1878, following the resignation of Joseph Stainsby through ill health, John Nicholson, who had joined the Borough Police in 1853, was appointed as Superintendent of the River and Borough Forces.

Stainsby had, in fact, been absent from duty since November, 1877, from which time Inspector Lakin had been vested by his Commissioners with the powers and duties of Superintendent of the River Police. It is questionable, however, whether such an appointment was lawful under the terms of the River Wear Watch Act.

It is of interest to note that Stainsby had styled himself as 'Chief Constable,' as opposed to 'Superintendent,' in his capacity of Chief Officer of both forces. This practice would be continued by his successors.

Nicholson, was succeeded, in November, 1885, by William Huntley, a native of Northumberland. As with his predecessor, Huntley had joined the Borough Police and risen through the ranks. He was to retire in 1897 owing to poor health and be replaced by a Yorkshireman, William Carter.

NEW PHYSICAL REQUIREMENTS

With effect from 28th October, 1880, it was decided that all new constables recruited to the force should be at least 5 feet 8 inches tall, with a minimum chest size of 33 inches and not be over thirty-five years of age.

PAY AND ALLOWANCES

A continuous rise in the cost of living lead to regular applications being submitted by members of the River Police for increases in their pay. Such claims would usually be treated by the Commissioners with as much sympathy as their limited financial resources would allow.

In December, 1881, following a pay review, a 'merit class' was introduced for constables and the following pay scale adopted:

Constables:

4th Class	**23s.**	**12 months without complaint or punishment before promotion to 3rd Class.**
3rd Class	**24s.**	**2 months without complaint or punishment before promotion to 2nd Class.**
2nd Class	**25s.6d**	
1st Class	**27s.6d**	**After 6 years service in 2nd Class.**
Merit Class	**29s.**	**On promotion by the Commissioners from any grade for meritorious conduct.**

Sergeants:

On promotion	**30s.**
After 1 year in rank	**31s.**

Sub-Inspector:

On promotion	**32s.**
After 1 year in rank	**33s.**

Inspector:

On promotion	**36s.**
After 1 year in rank	**38s.**

The 'merit' class for constables was relatively short-lived, having been dispensed with by 1893. In 1890, it was decided that ten per cent of the revenue earned from duties carried out in connection with land fires, salvage and other special assignments would be distributed amongst members of the force on a pro rata basis.

Another allowance was brought into being during 1893, when officers acting as enginemen on the firefloats and launches were granted an additional one shilling per week. This bonus was to remain in existence, without being increased, throughout the subsequent history of the Watch.

NEW CLERK TO THE COMMISSIONERS

In 1881, following the death in harness of the Clerk to the Commissioners, Charles Kidson, the office was 'kept in the family' with his brother, William A. Kidson being appointed as his successor.

PROPOSED TRANSFER OF THE WATCH

In 1885, having already weathered several previous attempts by Sunderland Corporation to take over responsibility for the Watch, the Commissioners again found themselves defending their very existence. The challenge, on this occasion, came in the form of the Borough of Sunderland Bill. Amongst its numerous provisions, Clause 27 proposed the absorption of the River Wear Watch Commissioners by Sunderland Corporation.

Eventually, the clause was dropped from the Bill following opposition from the shipowners and realisation by the Town Council of the financial implications for the Corporation.

By 1899, however, attitudes had changed, both on the part of the Watch Commission and the Corporation. Never again would the latter express a serious interest in taking over the Watch. On the other hand, the Watch Commissioners were beginning to consider that their existence as a separate entity had outlived its usefulness. They now turned to the River Wear Commissioners, some of whom were also Watch Commissioners, to relieve themselves of their responsibilities.

Matters were brought to a head early in February, 1899, with the arrival of the 7,575 gross tons San Francisco registered steamship, *Algoa* at Sunderland for bunker coal. Despite being in port for only a few hours, the vessel was charged £15 in respect of the prevailing River Wear Watch Rate of ³/4d per net registered ton. Naturally, the vessel's owners protested at the amount but were informed that as the charge was made under the Watch Commissioners' special Act of Parliament, it must stand.

At their quarterly meeting held on 9th February, 1889, the Commissioners discussed the matter at length and came to the conclusion that the Act was quite out of date and grossly unfair in the method by which rates were calculated. Initially, consideration was given to amending the Act or obtaining a new one in order to satisfy objectors.

In the meantime, the Traffic Committee of the River Wear Commission, which had also received complaints concerning the Watch Rate, had set up a subcommittee of its own to inquire into the subject of the River Wear Watch and its dues. Mr. Barwick of the Traffic Committee (who was also a member of the Watch Commission) stated his belief that most other port authorities in the kingdom had control over their police forces and that the time had now arrived for the R.W.C. to take over the Watch. Doubtlessly, uppermost in the minds of the R.W.C. was the fear of losing trade to other ports, especially the Tyne, through the additional charges imposed upon shipping in respect of the Watch.

On 9th March, 1899, at a special meeting of the Watch Commissioners, the following resolution was unanimously passed:

"That it is desirable that the duties and powers of the River Wear Watch Commissioners, under their Special Act, be transferred and handed over to the River Wear Commissioners, and that Messrs. T. W. Pinkney, Wm. Ritson, and John Hopper be appointed as a Committee for the purpose of arranging with the River Wear Commissioners as to the proceedings to be taken for carrying this Resolution into effect."

Despite initial enthusiasm on the part of the R.W.C., consideration of the motion dragged on for over a year. Eventually - primarily for financial reasons - the proposal was shelved and the River Wear Watch lived to fight another day.

FRICTION WITH THE BOROUGH POLICE

Signs of disharmony between members of the River Wear Watch and their opposite numbers in the Borough Police became evident during 1894. Although records do not provide examples of such discord, this was obviously a state of affairs which could not be allowed to continue. Accordingly, at the instigation of the Corporation Watch Committee, the following order was issued to both forces by Superintendent Huntley:

"Both the Borough Police and River Police have jurisdiction over all parts of the Borough, including the river, and it is incumbent on every member of one force to assist the other in discharge of duty and to obey the order of a superior officer of either force."

This instruction must have met with the desired effect, as no further references to this issue are recorded.

FIREFLOATS

The steam firefloat, *Fire Queen,* acquired in 1874, was to have a busy but relatively short working life. In 1877, the Commissioners' engineer, Charles R. Simey, reported that her boiler required extensive repairs as a result of water tubes giving way and that it had been necessary for a representative of her builders, Messrs. Merryweather and Son to travel to Sunderland to carry out the work.

To keep costs to a minimum, much of the repair work carried out upon the Commissioners' craft was usually undertaken by Watch personnel.

Although Mr. Simey resigned his position as engineer in 1878, the Watch Commissioners continued to retain consulting engineers to ensure that their vessels were maintained in a good state of repair.

Whilst the *Fire Queen* was usually moored in the river alongside one of the manual engines, with the other 'manual' being berthed in the docks, there were occasions when the *Fire Queen* was stationed inside Hudson Dock. In 1882, for instance, she was placed there during the winter at the request of the River Wear Commissioners due to their concern for the safety of the large volume of shipping present. Situations had arisen whereby the *Fire Queen* had been unable to gain access to the docks from the river due to the lock gates being closed when the tide was low.

On 22nd May, 1884, the River Wear Watch Commissioners imposed the following revised scale of charges for the services of their firefloats, which also indicates the variety of work being undertaken at that time:

FOR SERVICES OF THE FIRE QUEEN.

Engagement at land fires, pumping out ships in a sinking state, 'and sunk,' or other emergent work:-
First Hour £10 0s. 0d
Second and succeeding hours £5 0s. 0d

For pumping out tug boats, lighters, wrecks, & c., per hour, for every hour employed £4 0s. 0d

For filling ballast tanks of vessels on stocks, in shipbuilding yards, the existing charge (by weight) of 1s. per ton of water, inclusive of testing to remain.

For filling tanks of ships in graving docks, or afloat, the rate of charge to be 6d per ton.

For testing sailing vessels in graving docks, £2 2s. up to 500 register tons, and above 500 register tons, £3 3s.

When in compliance with a definite order, the Fire Queen proceeds to a fire on land or other engagement and commences work, and should complete such work in less than one hour, the full charge of £10 to be made.

Whenever an order for the services of the Fire Queen is given, and she proceeds in compliance with such order, and should not be required when she arrives, a charge of £2 2s. to be made.

FOR USE OF MANUAL ENGINE.

£2 2s. per hour, for every hour employed, 'exclusive of towage' with an allowance of 1s. per hour, per man, for pumping, the Inspector to employ a sufficient number of men for that purpose.

All engagements for service under any of the above heads, to be in writing, and signed by the person engaging, previous to the commencement of the work.

Application for use of the Fire Queen to be made to Inspector Lakin, Police Station, Bodlewell Lane.

THE SECOND 'FIRE QUEEN'

After being in service for little more than a decade, it became apparent that the *Fire Queen* was in urgent need of replacement due to the poor condition of her hull and boiler. Accordingly, Mr. F. W. Willcox, M.I.M.E., of the firm, Willcox and Wawn, 45 West Sunniside, Sunderland, was commissioned to design a new steam firefloat.

The vessel's hull, 50 feet in length with a beam of 11 feet 6 inches, was completed by S. P. Austin and Son at their Wear Dockyard and was launched on 22nd December, 1885. The two 25 horsepower propelling engines and pumping engine were removed from the old *Fire Queen* and refitted into the new vessel at John Dickinson's Palmers Hill Engineworks, whilst a new boiler, specially adapted for raising steam rapidly, was supplied by Merryweather and Sons.

It was decided that the new float would also be named *Fire Queen*. Having cost around £3,000 to construct, fitting out was quickly completed before she underwent acceptance trials on 28th January, 1886 on the Wear. Her trials were regarded as being extremely successful, during which she threw a water jet over the centre of Wearmouth Bridge.

Whilst her pumping rate of about 66,000 gallons of water per hour was similar to her predecessor, the leather screw-coupling hose with which she was originally equipped sometimes burst at full pressure. Following several trials during her early years of service, this type of hose was gradually replaced by superior canvas hose, fitted with instantaneous couplings.

STEAM LAUNCH, 'PATROL'

On 3rd September, 1896, the River Wear Watch Commissioners took delivery of their first steam launch for patrol duties. Hitherto, river patrols had been solely carried out using two rowing boats and acquisition of the launch now enabled officers to reach any desired part of the river within a few minutes. Rowing boats, however, continued to be used to supplement steam launches until 1928.

The new launch was named *Patrol*, having been built by Mr. F. T. Harker of Stockton-on-Tees at a cost of £160. Constructed from cedar wood and fitted with mahogany, she was 28 feet in length with a beam of 5 feet 6 inches Being an open boat, awnings were provided for wet or hot weather. Her boiler, tested to 260 pounds per square inch, had a working pressure of 120 pounds per square inch and was capable of being operated with fresh or salt water and with coal or coke, although coke was preferred. Her engine was of the compound surface condensing type giving a maximum speed of more than 10 knots.

Patrol had arrived in the Wear from the Tees under her own steam and despite having encountered heavy seas during the passage had proved herself thoroughly seaworthy. The following day, she underwent trials on the river. On board were Captain Butchart, representing the Watch Commissioners; Superintendent Huntley, Inspector Lakin, Sergeant Humble, and P.C. Wright; and Mr. Harker, the builder, together with one of his sons. The launch gave the greatest satisfaction, as the following extract from the Sunderland Daily Echo report of the trials shows:

*"Starting from beside the **Fire Queen**, off Scotia Wharf, the **Patrol** was taken down the river as far as the harbour entrance, turned and run up to Messrs. Short Bros. yard and back again. From the bridge to Messrs. Shorts' yard occupied about fifteen minutes and the craft ran wonderfully well and was remarkably easy to handle, being twisted here and there among the vessels on the river without the slightest trouble and working very smoothly all the time."*

23. The third *Fire Queen*, constructed in 1911, also by Henry Scarr, poses in the River Wear near J. L. Thompson and Sons Ltd. during the early years of her career. *Sunderland Museum (Tyne and Wear Museums).*

24. John William Arthur Rochford *(1869 - 1952)*, who held the position as Inspector of the River Wear Watch from 1913 until his retirement in 1949, then aged eighty. *Author's collection.*

25. Captain George Butchart *(1843 - 1916)*, a highly respected local maritime figure and ardent member of the River Wear Watch Commission from 1890 until his death. *Author's collection.*

26. The collier, *S.S. Corcrag (ex-Hornsey)*, *(built 1898 / 1,803 g.r.t.)* pictured under way during the period 1920 - 1924. On 10th November, 1918, whilst lying at buoys in the River Wear near Thornhill Quay, a serious fire which had broken out on board, threatening to engulf the ship's magazine, was heroically dealt with by members of the Watch. *National Maritime Museum.*

27a. A 12 pounder brass shell casing, from on board *S.S. Hornsey*, which was retained as a souvenir by Inspector Rochford. *Author's collection.*

27b. Markings on the base of the shell casing. Note the year of manufacturer - 1917. *Author's collection.*

28. Five brave men *(left to right)*: Inspector John William Arthur Rochford, Sergeant George William Jennings, P.C. Herbert Adams, Sergeant William Jackson and P.C. William Nichols Steel are pictured outside Shire Hall, Durham on 7th May, 1920 after receiving their Kings Medals for Gallantry from the Earl of Durham as a result of their actions on board ***S.S. Hornsey*** on 10th November, 1918.
Author's collection.

29. John Caffrey, V.C. *(1891 - 1953)*, who originated from Birr, Kings County, Ireland and served as a constable with the Watch in 1919, before transferring to Sunderland Borough Police.
Author's collection.

30. Viewed from the public stairs between S. P. Austin and Sons' shipyard and Scotia Quay are the River Station ***Manual***, the ***Fire Queen*** and a Watch rowing boat. The approximate date of the photograph can be ascertained from the France Fenwick and Co. Ltd. collier, ***Bearwood***, seen in the background, which was owned by that company between 1919 and 1927. *W. Bell collection.*

31. On parade at the Garrison Field, Gill Bridge Avenue, Sunderland, during the 1920's, members of the Watch are inspected by Superintendent Crawley and His Majesty's Inspector of Constabulary. *Author's collection.*

32. Watch personnel on board the *Fire Queen* during the 1920's. P.C. Jonathan Freeman is standing on the extreme left and Inspector Rochford is on the far right. *Author's collection.*

33. *Fire Queen* lies alongside the *Manual* in 1923.
Author's collection.

34.
John Edward Dawson *(1862 - 1942)*, who, as Chairman of
the River Wear Commissioners, conducted a campaign of
attrition against the Watch, after the passing of the River Wear
Watch Act in 1923. *Author's collection.*

35. Firefighters engaged at the scene of a fire which broke out on 6th November, 1923, amongst thousands of pit props stored on the east side of Hendon
Dock by George Horsley and Co. *Author's collection.*

36. *Fire King* engaged in pumping operations alongside the quay wall in Hendon Dock on 7th November, 1923. *Author's collection.*

37. Seventeen members of the Watch's establishment of twenty-two, pictured on 8th March, 1925: **Top row** *(left to right)*: Jonas S. Blakeston, George James Elstob, Alexander Knapp, George Thomas Tildon, Charles Peter Page and George William Jennings; **Centre row** *(left to right)*: John Mark Cartmer, *unknown*, John William Arthur Rochford, Robert F. Mustard and William Nichols Steel; **Bottom row** *(left to right)*: Gilbert J. Mellefont, *unknown*, Herbert Adams, Peter W. Atkinson, Thomas Swales and James Rich. *Author's collection.*

38. Motor launch, *Vigilante* which was acquired second-hand in 1928 and remained in service until 1933. Superintendent Ruddick is seated at the stern, with Inspector Rochford standing behind Constable Rich. *Author's collection.*

39. The *Fire Queen* makes a spectacular sight as she discharges five jets of water simultaneously at Claxheugh, South Hylton.
Northeast Press Ltd., Sunderland Echo.

40. An aerial view of the lower reaches of the Wear during the 1930's. The River Station, *Fire Queen* and other Watch craft are the lower group of vessels which can be seen in the bottom right hand corner of the picture. *Sunderland Museum (Tyne and Wear Museums).*

41. A pre-1932 photograph of the River Station, *Manual* with steam launch, *Patrol* moored on her port side and the *Fire Queen* on her starboard. *Northeast Press Ltd., Sunderland Echo.*

42. River Police sergeant passing the time of day with a cyclist on the Low Street near Wylam Wharf. *Author's collection.*

44.
P.C. John Patterson who served as a constable with the Watch between 1932 and 1961. As an army reservist, he was the only Watch member to see active service during World War 2. *Author's collection.*

43. John Thomas Burnop, who was elected as a River Wear Watch Commissioner in 1939 and also served as a shipowning representative on the River Wear Commission. *Author's collection.*

45. The scene at the junction of John Street
and Borough Road on the morning of
10th April, 1941, as firefighters tackle
the blaze at Binns' East side
Departmental Store, destroyed during
the previous night's air raid. For almost
fifteen hours, the *Fire Queen* had
pumped water half a mile, from the
river to Mowbray Park lake, to feed
pumps engaged at the incident.
Sunderland Museum
(Tyne and Wear Museums).

46. The collier, **S.S.** *Zealous* being pumped out by the *Fire Queen* at Hetton Quay on 5th June, 1942, after sustaining serious damage following the detonation of a delayed action bomb which had fallen into the river the previous night. *Sunderland Museum (Tyne and Wear Museums).*

47. A busy wartime scene on the Wear during the 1939 - 1945 conflict, looking north across the Wear from S. P. Austin and Sons' towards J. L. Thompson and Sons Ltd. Note the camouflage paintwork on the ship fitting out at Manor Quay and the barrage balloon aloft. *Northeast Press Ltd., Sunderland Echo.*

A RIVER PIRATE NAMED THOMPSON

Although many unsavoury characters frequented the River Wear and its docks, none was as infamous in the eyes of the River Wear Watch as a man named John Thompson. A powerfully built man, filled with hatred for the River Police, he would not hesitate in using extreme violence against them.

Thompson was in the habit of unmooring boats and going to sea or upriver in them, before allowing them to drift away. He was a terror to pilots and boatmen alike, the very sight of him causing law abiding citizens to shrink with fear.

His first violent encounter with the Watch took place on the evening of Saturday, 6th November, 1876, when Sergeant Thomas Howes and P.C. George Ranson, having received information that two cobles had been stolen, were making enquiries on the docks.

Whilst near Gladstone Bridge, the officers caught sight of Thompson and his brother James in a coble, which they moored as the policemen arrived. Pointing to John Thompson, Sergeant Howes observed "There's the man who does all the mischief with the pilots' cobles." Howes had scarcely spoken when John Thompson punched him violently in the eye, completely closing it. P.C. Ranson, on going to assist his sergeant was tripped and thrown to the ground so forcibly that his shoulder was dislocated by the impact.

Sergeant Howes then drew his truncheon which James Thompson attempted to wrench from his grasp. "Look out, he's got a knife," shouted Ranson, still on the ground. Howes turned to face John Thompson and saw that he was brandishing a knife threatening towards him. Bravely, the sergeant grappled with his assailant to prevent him from using the weapon. During the struggle he was dispossessed of his truncheon by James Thompson, who handed it to his brother. Still, Howes attempted to disarm John Thompson and in doing so was stabbed in the hand.

Eventually, owing to their injuries and the ferocity of the violence which had been directed towards them, the officers were forced to withdraw from the fray.

Warrants were subsequently applied for and both brothers were apprehended a few days later. On appearing before the magistrates, they were dealt with in a surprisingly lenient manner, in the circumstances, with John being sentenced to six months imprisonment and James being fined 20 shillings plus costs.

Following his release, John Thompson was frequently back behind bars, serving eighteen months for cutting and wounding a man and five years penal servitude for stealing sails and marine gear at Norwich.

His next desperate confrontation with the River Police took place ten years later, on the morning of Saturday, 21st August, 1886. At this time, P.C.'s John Hasker and George Thorn were on river patrol when they were informed by a foyboatman that John Thompson had stolen his coble. Soon the constables saw the coble in the distance and managed to overhaul it.

As the police coble pulled alongside, Thompson shouted, "I'll knock the first man's brains out who touches this boat." Undeterred, P.C. Thorn caught hold of the side of the stolen coble, whereupon Thompson brought an oar crashing down on the officer's hand. Thompson then took hold of the coble's mast, intending to use it against the police, but they managed to push him away. He next unshipped the tiller and struck Thorn so hard with it that he would be absent from duty for ten days. Picking up a pit prop from the bottom of the boat, he threw it at Hasker, shouting "You bastard, I'll not allow you to row anymore there."

Although the prop struck Hasker on the shoulder, the officers managed to keep Thompson's coble alongside their own by use of a boathook, upon which he cut his hand whilst trying to fend it off.

Eventually, a keel's mooring rope came within the reach of Thompson who grabbed it before swimming ashore and making good his escape.

He was able to elude the police until 8th October, that year, when he was arrested on warrant and brought before the magistrates the following day. Mr. W. A. Kidson, prosecuting, described him as "nothing better than a river pirate," and as "a terror to the port." Despite his previous record, Thompson again received another light sentence, this time of four months imprisonment with hard labour.

MURDER IN THE ROADS

At 8 p.m. on 26th June, 1878, on a beautiful summer's evening, a shocking murder took place on board the 415 net tons barque, **William Leckie** of Sunderland, whilst anchored in the roadstead about two miles off Sunderland Harbour.

The vessel had left the Wear at noon that day, bound for Montevideo in Uruguay, but due to her master, Captain Fletcher being ashore on ship's business at Newcastle, the ship was brought to anchor in the roads to await his return. A highly respected North Sea pilot named John Wallace was on board and it was to be his task to guide the barque down the east coast on the first leg of her voyage.

Captain Fletcher arrived on board at 4.30 p.m. and called a roll of the crew. He at once noticed that the ship's forty-nine years old cook and steward, Robert Vest, was somewhat the worse for liquor. Mindful of the long voyage ahead and the need to establish his authority from the outset, the captain immediately took Vest to task. Sternly he told him, "You have shipped as cook and steward and I find you the worse for drink. This will not suit me. You shall leave the cabin and go into the forecastle. I will not carry a drunken man." Standing next to the captain, Wallace nodded in agreement and said, "You are quite right Captain in bringing him up at once." Puffing on his pipe, the pilot then jocularly addressed the crew, saying "Lay aft boys and put him in irons."

Vest begged the captain to forgive him and promised that there would be no repetition of his behaviour. "Go away from me and tomorrow morning I will put you square," ordered Fletcher. Sulkily, Vest retired to the aft deckhouse without replying.

There being no wind by which to proceed, the barque remained at anchor. Wallace joined Captain Fletcher and his chief officer for tea in the captain's cabin. After a while, Wallace excused himself and made his way to the water closet.

Meanwhile, two apprentices, named Smith and Talbot, were amusing themselves on deck by playing the violin and accordion. The music ended abruptly as a desperate cry of "Boys, boys, I'm stabbed" echoed across the deck. The two apprentices ran to the water closet and there witnessed a most appalling scene. The cook, Vest, had hold of Wallace's collar with his left hand. In his right was a ten inch knife with which he, despite Wallace clutching his wrist, was in the process of cutting the pilot's throat.

Bravely, Talbot struck Vest's arm in an attempt to stop the progress of the knife and then tried to release a belaying pin with which to defend Wallace. Vest, however, continued with his murderous attack and plunged the knife, up to the hilt, into the pit of the pilot's stomach. Still with his trousers around his ankles, Wallace sank to his knees and pulled out the knife from his body, before keeling over, quite dead.

Calmly, Vest leaned against a rail saying only, "It's done."

Captain Fletcher, having been summoned from his cabin, immediately ordered the crew to seize Vest and to lash him to the deck. This being done, the cook was heard to say, "I hope the poor man is gone, his soul's in heaven." Later he said, "This last twenty-four years, something has told me I should be hung."

A signal for assistance was answered by the steamtug, **Champion**. Her master, having been informed of the murder, set off for the river and before long, had given the news to the River Police. Inspector Lakin, Sergeant Ranson and P.C. Smart at once boarded the tug, which returned to the **William Leckie**. There, Inspector Lakin told Vest that he was being placed under arrest on a charge of wilful murder, to which he replied, "It's all right, I plead guilty. I've done it." The officers then removed their prisoner from the ship and set off for harbour on board the tug.

What had caused Vest to carry out such a wicked act? Clearly, he had been incensed by the public rebuke given to him by Captain Fletcher and had been intensely irritated by the supportive stance adopted by Wallace.

As the tug neared the harbour, Vest turned to Sergeant Ranson and declared "Wallace was sitting in the water closet. He looked at me and I looked at him. I looked at the knife which was sticking in the galley and I walked along the deck a bit. Something said to me, go and finish him and I deliberately drew the knife out of the galley and did the deed. I am only sorry that I did not see the captain - he should have shared the same fate." The sergeant told Vest that it was a pity that he had done so. Vest answered "I am only sorry for my wife and five daughters," then added "I have read all kinds of books about all kinds of murders during the last twenty years and I always thought I would be hung."

The unfortunate Wallace, a quiet and inoffensive man, aged sixty-two, was buried at Bishopwearmouth Cemetery on 29th June. A huge crowd saw the departure of the cortege from his residence at 13 Peel Street, Sunderland.

Vest was subsequently committed to stand his trial at Durham Assizes which commenced on 12th July, 1878.

In his defence, Vest pleaded that the killing had been carried out during a moment of insanity. Great emphasis was placed upon a number of head injuries which he had received over the years. He had served in the Horse Artillery throughout the Crimean War, during which time he had been wounded in the forehead by a bayonet thrust. After leaving the army, he had received a severe cut to the head as a result of falling between two ships and on another occasion had been struck on the head with an iron bar during an altercation at Houghton-le-Spring. In addition, his brother testified to Vest having often talked about committing suicide.

The case for the defence was, at best, weak and few were surprised when the jury returned a guilty verdict. Although, they expressed a strong recommendation for mercy, the judge, Lord Justice Baggally, felt that he had little alternative but to don the black cap and sentence Vest to death.

Despite appeals for clemency, no reprieve was forthcoming and Vest was hanged at Durham Jail on 30th July, 1878, his executioner being the infamous William Marwood.

The execution aroused great sympathy for the murderer's wife and five young daughters who lived at Seaham Harbour. Such was public concern for their welfare following the loss of the family breadwinner, that donations flooded in to assist them in their plight.

SOME NOTABLE RESCUES

To the men of the River Wear Watch, lifesaving was almost a routine duty for which its members sought no recognition and received little. From the scores of occasions upon which they were instrumental in saving life, the following examples from the 1880's and '90's show the tremendous courage and initiative displayed by individual officers, often at great personal risk:

On a winter's afternoon early in January, 1888, P.C. Robert Agar was on duty on board the **Fire Queen** near to Bodlewell Lane Ferry Landing when he heard cries of "Boy overboard!" Jumping into a police coble, he carried out a search of the river in the vicinity of the steamtug, **Blacksmith** from where the boy had fallen. To his great disappointment, he found no trace of the child and was on the point of returning ashore for grappling irons when he noticed another small boy standing on the tug in an intense state of excitement. This boy had seen exactly where his friend had disappeared below the water and pointed this out to the officer. As it was low water and the depth was only about ten feet, Agar took hold of his boathook and began dragging it along the river bed. Within seconds he had pulled the victim to the surface and found, to his astonishment, that he was still alive. The constable quickly applied artificial resuscitation and soon the boy had recovered sufficiently to enable him to walk home.

Shortly after 11 p.m. on New Year's Eve, 1889, a man named Richard Baxter, employed on the **S.S. Glen Dochart**, walked over the edge of Hudson Dock near to No. 6 Coal Drop. Hearing the splash and cries for help, Sergeant Humble and P.C. Wright ran to give assistance. Fortunately, the River Wear Commissioners had recently gone to great expense in providing safety chains on the face of the dock wall to assist persons falling into the water. P.C. Wright slid down one of these and seized hold of Baxter, keeping him above the water until a life buoy and line had been obtained by the sergeant, thus enabling his removal from the dock.

On the afternoon of 31st August, the same year, Sergeant Humble effected a gallant rescue from the River Wear. A five years old boy, named Hughes, was fishing with some friends from the end of a wooden jetty projecting from the Commissioners' Quay when he overbalanced and fell into very deep water. Hearing cries for help, Sergeant Humble rushed to the end of the jetty and without even removing his watch, plunged into the river and swam towards the boy. Just as the officer was about to reach him, the boy sank below the surface. Nevertheless, Humble dove down after him and succeeded in bringing the frightened, cold and exhausted child to the ferry steps.

During the evening of 15th July, 1894, whilst a sailor named Thomas Rice was boarding the **S.S. Khio**, lying in Hudson Dock, his bag fell into the water. On attempting to recover it, he overbalanced and fell into the dock, striking his head on the ship's hull during his descent. Shouts of "Man overboard" immediately attracted P.C. William Avery to the scene. Without any thought for his own safety, he obtained a rope and lowered himself between the dock wall and the side of the ship - a hazardous thing to do. On reaching the waterline he managed to grab hold of Rice, who was rapidly losing consciousness and support his head above water. To add to the confusion, another sailor named Duffner, who had been trying to assist in the rescue, also fell into the dock. Despite already having hold of Rice, P.C. Avery managed to grab Duffner and keep him afloat too. Both sailors rapidly became exhausted and would certainly have drowned had it not been for the exertions of the officer. Eventually a boat containing the watchman from the **S.S. Lombard** and P.C. Nuttall of the Borough Police arrived and took all three on board.

Just before midnight on Saturday, 30th March, 1895, P.C. Thomas Parnaby was patrolling Hudson Dock, near to Laing Warehouse, when he heard a loud splash coming from the direction of the steamtug, *Northumberland* which was lying nearby. On running over to the quay edge he saw that the tug's watchman, Thomas Kish, had fallen between the vessel and quayside. The officer immediately entered the water and held Kish afloat. For some thirty minutes, P.C. Parnaby called for help but, as that part of the dock was deserted on a Saturday night, no-one came. Eventually, a pilot called Richard Gibbons heard the officer's shouts and with his assistance, Kish was removed from the water.

SAD DROWNING INCIDENT OFF ROKER

A particularly sad accident, deeply affecting the River Wear Watch, took place off the coast at Roker on Friday, 18th September, 1891, when a pleasant afternoon's sailing turned to tragedy.

That afternoon, Sergeant Henry Hawks, a member of the Watch since 1880, had arranged to spend his off duty time sailing in company with his son, John; a colleague, P.C. William Lance Snelgar; and a friend William Edward Marshall who was one of the Bodlewell Lane Ferry collectors.

Sergeant Hawks, an experienced sailor, was the proud owner of a 24 foot yacht named *Meteor* which was well renowned for her sailing qualities. The vessel had taken a first prize at the Roker Regatta and had also been successful at the recent Seaham Regatta.

Shortly after 2 p.m., the party boarded the *Meteor*, left the South Outlet and sailed south along the coast as far as Ryhope Snook. There, they turned and headed northwards once more. On passing Seaburn, the four men exchanged cheery waves with a local shipbuilder, Mr. John Crown who, together with his son, was also out enjoying a day under sail. Soon the *Meteor* had reached Whitburn Bay, at which point Henry Hawks altered course to shape for home. It was when the yacht was midway between Whitburn Bay and the new Roker Pier that disaster struck.

A sudden strong gust of wind off the land caught the sails and jammed the main sheet in the block. Sergeant Hawks got up to rectify the problem and as he did so the gunwale dipped, causing the craft to fill with water and capsize. In no time at all the *Meteor* had foundered.

The accident had been witnessed by John Crown who quickly brought his yacht to the scene, where he found all four crew members of the *Meteor* struggling in the sea. An oar was thrown to Henry Hawks who managed to grasp it and use it as a buoyancy aid. Next, a rope was thrown to Snelgar who, although only about a yard away from Crown's yacht, made no effort to catch it. Piteously he cried "Oh, my God!" before disappearing beneath the waves. About the same time, young John Hawks, who was a strong swimmer, also sank and was drowned. Marshall, who could scarcely swim a stroke, had taken off his cap and was using it as a paddle. He was completely exhausted and on the point of going down when a rope thrown to him by Crown, somehow became entangled around his head, enabling him to be hauled to safety. Finally, Henry Hawks, suffering badly from cramp, was picked up by two young men in a coble and taken ashore.

The bodies of John Hawks and Lance Snelgar were both later washed up on Whitburn Beach. At the subsequent inquests into their deaths, simple verdicts of 'accidental death by drowning' were returned in each case.

John Hawks had been employed as a labourer by the River Wear Commissioners and left a widow and two children. He had been a member of the East End Black Watch Football Club and of the Hartley Street Mission Brass Band. P.C. Snelgar, a quiet unassuming man, well respected by his colleagues, was survived by his wife and three children. He had completed three years service in the River Police.

One can only imagine the feelings of Henry Hawks over the deaths of his son and colleague.

EXPLOSION ON BOARD THE SCHOONER, 'THELMA'

At 1.20 a.m. on Friday, 15th September, 1899, the Swedish schooner, *Thelma* lay quietly in the tier off Mark Quay with her hatches battened down and her hold laden with gas coal, loaded at Bells Drops the previous day. Four of her crew remained on board, although her master and mate were ashore.

Being unable to sleep, one of the crew, Robert Andersen entered the cabin and struck a light to see the time. Immediately, a fearful explosion tore through the vessel and a sheet of flame and brilliant sparks shot high into the night sky. As Andersen lay writhing with horrific burns to his face and hands, the other crewmen who had been asleep in their hammocks, picked themselves up from the floor in a state of shock and confusion before stumbling on deck wearing only their night clothes.

The sound of the explosion had been heard throughout the town. Fortunately, P.C's John Arnold and William Johnson, who were patrolling the river in a coble, were nearby and quickly pulled to the scene. Upon arriving there, they found that the schooner was sinking rapidly due to her timbers having been forced apart by the blast. Without regard to their own safety, they quickly climbed aboard and assisted all four crewmen into their coble. As they rowed for the shore, the *Thelma* settled onto the river bed with half her stern blown out and listing towards the centre of the fairway.

Andersen, after having his injuries dressed by the police surgeon, Dr. Beattie, was despatched to the Infirmary in a serious condition. At low water, the decks of the ship became visible and the River Police went back on board to salvage what they could of the crew's possessions.

It was later ascertained that the hatches of the schooner had been secured before all the coal gas had been able to escape. As a result some of this gas had found its way into the cabin - hence the explosion.

As far as P.C's Arnold and Johnson were concerned, that would have been the end of the matter. The local press, however, took great interest in the story and discovered that, despite having saved countless lives, no member of the Watch had ever received an award for lifesaving. To rectify this shortcoming, much publicity was given to the *Thelma* incident.

As a result, at the quarterly meeting of the River Wear Watch Commissioners held on 30th November, 1899, P.C's Arnold and Johnson were presented with Royal Humane Society certificates on parchment in mahogany cases for their courageous conduct in saving the lives of the crew of the **Thelma**. Superintendent Carter, present at the meeting, stated that during the preceding thirty-four years, the River Police had saved no fewer that 345 lives, many of the rescues having been carried out a great personal risk. In addition, they had extinguished 191 fires on board ships. This was the first occasion upon which the bravery of his force had been so rewarded.

P.C. Arnold (who in the meantime had resigned to become Assistant Harbourmaster at Sunderland) and P.C. Johnson were also awarded the Swedish Royal Humane Certificate by the Royal Swedish Board of Commerce (Kommers Kollegum) for "meritorious services" in rescuing the schooner's crew. Each also received a gratuity of fifty shillings.

GREAT FIRES

During the final quarter of the Nineteenth Century, the Port of Sunderland saw a number of serious outbreaks of fire, many of which could only have been extinguished by the Borough Police Fire Brigade with the greatest of difficulty, had it not been for the presence of the River Wear Watch's firefloats. That the Watch possessed steam fire engines twenty-five years earlier than the Borough Brigade, demonstrates its importance as a firefighting body. Whilst the land-based brigade had to rely upon hose barrows and hydrants connected to the undependable town water supply, the steam firefloats were capable of pumping more than 60,000 gallons of water per hour onto a blaze. Even the manual firefloats were a formidable opponent to most outbreaks.

The following are accounts of some of the more notable fires attended by the River Wear Watch during this period:

THE DAY THE WEAR CAUGHT FIRE

Nowadays, stringent safety precautions are observed in the case of oil and petroleum tankers entering port for repair. During the last century, however, when the carriage of oil and its products was in its infancy, the hazards of doing so were not always fully appreciated, leading to grave deficiencies in measures to prevent occurrences of fire and pollution.

Such was the case on the morning of 8th January, 1890, as a busy scene presented itself on the River Wear at Manor Quay, just east of Wearmouth Bridge, where five steam vessels lay at their moorings.

Having moored in the tier off the seaward end of the quay, upon her arrival from Rouen earlier that day, the 2,657 gross tons oil tanker, **S.S. Wild Flower**, owned by Alfred Suart of London, was preparing to enter Bridge Graving Dock, operated by Robert Thompson and Sons who had built the ship the previous year. Upriver of her, also at the buoys, was the Lambton collier, **S.S. Douglas** (768 g.r.t.) which was waiting her turn for loading at the drops. Nearby, lay the steamtug, **Earl of Dumfries** awaiting orders. Undergoing repairs at the extreme west end of the quay, adjacent to an extensive timberyard, was moored the 1,663 gross tons Culliford and Clark steamer, **Deronda**. To the east of her lay the new steamship, **Parkfield** (2,607 g.r.t.), in the course of being fitted out by J. L. Thompson and Sons.

The 300 feet long **Wild Flower** had departed from Rouen after having discharged her cargo of crude petroleum oil which had been loaded at Philadelphia, U.S.A. During the voyage to England, all her cargo tanks had been filled with water to purge them of gas. Although four tanks had been pumped out, there had been insufficient time to discharge those forward and aft prior to entering the Wear. Despite an awareness that a residue of oil from the cargo would still be in those tanks, an order was given for their contents to be pumped into the river. Whilst to do such a thing today would render those responsible liable to the severest legal penalty, such actions were almost common practice in 1890.

At 11.50 a.m., without warning, the river around the five vessels erupted into a sea of flame. Frantic cries of "Fire, fire!" could be heard from those on board as they fled, jumping ashore, into nearby boats and even into the water, fearful of being burnt alive. It soon became apparent that that the remains of oil discharged from the **Wild Flower** had become ignited and had been carried upstream on the flooding tide. Sheets of flame shot into the air, leaping high up the side of the vessels, igniting their masts, rigging and decks, whilst clouds of dense black smoke billowed northwards.

Tragically, a twenty years old boilersmith, John Robert Thompson lost his life. He had been working in the engine room of the **Deronda** and, being unable to escape onto the quayside, had lowered himself into a boat at her stern, together with two others. On making for the shore the boat had become enveloped in flames, compelling its occupants to leap into the river. Although his companions reached safety, Thompson was drowned.

On the alarm being raised, the pumping apparatus at Manor Quay Engineworks was brought into operation, directing a stream of water from the river onto the flames. Next on the scene was a contingent of Borough policemen, under Sergeant Ross, from Barclay Street Police Station who arrived with the fire barrow and hose. It was only by their great skill and determination that the fire was prevented from taking hold on the quayside and in the timberyard.

Overlooking the scene, crowds of people lined Wearmouth Bridge directing anxious looks for the **Fire Queen**. To the great relief of all concerned, she arrived shortly after noon with Inspector Lakin in command. Utilising her power to the full, she had extinguished the remainder of the flames within the hour.

Damage to the **Wild Flower, Earl of Dumfries** and **Douglas** was severe, whilst the **Parkfield** and **Deronda** suffered less seriously. Ironically, had the unfortunate Thompson remained on board the **Deronda**, he would most probably have survived.

Besides the coroner's inquest into Thompson's death and civil proceedings instituted against the owners of the **Wild Flower**, the Board of Trade launched its own inquiry. The report of Mr. Mansel Jones, the Board of Trade inspector, condemned the practice of emptying 'slops' from the tanks of oil tankers into harbours busy with shipping as being extremely dangerous. The River Wear Commissioners' Petroleum Bye-laws did not appear to contemplate such a thing occurring and harbour authorities, in general, were recommended to take action to eradicate the habit.

Although many theories were suggested, the cause of the fire could not be positively ascertained. It was felt most likely, however, that a piece of burning oily waste had fallen overboard from either the **Deronda** or **Parkfield**, both of which had been using portable forges for repair purposes. It was later claimed that a rivet heater had been responsible by discarding red-hot ashes into the river.

THE WEAR PATENT FUEL WORKS FIRE OF 1891

The South Docks were the scene of many a great fire over the years, but probably the most notable of them all broke out at the Wear Patent Fuel Works, Hendon Dock on 27th July, 1891.

Erected in 1871 for the manufacture of tar products, the works covered an extensive area on the southern side of the dock and was the scene of a number of serious fires during its existence.

About 1 a.m., that morning, flames were seen to be issuing from the anthracene house. The alarm was quickly passed to Bodlewell Lane Police Station and soon fire barrows and policemen from all over town were concentrated at the scene. Valuable assistance was also provided by River Wear Commissioners' dock watermen and the fuel works' workforce. Steam was raised on the *Fire Queen* which, under the command of Inspector Lakin, proceeded to Hendon Dock and swiftly brought her jets into play.

Rivers of burning tar flowed from ruptured tanks, threatening to consume all in their path. The police were at first powerless to prevent the flames from spreading, their only answer being to pour gallons of water onto the burning mass. As flames ignited various chemicals stored in the works, the water reacted violently with some of these, serving only to exacerbate the situation. A lurid glow, accompanied by billowing green and black smoke, filled the night as explosions echoed through the air.

By 3 a.m., the conflagration covered an enormous area. As well as having destroyed a large part of the fuel works, the fire had caused great devastation elsewhere. Channelled by railway lines, the flaming mass of tar gutted about fifty railway trucks belonging to the North Eastern Railway Company. Vast stocks of timber stacked in the neighbourhood were consumed and a warehouse filled with esparto grass was burnt to the ground.

Intense heat, together with suffocating smoke and chemical fumes exacted a terrible toll upon the combined force of River and Borough Police. Several officers were temporarily blinded, the uniforms of many being irreparably damaged and their boots ruined by tar. In some cases the tar had eaten through uniforms, badly burning their wearers.

None rendered more valuable assistance than the members of the River Wear Watch. Besides those on board the *Fire Queen*, many of their number fought the fire from on shore, suffering greatly in the process. At one stage, the *Fire Queen* had pumped so much water out of Hendon Dock, that she was in danger of going aground and had to be locked into Hudson Dock from where she continued to provide her aid. It was later found that chemicals had damaged much of her hose beyond repair.

Two days after the initial outbreak, the ruins of the fuel works were still smouldering. A massive clearing up operation then began and it was some considerable time before production could be resumed. Due to the absence of wind and the tenacity of the firefighters, the fire had been prevented from spreading to the bulk of the fuel stocks. It was also fortunate that all the injured policemen recovered sufficiently to enable their return to duty.

DEATH OF TWO POLICE OFFICERS IN
EAST END WAREHOUSE COLLAPSE

In the event of a serious outbreak of fire in the town well away from the port, the River Wear Watch would often be called upon to support the Borough Police Fire Brigade, even though no assistance could be afforded by the firefloats.

Such was the case early on the morning of Monday, 4th November, 1895, the outcome of which was to be devastating for both forces. At 4.45 a.m., an alarm was raised that Joshua Wilson and Sons' warehouse, situated between Lombard Street and Walton Lane in the East End, was on fire. Fire barrows from Central, Monkwearmouth, West End and Bodlewell Lane Police Stations were promptly on the scene. Assisting with the latter was a contingent of the River Wear Watch.

On arrival, the police found the top floor to be well alight. The warehouse consisted of four storeys, the upper two being used for the manufacture of chicory, the first floor for the storage of groceries and the ground floor as a depository for packages. It was on the third floor, where a large quantity of machinery was situated, that the fire appeared to have originated. Owing to dry rafters and beams used in the construction of the old building and the combustible nature of its contents, the fire had soon spread throughout the structure.

By 6.30 a.m., the large quantity of water poured into the building had virtually subdued the flames. Cold and tired groups of policemen, many of whom had been detained on duty after performing night shift, stood around the perimeter of the warehouse awaiting orders.

River Police Sergeant John Hasker, together with Borough P.C's Jonathan Darling and William Dryden, who were in Lombard Street, decided to go to the other side of the building in Walton Lane to see if anything further could be done there. In order to do so, they entered a passageway through the warehouse, connecting the two streets, a decision which was to prove fatal.

Without warning and with a terrific crash, the entire building collapsed on top of them. Darling had a miraculous escape, being struck on the back by a falling timber and flung through a doorway. His companions, though, were less fortunate. Both were buried beneath tons of debris and were killed almost instantaneously.

With bare hands, their colleagues set about removing debris, but knew in their hearts that their efforts would be in vain. Lifting jacks were procured from the nearby Scotia Engineworks and after considerable toil, the broken bodies of Hasker and Dryden were extricated from the ruins.

It was only by good fortune that a disaster of greater magnitude had been averted, as up to forty of Joshua Wilsons' workforce had been passing to and fro' along the passage shortly before the officers had met their deaths. Many other police officers outside had also just managed to escape the falling rubble.

The following day, at the Rose and Crown Hotel, High Street, a searching inquest into the circumstances surrounding the deaths of the victims was held before Coroner Maynard.

The main question to be answered was "Why had the officers been allowed to go through the passageway?" It was revealed that no orders, either specific or general, had existed to prevent them from doing so. Senior officers had clearly been unaware of the disposition of some of their men and had not been aware of the presence of the officers in the passageway. Sub-Inspector Scarf of the Borough Police, could only claim that the men were expected to obey the orders of the officer in charge, but no order had been issued forbidding them to enter the passageway.

It appeared that the fire had first taken hold in the roof which had subsequently fallen in onto the top floor containing the furnaces and heavy machinery bedded into concrete. The beams supporting this floor, having been partially burnt through, had then given way under the sheer weight, thus precipitating the building's collapse.

In spite of being aware of the machinery, Sub-Inspector Scarf and other senior officers present had failed to appreciate the potential danger. Clearly, neither had the unfortunate victims. Although it was obvious why the premises had collapsed, the cause of the fire was not. The most likely source was the furnaces on the top floor, but these were supposed to have been extinguished for the weekend.

After retiring, the jury expressed the opinion that Hasker and Dryden had lost their lives in the execution of their duty as a result of the building's collapse.

P.C. Dryden, one of the tallest men in the Borough Police, was to be greatly missed from his beat in Monkwearmouth. He left a widow and two children. Sergeant Hasker, who had joined the River Wear Watch in 1880, before being promoted nine years later, also left a widow and children.

At what was befittingly, one of the largest police funerals ever held in the Borough, the two officers were laid to rest at Bishopwearmouth Cemetery on 6th November. The solemn procession commenced at Hendon Police Station at 1 p.m., before making its way to the residences of the deceased officers. Forces from throughout the Northeast were represented, the City of Newcastle, alone, sending more than fifty men. The entire establishment of the River Wear Watch was present under Inspector Lakin, as was every man from the Sunderland Borough Police Force who could be spared. In addition, a combined body of the Royal Naval Reserve and Coastguard took part.

Dense crowds, paying their final respects, lined the streets as the cortege passed by on its way to the cemetery. The sight of the police band in ceremonial dress leading scores of policemen well turned out in best uniform and firemen wearing beautifully polished brass helmets presented a fine, but melancholy spectacle.

If nothing else, the untimely and tragic deaths of John Hasker and William Dryden would serve as a cautionary reminder of the dangers to which firefighters were frequently exposed.

THE HAVELOCK HOUSE FIRE

During the late evening of Monday, 18th July, 1898, the most catastrophic fire to occur in Sunderland during the Nineteenth Century broke out at George Henry Robinson's Havelock House, situated at the junction of High Street West and Fawcett Street. The fire resulted in no fewer than forty-eight business premises and a Wesleyan chapel being either destroyed or seriously damaged.

After the fire, great criticism was directed towards the Town Council for their lack of a properly organised fire brigade and that they did not possess a single steam fire engine.

Had it not been for the attendance of the River Wear Watch's *Fire Queen*, the destruction would have been far greater. She had been taken upriver to Wearmouth Bridge shortly after the alarm was first raised. After encountering initial difficulties due to the low state of the tide, she contributed greatly to the fire extinguishing force. It was calculated that the firefloat had to pump water from the river some 150 feet up to street level and then to the scene of the fire about 275 yards away and was still able to provide a good strong jet. She could have done more, but the hose could not withstand her pumps working at maximum pressure for prolonged periods.

As a direct result of the blaze, the Borough Police Fire Brigade was completely reorganised and placed, in January, 1899, under the command of Superintendent Thomas Breaks who was responsible only to the Chief Constable. Two horse-drawn fire engines were purchased from Shand Mason in 1898, thus reducing reliance upon firefloats to combat land fires.

On 10th October, 1898, Robert Patterson, thirty years of age, the River Wear Police engineer in charge of the *Fire Queen* was appointed by the Borough Fire Brigade to supervise their new horse-drawn steamers. He was eventually to attain the rank of Superintendent of the Fire Brigade, a position which he held until his retirement in July, 1931.

SERIOUS FIRE ON BOARD GREEK STEAMER IN HENDON DOCK

Despite the age of the two old manual firefloats, *Wear Engines 'A'* and *'B'*, both continued to prove their worth into the Twentieth Century, especially within the docks.

What was almost certainly the final occasion upon which both were simultaneously engaged in action took place on 17th July, 1891, when fire broke out on board the 2,591 gross tons Greek steamship, *Eustathios Vlassopulo* which was loading coal at No. 31 Drop, Hendon Dock.

The fire was discovered amongst her bunkers shortly before noon and word was sent to the River Wear Watch, whose manual firefloat stationed in the docks was quickly at the scene with Inspector Lakin in charge. The Borough Fire Brigade under Sub-Inspector Scarf also attended.

In addition to the manual firefloat, the steamtug, *Electric* also went alongside and pumped water into the vessel's holds. It was soon determined that the fire had taken a firm hold in the cargo and it was decided to tow the burning ship into the centre of the dock away from other shipping and shore installations.

Onlookers expecting the arrival of the *Fire Queen* from the river were instead surprised to see the Watch's other manual float being towed through Hendon Gateway into the dock. The steam float was in fact undergoing maintenance with her boilers removed. The two manual engines, their pumps manned by dozens of volunteers, faced a formidable task in dealing with the fire and took several hours to defeat the outbreak.

Afterwards, the *Eustathios Vlassopulo* presented a sorry sight indeed. Many plates in her hull were severely buckled due to the intense heat and her paintwork was scorched and blistered. She had sustained extensive damage amidships and her deck fittings and stores had all been destroyed. Hydraulic cranes discharged the remains of her cargo before she was towed to one of the port's graving docks for lengthy repairs.

FIRES AT SOUTHWICK

Although the official jurisdiction of the River Wear Watch extended upriver only as far as Deptford, it became customary for the River Police to patrol as far as Hylton. In the event of fire, the firefloats would go wherever they were required. Getting to close quarters with outbreaks of fire on shore in the upper reaches often presented problems, especially when the tide was low. Such was the case at Southwick on the north side of the Wear, where dangerous mud banks skirted the riverside.

On 20th March, 1899, a disastrous fire broke out in a machinery shed at J. Priestman and Sons' shipyard, as the result of what was then a common cause, namely the hot end of a rivet falling from a ship under construction.

Personnel from the local Durham County Constabulary and Southwick Urban District Fire Brigade were assisted by the Sunderland Fire Brigade with one of their new horse-drawn fire steamers. Somewhat embarrassingly for the Borough Brigade, as there was no quay at the scene, their engine could not get its forty-five feet of suction hose within reach of the river. The fire, therefore, raged unchecked.

It was then decided to call upon the *Fire Queen*, the request for her services being received at Bodlewell Lane at 6.25 p.m. Manned by Inspector Lakin, Sub-Inspector Humble, Sergeant Peacock, and P.C's Wright and Jennings, the firefloat reached the scene at 7.10 p.m. and immediately commenced work.

A number of difficulties had to be contended with, not the least being the great distance of the steamer from the seat of the outbreak. She was brought as close as possible to the shore and her hose connected to others that had been laid on top of planks resting on the mud flats. Due to the distance involved - some 200 yards - only one jet was used, but to great effect. Utilising an unlimited supply of water, the *Fire Queen* soon had the blaze under control and was almost the sole means of extinguishing the flames and of preventing them from spreading to adjacent buildings.

In 1891, the *Fire Queen* had encountered similar problems in getting to close quarters with a fire at the same yard when the 697 gross tons *S.S. Menapia,* under construction for the Waterford S.S. Co., had been badly damaged on the stocks. The same difficulty had also beset her predecessor, the first *Fire Queen*, in 1874 at G. S. Gulston's shipyard at Southwick.

A strange situation arose in 1900, when about 3 a.m. on 29th December, a destructive fire broke out in the pattern shop at the George Clark engineworks at Low Southwick. Although having been engaged at Priestmans the previous year, the Sunderland Fire Brigade simply stood by and watched this blaze without making any effort to assist the local Southwick Brigade and police.

Apparently no agreement was then in force between Southwick U.D.C. and Sunderland Corporation regarding the deployment of the latter's fire brigade within Southwick. Despite being in telephone communication with their chief officer and Mr. George Clark (jun.) offering to be responsible for payment for their services, the crew of the Sunderland engine did not receive an order to commence pumping and returned to their station after about an hour.

About 4.30 a.m., as the fire raged unabated, it occurred to someone to send for the *Fire Queen* which soon arrived at the quay in charge of Sub-Inspector Humble. Shortly after 5 a.m., two jets had been deployed from the fireboat with dramatic effect. In less than an hour the fire was out with only the smouldering ruins of the pattern shop remaining.

THE ROLE OF SALVOR

For many years, the busy and crowded nature of the River Wear and its docks, together with their sometimes difficult seaward approaches, would occasionally lead to collisions or other accidents befalling shipping using the Port of Sunderland. Sometimes a vessel might founder, blocking a navigation channel or preventing the use of port facilities. On other occasions, a ship holed beneath the waterline would require prompt action to be undertaken to prevent her from sinking before she could be beached or dry docked.

In such instances, the services of the River Wear Watch's steam firefloats proved invaluable to the port and shipowner alike, with the salvage of numerous vessels being accomplished by means of their powerful centrifugal pumps.

There follow accounts of a number of such incidents that took place during the latter years of the Nineteenth Century and at which the *Fire Queen* was prominently engaged in salvage work.

A CHAPTER OF ACCIDENTS

Early in 1888, an extraordinary sequence of accidents, fortunately without loss of life, took place off the Port of Sunderland.

The story began on the morning of Sunday, 29th January, with the arrival of the *S.S. Linden*, owned by R. Thorman of Sunderland. Having arrived from London in ballast, the steamer engaged the Irwing tug, *General Gordon* to tow her into the South Docks via the South Outlet. Amidst a blinding snowstorm, whilst passing between the breakwaters shortly after 8 a.m., heavy seas forced the *Linden's* bow against the Southwest Breakwater roundhead. During efforts to tow her clear, the towline parted and the ship was driven onto rocks and holed.

Within a couple of days the *Linden* had become a complete wreck and, on the instructions of her underwriters, was cut into two and her bow section blown up. Before the channel could be cleared, the presence of the wreck caused great disruption to traffic using the South Outlet as the *S.S. Saltburn*, owned by J. S. Barwick, found to her cost on the night of 6th February.

Whilst proceeding to sea through the South Outlet, laden with coal for Rochefort, she strayed from the channel and struck the remains of the wreck. At first it was thought that no damage had been sustained but, whilst off Hartlepool, the *Saltburn* was found to be making water. Her Captain, William Knott, decided to return to Sunderland, taking a pilot off Seaham.

As she lay off port awaiting tugs, the vessel began to ship more water and it was decided to make a run for the main harbour entrance. Nevertheless, when only a quarter of a mile offshore, the 1,299 gross tons steamer went down by the head and took the ground on the southern approach to the harbour.

Adverse sea conditions caused attempts to refloat the *Saltburn* to be delayed. Owing to her hazardous position, danger lamps were hoisted on her rigging and upon the tug, *General Gordon*, which was stationed astern.

Such precautions were to prove inadequate as, in the early hours of 9th February, a third calamity took place. Inward bound from Hamburg, for a cargo of coal, the *S.S. Pinnas*, owned by J. H. Lorentzen and Co., approached the port with her skipper, Captain Mohr, apparently oblivious to the danger ahead. With great force, the bow of his 1,047 gross tons ship rammed the partially submerged *Saltburn* between her foremast and bridge, remaining fast. The *General Gordon* went to her aid without delay and, leaking badly, the German ship was towed towards the harbour mouth. As had occurred with the *Linden*, the tow rope broke and the *Pinnas* drifted helplessly onto the bar, with her bow to seaward, before sinking on the rocks near the South Pier end.

At the forefront of subsequent attempts to salve the two ships, was the *Fire Queen* under the command of Inspector Lakin. Her pumps worked tirelessly to expel gallons of sea water from the hulls of these stricken vessels after leaks had been temporarily sealed. The *Pinnas* was raised the following morning and beached at Polka's Hole, whilst the *Saltburn* was successfully refloated a day later and towed into harbour. The salvage operations were witnessed by crowds of spectators lining every available vantage point. The exertions of the fireboat together with the shouting of men, hooting of sirens and clouds of dense black smoke from attendant tugs straining to control their charges had combined to form some remarkable scenes.

SALVAGE OF 'S.S. LERO'

A little under two years later, the *Fire Queen* was requisitioned once more to assist another steamer that had run aground on attempting to enter harbour. On this occasion it was the 2,224 gross tons Neptune Steam Navigation Co. Ltd's *Lero* which was in trouble.

About 5 p.m. on Saturday, 18th October, 1890, the vessel, bound from Hamburg to the U.S.A. with general cargo, attempted to enter the port for bunker coals. As she approached the pier ends, strong seas drove her off course and she struck the harbour bar heavily.

Two local tugs, the *Severn* and *Lord Derby* succeeded in getting her off, but on reaching the harbour's outer basin, it was found that water was rushing into her hull near the engine room.

Whilst frogmen toiled to seal the leak, the *Fire Queen*, again under the direction of James Lakin, fought to save the ship. After almost twenty-four hours, the efforts of the fireboat's crew were rewarded, as she had been able to bring the *Lero* to a level trim, sufficient for her to be towed into dry dock to undergo repairs.

COLLISION INVOLVING 'S.S. SURBITON'

Early in the morning of 1st December, 1891, a serious collision occurred off Sunderland involving the 789 gross tons, three-masted screw steamer, *Surbiton* of London and the *S.S. Moray* of Aberdeen.

In dense fog, the *Surbiton* had put to sea from the river at 3.30 a.m., bound for Rochester was a cargo of coal from the Hetton Coal Company. Whilst abeam of the North Eastern Marine Engineworks, Hudson Dock she was in collision with the *Moray* which, having just left the docks by way of the South Outlet, was heading northwards in the opposite direction.

Not being badly damaged, the *Moray* was able to continue her voyage. The *Surbiton*, however, had received extensive damage to her starboard plates opposite the main hatchway, causing sea water to pour through the breach. The ship at once returned to the harbour entrance and was run up close to the North Pier to keep her out of the navigation channel, her head being jammed beneath the pier's protective woodwork.

The *Fire Queen* arrived shortly before 10 a.m. but, due to bad weather, was unable to go alongside to commence pumping operations. Returning later in the day, after efforts had been made to tow the *Surbiton* further across the channel to provide a lee for the firefloat, the *Fire Queen* began pumping and continued to do so whilst some of the steamer's cargo was discharged into lighters. Eventually, at 2 a.m. the following morning, the *Surbiton* was refloated by the steamtugs, *Electric* and *Lord Derby* and towed to the South Dock basin.

Although temporary repairs had been carried out on her damaged hull, these proved ineffective as the vessel foundered in the dock basin about 1 p.m.

The *Fire Queen* was re-engaged and worked throughout the night. Despite most of the *Surbiton's* cargo having been removed and additional pumps having been placed on board, she refused to float on the rising tide. Only the stern section, which was being kept buoyant by the fireboat, remained above the water.

It was not until 5th December that the *Surbiton* was completely refloated, but the saga was still far from being over. Before she could be dry docked, there was still a quantity of cargo to be removed from her holds and she was towed into the South Docks for this purpose. On 9th December, a plate below the waterline gave way and the ship began to sink again. Once more, the *Fire Queen* returned but this time was successful in keeping the collier afloat. The Dockmaster, fearful of what might happen next, then issued orders for the *Surbiton* to be removed from the docks. She was taken into the river and beached on the hard near Commissioners' Quay.

Two days later, it was with great relief that members of the River Wear Watch, going about their duties on the river, saw the patched up *Surbiton* being towed across to Crowns' slipway for repair.

SINKING OF THE 'COUNTY OF DURHAM'

Occasionally, even the best endeavours of the *Fire Queen's* crew could not prevent a ship from sinking. Such was the situation on 25th July, 1896, when the 673 gross tons passenger steamer, *General Havelock*, owned by R. M. Hudson of Sunderland, collided with the 787 gross tons Newcastle registered collier, *County of Durham* in Hudson Dock.

The *General Havelock* had passed through the South Outlet just before noon that day and entered the Sea Lock. As the tide had not then risen sufficiently to allow the lock gates to be opened, the majority of passengers left the ship whilst it waited there. About 2.30 p.m., the dock gates were opened and the *General Havelock* steamed through towards her berth.

To the horror of all concerned, instead of manoeuvring to port, she continued straight ahead towards the *County of Durham* which was lying under the spouts at No. 10 Coal Drop. The passenger ship's steering gear had failed and despite her engines being thrust hard astern, she struck the collier a fearful blow, cutting a huge hole in her side abaft the bridge and tearing open several plates.

The ***County of Durham*** began to sink rapidly and, in the hope of keeping her afloat, the services of the ***Fire Queen*** were requested. As the dock gates from the river were open, little time was wasted in the fireboat arriving at the drops. Pumping was commenced immediately and kept up with great vigour but it soon became manifest that her efforts would be to no avail. In a short time, the collier's stern was beneath the water and Inspector Lakin was forced to give the order for the firefloat to be withdrawn for her own safety.

The ***General Havelock*** had received only relatively slight damage, whilst the ***County of Durham*** was raised four days later and taken to be repaired at J. L. Thompson and Sons' shipyard.

Chapter 7

THE END OF THE LAKIN ERA

(1900 - 1913)

THE COMMISSIONERS LOOK TO THE FUTURE

As the Twentieth Century dawned and the Victorian era drew to a close, the future of the River Wear Watch Commissioners seemed uncertain. Negotiations with the River Wear Commissioners regarding the proposed take-over of the Watch had been dragging on for months. Eventually in March, 1900, with no signs of agreement in sight, the issue was shelved, leaving the Watch Commissioners to contemplate their position once more.

To their credit, the Commissioners did not allow the Watch to stagnate in the hope of alternative means being found of relieving them from their responsibilities. Instead, they looked to the future and set about planning the acquisition of the most modern equipment with which to protect the shipping of the port. The two old manual firefloats, one of which still maintained station, were well overdue for retirement. Although the *Fire Queen*, completed in 1886, was still performing fine work in the river, there was a great need for a second steam fireboat with which to protect the docks. As had frequently been demonstrated in the past, incidents in the docks requiring the attendance of the *Fire Queen* could not be relied upon to occur around high water when the entrance gates from the river were open.

THE 'FIRE KING'

In August, 1905, it was therefore decided to purchase a second steam firefloat, a subcommittee of the River Wear Watch Commission, comprising Captain George Butchart, Mr. John Ness, Mr. J. S. Barwick and Mr. W. A. Watson, being appointed to see the scheme through.

The new fireboat was constructed by Henry Scarr of Hessle-on-Humber at a cost of £2,907 16s. 11d, her twin propelling engines being manufactured and installed by Mr. F. T. Harker of Stockton-on-Tees. Named *Fire King*, she arrived at Sunderland during November, 1906 and entered service following impressive acceptance trials. The Commissioners could feel justifiably proud of their acquisition which was then one of the most powerful of such vessels afloat in the United Kingdom.

With her hull having been constructed from iron, the *Fire King* had an overall length of 60 feet (55 feet between perpendiculars) and a beam of 14 feet. Her maximum draught was 6 feet 6 inches, somewhat deeper than had been originally specified. Her twin propulsion engines, guaranteed to give a speed of 8 knots, each had cylinders of 7 and 12 inches diameter with an 8 inch stroke, working at 140 pounds per square inch.

Shand, Mason and Co. of London supplied the boiler and pumping machinery which was capable of pumping at the rate of 2,200 gallons per minute, twice the capacity of the existing *Fire Queen*.

In addition to a large gunmetal monitor fitted to the roof of the forward accommodation, which could direct a 2½ inch jet of water 220 feet skywards, the *Fire King* was equipped with nine delivery outlets capable of simultaneous operation. Three 6 inch suction pipes were also provided for salvage purposes. Nearly one mile of hose was supplied, together with all necessary branches, nozzles, breaking pieces, etc., by J. McGregor and Co. of Dundee.

On entering service, the new firefloat was stationed in the river, being berthed alongside one of the old manual engines, which had been relegated to the role of floating depot. The *Fire Queen* was, at the same time, transferred to the South Docks and the second manual float that had been moored in the docks was sold for £60. Never again would be witnessed the spectacle of dozens of men, stripped to the waist, rhythmically working the pumps of those manual engines, their perspiring faces reflecting the glow of a burning vessel.

In fact, the last recorded use of a manual float by the Watch had been on 25th July, 1905, when the dock engine had assisted the *Fire Queen* and Borough Brigade in quelling a serious outbreak of fire at H. Moller and Co's timberyard, Hendon Dock.

Little time would elapse before the *Fire King* was given the opportunity to prove herself and she was frequently in action during the early years of her career.

Between 1907 and 1911, six alarming fires broke out on board ships in the port, at which the *Fire King* or *Fire Queen*, or sometimes both, rendered invaluable service:

14th Feb., 1907	**S.S. El Argentino, North Eastern Marine, Hudson Dock**
7th Mar., 1907	**S.S. Ella Sayer, East Quay, Hendon Dock**
14th Oct., 1908	**S.S. Castle Eden, Lambton Drops, River Wear**
28th May, 1910	**S.S. Lavinia Westoll, Austins' Pontoon, River Wear**
6th Apr., 1911	**S.S. Lysaker, Lambton Drops, River Wear**
9th Aug., 1911	**S.S. Craigearn, Laing Wharf, Hudson Dock**

Accounts of three of these incidents follow:

ESPARTO GRASS FIRE ON BOARD 'S.S. ELLA SAYER'

About 5 a.m. on 7th March, 1907, a fire was discovered on board the Newcastle registered steamship, *Ella Sayer*, owned by the Ella Sayer Steamship Co. Ltd. of Newcastle, which was berthed at East Quay, Hendon Dock. The 2,549 gross tons vessel had arrived two days earlier from Tripoli with a cargo of esparto grass.

The fire involved bales of the esparto grass in the after part of No. 2 hold and the bunkers 'tween decks. The Dockmaster, Captain Leask soon had a party of R.W.C. gatemen and watermen at work fighting the blaze with a water jet. On arrival of the Borough Fire Brigade's horse-drawn steamer under Superintendent Yelland, the dockmen were experiencing difficulty extinguishing the flames which seemed to have taken hold well down in the middle of the bales. The fire had apparently been burning for some time and was extensive and spreading. The *Fire Queen* arrived shortly afterwards, some time later being joined by the *Fire King* from the river, both floats being under the command of Inspector Lakin.

By 8 a.m., no fewer than eight jets were at work on the holds and bunkers but these seemed to have little effect due to difficulties in getting right onto the burning mass. Eventually, a small plate in the deck was pulled up, through which aperture the men were able to work more effectually. By this time, owing to the combustible nature of the cargo, the fire had spread considerably and it was feared that the only way to save the ship would be to scuttle her. This extreme measure proved unnecessary as the morning progressed as by use of numerous jets, the efforts of the firefighters began to show signs of success. The heat was so extreme that it had actually caused the foredeck near the port bunker to buckle. Flooding in the vessel's fore hold had caused her to become very low in the water but the fire had been prevented from spreading to the after holds, Nos. 3 and 4, thereby saving the cargo contained there. At noon, although the fire was still raging in the 'tween deck bunkers and under the chartroom, it was slowly being extinguished.

Soon afterwards, the Borough Brigade left the scene, followed by the *Fire King*, leaving only the *Fire Queen* in attendance. The fire was by then completely under control and practically extinguished, with the bales only smouldering in places.

At the height of the operation, one jet from the horse-drawn steamer, one R.W.C. hydrant jet, two jets from the *Fire Queen* and six from the *Fire King* had been deployed. Firefighters had been present for over eight hours and damage valued in excess of £1,000 had been caused.

MEN ENTOMBED IN FIRE ON BOARD 'S.S. LAVINIA WESTOLL'

Three years later, on 28th May, 1910, the *Fire King* was present at a dramatic fire on board the 3,151 gross tons *Lavinia Westoll*, owned by James Westoll of Sunderland, and assisted in saving two workmen from a terrifying death.

Four men had been working in the forepeak of the steamer which was undergoing repairs on Austins' Pontoon near Wearmouth Bridge, when a hot rivet had accidentally fallen into a pile of oakum which immediately burst into flames, emitting dense volumes of smoke. Two of the men had managed to escape but the others, named Peter Mills and Jack Patterson, had found themselves trapped by the smoke and flames. Their colleagues outside, appreciating their workmates' predicament, pumped air through lines, pushed through rivet holes, which Mills and Patterson held to their mouths to enable them to breathe.

The Borough Fire Brigade, under the command of Superintendent Yelland, attended the scene, being joined shortly afterwards by the *Fire King*. Despite the use of a primitive form of breathing apparatus, the firemen were unable to gain access to the forepeak. As the condition of the entombed men was deteriorating rapidly, it was decided to cut a hole through the bulkhead from the fore hold into the peak.

After having been trapped for over an hour, the two workmen were eventually released in an extremely shocked and exhausted state. The firefighters were then able to turn their full attention to extinguishing the fire.

'S.S. CRAIGEARN' - ANOTHER ESPARTO FIRE

A fierce conflagration broke out on board the steamer, *Craigearn* at the South Docks at 10 p.m. on 9th August, 1911 and raged until the early hours of the following morning.

Belonging to Messrs. Bigart, Fulton and Grier of Cardiff, the 3,013 gross tons ship had arrived in the Wear from Sfax in Tunisia, laden with esparto grass which she was discharging at the Laing Wharf in Hudson Dock. Although stevedores had been working her until 5 p.m. that day, when the hatches had been closed, it had not been until five hours later that the fire had been discovered.

As the hatches of the after holds were hastily removed, a huge tongue of flame burst forth to a height of twenty feet. The Borough Fire Brigade was at once informed, arriving only eight minutes later with two horse-drawn steamers. The flames were found to have taken a firm hold of the combustible material in Nos. 3 and 4 holds, which were laden to just below the lower deck, part of the cargo having been discharged earlier.

The *Fire Queen*, commanded by Sub-Inspector Humble, also arrived expeditiously and in a short period a great volume of water was being pumped into the holds. Numerous jets fed from dock hydrants were also got into play but the flames seemed to defy all attempts to subdue them and continued to shoot out pertinaciously. By this time the heat and pungent smoke were becoming unbearable for the firefighters who had to remain close to the mouth of the holds. The deck plates became fearfully hot through the fire beneath, the interior of the holds being akin to roaring furnaces. The firemen were compelled to play a jet upon the deck to cool it for their feet. As the fire continued to burn ferociously, fears were entertained that plates in the ship's hull would buckle and that a dangerous leak would be sprung. Fortunately this did not occur.

There was, however, great danger of the flames spreading to the engine room and the fire did actually extend to a store there, where it ignited a quantity of waste and rubbish. A jet was quickly put to work on this as tanks containing about 100 gallons of paraffin were stored on the other side of the engine room and the area around the bulkhead was becoming red hot. Fortunately this outbreak was soon put out, allowing firefighting resources to be again fully directed against the burning grass in the holds.

Valuable aid arrived at 1 a.m. in the form of the *Fire King* which, ranging alongside the burning ship, soon had four large water jets playing into the holds. At this time, it was roughly computed that about 4,000 gallons per minute were being poured below and the water level could be seen steadily rising. The men were compelled to stand on planks and hatches, so hot was the deck. There were still fears of the *Craigearn* springing a leak and sinking in the dock but they were not fulfilled. Gradually, the flames were steadily subdued and by 4 a.m. they were totally out.

Great praise was bestowed upon the firefighters of both the Watch and Borough Brigade for the manner in which they had worked in the most arduous conditions. Steel plates on the top deck were afterwards found to have buckled due to the intense heat. Damage caused by the fire was later estimated at £7,000, the cause of which was attributed to spontaneous combustion.

Again, the perils associated with the importation of esparto, a commodity used widely in Sunderland's extensive rope making industry, had been vividly demonstrated.

THE THIRD 'FIRE QUEEN'

By 1910, the condition of the *Fire Queen's* hull and boilers was such that repairs had become uneconomical. It was therefore determined that a new fireboat would be built to replace her, the name *Fire Queen* again being chosen for the new vessel.

Owing to the success of the *Fire King*, Henry Scarr of Hessle was again selected to construct the new firefloat at a total price of £4,159 0s.9d. Although designed and equipped in a similar manner to the *Fire King*, the new *Fire Queen* was somewhat larger and more powerful, also being built of steel.

Her twin driving engines, each with a cylinder capacity of 7 and 14 inches with an 18 inch stroke, were supplied by the Vauxhall Hydraulic Engineering Co. of Luton. Shand, Mason and Co. provided the pumping engines which had the capability of pumping water at the rate of 2,600 gallons per minute.

The craft had a length of 65 feet, a beam of 15 feet and a moulded depth of 7 feet. Her maximum draught of 6 feet made her more suitable for use in the river than the *Fire King*.

The *Fire Queen* arrived in the Wear late in 1911 and after undergoing trials and receiving her final coat of paint, replaced the *Fire King* as the river fireboat early the following year. The Fire King was then transferred to the South Docks and the old *Fire Queen* sold for £350.

CRIME ON THE WEAR

During the early years of the Twentieth Century, crime was still widespread in the Port of Sunderland. In 1910, for instance, the River Wear Police charged seventy-seven persons with having committed felonies. In February of that year, the River Wear Commissioners expressed their concern over the amount of theft and pilfering which was taking place in the docks and on the river. It appeared that, on many occasions, the police were experiencing difficulties in persuading anyone to prosecute the offenders. There were always loafers about the docks, but the police had no powers to prevent them from being there, the docks then being a public thoroughfare.

The following year, Rear Admiral Hansen of the Royal Danish Navy complained bitterly that, whilst a passenger on a steamship at Wearmouth Drops, there had been no suitable places to disembark. In reply, the Wearmouth Coal Company had written *"... It is a lamentable fact that this river is so infested by thieves who carry out their nefarious practice from small boats, that it is positively dangerous to loose property lying on the quays to make easy landing places and we have purposely avoided doing so."*

Crews of visiting vessels also took a dim view of thieves and occasionally meted out their own justice before calling the police. In one case, in 1905, a larcenist caught rifling a tug's cabin was beaten senseless before being lashed to the mast to await the arrival of the Watch.

FATAL STABBING AT No. 21 STAITH

During the early hours of Sunday, 20th November, 1910, the 3,023 gross tons British registered steamship, **Lynfield**, owned by the Field Steamship Co. Ltd. of Stockton-on-Tees lay beneath the coal drops at No. 21 Staith on the west side of Hudson Dock. Although all of the officers and most of the crew were asleep in their bunks prior to the vessel's departure, all was not quiet.

Going about his business on the ship was George Harvey, a 40 years old master rigger, whose job it was to act as stevedore and ensure that the vessel was made ready for sea. A local tugboatman, John Swinhoe who had been engaged as ship's watchman whilst the vessel was in port was also present.

About 12.20 a.m. three men came on board. One was a crewman, another one of the ship's firemen and the third, a local 51 years old seaman named Benjamin Adair Caldwell who had no connection with the ship. All three, who were drunk and rowdy made their way into the forecastle where Caldwell, who was drinking from a bottle of beer, began singing loudly. He then said that he was going to the sailor's side of the ship to get some whiskey but returned shortly afterwards with a seaman named Handy who, on learning that Caldwell was not sailing with the ship, demanded that he went ashore and allow the crew to have some sleep. Caldwell took no notice of this request, whereupon George Harvey arrived and ordered him to leave the vessel.

Again, Caldwell declined to go. Harvey then seized Caldwell's collar and pulled him out of the forecastle before pushing him along the deck towards the gangway. A struggle then ensued, with Harvey calling for the assistance of the watchman, Swinhoe who unfortunately did not hear his shouts. Eventually, with some difficulty, Harvey was able to manhandle the struggling Caldwell across the gangway onto the quayside. Swinhoe, who by then had been attracted to the commotion, made his way down the gangway towards the two men. As he did so, Harvey cried "He has stabbed me!" Caldwell then ran off, pursued by Swinhoe and was detained near No. 19 Staith after being halted with a well aimed brick thrown by the latter. Within five minutes, P.C. Osborne Edward Sandy of the River Wear Watch who had been called from the Dock Police Station arrived and placed Caldwell under arrest. A thorough search of the prisoner and the surrounding area revealed no trace of a knife or other weapon.

Meanwhile, George Harvey was bleeding profusely from a deep stab wound to his lower left abdomen and was subsequently admitted to the Royal Infirmary in a critical condition.

Caldwell was taken to the Central Police Station, Gillbridge Avenue where he was charged by P.C. Sandy with 'cutting and wounding' to which he replied "That's all right, but that won't do."

On Monday, 21st November, Caldwell appeared before the magistrates at Sunderland Police Court charged with the offence and was remanded in custody for one week. The accused stated that he was unable to remember any of the events which had taken place at the docks.

Despite being subjected to surgery, Harvey lost his fight for life around 6 p.m. on the Monday night, his death being due to heart failure and peritonitis. In the presence of the prisoner, a dying declaration had been obtained from Harvey at the Infirmary in which he stated that Caldwell had been responsible for his injuries. P.C. Sandy later preferred a charge against the accused of 'causing death by stabbing' to which he answered "I cannot remember coming from the ship at all. I only remember drinking whiskey and beer from a white cup."

An inquest was held into the circumstances of Harvey's death on Tuesday, 22nd November at the Infirmary before Coroner Burnicle and a jury. After the evidence had been heard, the Coroner directed the jury on the options which they should consider in the case. The Coroner, himself, clearly favoured a verdict of 'manslaughter' as opposed to 'wilful murder' as he believed that the circumstances in which Caldwell had been hustled off the *Lynfield* had led to the deceased's injuries being inflicted in the heat of the struggle without legal malice. After having retired for only four minutes, the jury came back and returned a verdict of 'manslaughter.' Caldwell was duly committed to stand his trial at the next Durham Assizes and was taken back to the police station.

Evidently senior police officers were not in agreement with the verdict and P.C. Sandy was instructed to prefer a charge of 'wilful murder' against Caldwell. On being charged accordingly, he replied "I thought they said manslaughter. Will they hang me? I am sorry such a thing has happened to me. It is the first time I have been in a court for trial."

The trial of Benjamin Adair Caldwell took place at Durham Assizes on 2nd March, 1911 before Mr. Justice Avory. Mr. C. F. Lowenthal and Mr. Newbolt prosecuted on behalf of the Crown and a Mr. Hoare represented the defendant who entered a plea of 'not guilty' to the charge of 'wilful murder'.

Although not denying that he had inflicted the fatal wound upon Harvey, the defendant based his defence upon his lack of malice and intent to kill or inflict grievous bodily harm due to his intoxicated state; also upon the fact that he had been provoked by the rough treatment received from the deceased and that the stabbing had occurred before passions had time to cool.

In summing up, his Lordship stated that if the jury found at the time of commission of the act the prisoner was exceedingly drunk, they might come to the conclusion that being drunk he did not appreciate the natural consequence of stabbing a man in the stomach would either be to kill him or inflict grievous bodily harm. That, he believed was the only way in which drunkenness could be considered in reducing the charge from murder to manslaughter.

The jury, however, was not swayed and returned a verdict of 'guilty' to wilful murder but added a strong recommendation for mercy on the grounds of there having been no premeditation.

Before passing sentence, the judge asked Caldwell if he had anything to say. In an emotional address to the court, the accused emphasised his previous good character and drew attention to the conflicting nature of some of the evidence which had been given at the inquest. He also claimed to have a witness, a seaman from the ship *Rhodesia*, who could testify as to the violence used against him by the deceased. In conclusion he stated "I wish to give my life to atone for the sin I have committed."

His Lordship intimated that the jury had done their duty and had returned a proper verdict in accordance with the evidence. He therefore had no alternative but to don the black cap and sentence Caldwell to death, heedless to the protests and piteous groans of the defendant. The judge did, however, offer some hope to Caldwell by stating that the jury's recommendation for mercy would be forwarded to the proper quarter and that he concurred in their recommendation.

On 13th March, 1911, as Caldwell awaited his fate in Durham Prison, the Court of Criminal Appeal sat to hear an application for leave to appeal against his conviction. The Lord

Chief Justice, after considering the application, stated that there were no grounds upon which the original verdict could be reduced to manslaughter and therefore refused the appeal.

Four days later, the Home Secretary announced that he had commuted the death sentence imposed upon Caldwell to one of penal servitude for life.

So ended another tragic episode in which the River Wear Watch had played a part and which served to highlight the potential for drunken seamen to use extreme violence.

BIZARRE DROWNING CASES

Drownings continued to be commonplace in the early 1900's, sometimes being attended by bizarre circumstances.

In 1906, two small boys were fishing for crabs off the Panns Ferry landing when they fell into the river. One was drowned and the other, after having been rescued, ran home without telling his parents what had happened. Later that night his playmate's parents, concerned that their son had not arrived home, visited the home of the other boy. On being awakened and asked where his friend was, he merely replied "Oh, he's in the river."

Around midnight on 9th April, 1910, River P.C's Elstob and Avery were patrolling in their coble when they were informed that the watchman from the *S.S. Abchurch*, lying at Lambton Drops, had just fallen into the river and had been drowned. Whilst searching for his body they heard shouts from the nearby Hetton Staiths. Thinking that the watchman's body had been sighted, the officers made their way there only to learn that a Norwegian seaman had just been lost after falling overboard from his ship.

Occasionally, black humour crept into what was otherwise a tragic event. A wily old river constable named Thomas Hunter was once giving evidence at an inquest into the death of a man whose body he had recovered from the river. Although a half-brick and two pieces of pantile had been found in the deceased's pockets, they had not been heavy enough to keep the body down in the water. The coroner, rather perplexed by this, asked the officer why he thought they had been in the pockets. After pausing a moment, P.C. Hunter quick-wittedly replied "Well, the' couldn't 'ave bin pu'rin 'ees pockets t' keep 'im afloat."

Poor mastery of the English language cost the life of a German seaman in the South Docks one dark night. River P.C. Johnson had met the man, who asked for direction to his ship, the *Annie*, lying at No. 19 Drop. "You go down here and turn left," directed the officer, before bidding him goodnight. Seconds later, P.C. Johnson heard a loud splash. The seaman had turned right.

One afternoon, a riot almost broke out after onlookers crossing Wearmouth Bridge witnessed what they perceived as an extreme case of 'police brutality.' Members of the Watch had, in fact, recovered the badly decomposed body of a man from upriver and were, as was then the practice, towing it behind their steam launch to the Bodlewell Lane Ferry landing so that it could be removed to the nearby mortuary in Low Street. Some of those on the bridge actually thought that the River Police were towing a prisoner behind their launch and soon rumours to this effect had spread like wildfire down to the East End of the town.

As the boat was being made fast at the ferry landing, its crew was confronted by an angry mob who demanded that they release their 'prisoner.' Many would not be convinced that it was a corpse which was in police custody and to prove the point the officer in charge ordered that it be hauled ashore in full view of the crowd. Needless to say, the sight that met their eyes had the desired effect as men, women and children took to their heels, allowing the police to get on with their task.

MYSTERIOUS DEATH OF INSPECTOR JAMES LAKIN

After having served the River Wear Watch for almost half a century, their genial old Inspector, James Lakin met his death in 1913 in the most suspicious of circumstances.

It had become the habit of the old man, who some years previously had lost the sight of an eye whilst fighting a fire, to stand by the riverside at the Bodlewell Lane Ferry landing before the night shift paraded for duty. He would stand, gazing into the night, watching for anything untoward and perhaps reflecting upon his long career and the changes he had witnessed on the river.

Such was the case on Sunday, 23rd February, but on this occasion the Inspector failed to return to the police station, only a stone's throw away from the ferry landing. Inside the station, Lakin's colleagues became concerned and immediately organised a search after finding that he was not at the landing.

At 2 a.m. the following morning, River P.C's Middleton and Gifford, whilst searching in their coble saw a body floating face down in the water, only yards from the ferry landing. Their worst fears were confirmed as they lifted the corpse on board and found it to be that of their supervisor. The constables noticed that Lakin had a wound above his left eye and abrasions to his nose. With heavy hearts, the officers moored up and entered the station to report their discovery.

An inquest into Lakin's death was conducted before Coroner Burnicle at the Seamen's Mission later that day. Evidence was submitted that Lakin had been suffering from bronchial trouble and had not been in the best of health for some time. As there was no evidence to show how he came to be in the river, the jury returned a verdict of "found drowned." It was surmised that the Inspector had perhaps been taken ill or had slipped on the slimy steps causing him to fall into the water, striking his head in the process.

Lakin's funeral was held at Bishopwearmouth Cemetery on 26th February. As the cortege, led by the Borough Police band, made its way there, tokens of respect and appreciation for the dead Inspector were everywhere to be seen. Shop and house blinds were drawn and dense crowds lined the route with heads bowed, the men with hats and capes removed.

Soon after the funeral, however, events began to take a sinister turn. Rumours reached the ears of the C.I.D. that Inspector Lakin had intervened in a disturbance in Bodlewell Lane earlier in the day on which he had disappeared from the ferry landing. He had become involved in a run-in with those involved in the trouble, but eventually they had dispersed. It was suspected that those concerned had returned that night and attacked Lakin, either knocking him down and throwing him into the river, or striking him, causing him to fall in. It was suggested that his facial injuries had been caused with a knuckle-duster or similar weapon.

Despite extensive enquiries being conducted by the C.I.D., it was never discovered whether the rumours of foul play had any foundation. Certainly, no-one could ever imagine anyone wishing to harm an old man who was so much loved by everyone and who, before retiring at night, would seek out the homeless along the riverside, bringing them pennies for tea or a bed for the night.

APPOINTMENT OF INSPECTOR JOHN ROCHFORD

Pending a successor to Lakin being appointed, Sub-Inspector William Humble, a long and faithful servant of the Commissioners, took charge of the Watch. In all likelihood, had it not been for his advancing years, the Commissioners would have been content to promote him to the rank of inspector. In the event, forty-four years old John William Arthur Rochford, Inspector of the Manchester Ship Canal Dock Company Police, secured the post.

Had Rochford's wife had any say in the matter, they would have returned to Manchester on the next train after arriving in Sunderland. On leaving the Central Station, Rochford and his family began to make their way down the High Street towards the East End. As they did so, Mrs. Rochford became increasingly uneasy after seeing the squalor of that part of town and demanded to turn back at once. Meanwhile they were met by Sub-Inspector Humble, whose friendly welcome and assertions that things weren't as bad as they seemed, somewhat reassured her and led to a change of heart. In fact, she subsequently took up employment as matron at Bodlewell Lane Police Station.

John Rochford was to become, in his own right, as well respected on Wearside as Lakin before him. A native of Bristol, Rochford had joined the Manchester Dock Force in 1896, being promoted to sergeant in 1900 and to inspector in 1905. He was a man with considerable experience of shipping, having been engaged on all parts of the thirty-six miles of Ship Canal between Manchester and Eastham, on patrol, firefighting and salvage duties.

Before joining the police, he had undertaken a most interesting military career, having seen action with the East Yorkshire Regiment in the West Indies, South Africa and Egypt, being principally engaged in garrison and military police duties. During his service in South Africa, he had been employed as orderly to Major General Baden-Powell, then Captain and Military Secretary at Capetown and had also taken part in the first Bechuanaland Expedition of 1891. In Egypt, Rochford had been in charge of the river boat patrol of Memondah Canal at Alexandria, his duties having included the prevention of smuggling by native vessels coming down the Nile.

With the clouds of war now looming, any further thoughts of transferring the powers and responsibilities of the Watch Commissioners were forgotten for the time being. With a fine pair of firefloats and a first rate Inspector in command, the Watch prepared itself for what was to come.

Chapter 8

THE GREAT WAR PERIOD

(1914 - 1918)

On 4th August, 1914, Great Britain declared war upon Germany. Throughout the following four years, Sunderland was to contribute much of its manpower to the war effort, both at home and abroad.

During the war, the Wear shipyards were at their busiest and despite a general decrease in the volume of trade handled by the port, the River Wear and its docks were very active places indeed.

WAR RESTRICTIONS

In the eyes of the Government, security of port installations was paramount. As the war progressed, rumours of invasion became rife amongst the country's population. Strict orders, under the Defence of the Realm Regulations, were drawn up by the military authorities, placing severe restrictions upon vessels using the Port of Sunderland, curtailing the use of lights and prohibiting access to the South Docks by members of the public. Although admittance to the docks was to be restored after the war, permanent closure of their landward entrance to the general public would be re-imposed in 1923 as a crime prevention measure.

Pilotage for inward bound vessels (with some exceptions) became compulsory and navigation into the South Docks was permitted only from the river during daylight hours, the South Outlet being closed for the duration. No vessel was allowed to proceed upriver or into the docks until cleared to do so by H.M. Customs' officials and all craft were required to reply promptly when challenged by sentries.

The task of assisting the Borough Police and Military in enforcing these regulations fell upon the River Wear Watch. Its members, as the war continued, charged scores of persons with contravening the provisions of the new directives. In addition, numerous 'undesirables' were apprehended under the Aliens Act, many of whom were subsequently deported. The police, with the Special Constabulary, carried out many of the duties which were to be undertaken during the 1939 - 1945 conflict by civil defence organisations, such as wardens, air raid warnings, blackout inspectors and fireguards. By the end of the war, due to the additional responsibilities placed upon the force, the Watch's establishment would stand at thirty-two, the highest ever during its history.

From the early stages of the war, the Chief Constable directed that foot beats in the South Docks would be worked at the half-hour, each way, as follows:

Northwest Beat: From Gladstone Bridge to the Dock Police Station.
Southwest Beat: From the Dock Police Station to Hendon Bridge.
East Beat: From Gladstone Bridge to the Laing Warehouse.

In imposing orders upon shipping using the port, Brigadier General Baylay, Commanding Officer of the Tyne Defences, warned that any failure to comply would make vessels liable to be fired upon.

'S.S. STARTFORTH' FIRED UPON IN WEAR BY TERRITORIAL ARMY

The declaration of war was only five days old when a sensational incident occurred on the River Wear, demonstrating the seriousness of Baylay's warning.

About 10 p.m. on 9th August, 1914, the 167 gross tons 'scotch collier,' *S.S. Startforth,* inward bound from Alloa, was heading upriver with cargo for Fenwick's Brewery when she was challenged by a Territorial Army sentry posted on Thornhill Quay. With no response apparently being forthcoming from the vessel, the guard was turned out. After firing two shots across her bows, the soldiers then continued to rake the elderly steamer with gunfire. Miraculously, no fatalities were occasioned, although the captain, Matthew Ross, was slightly injured and a crewman, James Holmes Jackson, received serious wounds.

The *Startforth's* crew protested that the sentry's challenge had in fact been answered and pointed out that it was impossible to stop a ship instantly.

Although the incident led to questions being asked in the House of Commons and to a thorough investigation being conducted by military authorities, there can be no doubt that the episode served as a dire warning to the masters of other ships to exercise extreme caution in the future.

DETECTIVE SERGEANT GEORGE ROYAL - ALIEN ENEMY?

Vigorous enforcement of wartime regulations, requiring aliens to register with the police, and the prevailing anti-German sentiment in the country, combined to destroy the career of one of the River Wear Watch's most valued servants - Detective Sergeant George Royal.

Royal had been appointed as a constable on 6th June, 1907 and in less than seven years had been promoted to the rank of detective sergeant. His ability to converse in no fewer than five languages made him ideally suited to this unique position within the force, which entailed the investigation of crimes on board vessels of all nationalities visiting the port.

On 5th September, 1914, however, Royal's life began to fall apart around him as he stood before the magistrates at Sunderland Police Court, charged that "he being an alien, did unlawfully fail to register under the Aliens Registration Order."

The fact that he was an alien was indisputable, with Royal pleading guilty to the offence which was, as his solicitor, Edward Bell, termed it, "technical in nature." Royal's main problem was that the prosecution believed him to be a German subject, a fact that he strenuously denied.

Although having always considered himself an Englishman, Royal stated that he had been born about 1872 in British territorial waters, on board a Dutch ship, during a voyage from London to the Brazils. He claimed that his mother was a Dutch woman, the daughter of the ship's captain, and that his father was an Englishman, named William Royal, a London clerk. He had, however, never maintained contact with his father and knew nothing about him. He said that he had been put ashore in Holland together with his mother, before being brought up in Florida, U.S.A. by his mother's sister, eventually coming to England at the age of fourteen.

Despite his belief that he was a British subject, Royal had become uneasy on the outbreak of war and decided to resolve the issue of his nationality conclusively. Accordingly, he had sought advice from Mr. Bell who contacted the Home Office on his behalf. The Home Office had suggested that Royal apply to become a naturalised British citizen. As a result, papers had been drawn up and forwarded to the Home Office. Unfortunately for Royal, his application had still been pending upon his arrest as an alien.

Evidence was given that Royal had made conflicting statements to the police concerning his place of birth and nationality, but of greater significance, anonymous information - at that time not verified - had come to light relating to a man of German origin, named Rufus Royal, who was alleged to be the defendant's brother.

Despite the protests of Mr. Bell, George Royal was remanded in custody to allow for further enquiries to be made.

On 2nd September, 1914, he again appeared before the magistrates for the full hearing of his case and faced the additional charge that "he being an alien enemy, did reside in a prohibited area without a permit from the Registration Officer."

The Chief Constable, William Carter stated that the question of Royal's nationality had first arisen just after the outbreak of war, when certain anonymous letters had been received by his office alleging Royal to be a German subject. Mr. Carter testified that Royal had persistently maintained that he was not an alien and had no connection with Germany.

He had, however, later changed his story when confronted with the fact that Rufus Royal had been arrested at London. The defendant had admitted for the first time that he was an alien and that Rufus was his half brother.

Inspector Pinchen of the Borough Police then gave evidence that he had searched Royal's home and had found his shipping papers and discharge book, together with his marriage certificate. These documents gave his place of birth as Faversham, Kent and the marriage certificate showed his real Christian name to be Gustav. Royal stated that he had always given Faversham as his place of birth - presumably as this was the nearest place to where his birth on board the ship had taken place.

He had explained that before his marriage in 1897 to a Mary Larkin at Hartlepool Parish Church, he had written to his mother who was then living in Germany (having married a German citizen), requesting details of his father. It was then that he had been informed that his father was William Royal and that his own real name was Gustav.

The court was told that the German husband of Royal's mother bore the surname, Rohl and that Rufus Royal was the legitimate son of their marriage. Although initially having denied that he had been to Germany since working at sea, Royal now admitted that he had visited his mother there twice since joining the River Police. He also asserted that he had not had any contact with his half brother, Rufus.

The magistrates, however, must have found it difficult to believe that the similarity between Royal's surname and that of his mother's German spouse was purely coincidental, especially as Rufus had also adopted Royal as his surname. The prosecution went to great lengths to show that Rufus Royal was well known to the defendant and that they were brothers, not merely half brothers as had been claimed. Additionally, it was contended that George Royal had far greater connection with Germany than he was admitting to.

River Wear Watch colleagues and others were brought to give evidence that Rufus had been to Sunderland on several occasions and had been introduced to them by the defendant as his brother. It became clear that George and Rufus had lived together for a time and the latter had been secretary of the Sunderland Branch of the Sailors' and Firemen's Union. Inspector Rochford testified that Rufus had visited George at the police station only some six months earlier, on which occasion they appeared to have fallen out. Some witnesses alleged that the defendant had told them that his home was in Germany and a retired master mariner told the court that whilst George Royal had been employed as a seaman, he had been given permission to stay over in Germany to visit relatives.

Overall, the evidence against Royal was quite damning. There were too many discrepancies in what he had told investigating officers during several interviews. The testimonies of the witnesses tended to show that he was guilty of prevarication and there was every indication that Rufus was, in fact, his brother.

The magistrates had to decide whether Royal had, as he claimed, been born on a ship to an English father named William Royal, or if he was the son of a German named Rohl. Despite Royal's assertions that the former was true, the magistrates chose to believe the latter and he was ultimately convicted of both charges.

There was no dispute as to the hitherto excellent character of Royal, his superiors speaking highly of him. Undoubtedly he had been embroiled in circumstances beyond his control and had he been forthright from the beginning, he may have been treated with greater leniency than was to be the case. As it was, he was sentenced to six month's imprisonment and to be deported on his release.

Had the River Wear Watch a potential enemy agent in their midst, or was George Royal just an unfortunate individual whose past caught up with him in the lamentable circumstances of war? The truth of the matter will probably never be known. To which country Royal was deported, or what afterwards became of him unfortunately cannot be ascertained.

THE NEW STEAM LAUNCH, 'PATROL'

By 1914, the steam launch, *Patrol*, built in 1896, had reached the end of her useful working life. Consequently, in November of that year, a new steam launch was ordered from Mr. F. T. Harker of Stockton-on-Tees at a cost of £330. It was not until 1917 that the new launch was delivered, the delay presumably being attributable to heavy wartime production demands. The Commissioners were only too pleased to part with their £330, as they had already spent £250 on the hire of a launch since the demise of the original *Patrol*.

It was decided to transfer the name, *Patrol* to the new craft which, with a length of 32 feet and a beam of 6 feet 6 inches, was somewhat larger than her predecessor.

FREDERICK CRAWLEY APPOINTED SUPERINTENDENT

In 1915, Superintendent William Carter retired and was replaced by Frederick Crawley, then aged only thirty-five, the Chief Constable of Lincoln City Police. Although the substantial part of his duties would relate to his position as Chief Constable of Sunderland Borough Police, he would be responsible for rationalising the Watch and overseeing a number of innovations.

ENEMY ACTION AGAINST SUNDERLAND

During the Great War, many vessels were lost or damaged through enemy action within sight of the Port of Sunderland, with the River Police being actively engaged in assisting survivors on being landed there. Sunderland, itself, was subjected to a number of Zeppelin air raids during the war, the most severe occurring on the night of 1st April, 1916, when twenty-two people died and 105 were injured. Due to press censorship and the absence of River Wear Watch occurrence books for this period, the impact of the raid upon the Watch's resources is not known.

What would probably have been their greatest test was thankfully denied to the force. The threat of bombardment from the sea, such as had befallen Scarborough, Hartlepool and Whitby, was very real and came close to actually taking place during 1916. On 19th August, that year, the German High Seas Fleet sailed on a planned raid to bombard Sunderland but the Admiralty, becoming cognisant of German intentions, ordered the Royal Naval Grand Fleet to put to sea in force. The Germans soon became aware of the Grand Fleet's intentions and not wishing another encounter, as at Jutland, returned to harbour, not venturing out again until the surrender.

CAPTAIN GEORGE BUTCHART

Captain George Butchart, one of the most ardent of the River Wear Watch Commissioners and highly respected shipowners of Sunderland, died on 20th October, 1916, aged seventy-three years. Having been elected as a Watch Commissioner in 1890, he had for some years been the chairman of the Commission until 1912, when he was appointed treasurer, a post he held until his death. His most notable achievements on behalf of the Watch included his tireless work in connection with the acquisition of the two steam launches and the *Fire King* and *Fire Queen*.

Butchart had devoted most of his life to maritime affairs and was to be sorely missed by his colleagues and acquaintances. Having served his apprenticeship at sea, he had become an officer on ships belonging to Mr. E. T. Gourley, M.P. and afterwards on vessels of Glover Bros. of London, for whom, as a captain, he traded to China for eight or nine years. In 1882, after prior employment with Porteous and Senior of London, he entered the field of shipowning, carrying out his business from West Sunniside, Sunderland.

As well as holding office with the Watch Commission, Captain Butchart had, for twenty years, been a shipowners' representative on the Board of the River Wear Commission, a member of the local Pilotage Board and Lloyds' Agent for the Sunderland District for some fifteen years.

RECOGNITION OF BRAVERY OF
SUB INSPECTOR WILLIAM HUMBLE

It is a lamentable fact that the efforts of the Watch in saving human life often went unrewarded. This situation was somewhat righted at the quarterly meeting of the Watch Commissioners on 9th November, 1916, when Sub Inspector William Humble was presented with the Honorary Testimonial of the Royal Humane Society for, on 26th August, 1916, having gone to the rescue of two boys who were in imminent danger of drowning in the River Wear and gallantly saving their lives.

In making the presentation, the chairman of the Commissioners congratulated Sub Inspector Humble for having been awarded the testimonial and for the pluck and bravery which he had shown, not only on the occasion in question, but on fifteen others when his services had been instrumental in saving life. He was also awarded five guineas in appreciation of his meritorious conduct.

WILLCOX BROS. APPOINTED AS SUPERINTENDING ENGINEERS

In November, 1916, the River Wear Watch Commissioners appointed the Sunderland firm of Willcox Bros., established in 1896, as superintending engineers to oversee the upkeep of their firefloats and other vessels. It was an association which was to continue until dissolution came in 1961. Their advice and expertise were to prove invaluable to the Commissioners over the years, particularly with regard to maintenance of craft and the selection of replacement vessels when the need arose, in view of the limited financial resources which were available.

WARTIME FINANCES

Increases in the cost of living brought about by the war were felt deeply by Watch personnel who were granted a 'war bonus' of 2 shillings per week in February, 1916. This bonus was gradually increased until, at the end of the war, it stood at 12 shillings per week for all ranks.

To meet increased demands on their finances, the Commissioners took advantage of a clause in the Defence of the Realm Regulations which allowed them to levy dues over and above the statutory maximum. As a result, in 1917, authorisation was obtained from the Board of Trade to levy a rate of twopence per ton (an increase of one penny) and again, in 1918, authorising the rate to be increased to threepence.

At the end of 1918, the Watch's pay and allowances scale stood as follows:

	Years Service:	Shillings per Week:
Constables:	On appointment	40
	1	41
	2	42
	3	43
	4	44
	5	45
	6	46
	7	47
	8	48
	15	49
	20	50
Sergeants:	On appointment	53
	1	54
	2	55
	3	56
	4	57
Sergeant Engineer & Sub-Inspector:	On appointment	64
	1	65
	2	66
	3	67
Inspector:	On appointment	84
	1	85
	2	86
	3	87

Allowances:

Boot allowance:	1s.6d per week.
War Bonus:	12s. per week.
Children:	2s.6d per week (for each child living at home and not in paid employment).
Engineman:	1s. per week (for constables whilst acting as enginemen).
Detective:	£5 per annum (plain clothes allowance).
Gratuities:	10 per cent of earnings of firefloats to be distributed in shares amongst members of force.
Inspector:	Free housing, fire and light.

THREE MAJOR WATERSIDE FIRES

Three serious fires, each affecting waterside premises, were extinguished in the port with the aid of the Watch's firefloats during the war. None, however, were due to enemy action.

The first occurred shortly after 9.25 a.m. on 30th August, 1915, when smoke was discovered to be issuing from the Laing Warehouse, situated at the southeastern corner of Hudson Dock. Despite the prompt attendance of the Borough Fire Brigade and the *Fire King,* it soon became apparent that there was little chance of saving the building and great efforts were necessary to prevent the flames from spreading to the adjacent Fish Jetty and timberyard. It eventually took seven water jets to extinguish the blaze which gutted the warehouse. In addition to the warehouse machinery and equipment, its contents comprising large quantities of hemp, oats, barley, bran and oatmeal were destroyed. Three hydraulic dockside cranes also received serious damage. Fire investigation techniques of the time were not very advanced and the cause of the outbreak was recorded as 'spontaneous combustion,' a frequently used term. The loss of the warehouse's storage facilities at such an important time was to place a great strain upon the resources of the River Wear Commissioners.

Webster's Ropery, situated on the riverside at Deptford between Laings' shipyard and Queen Alexandra Bridge, was the scene of a huge blaze on the night of 21st November, 1917. About 9 p.m. that evening, shortly after the workforce had left for the day, fire was observed to have taken hold in the main building. Although the Borough Fire Brigade lost little time in despatching a motor fire pump and horse-drawn steamer, flames had soon reached all four storeys and spread to two adjacent buildings. With the firemen fighting a losing battle, the *Fire Queen* commanded by Inspector Rochford, was summoned to the scene and by 10 p.m. was directing her monitor and three jets onto the burning ropery. Difficulties were encountered in getting water onto the seat of the blaze due to the wire mesh which covered the ground floor windows. It was not until 2 a.m., the next morning, that fire was mastered. Damage was severe, with the main premises and one of the smaller buildings having been totally destroyed, although the firefighters had managed to save the warehouse and oil store. The incident was a severe blow to the company which had been extremely busy with production for the war effort, the cost of damage initially being estimated at between £10,000 and £20,000.

After some delay, Webster and Co. agreed to pay a sum of £70 for the *Fire Queen's* services, ten per cent of which was distributed amongst the Watch's establishment. Only two weeks before the fire, at the behest of the Commissioners, Superintendent Crawley had drawn up a revised scheme for the payment of gratuities to force members, whereby ten per cent of the firefloats' earnings would be paid on a quarterly basis to serving officers in the following proportions: **Inspector - three shares; Sub-Inspector and Sergeant Engineer - two shares; Sergeants and Assistant Engineers - one and a half shares; and Constables - one share.**

The *Fire Queen* was once more in action upriver shortly after 5 p.m. on 14th September, 1918, when she attended a serious outbreak of fire at W. Pickersgill and Sons' shipyard at Southwick, in support of the Urban District and Sunderland Fire Brigades. Despite the shipyard's joiners' shop being burnt to the ground, the combined efforts of the firefighters prevented the fire from spreading to adjoining structures.

THE WATCH'S FINEST HOUR - FIRE ON BOARD 'S.S. HORNSEY'

On 5th November, 1918, an urgent appeal was made by the Admiralty, on behalf of the War Office, for the Watch Commissioners to sell the **Fire King** and **Fire Queen** for use in France. Wisely, the Commissioners refused to entertain the request, considering it most imprudent to dispose of either firefloat. Within days, events were to prove their judgement sound.

With little more than twenty-four hours to elapse before the signing of the Armistice, the River Wear Watch's finest hour dawned. The courage displayed by five of its members on 10th November, 1918 would long be remembered throughout the town.

That morning, **S.S. Hornsey**, a 1,803 gross tons collier, owned by W. Cory and Sons Ltd. of London, lay at buoys in the River Wear near Thornhill Quay in the East End, laden with coal for the South. As her crew made sailing preparations, there can be little doubt that they were counting their blessings for having survived the war, unlike so many other of their colleagues in the Mercantile Marine. Perhaps they were also reflecting upon the occasion on 8th February, 1917, when their ship had come under gunfire from a German submarine in the North Sea and they had been lucky to escape with their lives.

As was the case with many other merchant vessels, the 268 feet long **Hornsey** was armed with a deck gun in an effort to defend herself from the U-boat menace. Additionally she was carrying about five tons of ammunition in her magazine, comprising one thousand rounds of 12 pounder armour piercing shells.

Suddenly, smoke was seen issuing from the aft part of the ship and before long the whole of this section, consisting of the saloon, officers' quarters and magazine was completely ablaze, with flames shooting up the companionway and through the skylights.

The River Wear Watch, on being informed of the outbreak, wasted no time in raising steam on the **Fire Queen** which was soon alongside the blazing collier. Crewing the firefloat that day were Inspector John Rochford, Sergeant George William Jennings, and Constables Herbert Adams, William Jackson and William Nichols Steel.

Upon their arrival the situation was critical, with the crew of the collier already having abandoned attempts to extinguish the fire and being in the process of taking to a lifeboat. Due to the dense volume of smoke, the police officers were unable to gain direct access to the magazine which was situated abaft the mess room. Consequently, a ladder was passed over the stern so that portholes could be smashed, thus enabling a jet of water to be played upon the ammunition cases, some of which by then were glowing red hot.

It appeared that a devastating explosion was imminent and with the evacuation of local inhabitants already in progress, no-one could have criticised Inspector Rochford had he then decided to withdraw his men. Nevertheless, being fully aware of the consequences of the magazine exploding, the men of the Watch maintained their positions and at incredible personal risk, eventually achieved mastery over the flames. The fire had destroyed the interior of the aft compartments, but the ammunition had been saved. So much water had been poured into the **Hornsey** by the time the fire had been extinguished, the **Fire Queen's** final task of the day was to pump her out.

For their extreme bravery, all five crew members of the **Fire Queen** were afterwards awarded the King's Police Medal for Gallantry. The medals were presented by the Earl of Durham at a ceremony held at the Shire Hall, Durham on 7th May, 1920. One of the recipients, William Jackson, had been promoted to sergeant since the incident and was to transfer to the Borough Police in 1921.

SERVICE TO KING AND COUNTRY

For a small force with a high average age, the River Wear Watch enjoyed a fine record of war service. On the declaration of war, two naval reservists and four members of the Fleet Reserve were immediately called up. In all, eleven force members served with the Royal Navy, the Army or the Mercantile Marine during the war. Two of them, Constables George Robson and Rowlandson Hardy Shotton were never to return, being killed on active service.

The following is a brief record of those members of the Watch - all constables - who served their country during the Great War:

ROYAL NAVY

Allan Ford Campbell	Served for the majority of the war on board the light cruiser, **H.M.S. Lowestoft**.
George James Elstob	As above.
Robert F. Mustard	Served with a trawler section on mine sweeping and anti-submarine duties.
Henry Pennington	Served on board the monitor, **H.M.S. Mersey**.
John William Race	Engaged on Channel patrol duties.
George Thomas Tildon	Engaged on secret naval work.
Rowlandson Hardy Shotton	Lost on board the cruiser, **H.M.S. Hawke** which was torpedoed by a German U-boat in the North Sea on 15th October, 1914.

MERCHANT NAVY

James Rich

ARMY

Arthur Lisle	Served with the Durham Light Infantry, losing a leg in their first action in 1915.
Charles Peter Page	Served throughout the East African campaign.
George Robson	Killed, after having previously been wounded on two occasions.

48. Alfred H. J. Brown, F.C.I.S., M.Inst.T., the General Manager and Clerk to the River Wear Commissioners, who also performed the duties of Clerk to the River Wear Watch Commissioners from 1946, until his death in 1957. *Author's collection.*

49. *S.S. Raloo* poses a major hazard to the navigation of the port, after sinking at North Quay buoys on 3rd February, 1946. *Northeast Press Ltd., Sunderland Echo.*

50. *S.S. **Raloo*** in trouble again, this time after running aground at North Sands in February, 1947.
Northeast Press Ltd., Sunderland Echo.

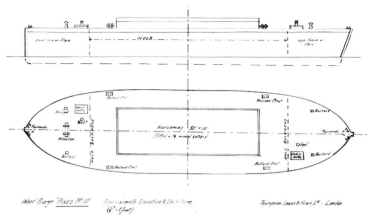

52. Plan of the dumb barge, ***Pikes' No. 10*** prior to her conversion as a floating headquarters for the Watch in 1949. *Author's collection.*

51. Robert Cyril Thompson, C.B.E., who was elected to the River Wear Watch Commission in 1948. He had headed the British merchant shipbuilding mission to the U.S.A. and Canada in 1940 and 1941. *Author's collection.*

53. Senior police officers of the West German *Wasserschutzpolizei* accompanied by Superintendent Tait of the Borough Police during their visit to the River Wear Watch on 9th March, 1950. *Northeast Press Ltd., Sunderland Echo.*

54. The *Fire King*, lying at her moorings at the entrance to the Sea Lock in Hudson Dock during the late 1950's. The Dock Police Station can be seen in the top left corner of the picture. *Northeast Press Ltd., Sunderland Echo.*

55. Sergeant Ernest Stark, with a party of visiting students from the Police College, on board the ***Fire Queen*** during the 1950's.
Author's collection.

56. River Police Constable dressed for maintenance duties on board the *Fire Queen* in the 1950's. Note the immaculate condition of the firefloat and launch moored alongside. *Author's collection.*

57. Members of the River Wear Watch are present at a memorial service held on board the paddle tug, *Eppleton Hall* on 12th February, 1951, for the four crew members of the steamtug, *Stag* who were lost a year previously when she capsized at sea. *Northeast Press Ltd., Sunderland Echo.*

58. The crew of motor launch, *Vigilant* observe attentively as tugs manoeuvre the newly launched stern portion of a ship towards the quayside. The occasion is either that of the launch, from John Crown and Sons Ltd., of the stern section of the Norwegian tanker, *Rondefjell* (15,067 g.r.t.), during 1951, or of another Norwegian tanker, *Ardvi* (12,315 g.r.t.), in 1954. *Author's collection.*

59. A view of *Fire Queen* alongside River Station, ***Pikes' No. 10***, in 1953. *Northeast Press Ltd., Sunderland Echo.*

60. In the cabin of the River Station, during 1953, Constable Richard Davison completes clerical work, watched by Constable Richard Swan *(left)* and Sergeant Thomas Hunter *(right)*. The occurrence book is also on the table. *Northeast Press Ltd., Sunderland Echo.*

61. Adjacent to Wearmouth Bridge, the six inch dry rising main is one of today's few existing reminders of the Watch. By this means, water was pumped from the river to street level by the ***Fire Queen*** during serious departmental store fires, at Binns in 1941, and at Joplings in 1954. *Author's collection.*

62. ***Fire King*** on John Crown and Sons' Strand Slipway on 12th May, 1955, undergoing what was to be her final overhaul. *Northeast Press Ltd., Sunderland Echo.*

Chapter 9

BETWEEN THE WARS

(1919 - 1939)

REORGANISATION OF WATCH DUTIES

As normality began to return following the long years of war, Superintendent Crawley embarked upon a reorganisation of the duties of the Watch. These changes, which took effect on 17th February, 1919, were so precisely calculated that out of a strength of twenty-seven, four and a half officers were left over for relief purposes after other duties had been allocated. How the two 'half' men in the force were deployed is not recorded!

JOHN CAFFREY V.C.

In May, 1919, the Watch was proud to appoint to its ranks, Constable John Caffrey V.C., a twenty-seven years old Irishman who had enlisted with the 2nd Battalion, The York and Lancaster Regiment in 1910, and in which he had served throughout the Great War.

His Victoria Cross had been earned for most conspicuous bravery on 16th November, 1916, near La Brique in France. A member of the West Yorkshire Regiment, having been badly wounded, was lying in the open and unable to move, in full view of and about 350 yards from the enemy's trenches. Together with a Corporal Stirk of the Royal Army Medical Corps, Private Caffrey had at once started out to rescue the man, but at the first attempt, had been driven back by shrapnel fire. Soon afterwards, under close sniping and machine-gun fire, the two succeeded in reaching and bandaging the wounded soldier. Just as Stirk had lifted him onto Caffrey's back, Stirk himself was shot in the head. Caffrey put down the man, bandaged Corporal Stirks's wounds and then helped him to safety. Finally, Caffrey returned and brought in the injured man from the West Yorkshire Regiment.

In all, Caffrey made three journeys across the open under close and accurate fire and had risked his life to save others with the utmost coolness and bravery.

During the war he was also awarded the Mons Star and the Cross of the Order of St. George, Fourth Class (Russia), the latter for bringing in, under heavy fire, a severely wounded officer.

Unfortunately, Caffrey's service with the Watch was short-lived as he transferred to the Borough Police at the end of 1919. He died in Derby on 26th February, 1953.

POST-WAR PAY AWARD

By 1919, the Watch Commissioners' financial position was giving great cause for concern, notwithstanding that the wartime Board of Trade Order, authorising the levy of a rate up to threepence per ton upon shipping, was still in force.

Sergeants and constables, anxious about re-establishing pay parity with the Borough Force, petitioned the Home Office on the issue, achieving some success. In consequence, the Home Office communicated with the Watch Commissioners, stating *"..... Though the Secretary of State is aware he has no authority in the matter, he would be glad to learn how far the Commissioners can meet the adjustment, which seems essential in this time of recent improved conditions given to the County and Borough Police."* The "recent improved conditions" referred to had stemmed from the Desborough Committee and the passing of the 1919 Police Act, following extreme discontent amongst many police officers throughout the country.

The Watch Commissioners, therefore, felt bound to grant as generous pay award as their finances would permit and at a special meeting held on 23rd October, 1919 to consider their financial position, the following pay scale was approved:

	Years Service:	Shillings per Week:
Constables:	**On appointment**	70
	1	72
	2	74
	3	76
	4	78
	5	80
	6	82
	7	84
	8	86
	9	88
	10	90
Sergeants:		95
Inspector:		117/6d

An additional 1s.6d per annum was to be paid to all ranks as a boot allowance, but all former allowances such as the war bonus and child allowance were abolished. The rank of sub-inspector was temporarily discontinued, the position having remained unfilled since the death of William Humble in March, 1919.

PROPOSED CORPORATION TAKEOVER OF THE WATCH

The Commissioners, anticipating that the Board of Trade Order, temporarily authorising the levy of an increased rate upon shipping, would be withdrawn at any time, were now of the opinion that they would be unable to carry out their functions on the reduced income. Consequently, the following resolution submitted by Mr. John Wallace Taylor was unanimously carried:

"That the time has now arrived when the River Wear Police should be taken over by the Sunderland County Borough Corporation, and merged in their police force."

Before arriving at their resolution, two alternative courses of action had been considered.

One was for the Watch Commissioners to obtain a new act of parliament to sanction the levy of increased dues upon shipping. This, at the time, had found little favour as it had been thought that shipowners and builders, together with the River Wear Commissioners, would have opposed such a measure.

The second possibility was for the River Wear Commissioners to take over the Watch, themselves, as had been unsuccessfully proposed in 1899. Owing to the lack of progress on that occasion, the Commissioners felt there was little point in again exploring that avenue.

Although lengthy negotiations ensued between the Watch Commissioners and the County Borough Watch Committee, it soon became evident that the latter was against the proposal for the Watch to merge with the Borough Police, despite the Home Office supporting such a plan.

It was not until October, 1922 - three years after the proposal had first been mooted - that the Watch Committee finally decided against taking over the Watch. It did suggest, however, that the Watch Commissioners should seek to overcome their difficulties by promoting a parliamentary bill that would include a clause to enable their functions to be transferred to the Corporation or the River Wear Commissioners in the future, in the event of all parties being mutually agreeable.

The Watch Commissioners, anticipating the Watch Committee's decision and being concerned over the lack of progress, had already turned their attention to such a course of action.

CONTRACTION OF THE FORCE

Fortunately for the Commissioners, the Board of Trade Order was not revoked until 31st August, 1921, on the official termination of the war, thus allowing them additional time to resolve their problems. With the expiry of the Order, however, the imposition of economies became essential. As often happens, it was the personnel that suffered. At a special meeting of the Commissioners, held on 9th February, 1922, the following measures were decided upon:

1. The authorised strength of the force would be reduced to twenty men (excluding the Superintendent);

2. Sergeants and constables would, in future, automatically retire at the age of sixty years;

3. Three months notice of termination of employment would be given to those force members then over the age of sixty. (Three constables, namely Charles Fenbow, William Thompson Chapman and William Avery, all being above the prescribed age limit, were each given notice and awarded a gratuity of £10);

4. The Superintendent would be responsible for the reorganisation of all police and fire duties at the depleted strength; and

5. It would be recommended to the Superintendent that he attempt to secure the transfer of three of the younger members of the Watch to the Borough Police. (Although five Watch members had transferred to the Borough Force in the intervening period since the end of the war, there is no record of the Superintendent acceding to the request for the transfer of further officers).

THE RIVER WEAR WATCH BILL

With no response having been forthcoming from the Town Council Watch Committee over the proposed takeover of the Watch by the Corporation, a series of meetings, commencing in August, 1922, were held by the Watch Commissioners to consider the promotion of a parliamentary bill.

The most important consideration was for any bill to derive greater income to finance the running of the Watch. This could only be effected by the levy of increased dues upon shipping. Initially, the draft Bill simply intended to retain the existing system by which vessels were charged on the first occasion they passed into or out of the Port of Sunderland each year and to increase the maximum permitted rate from one penny to twopence per ton.

Under the chairmanship of John Edward Dawson, the River Wear Commission's Emergency Committee - which had been set up due to the post-war financial difficulties of the R.W.C. - looked into the matter and strongly favoured charging for each voyage at the lowest possible rate. The existing method was considered to be obsolete and inequitable, it being felt that the only fair and correct basis would be to charge each vessel in respect of each voyage into and out of the port. As things stood, a vessel making one voyage would pay as much as one making forty.

Accordingly, in a resolution passed on 11th January, 1923, the R.W.C. reluctantly decided to petition against the Bill. However, five days later, on 16th January, a meeting took place between representatives of the Watch Commission and the R.W.C., as a result of which the former agreed to amend their Bill according to the wishes of the R.W.C. who then withdrew their opposition.

Hence, the Watch Commissioners now decided to levy a maximum rate of one penny per net registered ton, each time a vessel entered or sailed from the port. Naturally, the R.W.C. anticipated that the maximum would not be charged, but it became clear that they had not fully contemplated the consequences of the system of rating which they now advocated.

On the other hand, the Sunderland Shipowners' Society had. Following publication on 2nd March, 1923 of a public notice appertaining to the amended Bill, they urged the R.W.C. to continue their opposition and pointed out that shipping using the port most would be severely penalised. Having already made their stand, the R.W.C. initially attempted to distance itself from the controversy but, not having any representation on the River Wear Watch Commission at that time, began to make overtures to secure a majority representation to ensure that the Watch Rate was kept to a minimum. The Watch Commissioners, however, were opposed to such representation.

Although opposed to the Bill, the Shipowners' Society - which had long cast aside its affinity with the Watch Commission - failed to petition against it.

Due to the diminishing number of vessels being registered at Sunderland, the Bill also sought to abolish the qualification requirement for a Commissioner's shipping interests to be registered there.

The third major provision of the Bill was to facilitate the amalgamation of the Watch with the Borough Police, or its transfer to the River Wear Commissioners, with the mutual consent of the parties concerned, if at any time in the future this was deemed to be in the public interest.

The Watch Commissioners had also contemplated extending their jurisdiction and altering the status of their Superintendent. Records do not indicate what the Commissioners had in mind here, but in any event both proposals were dropped. As far as jurisdiction was concerned, they may have intended to extend this upriver beyond Deptford, the western limit as defined by the 1840 Act, possibility as far as Hylton and including Southwick. It seemed anomalous that some vessels berthing in the river above Deptford still paid Watch Dues but were not - according to the letter of the Act - entitled to protection from the Watch. Nevertheless, Watch personnel did have authority to act as constables throughout the Borough of Sunderland and it had become customary for them to patrol the River Wear beyond the Borough boundary as far as Hylton. Likewise, the Watch had never been constrained by the question of jurisdiction in despatching its firefloats to wherever they were required. It was therefore probably decided to maintain the status-quo, rather than invite further opposition to their Bill.

Consequently on 18th July, 1923, the Bill received its Royal Assent and the River Wear Watch Act, 1923 became law.

HOSTILE REACTION TO THE NEW WATCH RATE

If the Watch Commissioners thought that opposition to their new measures would abate with the passage of the Act, they were to be proved gravely mistaken.

At their annual meeting held on 9th August, 1923, newly acquired charging powers for their 1923/24 financial year commencing on 1st September, were put into effect. It was decided that three farthings per net registered ton would be levied on each occasion a vessel entered or sailed from the port, up to a maximum of twenty-five voyages.

Shipping companies whose ships traded regularly to the Port of Sunderland were outraged at the increased charges that they were now required to pay. Moreover, the River Wear Commissioners, fearful of loss of trade, expressed grave disquiet over the situation. The following comparison between dues paid by regular traders under the old method (i.e. one penny per n.r.t. for the first voyage only in each year), and those which would be levied under the new system (i.e. three farthings for each voyage, up to a maximum of twenty-five per annum), illustrates how justified shipowners and the R.W.C. were in their concern:

Vessel	N.R.T.	No. of voyages	Aggregate tonnage	Total Amount (£.s.d) New Rate	Old Rate	% inc.
ABERDALE	265	22	5,830	18. 4. 4	1. 2. 1	1,550
AFTERGLOW	482	25	12,050	37. 13. 1	2. 0. 2	1,775
BROMLEY	289	25	7,225	22. 11. 7	1. 4. 1	1,775
BOW	288	25	7,200	22. 10. 0	1. 4. 0	1,775
FLASHLIGHT	482	21	10,122	31. 12. 7	2. 0. 2	1,475
FERNHILL	1,457	22	32,054	100. 3. 4	6. 1. 5	1,550
FORD CASTLE	1,102	22	24,244	75. 15. 3	4. 11. 1	1,550
HOLYWOOD	965	25	24,125	75. 7. 10	4. 0. 5	1,775
KIRKWOOD	1,012	25	25,300	79. 1. 3	4. 4. 4	1,775
LONGHURST	1,042	25	26,050	81. 8. 1½	4. 6. 10	1,775
ST. AGNES	740	25	18,500	57. 16. 3	3. 1. 8	1,775
SPRAY	375	25	9,375	29. 5. 11	1. 11. 3	1,775
SUNNINGDALE	1,116	25	27,900	87. 3. 9	4. 13. 10	1,775
TYNEHOME	262	25	6,550	20. 9. 4	1. 1. 0	1,775

It will be seen that vessels completing the maximum twenty-five voyages, regardless of tonnage, could expect to pay a massive increase of 1,775 per cent. Even a vessel making only two voyages would pay a 50 per cent increase, whilst dues for ten voyages would increase by 650 per cent. If, in the future, the Watch Commissioners chose to levy the maximum permitted rate of one penny, ships completing twenty-five voyages would be subject to an astronomical increase of 2,400 per cent! Even if the minimum charge of one farthing was imposed, the increase would be 525 per cent. The sole beneficiaries of the new system would be those vessels making only one voyage per annum, whose dues would decrease by 25 per cent.

It is difficult to understand why the River Wear Commissioners had insisted upon the basis of rating which had been adopted. They seem not to have done their homework correctly. In effect, the Watch Commissioners were caught in an invidious position. Their expenditure for the year 1923/24 was estimated at £7,000. Clearly, their 1922/23 income of £4,674 13s.4d, derived from the levy of one penny upon 1,121,920 tons, indicated the need to increase rates. Had the method of rating which had originally been proposed - i.e. charging a maximum of twopence per ton for the first voyage in each year - been adopted, income would have been more than adequate to meet expenses. In fact, with such tonnage levels being maintained, only three ha'pence per ton need have been charged.

On the other hand, under the new system, the Watch Commissioners could not have charged less than three farthings per ton to meet expenditure. As it was, by the end of the 1923/24 financial year, £7,288 15s.2d had been collected by the levy of three farthings on 2,332,750 tons.

Some argued that it was only right that those vessels frequenting the port on a regular basis - and therefore being most liable to benefit from the services of the River Police - should pay the most. Others, however, were beginning to ask whether the continued existence of the Watch was necessary at all. Thus began a campaign of attrition against the Watch, led by the chairman of the River Wear Commissioners, John Edward Dawson.

Dawson had been a River Wear Commissioner since 1910, having been elected as one of the shipowners' representatives. As a result of the R.W.C's financial difficulties which had arisen following the end of World War One, he had been appointed chairman of the Emergency Committee which, in 1920, had negotiated a moratorium and later drawn up the constitution, on the basis of which the R.W.C. had been reconstituted in 1922. Dawson had succeeded Ralph Milbanke Hudson as chairman of the R.W.C. in 1921 and had been re-elected to the chair following reconstitution. Often outspoken, Dawson passionately believed in promoting the virtues of the town and port and would seize any opportunity to do so.

Besides his connection with the R.W.C., Dawson was managing director of the leading local tug company, France Fenwick Tyne & Wear Co. Ltd. and a director of Tyne and Wear Steamship Co., whose colliers operated from the port. It can be seen, therefore, that he had a vested interest in what was widely described as "the vexed question of the River Wear Watch levy," which he saw as a threat to the trade of the port as well as his own interests.

On 14th August, 1923, the subject of the levy was placed before the R.W.C. General Purposes Committee, where Dawson, together with Mr. J. R. D. Bell, chairman of the Traffic Committee, was appointed to confer with the River Wear Watch Committee and Sunderland Corporation with a view to resurrecting the proposal for the latter to take over responsibility for the Watch. One suggestion put forward by Dawson at this time was for firefighting and dock policing to be undertaken by the Corporation, leaving only the river to be policed by the Watch, financed by a much reduced levy upon shipping.

Meanwhile, some shipping companies were refusing outright to pay the new Watch Rate, whilst others were making payment "under protest and without prejudice to any claim which the owners may make for refund of the same." The British Steamship Owners' Association lent its weight to the crusade on 18th September, 1923, with the passing of the following resolution:

"The Directors of this Association protest against the dues on shipping imposed by the River Wear Watch Commission, which have lately been increased to such an extent against regular traders to the Port of Sunderland as to amount to an unjust burden and desire, moreover, to record their opinion that the policing of the River and Harbour should be taken over by Sunderland Corporation."

Initially, negotiations with the Corporation seemed to be progressing in Dawson's favour. On 3rd October, 1923, to reinforce his position, he wrote to the Mayor of the Borough, stating:

"In 1922, 3,386 vessels used the Port of Sunderland, whereas in 1862, there had been 12,097, which were nearly all sailing vessels and remained in port much longer, sometimes being laid up for the winter. The levy of Watch Duty once per annum was then feasible, but is now anomalous.

The Tyne has always been cheaper than the Wear and the new rate will accentuate the difference. If the rate was to be abolished, this would put the Wear on a par with the Tyne, which is desirable for successful competition. The town has an interest in vessels trading to the port due to contributions to the numerous businesses in the Borough.

We all need ships - and still more ships. Sunderland has two geese which lay golden eggs - coal and ships. Let us take great care of them.

One of the ways to entice more trade would be to cheapen the port and therefore abolish the Watch Rate.

I indicate the need for effective policing at the docks.

The town has a most efficient police organisation and it would be absurd for the River Wear Commissioners to attempt another police organisation with the town's at hand in the same geographical area.

It would be logical to unify policing under one control. This would be cheaper and more effective.

By the 1923 Act obtained by the River Wear Watch Commissioners, the R.W.C. and Sunderland Corporation have power to take over the Watch. If the R.W.C. were to take it over, the evils of dual control would be perpetuated.

I advocate that the Watch be abolished and its members made redundant, with the possibility that some might be re-engaged. I would suggest that the Corporation could take over the Watch at much less cost than that originally budgeted for, and that a Home Office grant might even by obtained."

FINE WORK BY FIREFLOATS AT SERIOUS TIMBER FIRE

Amidst all the antagonism being directed towards the Watch, the great value of its firefloats to the town was demonstrated at a huge fire that broke out 6th November, 1923 at the east side of Hendon Dock where hundreds of thousands of wooden pit props had been stacked to a height of sixty feet along the entire dockside by George Horsley and Co. of West Hartlepool.

The fire was discovered in the middle of the huge stack shortly after 10.30 p.m. and soon flames were leaping high into the air, being visible from miles around. On the arrival of the Borough Police Fire Brigade under Chief Constable Crawley and Superintendent Yelland, it was at once realised that a formidable task lay ahead.

Steam was raised on the *Fire King* which, after proceeding through Hendon Gateway from her berth in Hudson Dock, quickly got to work with her 2½ inch monitor. The creosote treatment of the pit props made them burn all the more fiercely and efforts were concentrated in containing the blaze to prevent it from reaching the Patent Fuel Works, the scene of a number of earlier conflagrations. The *S.S. Dagmar*, which had been discharging timber at the quay, was moved to safety. So severe was the outbreak, that it was also decided to bring the *Fire Queen* to the scene from the river as soon as the tide had risen sufficiently to allow the lock gates to be opened.

The efforts of the two fireboats, under the command of Inspector John Rochford, enabled them to pump water at a combined rate of some 6,000 gallons per minute through a total of fourteen jets. In ten hours, more than six feet of water had been drawn from Hendon Dock. So intense was the heat, that water running back into the dock was lukewarm. Firefighters on shore found it difficult to isolate the burning area due to the risk of pit props rolling down on top of them.

By 4 p.m., the following afternoon, although still burning, the fire was well under control. A sawmill in the vicinity and many of the pit props had been destroyed, although great quantities of the timber had been saved by the firemen's exertions.

There can be little doubt that without the presence of the firefloats, the fire would have assumed proportions which the Borough Brigade could have done little to contain.

CONTINUANCE OF ANTI-WATCH CRUSADE BY
JOHN EDWARD DAWSON

The success of the firefloats in tackling such a major blaze on land reinforced the argument that they should be under Corporation control. By January, 1924, however, with no progress having been made in that direction, Dawson found it impossible to conceal his frustration. "It is no use attempting further to seek to get the Watch taken over by Sunderland Corporation," he wrote to R.W.C. colleagues and added "We are up against a stone wall." He insisted that the Watch Rate must somehow be reduced.

Repudiating his previous stance on the R.W.C. taking over the Watch, Dawson arrived at the conclusion that this was now his only option and one which, at least, would give the R.W.C. absolute control.

In March, 1924, following a resolution by the Sunderland District of Chartered Ship-brokers condemning the Watch Rate, Dawson renewed his anti-Watch crusade with intense vigour. He now advocated a campaign against the Watch Commissioners by shipping interests. If successful, he believed, there would be no alternative but for the authorities concerned to take action to launch a parliamentary bill to abolish the Watch. In a crude and underhanded attempt to discredit the force, Dawson drafted a pro forma document which he intended to send to all local ship-brokers to be circulated to captains of ships entering the port. It read as follows:

"The dues payable to the River Wear Watch Commissioners in respect of my vessel, _____ which arrived in this port on _____, 192_ amount to £_____.

In my opinion the services rendered by the River Wear Watch do not justify such a payment.

The River Wear Watch was instituted in the year 1836 [sic] when vessels were in port for long periods and regularly laid up during winter months without adequate provision for watching.

In these circumstances, the Watch was formed to provide protection against pilfering and damage by fire, the latter being a greater risk in the case of wooden vessels than now. In these days there are no wooden vessels and ships are only in port for a few days, with either the whole or greater part of the crew on board. Practically every vessel is fitted with fire extinguishing appliances and I therefore consider that the purpose for which the River Wear Watch was formed no longer exists.

I protest against the charge for dues in respect of a service I do not desire, and the rendering of which is in present day circumstances totally unnecessary."

Dawson also intended that the owners of each vessel and the ship-brokers themselves should send a letter couched in similar terms to the Clerk and General Manager of the River Wear Commissioners, Mr. F. Humble.

Dawson's plan brought a swift condemnatory reaction from Humble who was only too well aware that it had been the R.W.C. who had been instrumental in forcing the Watch Commissioners to adopt the method of rating which was now the subject of so much criticism. Humble felt that if such a pro forma was to be distributed, it should originate from the Ship-brokers Association and not the R.W.C. Dawson angrily responded that the R.W.C. were "like ostriches hiding their heads in the sand, believing that no-one could see them."

Meanwhile, the R.W.C. continued to study the feasibility of taking over the Watch, but in May, 1925, with Superintendent Crawley shortly to leave to become Chief Constable of Newcastle City Police, Dawson saw another opportunity to persuade the Corporation to enter into negotiations to take over the Watch. Crawley had always favoured retaining the Watch as a separate entity - if for no other reason than the additional salary paid to him. Dawson conjectured that with Crawley out of the way, the matter might now be looked at differently.

Following his resignation on 1st July, 1925, the River Wear Watch Commissioners went to great lengths to show their appreciation of the services rendered to them by Crawley through his valuable reorganisation and administration of their force. In particular, they expressed their thanks for the happy relations which had always prevailed with him. It is a mark of the esteem in which he was held by the Watch Commissioners that at the time of his resignation, Crawley was receiving an annual salary of £160 in respect of his superintendency of the Watch, whilst his successor, John Ruddick would only receive £70.

In spite of Dawson's lengthy efforts to induce the Corporation to absorb the Watch into the Borough Force, neither they nor the River Wear Commissioners were eventually prepared to take on such a commitment. With the higher charges upon shipping being gradually and reluctantly accepted by shipowners, opposition evaporated and the River Wear Watch continued its tenuous existence.

During these years of uncertainty, the Watch Commissioners had little to say about the moves being made, outside their control, to shape the destiny of the Watch. Whilst most of them would have been only too pleased if Dawson's endeavours had come to fruition, they carried on regardless, discharging their functions in an exemplary manner and adopting a 'wait and see' attitude.

Yet with the passing of the Sunderland Corporation Act of 1927, there was still a chance that at some time in the future the Corporation might have a change of heart. Section 256 of the Act provided that, should the Watch be transferred to the Corporation in the future, the latter would be permitted to suspend the levy of dues upon shipping and meet the cost of its running from the general rate.

POLICE BOX SYSTEM APPLIED TO THE WATCH

The police box system, which was to be adopted by forces throughout the country, was pioneered in Sunderland by Chief Constable Crawley in 1923. By means of private telephone lines, each box was connected directly to the Borough Police Headquarters in Gill Bridge Avenue.

Realising the importance of including the River Wear Watch in the system, Crawley arranged for the *Fire Queen* (moored off the Low Street) and the *Fire King* (stationed in Hudson Dock South at the Sea Lock entrance) to be incorporated into the network.

FLOATING H.Q. FOR THE WATCH

On 13th May, 1925, the Watch Commissioners terminated their tenancy of the Bodlewell Lane Police Station which they had shared with the Borough Police since 1873.

From then on, the River Wear Watch's Headquarters was based on board the former manual firefloat, **Wear Engine 'B'** which for many years had been in use as a floating depot for the **Fire Queen**. Even as a floating police station, she continued to be affectionately known as the **Manual**.

The move from Bodlewell Lane also required Inspector Rochford to vacate his apartments in the building and he was subsequently granted a yearly allowance of £45 for rent, coal and light.

MOTOR LAUNCHES 'VIGILANTE' AND 'VIGILANT'

Although a steam launch had been in operation since 1896, river patrols were still being undertaken by rowing boat as late as 1928. In June of that year, the Commissioners' consulting engineers declared the last rowing boat in use for patrol work to be beyond repair and recommended its replacement by a motor launch.

Accordingly, the old boat was sold for £2 and a clinker-built open motor launch purchased second-hand for £75 from local marine engineers and salvage contractors, Lindsay, Swan and Hunter Ltd. Constructed from teak, the launch was named **Vigilante** and was 24 feet long, with a beam of 6 feet and a 1 foot 6 inch draught when light. She was propelled by a four cylinder, 16 b.h.p. petrol engine and fitted with Caledonia reverse gear and a three-bladed propeller.

In 1933, the **Vigilante** was sold for £10 and replaced by another petrol driven launch named **Bud**, bought from Messrs. Borwick of Bowness for the sum of £90 18s.1d (including delivery). Following successful trials on Lake Windermere, the 23 foot carvel-built craft, which had been constructed in 1926 by Courtney and Birkett of Southwick, Sussex, was transported to Sunderland by goods train where she entered service as **Vigilant**, a subtle name change from that of her predecessor. Although fitted with a cabin, her beam of 5 feet 4 inches was narrower than that of the **Vigilante**. Initially equipped with a six cylinder, 24 h.p. Studebaker engine, the little launch was to be re-engined on two occasions during her subsequent twenty-eight years of service with the Watch.

END OF THE KIDSON ERA

On 31st August, 1929, ninety years of association with the Watch Commissioners by the Kidson family came to an end with the resignation of their Clerk, William A. Kidson. He was succeeded by another Sunderland solicitor, Edward Cope who was to hold the position until 1946.

SPECIAL WATCHING AND FOAM GENERATORS FOR FIREFIGHTING

Another of Superintendent Crawley's innovations was the special watching of oil vessels arriving in port. Bye-laws required tankers loading or discharging oil products to be continuously supervised to minimise the risk from fire. Crawley saw this as an opportunity to create additional revenue for the Watch Commissioners and for police personnel to increase their earnings by performing overtime. Consequently, he entered into agreements with oil companies for members of the River Police to perform this duty, a practice which was to continue until the final days of the Watch.

In 1928, following a display by the Firefoam Company on board the **Fire King** of the effectiveness of 'Foamite', an agent used for fighting petro-chemical fires, it was decided to equip both fireboats with this apparatus. The 'Foamite' powder, when mixed with water, would expand ten-fold for each gallon of water used and was an important acquisition which enhanced the Watch's firefighting capability.

The importance of 'special watching' and 'Foamite' generators to the port was graphically illustrated on 12th January, 1931, when the Anglo-Saxon Petroleum Company's tanker, **Shell-Mex 1** was discharging ballast at Home Wharf in the South Docks, preparatory to loading 800 tons of benzol for Hull.

Suddenly, a spark from a dockside locomotive fell onto and ignited a residue of oil left on the deck of the 927 gross tons vessel from a previous discharge. As flames swept along the entire length of the ship and shot one hundred feet into the air, a member of the Watch, already in attendance on special watching duty, raised the alarm. Colleagues on board the **Fire King** immediately tackled the blaze with foam generators as the ship's crew, fearful that gas filled tanks would explode, were forced to run though a wall of flame to reach safety ashore.

Due to the Watch's prompt reaction, the fire was quickly extinguished and a catastrophic explosion averted. Although having been badly scorched, the vessel was fortunate only to sustain superficial damage.

THE RIVER WEAR WATCH RATE AGAIN

Late in 1932, it became known that the River Wear Commissioners, who for many years had collected dues on behalf of the Watch Commissioners, had for some time been failing to levy such dues upon certain vessels, namely those which paid the special watching charge of 2s.6d per hour and those entering port for repairs, bunkers and refuge. No-one within the employment of the River Wear Commissioners was prepared to admit for how long this practice had prevailed.

Irritated, by what he perceived as unwarranted interference by the R.W.C., the Clerk to the Watch Commissioners, Edward Cope warned them of the serious consequences that might arise through their setting aside of dues to which the Watch was legally entitled under its special parliamentary Act. The R.W.C., however, remained unrepentant and insisted that the categories of vessels subject of dispute should continue to be exempt from payment of the Watch Rate. The whole affair savoured of guile on the part of the R.W.C. and in particular, of involvement by John Edward Dawson.

Despite the protestations of Mr. Cope, the R.W.C., seeking to keep down port charges brought pressure to bear on the Watch Commissioners, forcing them to acquiesce. Accordingly at the quarterly meeting held in May, 1933, the following resolution was passed:

"That the resolution passed at the quarterly meeting of the River Wear Watch Commissioners, held on 25th August, 1932, fixing the rate for the ensuing year, be rescinded and that for the remainder of the ensuing year a rate be levied on each and every ship and

vessel passing into, or passing out of the port, at three farthings per net registered ton, subject to the following exemptions:

1) All vessels having made 20 voyages;

2) All vessels entering port for repairs, up to a maximum of 90 days;

3) All vessels entering port for bunkers only, up to a maximum of 96 hours;

4) All vessels entering port for refuge, except petroleum vessels; and

5) All petroleum vessels entering port and paying the special police charge of 2s.6d per hour for watching whilst the vessel in port.

SERGEANT ENGINEER HAMP

The death of Sergeant Engineer Francis William Hamp occurred during October, 1932. He had joined the Watch on 1st January, 1907 and had been appointed directly to his rank primarily due to his expert understanding of the types of boilers and mechanical equipment connected with firefloats. His knowledge was such that he was able to raise steam in the shortest possible time, thus enabling the fireboats to be used to their best advantage.

THE DEPRESSION YEARS

The uncertainties created by the post-war depression of the 1920's and subsequent slump of the early '30's undoubtedly had a profound effect on the men of the River Wear Watch who - as has been seen earlier - were quite justified in their fear of joining the ranks of the jobless at a time of great despair.

In September, 1921, members of the Watch had been ordered by Superintendent Crawley to assist the Borough Police on the streets of the town centre in the face of serious rioting by the unemployed.

In September, 1931, the Government decreed that police forces throughout the country would have their pay reduced by five per cent. Although not subject to Home Office control, the Watch Commissioners declared that the reduction would also apply to their force. A year later, a further five per cent reduction was applied nationally. On this occasion, however, the Commissioners felt unable to justify taking similar steps owing to the disparity between the pay of their men and that of the Borough Police, together with the fact that the Watch had no superannuation fund.

THE EMBARRASSING TALE OF THE 'J.E.D.'

One minor episode dealt with by the Watch in 1936 was probably a source of some embarrassment to the River Wear Commissioners, especially for their chairman and long time adversary of the Watch, John Edward Dawson.

On 21st January, that year, Sergeant Robert Mustard was on patrol in the outer basin when he noticed the River Wear Commissioners' motor launch, *J.E.D.* flying a defaced Red Ensign - a Red Ensign having the letters 'R.W.C.' in the fly. "Take that ensign down at once," Sergeant Mustard ordered the launchman, "you are contravening the Merchant

Shipping Act." Reluctantly, the launchman complied with the instruction before carrying on with his journey.

Two days later, the sergeant again saw the *J.E.D.* exhibiting the defaced ensign and demanded to know why it was still being flown after his previous warning against doing so. "Mr. Wake, the Dredging Superintendent has told me to continue flying the flag until he finds out whether the Commissioners have a warrant to fly it," replied the launchman. Sternly, Sergeant Mustard directed that the ensign must once more be removed and added "Please inform Mr. Wake that the Lords of the Admiralty do not issue warrants to private firms to deface ensigns in any way."

The matter was made a subject of a report, but fortunately for the R.W.C. did not end up in court. The motor launch *J.E.D.* was, of course, named after their illustrious chairman!

SUPERINTENDENT RUDDICK REPLACED BY
GEORGE HENRY COOK

Superintendent Ruddick, a member of the Borough Police since 1894, retired in 1937. He was replaced as Chief Constable and Superintendent of the Watch by George Henry Cook who was held in the highest esteem by men of both forces.

The 1930's were a fairly uneventful period for the Watch but, as the decade drew to a close, it was soon to face its greatest challenge.

Chapter 10

THE SECOND WORLD WAR YEARS

(1939 - 1945)

CONTROVERSY OVER ATTENDANCE OF FIREFLOATS AT LAND FIRES

Controversy over the manner in which income was generated by the Watch Commissioners seldom seemed to subside. During 1939, it was the practice of charging for the services of firefloats at land fires which was in contention.

The first six months of the year saw the firefloats being called to three separate timberyard fires in the port, the first of which broke out at Joseph Thompson and Co's sawmill on the east side of Hudson Dock South, shortly after midnight on 15th January. A patrolling River Police sergeant had discovered the blaze at which the *Fire King* was engaged for almost two hours.

On 23rd March, around 11 p.m., the *Fire Queen* steamed across the river to a fire at the premises of Armstrong, Addison and Co., North Dock, only to find that her services were no longer required, the Borough Brigade already having the outbreak under control.

George Horsley and Co., on the east side of Hendon Dock, was the scene of the final incident at which a stack of pit props had become ignited during the early hours of 8th June. Again, the alarm had been raised by a member of the Watch and the *Fire King* brought into play, utilising her powerful jets for three hours.

The presence of the *Fire King* at the Thompson and Horsley fires had been instrumental in the prevention of considerable damage and loss. The Commissioners, therefore, had every expectation of being compensated for the attendance of their floats at all three incidents, their accounts amounting to £22 10s., £5 5s. and £38 14s.6d, respectively.

In 1909, the Commissioners had resolved *"that in the event of any fire occurring in any yard, works or place of business adjacent to the river or docks, the services of the Fire Brigade and fire engines are not to be rendered unless the occupiers of such yard, etc. have signed the form of agreement authorising such services and have given an undertaking to be responsible for the same ....."*

Although all three companies had signed the form of agreement, their respective insurers refused to pay for the services rendered by the firefloats. Eventually, amidst the threat of legal action, the Thompson and Armstrong Addison accounts were settled but Horsleys' insurers steadfastly refused to do likewise and referred the matter to the Home Office Fire Officers Committee.

AGREEMENT WITH SUNDERLAND CORPORATION CONCERNING USE OF FIREFLOATS

In consequence of Horsleys' insurance company's stand, the Home Office communicated with Sunderland Corporation, stating that, in its opinion, a breach of the 1938 Fire Brigades Act was being occasioned. Under this Act, the Corporation, as the fire authority for the County Borough, was required to enter into arrangements with other bodies which maintained fire brigades, for the purpose of dealing with fires occurring in Sunderland that could not adequately be dealt with by the Borough Brigade. Clearly, the River Wear Watch fell within this category. Furthermore, the Act prohibited fire authorities from charging owners of properties for extinguishing fires.

Although the Clerk to the Watch Commissioners, Mr. Cope contended that the Fire Brigades Act did not apply to the Watch, his position was hopeless and on 18th June, 1940 an agreement was reached between the Corporation and Watch Commissioners, whereby the latter's firefloats would attend any fire occurring in premises adjacent to the river or docks when required to do so by the officer in charge of the Borough Brigade. It was also agreed that the senior Borough Brigade officer present would be in sole charge at the scene. Although an annual rental of £10 was to be paid by the Corporation for the services of the fireboats, the Commissioners lost a valuable source of incidental revenue owing to the cancellation of the agreements with the occupiers of premises - forty-four in all.

It is of interest to name those premises concerned:

Joseph L. Thompson & Sons Ltd.	Armstrong, Addison & Co.
The Rose Line Ltd.	Joseph Thompson & Co.
Pyman Bell & Co. Ltd.	F. Fenwick & Co. Ltd.
J. & W. Wilson & Sons	Richardson, Westgarth & Co. Ltd.
George Clark Ltd.	William Doxford & Sons Ltd.
S. P. Austin & Son Ltd.	The River Wear Commissioners.
Lambton, Hetton & Joicey Collieries Ltd.	Sir James Laing & Son.
Wearmouth Coal Co. Ltd.	James Hall
John Priestman & Co.	N. E. Marine Engineering Co. Ltd.
Bartram & Sons Ltd.	John Dickinson & Sons Ltd.
Short Bros. Ltd.	William Pickersgill & Sons Ltd.
Brotherton & Co. Ltd.	John Crown & Sons Ltd.
T. W. Greenwell & Co. Ltd.	Wearside Sailmaking Co.
Moor Engineering & Pipeworks Ltd.	James Deuchar Ltd.
East Coast Timber Co. Ltd.	William J. Logan & Son.
Shell-Mex Ltd.	The Wear Shipyard.
Thomas Young	Shell-Mex & B.P. Ltd.
Anglo-American Oil Co. Ltd.	Lloyds British Testing Co. Ltd.
Atkinson, Glover & Burnip & Co. Ltd.	Sir William Arrol & Co. Ltd.
National Benzola Co. Ltd.	Power Petroleum (North) Ltd.
Tyne-Tees Steam Shipping Co. Ltd.	British Oil Storage Co. Ltd.
Sunderland Oil Co. Ltd.	Steel & Co. Ltd.

It was, nevertheless, to be in the best interests of the town and port that the situation had been resolved prior to the commencement of German air raids in earnest.

R.W.C. AIR RAID PRECAUTIONS

In 1938, with the clouds of war looming over Europe, the Home Office had laid down details of measures to be adopted by dock authorities in preparing their Air Raid Precautions (A.R.P.) schemes. Although not of direct relevance to the River Wear Watch, it is meaningful to describe details of services provided by the River Wear Commissioners under their scheme for the Port of Sunderland:

SERVICE No.	DESCRIPTION OF SERVICE
1	Organisation and control.
2	Protection of property and materials.
3	Protection of workers.
4	First aid.
5	Fire precautions.
6	Rescue work.
7	Communication of air raid warnings.
8	Emergency communications.
9	Lighting restrictions.
10	Anti-gas organisation.
11	Gas detection.
12	Emergency maintenance and distribution of supplies.

Service number 5 was undertaken by the Chief Constable of the Borough Police, and number 6 by the Borough Engineer in the Town Council's A.R.P. scheme for the County Borough. Control and co-ordination of all twelve services were placed in the hands of the Clerk and General Manager of the R.W.C., acting as A.R.P. Officer for the port.

On the outbreak of war, the 'Sunderland Dock Area A.R.P. Scheme Emergency Fire Brigade', as it was officially named, was formed and recruited volunteers from the R.W.C. workforce who received training from the Borough Fire Brigade. Eventually, it was to have 120 men in its ranks and provide valuable assistance to the Borough Brigade and River Wear Watch.

The 'R.W.C. Heavy Mobile Firefighting Unit' was also formed and manned by a volunteer crew of seven men and a messenger. These men reported for duty on every alert and performed forty-eight hours fireguard duty each month. The unit would subsequently be engaged in fighting fires caused by enemy action and was to be in the forefront at the scene of the serious fire at T. W. Greenwell and Co. Ltd's shiprepair yard on the night of 16th May, 1943.

EFFECTS OF WAR

During the Second World War, Sunderland suffered gravely at the hands of the Luftwaffe, its civilian population and civil defence personnel bearing the brunt with almost three hundred fatalities being caused amongst them. It is said that the town was the most heavily bombed in the country, north of Hull.

Intense activity marked the industrial life of the port, particularly with regard to shipbuilding and repairing, together with related ancillary trades. During the period from the outbreak of war to the end of 1944, 249 merchant ships with an aggregate tonnage of 1,534,980 tons were built in the port, representing fifty per cent of merchant shipping produced in

England, or twenty-seven per cent of total United Kingdom output, this in addition to work carried out for the Admiralty.

During the early part of the war, however, there was a sharp decline in the tonnage of shipping and the quantity of cargo handled, partly due to the diversion of shipping to the west coast for strategic reasons.

Following heavy air attacks upon London and Liverpool, many ships were diverted to other ports, including Sunderland. From August, 1941 onwards, the Government decided to use the port for shipping cargoes of war materials. With traffic steadily increasing, thousands of tons of U.S. Army stores were landed at Sunderland. In addition, the ordinary trade of the port was being carried on, including the shipment of about 2,000,000 tons of coal per year to London and other U.K. ports.

In spite of being attacked on many occasions, the port itself escaped remarkably lightly, especially when its importance as a shipbuilding centre is taken into account. Nevertheless, some serious damage was caused to shipbuilding and repair yards, together with other port installations, as a result of at least twenty-four air raids.

As in the previous war, the River Wear Watch stood ready to protect the security of the port, working in close liaison with the Borough Police and military authorities. Constable John Patterson, as an army reservist, was the only Watch member to see military service, being called up early in 1939 and returning to his police duties following the cessation of hostilities.

DEATH OF CONSTABLE PAGE

The only fatality to befall the ranks of the Watch during the war was indirectly related to enemy action, when Constable Charles Peter Page, aged forty-nine, was killed in a collision involving his autocycle and a taxi at Elwin Terrace, Sunderland on 21st June, 1940. The officer had been on his way to report for duty in response to an air raid warning.

POWERS TO INCREASE WATCH RATE

As in the First World war, to alleviate financial problems brought about by wartime circumstances, the Watch Commissioners were provided with powers to charge an increased rate upon shipping on a temporary basis. Thus, under the River Wear Watch Commissioners (Increase of Charges) Order, 1940, the maximum rate authorised to be levied was increased from one penny to three ha'pence per net registered ton.

EXTRANEOUS DUTIES OF WAR

Besides those tasks routinely carried out by the Watch, such as the investigation of crime, recovery of bodies, involvement in rescues, dealing with breaches of the Merchant Shipping Act, extinguishing fires and attending shipboard accidents and disturbances, many extraneous duties became incumbent upon its members as a direct result of the war.

Blackout restrictions, preventing the use of unobscured lights, were vigorously enforced both in the docks and along the river, resulting in many prosecutions. Numerous persons were detained for contravening Defence Regulations by entering the docks and certain parts of the riverside which were prohibited areas, whilst attempts by seamen to take prostitutes on board ships would often be frustrated. In addition, dealing with contravention of other wartime regulations such as those concerning unauthorised photography, breaches of immobilisation orders upon small craft, wastage of fuel and absence of fire watchers from their places of duty was all in a day's work for the River Police.

With fear of sabotage and the threat from supposed fifth columnists being constantly in the minds of the entire population, it is not surprising that false alarms periodically arose. Such was the case on 13th May, 1940 when Sergeant Peter Atkinson and P.C. George Pickering, whilst engaged on river patrol, saw what appeared to be a suspicious box lying on an inspection gantry beneath Wearmouth Bridge. Thinking that they had discovered an attempt to blow up the bridge, the officers quickly returned to the River Station to inform Borough Police Headquarters. It was only when P.C. Pickering had been called from his home after unsuccessful attempts to locate the 'box' had been made by the Borough Police, that it was discovered to have been a warning notice attached to electricity cables which only became visible when the underside of the bridge was illuminated by the sun's reflection on the river.

Enemy air raids were an ever present menace. One officer, P.C. Thomas Davison, had a particularly chilling experience on the evening of 11th September, 1941 when he witnessed a German bomber fly low over Hudson Dock and drop a bomb directly into the dock not far from where he was standing. Miraculously, no damage was caused and the only casualties were the fish later found floating on the surface.

Other explosive devices, not necessarily enemy weapons, also presented a hazard. Whilst visiting the Gas, Light and Coke Company's collier, **Sir David**, lying at No. 31 Staith in Hendon Dock on 11th August, 1940, Sergeant Robert Mustard was badly injured as the result of the accidental detonation of a Mills bomb on board, with a crew member also being wounded.

A stray shell was recovered from a railway line near the North Eastern Marine Engineering works by P.C. Davison on 23rd May, 1944. The shell, which had failed to explode and narrowly missed some R.W.C. workmen, had been fired from **S.S. Empire Brutus** whilst engaged in gunnery trials about two miles offshore.

With magnetic and acoustic mines frequently being laid off the port by German aircraft and submarines, patrolling officers would occasionally spot or receive reports of such mines drifting perilously close to the foreshore abutting the docks. A careful watch would then be maintained upon their movement and their position reported to the naval authorities. At least one mine washed ashore in the darkness actually exploded, causing damage to the Monsanto chemical works at Hendon Dock on 9th January, 1941.

On 30th July, 1940, P.C. Harry Poulter was called to a shooting incident at the South Pier yard in which a private of the Essex Regiment had been fatally wounded after being accidentally shot by another soldier. The officer's attempts to investigate the matter were frustrated by the limited co-operation received from the lieutenant in charge.

Whilst the recovery of property was an everyday task, rather curious items would occasionally be taken into police possession. A number of parachutes used to drop mines from enemy aircraft were recovered, as were several barrage balloons, two of which were found snagged in a ship's superstructure and another that was taken in tow by a police launch after being observed drifting downriver. Other unusual finds included a quantity of live cartridges in a life buoy box at Leith Wharf, a life raft from an R.A.F. aircraft and several exhausted carrier pigeons.

Early in the morning of 13th March, 1940, P.C. Peter Cowe sighted an Admiralty Examination Vessel which had become stranded to the north of the New South Pier and subsequently assisted Roker Volunteer Life Brigade in the rescue by breeches buoy of her nine crew members.

Survivors from sunken allied vessels were frequently landed in the port, with Watch personnel often rendering first aid and arranging temporary accommodation upon their arrival.

Many outstanding feats of police work were performed by the River Police during the war. Once constable, in particular, named John Frederick Lowerson, a former War Reserve P.C. who had joined the Watch late in 1940, aged forty-two, seemed to be possessed with uncanny powers of observation and the ability to sense when a person had something to hide. Frequently, he would challenge individuals coming ashore from a ship in the docks and find them to have stolen property concealed about them or to be attempting to smuggle dutiable goods ashore.

RESCUES, DROWNINGS AND BODIES

During the period of the war, a notable increase was seen in the incidence of persons falling into the river and docks, frequently with fatal consequences. All too often, the victims were seamen, who whilst attempting to board or disembark from their ships, missed their footing during the blackout. Alcohol was often a contributory factor.

No fewer than fourteen persons were saved from drowning through the prompt action and vigilance displayed by members of the Watch, whilst many rescues were also accomplished by others before the arrival of the police at the scene.

Undoubtedly, their most unpleasant duty was the recovery of dead bodies from the water. A total of twenty-seven was recovered during the war, often in the most appalling state of decomposition. In general, the Watch maintained an excellent record in achieving the positive identification of such remains, a task made more difficult by the circumstances of war, especially when foreigners were involved. On several occasions, bodies that had lain in the river for months were brought to the surface by R.W.C. dredgers, the body of a seaman who had fallen overboard from the Iberian Shipping Company's **Baron Forbes** on 11th January, 1941 being found in such a manner some sixteen months later.

The most serious drowning incident to occur in the port during the war took place late on the night of 9th January, 1943, when a ship's boat returning six seamen to their vessels moored at White's Tier capsized, throwing its occupants into the river. River P.C's Ernest Stark and George Gibson were quickly on the scene in the motor launch, *Vigilant* and rescued three men who were found clinging to the piles of Corporation Quay. The remainder, however, were not so fortunate, having been swept away by the strong ebb tide and lost.

RESURGENCE OF THE 'FIRE KING' AND 'FIRE QUEEN'

Following years of moderate use, the *Fire King* and *Fire Queen* again came into their own as calls for assistance to combat land and shipboard fires, and to pump out flooded vessels, increased significantly. In fact, the fireboats were placed on stand-by or required to attend incidents, many as the result of enemy action, on about thirty occasions during the war.

Although the first air raid on the Port of Sunderland took place on 12th June, 1940, when Hendon Dock was bombed, it was some ten months later before a fire steamer was first employed due to German bombing.

BINNS' STORES GUTTED DURING AIR RAID

At 11.25 p.m. on 9th April, 1941, the wailing of air-raid sirens heralded what was to be a devastating attack upon both Wearside and Tyneside. As the fire steamers lay at their moorings with boilers warmed through, members of the Watch waited, wondering if this was to be their night for action.

With bombers droning overhead and sounds of explosions echoing through the night, an eerie glare lit up the sky to the south as hundreds of incendiaries rained down onto the town centre, turning Binns department stores on both sides of Fawcett Street into blazing infernos.

At 3 a.m., the following morning, as members of the Borough Brigade and the Auxiliary Fire Service struggled to subdue the flames, the call came for the assistance of the *Fire Queen.* Steam was at once raised and, under the command of John Rochford, she headed upriver to the Panns ferry landing below Wearmouth Bridge.

Connections were made to the 6 inch dry rising main beneath the bridge and further orders awaited. At 4 a.m., with instructions having been received to commence pumping, the powerful engines of the steamer sprang into life, pumping water from the river up to street level. From there, it was fed by relays of hose to Mowbray Park lake, almost half a mile distant, where trailer-pumps positioned around its perimeter supplied the water to firemen tackling the burning stores and other fires throughout the town centre. For almost fifteen hours, the *Fire Queen* continued to replenish the lake before returning to her moorings at 7.30 p.m. and making ready for further calls.

Although the fire was eventually overcome, only the burnt out shells of the stores remained. The *Fire Queen,* by means of her continuous pumping, had been the means of conserving much of the town's water supply.

FORMATION OF THE NATIONAL FIRE SERVICE (N.F.S.)

In respect of firefighting, the River Wear Watch had integrated well within the Borough's civil defence structure during the early years of the war.

The Borough Fire Brigade, still under the ultimate control of the Chief Constable, together with the Auxiliary Fire Service, were taken over by the National Fire Service upon its formation on 18th August, 1941. The Borough Brigade would never again return to police control, as an independent fire brigade for the town, under the command of a chief fire officer, was to be created on 1st April, 1948 under the provisions of the Fire Services Act, 1947.

The agreement which the River Wear Watch Commissioners and Sunderland Corporation had entered into during 1940, regarding the use of the Watch's firefloats, was transferred to the N.F.S., which continued to pay the annual rental of £10.

From 1941, the National Fire Service operated a small firefloat of its own. Sixteen firefighters were assigned to crew the vessel which was based at the Fish Quay. After the war, her services became superfluous but it was not until December, 1947 that she left the Wear, sailing for the Tyne to be sold. Her crew, whose annual salaries amounted to some £4,500, were then transferred to stations within the No. 1 Fire Force Area.

WARTIME SALVAGE DUTIES

Valuable assistance to ships attacked by enemy aircraft off the Northeast Coast was frequently rendered by the *Fire Queen*, with a number of such occurrences during 1941.

On 26th May, the 297 gross tons French steamer, *Gros Pierre*, on charter to the Ministry of Shipping, was bombed off Sunderland and, in a sinking condition, limped into the Wear before being beached on Potato Garth. Arriving on the scene shortly after 3.50 p.m., the **Fire Queen**, had, within the hour, pumped the stricken vessel's engine room dry, enabling her to be towed to John Crown's slipway for repair.

On 7th June, a similar incident occurred, this time involving the 220 gross tons H.M. Trawler, *Star of Deveron* which had also been bombed at sea. The trawler was able to reach Corporation Quay where the *Fire Queen* was brought alongside and engaged for four hours pumping water from her engine room and forepeak. After undergoing repairs, the *Star of Deveron* returned to service but was not to be so fortunate later the same year when, on 30th September, together with H.M. Trawler, *Eileen Duncan*, she was attacked and sunk by enemy aircraft at North Shields.

A further call for assistance was received on 2nd August from *S.S. Juta*, which required pumping out at the Lower Tier buoys after being hit by bombs off the port. On arrival of the *Fire Queen*, however, it was discovered that the inflow of water had been stemmed, her services no longer being required.

The next incident occurred on 12th August, when *S.S. Eaglescliffe Hall* was bombed two miles east of the Wear. Four badly injured crewmen were later landed at Corporation Quay and conveyed to hospital by the River Police. The 1,990 gross tons vessel was subsequently reported to be on fire and the *Fire Queen* was placed on stand-by to deal with the outbreak. By 2.30 a.m. the next morning, it had been confirmed that the fire had been extinguished at sea and that the ship would not be entering port until daylight. At 11.25 p.m. on 14th August, having entered the South Docks, the *Eaglescliffe Hall* was discovered to be making water. The *Fire King* was brought alongside, but it was found that the ingress of water was less than originally feared. River Police personnel gave constant attention until the following morning, when a portable pump which had been placed on board was found to be adequate in keeping her free from water.

On the evening of 13th April, 1942, the *Fire Queen* was called to provide assistance to the National Fire Service at an engine room fire on board the 2,569 gross tons steamer,

S.N.A. 8, berthed at Lambton Drops, the fire being extinguished after one hour's pumping. Whilst engaged on board the vessel, members of the Watch were required to work in dark and cramped conditions, having to wade through flooded compartments. Their task was hampered by the inexplicable lack of provision of basic equipment, such as rubber boots and electric torches, a fact that did not go unnoticed by the Superintendent Smith of the Borough Police who was present at the scene.

On 9th May, 1942, a further request was made for the *Fire Queen* to be placed in readiness to pump out a leaking minesweeper, *H.M.S. Ratapiko* which was making for Sunderland Harbour after being damaged by enemy action. By the time she reached the river, however, her own pumps had been found sufficient to cope and the fireboat was ordered to stand down.

A major effort was required on the morning of 5th June, 1942 to salvage *S.S. Zealous,* lying upriver at Hetton Drops. The collier had been seriously damaged by the detonation of a delayed action bomb, dropped into the river during the previous night's air raid. On arrival at the scene, the crew of the *Fire Queen* found that the *Zealous* had developed a heavy port list. Four lengths of suction hose were connected and led into the engine room which was flooded to the cylinder tops. Continuous pumping from 9.10 a.m. until 2 p.m. allowed workmen to gain access to effect temporary repairs. Meanwhile water from the engine room had leaked into No. 2 hold, necessitating the transfer of hoses from the engine room. The hold was eventually cleared, but further pumping was required to keep the engine room dry and enable the leaks there to be finally sealed. At 7.30 p.m., the vessel was taken under tow to Crown's slipway with the *Fire Queen* remaining alongside. Eventually, at 8.35 p.m., with the ship safely beached at the entrance to the slipway, suction hoses were removed and the firefloat returned to her moorings after having been working for a total of twelve hours, the charge for her services amounting to £105.

NIGHTS TO REMEMBER - MAY, 1943

Although a number of further incidents were attended by the firefloats, none were as a result of hostile action until May, 1943, when the men of the River Wear Watch were to experience the two greatest air raids unleashed upon Sunderland during the entire war - and live to tell the tale.

On the moonlit morning of 16th May, the alert was sounded at 1.44 a.m. For over an hour afterwards, bombs of every description - high explosive, parachute mines, firepots and hundreds of incendiaries - rained down upon the town. The blasts caused by the explosions produced a wind which blew burning embers in all directions as chandelier flares dropped from the German bombers turned night into day.

As anti-aircraft batteries across the town opened up skywards, Sergeant James Rich, together with Constables Frederick Lowerson and Thomas Hunter waited anxiously on board the River Station, *Manual*. Then, at 2.40 a.m., the officers braced themselves as they heard the awesome whistle of a high explosive bomb descending close by.

The bomb exploded in the river some thirty feet northwest of the station, causing her and the vessels moored alongside, consisting of the *Fire Queen, Patrol* and *Vigilant* to pitch so violently that they almost capsized. The whole of the superstructure and deck fittings of the River Station were severely damaged, with the starboard sides of her deck houses having been blown out by the blast. Her ancient hull was so badly shaken by concussion that it began to take in water at an alarming rate. Luckily, although badly shaken, the officers on board were unhurt.

Damage to the **Fire Queen** was extensive, her hull, superstructure, machinery and fittings all having been holed in many places by bomb splinters. In addition, a small fire had broken out aft but had quickly been extinguished. So severe was the overall damage, that she would be out of commission for a considerable period. As most of the bomb splinters had been absorbed by the **Fire Queen**, there is little doubt that her presence prevented serious casualties on board the **Manual**. Although both launches had been disabled, temporary repairs were soon effected.

The bomb blast had aggravated previous damage accidentally sustained by the **Patrol**, **Manual** and **Fire Queen**, just over a month earlier, on 8th April. The steam launch, whilst in attendance at Short Bros' shipyard at Pallion during the launch of steamship, had been crushed against the quayside by the ship, forcing the officers on board to jump for their lives. Then, twenty minutes later, **S.S. English Prince,** whilst being towed downriver, had collided with the River Station and firefloat as they lay at their moorings.

Returning to the events of 16th May, a tugboatman had been killed during the raid on board the paddle tug, **Wexford** at Manor Quay - only a short distance from the River Station. A huge fire was also raging at T. W. Greenwell and Co's shiprepair yard, where the contents of blazing oil storage tanks ruptured during the raid were spewing into the river, threatening to engulf the 2,723 g.r.t. Soviet vessel, **Bureya** in one of the company's dry docks. At one stage, flames were licking at the South Docks' entrance gateway, placing the whole complex in peril.

Being unable to operate the **Fire Queen**, members of the Watch made their way to the South Docks by launch but found that officers on board the **Fire King** had not raised steam and had made their way to Greenwell's, expecting the **Fire Queen** to be there. With telephone communication having been cut, there was no way in which they could have known her fate. After some delay, the **Fire King** was got under way and locked into the Half-Tide Basin, where she steamed to the inside of No. 1 Gateway, only yards from the burning tanks and directed five jets onto the flames. As daylight broke, a column of smoke could be seen drifting as far south as Hartlepool, but by 7 a.m., the outbreak had finally been extinguished. After her equipment had been made up, the **Fire King** proceeded upriver to the River Station to deputise for the **Fire Queen**.

During the height of the fire, a firefloat maintained by Doxford's shipyard had become trapped amidst the burning oil and had been saved only by the timely intervention of France, Fenwick Tyne and Wear Company Ltd's steamtug, **Roker** which had manoeuvred through the flames to pull her to safety. Throughout the town, great devastation had resulted from the raid, with over seventy fatalities having occurred.

Continuous use of the pumps was required to keep the **Manual** afloat before some of the leaks could be sealed and tarpaulin covers placed over the wrecked cabin to allow the craft to remain in use. A subsequent appeal to Sunderland Corporation to provide a police box on shore, as temporary accommodation for the Watch, was surprisingly turned down.

In little more than a week, events were to be repeated. With even greater ferocity, the bombers returned during the early hours of Monday, 24th May.

With bombs falling all around, the **Fire King** had little distance to travel as fire, caused by the dropping of parachute mines, enveloped part of J. L. Thompson's premises at Manor Quay. As had been so during the raid of 16th May, fifteen Watch personnel were engaged in firefighting duties who, in conjunction with the N.F.S. and volunteers from the shipyard, had doused the flames by 5 a.m., the *Fire King* having deployed seven water jets for ninety minutes.

During the raid, accredited with being the worst of the war for the port, a new 7,241 gross tons ship named *Denewood*, which was fitting out near the firefloat received a direct hit and sank to the river bed. Bomb shrapnel penetrated the *Fire King's* hull, fortunately causing little harm, whilst further slight damage was caused to the *Fire Queen* which lay idle across the river.

Elsewhere, a bomb fell through the hatchway of a collier lying at a coal belt in Hudson Dock, passing clean though the bottom of her hull, but without sinking her. Two concrete hulks in Hendon Dock and two water boats in Hudson dock were sunk, with nine other craft being damaged. The Corporation Quay oil installation and the grain warehouse at the northwest corner of Hudson Dock received remarkable escapes as incendiaries and firepots landed close by. Over forty buildings were damaged in the dock area alone, together with six of the coal staiths and the New South Pier. Dock roads and railways also suffered, with a number of railway wagons being destroyed. As fires broke out within the South Dock estate, the *Fire King* was badly missed due to her enforced transfer to the river. The town again had suffered badly, with around eighty-five inhabitants having lost their lives.

As the River Wear Watch prepared for what might follow on nights to come, its members could not have known that the bombers would never again return to Sunderland.

Yet, before the war ended, the Watch still had many important duties to perform and did not relax its vigilance for one moment. The fireboats continued to be regularly engaged, with their services being requested in connection with the salvaging of the Lambton, Hetton and Joicey Collieries' paddle tug, *Eppleton Hall* at Hetton Quay and a tank landing craft in Hendon Dock, together with outbreaks of fire at Dickinson's Engineworks, the Shipbuilding Corporation's yard at Southwick, on board the *S.S. Empire Crest* berthed at Scotia Quay and the steamships, *Empire Gain*, *Nandi* and *Empire Wyclif*, all at Dickinson's Quay.

Chapter 11

THE EARLY POST-WAR PERIOD

(1945 - 1953)

It can be argued that the River Wear Watch reached its zenith during the 1940's. With the onset of war, any fresh notions regarding the cessation or transfer of the Commissioners' powers had been held in abeyance, a state of affairs which was to continue until the end of the decade. Indeed, the existence of the force was, in all likelihood, perpetuated due to its first class work during the war, together with a number of practical measures undertaken by the Commissioners in the years immediately afterwards.

A NEW CLERK TO THE COMMISSIONERS

In January, 1946, the Clerk to the Watch Commissioners, Mr. Edward Cope resigned his position due to ill health. In a resourceful move, the Commissioners chose to dispense with their tradition of appointing a practising solicitor as Clerk and instead requested that the River Wear Commissioners consider providing Cope's successor from within their own ranks.

Consequently, Mr. A. H. J. Brown, the R.W.C. General Manager and Clerk was appointed Clerk to the Watch Commissioners as an additional capacity. In practice, the onerous clerical duties appertaining to the office were discharged by Brown's deputy, Mr. E. Lonsdale who also received the annual salary of £110 attached to the post.

LAUNCH FACILITIES GRANTED TO THE PORT HEALTH AUTHORITY

In May, 1946, an agreement was reached between the Watch Commissioners and Sunderland Port Health Authority, whereby police launch facilities were to be accorded, free of charge, to health inspectors to remove sick and injured seamen from vessels lying at buoys in the river and docks. Interestingly, the Watch Commissioners had turned down a similar request by the Port Health Authority in 1917.

A comparable agreement, by which H.M. Customs and Excise officers were conveyed to ships when their own launch was unavailable was already in operation.

THE SEARCH FOR A NEW HEADQUARTERS

As peace followed war, a major priority for the Commissioners was to replace their decrepit and timeworn River Station, ***Manual***, together with the elderly steam launch, ***Patrol***.

Owing to her great age and the battering that she had sustained during 1943, the *Manual* was in urgent need of replacement. In November, 1945, Willcox Bros., the Commissioners' superintending engineers had described her hull as being *"in a very porous and rotten condition, having long passed the stage where satisfactory repairs could be carried out."* Indeed, John Crown and Sons had refused the responsibility of placing the craft on their slipway for fear that she might disintegrate.

Two choices were available to the Commissioners; either to acquire another floating station or to move to premises on shore. Although both options were explored, several years would elapse before a satisfactory solution was arrived at.

In August, 1946, a request by the Watch Commissioners to the R.W.C. to ascertain whether the latter could provide a riverside site for the erection of a shore station, with suitable moorings for the *Fire Queen* and launches, met with an unfavourable response. Captain Chapman, the Superintendent Harbour and Dockmaster, felt it to be in the Watch's best interests for a replacement floating station to be provided in the same berth as the *Manual*. He considered this location to be the finest in the river as it was in a central position, out of reach of the worst effects of the sea and could be used at all states of the tide by launches and fireboats. In any event, no shore site was available to the east of Wearmouth Bridge, although it might have been possible to provide one at Hetton Quay.

Accordingly, the Commissioners continued with their endeavours to find a craft suitable for conversion into a floating station. Despite numerous vessels being inspected, none were deemed adequate for the purpose required.

It had been hoped that the Director of Small Craft Disposals at the Admiralty would have been able to provide a vessel. The most acceptable which could be offered from this source was an ex-barrage vessel, *B.V. 18* which, at a length of 98 feet, was too large for the Commissioners' purposes. Other craft considered were one of twenty-eight steel nesting barges at Bidstone Dock, Liverpool; a steel hulled vessel named *Meadows*, lying in the Forth; the water boat, *Renora* and the *S.S. Fairy Queen*, both on the Tyne; and the Admiralty dumb barge, *Spider (W.D. 148)*. This latter vessel had been towed into Sunderland on 4th April, 1948 by the Admiralty tug, *Earner*, together with a similar barge named *Wasp*, after developing a leak whilst on passage from Chatham, and had been pumped out by the *Fire Queen*. Afterwards, the *Earner* had left port with the *Wasp* in tow, leaving the *Spider* behind in the South Docks. Regrettably for the Commissioners, on enquiring whether the barge was for sale, they were informed that it was still required for service as a coal lighter.

Consideration was even given to constructing a new floating station, with John Crown and Sons drawing up plans for a pontoon design. The idea, however, was soon rejected on the grounds of prohibitive cost.

ACQUISITION OF 'PIKES' No. 10'

With the need to replace the *Manual* becoming more urgent by the day, information was received concerning two dumb barges, the *C.160* and *Pikes' No. 10*, which were being offered for sale by Risdon Beazley Ltd. of Southampton.

Preliminary examination of the craft by marine surveyors, Thompson, Lewis and Howie Ltd. proved encouraging and in October, 1948, Theo. Willcox and Sub-Inspector Pennington travelled to Southampton to conduct their own inspection.

Whilst the ***C.160*** was deemed to be too large, ***Pikes' No. 10*** seemed to be just what the Commissioners had been looking for. She had been built in 1943 by clay merchants, Messrs. Pike of Wareham, Dorset and had been requisitioned by the Government during the war as an armaments carrier. The barge had ultimately been used for diving purposes before being put up for sale and had a length of 70 feet with a 17 feet 9 inch beam. Her hull was constructed from Oregon pine and her frames of oak.

A price of £1,250 (including delivery), plus £14 for coating her bottom with tar, was agreed upon, the contract being signed on 15th October, 1948. Five days later, ***Pikes' No. 10*** arrived in the Wear under tow by the tug, ***Topmast 10*** and was berthed at Scotia Quay.

The contract for her conversion into a floating police station was awarded to John Crown and Sons Ltd., the craft being placed on their slipway on 15th March, 1949. Work progressed speedily and at 6 a.m. on 12th May, 1949, the new station entered commission. Conversion work had been undertaken at a cost of £875 with an additional £222.15s. being spent on fitting out and necessary hull repairs.

Pikes' No. 10 was a great improvement for River Police personnel, although the straight sides and low freeboard of the ***Manual*** had made that craft more suitable for mooring alongside. The hull of the new station was coated with black varnish and fitted with a cabin measuring 12 feet by 10 feet, inside which were provided a lavatory, lockers, seats, cushions and a coal burning stove, together with a 9 feet by 6 feet office which contained a desk, telephone facilities and a washbasin. The hold, measuring 42 feet 7 inches by 14 feet 10 inches had been converted for use as a store and workshop and contained a half-ton fresh water tank.

An overhead electricity connection was made with the shore and the opportunity also taken to equip the ***Fire Queen*** with this facility. Special permission had to be obtained from the Ministry of Transport for a flexible cable to be suspended over the river between the premises of S. P. Austin and Sons and the station.

THE END OF THE ROAD FOR THE 'MANUAL'

As for the ***Manual***, her days were now over with £10 scrap value having been paid by Crowns. At 11.45 a.m. on 12th May, 1949, after removal of serviceable fittings, the vessel, in the charge of two men employed by Thomas Young and Sons (Shipbreakers) Ltd., proceeded upriver under tow by Crowns' launch, with a police launch assisting at the stern. She was taken to the south shore of the river just above John Wigham and Sons' winch works at South Hylton and placed in charge of a Mr. Russell who commenced breaking her up and removing her oak timbers and copper bottom on behalf of Youngs. It was a sad end for a vessel which had served the Watch so well for a century.

STEAM LAUNCH REPLACED BY NEW MOTOR LAUNCH

After more than twenty-eight years of service with the Watch, the steam launch, ***Patrol*** had finally been placed out of commission on 30th October, 1945, as her boiler had been condemned by the National Boiler and General Insurance Co. Ltd's inspector.

It was subsequently decided to place an order for a new motor launch with the Wearside Boatbuilding Co. at Monkwearmouth Shore.

The launch was built at a cost of £715 and was similar in appearance to the standard pattern of police launch used for many years on rivers such as the Thames and Tyne. She was clinker-built from timber with a length of 26 feet and a beam of 7 feet 6 inches A maximum speed of ten knots was provided by a Morris Marine Commodore six cylinder, 20 h.p., petrol driven engine which had been supplied by Morris Engines Ltd. of Coventry.

The name *Patrol* was transferred to the new launch, which entered service on 4th August, 1947. The old steam launch had been sold for £60 to a Mr. J. Hudson of Wear Street, South Hylton in August, 1946, on condition that she would be renamed.

RETIREMENT OF INSPECTOR ROCHFORD

On 30th March, 1949, owing to his great age and failing health, Inspector John William Arthur Rochford, then eighty years old, regretfully relinquished his position with the River Wear Watch.

His police career had spanned fifty-three years, the last thirty-six as Inspector of the Watch. Despite his long service, he received no pension as it had not been possible, in spite of several short-lived attempts, to formulate a successful superannuation scheme for the force. Everyone was sorry to see him leave and in recognition of his long and faithful service he was awarded a handsome gratuity by the Watch Commissioners. He was to enjoy only a short retirement, living at his Nelson Street home until his death on 12th February, 1952.

Rochford was succeeded as Inspector by James Laws Pennington who had joined the Watch as a constable in 1925, before being promoted to sergeant in 1932 and to sub-inspector three years later.

VISIT OF GERMAN WATERWAYS POLICE CHIEFS

After the war, the entire German police structure was gradually reorganised. In 1950, following the creation of the Federal Republic of Germany the previous year, five chiefs of West German waterways police forces *(Wasserschutzpolizei)* visited the United Kingdom on a fact-finding tour. The officers were eager to learn about British marine policing practices in order that some might be adopted in West Germany.

On 9th March, the Germans visited Sunderland and were hosted by Superintendent Tait of the Borough Police and members of the River Wear Watch, being taken on a most enlightening tour of the port.

POST-WAR SALVAGE DUTIES

The years from 1946 to 1953 saw a marked reduction in the number of incidents attended by the Watch's firefloats, salvage duties becoming their predominant function.

For several weeks early in 1946, the sight of the sunken 1,368 gross tons steam collier, *Raloo*, owned by Austin Friars Steam Shipping Co. Ltd., at North Quay Buoys was a familiar one to Wearsiders crossing Wearmouth Bridge. Yet, had the advice of the River Wear Watch been heeded, the situation might never have arisen.

At 7.40 p.m. on 2nd February, information had been received at the River Station that the *Raloo*, then lying alongside Austins' Pontoon, was making water rapidly after being involved in a collision with the 8,398 gross tons motor tanker, *Derwentdale*, near Corporation Quay. *The Fire Queen*, with Sub-Inspector Pennington in charge, was quickly alongside the ship, which was fully laden and well down by the head due to water leaking into the forward hold. Sizing up the situation, the Sub-Inspector pointed out to the vessel's master and chief engineer that there was no way in which to deal with the ingress of water unless a hole was cut through the bulkhead between the forepeak and hold to allow pumping to be carried out from there. The ship's own pumps, the sub-inspector judged, could adequately deal with the water running aft towards the engine room.

Undoubtedly feeling that they had good cause, the captain and chief engineer declined to act upon the Sub-Inspector's suggestion and dispensed with the fireboat's services. At 11.30 p.m., the *Raloo* was towed across the river to the North Quay Buoys, where she sank to the river bed at 8 a.m. the following morning.

Salvage operations were subsequently undertaken by the Admiralty, in which the River Wear Watch played no part, necessitating the off-loading of most of the sunken vessel's cargo of coal. Navigation within the river was severely impeded, with the launch of the collier, *Sir Alexander Kennedy* from S. P. Austin and Sons' shipyard having to be postponed. It was not until 2nd April, 1946 that the *Raloo* was finally raised and berthed alongside Dickinson's Quay.

The Wear was indeed an unlucky river for the *Raloo* as, almost exactly a year later, on 5th February, 1947, she broke her moorings during a blizzard and ran aground at North Sands. Although refloated the following day, she began to leak and a repetition of the previous year's foundering was feared. Fortunately, the leak was sealed without further mishap.

On 14th October, 1947, the *Fire Queen* was again called to Austins' shipyard to pump out another leaking collier. This time it was the Gas, Light and Coke Company's 2,136 g.r.t. Stelling. It was a lengthy task, with the firefloat being engaged for over eleven hours.

Following the salvaging of the lighter, *Spider* in 1948, previously referred to, the *Fire Queen* was next in action on 8th September, 1949 when the 158 g.r.t. coaster, *Oceanic,* owned by the Vectis Shipping Co., Isle of Wight, arrived at Corporation Quay with a flooded engine room. The situation, which had been caused by a faulty discharge valve, was quickly dealt with in only thirty minutes.

An unusual request for the services of the *Fire Queen* was received in 1950, when the Demolition and Construction Co. Ltd. engaged her services to pump water at high pressure to remove mud and other debris from the base of new iron piles at the entrance to the new Greenwells' No. 1 Dry Dock.

Wear Dredger No. 2, of 1902 vintage, which was found to be in a leaking condition whilst lying at the Lower Buoys in the river, was pumped out by the *Fire Queen* during the early hours of 3rd October, 1951 in an operation lasting four and a half hours.

Finally, in 1952, the *Fire Queen*, under the command of Inspector Pennington, was engaged in a protracted operation when the salvage vessel, *Airmoor II* struck a submerged object at sea and put into port in a leaking condition on 27th November. The fireboat was quickly alongside, with suction hose being coupled up and led into the vessel's engine room which was flooded up to deck level. Before the pumps could be started, however, the *Airmoor II* sank rapidly by the stern, making necessary the prompt evacuation of her crew to the

Fire Queen. Attempts to refloat the salvage vessel were made on 5th December, 1952 when the *Fire Queen* was recalled to the scene. By 4 a.m. the next day, after almost eight hours of pumping at full pressure, the *Airmoor II* was found to be on an even keel and practically free of water. She was then towed to Crowns' slipway with the fireboat remaining alongside with pumps still active. On reaching the slipway, all suction hoses were disconnected, but almost immediately the *Airmoor II* again began to fill with water. Once more, pumping was recommenced but after an hour, it was decided to allow the vessel to settle at the foot of the slipway. Although the *Fire Queen* returned later that afternoon and stood by whilst slipping operations were undertaken, her services were not required.

FIRE AT R.W.C. WORKSHOPS, SOUTH DOCKS

A rare appearance of the *Fire King* was seen on 12th October, 1949 when a huge fire broke out in the River Wear Commissioners' workshops, situated on the east side of the Half-Tide Basin, South Docks.

As if to demonstrate the steamer's powerful capability, the crew of the *'King'* immediately deployed her 2¹/₂ inch monitor with shattering effect. Pit props on the quayside were scattered like matchsticks as walls and the roof of the workshops were demolished by the sheer force of the water jet. Within thirty minutes of the fireboat's arrival the flames had been subdued and prevented from spreading to a nearby dredger and other premises.

Afterwards, criticism was directed towards the Watch, as members of the Borough Fire Brigade engaged at the scene had been placed in mortal danger through the use of the monitor.

FIRE ON BOARD 'M.V. BRITISH NAVIGATOR' AT MANOR QUAY

The final occasion upon which a River Wear Watch firefloat was engaged at the scene of a shipboard fire took place on 12th December, 1950 - almost eleven years before the Watch finally went out of existence.

At 8.50 a.m., that day, information was received at the River Station that fire had broken out on board the 6,135 g.r.t. motor tanker, *British Navigator*, a new vessel which had been launched by J. L. Thompson and Sons Ltd. for the British Tanker Co. Ltd. and which was fitting out at Manor Quay.

Accompanied by Sergeant Davison and P.C. Dodsworth, Inspector Pennington crossed the river by launch to ascertain the extent of the outbreak. On boarding the ship, smoke was seen to be pouring from the aft alleyways and ports as the result of a fire within the refrigerating compartment. Steam was raised on the *Fire Queen* and at 9.15 a.m., the steamer made her way to Manor Quay and moored astern of the tanker, where Borough Fire Brigade personnel had made ready a 2¹/₂ inch hose to connect to the fireboat.

The *Fire Queen* commenced pumping at 9.25 a.m. and later another line of 2¹/₂ inch hose was passed on board the ship. Pumping was maintained until 10.15 a.m., when Deputy Chief Fire Officer Allinson announced that the fire had been extinguished and that the services of the fireboat would no longer be required. Fortunately, extensive damage had been prevented, although wooden and cork insulation had been destroyed, electrical wiring burnt out and some plating buckled.

ASSISTANCE TO SHIPWRECKED SURVIVORS

Following the war, it was still not uncommon for vessels to come to grief off the local coastline. In such instances, the River Wear Watch would always be available to assist survivors who were brought ashore in the port.

Such was the case on 18th March, 1947, when the 8,146 g.r.t. motor tanker, *Diloma*, owned by the Anglo-Saxon Petroleum Co. Ltd., ran aground on rocks off Hendon whilst on passage from Haifa to Jarrow with a cargo of benzine. Sunderland lifeboat, *Edward and Isabella Irwin* and one of the port's pilot cutters were soon on the scene to assist the tanker's crew of forty-nine who had taken to the lifeboats.

Tragically, a lifeboat being towed by the pilot cutter capsized, throwing all its occupants into the sea. Although the lifeboat and pilot cutter were successful in recovering all of the men from the water, two Chinese seamen lost their lives and many others suffered injury and the effects of exposure. As the survivors were landed at Corporation Quay, members of the Watch were present to look after their welfare. Their priority was to render first aid and organise the removal of casualties to hospital. When this had been accomplished, arrangements were made for uninjured crewmen to be accommodated at the local Seamen's Mission.

Similar support was provided on 11th February, 1950, after the France, Fenwick Tyne and Wear Co. Ltd. steamtug, *Stag* keeled over and sank whilst assisting in the towage of the new Ellerman Lines', *City of Manchester* towards Sunderland in a fearful offshore wind. Four of the tug's crew of six were drowned, but her captain and fireman were rescued and brought ashore at Corporation Quay by the steamtug, *Fulwell*. They were accompanied to hospital by River Police officers who also provided first aid during the journey. A year later, the Watch was represented on board the paddle tug, *Eppleton Hall* during a moving memorial service at sea for those who had been lost.

OFFBEAT DUTIES

Routine duties carried out by the Watch were occasionally interspersed with somewhat unusual occurrences. On 18th January, 1947, for instance, P.C. Frederick Lowerson gave chase to a riderless horse and cart seen galloping furiously along the west side of Hudson Dock. Upon the officer catching up with them on Gladstone Bridge, the horse bolted, overturning its cart, and ran towards Greenwells' Dry Docks. Again the P.C. took up the pursuit and was eventually able to capture the frightened animal.

Another serious mishap was prevented by P.C. George Gibson on 14th June, 1948, when he brought a set of runaway railway wagons to a standstill as they approached the Sea Lock bridge, by applying their brakes at great personal risk.

An occurrence which afterwards must have been regarded with great hilarity, took place at Scotia Quay on 23rd December, 1948, when *S.S. Colville* which was engaged in quayside engine trials, had her propeller fouled by a baulk of timber, some thirty feet long. Sub-Inspector Pennington and P.C's Swan and Dodsworth kindly offered their services to

138

remove the obstruction, on the strict understanding that the ship's engines would not be started. With such an undertaking having been given, the three officers set off in a rowing boat to remove the timber. Whilst engaged in doing so and without warning, the propeller began to turn and struck the stern of the rowing boat slightly. Apprehending that the engines were about to be started and being in fear for their lives, P.C. Dodsworth jumped into the river and P.C. Swan leapt on top of the ship's rudder. In fact, the propeller had only turned about a quarter of a revolution by virtue of the engines moving through their own momentum. Apparently, the officers concerned took some convincing of this, being intent upon offering pieces of their minds to those on board the ship whom they believed had attempted to start the engines.

Whilst it was rare for members of the River Police to go to sea in the course of their duties, this was the case on 15th August, 1951 when, at 4.30 p.m., a report was received of a fishing vessel being on fire off the port. Initially, Sergeant Stark and P.C. Renwicks headed downriver to the harbour bar, from where they espied a vessel burning furiously out at sea. They returned directly to North Dock, where the sergeant boarded a pilot cutter together with Fire Officer Stoddart of the Borough Fire Brigade and a pilot, before setting off to investigate the fire. Whilst about one mile from Ryhope Dene, the cutter reached the fishing yawl, *Volga* which was blazing fiercely from stem to stern. Despite the flames, Sergeant Stark and the fire officer were able to board the vessel to ensure that no-one remained on board. As it was considered too dangerous to take the yawl in tow, the cutter commenced a search of the area for survivors and eventually came upon the coble, *Treasure* which had picked up the *Volga's* crew, unharmed. Later that night, the burnt out hulk of the yawl was seen drifting off the harbour and brought into port and beached by the pilot cutter.

FINANCIAL MATTERS

During the latter stages of the war and until the early 1950's, the Watch Commissioners' financial state had been healthier than for some years. Besides purchasing a new river station and motor launch, it had been possible to set aside cash, in the form of investments, for renewals and repairs to other craft. Uppermost in the minds of the Commissioners was the age of the two firefloats, which although performing satisfactorily, would require replacement in the future.

Dues levied upon shipping peaked during the Commissioners' 1952/53 financial year, when £11,439.12.9d was collected on 1,830,786 tons. In fact, each year between the end of the war and 1954, with the exceptions of 1947 and 1949 when considerable outlay had been required to buy new craft, the Watch Commissioners operated at a surplus.

The 1940 Order, authorising the levy of an additional rate of one ha'penny over and above that which they were allowed to impose by the River Wear Watch Act, 1923, was terminated in October, 1950. Not wishing to return to a statutory maximum of only one penny per ton, the Watch Commissioners came to an agreement with the R.W.C. for the insertion of a clause in their pending Wear Navigation and Sunderland Dock Bill, 1950, whereby the maximum rate would be increased to twopence per n.r.t. Ten per cent of the costs of obtaining this Act was met by the Watch Commissioners. In the event, a rate of three ha'pence per ton continued to be levied until 1959, without the furore which had accompanied the implementation of new charging powers under the 1923 Act.

REPORT OF THE DOCKS AND INLAND WATERWAYS EXECUTIVE

Despite its immediate future appearing secure, August, 1951 saw the beginning of the long drawn out end for the River Wear Watch.

The Transport Act of 1947 required the British Transport Commission to keep trade harbours under review, this duty having been delegated to the Docks and Inland Waterways Executive. Accordingly, the Executive visited Sunderland during February, 1949 and on publication of its report in August, 1951, there seemed little doubt that the writing was on the wall for the Watch. The section of the report referring to the force read as follows:

"A curious arrangement survives whereby the policing of the river is undertaken by the River Wear Watch Commissioners who are authorised to levy charges for this service on shipping using the port. The River Wear Watch Act, 1923 authorises the transfer of the Watch to the Sunderland Corporation or to the River Wear Commissioners by agreement, and the Sunderland Corporation Act, 1927 provides that if the Watch is transferred to the Corporation, the special watching charge levied on shipping may be suspended and the cost of the service borne out of the Borough rates. As the River Wear Police Force is already superintended by the Chief Constable of Sunderland, there is no evident need for the continued existence of the Watch Commission, and shipping might well be relieved of the additional charge raised for this service."

In the course of their consideration of the report, the R.W.C. asked the Watch Commissioners for their views on the comments of the Executive. Objectively, the Watch Commissioners confirmed the view of their predecessors who, in 1919, had first expressed the desire that the Watch should be taken over by the Corporation. They believed that the services provided by the force were very necessary and in the interests of the community as a whole, but felt that there was no need for the continued existence of the Watch Commissioners as a body, as their functions could very well be performed by the Corporation.

A meeting was held on 13th February, 1952, between representatives of the Corporation and the R.W.C. to discuss the wider implications of the Executive's report in relation to the port as a whole, the views of the Watch Commissioners then being conveyed to the Corporation. The Corporation representatives, however, requested that the question of the Watch be held in abeyance as a number of other matters of greater significance arising from the report still had to be discussed by the R.W.C. and Corporation.

There the matter rested for the time being, but the Watch Commissioners would not allow it to remain dormant for ever.

63. Watched by a constable on board the *Fire Queen*, motor launch, *Patrol* leaves her moorings in 1959. The tugs, *Cleadon*, *Prestwick* and *Ryhope*, belonging to France, Fenwick Tyne & Wear Co. Ltd. provide an interesting background. *Northeast Press Ltd., Sunderland Echo.*

64. Walter Beattie Allan, a partner in Allan, Black & Co. and a director of the Albyn Line, who, on 28th October, 1959, was the last shipowner to be appointed to the River Wear Watch Commission. *Author's collection.*

65. This 1959 photograph shows that the Wear was still a hive of activity with colliers undergoing repair at, what was by then, Austin and Pickersgill Ltd's Wear Dockyard and new ships fitting out on the north side of the river at Manor Quay. *Northeast Press Ltd., Sunderland Echo.*

66. The firefloat, *Fire Queen* and motor launch, *Patrol* lie quietly alongside the River Station, *Pikes' No. 10*, in 1959. *Northeast Press Ltd., Sunderland Echo.*

67. Ernest Alfred Stark, who was promoted to Inspector of the River Wear Watch on 30th May, 1957 and served in that capacity until dissolution in 1961. *Author's collection.*

68. Sergeant 'No. 2' Thomas James Hunter, a member of the Watch between 1930 and 1961. *Author's collection.*

69. P.C. William Henry Dodsworth, who served with the Watch from 1928 until 1961. *Author's collection.*

70. Sergeant Robert F. Mustard on board the pristine *Fire Queen*, together with an unknown gentleman. *Author's collection.*

24

I beg to report at 2·20³·¹⁷ Wed 12th Oct 1960 while on duty at the River Station, a telephone message was received that a body was floating in the River at the Corporation Quay accompanied by P.C. 13 Chicken I proceeded to the spot in the Police launch & took possession of a badly decomposed body which was disintegrating on being brought alongside of the launch. On the body being lifted into the launch it was found to consist of a torso & leg from the thigh to the knee. It was then brought to the River station. The ambulance was sent for at 2·40 P.M. & on its arrival at 3·40 P.M. drawn by F. Glendenning the body was taken to the R.I. where it was examined by

Dr. Shanker who stated it was a torso of a human being but the sex could not be determined until further examination. It was then transferred to the Gen. Hos. mortuary. The body was badly decomposed & void of clothing except for some strands of fine white elastic around the hip. The length of the torso was approx 28" in length. C.I. informed at 4·15 P.M.

71. The entry in P.C. Dodsworth's note book concerning the recovery of an unidentified torso from the River Wear at Corporation Quay on 12th October, 1960. *Author's collection.*

72. The River Wear Watch's 'Foul Anchor' cap badge. *Author's collection.*

73.
River Wear Watch Inspectors' cloth cap badge. *Author's collection.*

74. River Wear Watch uniform button. *Author's collection.*

75. River Wear Police whistle. *Author's collection.*

76. Lying forlorn and forgotten in a corner of Hudson Dock, the *Fire King* and *Fire Queen* present a sorry sight in this 1962 picture as they await their fate. The superstructure of the *Fire Queen* has already been partially dismantled. *Northeast Press Ltd., Sunderland Echo.*

77. Motor launch, *Patrol*, pictured in May, 1962 in the service of Sunderland Borough Police River Section. Note her immaculate condition. *Northeast Press Ltd, Sunderland Echo.*

78. Constables Malcolm Donkin and Albert Swinbank of the Borough Police River Section on board the *Patrol*, in 1962, operating her new two-way v.h.f. wireless. *Northeast Press Ltd., Sunderland Echo.*

79. Another view of the *Patrol*, taken in 1964, showing the launch's white livery. *Northeast Press Ltd., Sunderland Echo.*

80. Grim faced Borough firemen at the scene of the fatal fire on board *M.V. Toronto City* at Doxford's Quay on 30th October, 1966, when seven men lost their lives. *Northeast Press Ltd., Sunderland Echo.*

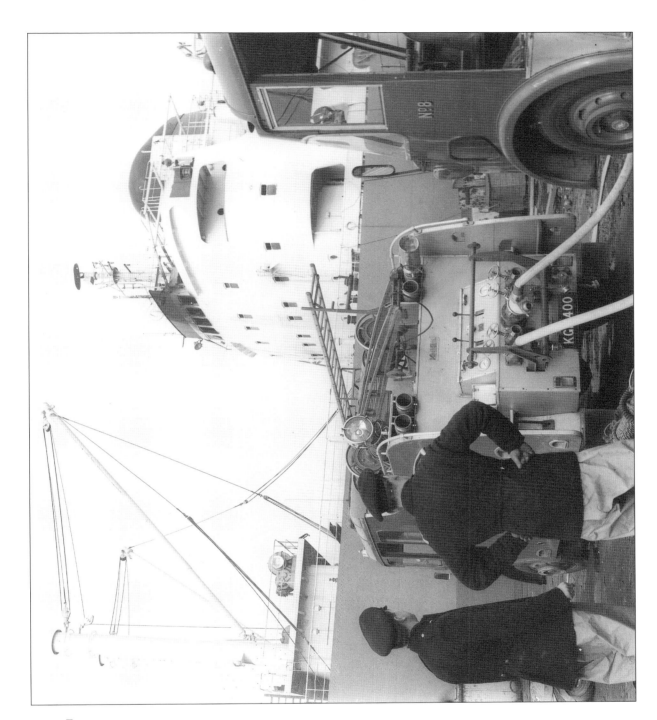

81. Members of Sunderland Borough Fire Brigade tackling the blaze on board *M.V. Landwade* at T. W. Greenwell and Co. Ltd's quay on 15th April, 1967. The blackened superstructure where four persons died is evident. *Northeast Press Ltd., Sunderland Echo.*

82. The Borough Brigade's new smoke extraction unit is used to good effect at a fire on board the West German collier, *Hanngrid*, at Hudson Dock, also in April, 1967.
Northeast Press Ltd., Sunderland Echo.

83. Members of the Auxiliary Fire Service exercising with a Bikini Raft Unit on the River Wear in 1964. Normally, each craft carried a crew of two.
Northeast Press Ltd., Sunderland Echo.

84. A Northumbria Police diver working with lifting bags at Hudson Dock in 1981 following the sinking of Lawson-Batey Tugs Ltd's motor tug, *Alnwick*.
L. G. Britton.

85. Northumbria Police Marine Sub Division's *Wear Station, North Dock, December, 1980. Police launches, *No. 4 (nearest camera)* and *No. 5* are moored to the pontoon in the corner of the dock, whilst a Watercraft launch is undergoing refurbishment on the quayside. Four U.S.U. vehicles can be seen inside the compound together with an assortment of portacabin accommodation. *Author's collection.*

86. Tyne and Wear Metropolitan Fire Brigade's fireboat, *Vedra*. *Tyne and Wear Metropolitan Fire Brigade.*

87. Members of the Northumbria Police Underwater Search Unit prepare their equipment before undertaking a search for two children thought to be missing near the Old North Pier in April, 1995.
Northeast Press Ltd, Sunderland Echo.

88. A popular duty for Northumbria Marine officers is attendance at the Sunderland International Air Show, held annually off the coast of Seaburn. Here, police launch. *Northumbria* keeps spectator craft at a safe distance during the touchdown of a Catalena flying boat. *L. G. Britton.*

89. *M.V. Viking*, formerly the firefloat, *Fire King* pictured at Grimsby Marina with all sails fully rigged. *Author's collection.*

Chapter 12

DEMISE OF THE WATCH

(1954 - 1959)

NEW MOVES TO SECURE CORPORATION TAKEOVER OF THE WATCH

Towards the end of 1954, with no further progress having been achieved in implementing the suggestions embodied in the Docks and Inland Waterways Executive's report regarding the transfer of the Watch to Sunderland Corporation, the Watch Commissioners decided to stimulate matters themselves.

Accordingly, at a meeting held on 24th November, 1954, the Commissioners resolved to reopen negotiations with the Corporation to secure the transfer of the Watch to the latter, under powers granted by Section 6 of the River Wear Watch Act, 1923. In reaching their decision, the Commissioners had in mind three main considerations:

Firstly, it had become increasingly difficult to find suitably qualified shipowners prepared to act as Commissioners. The time was fast approaching when a properly constituted meeting, requiring a quorum of five, might be unable to be conducted. By 1955, only five Commissioners were still active, namely Messrs. Burnop, Black, Irving, Rose and Marshall.

Secondly, the Home Office had indicated that upon the retirement of Superintendent Cook, it would be unwilling to permit his successor to carry out the functions of Superintendent of the Watch besides his duties as Chief Constable of the Borough Police. This, of course, was at odds with the 1840 River Wear Watch Act that stipulated that this must be the case. In the event, such fears were to prove unfounded as William Tait, who succeeded Cook in 1955, was authorised to perform such duties and to continue to receive an additional salary for doing so.

Thirdly, was the problem of the Commissioners' limited financial resources which appeared sounder than was actually the case. For four years, the actual strength of the force had been nineteen, three constables short of authorised establishment. Although difficulties had been experienced in recruiting suitable men, the Commissioners had remained in no hurry to fill these vacancies. The trend was one of increased expenditure and were the vacancies to be filled, the Commissioners would have to defray costs from their investments that had been set aside for the replacement of craft, particularly the firefloats. It was judged most imprudent to do such a thing as these reserves fell far short of the actual purchase price of new vessels. In addition, although trade in the port was booming, there was always the concern that a recession would adversely affect the amount of dues received from shipping.

REJECTION OF WATCH COMMISSIONERS' PROPOSAL BY SUNDERLAND CORPORATION

In October, 1955, following consideration of the Commissioners' resolution, the Town Clerk, Mr. G. S. McIntire replied on behalf of Sunderland Corporation:

"After full and careful consideration has been given by the committees of the Council to the proposed transfer .... they are unable to enter into an agreement under Section 6 of the River Wear Watch Act, 1923 for the transfer of the powers and duties of the River Wear Watch Commissioners."

THE RIVER WEAR COMMISSIONERS BECOME INVOLVED

Following this curt rejection of their proposal, the Watch Commissioners began to consider in earnest making an approach to Parliament to seek relief from their statutory duties. Before doing so, nevertheless, they wished to explore every possibility and therefore turned to the River Wear Commissioners, requesting their advice and co-operation to find the best solution to their difficulties.

The Clerk to the Watch Commissioners, Mr. Alfred H. J. Brown, acting in his capacity of General Manager and Clerk of the R.W.C., explained the situation to a meeting of the R.W.C. General Purposes and Finance Committee on 13th December, 1955. In consequence, a subcommittee was appointed, which reported back on 10th January, 1956.

Whilst not at that stage contemplating a R.W.C. takeover of the Watch, the subcommittee's report was sympathetic to the position of the Watch Commissioners and expressed an appreciation of their decision to consult with them on the matter. The subcommittee was of the opinion that the services rendered by the Watch to the port were of considerable value and hoped that a way could be found by which they could be kept in being. It was felt that the situation called for discussions between representatives of Sunderland Corporation, the River Wear Commissioners and the River Wear Watch Commissioners to enable the facts and possibilities to be made clear to all the parties involved.

TRIPARTITE MEETING

On 20th March, 1956, a tripartite meeting of the delegates of the three bodies was held at Sunderland Town Hall, the following being present:

River Wear Commissioners: Mr. R. A. Bartram (Chairman of the Board), Col. F. Dawson, Col. T. G. Greenwell, Mr. J. H. Short and Ald. A. H. Suddick.

R.W.C. Officials: Mr. A. H. J. Brown (Clerk and General Manager, also Clerk to the River Wear Watch Commissioners), Mr. E. Lonsdale (Deputy to Brown) and Mr. R. H. Middleton (Solicitor to the R.W.C.).

River Wear Watch Commissioners: Mr. N. R. Rose (Chairman of the Watch Commission), Mr. T. G. Irving and Mr. A. Marshall.

Sunderland Corporation: Ald. Miss. E. E. Blacklock (Mayor), Ald. N. L. Allinson, Ald. J. Hoy, Cllr. T. M. Carr and Cllr. R. Wilkinson.

Corporation Officials: Mr. G. S. McIntire (Town Clerk), Mr. J. Storey, Mr. L. Smith and Mr. W. Tait (Chief Constable of the Borough Police and Superintendent of the Watch).

In opening the discussions, Mr. Bartram expressed the view of the River Wear Commissioners that the Watch should be kept alive, albeit under the control of Sunderland Corporation. He was of the opinion that when the matter had been considered in the past, the Corporation had looked upon it as an additional expense without any income against it, but pointed out that he saw no reason why shipping dues could not continue to be levied and handed over to the Corporation.

Mr. Rose, for the River Wear Watch Commissioners agreed and expressed a hope that the Watch could be taken over along these lines. The Watch Commissioners were, he stated, short of Commissioners, short of men and short of money. They were labouring under an out of date constitution with the force then being five members below authorised strength. He added that they were trying to do the best they could for police personnel in the matter of wages but could not keep pace with the Borough Police. In addition, his men had no superannuation scheme and no rent allowance.

Alderman Allinson, the chairman of the meeting, enquired whether the Watch Commissioners had considered altering their constitution so as to appoint additional Commissioners. In reply, Mr. Rose stated that they had, but this was only part of the problem as it would also be necessary to apply for powers to increase the Watch Rate. This, they did not wish to do as port charges were already high enough at a time when Sunderland was one of the most expensive ports on the Northeast coast.

The Town Clerk, Mr. McIntire revealed that the Chief Constable had recently stated that if the Corporation was to take over the Watch, the estimated annual cost would be £13,731. This figure had, however, been calculated before a recent increase in police pay and was based on a strength of twelve firemen to maintain one firefloat in the river and nine constables for patrol duties. The second firefloat in the docks would, according to the Chief Fire Officer, become redundant as it was deemed superfluous to requirements.

Alderman Allinson, on enquiring with Mr. Brown whether the R.W.C. had considered taking over the Watch themselves, was informed that they had not. Mr. Brown felt that there seemed to be a natural affinity between the Borough and Watch services, as the River Police carried out certain duties that would be a matter for the Borough Police if the Watch did not exist. He further pointed out the close ties between the two forces brought about through the dual capacity of the Chief Constable.

Another stumbling block to a Corporation takeover was the question of policing the South Docks. The docks, as was pointed out by the Town Clerk, were private property and as such it was not the duty of the Corporation to police them. He conjectured that if the Corporation did so, the British Transport Commission, for example, might ask the Corporation to police the railways on their behalf.

The chairman stated, quite frankly, that the Corporation took the view that it was for the River Wear Commissioners to takeover the Watch.

Eventually, in the light of these discussions, it was agreed by the Corporation and R.W.C. representatives that each body would give further consideration to taking over the Watch and that the Watch Commissioners would study the possibility of amending their own constitution.

MEETING OF CORPORATION AND R.W.C. REPRESENTATIVES

A further meeting between representatives of the Corporation and R.W.C. took place at the Town Hall on 16th October, 1956. Again, the Corporation maintained a position of intransigence over the question of the future of the Watch, maintaining that if anyone was going to take it over then it should be the R.W.C. In general, it appeared that in other ports, firefighting duties were undertaken by local authorities, whilst port authorities were responsible for policing. To support this view, details were submitted of policing and firefighting arrangements then in being on the Rivers Tees and Tyne.

Following argument and counter argument between the two parties, the chairman of the meeting, Alderman Hoy stated that two points appeared to be in issue: Firstly, were the River Police really necessary? Secondly, if so, who should bear the financial burden?

On the initial point, reference was made to the memorandum of the Chief Officials of the R.W.C., dated 9th October, 1956, in which was stated:

"In the opinion of the officials of the River Wear Commissioners, all of the existing services supplied by the Wear Watch are essential and should continue in being.

It is considered that both firefloats - one in the river and one in the docks - should always be available for fighting ship fires and for salvage purposes.

The Commissioners' officials are also of the opinion that the presence of a waterborne police force to deal with any incidents on board ships, particularly those moored in tiers or on the riverside, is a useful service and should be kept in being ...."

On the second point, the chairman said that it was the opinion of the Corporation that the Watch should be taken over by the R.W.C., who should continue to collect dues from shipping. In effect, the Corporation maintained the view that if the R.W.C. wished to retain a river police force, then it should be they who would be responsible for it. Thus, the ball was placed firmly in the R.W.C's court, whose delegates once more agreed to further deliberation on the subject.

COUNSEL'S OPINION SOUGHT BY R.W.C.

Throughout 1957, the future of the Watch remained uncertain, with little progress being made with negotiations until March, 1958 when, following certain proposals from the Corporation, the R.W.C. seriously began to study how they would stand if they were to take over the Watch under Section 6 of the River Wear Watch Act, 1923. In particular, they wished to ascertain their liability for maintaining existing Watch functions if they decided to assume such a responsibility.

The persuasion of the R.W.C. at that time was they might be very likely disposed to take the force over, provided that they would be under no obligation to continue any firefighting functions as they strongly believed that such duties should be performed by the Corporation by virtue of their obligations under the Fire Services Act of 1947. On this basis, the R.W.C. might have been prepared to assume control of the Watch and provide a police patrol of the river and possibly the docks, at any rate until the assets of the Watch were exhausted. On the other hand, the R.W.C. were still reluctant to proceed with this course of action if they would be under a legal obligation to maintain police and/or fire services which would necessitate statutory powers to abandon.

Another important issue was the provision of salvage functions by the *Fire King* and *Fire Queen*. Whilst such services were viewed as being of great value to the port, the R.W.C. were unsure, if they disposed of the fireboats, whether they would be legally entitled to enter into an agreement with a local tug company, for instance, to perform salvage duties on their behalf.

It soon became apparent that a number of complex legal questions were involved and it was therefore decided to obtain the opinion of counsel on certain points. Initially, advice was sought from Mr. Ralph Instone of Lincoln's Inn but upon receipt of his opinion, doubts were expressed over some of his conclusions. It was consequently decided to obtain a 'second opinion' on the same points from Sir Milner Holland Q.C. It was subsequently found that, on the principal points in issue, Sir Milner took an entirely different view to that of Mr. Instone. The R.W.C. therefore decided that they must be guided, as to points of law, by Sir Milner Holland's opinion and take into account his view that the R.W.C. would be bound to maintain existing police and fire services if they were to assume responsibility for the Watch.

After consideration of counsel's opinion on 14th April, 1959, the R.W.C. General Purposes and Finance Committee concluded that they would not agree to a takeover of the Watch but proposed further talks to consider the matter in light of what had transpired.

DRASTIC ECONOMIES

In the meantime, with expenditure by far exceeding income, the River Wear Watch Committee met on 27th May, 1959 to discuss their financial situation. Although it was clear that drastic economies had to be effected, the Superintendent advised against any redundancies as the Watch was already well below strength. It was decided that the *Fire King*, which already required major boiler repairs, would be laid up immediately on a care and maintenance basis and that her crew would be transferred to patrol duties. As an additional saving, the circulating boiler of the *Fire Queen* which was always kept warmed through to enable the raising of steam within seven or eight minutes, would be put out of operation and steam raised only when required. In future, it would take about thirty minutes to do so after the fire beneath the main boiler had been lit.

It was reluctantly decided to realise a substantial part of the Commissioners' investments to meet expenses, with £500 worth being sold at once and others to a value of £1,000 being sold within a few weeks. The last pay rise granted to Watch members had been on 5th September, 1957 and no further increases were to be awarded in the future. Neither were any new uniforms were to be purchased for Watch personnel, their last issue having been in 1958.

Finally, at their quarterly meeting on 26th August, 1959 the Commissioners had little option but to increase the Watch Rate from three ha'pence per net registered ton to the statutory maximum of twopence.

THE FINAL NAIL IN THE COFFIN

Further moves by the Watch Commissioners to renew talks with the Corporation were to prove fruitless and on 18th December, 1959, a letter received by the Clerk to the Commissioners from the Town Clerk placed the final nail in the River Wear Watch's coffin. In a clear and unequivocal manner, the Watch Commissioners were left in no doubt that any further attempt to secure a Corporation takeover of the Watch would be futile. The text of the correspondence read as follows:

"....... *Apart from their statutory functions and duties under the provisions of the Fire Brigades and Police Acts in relation to the provision of firefighting and police services, respectively, within the Borough, which includes the portion of the River Wear within the Borough Boundaries, the Corporation are not prepared to carry out any other police or firefighting functions or duties of any other character previously performed by the River Wear Watch Commissioners, including duties in connection with the policing of the docks. Furthermore, the Corporation will not take over and maintain the existing two firefloats, the floating station or any of the Watch personnel.*"

With the River Wear Commissioners having already declared that they would not take control of the Watch, there was now no option for the Watch Commissioners but to seek parliamentary approval to wind up their affairs.

With so much uncertainty over the future of the Watch after 1953, morale of the men must have been adversely affected. Even so, there can be no doubt that they carried on with their duties in the highly professional manner always associated with the force.

PAY AND ALLOWANCES

Although the members of the Watch had received four pay increases between 1950 and 1954, by 1955 they lagged far behind the rate being paid to the Borough Force. As well as higher pay, the Borough men received a rent allowance and superannuation, neither of which (with the exception of the Watch Inspector as regards a rent allowance) was payable to the River Force.

The following is a comparison of weekly remuneration received by each of the two forces in January, 1955:

	River Wear Watch	Borough Police
Inspectors		
On appointment	£12.14s. 3d	£13. 8s. 4d
After 1 year	-	£13.14s. 1d
After 2 years	-	£13.19s.10d
After 3 years	-	£14. 5s. 7d
Sergeants		
On appointment	£9.12s.4d	£11. 6s. 2d
After 1 year	-	£11.10s. 0d
After 2 years	-	£11.13s.10d
After 3 years	-	£11.17s. 8d
After 4 years	-	£12. 3s. 5d

Constables

On appointment	£7.	9s.	6d	£ 8. 10s. 7d	
After 1 year	£7.	11s.	8d	-	
After 2 years	£7.	13s.	10d	£ 8. 14s. 5d	
After 3 years	£7.	16s.	1d	£ 8. 18s. 3d	
After 4 years	£7.	18s.	3d	£ 9. 2s. 1d	
After 5 years	£8.	1s.	7d	£ 9. 5s. 11d	
After 6 years	£8.	4s.	10d	£ 9. 9s. 9d	
After 7 years	£8.	8s.	2d	£ 9. 13s. 7d	
After 8 years	£8.	11s.	6d	-	
After 9 years	£8.	14s.	9d	-	
After 10 years	£8.	18s.	7d	£ 9. 17s. 5d	
After 15 years	-			£10. 1s. 3d	
After 22 years	-			£10. 5s. 1d	
After 25 years	-			£10. 10s. 10d	

Rent Allowance

Inspectors		17s. 4d	Up to £1.12s. 0d max.
Sergeants	(Married)	-	Up to £ 1.12s. 0d max.
	(Single)	-	Up to 15s. 0d max.
Constables	(Married)	-	Up to £ 1.10s. 0d max.
	(Single)	-	Up to £ 15s. 0d max.

Boot & Lamp Allowance

	3s. 0d		3s. 6d

Weekly superannuation deductions were made from the pay of the Borough Police, ranging from 14s.4d for an inspector with over four years service, to 7s.5d for a constable in his first year.

NEW INSPECTOR AND CLERK TO THE WATCH

On 30th May, 1957, James Pennington was succeeded as Inspector of the River Wear Watch by Alfred Ernest Stark. Stark had joined the force in 1932 as a constable and had been promoted to sergeant in 1946. Initially, due to the uncertainties surrounding the future of the Watch, his appointment was one of Temporary Inspector.

Also in 1957, Alfred Brown, the Clerk to the Watch Commissioners and General Manager and Clerk to the R.W.C. died in harness. He was replaced in both offices by his deputy, Mr. E. Lonsdale.

STATISTICS OF OCCURRENCES, 1954 - 1959

The duties carried out by the Watch during its final years were a far cry from those performed during the previous century. Gone were the days of barques and brigs being found, almost daily, adrift from their moorings. Crime, once widespread in the port, had greatly diminished and although the danger to shipping from fire was always present, improvements in technology and safety standards had made its occurrence almost a rarity. Likewise, the incidence of vessels requiring salvage in the port was relatively uncommon and greater awareness of safety had reduced drowning fatalities dramatically. Nevertheless such things did still occur and the need to be able to deal effectively with them remained. An illustration of the duties performed by the River Police during its final years is provided by the following summary of occurrences:

	1954	1955	1956	1957	1958	1959
Persons apprehended & convicted of larceny from ships	2	-	-	-	-	-
Persons apprehended & convicted of larceny - other	-	3	6	-	3	3
Cases of larceny reported & investigated - ships	1	2	2	2	1	4
Cases of larceny reported & investigated - other	-	-	-	1	-	-
Attempted suicide	-	-	-	1	-	-
Persons apprehended for canteen breaking, etc	-	-	2	-	-	-
Persons summonsed & fined for trespass at South Docks	19	3	-	-	4	18
Seamen apprehended & convicted under Merchant Shipping Act for wilful disobedience to master's lawful commands	2	-	-	-	-	-
Seamen arrested on warrant	1	4	-	1	1	-
Service of summons on board ships	-	4	-	3	2	-
Service of summons on dock tenants	2	-	-	-	-	-
Police called to quell disturbances on board ships	-	5	3	2	-	-
Police called to cases of assault on board ships	1	-	1	-	1	1
Women of undesirable character removed from ships	-	7	2	3	2	1
Persons in possession of uncustomed goods reported to Customs	-	-	1	-	1	3
Offences under Oil in navigable Waters Act reported	-	4	2	1	-	-
Convictions under Oil in Navigable Waters Act	-	1	-	-	-	-
Police called to accidents/assist persons taken ill on board ships	2	4	2	3	6	15
Police called to accidents or to assist persons taken ill on shore	-	1	3	6	8	3
Attendance of police at fires on board ships (without firefloats)	-	1	1	1	1	1
Firefloats called to fires on board ships	-	-	-	-	-	-
Attendance of police at fires on shore (without firefloats)	-	-	3	3	2	-
Firefloats called to fires on shore	2	1	-	-	-	-
Police called to drowning fatalities - seamen	2	-	-	1	2	-
Police called to drowning fatalities - others	3	1	1	3	-	-
Persons rescued from water, river & docks - seamen	4	-	1	2	-	-
Persons rescued from water, river & docks - others	1	-	2	3	1	-
Bodies recovered from river & docks - seamen	1	-	-	2	2	-
Bodies recovered from river & docks - others	5	3	1	2	6	-
Collisions, foundering or damage to vessels reported	-	2	-	-	-	-
Firefloats engaged in salvage duties	2	2	1	-	-	1
Assistance to remoor ships which had broken moorings in river	-	2	2	-	-	-
Attendance of river patrol at launching of new ships	25	29	29	28	30	26
Visits to ships re. Diseases of Animals Act	38	30	22	55	40	47
Occasions on which police launch assisted Customs Waterguard	4	17	10	4	2	6
Occasions on which police launch assisted Port Health Authority	3	5	4	3	19	12
Hours of Special Duty performed on board ships loading or discharging petroleum spirit in the port	2495	2459	2654	2872	2472	1647

ROYAL HUMANE SOCIETY CERTIFICATE AWARDED TO
P.C. JOSEPH DUNN

In terms of saving life, one of the most hazardous situations in which a river policeman might find himself was when a person fell between a ship and the quayside; both victim and rescuer at risk of being crushed between the vessel's hull and the quay wall. Many such rescues had been effected by Watch officers over the years and in 1954, a constable received official recognition of his involvement in such an incident.

About 3.45 p.m. on 30th August, that year, P.C. Joseph Dunn was on duty on board the **Fire King** at the Sea Lock, Hudson Dock when his attention was directed to a shout of "Man overboard" coming from the **S.S. Greathope** which was berthed nearby at East Quay South. On reaching the ship, the constable learned that the ship's 60 years old wireless operator, a man named Daniel Glen had slipped from the gangway and fallen into the dock between the side of the vessel and quay wall.

Two dockers had already bravely gone to Glen's assistance, one being suspended from the hook of a crane and the other having been lowered by rope. Without regard for his personal safety, P.C. Dunn climbed onto the **Greathope's** wooden fender to assist the dock workers who were supporting the unconscious seaman's head above the water. After helping to secure a line around Glen and assisting in his removal onto the quay, P.C. Dunn then successfully applied artificial resuscitation.

For his actions that day, P.C. Dunn was awarded the Certificate of the Royal Humane Society, an honour which presumably was also presented to the two dock workers.

SERIOUS OUTBREAKS OF FIRE AT BARTRAMS AND JOPLINGS

1954 saw what turned out to be the final deployment of each of the fireboats in connection with fire, although on 3rd September, 1955, the **Fire Queen** was called out to a large fire at Aiton and Co. Ltd's pipeworks, Southwick which had been extinguished before her arrival.

On 25th May, that year, a serious fire broke out in the joiners' shop at Bartrams and Sons Ltd's shipyard, South Docks when the assistance of the **Fire King** was requested by the Borough Fire Brigade. The firefloat made short work of her task, as after being engaged for only about thirty minutes directing her monitor jet onto the flames, the outbreak was sufficiently under control to permit her withdrawal.

What was one of the greatest peacetime fires in Sunderland, occurred during the early hours of 14th December, the same year, when Joplings Departmental Store in High Street West was completely gutted. At the height of the conflagration, twenty pumps, two turntable ladders and one hundred firemen from various brigades through Durham and Northumberland were engaged at the scene.

Such was the magnitude of the blaze, that the Chief Fire Officer requested the **Fire Queen** to make her way to Wearmouth Bridge and feed the six inch dry riser main to supply land units with additional water. The fireboat was employed in pumping operations for over three hours and stood by for a further two before being ordered to return to her moorings.

SALVAGE OF THE 'CORNHILL' AND 'WEAR HOPPER No. 34'

Between 1954 and 1956, five requests were made for the attendance of the fire steamers to pump out leaking vessels, though in the event, their pumps were only put into operation on two of these occasions, both during 1955.

France, Fenwick Tyne and Wear Co. Ltd's 176 g.r.t. motor tug, *Cornhill* was the recipient of the *Fire Queen's* services on 30th July, that year, when a defective stern gland caused the tug's engine room to flood, requiring her to be beached on North Sands.

Then on Christmas Day, later the same year, the *Fire King* was called out to salve her last vessel. Shortly after 1.50 p.m., she made her way across Hudson Dock to No. 19 Staith, where the elderly *Wear Hopper No. 34* was lying with a severe port list, her deck plating being flush with the surface of the water. Eight lengths of suction hose were coupled up and pumping continued until 6 p.m., by which time the hopper was at last on an even keel. It was discovered that the ingress of water had resulted from a bolt on the quay wall rubbing against the vessel's hull plating.

UNORTHODOX DUTIES

A number of unorthodox duties were also performed by the Watch which, although having little in common with police work, served to provide much needed additional revenue for the Watch Commissioners.

During December, 1957, both firefloats were engaged in work reminiscent of the days in which their predecessors had been used to fill the hulls of sailing ships to test for leaks. On this occasion their task involved pumping of water, for testing purposes, from the river into a new petroleum storage tank that had been constructed for the Petrofina Corporation at Corporation Quay. Owing to the *Fire Queen* becoming defective, what should have been a fairly routine operation turned into a protracted affair and provided the *Fire King* with what was to be her final engagement on behalf of the River Wear Watch.

The *Fire Queen* was moored alongside the west wall of the Outer Basin at 9.30 a.m. on 4th December and two lines of 3½ inch hose, having a combined length of 700 feet were led into the top of the storage tank.. Pumping started at 10.50 a.m. but shortly afterwards the first problem was encountered. Several lengths of hose, unable to withstand the high pressure required to maintain the flow of water into the tank, burst and had to be replaced. A steady average flow of 2 feet of water per hour was then maintained, but at 5.40 p.m., with only 13 feet of water in the tank, the main boiler joint of the fireboat began to blow. In spite of all efforts to rectify this problem, steam pressure could not be maintained. There was no option but to disconnect the hose to enable the *Fire Queen* to limp back to her station whilst sufficient steam remained.

As the biannual overhaul of the vessel was due the following May, it was determined to bring this forward and to effect boiler repairs at the same time.

It was then decided to complete the testing of the storage tank by having recourse to the *Fire King* which languished in Hudson Dock. She began pumping at 7.15 a.m. the next morning and continued until 8 p.m. Operations resumed at 6 a.m. on 6th December, before being discontinued at 12.30 p.m. the same day, by which time approximately 4,000 gallons had been discharged into the tank. Great satisfaction was expressed with the performance of the

Fire King which, on completion of her task, was taken to the River Station to deputise for the *Fire Queen*.

On the morning of 17th December, 1957, the *Fire Queen* returned to service following overhaul and the *Fire King* steamed back to her berth in the South Docks. She had sailed her last on behalf of the River Wear Watch.

During the night of 30th December, 1959, the *Fire Queen* was again called out to carry out an unusual duty when, due to an abnormally high tide, Austin and Pickersgill Ltd's Wear Dry Dock became flooded. Portable pumps already at the scene proved no match for those of the firefloat which cleared the dock of water in about seven hours. As a precautionary measure, steam was again raised on the *Fire Queen* the following evening, as similar conditions had been forecast. In the event, however, her services were not required.

Special duties were also undertaken by River Police launches. In 1956, for example, assistance was provided to the North East Electricity Board whilst electricity cables were suspended across the river near Wearmouth Railway Bridge. In March, 1958, a request from the Port Health Authority for the use of a police launch to obtain samples of river water during the subsequent twelve months was approved.

POLICE, FIRE AND SALVAGE SERVICES ON THE TEES AND TYNE

During attempts to secure the transfer of the Watch to Sunderland Corporation or the River Wear Commissioners during the 1950's, much research was conducted into the policing, firefighting and salvage arrangements which were then in existence in other United Kingdom ports. It is of relevance to outline here, details of such organisations which existed at that time in the other major Northeast ports, namely the Tees and Tyne:

RIVER TEES

Police: The River Tees Police, originally formed in 1904, under powers granted by the Tees Conservancy Act, 1884; the Harbours, Docks and Piers Clauses Act, 1847; and the Town Police Clauses Act, 1847 was maintained by the Tees Conservancy Commissioners (T.C.C.) from funds borne out of their ordinary revenue. The Tees Harbour Master acted as Chief Officer of the force which had only a small establishment of police officers, although other personnel within the Harbour Master's Department were sworn as constables to allow them to deputise when necessary and to act as watchkeepers at Teesport oil berths.

The duties of the force were: to ensure that the port bye-laws and Oil in Navigable Waters Act were observed; patrols of the river banks; inspection of outlets for oil pollution; maintaining a general watch on T.C.C. property; gateman, watchkeeping and ship and shore service duties at Teesport; prevention and detection of crime; relief duties in other sections of the Harbour Master's Department; and supervision of road closures at South and North Gare Breakwaters. The force, to a large extent, existed to ensure that petroleum oil and spirit cargoes, explosives and other hazardous substances were handled in accordance with bye-laws and other regulations.

No designated police launches were operated by the force, although the Harbour Master's launch could be utilised if required. Personnel were issued with uniform based upon the standard pattern worn by members of the Harbour Master's Department, though a distinctive cap badge was worn.

The T.C.C. has since been superseded by the Tees and Hartlepool Port Authority Ltd., which today operates the Tees and Hartlepool Harbour Police.

Fire / Salvage: A firefloat and river fire station were maintained by Middlesbrough Borough Fire Brigade, the cost of which was equally shared between Middlesbrough Corporation, North Riding County Council and Durham County Council. Certain of the Tees Conservancy Commissioners' craft were also capable of acting as firefighting vessels and first aid extinguishing equipment was maintained. At Teesport, specialised foam firefighting appliances were provided.

For salvage work the Commissioners' general purpose vessel, **Wilton** was equipped with a 4 inch pump and suction hose, together with a 2¹/₂ inch sea water or bilge pump. The Tees Towing Company's steamtug, **Euston Cross** was fitted with a 7 inch pump, with four 3 inch deliveries. Both of these vessels also had a firefighting capability.

RIVER TYNE

Police: The River Tyne Police, originally formed in 1845 under powers granted by the Newcastle upon Tyne Port Act of that year, had been maintained by the Tyne Improvement Commissioners (T.I.C.) since 1852. With a strength of some seventy-eight men, it was responsible for policing the navigable section of the River Tyne - a distance of approximately 19¹/₂ miles - together with its docks. Whilst the force was subject to Home Office regulations and scales of pay, it did not receive a grant from the Home Office towards its running costs which were financed solely from T.I.C. income. Accounts for 1956, show the cost of maintaining the force as being £52,642, as set against River Police income of £8,668.

Until 1st September, 1949, an additional force under T.I.C. control, the Tyne Improvement Commission Docks and Piers Police, which had been established in 1874 under the Harbours, Docks and Piers Clauses Act of 1847, had jurisdiction over the policing of the docks, piers and other T.I.C. property. The force had then been disbanded and its members transferred to the T.I.C. Traffic and Engineering Department as uniformed watchmen, no longer being sworn as constables. Former members of the police force with over five years service were retained without suffering reduction in their rate of pay, but subsequent employees received lower remuneration.

Fire / Salvage: The Tyne Improvement Commission maintained shore based voluntary fire brigades in their dock estates, their members being paid a retaining fee subject to the appropriate number of drills being attended. At each dock, there was a full-time residential fireman whose responsibilities included looking after dock fire equipment and ensuring that hydrants were kept clear and in working order. When off duty, these men were subject to being called out. A permanently manned steam harbour master's launch, fitted with a monitor pump, was also available to assist with firefighting, as was a similar launch operated by the River Tyne Police. Two tugs, each equipped with firefighting apparatus, had been based at Tyne Dock but their use had been discontinued during the early 1950's. Permanently manned firefloats were maintained by the Newcastle and Gateshead Fire Brigade at Walker, and by South Shields County Borough Fire Brigade at South Shields. These floats were occasionally used for salvage work, with shipowners being charged for this service. Whilst the T.I.C. did not possess salvage craft as such, their **Screw Keel No. 4**, used for work on moorings, was fitted with a powerful salvage pump. A further salvage pump was carried on board one of the harbour master's launches.

Chapter 13

DISSOLUTION OF THE WATCH

(1960 - 1966)

WHEELS OF DISSOLUTION SET IN MOTION

The years of uncertainty over the future of the Watch finally came to an end on 25th November, 1959 when, at the quarterly meeting of the Watch Commissioners, approval was given for the preparation of a draft parliamentary bill to wind up their affairs. In formulating the Bill, the Commissioners were eager to avoid any objections that might delay its progress.

In the event, the only opposition forthcoming was from the Town Council, which was unhappy with the portion of the preamble which stated that the part of the port or haven under jurisdiction of the Watch and the docks were "...... *entitled to the protection and benefit of the Borough Police Force and the Borough Fire Services provided and maintained by the Mayor, Aldermen and Burgesses of the said County Borough."*

Rightly, the Council felt that this seemed to suggest that the docks and other R.W.C. private property in the port were entitled to greater protection from the Borough Police and Fire Brigade than they actually were. In reality, R.W.C. property, including the docks, qualified only for the same treatment as any other private property in the town, which was quite limited in nature.

After much wrangling, a compromise was reached whereby the offending clause was amended to read that the River Wear (within the jurisdiction of the Watch) and the docks were "...... *entitled to the general services provided and maintained in and for the said County Borough by the police and fire authorities, respectively thereof."*

THE RIVER WEAR WATCH (DISSOLUTION) ACT, 1961

Accordingly, on 19th July, 1961, the River Wear Watch (Dissolution) Act, 1961 became law. It was stipulated that on and from 1st October, 1961, the powers, privileges, duties and obligations of the Watch Commissioners to maintain a police force would cease to exist. The Commissioners were to remain in office afterwards for the sole purpose of carrying out the Act's provisions as to the winding-up of their affairs.

Following the realisation of their assets, the remaining proceeds were to be used for the following purposes, in order of priority:

(1) Payment of expenses incurred in the acquisition of the Dissolution Act;

(2) Payment of any debts owed by the Commissioners and of any expenses incurred in the winding-up of their affairs;

(3) Provision of compensation to employees of the Watch made redundant as a result of dissolution; and

(4) Donation to a local charity and for any other purpose approved by the Minister of Transport.

PREMATURE RESIGNATIONS

Following the deposit of the Dissolution Bill with Parliament during late November, 1960, it was only natural that some of the Watch's fifteen remaining members should seek alternative employment immediately, rather than wait until disbandment came. Accordingly, seven officers resigned during this period and another (P.C. Cowe) died, leaving only seven members extant at the end.

In spite of being hampered by lack of manpower, the Watch continued to perform its statutory duties as best as could be done in the circumstances. By the end of January, 1961, with its strength down to nine men, it was decided to reorganise duties so as to require each officer to work a forty-eight hour week, to include four hours overtime. The practice of granting time off in lieu of overtime ceased and payment at time and a half was made instead, with rest day allocation being changed from three per fortnight to one per week. Certain duties were severely curtailed, in particular the dock foot patrol.

RESCUE OF THE CREW OF FISHING VESSEL, 'JANET'

Whilst patrolling the South Docks, River Policemen would always keep a watchful eye to seaward for any vessel that might be in distress. Such was the case about 9 p.m. on 2nd October, 1960, when the local fishing vessel, *Janet (SD 126)* suffered engine failure off the sea wall at Hendon. With the wind increasing in strength and her engine flooded, the *Janet* was driven inshore towards dangerous rocks. Attempts to anchor her proved abortive and in desperation, one of the crew of three flashed a distress signal towards the shore. Fortunately, the flashing light was observed by P.C's Barr and Chicken who unsuccessfully attempted to throw a line to the disabled craft which had become stranded on rocks close to shore.

The officers, after first alerting Roker Volunteer Life Brigade, sought help from the crew of the *M.V. Oarsman* which was berthed in the docks. Willing assistance was provided by the ship's master, mate and chief engineer who accompanied the officers to the breakwater, bringing with them a Schermuly line-throwing pistol. The pistol was used to good effect, with a line being fired across the fishing vessel, thus enabling the police and ships' officers to haul the shocked fishermen to safety by use of a life buoy.

THE MYSTERY OF THE ROTTING TORSO

Only twenty minutes had elapsed into the two 'til ten shift on Wednesday, 12th October, 1960, when the telephone rang on board the River Station informing the Watch that a body had been sighted in the water near to Corporation Quay. Without delay, P.C's William Dodsworth and Norman Chicken prepared one of the launches and made the short journey downriver to the scene.

Upon their arrival a ghastly sight met their eyes, for floating in the river was the badly decomposed remains of a human body. As it was brought alongside the launch, the corpse began to disintegrate and it was with some difficulty that it was lifted on board. The officers knew that identification of the body would be extremely difficult, if not impossible, as only the torso, about twenty-eight inches in length and one leg down to the knee remained. Being devoid of clothing, no clue as to the body's identity would be forthcoming from that source, although some strands of fine white elastic were present around the hips.

Eventually, the remains were transported to the Royal Infirmary, where the casualty doctor was unable to determine their sex. A post-mortem examination at Sunderland General Hospital later revealed the body to be that of a female, aged between twenty-five and fifty, approximately 5 feet 3 inches tall and who had been dead for a number of years. The cause of her death could not be ascertained.

Despite extensive enquiries being conducted, police were never able to establish the true identity of the cadaver. It was, however, strongly suggested that the torso may have been that of one Mary Burslem, a dancer and entertainer, who had been on Sunderland Police's missing person files since 1949. Better known under her stage name of Molly Moselle, she had left her lodgings in Sunderland, during a period of engagement at the Empire Theatre, then aged thirty-three, and had never been seen since.

Officially, the files relating to Mary Burslem and the unidentified torso remain open, but it is unlikely that either mystery will ever be solved.

ASSISTANCE TO 'M.V. MOGEN' BY 'FIRE QUEEN'

The final engagements of the *Fire Queen* on behalf of the Watch took place at the end of May and beginning of June, 1961 when she pumped 3,000 tons of water out of a flooded ship and a week later, pumped almost the same amount back in again!

On 29th May, a new 14,661 gross tons bulk carrier, *M.V. Mogen* which had been built for Norwegian owners by Sir James Laing and Sons Ltd., Deptford was found to be flooded due to a main inlet valve having been left open whilst the vessel was fitting out at the Southwick Quay of George Clark (1938) Ltd.

Initially, the Borough Fire Brigade had been called out to deal with the flooded engine room, but after pumping for twelve hours with portable pumps, the level of water had fallen only by about two feet. As so often had been the case during the heyday of the Watch, it had then been decided to call upon the services of the *Fire Queen*.

The elderly fire steamer was brought alongside the *Mogen* and suction hoses led through an aperture cut in the ship's shell plating. Pumping commenced at 1 a.m. on 30th May, at which time some fifteen feet of water flooded the engine room. With the firefloat's ageing machinery being operated with great care, pumping continued until 2.30 p.m., the following day, by which time it was reckoned that 3,000 tons of water had been discharged. This was sufficient for the ship to be refloated at half flood tide and to allow her to be towed away from the quay.

Despite her great age, the *Fire Queen* gave every satisfaction during the fifteen hours she was in service, with all available Watch personnel being engaged during the proceedings. It was suspected that the inlet valve had been deliberately left open by some unknown person, resulting in an extensive investigation by the Borough C.I.D. into a case of malicious damage, the value of which was estimated at £26,000.

On 8th June, the **Fire Queen** was recalled to Clark's Quay, this time to ballast the **Mogen** to bring her into correct trim for dry-docking. It had been found that the vessel was too far down by the stern, necessitating the ballasting of her forward double bottom and upper tanks. The fireboat maintained pumping for eleven hours, through two lines of 3½ inch and one line of 2½ inch hose, after which it was calculated that 2,700 tons of water had been pumped on board, bringing the bulk carrier's trim well within the limits for dry-docking.

At 8.40 p.m., the same day, after her hoses had been uncoupled and stowed, the **Fire Queen** headed slowly downriver to the River Station and made fast, her work now finished for ever.

THE FINAL RESCUES

The importance of retaining river police on the Wear was aptly demonstrated during July, 1961, when members of the Watch were responsible for saving the lives of three people in three separate incidents.

The first occurred shortly before 4 p.m. on 16th July, whilst P.C. Lawrence Barr was performing special watching duty on board the coastal tanker, **Agility** in Hendon Dock. His attention was drawn to a River Wear Commissioner's employee in the dock, holding onto a ladder and supporting an elderly man's head above the surface of the water. The officer immediately ran to the spot and passed down a rope, by means of which the old man was hauled onto the quayside. Seeing no signs of life, P.C. Barr applied artificial respiration and succeeded in restoring the victim's breathing.

Having regard to the River Wear Watch's proud record of having saved innumerable lives throughout its history, it is befitting that one of its final accomplishments was the rescue of one of its own number. Reporting for night duty on 30th July, P.C's Barr and Dodsworth arrived at the landing opposite the River Station and as was normal practice, hailed the man on board - Hector Clazey - to come across with the coble. On this occasion, however, they received no reply but did hear shouting which appeared to come from the north side of the river. Concerned for the safety of his colleague, P.C. Dodsworth made his way to a nearby police box to enquire with Police Headquarters in Gill Bridge Avenue whether P.C. Clazey had reported leaving the River Station for any reason. On learning that he had not, the officer hurried to the Fish Quay where he commandeered a dingy. Rowing as quickly as his arms would allow, Dodsworth arrived at the River Station to find P.C. Clazey in the water, barely managing to hold onto a fender between the **Fire Queen** and **Vigilant**. With some difficulty the unfortunate officer, suffering from shock and exposure, was assisted on board the River Station before being taken to hospital. It was learned that P.C. Clazey had been checking the police launch when he had overbalanced and fallen into the river. Due to an attack of cramp, he had been prevented from climbing back on board. Because of the acute manpower situation, the officer had been on duty alone and had almost paid with his life.

Just after midnight, the following night, P.C's Barr and Dodsworth effected the Watch's final rescue. After receiving a report of a man being in the river near the south ferry landing, the officers made they way to the scene by launch, at first finding nothing. On continuing their search downriver, the body of the man was seen floating face down near the west end of Corporation Quay and lifted on board the launch. Again, the Watch's expertise in the application of artificial resuscitation proved inestimable and before long the thirty-nine years old Shiney Row man had been revived and despatched to hospital for treatment.

THE CLOSING DAY

So it transpired, that at midnight on Saturday, 30th September, 1961, the River Wear Watch unceremoniously ceased to exist and a melancholy day for those officers who had performed their final shift drew to a close.

How the men spent that closing day must remain a matter for conjecture. It had been an uneventful day, as no incidents are recorded in the occurrence book. Perhaps a final river patrol had been undertaken, with the crew of the police launch reminiscing over past events or reflecting upon changes they had seen in the port, which was already showing traces of decline. Probably, time had been spent on cleaning the *Patrol*, soon to be taken over by the Borough Police, so that no-one would have cause for complaint over her condition. Members of the Borough Force, who would soon form their own river section, may have visited the River Station to be shown over the launch and to be told some of the secrets of the Wear. Possibly the opportunity had also been taken to bid farewell to some of the many acquaintances made over the years, such as the tugboatmen, fishermen, pilots, customs officers, River Wear Commissioners' staff and others who were part of the day-to-day activity within the port.

And after having rowed ashore from the River Station for the very last time and whilst walking along the pathway towards the Low Street, perhaps those River Policemen had taken one final glance back towards the river to behold the *Fire Queen* and other craft which had served the Wear so well and realised that a chapter in the history of Sunderland had drawn to a close.

DISPOSAL OF CRAFT

In a remarkable change of attitude, the Watch Committee of the Town Council had decided to form a River Section within Sunderland Borough Police to take over some of the Watch's former duties. Consequently, it was decided to purchase the motor launch, *Patrol* for use by the section. Following an independent survey by M. Wawn and Son, Marine Surveyors, a price of £350 was agreed.

The remainder of the Commissioners' craft, comprising the firefloats, *Fire King* and *Fire Queen*; the motor launch, *Vigilant;* the floating police station, *Pikes' No. 10*; a 17 foot rowing boat; a 12 foot 6 inch rowing boat and a coble, were all advertised for sale in August, 1961. A great deal of interest was aroused by the sale, with a wide variety of offers being tendered by prospective purchasers.

The Watch Commissioners met on 4th October, 1961 to decide upon which of the bids to accept and were told that a further offer of £2,000 for all of the vessels (excluding the coble) had been submitted after the closing date by John Brent (Ship-brokers) Co. Ltd. of London. After a full discussion, the Commissioners resolved to accept Brent and Co's offer, although this was over £100 less than the sum which could have been raised had other bids been accepted. Perhaps the Commissioners felt that the deal would proceed more smoothly by dealing with only one purchaser. If this was the case, they were to regret their decision.

The coble, which had been built around 1912 and latterly used to ferry police personnel to and from the River Station, was sold to a representative of Seaham Boatowners Association for the sum of £10.

The sale of the other craft to John Brent (Ship-brokers) Co. Ltd. was, however, beset with difficulties. Completion was originally set for 12th October, 1961, but postponed until 26th October, at the company's request, when it again failed to complete. Further correspondence resulted in a cheque being received by the Commissioners on 9th November, 1961, but this was returned by the bank, marked 'refer to drawer'. After receipt of the cheque, Brent's representatives had removed hose pipes and other fittings from the firefloats but had not been allowed to take these away until a deposit had been made into the Commissioners' bank account.

On 15th November, 1961, the floating station and remaining craft were moved into Hudson Dock, whereupon Inspector Stark, who had been retained in the service of the Commissioners to oversee the disposal of craft, terminated his employment.

It appeared that a Dutch company had agreed to purchase the two firefloats from Brent and Co., but a dispute had arisen concerning the removal of equipment from the vessels by Brent's representatives. Alarm bells began to sound when a search of the Companies Register disclosed that Brent and Co. had only an authorised capital of £100 and an issued capital of £2. With payment still not forthcoming, the matter was placed in the hands of the Commissioners' solicitor before it was ultimately decided, at a special meeting of the Watch Commissioners held on 26th January, 1962, to give notice to John Brent and Co. that the craft would be resold if payment in full was not received within three months. Eventually, after almost nine months, Brent and Co. finally paid the full purchase price for the craft. The company was clearly in financial difficulties and subsequently went into liquidation resulting in the resale of the vessels which they had acquired.

What became of *Pikes' No. 10*, *Vigilant* and the two remaining rowing boats unfortunately is not known. The two fireboats, however, were to have widely differing fates.

The *Fire King* was eventually sold, stripped of her steam machinery and found use as a houseboat at Scarborough in the North Riding of Yorkshire. Following further changes in ownership, she was acquired in 1975 by a Mr. G. F. Spink and berthed at Grimsby Marina on the Humber, having been renamed *Viking.* At that time she was in a terribly dilapidated state but over the subsequent years, Mr. Spink set about her conversion into a beautiful motor cruiser, rigged with sails.

Regrettably, the *Fire Queen* was to have an ignominious end. In August, 1964, still languishing in Hudson Dock, she was the subject of interest by Hylton Red House Comprehensive School, Sunderland which was considering her purchase for a headquarters for its nautical section and newly formed yacht club. This did not, in fact, materialise and in October, the same year, the vessel was bought by a Mr. W. Darnton of Monkwearmouth who intended to scrap her. Yet, there was still hope for the elderly craft as she was later resold for conversion into a houseboat on the River Ouse at York. Owing to difficulties in making her seaworthy for the voyage, she was sold again, this time for use as a floating dance platform on the Ouse. Certain regulations prevented this from taking place and in 1966, the *Fire Queen* was bought by a Newcastle scrap dealer. This time there was to be no reprieve, as she was subsequently broken up on the west side of Hudson Dock near Nos. 1 and 2 Coal Belts, without ever leaving the port she had served throughout her life.

Motor launch, *Patrol*, which had been taken over by the Borough Police River Section, was transferred into the ownership of Durham Constabulary on amalgamation of the two forces on 1st April, 1967. She continued in use as a police launch until 4th December, 1968 when, designated as *Boat 'E'*, she was involved in a collision and written off by her insurers. She was replaced by a new launch in 1969 and was subsequently sold and repaired.

After bearing the name, *Cocoon,* the boat was acquired in 1976 by a Mr. J. Hutchinson who renamed her *Jill 1*. She can still be seen moored in the North Dock, although substantially altered in appearance.

THE COMPENSATION ISSUE

Settlement of the question of compensation for former members of the Watch was a protracted business, provoking a great deal of anger and public interest over the time it took to resolve. It must be said, however, that the Watch Commissioners and their Clerk, Mr. Lonsdale who worked tirelessly to bring matters to a conclusion, were irreproachable in the affair. Initially, the delay had been caused by the difficulties encountered through the sale of the Commissioners' floating property to John Brent (Ship-brokers) Co. Ltd.

On 25th June, 1963, following involved discussions with the Ports Division of the Ministry of Transport, a special meeting of the River Wear Watch Commissioners was convened in the offices of the River Wear Commission, at which a provisional winding-up statement and several alternative schemes of compensation were submitted by Mr. Lonsdale and passed by the Commissioners.

In considering the schemes of compensation, the Commissioners also made provision for those Watch members who had resigned to take up other employment between the dates of the Dissolution Bill being lodged with Parliament and its Royal Assent. Because of the reduction in the strength of the force, the wage bill had been considerably reduced and in consequence, a far greater sum of money than originally anticipated was available for the payment of compensation.

The Commissioners felt, therefore, that those officers who had left prematurely, though not specifically entitled to compensation under the Act, should receive as generous an ex gratia payment as possible. Such payments could be authorised by the Minister of Transport, as the Dissolution Act allowed for the residue of any money remaining, after other payments had been made, to be used for charitable or 'other purposes'.

On 30th April, 1964, formal approval was given by the Minister of Transport to the compensation scheme which had been submitted, with cheques totalling almost £9,500 being forwarded to former personnel the following month. The Commissioners had previously agreed that they, themselves, should not benefit from any such payment through loss of office. Unhappily, Sergeant Robert Mustard who had joined the Watch in 1914 and reached the age of 73 at the time of disbandment, had died in May, 1963 before being able to benefit from the disbursement.

FINAL MEETING OF THE RIVER WEAR WATCH COMMISSION

Having been kept alive, solely for the purpose of winding up its affairs, the final meeting of the River Wear Watch Commission was held at the River Wear Commissioners' Offices, St. Thomas Street, Sunderland on Friday, 15th April, 1966, more than four and a half years after the disbandment of its force. All surviving Commissioners, namely Messrs. W. B. Allan, K. W. Black, A. Marshall, R. C. Thompson and N. R. Rose were in attendance, the latter chairing the meeting.

The Clerk, Mr. Lonsdale outlined details of compensation which had been awarded to former Watch members and particulars of additional payments incurred in connection with dissolution.

After all disbursements had been made, a credit balance of £152 1s.9d remained. This, it was agreed, would be donated to the Royal National Lifeboat Institution, with the stipulation that the cash must be used for the Institution's work in the Sunderland area.

A request from the Town Clerk, concerning the records of the River Wear Watch, was then considered, resulting in the Commissioners resolving to approve the transfer of those documents which might be of historical interest, to the Sunderland Public Libraries, Museum and Art Gallery for preservation. Without such a magnanimous gesture on the part of the Commissioners, this book could not have been written in its present form.

With no further business to transact, it then fell to the Watch Commissioners to perform their final act by passing the following resolution:

"That the winding-up of the affairs of the River Wear Watch Commissioners having been completed, the Commissioners do go out of office and are hereby finally dissolved pursuant to Section 6 of the River Wear Watch (Dissolution) Act, 1961."

Chapter 14

POST-WATCH POLICING AND FIREFIGHTING ON THE WEAR

(1961 - 1998)

This final chapter sets out to review briefly the manner in which the provision of police and fire services within the Port of Sunderland has evolved since the cessation of the activities of the River Wear Watch. During the period in question the method of marine policing, in particular, has been subject to marked changes that have been felt no less at Sunderland than elsewhere. To reflect broader developments brought about through amalgamations within the police and fire services, it has been necessary to include additional references relating to both marine policing and firefighting within the Tyne and Wear area and beyond.

SUNDERLAND BOROUGH POLICE (1961 - 1967)

Upon the disbandment of the Watch, a river section was formed within Sunderland Borough Police to police the Wear within the Borough boundaries. Competition amongst force members to obtain a posting within the section was keen and initially six officers, all with previous seagoing or R.A.F. experience, were selected.

Motor launch, *Patrol* was removed from the water and refitted at the Sunderland Corporation Central Repair Depot in Monkwearmouth. A new four cylinder, 2¹/₂ litre B.M.C Commander diesel engine was installed, increasing the launch's maximum speed to around thirteen knots. Accommodation was later provided for her crew in the ambulance room of Austin and Pickersgill Ltd's Wear Dockyard where the *Patrol* could often be seen moored in the dry dock. In 1962, the launch was equipped with a modern police v.h.f. wireless, providing two-way communication with headquarters information room. Wireless was an amenity that had never been afforded the Watch.

Duties of the River Section remained comparable to those which had been performed by the Watch on the river, with the exception of firefighting which was now wholly the domain of the Borough Fire Brigade. Unlike the Watch, the Borough Police had no special authority within the docks and was required to exercise its functions in accordance with its limited powers of entry onto private premises.

Whilst assisting at ship launchings was a regular duty performed by the section, no such occasion had been as memorable or presented such a hazard to public safety as the launch of the 49,054 g.r.t. Norwegian tanker, *Borgsten* from the slipways of J. L. Thompson and Sons Ltd. on 1st November, 1963. The vessel, which then was by far the largest built on the Wear, entered the river in extremely poor visibility, with thousands of spectators cramming the riverbanks and quays.

DURHAM CONSTABULARY (1967 - 1974)

On 1st April, 1967, Sunderland Borough Police amalgamated with Durham County Constabulary to form Durham Constabulary which then assumed responsibility for policing the River Wear. The twenty years old *Patrol* continued in use, albeit for a short time, before being withdrawn from service following her accident in December, 1968.

Upon the merger of South Shields and Gateshead Borough Police Forces with Durham Constabulary on 1st October, 1968, a Marine Division, which included the Underwater Search Unit (U.S.U.) and a small C.I.D. section, was formed to police the Rivers Tyne and Wear. It should be explained that the old River Tyne Police (referred to in Chapter 12) had ceased to exist on 1st August, 1968, when its members and responsibilities - in relation to the River Tyne - were transferred to South Shields Borough Police under the Port of Tyne Reorganisation Scheme, 1967 - Confirmation Order, 1968. The River Division of South Shields Borough Police was only intended as a temporary measure pending the planned amalgamation of the force with Durham Constabulary.

The Marine Division was designated as 'I' Division of Durham Constabulary and held a territorial responsibility for crimes and other incidents occurring on the Tyne and Wear. For a short period, Mill Dam at South Shields continued in use as Divisional Headquarters until the former Harbour Master's office at Pipewellgate, Gateshead, previously shared with the River Tyne Police, had been renovated solely for police use. Five police launches were inherited by the Marine Division. With the exception of the *Patrol,* these launches were 30 foot craft built between 1950 and 1967 for the Tyne Improvement Commission, for use by the River Tyne Police. They were so badly maintained and in such poor condition that it was immediately apparent that a programme of replacement would have to be undertaken.

It was decided that launches should be deployed over a twenty-four hour period, with one patrol boat each being based at the Gateshead (Pipewellgate), South Shields (Mill Dam) and Sunderland (North Dock) stations. In addition, the increase in small pleasure craft using the lower reaches and harbour mouths of both rivers necessitated the purchase of a larger launch capable of operating in rough weather and being able to sail between the Tyne and Wear as required. Such a craft could also be utilised as a supervision vessel. Two reserve boats were also required - one for each river - to provide additional cover at special events, such as ship launches and for deputising for other craft requiring maintenance. To ensure operational efficiency, the total number of launches required was therefore six. Appreciating the need for an effective waterborne police presence, the Police Authority agreed to a programme of replacement of the older boats by modern glass fibre craft and thereafter, to their replacement following twelve years in service.

The first new launch to be purchased under the programme was a 30 foot vessel, constructed by Watercraft Ltd. of Shoreham, Sussex and delivered in July, 1969. She was based at Sunderland as a replacement for the *Patrol* and was allocated the radio call sign 'Alpha India 21'. The launch was supplemented by a 13 foot outboard powered 'Dory' which enabled members of the Marine Division to operate in the upper reaches of the Wear when tidal conditions prevented a conventional launch from doing so.

Two further Watercraft launches were acquired in November, 1970 and February, 1971, respectively, for service on the Tyne. March, 1971 saw the purchase of a twin screw seagoing Nelson launch, capable of $18\frac{1}{2}$ knots, constructed by Adams and Son of Gourock. She was named *Alec Muir* after the renowned Chief Constable of Durham Constabulary who had retired the previous year and had done so much to secure the future of the Marine Division.

Finally, it is also of note that, in 1972, the functions of the long established River Wear Commissioners were placed under local authority control with the creation of the Port of Sunderland Authority, a body with which the Marine Division and its successors continued to enjoy a fine working relationship.

NORTHUMBRIA POLICE (1974 - 1998)

On 1st April, 1974, those parts of Durham Constabulary (namely the Boroughs of Sunderland, South Tyneside and Gateshead) which fell within the boundaries of the newly created Metropolitan County of Tyne and Wear were amalgamated with Northumberland Constabulary, to form Northumbria Police.

Consequently, the Marine Division of Durham Constabulary became 'K' or Marine Division of Northumbria Police, with its Divisional Headquarters remaining at Gateshead. The policy of launch replacement continued with the acquisition, during April, 1974, of a new vessel built by Cheverton Workboat Ltd. to replace one of the older craft. Initially, there were few changes, with the Division retaining territorial jurisdiction over all incidents occurring on the Tyne and Wear, together with the maintenance of the Underwater Search Unit. The Division's authorised establishment continued at eight-two officers until mid-1975, when it was reduced to forty-eight. This figure included the strength of sixteen officers, comprising one inspector, five sergeants and ten constables, which then constituted the Wear Section, but which, for administrative reasons was included in the establishment of the newly formed Sunderland North Sub Division. For all practical purposes, these men remained under the command of the officer in charge of the Marine Division and were not utilised for sub divisional duties.

In 1977, the Marine Division lost its territorial status, becoming a sub division of the newly formed Operations (later Support Services) Division which was composed of specialist departments such as Dogs/Horses, Communications, Special Patrol Group, Club & Vice, Communications and Scientific Aids which provided support to the force as a whole.

During 1981, cover of the Port of Sunderland by officers working from the Wear Station at North Dock was reduced from twenty-four to sixteen hours. The following year, it was decided to transfer all boat crews stationed there to the Tyne, with the result that, for the first time since 1840, the River Wear was without a permanent operational police presence. This decision had been made on the grounds that, owing to the decline in activity on the river, such a presence could no longer be justified. In future, river patrols were to be concentrated on the Tyne on a round-the-clock basis, with occasional patrols being undertaken on the Wear when necessary, using the launch which had been retained at North Dock, primarily for utilisation by the U.S.U. In an emergency, Tyne based crews would travel to Sunderland by road before going afloat.

At Tyne Dock, South Shields, where temporary accommodation had been erected in 1980 to replace the ageing Mill Dam station, a coastal patrols section was inaugurated in 1982, using police launch, *Northumbria*, a 13.5 metre Fairey Sword fast patrol craft, also purchased that year. The acquisition of this vessel represented a departure from the sub division's traditional role as 'river police' and opened up a new sphere of activity in marine policing. The introduction of coastal patrols enabled the sub division to police territorial waters between Berwick-upon-Tweed and Ryhope Dene (on the Northumbria/Durham boundary) and to continue to provide a limited presence on the Wear, in addition to small ports on the Northumberland coast.

Since 1981, largely due to periods of increased criminal activity within the Port of Sunderland, it has been found necessary, on more than one occasion, to reinstate cover at North Dock on a semi-permanent basis. At other times, Tyne based marine officers have regularly visited the port to carry out routine launch, mobile and foot patrols, and to deal with the wide variety of marine related incidents which regularly occur.

A long-standing proposal to centralise all Marine Sub Divisional activities, namely: administration, operational marine patrols, craft repair and maintenance, the Underwater Search Unit and the National Diving and Marine School came a step nearer to fruition early in 1991 with the transfer of coastal patrol, diving, training and maintenance facilities to a prime site on the south bank of the Tyne at Viking Park Industrial Estate, Jarrow. Initially, a temporary complex was provided, pending the completion of the adjacent purpose-built structure which was officially opened on 7th October, 1994, having cost in excess of £1.5 million. All remaining staff and facilities based at Pipewellgate were transferred to Viking Park and the old building closed before eventually being sold for use as a restaurant.

With the removal of diving and launch maintenance functions from North Dock, the facility was demolished as part of a major housing and marina development of the area. Prudently, it was decided to retain a launch and moorings at North Dock, with a temporary office being provided on site by the Tyne and Wear Development Corporation (T.W.D.C.). On 29th November, 1994, the brand new Marine Activities Centre at North Dock, incorporating accommodation shared by Northumbria Police Marine and Dogs Units, was officially opened by round-the-world yachtsman, Chay Blyth, C.B.E.

Whilst six displacement launches and a variety of smaller inflatable and other craft have been in service with Northumbria Police during recent years, there has been an increasing trend to purchase rigid hulled inflatable craft (R.H.I.B's) to meet training, diving and operational needs.

At present, the fleet includes seven R.H.I.B's, details of which follow:

Name	**Make**	**Length**	**Engine(s)**
Scimitar	Halmatic Arctic 24	7.6 metres	Twin 150 h.p. outboard
Sabre	Delta	7.7 metres	Twin 135 h.p. outboard
Sword	Avon	6.0 metres	Twin 75 h.p. outboard
Dart	Avon	5.4 metres	Single 75 h.p. outboard
Rapier	Avon	5.4 metres	Single 75 h.p. outboard
-	Details unavailable	4.0 metres	Details unavailable
-	Details unavailable	4.0 metres	Details unavailable

With the exception of *Northumbria*, referred to earlier, all of the displacement launches have been based at Sunderland for various periods. Police launch, *Aidan (ex-No. 1)*, which replaced the *Patrol* in 1969, is still part of the fleet, as are the Cheverton launch, *Egbert (ex-No. 5)* and high speed cathedral-hulled Watercraft launch, *Bede (ex-No. 2)*, purchased in 1983, which is propelled by twin Volvo inboard engines with outboard drives. The Watercraft launch, *Cuthbert (ex-No. 3)*, in service since 1970, was sold early in 1992 and the seagoing Nelson, *Dunelm (ex-Alec Muir* and *No. 4)* was disposed of during 1996.

In April, 1993, as part of an extensive review of Northumbria Police, conducted following the appointment of John Stevens as Chief Constable, the establishment of the Marine Sub Division was cut back from forty to seventeen police personnel and its designation changed to that of Marine Unit. The Unit, which now forms part of the force's Operations Support Department and has basically retained its predecessor's responsibilities and acquired others, continues to function in its depleted form.

In its most recent service level agreement, the Marine Unit undertakes to provide services which:

a) Support the strategic aims and positively promote the image of Northumbria Police;

b) Proactively contribute to the reduction of crime and disorder;

c) Provide specialist surface and sub-water capacity to all ports, rivers and coastal and inland waterways within the force area;

d) Provide resources, when available, to assist other Operations Support sections;

e) Comply with the standards laid out in the Force Charter; and

f) Generate revenue through training, subcontracting to other forces, law enforcement agencies and regional health authorities.

Eight basic services are provided in support of the foregoing objectives:

1) Operational support for incidents involving waterways;

2) The collation of intelligence relating to marine property crimes;

3) Specialist searches (water and non-water related);

4) Diver and marine training;

5) Proactive patrols;

6) Emergency recompression treatment;

7) Ad-hoc advice and guidance; and

8) Maintaining details of Marine Safety Agency (M.S.A.) passenger counting and recording systems approvals for marine vessels.

In addition to assisting area commands within the Northumbria Police area, surface and underwater incident support is provided on request to Durham and Cleveland Constabularies.

Although, in the past, the Department consisted of four distinct branches, namely marine patrols, underwater search unit, diving training and marine training, it is now difficult to make such distinctions. All training comes under the umbrella of the National Diving and Marine School and whilst the primary role of officers attached to the Marine Unit is that of an operational police officer, such personnel are encouraged to develop a multi-skilled approach to their work, with all being skilled in diving and/or training duties.

With regard to operational marine policing, there is a high level of demand for the Marine Unit to deal with incidents occurring at sea, on rivers or upon other waterways and to provide specialist support to the area commands which have replaced the old divisional structure within Northumbria Police. In particular, great emphasis is placed upon the prevention and investigation of marine orientated crime.

Besides the general duties of an operational police officer, specific areas of responsibility appertaining to the marine environment are entrusted to members of the Unit. These include the protection of life and property; investigation of sudden deaths; prosecution of offences, in particular those contravening the Merchant Shipping Acts, port and local authority bye-laws, and poaching, pollution and rabies legislation; boarding of ships; advice upon crime prevention to the marine community; and recovery of stolen motor vehicles from rivers. Another important function of the Unit is to liaise with and provide support to a host of outside agencies, such as H.M. Customs and Excise, H.M. Immigration Service, H.M. Coastguard, port authorities, Marine Safety Agency, Environment Agency and the Royal Naval Explosive Ordnance Disposal Unit, to name but a few.

Whilst there is still a strong accent upon traditional marine policing duties, the variety and scope of work now undertaken have expanded to such an extent as to be almost beyond the comprehension of the old-time river policeman.

The importance of marine training, initially commenced some years ago under the auspices of the Marine Sub Division and now undertaken by the prestigious National Diving and Marine School, under Department of Transport recognition, cannot be overstated. Before 1979, officers transferring to the Sub Division received no formal marine training. Since then a variety of courses have been introduced, leading to the establishment and development of the marine training role of the School.

These courses have been organised, not only for the benefit of Northumbria Police officers, but for students from other United Kingdom forces having a marine facility; overseas law enforcement agencies from Bahrain, Qatar, Brunei, Oman, Malaysia, Zimbabwe, United States of America and Hong Kong; and non-police organisations, such as H.M. Customs and Excise, National Rivers Authority, fire brigades and local authorities.

A wide range of marine courses are currently provided and include the following:

Coastal Patrol, Basic Patrol Launch, Offshore Rigid Inflatable Boat, Advanced Rigid Inflatable Boat, Basic Small and Rigid Inflatable, together with refresher training in respect of each of these disciplines. In addition, Marine V.H.F. Radio Licence (Operator), Basic Sea Survival and Marine Officer Law courses are undertaken.

Although recent restructuring of marine policing within Northumbria Police has resulted in a leaner organisation, every effort is being made to develop its potential to the full and meet the challenges of the future.

UNDERWATER SEARCH UNIT AND DIVER TRAINING (1959 -1997)

Having regard to its long association with the River Wear and the importance of its role within the police service, it is appropriate that a section of this chapter be devoted to the development of the Underwater Search Unit, from its modest origins within Durham County Constabulary to the prominent position which it now occupies.

Initially formed in 1959, on a part-time basis under the auspices of the Organisation and Training Department of Durham County Constabulary, the Unit comprised sixteen volunteers, from various branches of the force, to provide a police operational diving team. Its terms of reference were to assist in the recovery of bodies, stolen property, weapons used in crime and lost property of an extremely valuable nature.

Following the amalgamation of Gateshead and South Shields Borough Police Forces with Durham Constabulary, the U.S.U. became an integral part of the newly created Marine Division, becoming a specialist full-time unit in November, 1969 based at the force's Aykley Heads headquarters, where purpose-built accommodation was provided. The authorised strength of the Unit then was one inspector, one sergeant and six constables. A specially constructed vehicle was utilised to transport personnel, carry equipment, and provide wet and dry storage compartments together with refreshment facilities.

Throughout the years, the Unit continued to develop operational techniques which became recognised and accepted by many other police forces, as a result of which, in 1970, courses commenced for the training of police divers throughout the North East (No. 2) Region. The Wear Station was regularly used as a base for training courses whilst engaged in diving instruction.

On 1st April, 1974, Unit members were transferred to the newly formed Northumbria Police as part of its Marine Division and were permanently based at North Dock. Despite additional portacabins being erected to facilitate the U.S.U., it was hoped that permanent buildings would be constructed on the site in due course. Unfortunately this did not materialise, but North Dock was to remain the home of the Unit until October, 1991.

In 1976, the Chief Constable agreed to a request from the A.C.P.O. Training Committee to make training courses available for police divers on a national scale, resulting in considerable expansion of the training programme and subsequent increases in establishment.

The evolution of the Underwater Search Unit and diver training as an integral part of the Northumbria Marine Unit and National Diving and Marine School has been detailed within the previous section of this book.

Officers carrying out U.S.U. duties receive extensive training to qualify as police divers in accordance with the Police Diving Rules and Codes of Practice. In general, such officers are drawn from the ranks of the Marine Unit, although 'reserve divers' (officers who have received the requisite training but are not current Marine Unit members) are sometimes seconded for specific operations.

The terms of reference for the Underwater Search Unit, whose members are trained to conduct diving operations to a maximum depth of fifty metres, are wide ranging and include the following duties:

Provision of support to police officers investigating crime; searching for and the recovery of bodies, property, weapons and other items subject of police investigation; rescue situations when the rescue is to be effected underwater; the search for and recovery of lost property of high value or of particular significance; assisting in the investigation of certain reports of missing persons; the preservation of evidence; security searches associated with special events and visits by V.I.P's; and providing assistance during instances of flooding.

The National Diving and Marine School is responsible for the provision of training to all United Kingdom police divers. In addition, training is provided to students from overseas law enforcement agencies and to certain domestic fire brigades. The training programme, recognised by the Health and Safety Executive, meets standards of competence specified in Diving Operations at Work Regulations and is of an extremely comprehensive nature.

The present syllabus embraces the following courses which are conducted by qualified police divers, who are members of the Marine Unit and who have progressed to become qualified diving instructors:

Basic Air Diving, Air Diving (Refresher), Diving Supervisor, Diving Supervisor (Refresher), Air Chamber Operator, Diving Contractor, Basic Diver Medic (Inshore), Diving First Aid and Diving First Aid (Refresher).

The National Diving and Marine School is also a member of the Association of British Diving Schools, the Society of Underwater Technology and the British Hyperbaric Association.

A two-compartment decompression chamber, primarily for use in diver training, has been located at the training school since 1981. Formal arrangements have since been entered into with the National Health Service to provide emergency recompression treatment for divers suffering from decompression illness, known as "the bends."

Over the years, diving personnel have striven to promote 'best practice' in diving techniques by identifying alternative methods and procedures. The National Diving and Marine School has long been recognised as a world leader in the sphere of police diving and the showpiece Viking Park complex will undoubtedly serve to preserve this standing well into the next century.

AIR SUPPORT UNIT (1989 - 1998)

Whilst not directly related to marine policing, the work carried out by the Marine Sub Division of Northumbria Police in establishing the force's Air Support Unit (A.S.U.) is worthy of note.

Inaugurated on 1st November, 1989, the Air Support Unit was for some time an integral part of the sub division. Based at Newcastle International Airport, the Unit soon became indispensable in supporting territorial officers in combating crime, assisting with searches and carrying out aerial surveillance. Two helicopters, a German built MBB Bolkow 105 and French made Aerospatiale Squirrel, supplied under contract by Police Aviation Services Ltd. of Devon, were each placed on trial for six months, before it was decided to retain the latter aircraft and continue with the provision of an air support unit for the force.

After a period as the Helicopter Support Unit under the Traffic Division and later Operations Support Department, the Unit has now been regionalised. In addition to the helicopter, a fixed-wing Islander aircraft is in service with the North East Air Support Unit which serves the police areas of Northumbria, Durham and Cleveland.

The helicopter, in particular, is often seen in the skies above Sunderland and is at times deployed to assist at the scenes of marine related incidents. It is now equipped with life saving apparatus to assist persons in difficulty in the water.

It is also of note to relate that as early as January, 1978, the acquisition of a helicopter by the Marine Sub Division had first been mooted - although the idea never got off the ground! It had been suggested that an ex-military aircraft might be purchased, as a replacement for a river launch at a cost of around £20,000, to afford greater flexibility to river and sea patrols and to assist other divisions.

SUNDERLAND BOROUGH FIRE BRIGADE (1961 - 1974)

The history of the Borough Fire Brigade is another story in itself. The demise of the River Wear Watch in 1961 had little effect upon the manner in which the Brigade carried out its firefighting responsibilities towards the port and shipping in general. It should be remembered that neither firefloat had been engaged in fighting a shipboard fire since 1950 and that on only a handful of occasions since then had they assisted at scenes of fires ashore. There were few incidents with which the Brigade's modern appliances could not adequately deal from onshore, although if the situation warranted, assistance of craft operated by the port authority, river police or local tug company could be procured.

Two major fires which occurred on board ships in the Wear during the 1960's, less than six months apart, did have grave consequences and served to emphasise the hazards of such outbreaks and the need to have effective means by which to combat them.

The first occurred on 30th October, 1966, on board Bibby Lines Ltd's **Toronto City**, a 7,643 gross tons cargo ship which, having been launched by Doxford and Sunderland Shipbuilding and Engineering Co. Ltd., was fitting out at Pallion Quay. Seven men who had been working in the propeller shaft lost their lives when oil, which sprayed out under pressure when a pipe became disconnected, was ignited by an oxy-acetylene burner. It took the efforts of the crews of seven fire appliances, working alongside shipyard employees in the most arduous of conditions, to recover the bodies of the unfortunate men.

Then, on 15th April, 1967, disaster struck again, this time on board the 7,856 gross tons motor ship, **Landwade**, owned by the Atlantic Shipping and Trading Co. Ltd., which was undergoing repairs at T. W. Greenwell and Co. Ltd's quay. Without warning, fire - later found to have been caused accidentally - swept through the ship's superstructure, engulfing the officers' accommodation, bridge and chartroom. The master and his wife, and the third mate and his wife were all killed in the inferno, which at one time had threatened to spread to the engine room and cause a serious explosion. At the height of the fire, forty firemen were engaged at the scene, with valuable assistance being provided by two tugs in the absence of fireboats.

Less than a week later, another fire, fortunately without casualties, broke out on board the West German collier, **Hanngrid** which was berthed in Hudson Dock. A new smoke extractor, used for the first time by the Brigade, proved to be highly effective.

The Borough Fire Brigade survived, serving the Port of Sunderland, until 1st April, 1974, when it was merged into the newly formed Tyne and Wear Metropolitan Fire Brigade.

AUXILIARY FIRE SERVICE (1949 - 1968)

Until its disbandment in 1968, the Auxiliary Fire Service (A.F.S.), which had been reformed under the Civil Defence Act, 1949, maintained a strong presence in Sunderland.

Of particular interest is the Transportable Water Unit, familiarly known as the 'Bikini Raft Unit', which was specifically designed for use with A.F.S. Mobile Fire Columns to provide water from rivers, seas or lakes in the event of land sources being unavailable. Occasionally, a 'Bikini' unit could be seen exercising in the South Docks or on the River Wear at Sunderland.

Each unit comprised three inflatable rafts, each being equipped with three lightweight portable Godiva pumps and having a crew of two. Together, the pumps were capable of delivering about 1,000 gallons of water per minute at 100 pounds per square inch. Propulsion and steerage were provided by jet reaction from one of the pumps, working through a swivel-mounted branch pipe. A Commer or Bedford lorry, fitted with a crane, was provided to transport the full complement of each unit's equipment.

TYNE AND WEAR METROPOLITAN FIRE BRIGADE (1974 - 1998)

Since 1st April, 1974, responsibility for firefighting within the Port of Sunderland has been vested with the Tyne and Wear Metropolitan Fire Brigade. Besides normal fire appliances, the Brigade possesses two highly manoeuvrable purpose-built firefighting craft, designed for use on both rivers and inland waterways.

Two training courses, each of three weeks duration, were initially provided, early in 1990, by Northumbria Police National Marine School for selected Brigade officers who have subsequently conducted further in-house training in the use of the craft for other Brigade members.

The need for such craft was accentuated with the implementation of the Pilotage Act, 1987, which transferred the responsibility for the provision of pilotage services from pilotage to harbour authorities. Hitherto, notably on the River Tyne, the Brigade had been able to utilise the services of port authority launches in connection with firefighting. However, with their new obligations, ports authorities became unable to guarantee the availability of their craft to the Brigade.

The two fireboats were delivered in 1990, having been constructed by Campbells' Boatyard at Blyth, Northumberland. Named *Vedra* and *Tinea* (the Roman names for the Wear and Tyne), the craft were shore-based at the Central Fire Station, Sunderland and the Fossway Fire Station, Newcastle, respectively. When required, they are towed to a suitable launching site on a conventional trailer by a Brigade rescue tender and can either be launched directly from the trailer. or hoisted into the water by a turntable ladder. In 1996, however, owing to financial constraints within the Brigade, the *Vedra* was withdrawn from operational service and placed in reserve.

Each fireboat has a minimum crew of three firefighters, who have undergone extensive training in seamanship and navigational skills. When fully laden, the vessels can carry up to twelve firefighters, together with full firefighting kit and equipment. In built fire pumps, capable of delivering up to 1,000 gallons of water per minute, are fitted and twin 65 h.p. outboard engines provide a maximum speed of about thirty knots.

Whilst primarily for use in connection with firefighting, the fireboats have occasionally been deployed to rescue situations on the Rivers Tyne and Wear when necessary.

In October, 1996, the Brigade announced plans to replace both fireboats with lighter, more cost effective models, having less onerous training implications.

Appendix 1

RIVER WEAR WATCH - POLICE PERSONNEL

(1840 - 1961)

The following is a record of police officers who served with the River Wear Watch during its 121 years history. Unfortunately, due the absence of records for certain periods, predominantly during the Nineteen Century, it has not been possible to compile a complete listing of all officers so employed and of their dates of service.

Italicised dates shown in the remarks column indicate that an officer is known to have served during the year or years referred to.

Name of Officer	Force No(s).	From	To	Remarks
ADAMS, Herbert	22/6	1914	1934	
AGAR, Robert	15/1	1867	1910	Promoted Sergeant 1888.
ALDERSON, James	7	?	?	*1847 - 1852.*
ALLAN, Nathaniel	-	1860	1875	Appointed as Inspector / Required to resign.
ANDERSON,	?	?	?	*1873.*
ANNISON, Ralph	-	1840	1854	Appointed as Inspector.
ARMSTRONG, William	29	1916	1916	
ARNOLD, John	5	1891	1900	Resigned to become RWC Assistant Harbour Master.
ARNOLD, John William	19	1882	1901	
ATCHINSON, Robert	17	?	?	*1852.*
ATKINSON, Christopher	6	1872	1919	
ATKINSON, Peter William	16/5/3	1901	1946	Promoted Sergeant 1915.
AVERY, William	24	1891	1922	
BAILES, Charles	15	1919	1920	Transferred to Sunderland Borough Police.
BAKER, H. H.		1882	?	*1887.*
BARR, Lawrence	14	1948	1961	
BEE, William	10	?	1882(3)	
BELL, George Robert	15	1920	1921	Transferred to Sunderland Borough Police.
BEWICK, John Henry	17	1916	?	
BLACKETT, John	?	1902	?	
BLACKHURST, Thomas B.	17	1932	1946	
BLAKESTON, Jonas S.	28/9	1914	1945	
BOWHILL, James	?	?	?	*1880.*
BOWEY,	?	?	?	*1873.*
BOYES,	?	?	?	*1855.*
BOYS, John J.	?	1887	?	
BOYS, William J.	?	1883	1885	
BURDON, Robert	20/13	?	?	*1849 - 1853.*
BURTON, William	?	?	1888	Promoted Sergeant 1880.
BURN, Z.	?	?	?	*1866.*
CAFFREY, John	26	1919	1919	Transferred to Sunderland Borough Police.
CAMPBELL, Allan Ford	8	1902	1937	Engaged on active service during World War 1.
CAMPION, Charles	7	1950	1955	
CARLSON, Edward John	13	1904	1914	
CARTMER, John Mark	5/7	1906	1941	Promoted Sergeant 1911.
CHAPMAN, William Thompson	14	1891	1922	
CHICKEN, Norman	13	1948	1961	
CHILD, Richard	?	?	?	*1849.*

CLAZEY, Hector	12	1948	1961	
COWE, Peter	10	1930	1961	Died whilst serving.
CROZIER,	?	?	?	*1882.*
CRISP, Lawrence	5	1915	1916	
CURTIS, L. F.	7	1949	1950	
DABNES, William	?	?	?	*1880.*
DANKISS, Robert	?	?	?	*1880.*
DAVISON, James W.	5	1915	?	
DAVISON, Leslie	21/12	1946	1948	
DAVISON, Richard	25	1950	1955	
DAVISON, Thomas	13/3	1930	1956	Promoted Sergeant 1946.
DEN BOGERT, Henry	?	?	?	*1876 - 1880.*
DITCHBURN, John	10	?	?	*1853.*
DIXON,	?	1840	?	Appointed as Captain.
DIXON, James	18	?	?	*1849.*
DODSWORTH, Henry B.	5	1885	?	
DODSWORTH, William Henry	11	1928	1961	
DONKIN,	?	?	?	*Sergeant in 1868.*
DONKIN, Nixon	19/14	?	?	*1850 - 1853.*
DOWNES, Charles	16	?	1868	*1851.*
DUNHAM, John Speight	8	1891	1902	
DUNN, Joseph	9	1946	1961	
DUNNING,	?	?	?	*1900.*
ELSTOB, George James	21/5	1902	1948	Engaged on active service during World War 1.
ELSTOB, George	10	1882	?	
ELSTOB, William	21	1883	?	
FANNEN, John	13	1880	?	*1900.*
FENBOW, Charles	18	1882	1922	
FRANCIS,	?	?	1884	
FREEMAN, Jonathan	19	1901	1930	
GIBSON, George Dawson	7	1941	1949	
GIFFORD, James	17	1905	1913	
HALL, Thomas	5	?	?	*1846 - 1852.*
HAMP, Francis William	2	1907	1932	Appointed as Engineer Sergeant.
HASKER, John Staff	12	1882	1895	Promoted Sergeant 1889 / Killed on duty at fire.
HAWKS, Henry	2	1880	?	Promoted Sergeant 1889.
HEBNER, Charles	10	1916	1919	
HIRD, William	?	?	1866	Killed on duty at South Dock.
HEIRD, Robert	7/10	?	1852	Drowned on duty at North Dock.
HOPE, Alan	15	1949	1950	
HOWES, Thomas	?	?	?	Promoted Detective Sergeant 1865.
HUMBLE, William	10/2	1879	1919	Promoted Sergeant 1882 & Sub-Inspector 1896.
HUNTER, Thomas	12	1863	1903	
HUNTER, Thomas James	19/2	1930	1961	*Sergeant in 1961.*
HUNTLEY, John	29	1916	1916	
HUTCHINSON, James Henry	17	1946	1946	
INNES, John	17	1947	1961	
JACKSON, William	15/3	1912	1921	Promoted Sergeant 1919 / Transferred to Bor. Police.
JEFFERSON, Lancelot	1	1840	1860	Appointed as Captain / Promoted Inspector 1854.
JENNINGS, George William	7/1	1890	1930	Promoted Sergeant 1910 & 1925.
JOHNSON, William	23	1883	?	*1901.*
KEELER, Richard Allan	13	1946	1946	
KNAPP, Alexander	15/25	1903	1940	
LAKIN, James	-	1865	1913	Appointed as Sub-Inspector / Promoted Inspector 1875 / Drowned River Wear on duty.
LARAMAN, Sydney Stead	?	1889	1891	
LEIGH,	?	?	?	*1870.*
LOW, Thomas S.	?	?	?	Promoted Sub-Inspector from Sergeant 1880.
LILISTON, George	11	1896	1928	
LINDSEY,	4	?	?	*1846.*

172

LISLE, Arthur	27	1914	?	Engaged active service in World War 1, losing leg.
LONGRIDGE, William Richard	15	1880	?	*1911.*
LORD,	6	?	1872	*1864.*
LOWERSON, John Frederick	15	1940	1949	Former War Reserve P.C.
MACHIN, Alexander	15	1919	1919	
MARKWELL, David	?	?	?	*1846.*
METCALF, Robert	?	?	?	*1850 - 1852.*
METCALFE, Thomas	?	1840	?	Appointed as Captain.
MELLEFONT, Gilbert J.	16	1919	1942	Rejoined after break in service.
MIDDLETON, John	9	1882	1917	
MILLER, George	?	?	?	*1870 - 1877.*
MITCHELL, John Robert	6	1920	1921	Transferred to Sunderland Borough Police.
MUSTARD, Robert F.	17/14	1914	1961	Engaged active service World War 1 / Promoted Sgt.
OATES, George	?	?	?	*1880.*
PAGE, Charles Peter	14/26	1914	1940	Engaged in active service during World War 1/Killed during air raid whilst reporting for duty.
PALLAS, George	6	?	?	*1848 - 1852.*
PARNABY, Thomas	22	1883	?	*1899.*
PATTERSON, Robert J.	?	?	1898	Sergeant Engineer / Transferred to Sunderland Borough Police (Fire Brigade).
PATTERSON, John	20	1932	1961	Engaged on active service during World War 2.
PEACOCK, William K.	16/4/3	1880	?	Promoted Sergeant 1895. *1911.*
PEARS, Thomas	18	1872	?	
PENNINGTON, Henry	12	1914	1925	Engaged on active service during World War 1.
PENNINGTON, James Laws	12	1925	1957	Promoted Sergeant 1932, Sub-Inspector 1935 & Inspector 1949.
PICKERING, George Wright	6	1934	1960	
POULTER, Harry	14	1940	1948	
RACE, John William	5	1914	?	Engaged on active service during World War 1.
RANSON, George	17/12	?	?	*P.C. in 1846 / Sergeant in 1878.*
REICHARD, Jack L.	5	1948	1950	
RENWICKS, Ralph Stafford	8	1937	1961	
RICH, James	10/1	1913	1946	Engaged active service World War 1 / Sergt. in 1946.
RICHARDSON, John	?	1856	1873	
RICHARDSON, William	18/9	?	?	*1846 - 1852.*
RITCHIE,	?	?	?	*1855 - 1877.*
ROBINSON, William	18/11	?	?	*1847 - 1849.*
ROBSON,	?	?	?	*1913.*
ROBSON, George	29	1914	1916	Killed on active service during World War 1.
ROCHFORD, John William Arthur	-	1913	1949	Appointed as Inspector.
ROYAL, George	22	1907	1914	Promoted Detective Sergeant 1913 / Imprisoned & deported after conviction as enemy alien.
SANDY, Osborne Edward	12	1903	1914	
SCOTT, Thomas	18	?	1872	
SCOTT, Peter	?	1889	1891	
SHARP,	?	?	?	*1869.*
SHOTTON, Rowlandson Hardy	?	1914	?	Killed on active service during World War 1.
SINCLAIR,	?	?	?	*1868.*
SIMPSON,	?	?	?	*1863.*
SMART, John	?	?	?	*1864 - 1878.*
SNELGAR, William Lance	?	1888	1891	Drowned in yachting accident at sea.
SNOWDON, Thomas	?	1884	?	*1887.*
SOFTLEY,	?	?	?	*1873.*
SOFTLEY, Robert William	?	1901	?	
STARK, Ernest Alfred	12/1	1932	1961	Promoted Sergeant 1946 & Inspector 1957.
STEEL, William Nichols	20	1898	1932	
STEPHENSON, Joseph	?	?	1880	
STEWART, William Thomas Moffatt	16	1895	1901	
STOKOE, Norman	13	1947	1948	
STRUTT, Harry	5	1916	?	
SUDDICK, William	?	?	?	*1846 - 1847.*
SWALES, Thomas	18/23	1902	1948	

SWAN, Richard Maurice	16	1942	1960	
TAYLOR, Michael	8	?	?	*1846 - 1852.*
THIRKELL, Nylam	25	1893	?	
THORN, George	?	?	?	*1886 - 1893.*
THURSTON,	23	?	?	*1873.*
TILDON, George Thomas	13	1914	1930	Engaged on active service during World War 1 / Died on quayside after terminating tour of duty.
TINMOUTH,	2	1840	?	Appointed as Captain / Sergeant in 1861.
TODD, Lindsey	?	?	?	*1846.*
TODD, Robert	14/19	?	?	*1850 - 1853.*
TOPHAM, Albert Fisher	25	1956	1961	
WARREN, William Henry	?	?	1880	Murdered in Bridge Street, Sunderland by an unknown man following an altercation - two weeks after his dismissal from the River Wear Watch.
WAYMAN, William T.	27	1915	1916	
WILLIAMS, Charles James	7	1910	1913	
WILLIAMSON, Ernest	27	1914	?	
WILSON, John	?	?	1849	Dismissed for indecently assaulting a colleague.
WILSON, Newby	10	?	1849	Died on duty at Wylam Wharf.
WILTON, Benjamin	?	1862	1863	Drowned on duty at South Dock.
WINGATE,	?	?	?	*1869.*
WRIGHT, Frederick	17/3	1883	1919	Promoted Sergeant 1905.

NOTES:

1. Until 1859, the strength of the force was reduced during the summer months. Some constables, therefore, were employed on a seasonal basis only between 1840 and 1859.

2. The collar numbers allocated to individual officers do not necessarily indicate the strength of the Watch at any particular time.

3. Collar numbers 1 - 4 (and sometimes no. 5) were allocated to Captains/Sergeants. Sub-Inspectors and Inspectors were not numbered. The title 'Captain' was substituted by 'Sergeant' in 1861.

4. Unless otherwise stated, references are to officers' service as Boatmen/Constables.

Appendix 2

RIVER WEAR WATCH COMMISSIONERS

(1840 - 1961)

Many notable Sunderland shipowners held office as Commissioners of the River Wear Watch. The following is a complete record of these men, showing the year in which they signed the declaration to become Commissioners:

1840: (Inaugural meeting) William ORD, William NICHOLSON, George SPARK, Turner THOMPSON, Andrew WHITE, George BOOTH, Caleb WILSON, John CROPTON, Henry MOON, George PAULL, John MURRAY, John ATKIN, Robert TATE, Joseph LUMDSON, Thomas PARKER, Hill PARKER, John HUTCHINSON, George MOON, Robert ORD (the younger), Thomas Bell ORD, John WILKINSON, Henry TANNER, James PARKER, George COOK, Thomas BLAIR, Thomas REED (Nicholson Street), Andrew MUIR, Joseph Norman WILSON, John CROZIER, Thomas WALKER, Edward SMITH, Robert FRENCH, William HOLMES, Albany BAKER, George RICHARDSON, John STOREY, Thomas REED, Philip LAING, Martin LONIE, Richard VIPOND, Robert SCURFIELD, Robert BROWN, Thomas BROWN (the younger), Thomas SPEEDING, William SNOWBALL, George BOLAM, George HUTCHINSON, Robert MITCHINSON, John ROBINSON.

1840: Richard WHITE, David JONASSOHN, James Wilkie COLLINGWOOD, Thomas HUNTER.

1841: Thomas WOOD.

1842: George HUDSON.

1843: Charles TAYLOR, Henry Alexander MOON, Samuel ALCOCK.

1844: William NICHOLSON (the younger), John NICHOLSON, George REED.

1846: Joshua WILSON, Thomas Boyes SIMEY, George HARRISON.

1847: Sanderson HOWE, John RITSON, Joshua Thomas ALCOCK, James LAING, John CLAY.

1848: Thomas OLIVER, Robert HOLMES, Martin MOORE, Joseph SPENCE, John Ibbotson COOPER.

1851: John ROBINSON, Richard ROBINSON.

1855: William DIXON.

1856: Robert DIXON, John LINDSAY.

1858: Edward Temperley GOURLEY.

1860: John George RITSON, Francis RITSON, William ORD (the younger).

1861: Thomas Charles SIMEY, William Ash ORD, Martin LONIE (the younger), Robert ELWIN.

1862: William THOMPSON.

1863: George Robert BOOTH.

1865: John CANDLISH, Allison WHITFIELD, William BRIGGS, Cuthbert HODGSON, Thomas REED (the younger), Henry HOLMES, John James CLAY.

1866: James AYRE, Ralph Milbanke HUDSON, Charles TAYLOR, William RITSON, Martin WEINER.

1867: George C. PECKET.

1868: Francis ROBINSON, John Hunter WATSON.

1870: Robert Scott BRIGGS, Charles James BRIGGS.

1871: Richard HUMBLE.

1872: Henry O. BOWMAN, George BOWMAN.

1873: George FOREMAN, Robert Heydon GAYNER.

1874: Thomas John TAYLOR, Charles John RICHES.

1876: Isaac WHITFIELD, John CROSSBY, William COULSON, James BAMBOROUGH.

1877: Leopold Anton Victor RUDOLPHI, Robert Todd NICHOLSON, William Bramwell FERGUSON, William Henry DIXON.

1878: Charles LILBURN, John Storey BARWICK.

1879: John HOPPER, James HORAN.

1882: Thomas PINKNEY, Thomas STOCKDALE.

1884: John FIRTH.

1885: John SANDERSON.

1886: Robert SHADFORTH, James CHRISP.

1887: James Henry A. CULLIFORD.

1889: John HOPPER.

1890: William Jopling BRANFOOT, George BUTCHART.

1891: Thomas NICHOLSON, Thomas William PINKNEY.

1899: William Anthony WATSON.

1902: Arthur RITSON, Cuthbert WILKINSON, Thomas Anderson HORAN, John NESS, John Weston ADAMSON.

1904: Herbert WEBSTER.

1911: John Joseph ROBSON, Thomas SPEEDING, John Wallace TAYLOR (the younger).

1915: Henry Allison COCHRANE, William BLACK, John DIXON, William HANDY.

1925: Stanley McKenzie RITSON, Henry ARMSTRONG, Andrew COMMON.

1929: Joseph William COTTEE, Ernest Frederick DIX.

1939: Septimus MARSHALL, John Thomas BURNOP, Kenneth William BLACK.

1945: Thomas George IRVING.

1946: Norman Reginald ROSE, Harry SOUTER.

1948: Robert Cyril THOMPSON.

1952: Andrew MARSHALL.

1953: Frank DAWSON.

1959: Walter Beattie ALLAN.

Appendix 3

SUPERINTENDENTS AND INSPECTORS OF THE WATCH

(1840 - 1961)

SUPERINTENDENTS

William BROWN	1840	-	1855
Robert GIFFORD	1855	-	1858
Joseph STAINSBY	1858	-	1878
John NICHOLSON	1878	-	1885
William HUNTLEY	1885	-	1897
William CARTER	1897	-	1915
Frederick CRAWLEY	1915	-	1925
John RUDDICK	1925	-	1937
George Henry COOK	1937	-	1955
William TAIT	1955	-	1961

INSPECTORS

Ralph ANNISON	1840	-	1854
Lancelot JEFFERSON	1854	-	1860
Nathaniel ALLAN	1860	-	1875
James LAKIN	1875	-	1913
John William Arthur ROCHFORD	1913	-	1949
James Laws PENNINGTON	1949	-	1957
Ernest Alfred STARK	1957	-	1961

Appendix 4

CLERKS TO THE RIVER WEAR WATCH COMMISSIONERS

(1840 - 1966)

John Pexall KIDSON	840	-	1854
John KIDSON	1854	-	1874
Charles KIDSON	1874	-	1881
William A. KIDSON	1881	-	1929
Edward COPE	1929	-	1946
Alfred H. J. BROWN	1946	-	1957
E. LONSDALE	1957	-	1966

NOTES:

1. Messrs. Brown and Lonsdale performed the office of Clerk as an additional capacity whilst they were employed as General Manager and Clerk to the River Wear Commissioners.

2. E. Lonsdale continued in office until 1966, pending the winding up of the affairs of the River Wear Watch Commissioners.

Appendix 5

MEDICAL OFFICERS
TO THE RIVER WEAR WATCH

(1883 - 1958)

A police surgeon was retained by the River Wear Watch Commissioners to attend to members of the force and to carry out other medical duties as required, such as the examination of bodies recovered from the river or docks. The position of Medical Officer was abolished upon the retirement of Dr. Robinson in 1958.

The following are those doctors who are known to have held the position, although particulars of Medical Officers before Dr. Francis are not known:

Dr. FRANCIS	?	-	1883
Dr. BEATTIE	1883	-	1908
Dr. Robert Stephen HUBBERSTY	1908	-	1939
Dr. G. S. ROBINSON	1939	-	1958

Appendix 6

RIVER WEAR WATCH FLOATING PROPERTY

(1841 - 1961)

The following is a brief record of craft operated by the River Wear Watch during its history. The dates shown are those between which vessels were owned by the Watch Commissioners, but not necessarily the period during which they were in commission. Full details of each vessel are given in the relevant preceding chapter:

FIREFLOATS

WEAR ENGINE 'A'	Manual firefloat	1841 - 1907	*1.*
WEAR ENGINE 'B'	Manual firefloat	1850 - 1906	*2.*
FIRE QUEEN	Steam firefloat	1874 - 1886	
FIRE QUEEN	Steam firefloat	1886 - 1912	
FIRE KING	Steam firefloat	1906 - 1962	
FIRE QUEEN	Steam firefloat	1911 - 1962	

LAUNCHES   *3.*

PATROL	Open steam launch	1896 - 1915	
Unknown	Unknown	1915 - 1916	*4.*
PATROL	Enclosed steam launch	1917 - 1946	
VIGILANTE	Open motor launch	1928 - 1933	
VIGILANT	Enclosed motor launch	1933 - 1962	
PATROL	Enclosed motor launch	1947 - 1961	

FLOATING POLICE STATIONS

| MANUAL | Converted manual firefloat | 1925 - 1949 | *5.* |
| PIKES' No. 10 | Converted dumb barge | 1948 - 1962 | |

NOTES:

1. Prior to the acquisition of *Wear Engine 'B'* in 1850, *Wear Engine 'A'* was known simply as *Wear Engine*.

2. Although **Wear Engine 'B'** is believed to have ceased her firefighting capability in 1906, she had, for a number of years previously, been stationed as a floating depot for the steam firefloats. She continued in this role from 1906 until 1925, when her status was upgraded to that of floating H.Q. (See also note 5.)

3. Besides steam and motor launches, a number of rowing boats were utilised for patrol work, transport and attending occurrences. Between 1840 and 1896, patrol duties afloat were undertaken solely by such means, with a rowing boat remaining in use for river patrols until 1928 to supplement the steam launch.

4. This launch was hired by the Watch Commissioners due to the unserviceability of their steam launch.

5. Upon the Watch's vacation of Bodlewell Lane Police Station in 1925, the **Manual's** function was upgraded from floating depot to floating H.Q. The name, **Manual** was unofficial but had always been and continued to be used to refer to the craft.

Appendix 7

RIVER WEAR WATCH - HONOURS

(1840 - 1961)

At first glance, the list of awards presented to members of the River Wear Watch for saving life during its history appears sparse. However, numerous instances are well documented in which its members performed outstanding acts of bravery which resulted in lives being saved and which, by today's standards, would surely have met with official recognition. It is difficult to understand why Watch members were not recommended for awards more frequently.

The following is a list of honours which are known to have been received by force members over the years:

Date of Incident.	Officers Involved.	Nature of Award.	Location of Incident and Circumstances.
15/9/1899	P.C. John Arnold & P.C. William Johnson	R.H.S. Certificate on Parchment & Swedish R.H.S. certificate.	Rescue of crew of schooner, *Thelma* after explosion on board near Mark Quay, River Wear.
26/8/1916	Sub Ins. William Humble	R.H.S. Honorary Testimonial on Vellum.	Rescue of two boys from River Wear.
10/11/1918	Ins. John W. A. Rochford, Sgt. Geo. Wm. Jennings, P.C. Herbert Adams, P.C. William Jackson & P.C. William Nichols Steel.	Kings Police Medal for Gallantry.	Extinguishing fire involving ammunition magazine on board *S.S. Hornsey* near Thornhill Quay, River Wear.
30/8/1954	P.C. Joseph Dunn.	R.H.S. Certificate	Rescue and resuscitation of wireless operator of *S.S. Greathope* at East Quay South, Hudson Dock.

Appendix 8

RIVER WEAR WATCH - ROLL OF HONOUR

(1840 - 1961)

The following Watch members are known to have lost their lives either in the execution of their duty or in service to their country:

Date	Name of Officer	Place of Death	Cause of Death
6/9/1849	P.C. Newby Wilson	Wylam Wharf	Fell over quayside into river after being taken ill and was drowned.
19/10/1852	P.C. Robert Heird	Wearmouth Dock	Tripped on broken kerbstone, fell into dock and was drowned.
17/3/1863	P.C. Benjamin Wilton	Half-tide Basin, South Dock	Tripped on length of chain, fell into dock and was drowned.
29/11/1866	P.C. William Hird	Londonderry Drops, South Docks	Missed footing, fell into dock and sustained a broken neck.
4/11/1895	Sergeant John Hasker	Joshua Wilson and Sons' warehouse, Lombard St. / Walton Lane, East End	Died from multiple injuries during building collapse whilst whilst engaged at scene of serious fire. (Borough P.C. also died).
23/2/1913	Inspector James Lakin	Bodlewell Lane Ferry Landing	Fell into river and was drowned in mysterious circumstances.
15/10/1914	P.C. Rowlandson Hardy Shotton	North Sea, off Aberdeen	Killed on active service with the Royal Navy when the cruiser, *H.M.S. Hawke* was torpedoed by U-9.
1914-18	P.C. George Robson	Unknown	Killed on active service with the Army.
21/6/1940	P.C. Charles Peter Page	Elwin Tce., Pallion	Whilst reporting for duty in response to an air raid warning, was killed when his auto cycle was in collision with a taxi.